КРЕМЛЬ

«МОСКВА»

ГОСУДАРСТВЕННЫЙ
ИСТОРИЧЕСКИЙ МУЗЕЙ

МАНЕЖНАЯ ПЛОЩАДЬ

ГУМ (ГОСУДАРСТВЕННЫЙ
УНИВЕРСАЛЬНЫЙ МАГАЗИН)

КРАСНАЯ ПЛОЩАДЬ

МАНЕЖ

МАВЗОЛЕЙ ЛЕНИНА

АРСЕНАЛ

ЗДАНИЕ СОВЕТА МИНИСТРОВ
СССР

СПАССКАЯ
БАШНЯ

ДВОРЕЦ СЪЕЗДОВ

ПОКРОВСКИЙ СОБОР
(ХРАМ ВАСИЛИЯ
БЛАЖЕННОГО)

УСПЕНСКИЙ
СОБОР

ЦАРЬ-
ПУШКА

ЦАРЬ-КОЛОКОЛ

ГРАНОВИТАЯ
ПАЛАТА

КОЛОКОЛЬНЯ
ИВАНА ВЕЛИКОГО

АРХАНГЕЛЬСКИЙ
СОБОР

БЛАГОВЕЩЕНСКИЙ
СОБОР

БОЛЬШОЙ
КРЕМЛЕВСКИЙ
ДВОРЕЦ

МОСКВА

МОСКВА

1 СТАДИОН «ДИНАМО»
2 САВЕЛОВСКИЙ ВОКЗАЛ
3 «СОВЕТСКАЯ»
4 ЦЕНТРАЛЬНЫЙ ТЕАТР СОВЕТСКОЙ
АРМИИ
5 РИЖСКИЙ ВОКЗАЛ
6 ИППОДРОМ
7 БЕЛОРУССКИЙ ВОКЗАЛ
8 «ЛЕНИНГРАДСКАЯ»
9 ЛЕНИНГРАДСКИЙ ВОКЗАЛ
10 ЯРОСЛАВСКИЙ ВОКЗАЛ
11 КАЗАНСКИЙ ВОКЗАЛ
12 ВЫСОТНЫЕ ЗДАНИЯ
13 МОСКОВСКИЙ ЗООЛОГИЧЕСКИЙ САД
14 «ПЕКИН»
15 ЦЕНТРАЛЬНЫЙ ТЕАТР КУКОЛ
16 МОСКОВСКАЯ КОНСЕРВАТОРИЯ
ИМЕНИ П. И. ЧАЙКОВСКОГО
17 ПЛАНЕТАРИЙ
18 МОССОВЕТ
19 БОЛЬШОЙ ТЕАТР
20 ПОЛИТЕХНИЧЕСКИЙ МУЗЕЙ
21 «КОЛИЗЕЙ»
22 МОСКОВСКИЙ ГОРОДСКОЙ ДОМ
ПИОНЕРОВ
23 КУРСКИЙ ВОКЗАЛ
24 КИЕВСКИЙ ВОКЗАЛ
25 «УКРАИНА»
26 МУЗЕЙ ИЗОБРАЗИТЕЛЬНЫХ
ИСКУССТВ ИМЕНИ А. С. ПУШКИНА

27 ОТКРЫТЫЙ ПЛАВАТЕЛЬНЫЙ
БАССЕЙН «МОСКВА»
28 НОВО-ДЕВИЧИЙ МОНАСТЫРЬ
29 МУЗЕЙ-УСАДЬБА ЛЬВА Н. ТОЛСТОГО
30 МУЗЕЙ Л. Н. ТОЛСТОГО
31 ВДНХ, РАЗДЕЛ «СТРОИТЕЛЬСТВО И
АРХИТЕКТУРА»
32 ЦЕРКОВЬ НИКОЛЫ В ХАМОВНИКАХ
33 ЦЕНТРАЛЬНЫЙ ПАРК КУЛЬТУРЫ И
ОТДЫХА ИМЕНИ ГОРЬКОГО
34 ЦЕРКОВЬ ИОАННА ВОИНА
35 ЦЕРКОВЬ «ВСЕХ СКОРБЯЩИХ»
36 ТРЕТЬЯКОВСКАЯ ГАЛЕРЕЯ
37 ПАВЕЛЕЦКИЙ ВОКЗАЛ
38 ЦЕРКОВЬ КРУТИЦКОГО
39 МГУ (МОСКОВСКИЙ
ГОСУДАРСТВЕННЫЙ УНИВЕРСИТЕТ)
40 ЦЕНТРАЛЬНЫЙ СТАДИОН ИМЕНИ
В. И. ЛЕНИНА
41 АКАДЕМИЯ НАУК СССР
42 МУЗЕЙ АРХИТЕКТУРЫ
43 ВСЕСОЮЗНАЯ БИБЛИОТЕКА ИМЕНИ
В. И. ЛЕНИНА
44 ТЕЛЕЦЕНТР
45 ДВОРЕЦ ПИОНЕРОВ НА ЛЕНИНСКИХ
ГОРАХ

НАБ.	НАБЕРЕЖНАЯ	Б.	БОЛЬШАЯ
ПЛ.	ПЛОЩАДЬ	М.	МАЛАЯ
ПР.	ПРОСПЕКТ		
УЛ.	УЛИЦА		МЕТРО

ПАРК КУЛЬТУРЫ
И ОТДЫХА «СОКОЛЬНИКИ»

КУЙБЫШЕВСКИЙ

КОМСОМОЛЬСКАЯ ПЛ.

ПЕРВОМАЙСКИЙ

КАЛИНИНСКИЙ

КРЕСТЬЯНСКАЯ
ПЛ.

ЖДАНОВСКИЙ

ПРОЛЕТАРСКИЙ

Modern Russian I

A Project of Syracuse University
under contract with the United States Office of Education

In February 1960 the University of Michigan sponsored a conference of scholars to "develop criteria for a two-year college sequence of specialized materials for learning the Russian language." In its proposal to the U.S. Office of Education for funds to support the conference, the University of Michigan stated its view that "The urgency of our national need to improve and increase the study of the Russian language in our schools and colleges and the comparative dearth and inadequacy of existing materials for this purpose dictate the collaboration of the U.S. Office of Education with the Russian language specialists . . . in the production of a complete two-year college level course in Russian." The proposal advised that "pertinent decisions regarding personnel, institutional sponsorship, and methodology for the production of such a course should be made only on a broadly established basis of consensus among a widely representative group of scholars and specialists in this field." The twenty-seven scholars and specialists listed on the page opposite collaborated at the conference to achieve that consensus, and designated nine persons, similarly listed, as an Advisory Committee to the project.

Recommendations arising from the February 1960 conference and from the Advisory Committee resulted in the naming and empowering of the Working Committee: Dr. Clayton L. Dawson, Professor and Chairman of the Slavic Department at Syracuse University (project coordinator); Dr. Charles E. Bidwell, Associate Professor and Chairman of the Department of Slavic Languages and Literatures, University of Pittsburgh; and Dr. Assya Humesky, Associate Professor of Russian Language and Literature, University of Michigan. Syracuse University undertook to house and administer the entire project, and assumed responsibility for the preparation of the new materials. Both the University of Michigan conference and the University of Syracuse project to produce the two-year course were supported by the U.S. Office of Education, under authority of Title VI of the National Defense Education Act.

The University of Michigan, the University of Pittsburgh, and Syracuse University cooperated by granting leaves of absence to Drs. Humesky, Bidwell, and Dawson respectively. Along with these universities, The American University, the Foreign Service Institute, Georgetown University, Indiana University, St. John's University, the State University College at New Paltz, New York, and the University of Washington participated in the field testing of materials prior to publication, providing helpful suggestions and encouragement. Generous help was provided in typing, advising, and recording by a large group of native Russians teaching in the Slavic Department of Syracuse University. Professors Robert L. Baker of Indiana University and Tatiana Cizevska of the University of Illinois contributed timely information on culture and current usage out of their recent experience in the Soviet Union. Finally, special critical evaluations and recommendations were provided by Professors Baker, Richard Burgi of Princeton University, Kurt Klein of the University of Illinois, and Laurence Thompson of the University of Washington.

Modern Russian, together with the recordings and the teacher's manual prepared to accompany it, unique in both content and techniques in the Russian field, is the fruition of this cooperative group effort.

Modern Russian I

A Project of Syracuse University
under contract with the United States Office of Education

Clayton L. Dawson *Coordinator, Syracuse University*

Charles E. Bidwell *University of Pittsburgh*

Assya Humesky *University of Michigan*

 Harcourt, Brace & World, Inc. *New York / Chicago / San Francisco / Atlanta*

SOURCES OF PHOTOGRAPHS

Title page: View of Red Square, the Kremlin, and Lenin's Tomb.
George Holton from Photo Researchers

  2 Marc Riboud from Magnum Photos
 18 Pressehuset from P.I.P.
 34 Marc Riboud from Magnum Photos
 48 George Holton from Photo Researchers
 60 Marc Riboud from Magnum Photos
 82 Marc Riboud from Magnum Photos
108 Jerry Cooke from Photo Researchers
138 William Vandivert
166 V. Shustov
194 Cornell Capa from Magnum Photos
224 Jerry Cooke from Photo Researchers
252 TASS
278 William Vandivert
308 Marc Riboud from Magnum Photos
334 E. Shulepov from Sovfoto
360 Cornell Capa from Magnum Photos
388 Jerry Cooke from Photo Researchers
418 Marc Riboud from Magnum Photos

Endpaper maps of Moscow and the Soviet Union by Klaus Grutzka

© 1964 by Harcourt, Brace & World, Inc.

This work was produced pursuant to a contract between Syracuse University and the U.S. Office of Education, Department of Health, Education and Welfare.

ISBN: 0-15-562860-7

Library of Congress Catalog Card Number: 64–13285

Printed in the United States of America

Introduction: Using *Modern Russian*

The materials of *Modern Russian*, like those of its prototype, the Modern Language Association's *Modern Spanish*, provide a new kind of language course based on audio-lingual principles and aimed at speaking proficiency within the framework of the traditional language program. *Modern Russian* consists of two volumes of eighteen lessons each, designed for a two-year course meeting from three to five hours a week.

Stressing the fundamental structural features of the contemporary spoken language, the thirty-six lessons present a total vocabulary of some 2700 items. Magnetic tape recordings, available to accompany the written materials, are an integral part of the two-year program. In addition, long-playing disk recordings of basic portions of the lessons are obtainable for home study.

Audio-lingual principles assume that fluency in a foreign language is acquired less by intellectual analysis than by intensive practice. Awareness of structure is acquired not by memorizing rules and paradigms but by imitation and repetition of basic language patterns and by performance of drills carefully constructed to capitalize on the learner's natural inclination to analogize from material already learned. Language learning thus properly begins with listening and repeating and only later proceeds to reading and writing. These first two stages are of primary importance if the student is to gain even a minimum control of spoken Russian; for this reason we recommend strongly that most material be presented and practiced with books closed, both in class and in the laboratory.

A lesson consists of the following parts designed to be used as suggested:

Preparation for Conversation. Anticipating the Conversation to follow, this part presents the basic elements of the Conversation in the order of their appearance, together with parallel English equivalents and, where needed, with phonetic transcription. This material provides a basis for understanding and assimilating the Conversation. Supplementary related words and phrases are also given here.

Conversations. Simulating situations of contemporary Soviet life, these introduce the basic lexical and structural items of the lesson in dialogue form and in colloquial Russian. The first four lessons contain a single Conversation each; the remaining lessons each contain a pair of Conversations. **Notes** explain points of cultural difference and of usage and style. For the first five lessons a parallel English equivalent of each Conversation is provided. A phonetic transcription of the Russian is also given as an aid to proper pronunciation in learning the materials; this is presented consistently in the first ten lessons, but only to clarify special problems thereafter. The Conversations, basic to each lesson, are best assimilated to the point of complete memorization. These are recorded on the tapes—and on the records as well—for individual repeated listening and imitation. They are presented in four stages: (1) the entire dialogue at natural speed without pauses; (2) the individual sentences, broken down from the end, with pauses for student repetition; (3) complete utterances, again with pauses for student repetition; and (4) the entire dialogue once again at natural speed without pauses.

Basic Sentence Patterns. These are sets of patterned sentences, deriving from the Conversations and illustrating the major structural points of the lesson with the use of new and review vocabulary. They are to be mastered through repeated practice. The Basic Sentence Patterns are paralleled by English equivalents.

Pronunciation Practice. To instill habits of correct pronunciation, every lesson provides pronunciation drills, frequently contrastive ones. Additional pronunciation drills, not appearing in the text, are given in the *Teacher's Manual* and on the tapes. Lessons 6 through 11 each present an **Intonation Practice** treating the fundamental patterns of simple sentences.

Structure and Drills. These form the grammatical heart of the course, generally treating four or five major structural points per lesson. Each structural point is developed in five to twelve different drills, with an average of ten responses. The student imitates the models given (generally there are two, the first with an English equivalent), by responding orally to sentences, questions, and/or cues in Russian provided by the teacher. The drills are widely varied: repetition, substitution, question-answer, subject reversal, transformation, structure replacement, integration, expansion, and progressive substitution. All drills are fully recorded on the tapes with appropriate pauses for student responses, followed by the confirming responses. To make the procedure clear, the desired responses for the first two lessons are printed in full. A discussion of a structural point generally follows the drills in which it has been developed.

Reading and Writing. Essentially a recapitulation of the lexical and structural items in the lesson and a review of past items, this part is a reworking of the Conversation materials and provides practice in reading. The portions presented in handwritten form invite practice in dictation or copying (easily self-corrected), as well as in reading a cursive script. Translation of the readings is *not* recommended; comprehension can best be checked by questions in Russian as provided in the *Teacher's Manual.*

Experience suggests that presentation of dialogues is most effective when delivered at a normal conversational speed in natural word groupings (not as words in isolation), with a natural intonation. Class choral repetition is helpful in presenting new Conversations in order to bring the class into active participation, and choral recitation of the parts of the dialogue by designated groups of the class provides a useful check on memorizing the Conversations. Memorizing the Conversations, though not indispensable, does result in higher achievement in the structural drills. Intensive drill on the Preparation for Conversation and class practice on the Conversation, followed by the use of the tape in the language laboratory and/or the records at home, can make memorizing the Conversation a relatively simple task.

Practice in writing—whether mere copying or writing out drill responses specifically assigned for that purpose—should not be neglected, despite the strong oral emphasis of *Modern Russian*. The writing of selected drills tends to reinforce mastery of the structure and to check on progress being made.

Normally a lesson will take five meetings to cover, though clearly the longer the time spent on a lesson, the more complete the mastery of it is likely to be. The first four lessons are shorter and may therefore be covered in four sessions each. Where classes meet only three hours a week, drills which cannot be covered in class may be assigned for performance in a language laboratory. A course of three class hours a week has been successfully given by Syracuse University with these materials on just such a basis.

Contents

Modern Russian I

A Project of Syracuse University
under contract with the United States Office of Education

The Russian sound system

Russian sounds may be divided into two basic groups: vowels and consonants.

A. The vowels

Russian has five basic vowel sounds, all of them shorter than the very approximate English vowels given here for the sake of a rough comparison.[1]

[a]	star	[tám, vás]
[o]	port	[ón, nós]
[e]	met	[étu, jél]
[i]	machine	[i, iván]
[u]	lunar, soon	[nú, kúm]

As aids to pronunciation, we also give two additional symbols to represent positional variants of [a] and [i].

| [ə] | sofa, about | [pápə, ókələ] |
| [ɨ] | ship, weary | [bɨk, sɨn] |

> Sound Drill 1: Practice the Russian examples illustrating the vowel sounds, imitating your instructor (or the tape) as accurately as you can.[2]

B. The consonants

Russian consonants fall into two main groups, which we call "hard" and "soft." Hard consonants are pronounced with the main body of the tongue flattened, creating a hollow, open, mouth cavity. Soft consonants, conversely, are pronounced with the tongue raised in an arc, creating a narrowed mouth cavity and a restricted passage of air.

The consonants may be divided into four subgroups: those which occur in both soft and hard varieties regardless of what sound follows, those whose hardness or softness depends on the sound that follows, those which are only hard, and those which are only soft.

---

[1] In illustrating the sounds we use a transcription based on Latin characters, some slightly modified in form.
[2] Sound Drills 1–5 are recorded on tape and printed in the Teacher's Manual.

1. Consonants which occur in both hard and soft varieties regardless of the sound that follows.[1]

[m]	**m**oose	[móst, tám]
[m̦]	a**m**use	[m̦éstə, m̦átə]
[b]	**b**oots	[bábə, búdu]
[b̦]	**b**eauty	[b̦ít, ab̦édə]
[p]	**p**oor	[pápkə, sláp]
[p̦]	**p**ure	[sp̦í, p̦ós]
[v]	**v**oice	[vám, slóvə]
[v̦]	**v**iew	[v̦ízə, v̦étkə]
[f]	**f**ood	[fú, slóf]
[f̦]	**f**eud	[f̦ín, astáf̦]
[n]	**n**ow	[nós, vón]
[n̦]	me**n**u	[n̦ós, n̦ét]
[d]	**d**o	[dá, dímə]
[d̦]	a**d**ieu, shoul**d** you	[d̦ád̦ə, d̦ímə]
[t]	s**t**ool	[tót, tút]
[ț]	cos**t**ume, wha**t** youth	[țók, máț]
[z]	**z**oom	[zónə, vázə]
[z̦]	pre**s**ume (British), he'**s** young	[z̦imá, vaz̦mú]
[s]	**s**wim	[sók, vús]
[ș]	a**ss**ume, thi**s** youth	[șádu, p̦ișmó]
[r]	trilled r (as in Spanish or Italian)	[ruká, urók]
[r̦]	soft trilled r (no equivalent)	[r̦iká, gəvar̦ú]
[l]	be**l**t	[lámpə, stól]
[l̦]	mi**ll**ion	[l̦águ, stál̦]

> Sound Drill 2: Practice the Russian examples illustrating these hard and soft consonant pairs, imitating your instructor (or the tape) as accurately as you can. Note that Russian consonants do not have the slight puff of breath characteristic of such English consonants as p, t, and k in certain positions.

2. Consonants whose hardness or softness ordinarily depends on the sound that follows.

The consonants [k], [g], and [x] are ordinarily pronounced hard, but are replaced by their soft alternates [k̦], [g̦], and [x̦] respectively when followed by the vowels [e] and [i]:

[k]	**sk**ill, **sc**at	[kák, drúk]
[k̦]	a**c**ute, **c**ure	[k̦inó, k̦ém]
[g]	**g**o	[gúm, góləs]
[g̦]	ar**g**ue	[nóg̦i, nag̦é]
[x]	(no English equivalent; something like the Scotch or German **ch** in lo**ch** or a**ch**)	[xudój, áx]
[x̦]	(soft variety; no equivalent)	[x̦ím̦ik, branx̦ít]

> Sound Drill 3: Practice the Russian examples illustrating these sounds, imitating your instructor (or the tape) as accurately as you can.

---

[1] In the transcription, a small hook under the letter marks the soft consonant. Notice that the soft consonant has somewhat the effect of a "y-like" glide following the consonant.

3. Consonants which occur only in a hard variety regardless of the sound that follows:

[c]	**its, waltz**	[caŗícə, aṭéc]
[š]	**sh**rimp	[škáf, šútkə]
[ž]	a**z**ure, lei**s**ure	[žúk, užé]

> Sound Drill 4: Practice the Russian examples illustrating these sounds, imitating your instructor (or the tape) as accurately as you can. Note that the Russian [c] is a single sound unit, and that both [š] and [ž] are articulated farther back in the throat than the comparable English sounds.

4. Consonants which occur only in a soft variety, regardless of the sound that follows:

[č]	**ch**eap	[čás, dóč]
[šč]	fre**sh ch**eese or wa**sh sh**eets (pronounced as a single sound unit)	[ščí, jiščó]
[j]	**y**es, bo**y**	[já, mój]

> Sound Drill 5: Practice the Russian examples illustrating these sounds, imitating your instructor (or the tape) as accurately as you can.

The Russian (Cyrillic) alphabet and the writing system

Russian does not use the Latin alphabet employed by English and such Western European languages as French, German, Spanish, and Italian. Rather, Russian uses another alphabet, called the Cyrillic. It is basically modeled after the Greek alphabet, but is supplemented by additional symbols for certain sounds occurring in the Slavic languages but not in Greek. Other Slavic peoples using the Cyrillic alphabet include the Ukrainians, Byelorussians, Bulgarians, Macedonians, and Serbs; while the Czechs, Poles, Slovaks, Slovenes, and Croats use the Latin alphabet.

The Russian (Cyrillic) alphabet is given below in its conventional order, together with typical pronunciations of the letters and illustrative examples. Note that most letters are pronounced in more than one way, depending upon where they occur or the place of stress in the word.[1]

THE ALPHABET	TYPICAL PRONUNCIATION	EXAMPLES
А а	[a]	**а**, т**á**м
	[ə]	м**á**м**а**
Б б	[b]	**б**áк, **б**á**б**а
	[b̦]	ó**б**е, те**б**é
	[p]	бó**б**, бá**б**ка
В в	[v]	**в**áм, **в**óт
	[ɣ]	**в**éк
	[f]	**в** тóм
Г г	[g]	**г**отóва, тó**г**а
	[g̦]	бé**г**е, тó**г**е
	[k]	бé**г**, мó**г**
	[v]	то**г**ó, какó**г**о

---

[1] Stress is marked with an acute (´) accent over the vowel.

Д д	[d]	дá, дóм
	[ḍ]	гдé, водé, одéт
	[t]	обéд, гóд, вóдка
Е е	[e]	обéд, вéтка, тé
	[je]	éм, éдет
	[i]	дóме, бедá
	[ji]	едá, егó
Ё ё	[o]	мёд, тёте
	[jo]	её, моё
Ж ж	[ž]	дáже, жáба
	[š]	ёж, одёжка
З з	[z]	завóд, бáза
	[ẓ]	зевóк, везёт
	[s]	вóз, гáз
И и	[i]	и́, зимá, ги́д
	[ji]	мои́, твои́
	[ɨ]	живёт
Й й	[j]	мóй, такóй, мáйка, йóд
К к	[k]	кáк, вóдка
	[ḳ]	кéм, Китáй
Л л	[l]	лóжка, ви́лка, ви́дел
	[ḷ]	лёд, лéто, болéли
М м	[m]	мóй, тáм
	[ṃ]	мéл, тéми
Н н	[n]	но, онá
	[ṇ]	нéт, они́
О о	[o]	дóм, завóд, вóдка
	[a]	окнó, словá
	[ə]	мáло, молокó
П п	[p]	пойдём
	[ṗ]	пи́л, пéние
Р р	[r]	рукá, ми́р
	[ṛ]	рекá, мóре
С с	[s]	скажи́, вáс, доскá
	[ṣ]	сéл, Семён, неси́
Т т	[t]	тáм, привéт
	[ṭ]	тéм, тёк
У у	[u]	у́тро, кудá, иду́
Ф ф	[f]	фóрма, фáкт
	[ḟ]	Фёкла, Фили́пп
Х х	[x]	áх, хóлодно, хлéб
	[x̣]	хи́мик, Хитрóв

Ц ц	[c]	отéц, цари́ца
Ч ч	[č]	чáй, пóчта, врáч
Ш ш	[š]	шáр, шýм, хорошó
Щ щ	[šč]	щи́, бóрщ, ещё
Ъ ъ	(hard sign)[1]	
Ы ы	[ɨ]	ты́, вы́, бы́ло, рáды
Ь ь	(soft sign)[1]	
Э э	[e]	э́то, э́тот, э́ти, поэ́т
Ю ю	[u]	Вáню, всю́, бюрó
	[ju]	ю́бка, свою́, мою́
Я я	[a]	пя́ть, опя́ть, говоря́т
	[i]	пяти́, тяжелó
	[ja]	я́, твоя́, стоя́л
	[ji]	язы́к
	[jə]	пéния, до свидáния

Remarks on stress

A. Stress in the word

A stressed vowel is one pronounced with greater intensity or loudness than an unstressed vowel. Words of more than one syllable can have only one syllable which is stressed in Russian. This contrasts sharply with English, where many words have more than one stress, for example:

> ENGLISH pròpagánda
> RUSSIAN пропагáнда [prəpagándə]

When words are combined in a sentence in Russian, certain short words may receive no stress. For example, prepositions such as **у** and **на**, and the negative particle **не** are normally pronounced as though they were part of the following word:

> у неё [uɲijó]
> на пóчту [napóčtu]
> не ви́дел [ɲiɣídil]

B. The major segment

A Russian sentence may consist of a single word or of one or more groups of words. Each group contains one word which has an even stronger stress than any of the other stressed words in the group. We call the groups *major segments* and the strongest stress in each group the *major stress*. We call the remaining word stresses in the major segment *secondary stresses*. The boundary between major segments represents a point where a short slowing up or pause may be made in speaking. In our transcription, the major sentence stress will be indicated by a double accent mark (″), and the secondary or word stress will have a single acute accent mark (′). On the material printed in Cyrillic, only the single accent mark will be used for both major sentence stress and word stress.

---

[1] The hard sign **твёрдый знáк** and soft sign **мя́гкий знáк** have no sound value. For a description of their function, see page 9.

Division of a sentence into major segments will often depend on the individual speaking style and tempo. A given sentence in rapid speech will be spoken with fewer major segments than the same utterance in slow deliberate speech. But the segmentation is not arbitrary—there are some places where a major segment boundary may be made and others where it will be rare or nonexistent. For example, a major segment boundary does not occur between a preposition and the following word, and it rarely occurs between an adjective and the noun it qualifies.

In neutral, unemphatic style, the major stress usually falls on the last word of each major segment. In statements, a shift of the major stress to another word in the segment shifts the emphasis to that word:

NEUTRAL Я иду́ домо́й. [já idú damój] I'm going *home*.
SPECIAL Я иду́ домо́й. [já idǘ damój] I *am* going home.
or Я иду́ домо́й. [já idú damój] *I'm* going home.

To sum up, we indicate the degrees of stress (loudness) as follows:

1. Major stress (one per major segment)—double accent mark on transcription, single accent mark on Cyrillic.
2. Secondary or word stress (no more than one per word)—single acute accent mark.
3. No stress—no accent mark.

EXAMPLE Я иду́ на по́чту. [já idú napóčtu]

Above all, the student should bear in mind that the best guide to accurate pronunciation is the way a native speaker actually pronounces the words, not the written representation of stress.

Discrepancies between the sound system and the writing system

A. Use of the same consonant letter to write both hard and soft consonant varieties

As we know, most Russian consonant sounds come in hard and soft varieties. It is a peculiarity of the writing system and the alphabet, however, that the same letter often represents both a hard and soft consonant in writing. For example, both hard [n] and soft [ņ] are written н in Cyrillic; only the following letter can tell us whether it is hard or soft. Compare нóс [nós] with нёс [ņós].

B. Double set of vowel letters in the writing system

To preserve the distinction between hard and soft consonants in the writing system, the Russian alphabet employs a double set of vowel letters which may be termed "hard-" and "soft-series" vowel letters. In themselves the vowels are neither hard nor soft; rather, they indicate the hardness or softness of the preceding consonant. Thus "hard-series" vowel letter **a** typically follows a hard consonant, and "soft-series" vowel letter **я** typically follows a soft consonant.

HARD SERIES	SOFT SERIES
а	я
э	е
ы	и
о	ё
у	ю

	HARD CONSONANT PLUS VOWEL					SOFT CONSONANT PLUS VOWEL				
WRITTEN	ба	бо	бу	бэ	бы	бя	бё	бю	бе	би
PRONOUNCED	[ba	bo	bu	be	bɨ]	[ba̦	bo̦	bu̦	be̦	bi̦]
WRITTEN	да	до	ду	дэ	ды	дя	дё	дю	де	ди
PRONOUNCED	[da	do	du	de	dɨ]	[d̦a	d̦o	d̦u	d̦e	d̦i]
WRITTEN	ма	мо	му	мэ	мы	мя	мё	мю	ме	ми
PRONOUNCED	[ma	mo	mu	me	mɨ]	[m̦a	m̦o	m̦u	m̦e	m̦i]
WRITTEN	та	то	ту	тэ	ты	тя	тё	тю	те	ти
PRONOUNCED	[ta	to	tu	te	tɨ]	[ța	țo	țu	țe	ți]

The special symbol **ь** indicates the softness of a preceding consonant when no vowel letter follows.[1] Remember that this sign is not a vowel, i.e., it has no independent sound value. It is merely an alphabetic device to show that the preceding consonant is soft. It is written principally at the end of a word or between consonants.

	HARD CONSONANT NOT FOLLOWED BY VOWEL		SOFT CONSONANT NOT FOLLOWED BY VOWEL	
WRITTEN	сто́л	table	сто́ль	so much
PRONOUNCED	[stól]		[stól̦]	
WRITTEN	бра́т	brother	брать	to take
PRONOUNCED	[brát]		[bráț]	
WRITTEN	у́гол	corner	у́голь	coal
PRONOUNCED	[úgəl]		[úgəl̦]	
WRITTEN	по́лка	shelf	по́лька	polka
PRONOUNCED	[pólkə]		[pól̦kə]	

C. Soft-series vowel letters at the beginning of a word or following another vowel letter

The soft-series vowel letters **я**, **ё**, **е**, and **ю**, also serve another function. At the beginning of a word following another vowel letter, they are written to represent the consonant sound [j] (written elsewhere **й**) plus a vowel. Thus **я** in these positions is equivalent to **й** plus **a**; **ё** is equivalent to **й** plus **o**; **e** is equivalent to **й** plus **э**, and **ю** is equivalent to **й** plus **y**.

WRITTEN	я́ма	моя́	ёж	моё	е́сть	мое́й	юг	мою́
PRONOUNCED	[jámə	majá	jóš	majó	jésț	majéj	júk	majú]

The soft-series vowel letter **и** differs from the others in that there is usually no preceding [j] sound in initial position, and there is a rather weak [j] between vowels:

и́мя	мой
[ím̦ə]	[mají] *or* [maí]

D. The hard sign ъ and soft sign ь

There are two letters in the Russian alphabet with no independent sound value. They are called **твёрдый знак** *hard sign* **ъ** and **мягкий знак** *soft sign* **ь**.

---

[1] See item D below, for fuller treatment of this symbol.

1. THE SOFT SIGN

Of the two symbols, the soft sign ь is much more frequently encountered and serves two major purposes:

a. To indicate consonant softness at the end of a word or before another consonant: пять [p̣át] *five*, то́лько [tólkə] *only*, чита́ть [čitát] *to read*.

b. To indicate that a preceding consonant is soft *and* that the next vowel is preceded by the sound [j]: семья́ [s̨im̨já] *family*, пьёт [p̨jót] *he drinks*.

Note: Although the soft sign is sometimes written after the consonants ж and ш for historic reasons, these consonants are nevertheless pronounced hard: мужья́ [mužjá] *husbands*, идёшь [iḍóš] *you're going*.

2. THE HARD SIGN

The hard sign ъ in modern Russian is only used after prefixes ending in a consonant followed by a soft-series vowel. It indicates that a [j] sound precedes this vowel: съе́л [sjél] *he ate up*, отъе́зд [atjést] *departure*.

PREPARATION FOR CONVERSATION   **Студе́нт и студе́нтка**

Except in certain fixed expressions, nouns are first given in their nominative case form. The nominative case is primarily used to indicate the subject of a sentence or clause. Russian nouns are of three genders: masculine, feminine, and neuter. Masculine nouns usually terminate in a consonant letter, feminine ones in –a or –я, and neuters in –o or –e. The gender of nouns will be indicated in the Preparation for Conversation only where it is not obvious from the nominative form, as for example: две́рь (f) *door*, де́нь (m) *day*. For the time being verbs and adjectives will be given only in the form in which they occur in the conversation.

студе́нт [stuḍént]	student
и [i]	and
студе́нтка [stuḍéntkə]	girl student, coed
Евге́ний [jivgéṇij]	Evgeny
Ни́на [ṇínə]	Nina
приве́т [p̣riɣét]	greetings! regards! hi!
Приве́т, Ни́на![1]	Hi, Nina!
вы́ идёте [ví iḍoṭi]	you're going, you're on your way
куда́ [kudá]	where, where to, to what place
Куда́ вы́ идёте?	Where are you going?
уро́к [urók]	lesson, a lesson, the lesson[2]
на уро́к [nəurók]	to the lesson, to class
пе́ние [p̣éṇijə]	singing
уро́к пе́ния [urók p̣éṇijə]	singing class, a singing lesson
На уро́к пе́ния.	To a singing lesson.
я иду́ [já idú]	I'm going, I'm on my way
Я иду́ на уро́к пе́ния.	I'm going to a singing lesson.
а [a]	and, but, by the way, how about
домо́й [damój]	home, homeward
А вы́ домо́й?	And are you on your way home?

---

[1] Boldface sentences in the Preparation for Conversation are those that appear in the Conversation itself.
[2] Notice that Russian does not have definite or indefinite articles corresponding to English *the, a, an.*

10   LESSON 1

нét [ņét] — no
пóчта [póčtə] — post office
на пóчту [napóčtu] — to the post office
Нéт, я идý на пóчту. — No, I'm on my way to the post office.
письмó [ṕişmó] — a letter
послáть письмó [paslát́ ṕişmó] — to send a letter
Я идý на пóчту послáть письмó. — I'm going to the post office to send a letter.

собрáние [sabráņjə] — meeting, a meeting, the meeting
бы́ло [bílə] — was, there was
вчерá [fčirá] — yesterday
Вчерá бы́ло собрáние? — Was there a meeting yesterday?
скажи́те [skažíţi] — say! tell [me]!
Скажи́те, вчерá бы́ло собрáние? — Say, was there a meeting yesterday?

бы́ло [bílə] — there was
нé было [ņébilə] — there wasn't
Нéт, нé было. — No, there wasn't.
клýб [klúp] — club
в клýбе [fklúb̦i] — in the club, at the club
В клýбе? Нéт, нé было. — At the club? No, there wasn't.

завóд [zavót] — plant, factory
на завóде [nəzavód̦i] — at the plant, at the factory
А на завóде? — How about at the plant?

тáм [tám] — there
я нé был [já ņébil] — I wasn't
Я тáм нé был. — I wasn't there.
но [no] — but
Бы́ло, но я тáм нé был. — There was [a meeting], but I wasn't there.

нý [nú] — well
извини́те [izɣiņíţi] — excuse [me]
Нý, извини́те. — Well, excuse [me].

автóбус [aftóbus] — bus
мóй автóбус [mój aftóbus] — my bus
вóт идёт [vót id̦ót] — here comes, there goes
Вóт идёт мóй автóбус. — Here comes my bus.

до свидáния [dəsɣidáņjə] — good-bye, I'll be seeing you
До свидáния. — Good-bye.

SUPPLEMENT

я идý [já idú] — I'm going
ты́ идёшь [tí id̦óš] — you're going[1]
óн идёт [ón id̦ót] — he's going
онá идёт [aná id̦ót] — she's going
мы́ идём [mí id̦óm] — we're going
вы́ идётè [ví id̦óţi] — you're going[1]
они́ идýт [aņí idút] — they're going

---

[1] **Ты́** *you* is used in addressing a close friend or a member of one's family. **Вы́** *you* is used in addressing a person where a more formal relationship exists, and it is also used whenever more than one person is addressed.

CLASSROOM EXPRESSIONS

The following are some of the classroom words and expressions your instructor will be using. Be sure you are able to recognize them when you hear them.

ещё ра́з [jiščó rás]	once again, once more
повтори́те [pəftaŗíţi]	repeat!
пожа́луйста [pažáləstə]	please
говори́те [gəvaŗíţi]	speak! talk!
гро́мче [grómči]	louder
все́ вме́сте [fşé vm̧éşţi]	all together
чита́йте [čitájţi]	read!
хорошо́ [xərašó]	good, fine, all right
пло́хо [plóxə]	bad, poor, not good
лу́чше [lúčšɨ]	better

Студе́нт и студе́нтка*[,1]

Boy student and girl student

The following symbols are used in the transcription of the conversations to give the student some notion of the inflection of the voice at the end of a phrase or sentence:

↓ indicates a dropping off of the voice
↑ indicates a rise of the voice
| indicates voice level sustained

Е. — Евге́ний (студе́нт) Evgeny (a student)
Н. — Ни́на (студе́нтка) Nina (a girl student)

Е.	1	Приве́т, Ни́на! Куда́ вы́ идёте?	p̧ŗiy̧e̋t ņínə ↓ kudá vɨ́ iḑőţi ↓	Hi, Nina! Where are you going?
Н.	2	На уро́к пе́ния. А вы́ домо́й?	nəurók p̧e̋ņijə ↓ a vɨ́ damőj ↑	To a singing lesson. And you're on your way home?[2]
Е.	3	Не́т, я иду́ на по́чту посла́ть письмо́.	ņe̋t ↓ já idú napőčtu | pasláţ p̧işmő ↓	No, I'm on my way to the post office to send a letter.
Н.	4	Скажи́те, вчера́ бы́ло собра́ние?	skažı̋ţi ↓ fčirá bɨ̋lə sabráņjə ↓	Say, was there a meeting yesterday?
Е.	5	В клу́бе? Не́т, не́ было.	fklűb̧i ↑ ņe̋t ↓ ņe̋bɨlə ↓	At the club?[3] No, there wasn't.
Н.	6	А на заво́де?	a nəzavőḑi ↑	How about at the plant? [4,5]
Е.	7	Бы́ло, но́ я та́м не́ был.	bɨ̋lə | nó já tám ņe̋bɨl ↓	There was, but I wasn't there.

* Superscript numerals in the Conversation refer to the Notes immediately following.

H.	8	Ну́, извини́те.	nű | izɣiṇíţi ↓	Well, excuse me. Here comes my
		Во́т идёт	vót iḍót	bus.
		мо́й авто́бус.	mój aftŏbus ↓	
E.	9	До свида́ния.	dəsɣidáṇjə ↓	I'll be seeing you.
H.	10	До свида́ния.	dəsɣidáṇjə ↓	Good-bye.

NOTES

[1] The terms **студе́нт** and **студе́нтка** refer only to university students, as compared with **учени́к** and **учени́ца** which designate pupils or students below university level. Russians make a much sharper distinction than we in the terms used for university level as opposed to pre-university level, for example:

UNIVERSITY LEVEL		PRE-UNIVERSITY LEVEL		
профе́ссор	*professor*	учи́тель (m) учи́тельница (f)		*teacher*
университе́т	*university*	шко́ла		*school*
ле́кция	*lecture*	уро́к		*lesson, class*

[2] Russian has two words **и** and **а** both meaning *and*. **И** is used as a simple connector:

студе́нт **и** студе́нтка   boy *and* girl student

whereas **а** is used to point up a contrast or to introduce a new topic:

Я иду́ на уро́к. **А** вы́ домо́й?   I'm going to a lesson. *And* you,
                                             are you going home?

[3] **Клу́б** means *club* in the sense of a group of working associates who meet for recreational or informal educational purposes. Clubs in the Soviet Union play a political-educational role in encouraging useful hobbies such as radio, photography, or airplane modeling; or in the study of technical subjects, mathematics, botany, zoology, and so forth. Recreational activities include amateur performances, dances, and games such as chess.

[4] It is not uncommon in the Soviet Union for university students to work in a factory during the day and attend classes in the evening. Unless they are excellent students, secondary school graduates generally must work for two years before entering the university.

[5] Notice that *at* in Russian is **на** in **на заво́де** *at the plant*, but **в** in **в клу́бе** *at the club*. Certain nouns require the preposition **на** in this meaning, while other nouns require **в**. In the same way, when these prepositions are used in the meaning *to*, **на** must be used with **заво́д** (**на заво́д** *to the plant*) and **в** must be used with **клу́б** (**в клу́б** *to the club*).

Basic sentence patterns

The material in this section gives some of the possible variants of utterances found in the conversation. It is designed to provide the student with certain basic patterns before an analysis of the structure is given and before he is asked to manipulate the specific grammatical items. In this way it is hoped that he will not only be able to observe the over-all structural patterns of Russian, but also have some ready-made utterances for active use when he begins to converse. The material should be thoroughly drilled as repetition practice with books closed as the first step. After this, it may be used for reading practice.

1. Куда́ вы́ идёте?
   — На уро́к пе́ния.
   — Я́ иду́ на уро́к пе́ния.
   — На по́чту.
   — Я́ иду́ на по́чту.
   — На собра́ние.
   — Я́ иду́ на собра́ние.
   — На заво́д.
   — Я́ иду́ на заво́д.

Where are you going?
To a singing lesson.
I'm going to a singing lesson.
To the post office.
I'm going to the post office.
To a meeting.
I'm going to a meeting.
To the plant.
I'm going to the plant.

2. Куда́ ты́ идёшь?
   — На по́чту посла́ть письмо́.
   — Я́ иду́ на по́чту посла́ть письмо́.
   — Домо́й.
   — Я́ иду́ домо́й.
   — В клу́б.
   — Я́ иду́ в клу́б.

Where are you going?
To the post office to send a letter.
I'm going to the post office to send a letter.
Home.
I'm going home.
To the club.
I'm going to the club.

3. Во́т идёт мо́й авто́бус.
   _____ Евге́ний.
   _____ Ни́на.
   _____ студе́нт.
   _____ студе́нтка.
   Во́т иду́т Евге́ний и Ни́на.
   _____ студе́нт и студе́нтка.

Here comes my bus.
_____ Evgeny.
_____ Nina.
_____ a student.
_____ a girl student.
Here come Evgeny and Nina.
_____ a boy and a girl student.

STRUCTURE AND DRILLS

The present tense of the first conjugation verb идти́

я́ иду́	I'm going, I'm on my way, I'm coming
ты́ идёшь	you're going, you're on your way, you're coming
о́н идёт	he's going
она́ идёт	she's going
мы́ идём	we're going
вы́ идёте	you're going
они́ иду́т	they're going

■ REPETITION DRILL

Listen to your instructor (or the tape) and repeat the above pronoun-verb model until you can say it perfectly.

■ REPETITION-SUBSTITUTION DRILL

Repeat after your instructor (or the tape) as accurately as you can, imitating both the individual words and the sentence intonation. Then, on hearing only the subject pronoun, give the full sentence.[1]

---

[1] Complete student answers are given in the first two lessons only. Although instructions for the drills are addressed to the student, he is advised to perform them without looking at the printed page, preferably with his book closed. Boldface type always indicates the "model" sentence to be spoken by the student; the corresponding lightface sentence is the "model" to be spoken by the teacher. The English translation appears in italic type.

TEACHER	STUDENT
I'm going home	*I'm going home.*
Я́ иду́ домо́й.	**Я́ иду́ домо́й.**
Ты́ идёшь домо́й.	Ты́ идёшь домо́й.
Óн идёт домо́й.	Óн идёт домо́й.
Она́ идёт домо́й.	Она́ идёт домо́й.
Мы́ идём домо́й.	Мы́ идём домо́й.
Вы́ идёте домо́й.	Вы́ идёте домо́й.
Они́ иду́т домо́й.	Они́ иду́т домо́й.

■ QUESTION-ANSWER DRILL

Answer the question, using **на по́чту** with both short and full answers. (In class two students may participate.)

TEACHER	STUDENT
Where are you going?	*To the post office.*
Where are you going?	*I'm going to the post office.*
Куда́ вы́ идёте?	**На по́чту.**
Куда́ вы́ идёте?	**Я́ иду́ на по́чту.**
Куда́ ты́ идёшь?	На по́чту.
Куда́ ты́ идёшь?	Я́ иду́ на по́чту.
Куда́ о́н идёт?	На по́чту.
Куда́ о́н идёт?	О́н идёт на по́чту.
Куда́ мы́ идём?	На по́чту.
Куда́ мы́ идём?	Мы́ идём на по́чту.
Куда́ она́ идёт?	На по́чту.
Куда́ она́ идёт?	Она́ идёт на по́чту.
Куда́ вы́ идёте?	На по́чту.
Куда́ вы́ идёте?	Я́ иду́ на по́чту.
Куда́ они́ иду́т?	На по́чту.
Куда́ они́ иду́т?	Они́ иду́т на по́чту.

■ QUESTION-ANSWER DRILL

Answer the question, using **на собра́ние,** with both short and full answers.

TEACHER	STUDENT
Where are you going, home?	*No, to a meeting.*
Where are you going, home?	*No, I'm going to a meeting.*
Куда́ вы́ идёте, домо́й?	**Не́т, на собра́ние.**
Куда́ вы́ идёте, домо́й?	**Не́т, я́ иду́ на собра́ние.**
Куда́ о́н идёт, домо́й?	Не́т, на собра́ние.
Куда́ о́н идёт, домо́й?	Не́т, о́н идёт на собра́ние.
Куда́ она́ идёт, домо́й?	Не́т, на собра́ние.
Куда́ она́ идёт, домо́й?	Не́т, она́ идёт на собра́ние.
Куда́ мы́ идём, домо́й?	Не́т, на собра́ние.
Куда́ мы́ идём, домо́й?	Не́т, мы́ идём на собра́ние.
Куда́ они́ иду́т, домо́й?	Не́т, на собра́ние.
Куда́ они́ иду́т, домо́й?	Не́т, они́ иду́т на собра́ние.
Куда́ ты́ идёшь, домо́й?	Не́т, на собра́ние.
Куда́ ты́ идёшь, домо́й?	Не́т, я́ иду́ на собра́ние.

Answer two ways, using **на уро́к пе́ния.**

TEACHER	STUDENT
Where's Nina going?	*To a singing lesson.*
Where's Nina going?	*Nina's going to a singing lesson.*
Куда́ идёт Ни́на?	**На уро́к пе́ния.**
Куда́ идёт Ни́на?	**Ни́на идёт на уро́к пе́ния.**
Куда́ идёт Евге́ний?	На уро́к пе́ния.
Куда́ идёт Евге́ний?	Евге́ний идёт на уро́к пе́ния.
Куда́ идёт студе́нт?	На уро́к пе́ния.
Куда́ идёт студе́нт?	Студе́нт идёт на уро́к пе́ния.
Куда́ идёт студе́нтка?	На уро́к пе́ния.
Куда́ идёт студе́нтка?	Студе́нтка идёт на уро́к пе́ния.

■ SUBSTITUTION DRILLS

Items to be cued by the teacher are indicated in parentheses.

1. *The student is going to a meeting.*

Студе́нт идёт на собра́ние.	**Студе́нт идёт на собра́ние.**
(Студе́нт и студе́нтка) ____.	Студе́нт и студе́нтка иду́т на собра́ние.
(Óн) _____.	Óн идёт на собра́ние.
(Она́) _____.	Она́ идёт на собра́ние.
(Они́) _____.	Они́ иду́т на собра́ние.
(Евге́ний) _____.	Евге́ний идёт на собра́ние.
(Ни́на) _____.	Ни́на идёт на собра́ние.
(Евге́ний и Ни́на) _____.	Евге́ний и Ни́на иду́т на собра́ние.

2. *Here comes my bus.*

Вóт идёт мóй авто́бус.	**Вóт идёт мóй авто́бус.**
Вóт идёт Ни́на.	**Вóт идёт Ни́на.**
_____ (Евге́ний).	Вóт идёт Евге́ний.
_____ (студе́нт).	Вóт идёт студе́нт.
_____ (студе́нтка).	Вóт идёт студе́нтка.
_____ (мóй авто́бус).	Вóт идёт мóй авто́бус.
_____ (Евге́ний и Ни́на).	Вóт иду́т Евге́ний и Ни́на.
_____ (студе́нт и студе́нтка).	Вóт иду́т студе́нт и студе́нтка.

■ QUESTION-ANSWER DRILL

Answer the following questions, using a pronoun and **в клу́б** in the answer.

TEACHER	STUDENT
Where's the student going?	*He's on his way to the club.*
Куда́ идёт студе́нт?	**Óн идёт в клу́б.**
Куда́ иду́т студе́нтка и студе́нт?	Они́ иду́т в клу́б.
Куда́ идёт Евге́ний?	Óн идёт в клу́б.
Куда́ иду́т Ни́на и Евге́ний?	Они́ иду́т в клу́б.
Куда́ идёт Ни́на?	Она́ идёт в клу́б.
Куда́ иду́т студе́нт и студе́нтка?	Они́ иду́т в клу́б.

As you have noticed, the endings of the verb **идти́** in the present tense change for each person in the singular and plural. Thus the first person singular is **я иду́**, second person singular **ты́ идёшь**, third person singular **о́н** (*or* **она́**) **идёт**, and so forth.

The present stem of the verb is **ид–**, and the stress is on the endings throughout the conjugation. Note that the stem consonant **д** is hard in the first person singular and third person plural, but is soft in all the other forms.

	SINGULAR			PLURAL	
1	ид–у́	[id–ú]		ид–ём	[iḏ–óm]
2	ид–ёшь[1]	[iḏ–óš]		ид–ёте	[iḏ–óṭi]
3	ид–ёт	[iḏ–ót]		ид–у́т	[id–út]

This pattern of endings is typical of first conjugation verbs with the stress on the endings. There are only two conjugations in Russian; the second will be discussed later.

It is important to note that **идти́** means both *to be going* and *to be coming*. It describes motion in process and is generally restricted to going on foot.

---

[1] It is a convention in Russian to spell the second person singular ending with a **ь**, even though the consonant **ш** cannot be pronounced soft. Notice also that since the letter **ё** *always* carries the stress, it is unnecessary to mark the stress further.

PREPARATION FOR CONVERSATION

Давно́ ва́с не ви́дел

не ви́дел [ṇiɣíḍil]	haven't seen, didn't see
ва́с [vás]	you (dir obj)
давно́ [davnó]	for a long time, a long time ago
Давно́ ва́с не ви́дел.	I haven't seen you for a long time.
всю́ зи́му [fṣú ẓímu]	all winter, all winter long
Всю́ зи́му ва́с не ви́дел.	I haven't seen you all winter.
ка́к дела́ [kág ḍilá]	how is everything
а́ *long* [á]	ah, oh
А́, Кири́лл Па́влович! Ка́к дела́?	Ah, Kirill Pavlovich! How is everything?
хорошо́ [xərašó]	well, fine, good
спаси́бо [spaṣíbə]	thanks, thank you
Хорошо́, спаси́бо.	Fine, thanks.
больны́ [baḷṇí]	sick, ill
вы́ бы́ли [ví bíḷi]	you were
Вы́ бы́ли больны́.	You were sick.
я́ слы́шал [já slíšəl]	I heard
Я́ слы́шал, вы́ бы́ли больны́.	I heard you were sick.
здоро́в [zdaróf]	healthy, well, recovered
тепе́рь [ṭiṛéṛ]	now
Тепе́рь я́ здоро́в.	I'm well now.
вполне́ [fpalṇé]	completely, fully, quite
уже́ [užé]	already, by now
Тепе́рь я́ уже́ вполне́ здоро́в.	I'm completely well now. (*Lit.* Now I already completely well.)
но [no]	but
да́ [dá]	yes
Да́, но тепе́рь я́ уже́ вполне́ здоро́в.	Yes, but now I'm completely well. (*Lit.* Yes, but now I already completely well.)
горсове́т [gorsaɣét]	gorsovet (city council)
в горсове́те [vgorsaɣéṭi]	at the gorsovet
вы́ рабо́таете [ví rabótəjiṭi]	you work, you've been working

◄ **Моско́вский кремль. Вид на реку Москву.**   **19**

Вы́ рабо́таете в горсове́те?	Do you work at the gorsovet?
всё ещё [fšó jiščó]	still, yet
Вы́ всё ещё рабо́таете в горсове́те?	Do you still work at the gorsovet?
я рабо́таю [já rabótəju]	I work
Да́, я всё ещё рабо́таю в горсове́те.	Yes, I still work at the gorsovet.
то́же [tóži]	too, also
жена́ [žiná]	wife
Да́, и жена́ то́же.	Yes, and my wife [does] too.
она́ рабо́тает [aná rabótəjit]	she works
Да́, и жена́ то́же рабо́тает.	Yes, and my wife works too.
слы́шать [slíšəṭ]	to hear
э́то [étə]	that, it, this
ра́д [rát]	glad
Ра́д э́то слы́шать.	Glad to hear it.
Давно́?	For a long time?
о́сень (f) [óṣiṇ]	fall, autumn
с о́сени [sóṣiṇi]	since autumn, since fall
Да́, с о́сени.	Yes, since fall.
я спешу́ [já spišú]	I'm hurrying, I'm in a hurry
на авто́бус [nəaftóbus]	for the bus, to catch a bus
Я́ спешу́ на авто́бус.	I'm in a hurry to catch a bus.
Извини́те, я спешу́ на авто́бус.	Excuse me, I'm in a hurry to catch a bus.
приве́т жене́ [pṛiɣéd žiṇé]	regards to your wife, say hello to your wife
До свида́ния. Приве́т жене́.	Good-bye. [Give my] regards to your wife.
всего́ хоро́шего [fṣivó xaróšivə]	good-bye
спаси́бо [spaṣíbə]	thanks, thank you
Спаси́бо. Всего́ хоро́шего.	Thank you. Good-bye.

SUPPLEMENT

му́ж [múš]	husband
му́ж и жена́ [múš i žiná]	husband and wife
ты́ рабо́таешь [tí rabótəjiš]	you work, you've been working, you're working, you do work
где́ [gḍé]	where, at what place[1]
Где́ ты́ рабо́таешь?	Where do you work?
— Я́ рабо́таю в клу́бе.	I work at the club.
они́ рабо́тают [aṇí rabótəjut]	they work
Где́ они́ рабо́тают?	Where do they work?
— Они́ рабо́тают на заво́де.	They work at a plant.
мы́ рабо́таем [mí rabótəjim]	we work
Мы́ рабо́таем на по́чте.	We work at the post office.

---

[1] There are two words for *where* in Russian: где́ and куда́. Где́ means *where* in the sense *at what place* as opposed to куда́ *to what place*.

Compare	**Где́ вы́ рабо́таете?**	— **На заво́де.**	**В клу́бе.**	**На по́чте.**
with	**Куда́ вы́ идёте?**	— **На заво́д.**	**В клу́б.**	**На по́чту.**

Давно́ ва́с не ви́дел

I haven't seen you for a long time

K.П. — Кири́лл Па́влович Цара́пкин
C.Ф. — Семён Фили́ппович Хитро́в

K.П.	1	Семён Фили́ппович! Всю зи́му ва́с не ви́дел.	şiṃón fiḷípič ↓ fşú ẓímu vás ṇiɣíḍil ↓	Semyon Filipovich![1] I haven't seen you all winter.
C.Ф.	2	А́, Кири́лл Па́влович! Ка́к дела́?	ắ ↓ ķiŗíl pắlič ↓ kág ḍilắ↓	Ah, Kirill Pavlovich![1] How is everything?[2]
K.П.	3	Хорошо́, спаси́бо. Я слы́шал, вы́ бы́ли больны́.	xərašṍ | spaşíbə ↓ já slíšəl | ví bíḷi baḷṇí ↓	Fine, thanks. I heard you were sick.
C.Ф.	4	Да́. Но тепе́рь я уже́ вполне́ здоро́в.	dắ ↓ no ṭiṗéŗ | já užé fpalṇế zdarṍf ↓	Yes. But now I'm completely well.[2]
K.П.	5	Вы́ всё ещё рабо́таете в горсове́те?	ví fşó jiščó rabótəjiṭi vgorsaɣếṭi ↓	Are you still working at the gorsovet?[3]
C.Ф.	6	Да́, и жена́ то́же.	dắ ↓ i žiná tṍži ↓	Yes, and my wife is too.
K.П.	7	Да́? Ра́д э́то слы́шать. Давно́?	dắ ↑ rát étə slíšəṭ ↓ davnṍ ↑	Is that so? Glad to hear it. For a long time?
C.Ф.	8	С о́сени. Извини́те, я спешу́ на авто́бус.	sṍşiṇi ↓ izɣiṇíṭi ↓ já sṛišú nəaftṍbus ↓	Since fall. Excuse me, I'm hurrying to catch a bus.
K.П.	9	До свида́ния. Приве́т жене́.	dəsɣidắṇjə ↓ pṛiɣéd žiṇế ↓	Good-bye. [Give my] regards to your wife.
C.Ф.	10	Спаси́бо. Всего́ хоро́шего.	spaşíbə ↓ fşivó xarṍšivə ↓	Thank you. Good-bye.[4]

NOTES [1] Adult Russians commonly address each other by the first name and a middle name derived from the father's first name. **Па́влович** and **Фили́ппович** are middle names, or patronymics, formed by adding the suffix **-ович** to the stem of first names **Па́вел** *Paul* and **Фили́пп** *Philip*. Daughters of **Па́вел** and **Фили́пп** have patronymics **Па́вловна** and **Фили́пповна** respectively, with the feminine suffix

–овна. If the father's first name ends in **–й**, the patronymic suffix is spelled **–евич** (for the son) and **–евна** (for the daughter).

FATHER'S FIRST NAME		SON'S PATRONYMIC	DAUGHTER'S PATRONYMIC
Никола́й	Nicholas	Никола́евич	Никола́евна
Евге́ний	Eugene	Евге́ниевич	Евге́ниевна
Ива́н	John	Ива́нович	Ива́новна
Кири́лл	Cyril	Кири́ллович	Кири́лловна
Семён	Simon	Семёнович	Семёновна

Patronymics are usually shortened in speech, for example: **Семён Фили́ппович** is usually pronounced [şiṃón fiḷípič]; **Кири́лл Па́влович** [ķiŗíl páḷič]; **Ни́на Семёновна** [ṇínə şiṃónnə].

[2] Observe that the present tense forms of the verb *to be* (corresponding to English *am*, *is*, *are*) are usually not expressed in Russian:

Ка́к дела́?	How is everything? (*Lit.* How things?)
Я́ вполне́ здоро́в.	I'm completely well. (*Lit.* I completely well.)

[3] **Горсове́т** (short for **городско́й сове́т**) means city council and includes all of the administrative offices necessary to run a city.

[4] **Всего́ хоро́шего** and **до свида́ния** are used more or less interchangeably in saying *good-bye*. Note that both **всего́** and **хоро́шего** spell their last consonant with a **г** but pronounce it [v]: [fşivó xaróšivə]. This pronunciation of **г** as [v] is regular for adjective and pronoun endings spelled **–ого** and **–его**.

Basic sentence patterns

1. Где́ ты́ рабо́таешь?   Where do you work?
   — Я́ рабо́таю в горсове́те.   I work at the gorsovet.
   _____ в клу́бе.   _____ at the club.
   _____ на заво́де.   _____ in a plant.
   _____ на по́чте.   _____ at the post office.

2. Ты́ давно́ та́м рабо́таешь?   Have you been working there long?
   — Да́, давно́.   Yes, I have.
   — Да́, уже́ давно́.   Yes, for a long time now.
   — Да́, с о́сени.   Yes, since fall.
   — Да́, и жена́ то́же.   Yes, and my wife too.
   — Да́, и му́ж то́же.   Yes, and my husband too.

3. Я́ всю́ зи́му ва́с не ви́дел.[1]   I haven't seen you all winter.
   Я́ давно́ ва́с не ви́дел.   I haven't seen you in a long time.
   Я́ вчера́ ва́с не ви́дел.   I didn't see you yesterday.
   — Я́ то́же ва́с не ви́дел.   I didn't see you either.

[1] The past tense form **ви́дел** is used only when the subject is masculine. It is replaced by **ви́дела** when the subject is feminine: **Я́ всю́ зи́му ва́с не ви́дела. Я́ давно́ ва́с не ви́дела. Я́ вчера́ ва́с не ви́дела. Я́ то́же ва́с не ви́дела.**

4. Извини́те. Я спешу́.	Excuse me, I'm in a hurry.
Я спешу́ на авто́бус.	I'm hurrying to the bus.
_____ на заво́д.	_____ to the plant.
_____ на по́чту.	_____ to the post office.
_____ в клу́б.	_____ to the club.
_____ в горсове́т.	_____ to the gorsovet.
_____ домо́й.	_____ home.

Correspondence between cyrillic vowel letters and the vowel sounds

The Russian vowel letters have already been discussed, particularly with reference to their functions as indicators of softness or hardness of the preceding consonant. We have also discussed the particular function of the soft-series vowel letters, **я, е, и, ё, ю**, as indicators of the presence of a preceding [j] sound under certain conditions.

In the following paragraphs the Cyrillic vowel letters will be presented, with examples of their occurrence in both stressed and unstressed syllables. Observe carefully the correspondence between the Cyrillic vowel *letters* and their *sound values*, noting particularly that the position of a vowel in relation to the stressed syllable often determines its sound value.

A. The Cyrillic letters **и** and **ы** have approximately the same vowel sound in unstressed syllables as in stressed syllables, [i] and [i] respectively. Except for **ш, ж**, and **ц**, all consonants before **и** are pronounced soft; all consonants before **ы** are pronounced hard.

и́ли	[íļi]	or	высо́кий	[visóķij]	high
име́ть	[iṃéţ]	to possess	но́вый	[nóvij]	new
лю́ди	[ļúḓi]	people	была́	[bilá]	was
мину́та	[ṃinútə]	minute			
ты́	[tí]	you			

B. The Cyrillic letters **ю** and **у** have the same vowel sound in unstressed syllables as in stressed syllables: [u].

At the beginning of a word and after **ъ, ь,** or a vowel, however, the letter **ю** is pronounced [ju]. Consonants preceding **ю** are always pronounced soft; except for **ч** and **щ**, all consonants before **у** are pronounced hard.

у́лица	[úļicə]	street	говорю́	[gəvaṛú]	I speak
ми́нус	[ṃínus]	minus	зна́ю	[znáju]	I know
друго́й	[drugój]	other	пью́т	[pjút]	they drink
рубли́	[rubļí]	rubles	ю́га	[júgə]	of the south
пи́шут	[p̣íšut]	they write			
зву́к	[zvúk]	sound			
у́ксус	[úksus]	vinegar			
ую́тно	[ujútnə]	cozy			
мо́рю	[móṛu]	to the sea			
люби́ть	[ļuḅíţ]	to love			

C. The Cyrillic letter **ё** occurs only in stressed syllables and is consistently pronounced with the vowel sound [o].

At the beginning of a word and after **ь**, **ъ**, or a vowel, the letter **ё** is pronounced [jo]. Except for **ш** and **ж**, consonants preceding **ё** are pronounced soft.

нёс	[n̦ós]	he was carrying		ёлка	[jólkə]	spruce
тёмный	[țómnɨj]	dark		приём	[pr̦ijóm]	reception
идёт	[id̦ót]	he's going		пьёт	[p̦jót]	he drinks

Note: In our text **ё** will be consistently written with two dots to keep it distinct from **e**. Except in textbooks and dictionaries, Russians do not normally make a distinction between **e** and **ё** in writing.

D. The Cyrillic letter **o** has the sound value [o] only in stressed syllables. In the syllable immediately before the stress and at the very beginning of a word it is pronounced [a]. In all other positions the Cyrillic letter **o** is pronounced [ə]. Except for **ч** and **щ**, consonants before **o** are always pronounced hard.

оборо́т	[abarót]	turn		оно́	[anó]	it
хорошо́	[xərašó]	good		вопро́с	[vaprós]	question
городо́к	[gəradók]	small town				
о́лово	[óləvə]	tin				
молоко́	[məlakó]	milk				
то́лько	[tól̦kə]	only				

E. The Cyrillic letter **e** has the sound [e] only in stressed syllables. In other positions it is pronounced as [i], varying in value from the sound of the English *e* in *e*mit or *re*act to a shorter, more obscure sound as in the first syllable of d*i*spatch.

In certain grammatical endings it is pronounced by some speakers as short [i] and by others as [ə], for example, **по́ле** [pól̦i] or [pól̦ə]. Remember that at the beginning of a word, or following **ь**, **ъ**, or a vowel, the letter **e** is pronounced with a preceding [j] sound. Except for **ш**, **ж**, and **ц**, consonants before **e** are pronounced soft.

челове́к	[čilaɣék]	person		бо́лее	[ból̦iji]	more
мое́й	[majéj]	my		съе́ли	[sjél̦i]	they ate up
де́ло	[d̦élə]	business		отъе́зда	[atjézdə]	of the departure
тепе́рь	[țip̦ér̦]	now		чье́й	[čjéj]	whose
переведи́те	[p̦ir̦iɣid̦íți]	translate				
меня́	[m̦in̦á]	me				
е́сли	[jésl̦i]	if				
ещё	[jiščó]	yet, still				

F. The Cyrillic letter **э** occurs chiefly in words of non-Russian origin and almost always at the beginning of a word. When stressed it has the sound value [e]; when unstressed it is heard as [i].

э́то	[étə]	this		эне́ргия	[in̦érgijə]	energy
э́ти	[éți]	these		этажи́	[itaží]	floors
э́хо	[éxə]	echo				
экза́мен	[igzám̦in]	examination				
элеме́нт	[il̦im̦ént]	element				

Some Russian speakers, however, tend to pronounce **э** as [e] wherever it occurs, for example, **эта́ж** [etáš] or [itáš].

G. The Cyrillic letter **я** has the vowel sound [a] in stressed syllables and the vowel sound [i] in unstressed syllables except for certain endings, where it has the value [ə]. Consonants preceding **я** are always pronounced soft. At the beginning of a word and after **ь**, **ъ**, or a vowel, the letter **я** is pronounced with a preceding [j] sound.

пять	[pát̠]	five		ясно	[jásnə]	clearly
поля	[paļá]	fields		Ялта	[jáltə]	Yalta
меня	[miṇá]	me		язык	[jizík]	language
моря	[maŗá]	seas				
пяти	[piṭí]	five				
глядеть	[gļiḍét̠]	to gaze				
я	[já]	I				

STRUCTURE AND DRILLS

The present tense of the first conjugation verb работать

я работаю	I work, I'm working, I've been working
ты работаешь	you work, you're working, you've been working
он работает	he works
она работает	she works
мы работаем	we work
вы работаете	you work
они работают	they work

■ **REPETITION DRILL**

Listen to your instructor (or the tape) and repeat the above pronoun-verb model until you can say it perfectly.

■ **REPETITION-SUBSTITUTION DRILLS**

Repeat after your instructor (or the tape) as accurately as you can, imitating both the individual words and the sentence intonation. Then, on hearing only the subject cue, give the full sentence.

TEACHER	STUDENT
1. *I'm working now.*	*I'm working now.*
Я теперь работаю.	**Я теперь работаю.**
Они теперь работают.	**Они теперь работают.**
Ты теперь работаешь.	Ты теперь работаешь.
Вы теперь работаете.	Вы теперь работаете.
Мы теперь работаем.	Мы теперь работаем.
Он теперь работает.	Он теперь работает.
Она теперь работает.	Она теперь работает.

2. *I work too.*

　Я то́же рабо́таю.

　Вы́ то́же рабо́таете.

　Ты́ то́же рабо́таешь.

　Жена́ то́же рабо́тает.

　Она́ то́же рабо́тает.

　Му́ж то́же рабо́тает.

　О́н то́же рабо́тает.

　Мы́ то́же рабо́таем.

　Они́ то́же рабо́тают.

I work too.

Я́ то́же рабо́таю.

Вы́ то́же рабо́таете.

Ты́ то́же рабо́таешь.

Жена́ то́же рабо́тает.

Она́ то́же рабо́тает.

Му́ж то́же рабо́тает.

О́н то́же рабо́тает.

Мы́ то́же рабо́таем.

Они́ то́же рабо́тают.

■ QUESTION-ANSWER DRILLS

Answer the questions in the negative according to the models given.

TEACHER	STUDENT
Do you work?	*No, I don't.*
Ты́ рабо́таешь?	**Не́т, не рабо́таю.**
Вы́ рабо́таете?	**Не́т, не рабо́таю.**
Жена́ рабо́тает?	Не́т, не рабо́тает.
Му́ж рабо́тает?	Не́т, не рабо́тает.
Они́ рабо́тают?	Не́т, не рабо́тают.
Она́ рабо́тает?	Не́т, не рабо́тает.
О́н рабо́тает?	Не́т, не рабо́тает.

Using **на по́чте,** answer with both short and full answers according to the models given.

Where do you work?	*At the post office.*
Where do you work?	*We work at the post office.*
Где́ вы́ рабо́таете?	**На по́чте.**
Где́ вы́ рабо́таете?	**Мы́ рабо́таем на по́чте.**
Где́ она́ рабо́тает?	На по́чте.
Где́ она́ рабо́тает?	Она́ рабо́тает на по́чте.
Где́ ты́ рабо́таешь?	На по́чте.
Где́ ты́ рабо́таешь?	Я́ рабо́таю на по́чте.
Где́ они́ рабо́тают?	На по́чте.
Где́ они́ рабо́тают?	Они́ рабо́тают на по́чте.
Где́ о́н рабо́тает?	На по́чте.
Где́ о́н рабо́тает?	О́н рабо́тает на по́чте.

■ SUBSTITUTION DRILL

He's been working there for a long time.	*He's been working there for a long time.*
О́н давно́ та́м рабо́тает.	**О́н давно́ та́м рабо́тает.**
Жена́ давно́ та́м рабо́тает.	**Жена́ давно́ та́м рабо́тает.**
(Евге́ний) ——————.	Евге́ний давно́ та́м рабо́тает.
(Ни́на) ——————.	Ни́на давно́ та́м рабо́тает.
(Она́) ——————.	Она́ давно́ та́м рабо́тает.
(Семён) ——————.	Семён давно́ та́м рабо́тает.
(Они́) ——————.	Они́ давно́ та́м рабо́тают.
(Кири́лл и Семён) ———.	Кири́лл и Семён давно́ та́м рабо́тают.
(Му́ж) ——————.	Му́ж давно́ та́м рабо́тает.

Following the models, give both short and full answers.

TEACHER	STUDENT
Have you been working at the club long?	*Yes, for a long time, since fall.*
Have you been working at the club long?	*Yes, I've been working there since fall.*
Вы́ давно́ рабо́таете в клу́бе?	**Да́, давно́, с о́сени.**
Вы́ давно́ рабо́таете в клу́бе?	**Да́, я рабо́таю та́м с о́сени.**
О́н давно́ рабо́тает в клу́бе?	Да́, давно́, с о́сени.
О́н давно́ рабо́тает в клу́бе?	Да́, о́н рабо́тает та́м с о́сени.
Они́ давно́ рабо́тают в клу́бе?	Да́, давно́, с о́сени.
Они́ давно́ рабо́тают в клу́бе?	Да́, они́ рабо́тают та́м с о́сени.
О́на давно́ рабо́тает в клу́бе?	Да́, давно́, с о́сени.
О́на давно́ рабо́тает в клу́бе?	Да́, она́ рабо́тает та́м с о́сени.
Кири́лл давно́ рабо́тает в клу́бе?	Да́, давно́, с о́сени.
Кири́лл давно́ рабо́тает в клу́бе?	Да́, о́н рабо́тает та́м с о́сени.
Ты́ давно́ рабо́таешь в клу́бе?	Да́, давно́, с о́сени.
Ты́ давно́ рабо́таешь в клу́бе?	Да́, я рабо́таю та́м с о́сени.

DISCUSSION

Like **идти́**, the verb **рабо́тать** belongs to the first conjugation. It differs from **идти́** in that its present stem appears to end in a vowel (**рабо́та–**), whereas that of **идти́** ends in a consonant (**ид–**). This is only a convention of the writing system, however, since the actual present stem of **рабо́тать** ends in the consonant *sound* [j]. As we know, when [j] occurs between vowels it is expressed through the "soft-series" vowel letters which follow. Thus we may contrast the written stem and endings in the chart below with those of the transcription, which show the real division of stem and ending.

		WRITTEN FORMS	TRANSCRIPTION
STEM		**рабо́та–**	rabótəj–
SINGULAR	1	**рабо́та–ю**	rabótəj–u
	2	–ешь	–iš
	3	–ет	–it
PLURAL	1	–ем	–im
	2	–ете	–iţi
	3	–ют	–ut

It is only in the imperative forms that the [j] of the stem is written with a separate letter **й**: **рабо́тай (рабо́тайте)**! *work!*

Рабо́тать is typical of the "j-stem" verbs in that it has a fixed stress which falls on the same syllable of the stem in all forms.

The Russian handwriting system

A. The alphabet

PRINTED	WRITTEN	PRINTED	WRITTEN	PRINTED	WRITTEN
А а	*А а*	К к	*К к*	Х х	*Х х*
Б б	*Б б*	Л л	*Л л*	Ц ц	*Ц ц*
В в	*В в*	М м	*М м*	Ч ч	*Ч ч*
Г г	*Г г*	Н н	*Н н*	Ш ш	*Ш ш*
Д д	*Д д*	О о	*О о*	Щ щ	*Щ щ*
Е е	*Е е*	П п	*П п*	Ъ ъ	*ъ*
Ё ё	*Ё ё*	Р р	*Р р*	Ы ы	*ы*
Ж ж	*Ж ж*	С с	*С с*	Ь ь	*ь*
З з	*З з*	Т т	*Т т*	Э э	*Э э*
И и	*И и*	У у	*У у*	Ю ю	*Ю ю*
Й й	*Й й*	Ф ф	*Ф ф*	Я я	*Я я*

B. Reading practice

Conversations from Lessons 1 and 2 are given below in handwritten form as an introduction to the handwriting system. Now that you are familiar with the conversations, you should have no real difficulty reading them. Refer to the printed versions if necessary.

Студент и студентка.

— Привет, Нина! Куда вы идёте? — На урок пения. А вы домой? — Нет, я иду на почту послать письмо. — Скажите, вчера было собрание? — В клубе?

Нет, не было. – А на заводе? – Было, но я там не был. – Ну, извините. Вот идёт мой автобус. – До свидания! – До свидания!

Давно вас не видел.
– Семён Филиппович! Всю зиму вас не видел.
– А, Кирилл Павлович! Как дела? – Хорошо, спасибо. Вы, я слышал, были больны? – Да. Но теперь я вполне здоров. – Вы всё ещё работаете в горсовете? – Да, и жена тоже. – Да? Рад это слышать. Давно? – С осени. Извините, я спешу на автобус. – До свидания! Привет жене! – Спасибо. Всего хорошего!

C. How the letters are formed

1. SMALL LETTERS

o   a   д   б   ф

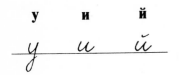

The first three letters are formed in practically the same way as in English. The letters **б** and **ф** begin the same way as **o**. In **б**, a vertical line then goes upward and curves at the top to the right. In **ф**, after the first circle, a straight vertical stroke goes downward and then back up along the same line, returning to the initial point and continuing up and clockwise to form another circle.

у   и   й

The letters **у** and **и** are formed like the English handwritten *y* and *u*; **й** is the same as **и**, but with the addition of a short half circle above. (Write it immediately lest you forget.)

ц   ш   щ

The letter **ц** is also written like **и**, except that it ends in a small loop below the line. Handwritten **ш** and **щ** consist of three vertical lines of equal height with a final drop to the line (unlike the English written *w*). The **щ** has a small tail loop like **ц**.

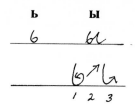

ь   **ы**

Make a small figure 6 to form the soft sign. The written **ы** starts with the same downstroke and loop as **ь**, swings up to a sharp peak, goes down again, and then curves to the right. Both letters are short compared with the handwritten **в**.

Любовь, вы

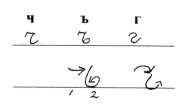

ч   **ъ**   **г**

The first letter is written like one variant of the English handwritten *r*. The second is similar, but ends in a small circle, resembling a combination of **ч** and **ь**. (Some Russians replace **ъ** with an apostrophe.) The third differs from the first in that it does not have the short horizontal line at the top, but is rounded.

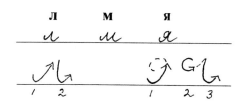

л   **м**   **я**

These three letters begin with a small hook slightly above the line (remember this when joining these letters to others). To form **я**, begin with the same upward stroke as in **л** and **м**. Then make a small counterclockwise circle at the top, returning to the same point and ending in a line down (**я** looks like **л** with a small loop to the left of its top). Do not make the Russian **л** as tall as an English *l*.

п   **т**   **к**

The first two letters, **п** and **т**, are formed much like the English handwritten *n* and *m*. The Russian **к** is written like the printed English *k*; it is never tall with a loop as in the English written *k* (*к* not *k*).

н   **ю**

For **н**, start from the top down, then go back halfway up the same line, turning to the right and upward, then finally coming back down to the line. To form **ю**, follow the directions for **н**, but continue the last stroke back upward to form a circle.

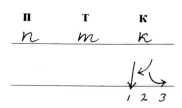

э   **ж**

For handwritten **э**, begin at the top and make a half circle clockwise, then cut it in half by a small horizontal line. For **ж**, start at the top and make the same half circle, then slant back up to the right, then straight down and again up to the right; finish with another half circle (like the English written *c*) going in the opposite direction.

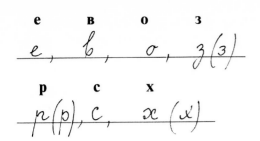

These letters are all formed much the same way as in English. The letter **e** must be written _e_ (never _ε_); the letter **в** must be written tall and kept distinct from **ь** (_ƅ_ versus _б_).

Note: Russians do not print words, even when they fill out official forms by hand.

■ HANDWRITING DRILL

Practice copying the small letters above until you can write them easily and accurately.

2. CAPITAL LETTERS[1]

А	В	Д	К

These are similar to the English letters with corresponding shapes.

Н	О	С	Х

Ж	И	Й	Л	М

These are the same as their corresponding small letters but taller and larger.

Ш	Щ	Ц	Э	Ю	Я

Г	П	Б	Ф

All four letters start with a basic line that curves downward, turning to the left. The fourth letter differs from the others only in that it starts with a small flourish at the top. The same stroke in the first, second, and third is the curved line from left to right that caps each letter. The second has another downward stroke, ending toward the right before the cap is added. The third letter has as its third stroke a large loop at the bottom (like a closed, looped figure 2). The fourth has two loops on either side of the down stroke which resemble a figure 8 on its side.

---

[1] Russian capital letters are used only at the beginning of the sentence, in proper names, and in the first word of a title. Russians do not capitalize the names of months, nationalities, centuries, professions, or ranks; nor do they capitalize the personal pronoun **я** within a sentence.

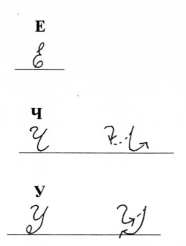

E

Ч

У

Certain varieties of the English written capital *E* are acceptable. Start outside and make the small top loop; the bottom half circle must be larger than the upper one.

For **Ч**, begin with an upward, clockwise curve, then make a downward, "u-shaped" curve, slanting back and down, finally curving to the right *on the line*.

Capital **У** is like the preceding letter, except that the curved downward stroke goes to the left. Unlike its small counterpart, capital **У** starts high above the base line and must not extend below the line.

■ HANDWRITING DRILL

Practice copying the capital letters until you can write them easily and accurately.

D. Summary remarks on the handwriting system

1. All Russian capital letters except **Щ** and **Ц** have their base on the line and extend above it; **Щ** and **Ц** each has a small loop which extends below the line.

2. Small handwritten letters are of two types: long and short.

a. *Long letters*
Three long letters have their base on the line and extend above it.

and

Five long letters have their base on the line and extend below it.

and

b. *Short letters*
All the remaining letters are of the same height and are written on the line except **щ** and **ц**, each of which has a short loop below the line.

3. Most letters are joined together in writing; however, and are usually not connected to the following letter.

4. The letters з, д, р, т, and х, may be handwritten in two ways.

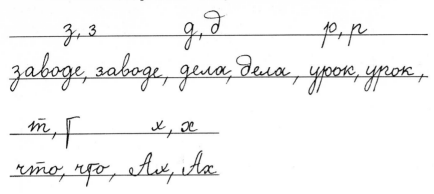

The first variant in each pair is the one used more frequently. Some Russians draw a horizontal line above _т_ and below _ш_ to make these letters stand out better. The student is advised to use the first variant of _т_ because he cannot substitute the usual English written _t_ for Russian _т_.

каши   _хотите_

■ COPYING AND HANDWRITING PRACTICE

1. Copy the handwritten versions of the first two conversations, being careful to observe the connections of the letters. 2. Return to the first two conversations in printed form and copy each in handwriting.

Syllabification of words in Russian

Both in pronouncing words by syllable and in dividing them at the end of a written line, there are certain important principles that should be followed.

In pronunciation, the basic pattern is to end a syllable with a vowel wherever possible.

спа–си́–бо	[spa–şí–bə]	thanks
ра–бо́–та–е–те	[ra–bó–tə–ji–ţi]	[you] work
пи–сьмо́	[ṇi–şmó]	letter
ска–жи́–те	[ska–ží–ţi]	tell [me]! say!
по–вто–ри́–те	[pə–fta–ŗí–ţi]	repeat!

Consonant clusters beginning with р, л, н, and й are usually divided after these consonants. Final consonants are, of course, treated as part of the syllable which they end.

ка–ран–да́ш	[kə–ran–dáš]	pencil
чи–та́й–те	[či–táj–ţi]	read!
по́л–ка	[pól–kə]	shelf
у–ни–вер–си–те́т	[u–ṇi–γir–şi–ţét]	university

In dividing written words at the end of a line, these same general rules apply, but there is slightly more leeway in the division of clusters of consonants. For example, сестра́ may be divided се–стра́ (as in pronunciation), сес–тра́, or сест–ра́. Doubled letters are always divided when carried over to the next line, for example, Áн–на and под–да́ть. Single letters are never left at the end of one line or at the beginning of the next.

PREPARATION FOR CONVERSATION　　Лу́чше по́здно, чём никогда́

лу́чше [lúčši]	better
по́здно [póznə]	late
чём [čém]	than
никогда́ [n̢ikagdá]	never
Лу́чше по́здно, чём никогда́.	Better late than never.
здра́вствуйте [zdrástujt̢i] [1]	hello
Лёв, здра́вствуйте!	Hello, Lev!
вы́ спеши́те [ví sp̢iší̢t̢i]	you're hurrying
Куда́ вы́ спеши́те?	Where are you hurrying to?
университе́т [un̢iɣirşit̢ét]	university
в университе́т [vun̢iɣirşit̢ét]	to the university
Я́ спешу́ в университе́т.	I'm hurrying to the university.
конце́рт [kancért]	concert
на конце́рт [nəkancért]	to a concert
В университе́т, на конце́рт.	To the university, to a concert.
Я́ спешу́ в университе́т, на конце́рт.	I'm hurrying to the university, to a concert.
интере́сно [int̢iŗésnə]	that's interesting
беспла́тно [b̢isplátnə]	free
Интере́сно. Это беспла́тно?	That's interesting. Is it free?
пойти́ [pajt̢í]	to go
[вы] хоти́те [ví xat̢í̢t̢i]	you want
Хоти́те пойти́?	Do you want to go?
удово́льствие [udavól̢st̢ɣijə]	pleasure
С удово́льствием! [sudavól̢st̢ɣijəm]	With pleasure! *or* I'd love to!

---

[1] **Здра́вствуйте** is simplified in pronunciation to something that ranges from [zdrástujt̢i] to [zdrás̢s̢t̢i], depending on the tempo of speech and the informality of the speaker. Note also that **по́здно** is pronounced without д : [póznə]. Clusters of three or more consonants are usually simplified, and д and т are usually omitted between consonants except at the beginning of a word: **пра́здник** [prázn̢ik] *holiday*.

◀ **Вестибюль главного здания МГУ.**

вы́ де́лаете   [ví ḑéləjiți] you're doing
что́   [štó] what
Что́ вы́ де́лаете? What are you doing?
кста́ти   [kstáți] by the way, incidentally
Кста́ти, что́ вы́ тепе́рь де́лаете? By the way, what are you doing now?

лаборато́рия   [ləbəratóŗijə] laboratory
в лаборато́рии   [vləbəratóŗiji] in a laboratory
Я рабо́таю в лаборато́рии. I work in a laboratory.

та́к ску́чно   [ták skúšnə]¹ [it's] so dull, [it's] so boring
Там та́к ску́чно. It's so boring there.

поступа́йте в университе́т enroll at the university! enter the univer-
   [pəstupájți vuņiɣirşiţét]   sity!
так   [tək] in that case, then
Так поступа́йте в университе́т. Then enroll at the university.

Что́ вы́! You can't mean it! or You're not serious!

уже́ по́здно   [užé póznə] it's already late, it's too late
мне́   [mņé] for me, to me
Мне́ уже́ по́здно. It's too late for me.
Мне́ тепе́рь уже́ по́здно. It's too late for me now.

говоря́т   [gəvaŗát] they say, people say
[вы] зна́ете   [ví znájiți] you know
зна́ете, говоря́т...   [znájiți gəvaŗát] you know [what] they say . . .
Зна́ете, говоря́т: "Лу́чше по́здно, чём You know [what] they say: "Better late than
никогда́".   never."

SUPPLEMENT

ра́но early
Ещё ра́но. It's early yet or It's too early.
за́нят (m) he's busy, occupied, tied up
занята́ (f) she's busy, occupied, tied up
за́няты (pl) we're busy, occupied, tied up
Вы́ за́няты? Are you busy?
— Да́, я́ за́нят (or занята́). Yes, I am.
ча́сто often
Я́ ча́сто рабо́таю в лаборато́рии. I often work in the laboratory.
ре́дко rarely, seldom
Я́ ре́дко рабо́таю в лаборато́рии. I rarely work in the laboratory.
иногда́ sometimes
Я́ иногда́ рабо́таю в лаборато́рии. I sometimes work in the laboratory.
никогда́ не never
Я́ никогда́ не рабо́таю в лаборато́рии. I never work in the laboratory.

ADDITIONAL CLASSROOM EXPRESSIONS

отвеча́йте   [atɣičájți] or отве́тьте answer!
   [atɣéțți]
Откро́йте кни́ги.   [atkrójți kņígi] Open your books.

---

¹ **Ску́чно** is pronounced [skúšnə] by some speakers, [skúčnə] by others.

Закро́йте кни́ги. [zakrójţi kņígi]	Close your books.
пра́вильно [práɣiļnə]	right, that's right
непра́вильно [ņipráɣiļnə]	wrong, that's wrong
господи́н [gəspaḑín]	Mr.
госпожа́ [gəspažá]	Miss, Mrs.
господа́ [gəspadá]	ladies and gentlemen, everybody, everyone

Закро́йте кни́ги, господа́.	Close your books, everyone.
Вы́ понима́ете? [ví pəņimájiţi]	Do you understand?
— Я понима́ю. [já pəņimáju]	I understand.

Лу́чше по́здно, чём никогда́

Better late than never

М. — Ми́ла   Л. — Лёв

М.	1	Лёв, здра́вствуйте! Куда́ вы́ спеши́те?	ļĕf ↓ zdrắstujţi ↓ kudá ví sṗiši̇̌ţi ↓	Hello Lev. Where are you hurrying to?
Л.	2	В университе́т, на конце́рт.	vuņiɣirşiţĕt ↓ nəkancĕrt ↓	To the university, to a concert.
М.	3	Интере́сно. Э́то беспла́тно?	inţiṛĕsnə ↑ étə ḅisplắtnə ↑	That's interesting. Is it free?
Л.	4	Да́. Хоти́те пойти́?	dắ ↓ xaţíţi pajţí ↑	Yes. Do you want to go?[1]
М.	5	С удово́льствием!	sudavǒļstɣijəm ↓	I'd love to!
Л.	6	Кста́ти, что́ вы́ тепе́рь де́лаете?	kstắţi ↓ štó ví ţiṛĕṛ ḑĕləjiţi ↓	By the way, what are you doing now?[2]
М.	7	Рабо́таю в лаборато́рии. Та́м та́к ску́чно!	rabótəju vləbəratǒṛiji ↓ tám tắk skúšnə ↓	I work in a laboratory. It's so dull there!
Л.	8	Так поступа́йте в университе́т.	tək pəstupájţi vuņiɣirşiţĕt ↓	Enroll at the university then.[3]
М.	9	Что́ вы́! Мне́ тепе́рь уже́ по́здно.	štǒ ví ↓ mņé ţiṛĕṛ užé pǒznə ↓	You're not serious! It's too late for me now.
Л.	10	Зна́ете, говоря́т: «Лу́чше по́здно, чём никогда́».	znắjiţi ↓ gəvaṛắt | lúčši põznə ↑ čĕm ņikagdắ ↓	You know what they say: "Better late than never."

¹ Verbs in Russian almost always come in pairs called "imperfective" and "perfective." **Пойти** is the perfective member of the imperfective-perfective pair of verbs **идти** and **пойти**. The imperfective member of the verbal pair usually describes an action viewed as a process (**идти** *to be going*); the perfective usually describes an action in terms of its accomplishment or result (**пойти** *to go*). Verbal pairs usually have the same root, but differ in their prefix or in their stem. The system of paired verbs is called "aspect," and the choice of which verb to use—imperfective or perfective—depends on how the Russian speaker views the action.

In these early lessons, the student will encounter verbs of both aspects and will practice them as he meets them, without being expected to know both members of a particular pair or how one is formed in relation to the other.

² Russian adverbs, unlike those in English, are usually placed before the verb:

Что вы **теперь** делаете?	What are you doing *now*?
Вчера было собрание?	Was there a meeting *yesterday*?
Я **там** нé был.	I wasn't *there*.

It is also normal to place direct object pronouns before the verb.

Я всю зиму **вас** не видел.	I haven't seen *you* all winter.
Я давно **вас** не видел.	I haven't seen *you* in a long time.
Рад **это** слышать.	Glad to hear *it*.

³ The stressed word **так** in **так скучно** means *so* and differs from the unstressed **так** [tək] in **Так поступайте в университет,** which means *then, in that case.*

Basic sentence patterns

1. Куда ты спешишь?	Where are you hurrying to?
— В университет.	To the university.
— В клуб.	To the club.
— На собрание.	To a meeting.
— На почту.	To the post office.
— На концерт.	To a concert.
— На урок.	To class.
— На урок пения.	To a singing class.
— На автобус.	To the bus.
— На завод.	To the plant.
— Домой.	Home.

2. Куда вы спешите?	Where are you hurrying to?
— Я спешу в клуб.	I'm hurrying to the club.
_____ в университет.	_____ to the university.
_____ на собрание.	_____ to the meeting.
_____ на почту.	_____ to the post office.
_____ на урок.	_____ to class.
_____ на урок пения.	_____ to a singing class.
_____ на автобус.	_____ to the bus.
_____ на завод.	_____ to the plant.
_____ домой.	_____ home.

3. Хотите пойти на концерт?
_____ на собрание?
_____ на почту?
_____ в клуб?
_____ в университет?
_____ в университет, на концерт?

Want to go to the concert?
_____ to the meeting?
_____ to the post office?
_____ to the club?
_____ to the university?
_____ to the university, to a concert?

4. Хотите пойти в клуб?
— С удовольствием.
— Да. Я давно там не был.
— Да. Я давно там не была.[1]
— Нет, я занят.
— Нет, я занята.[1]
— Нет, я уже там был.
— Нет, я уже там была.[1]
— Нет, там так скучно.
— Нет, уже поздно.
— Нет, ещё рано.

Want to go to the club?
I'd love to.
Yes, I haven't been there for a long time.
Yes, _____.
No, I'm busy.
No, _____.
No, I was already there.
No, _____.
No, it's so boring there.
No, it's [too] late.
No, it's still early.

5. Что вы теперь делаете?
— Работаю в лаборатории.
_____ на заводе.
_____ в клубе.
_____ в горсовете.
_____ в университете.
_____ на почте.

What do you do now?
I work in a laboratory.
_____ at the plant.
_____ at the club.
_____ at the gorsovet.
_____ at the university.
_____ at the post office.

6. Куда спешит Лев, на завод?
— Нет, на собрание.
— Нет, на урок пения.
Куда спешат Нина и Кирилл?
— Они спешат в клуб.
— Они спешат в лабораторию.
Куда вы спешите, Евгений?
— Я спешу в университет.
— Я спешу на концерт.

Where's Lev hurrying to, the plant?
No, to a meeting.
No, to a singing lesson.
Where are Nina and Kirill hurrying to?
They're hurrying to the club.
They're hurrying to the laboratory.
Where are you hurrying to, Evgeny?
I'm hurrying to the university.
I'm hurrying to a concert.

The alternation of voiced and voiceless consonants

Besides the important feature of hardness and softness, the Russian consonant system is dominated by another significant element: the presence or absence of what is called "voice."

A *voiced* consonant is one pronounced with an accompanying vibration of the vocal cords. For example, the Russian [b, b̦; v, ɣ; d, d̦; z, z̦] are all considered *voiced* consonants. So, too, are the English *b* in *boys*, *v* in *view*, *d* in *dog*, and *z* in *zip*.

In contrast, a *voiceless* (or *unvoiced*) consonant is one pronounced without this accompanying vibration of the vocal cords. For example, the Russian [p, p̦; f, f̦; t, ț; s, ș] are all considered *voiceless* consonants in the system. Similarly, the English *p* in *poise*, *f* in *few*, *t* in *togs*, and *s* in *sip* are voiceless consonants.

The main difference between the Russian and English treatment of the voiced and voiceless consonants is that in Russian there is a systematic replacement of one by the other under prescribed circumstances while in English there is not. We can pronounce the English *gooseberry* with either

---

[1] Feminine speaker.

an [s] or a [z] sound, and both are acceptable. Russian, however, requires that the written д of **во́дка** be pronounced [t] because it occurs before [k], an unvoiced consonant: [vótkə].

Although all Russian consonant sounds may be characterized as voiced or voiceless, not all occur in opposed pairs. The following chart shows the regularly opposed pairs.

SOUNDS	*Voiced*	b	ḅ	v	γ	d	ḍ	z	ẓ	ž	g
	Voiceless	p	ṛ	f	ḟ	t	ṭ	s	ṣ	š	k

The consonants [x, x̣, c, č, šč] are all voiceless, but do not have voiced counterparts that operate independently in the system. They can, however, affect the pronunciation of a preceding consonant. The consonants [r, ṛ, l, ḷ, m, ṃ, n, ṇ, j] possess voice, but have no corresponding voiceless counterparts. They are considered "neutral" because they do not determine the pronunciation of other consonants occurring in combination with them.

In terms of the Russian writing system, the paired voiced and voiceless consonants may be indicated as follows:

Voiced	б	бь	в	вь	д	дь	з	зь	ж	г
Voiceless	п	пь	ф	фь	т	ть	с	сь	ш	к

Since the writing system does not accurately reflect the spoken language, it is essential for the student to know which consonants are voiced, which are voiceless, and, especially, which are paired in terms of voice or absence of voice. This is important because, in certain positions, only consonant sounds of one or the other series are spoken, regardless of the spelling. The automatic alternation of voiced and voiceless consonant sounds operates, under the following conditions, within a word or combination of words spoken together as a unit.[1]

A. At the end of a word, consonants ordinarily voiced are replaced automatically by their unvoiced counterparts.

FINAL POSITION

гото́в	[gatóf]	ready
заво́д	[zavót]	plant
гри́б	[gṛíp]	mushroom
о́чередь	[óčiṛiṭ]	line

NON-FINAL POSITION

гото́ва	[gatóvə]	ready
заво́ды	[zavódi]	plants
грибы́	[gṛibí]	mushrooms
о́череди	[óčiṛiḍi]	lines

B. Consonants in clusters, either within one word or in adjacent words pronounced without a break, are assimilated to the extent that the entire cluster is pronounced either voiceless or voiced.

Note, in the following examples, that it is the *second or last* voiced or voiceless consonant in the series that determines how the preceding consonant(s) will be pronounced.

1. VOICELESS CLUSTERS

	SPELLED			PRONOUNCED		
вч	in	**вч**ера́	yesterday	[fč]	in	[fčirá]
зд		по́ез**д**	train	[st]		[pójist]
бк		коро́**бк**а	box	[pk]		[karópkə]
вст		**в ст**оле́	in the desk	[fst]		[fstaḷé]
дк		во́**дк**а	vodka	[tk]		[vótkə]
вк		**в к**лу́бе	at the club	[fk]		[fklúḅi]

---

[1] Since the neutral consonants **р, л, н, м,** and **й** do not play a part in the alternation of voiced and voiceless consonants, they will be excluded from this discussion.

2. VOICED CLUSTERS

кд	in	ка́к дела́	how are things	[gd̦]	in	[ká g̦ḍilá]
сьб		про́сьба	request	[ẓb]		[pró ẓbə]
кж		та́кже	likewise, too	[gž]		[tá gži]

The consonant **в (вь)** must be considered a special case. Although it undergoes unvoicing (i.e., it is pronounced as [f] or [f̦] either in final position or when followed by an unvoiced consonant), it does not cause a normally voiceless consonant preceding it to become voiced. Thus, both **зва́ли** (with cluster [zv]) and **свали́** (with cluster [sv]) exist in Russian.

To summarize, we may say that the assimilation of consonants is a regressive process in Russian: the last element affects that which precedes it. Thus, in the following series, Position 2 determines the quality of Position 1 in terms of voice or its lack.

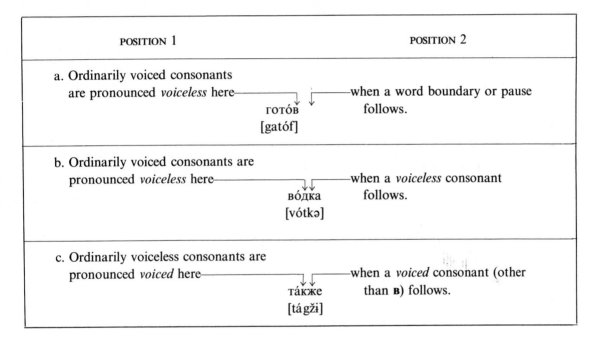

POSITION 1	POSITION 2
a. Ordinarily voiced consonants are pronounced *voiceless* here — гото́в [gatóf]	when a word boundary or pause follows.
b. Ordinarily voiced consonants are pronounced *voiceless* here — во́дка [vótkə]	when a *voiceless* consonant follows.
c. Ordinarily voiceless consonants are pronounced *voiced* here — та́кже [tá gži]	when a *voiced* consonant (other than **в**) follows.

■ VOICING AND UNVOICING DRILLS

Read the following Cyrillic words, noting the automatic changes in pronunciation that take place in certain positions.

1. UNVOICING AT END OF WORDS

б pronounced [p]

ра́б	[ráp]
сла́б	[sláp]
гри́б	[gr̦íp]
сто́лб	[stólp]
ло́б	[lóp]
зу́б	[zúp]
ду́б	[dúp]
ря́б	[r̦áp]

бь pronounced [p̦]

скорбь	[skór p̦]
зя́бь	[ẓá p̦]
дробь	[dró p̦]
го́лубь	[gólu p̦]
зы́бь	[zí p̦]
ря́бь	[r̦á p̦]
грабь	[grá p̦]
О́бь	[ó p̦]

в pronounced [f]

Хрущёв	[xruščóf]
Лёв	[l̦éf]
Турге́нев	[turgé ṇif]
жи́в	[žíf]
но́в	[nóf]
сло́в	[slóf]
о́стров	[óstrəf]
не́рв	[ṇérf]
рёв	[r̦óf]
обры́в	[abríf]
сня́в	[sṇáf]

вь pronounced [f̡]		г pronounced [k]		д pronounced [t]	
прибавь	[pr̡ibáf̡]	шаг	[šák]	рад	[rát]
заставь	[zastáf̡]	снег	[sn̡ék]	сад	[sát]
бурав́ь	[buráf̡]	берег	[b̡ér̡ik]	обед	[ab̡ét]
любо́вь	[l̡ubóf̡]	лёг	[l̡ók]	лёд	[l̡ót]
морко́вь	[markóf̡]	книг	[kn̡ík]	вид	[v̡ít]
бровь	[bróf̡]	пирог	[p̡irók]	год	[gót]
кровь	[króf̡]	друг	[drúk]	город	[górət]
новь	[nóf̡]	круг	[krúk]	ряд	[r̡át]
червь	[čérf̡]	юг	[júk]	стыд	[stít]
обувь	[óbuf̡]				

дь pronounced [t̡]		ж pronounced [š]		з pronounced [s]	
кладь	[klát̡]	гараж	[garáš]	раз	[rás]
гладь	[glát̡]	этаж	[itáš]	глаз	[glás]
тетрадь	[t̡itrát̡]	нарежь	[nar̡éš]	газ	[gás]
лошадь	[lóšit̡]	ёж	[jóš]	рассказ	[raskás]
площадь	[plóščit̡]	стриж	[str̡íš]	вниз	[vn̡ís]
медь	[m̡ét̡]	нож	[nóš]	колхоз	[kalxós]
очередь	[óčir̡it̡]	уж	[úš]	мороз	[marós]
будь	[bút̡]	муж	[múš]	союз	[sajús]
		замуж	[zámuš]		

зь pronounced [s̡]

мазь	[más̡]	сузь	[sús̡]
лазь	[lás̡]	грязь	[gr̡ás̡]
слезь	[sl̡és̡]	связь	[sv̡ás̡]
резь	[r̡és̡]	князь	[kn̡ás̡]
слизь	[sl̡ís̡]	бязь	[b̡ás̡]
врозь	[vrós̡]		

2. UNVOICING BEFORE AN UNVOICED CONSONANT

в pronounced [f]		б pronounced [p]		г pronounced [k]	
всю	[fs̡ú]	общий	[ópščij]	бегство	[b̡ékstvə]
вчера	[fčirá]	рыбка	[rípkə]	когтя	[kókt̡ə]
вход	[fxót]	рябчик	[r̡ápčik]	ногтя	[nókt̡ə]
автобус	[aftóbus]	удобство	[udópstvə]	жёгший	[žókšij]
овца	[afcá]	хлебца	[xl̡épcə]	ЗАГС	[záks]
продавщица	[prədafščícə]	коробка	[karópkə]	дёгтя	[d̡ókt̡ə]
в час	[fčás]	вообще	[vəapščé]	лягте	[l̡ákt̡i]
в коробке	[fkarópk̡i]			постригши	[pastr̡íkši]
вполне	[fpaln̡é]				

д pronounced [t]		ж pronounced [š]		з pronounced [s]	
ло́дка	[lótkə]	кни́жка	[kņíškə]	бли́зко	[bḷískə]
похо́дка	[paxótkə]	неу́жто	[ņiúštə]	ска́зка	[skáskə]
блю́дце	[bḷútcə]	ло́жка	[lóškə]	по́езд	[pójist]
молодцы́	[məlatcí]	наде́жд	[naḍéšt]	визг	[ɣísk]
во́дка	[vótkə]	нужд	[núšt]	мозг	[mósk]
зага́дка	[zagátkə]	немно́жко	[ņimnóškə]	дрозд	[dróst]
на́дпись	[nátpiş]			из та́нка	[istánkə]
под сне́гом	[patsņégəm]			слёзка	[sḷóskə]
над собо́й	[nətsabój]				

3. VOICING BEFORE A VOICED CONSONANT

к pronounced [g]		с pronounced [z]		т pronounced [d]	
та́кже	[tágži]	сгора́ть	[zgaráţ]	от го́рода	[adgórədə]
как дела́	[kagḍilá]	сбить	[zḅíţ]	от бра́та	[adbrátə]
вокза́л	[vagzál]	сго́вор	[zgóvər]	отбо́й	[adbój]
экза́мен	[igzáṃin]	сбор	[zbór]	отжа́ть	[adžáţ]
анекдо́т	[aṇigdót]	сбо́рник	[zbórņik]	о́тзыв	[ódzɨf]
к жене́	[gžiņé]	сда́ча	[zdáčə]	от за́висти	[adzáɣişţi]
к зиме́	[gẓiṃé]	с горы́	[zgarí]	о́тжил	[ódžil]
к ба́бе	[gbáḅi]			отбро́сы	[adbrósi]
к до́му	[gdómu]			от жены́	[adžiní]
ка́к бы	[kágbɨ]			отгада́ть	[adgadáţ]

сь pronounced [ẓ]		ть pronounced [ḍ]	
про́сьба	[próẓbə]	сели́тьба	[şiḷíḍbə]
косьба́	[kaẓbá]	жени́тьба	[žiņíḍbə]
		молотьба́	[məlaḍbá]

STRUCTURE AND DRILLS

The present tense of the second conjugation verb спеши́ть

я спешу́	I'm hurrying, I'm in a hurry
ты́ спеши́шь	you're hurrying, you're in a hurry
о́н спеши́т	he's hurrying
она́ спеши́т	she's hurrying
мы́ спеши́м	we're hurrying
вы́ спеши́те	you're hurrying
они́ спеша́т	they're hurrying

■ REPETITION DRILLS [1]

1. Listen to your instructor (or the tape) and repeat the preceding pronoun-verb model until you can say it perfectly.

2. *I'm hurrying to a lesson.*
   т: Я спешу́ на уро́к.
   s: **Я спешу́ на уро́к.**
   Они́ спеша́т на уро́к.
   Вы́ спеши́те на уро́к.
   Она́ спеши́т на уро́к.
   Мы́ спеши́м на уро́к.
   Óн спеши́т на уро́к.
   Ты́ спеши́шь на уро́к.

■ QUESTION-ANSWER DRILLS

1. *Where are you hurrying to?*
   We're hurrying to a concert.
   т: Куда́ вы́ спеши́те?
   s: **Мы́ спеши́м на конце́рт.**
   т: Куда́ о́н спеши́т?
   s: **Óн спеши́т на конце́рт.**
   Куда́ они́ спеша́т?
   Куда́ ты́ спеши́шь?
   Куда́ она́ спеши́т?
   Куда́ мы́ спеши́м?

   Using **в университе́т**, Student 1 first replies with a short answer, then Student 2 replies with a full answer.

3. *Where are you hurrying to?*
   To the university.
   I'm hurrying to the university.
   т: Куда́ вы́ спеши́те?
   s₁: **В университе́т.**
   s₂: **Я спешу́ в университе́т.**
   Ни́на, Кири́лл, куда́ вы́ спеши́те?
   Куда́ ты́ спеши́шь?
   Куда́ о́н спеши́т?
   Куда́ она́ спеши́т?
   Куда́ они́ спеша́т?

5. *Where are you hurrying to, the laboratory?*
   No, I'm hurrying to the club.
   т: Куда́ вы́ спеши́те, в лаборато́рию?
   s: **Не́т, я спешу́ в клу́б.**
   т: Куда́ ты́ спеши́шь, в лаборато́рию?
   s: **Не́т, я спешу́ в клу́б.**

2. *Where are you hurrying, home?*
   No, I'm hurrying to the post office.
   т: Куда́ вы́ спеши́те, домо́й?
   s: **Не́т, я спешу́ на по́чту.**
   т: Куда́ она́ спеши́т, домо́й?
   s: **Не́т, она́ спеши́т на по́чту.**
   Куда́ они́ спеша́т, домо́й?
   Куда́ о́н спеши́т, домо́й?
   Куда́ ты́ спеши́шь, домо́й?

   Using **на авто́бус,** answer the question with both short and full answers.

4. *Where are you going in such a hurry?*
   To catch a bus.
   I'm hurrying to catch a bus.
   т: Куда́ вы́ та́к спеши́те?
   s₁: **На авто́бус.**
   s₂: **Я спешу́ на авто́бус.**
   Куда́ о́н та́к спеши́т?
   Куда́ они́ та́к спеша́т?
   Куда́ мы́ та́к спеши́м?
   Куда́ ты́ та́к спеши́шь?
   Куда́ она́ та́к спеши́т?

   Куда́ о́н спеши́т, в лаборато́рию?
   Куда́ они́ спеша́т, в лаборато́рию?
   Куда́ ты́ спеши́шь, в лаборато́рию?
   Куда́ она́ спеши́т, в лаборато́рию?
   Куда́ вы́ спеши́те, в лаборато́рию?

---

[1] Beginning with this lesson, both the teacher and student sentences are included in the same column.

Спеши́ть is a second conjugation verb with the stress on the endings.

	SINGULAR	PLURAL
1	спеш–у́	спеш–и́м
2	–и́шь	–и́те
3	–и́т	–а́т

Second conjugation verbs have linking vowel и, (спеши́шь, спеши́т, спеши́м, спеши́те) where first conjugation verbs have е or ё (рабо́таешь идёшь). Where first conjugation verbs have the third person plural ending in –ут or –ют (иду́т рабо́тают), second conjugation verbs have –ат or –ят (спеша́т, говоря́т). It is only in the first person singular that first and second conjugation verbs share the common ending –у or –ю.

Examples of other second conjugation verbs so far encountered:[1]

> **слы́шать**   *to hear*
> слы́ш–у, слы́ш–ишь, слы́ш–ит, слы́ш–им, слы́ш–ите, слы́ш–ат
> **говори́ть**   *to speak, say*
> говор–ю́, говор–и́шь, говор–и́т, говор–и́м, говор–и́те, говор–я́т
> **стоя́ть**   *to stand*
> сто–ю́, сто–и́шь, сто–и́т, сто–и́м, сто–и́те, сто–я́т

Masculine, feminine, and plural endings of short-form adjectives

MASCULINE SUBJECT	Я (ты́, о́н) за́нят.	I'm (you're, he's) busy.
	_____ ра́д.	_____ glad.
	_____ здоро́в.	_____ well.
	_____ бо́лен.	_____ sick.
FEMININE SUBJECT	Я (ты́, она́) занята́.	I'm (you're, she's) busy.
	_____ ра́да.	_____ glad.
	_____ здоро́ва.	_____ well.
	_____ больна́.	_____ sick.
PLURAL SUBJECT	Мы́ (вы́, они́) за́няты.	We're (you're, they're) busy.
	_____ ра́ды.	_____ glad.
	_____ здоро́вы.	_____ well.
	_____ больны́.	_____ sick.

■ REPETITION DRILL

Listen to your instructor (or the tape) and repeat the above models until you can say them perfectly.

---

[1] These verbs are given here primarily to show ending and stress patterns. They will be drilled later.

Repeat after your instructor (or the tape) as accurately as you can, imitating both the individual words and the sentence intonation. Then, on hearing only the subject cue, supply the full utterance according to the given model.

1. *I'm busy now.*
   т: Я́ тепе́рь за́нят.
   s: **Я́ тепе́рь за́нят.**
   т: Она́ тепе́рь занята́.
   s: **Она́ тепе́рь занята́.**
      (они́, вы́, Ни́на, жена́, му́ж, мы́, Ми́ла)

2. *Are you glad to hear it?*
   т: Ты́ ра́д э́то слы́шать?
   s: **Ты́ ра́д э́то слы́шать?**
   т: Она́ ра́да э́то слы́шать?
   s: **Она́ ра́да э́то слы́шать?**
      (Семён, они́, Цара́пкин, вы́, Ми́ла)

3. *I'm completely well.*
   т: Я́ вполне́ здоро́в.
   s: **Я́ вполне́ здоро́в.**
   т: Они́ вполне́ здоро́вы.
   s: **Они́ вполне́ здоро́вы.**
      (вы́, жена́, она́, Евге́ний)

4. *I'm sick.*
   т: Я́ бо́лен.
   s: **Я́ бо́лен.**
   т: Она́ больна́.
   s: **Она́ больна́.**
      (Ми́ла и Семён, вы́, Евге́ний, мы́, Ни́на)

■ QUESTION-ANSWER DRILLS

1. *Lev, are you busy?*
   No, I'm not busy.
   т: Лёв, ты́ за́нят?
   s: **Не́т, я́ не за́нят.**
   т: Ни́на, ты́ занята́?
   s: **Не́т, я́ не занята́.**
      (Ми́ла, Хитро́в, Кири́лл Па́влович, Ни́на Семёновна, Семён)

2. *Nina, are you still sick?*
   No, I'm completely well now.
   т: Ни́на, вы́ всё ещё больны́?
   s: **Не́т, я́ тепе́рь вполне́ здоро́ва.**
   т: Кири́лл, ты́ всё ещё бо́лен?
   s: **Не́т, я́ тепе́рь вполне́ здоро́в.**
   Семён Фили́ппович, вы́ всё ещё больны́?
   Ми́ла, ты́ всё ещё больна́?
   Евге́ний, ты́ всё ещё бо́лен?
   Кири́лл Па́влович, вы́ всё ещё больны́?

■ SUBSTITUTION DRILL

I'm glad to hear that.
т: Я́ ра́д э́то слы́шать.
s: **Я́ ра́д э́то слы́шать.**
т: (Мы́) _____.
s: **Мы́ ра́ды э́то слы́шать.**
   (они́, Кири́лл, жена́, Семён
   Фили́ппович, она́, Ни́на и Ми́ла, о́н)

MASCULINE	FEMININE	PLURAL
–	–a	–ы

The short-form adjectives agree with their subject in gender or number. Note that those used with masculine subjects have no ending, those used with feminine subjects end in –a, and those used with plural subjects end in –ы.[1]

Note that the stress may shift to the ending, particularly in the feminine form: **Она́ занята́.** (Compare it with **Óн за́нят.**)

If the stem ends in more than one consonant, the masculine form may contain a vowel that does not appear in the other forms. This vowel appears between the last two consonants of the stem. Compare **он бóлен** with **она́ больна́, вы́ больны́.** The soft sign is written in the feminine and plural forms to indicate that the л is soft.

ЧТÉНИЕ И ПИСЬМÓ   READING AND WRITING

The conversation for Lesson 3 is presented here in handwritten form for reading and copying practice.

Лучше поздно, чем никогда

— Лев! Здравствуйте! Куда вы спешите?
— В университет, на концерт. — Интересно. Это бесплатно? — Да. Хотите пойти? — С удовольствием. — Кстати, что вы теперь делаете? — Работаю в лаборатории. Там так скучно. — Так поступайте в университет. — Что вы! Мне теперь уже поздно! — Знаете, говорят: „Лучше поздно, чем никогда."

---

[1] The neuter short adjective ending –o is excluded from this discussion for practical reasons since the subjects used with these adjectives are mostly masculine, feminine, or plural.

PREPARATION FOR CONVERSATION   **Разгово́р в общежи́тии**

общежи́тие   [apščiží̱t̢ijə]   dormitory
в общежи́тии   [vəpščiží̱t̢iji]   in the dormitory
разгово́р   [rəzgavór]   conversation
Разгово́р в общежи́тии.   Conversation in the dormitory.
войти́ (pfv)[1]   [vajt̢í]   to enter, come in, go in
мо́жно   [móžnə]   it's possible, one may
Мо́жно войти́?   May I come in?

коне́чно   [kaṇéšnə] [2]   of course, certainly
заходи́ть   [zəxaḑít̢]   to drop in, stop by, call [on someone]
заходи́   [zəxaḑí]   come in!
заперта́   [zəp̢irtá] [3]   locked
дверь (f)   [dv̢ér̢]   door
Дверь не заперта́.   The door isn't locked.
Заходи́! Дверь не заперта́.   Come in! The door isn't locked.

бы́ть   [bít̢]   to be
я была́   [já bilá]   I (f) was, I've been
зна́ть   [znát̢]   to know
ты зна́ешь   [tí znájiš]   you know
Зна́ешь, где я была́?   Know where I've been?
всё у́тро   [fṣó útrə]   all morning
Зна́ешь, где я была́ всё у́тро?   Know where I've been all morning?

го́род   [górət]   city, town
в го́роде   [vgórəḑi]   in the city, in town, downtown
Я была́ в го́роде.   I've been downtown.

пода́рок   [padárək]   gift, present
я покупа́ла   [já pəkupálə]   I (f) was buying
покупа́ть   [pəkupát̢]   to buy, to be buying

---

[1] The abbreviation *pfv* will be used for the perfective aspect and *ipfv* for the imperfective.
[2] **Коне́чно** is pronounced [kaṇečnə] by many speakers.
[3] Two pronunciations are possible: [zəp̢irtá] and [záp̢irtə].

Я покупа́ла пода́рок.	I was buying a present.
Ни́не [ɲíɲi]	[for] Nina
Я покупа́ла пода́рок Ни́не.	I was buying Nina a present.
а́х [áx]	oh!
А́х, да́!	Oh, yes!
де́нь (m) [ḍéṇ]	day
де́нь рожде́ния [ḍéṇ ražḍéṇijə]	birthday (*lit.* day of birth)
у неё [uṇijó]	she has (*lit.* by her)
У неё де́нь рожде́ния.	She has a birthday *or* It's her birthday.
за́втра [záftrə]	tomorrow
У неё за́втра де́нь рожде́ния.	She has a birthday tomorrow.
купи́ть (pfv) [kuṗíṭ]	to buy
ты́ купи́ла [tí kuṗílə]	you (f) bought
Что́ ты́ купи́ла?	What did you buy?
посмотре́ть (pfv) [pəsmatṛéṭ]	to take a look
[ты́] хо́чешь [tí xóčiš]	you want
Хо́чешь посмотре́ть?	Want to take a look?
коро́бка [karópkə]	box (cardboard)
в коро́бке [fkarópḳi]	in the box
ту́т [tút]	here
Во́т ту́т, в коро́бке.	It's here in the box.
портфе́ль (m) [partḟéḷ]	briefcase
доста́ть (pfv) [dastáṭ]	to get
ты́ доста́ла [tí dastálə]	you (f) got
Где́ ты́ доста́ла?	Where'd you get [it]?
Портфе́ль! Где́ ты́ доста́ла?	A briefcase! Where'd you get it?
ГУ́М [gúm]	GUM (State Department Store)
в ГУ́Ме [vgúṃi]	at GUM
краси́вый [kraṣívij]	handsome, pretty, lovely
пра́вда [právdə]	isn't it (*lit.* truth)
Пра́вда, краси́вый?	Handsome, isn't it?
В ГУ́Ме. Пра́вда, краси́вый?	At GUM. Handsome, isn't it?
о́чень [óčiṇ]	very
О́чень краси́вый.	Very handsome.
до́лго [dólgə]	long, a long time
стоя́ть [stajáṭ]	to stand, to be standing
ты́ стоя́ла [tí stajálə]	you (f) stood
Ты́ до́лго стоя́ла?	Did you stand for a long time?
о́чередь (f) [óčiṛiṭ]	line, turn
в о́череди [vóčiṛiḍi]	in line
Ты́ до́лго стоя́ла в о́череди?	Did you stand in line a long time?
Не́т, не о́чень.	No, not very [long].

де́лать [ḍélət]	to do, to be doing
Что́ вы́ де́лали?	What did you do? *or* What were you doing?
— Ничего́. ṇičivó]	Nothing.
Где́ вы́ бы́ли?	Where were you?
слу́жба [slúžbə]	job, work, service
— На слу́жбе.	At work.
Что́ вы́ купи́ли?	What did you buy?
материа́л [məṭirjál]	material
пла́тье [pláṭjə]	dress
— Материа́л на пла́тье.	Material for a dress *or* Dress material.
костю́м [kasṭúm]	suit
— Материа́л на костю́м.	Material for a suit *or* Suit material.

ADDITIONAL CLASSROOM EXPRESSIONS

да́льше [dáḷši]	continue! go on! (*lit.* further)
Чита́йте да́льше!	Go on reading!
пиши́те [ṛišíṭi] *or* напиши́те [neṛišíṭi]	write!
на доске́ [nədasḳé]	on the board
Напиши́те на доске́!	Write on the board!
иди́те [iḍíṭi]	go!
к доске́ [gdasḳé]	to the board
Иди́те к доске́!	Go to the board!
измени́те [izṃiṇíṭi]	change! make a change!
замени́те [zəṃiṇíṭi]	substitute! make a substitution!

Разгово́р в общежи́тии

Conversation in the dormitory

C. — Са́ша (студе́нт)
O. — О́ля (студе́нтка)

C.	1 Кто́ та́м?	któ tắm ↓	Who's there?
O.	2 Э́то я́, О́ля. Мо́жно войти́?	étə jắ ↓ őḷə ↓ móžnə vajṭí ↓	It's me, Olya. May I come in?
C.	3 Коне́чно. Заходи́. Две́рь не заперта́.	kaṇḗšnə ↓ zəxaḍí ↓ dγéṛ ṇizəṛirtắ ↓	Of course. Come in. The door isn't locked.
O.	4 Зна́ешь, где́ я́ была́ всё у́тро? В го́роде. Покупа́ла пода́рок Ни́не.	znájiš gḍé já bɨlắ ↓ fşó űtrə ↓ vgőrəḍi ↓ pəkupálə padắrək ṇíṇi ↓	Know where I've been all morning? Downtown. I was buying a present for Nina.

C.	5	Áх, дá! У неё зáвтра дéнь рождéния. А чтó ты́ купи́ла?	áx dã ↓ uɲijó záftrə ɟéɲ raʐɟéɲijə ↓ a štő tí kupílə ↓	Oh, yes! It's her birthday tomorrow. And what did you buy?
O.	6	Хóчешь посмотрéть? Вóт тýт, в корóбке.	xóčiš pəsmatr̝éʦ̬ ↑ vót tűt ↓ fkarőpḳi ↓	Want to take a look? It's here in the box.
C.	7	Портфéль! Гдé ты́ достáла?	partf̝él̝ ↓ gɟé tí dastắlə ↓	A briefcase! Where did you get it?
O.	8	В ГУ́Ме. Прáвда, краси́вый?	vgűm̝i ↓ právdə kraʂívij ↑	In GUM.[2] Handsome, isn't it?
C.	9	Óчень. Ты́ дóлго стоя́ла в óчереди?	őčiɲ ↓ tí dőlgə stajálə vóčir̝iɟi ↓	Very. Did you stand in line a long time?
O.	10	Нéт, не óчень.	ɲét ↑ ɲiőčiɲ ↓	No, not very.

NOTES

[1] Informally Russians address each other using nicknames based on the first name, for example: **Сáша** for **Алексáндр**, **Óля** for **Óльга**. Such names are comparable to our Bob for Robert, Gene for Eugene, Betty for Elizabeth, and so forth. Others are:

Жéня	*for*	Евгéний	Eugene	Ми́ла	*for*	Людми́ла	Ludmilla
Вáня		Ивáн	John	Гáля		Гали́на	Galina
Лёва		Лéв	Leo	Тáня		Татья́на	Tatiana
Кóля		Николáй	Nicholas	Кáтя		Екатери́на	Katherine
Пéтя		Пётр	Peter	Зи́на		Зинаи́да	Zinaida
Алёша		Алексéй	Alexis	Лю́ба		Любóвь	Amy
Сéня		Семён	Simon	Мáша		Мари́я	Mary
Бóря		Бори́с	Boris	Лéна		Елéна	Helen
Волóдя		Влади́мир	Vladimir	Ли́за		Елизавéта	Elizabeth

[2] **ГУМ (Госудáрственный универсáльный магази́н)** is the State Department Store, which is located in Red Square opposite the Moscow Kremlin. Note that, although GUM itself is written with capital letters, its declensional endings are written with small letters: **в ГУ́Ме** *in GUM*.

Basic sentence patterns

1. Ктó тáм?
   — Это я́, Óля.
   _____ Евгéний.
   _____ Ни́на.
   _____ Кири́лл Пáвлович.
   _____ Семён Фили́ппович.

Who's there?
It's me, Olya.
_____ Evgeny.
_____ Nina.
_____ Kirill Pavlovich.
_____ Semyon Filippovich.

_____ Царáпкин.	_____ Tsarapkin.
_____ Хитрóв.	_____ Khitrov.
_____ Мѝла.	_____ Mila.
_____ Лёв.	_____ Lev.

2. Сáша, гдé тѝ бы́л всё ýтро? — Where were you all morning, Sasha?
   — Я бы́л на собрáнии. — I've been at a meeting.
   _____ на урóке пéния. — _____ at a singing lesson.
   _____ на завóде. — _____ at the plant.
   _____ на пóчте. — _____ at the post office.
   _____ на концéрте. — _____ at a concert.

3. Óля, гдé тѝ былá всё ýтро? — Where were you all morning, Olya?
   — Я былá в гóроде. — I was in town.
   _____ в ГУ́Ме. — ____ at GUM.
   _____ в общежѝтии. — ____ in the dormitory.
   _____ в университéте. — ____ at the university.
   _____ в горсовéте. — ____ at the gorsovet.
   _____ в клýбе. — ____ at the club.
   _____ в лаборатóрии. — ____ at the laboratory.

4. Чтó тѝ дéлал в гóроде, Сáша? — What were you doing in town, Sasha?
   — Я покупáл подáрок. — I was buying a present.
   — Я покупáл подáрок Нѝне. — I was buying Nina a present.
   — Я стоя́л в óчереди. — I was standing in line.
   — Я покупáл портфéль. — I was buying a briefcase.
   — Я покупáл материáл на костю́м. — I was buying suit material.

5. А чтó тѝ дéлала, Óля? — And what were you doing, Olya?
   — Я тóже былá в гóроде. — I was in town, too.
   — Я тóже покупáла подáрок. — I was buying a present, too.
   — Я тóже стоя́ла в óчереди. — I was standing in line, too.
   — Я покупáла плáтье. — I was buying a dress.
   — Я покупáла материáл на плáтье. — I was buying dress material.
   — Я покупáла материáл на костю́м. — I was buying suit material.

6. Гдé вѝ э́то достáли? — Where did you get that?
   — В гóроде. — In town.
   — В ГУ́Ме. — At GUM.
   — В университéте. — At the university.
   — В общежѝтии. — At the dormitory.
   — В клýбе. — At the club.
   — В лаборатóрии. — At the laboratory.

Introductory remarks on the Russian case system

By now you have noted that Russian nouns may vary their endings in accordance with the way they function in a sentence. Thus, in the following examples, the Russian word for *laboratory* changes its ending according to whether it indicates location or destination.

| LOCATION | Онá рабóтает в лаборатóри**и**. | She works in a laboratory. |
| DESTINATION | Онá идёт в лаборатóри**ю**. | She's on her way to the laboratory. |

Compare the examples with English, where the word *laboratory* does not change but a different preposition is used: *in* for location and *to* for destination.

In Russian the same preposition (в) is used but a different "case" form of the noun is required: prepositional case for location and accusative case for destination.

There are six cases in Russian, used in both the singular and the plural. They are given below together with a brief comment on their primary function.

CASE NAME	ABBREVIATION	PRIMARY FUNCTION TO INDICATE
NOMINATIVE	NOM or N	grammatical subject of sentence
ACCUSATIVE	ACC or A	direct object, complete goal of action
GENITIVE	GEN or G	possession, absence, limitation
PREPOSITIONAL[1]	PREP or P	location or focus of activity
DATIVE	DAT or D	indirect object, person affected (in impersonal constructions)
INSTRUMENTAL	INSTR or I	instrument or means of accomplishment of activity

The nominative form is customarily used in citing nouns, pronouns, and adjectives in dictionaries or otherwise out of context.

Remarks on stems and endings: the concept of "zero" ending

Since Russian, like Latin and German, relies heavily on changes in the forms of its nouns, adjectives, and verbs for grammatical purposes, the student must be able to identify and manipulate both stems and grammatical endings.

Briefly stated, the stem is the part of a word that remains relatively constant; the ending is the part that varies to show grammatical changes. Compare the following sets, observing that both existent endings and the absence of endings provide important grammatical information.

Москва́	Moscow	в Москву́	to Moscow
окно́	window	на окне́	on the window
одно́ сло́во	one word	мно́го слов	many words
сто́л	table	на столе́	on the table
о́н здоро́в	he's well	она́ здоро́ва	she's well
о́н бы́л	he was	она́ была́	she was

The concept of the nonexistent or "zero" ending is a very important one for Russian. Nouns, verbs, adjectives, and numerals all have forms where a "zero" ending contrasts with explicit endings.

---

[1] The prepositional case is also frequently called the *locative* case. It is the one case in Russian that is *never* used *without* a preposition.

For example, most masculine nouns have a "zero" ending in their nominative singular case form. A "zero" ending also occurs after the suffix **л** in the masculine past tense form, contrasting with the feminine ending **–a**, the neuter ending **–o**, and the plural ending **–и**. Furthermore, most feminine and neuter nouns have a "zero" ending in the genitive plural, in contrast with all of their case forms that occur with an ending. Compare **сло́во** *word*, **слова́** *words* with **сло́в** *of the words*; and **кни́га** *book*, **кни́ги** *books* with **кни́г** *of the books*.

STRUCTURE AND DRILLS

Past tense of the verb бы́ть *to be*

MASCULINE SUBJECT	Я́ бы́л та́м.	I was there.
	Ты́ бы́л та́м.	You were there.
	О́н бы́л та́м.	He was there.
	Портфе́ль бы́л та́м.	The briefcase was there.
FEMININE SUBJECT	Я́ была́ та́м.	I was there.
	Ты́ была́ та́м.	You were there.
	Она́ была́ та́м.	She was there.
	Коро́бка была́ та́м.	The box was there.
NEUTER SUBJECT	Собра́ние бы́ло та́м.	The meeting was there.
PLURAL SUBJECT	Мы́ бы́ли та́м.	We were there.
	Вы́ бы́ли та́м.	You were there.[1]
	Они́ бы́ли та́м.	They were there.
	Ле́в и Ни́на бы́ли та́м.	Lev and Nina were there.

■ REPETITION DRILL

Listen to your instructor (or the tape) and repeat the above models until you can reproduce them accurately.

■ REPETITION-SUBSTITUTION DRILL

I was at the plant.

т: Я́ бы́л на заво́де.

s: **Я́ бы́л на заво́де.**

(о́н, они́, Са́ша, Ни́на, О́ля и Ле́в, вы́,

она́, мы́)

---

[1] Note that **вы́**, the plural-polite pronoun *you*, is treated grammatically as a plural even when it refers to a single person. Thus, **Где́ вы́ доста́ли?** can be addressed to one person who is not an intimate friend, or to more than one person. **Ты́**, on the other hand, can only be addressed to one person.

1. *Were they in the dormitory too?*
   Yes, they were.
   т: Они́ то́же бы́ли в общежи́тии?
   s: **Да́, бы́ли.**
   т: О́н то́же бы́л в общежи́тии?
   s: **Да́, бы́л.**
   (Ле́в и Кири́лл, она́, Са́ша, О́ля)

2. *Have you already been to the club, Nina?*
   Yes, I have.
   т: Вы́ уже́ бы́ли в клу́бе, Ни́на?
   s: **Да́, была́.**
   т: Вы́ уже́ бы́ли в клу́бе, Ле́в?
   s: **Да́, бы́л.**
   Ты́ уже́ была́ в клу́бе, Ми́ла?
   Ты́ уже́ бы́л в клу́бе, Са́ша?
   Вы́ уже́ бы́ли в клу́бе, О́ля?

3. *Where were you, Sasha?*
   I was in the laboratory.
   т: Где́ ты́ бы́л, Са́ша?
   s: **Я́ бы́л в лаборато́рии.**
   т: Где́ ты́ была́, Ни́на?
   s: **Я́ была́ в лаборато́рии.**
   Где́ вы́ бы́ли, Кири́лл?
   Где́ вы́ бы́ли, Ми́ла?
   Где́ о́н бы́л?
   Где́ она́ была́?
   Где́ мы́ бы́ли?
   Где́ они́ бы́ли?

4. *Nina, where have you been all morning?*
   I've been in town.
   т: Ни́на, где́ вы́ бы́ли всё у́тро?
   s: **Я́ была́ в го́роде.**
   т: Са́ша, где́ ты́ бы́л всё у́тро?
   s: **Я́ бы́л в го́роде.**
   О́ля, где́ ты́ была́ всё у́тро?
   Кири́лл, где́ ты́ бы́л всё у́тро?
   Ле́в, где́ вы́ бы́ли всё у́тро?
   О́ля и Ни́на, где́ вы́ бы́ли всё у́тро?
   Ле́в и Кири́лл, где́ вы́ бы́ли всё у́тро?

5. *Was she at work?*
   Yes, she was.
   т: Она́ была́ на слу́жбе?
   s: **Да́, была́.**
   т: Они́ бы́ли на слу́жбе?
   s: **Да́, бы́ли.**
   Му́ж бы́л на слу́жбе?
   Они́ бы́ли на слу́жбе?
   Кири́лл бы́л на слу́жбе?
   Жена́ была́ на слу́жбе?
   Кири́лл и Ле́в бы́ли на слу́жбе?

DISCUSSION

The past tense differs from the present and future in Russian in that it is not based on personal endings but on gender-number endings. The past tense of the verb **бы́ть** *to be* illustrates this principle.

SINGULAR			PLURAL
Masculine	*Feminine*	*Neuter*	
бы́л	бы́л-**а́**	бы́л-**о**	бы́л-**и**

Я та́м не́ **был**.   I (*m*) wasn't there.
Вы́ **бы́ли** больны́. You were sick.
Она́ **была́** в го́роде. She was in town.
Вчера́ **бы́ло** собра́ние. There was a meeting yesterday.

In the last example, **бы́ло** agrees with the neuter noun **собра́ние**.

The accusative form of inanimate masculine and neuter nouns

MODELS

Я спешу́ на уро́к.   I'm hurrying to a lesson.
_____ на уро́к пе́ния. _____ to a singing lesson.
_____ на конце́рт.   _____ to a concert.
_____ на авто́бус.   _____ to the bus.
_____ на заво́д.   _____ to the plant.
_____ на собра́ние.   _____ to a meeting.

Я иду́ в университе́т.   I'm on my way to the university.
_____ в клу́б.   _____ to the club.
_____ в горсове́т.   _____ to the gorsovet.
_____ в го́род.   _____ to town.
_____ в ГУ́М.   _____ to GUM.
_____ в общежи́тие.   _____ to the dormitory.

Ты́ уже́ ви́дел го́род?   Have you already seen the city?
_____ пода́рок?   _____ the present?
_____ портфе́ль?   _____ the briefcase?
_____ клу́б?   _____ the club?
_____ ГУ́М?   _____ GUM?
_____ университе́т? _____ the university?
_____ письмо́?   _____ the letter?
_____ общежи́тие?   _____ the dormitory?

Где́ вы́ доста́ли пода́рок? Where did you get the present?
_____ портфе́ль?   _____ the briefcase?
_____ письмо́?   _____ the letter?

■ **REPETITION DRILLS**

Repeat the models after your instructor (or the tape), noting that the accusative form is like the nominative for these masculine and neuter nouns referring to inanimate things. Note also that certain nouns require the preposition **в** and others require **на.**

1. *She's going to class.*
   т: Она́ идёт на уро́к.
   s: **Она́ идёт на уро́к.**
   т: _____ (на по́чту).
   s: **Она́ идёт на по́чту.**
   (на конце́рт, на заво́д,
   на собра́ние, на уро́к пе́ния)

2. *She's going to the club.*
   т: Она́ идёт в клу́б.
   s: **Она́ идёт в клу́б.**
   т: _____ (в горсове́т).
   s: **Она́ идёт в горсове́т.**
   (в ГУ́М, в го́род, в общежи́тие,
   в университе́т, в клу́б)

3. *We're hurrying to the bus.*
   т: Мы́ спеши́м на авто́бус.
   s: **Мы́ спеши́м на авто́бус.**
   т: _____ (в ГУ́М).
   s: **Мы́ спеши́м в ГУ́М.**
   (на уро́к, в общежи́тие,
   на конце́рт, в университе́т,
   на заво́д, в го́род, на собра́ние,
   в клу́б)

4. *I've already seen the present.*
   т: Я́ уже́ ви́дел пода́рок.
   s: **Я́ уже́ ви́дел пода́рок.**
   т: _____ (общежи́тие).
   s: **Я́ уже́ ви́дел общежи́тие.**
   (го́род, ГУ́М, письмо́, клу́б,
   университе́т, портфе́ль)

DISCUSSION

Masculine and neuter nouns such as **уро́к**, **портфе́ль**, **собра́ние**, and **письмо́**, which refer to other than living beings, have the same form in the accusative case as in the nominative. The accusative case is used in Russian for the direct object of a verb, or for the object of certain prepositions such as **в** or **на**, used in conjunction with verbs of motion. It is important to remember that in the meaning *to*, certain nouns require the preposition **в** while others require the preposition **на**.

в го́род	to town	на конце́рт	to the concert
в ГУ́М	to GUM	на авто́бус	to the bus
в общежи́тие	to the dormitory	на уро́к	to class
в клу́б	to the club	на по́чту	to the post office
в университе́т	to the university	на собра́ние	to the meeting

Разговор в общежитии

— Кто там? — Это я, Оля. Можно войти? — Конечно. Заходи. Дверь не заперта. — Знаешь, где я была всё утро? В городе. Покупала подарок Нине. — Ах да! У неё завтра день рождения. А что ты купила? — Хочешь посмотреть? Вот тут в коробке. — Портфель? Где ты достала? — В ГУМе. Правда красивый? — Очень. Ты долго стояла в очереди? — Нет, не очень.

PREPARATION FOR CONVERSATION   **Чтó на обéд?**

обéд [ab̧ét]		dinner
на обéд [nəab̧ét]		for dinner
Чтó на обéд?		What's for dinner?
кáк насчёт [kák naščót]		how about
Кáк насчёт обéда?		How about dinner?
Кáк насчёт обéда, Олéг?		How about dinner, Oleg?
откры́та [atkrítə]		open
столóвая [stalóvəjə]		dining hall, cafe, restaurant, dining room
Столóвая откры́та.		The dining hall's open.
Столóвая давнó откры́та.		The dining hall's been open for a long time.
обéдать [ab̧édəţ]		to dine, eat dinner
идём [iḓóm]		let's go!
Идём обéдать!		Let's go eat dinner!
Хорошó. Идём обéдать.		Fine. Let's go eat dinner!
гóлоден [góləḓin]		hungry
Я́ ужé гóлоден.		I'm already hungry.
сегóдня [şivódņə][1]		today
Чтó сегóдня на обéд?		What's for dinner today?
интерéсно [inţiŗésnə]		I wonder (*lit.* [it is] interesting [to me])
Интерéсно, что сегóдня на обéд?		I wonder what's for dinner today.
смотрéть [smaţŗéţ]		to look
Ты́ смотрéл?		Did you look?
всегдá [ˈşigdá]		always
Как всегдá.		[Same] as always.
пи́ща [p̧íščə]		fare, food, diet
нáша [nášə]		our

---

[1] Note that г is pronounced [v] in **сегóдня** [şivódņə] *today*.

щи́ (pl) [ščí]	schi (sauerkraut soup, cabbage soup)
да [də][1]	and
ка́ша [káša]	kasha (cooked cereal, porridge)
«Щи́ да ка́ша — пи́ща на́ша».	"Schi and kasha is our diet."
бо́льше [bóļši]	more, bigger
бо́льше не́т [bóļši ņét]	there isn't any more, it's all gone
ры́ба [rɨ́bə]	fish
Была́ ры́ба, но бо́льше не́т.	There was fish, but it's all gone.
доса́да [dasádə]	annoyance, aggravation, disappointment, vexation
Во́т доса́да!	How annoying! *or* What a nuisance!
не хо́чется [ņixóčitcə]	[one] doesn't feel like
туда́ [tudá]	there, to that place
Не хо́чется идти́ туда́.	I don't feel like going there.
да́же [dáži]	even
Да́же идти́ туда́ не хо́чется.	I don't even feel like going there.

SUPPLEMENT

голодна́ (f) [gəladná]	hungry
Ни́на, ты голодна́?	Nina, are you hungry?
го́лодны (pl) [gólədnɨ]	hungry
Вы́ го́лодны?	Are you hungry?
бо́рщ [bóršč]	borsch (beet soup)
Что́ на обе́д, бо́рщ?	What's for dinner, borsch?
ко́фе (m) [kófi][2]	coffee
Хо́чешь ко́фе?	Want some coffee?
пи́ть [ṕíţ]	to drink
Я́ пи́л ко́фе.	I was drinking (*or* drank) coffee.
ча́й (m) [čáj]	tea
Я́ пи́л ча́й.	I was drinking (*or* drank) tea.
неда́вно [ņidávnə]	awhile ago, recently, not long ago
Я́ неда́вно пи́л ча́й.	I drank tea awhile ago.
молоко́ [məlakó]	milk
Я́ неда́вно пи́л молоко́.	Awhile ago I drank some milk.

---

[1] Do not confuse unstressed **да** [də] *and* with stressed **да́** [dá] *yes.*

[2] **Ко́фе** is considered a masculine noun by some speakers; others treat it as a neuter. It is one of a small number of indeclinable nouns, i.e., nouns that use the same form in all cases.

Чтó на обéд?

What's for dinner?

О. — Олéг

Л. — Лéв

Л. 1	Кáк насчёт обéда, Олéг? Столóвая давнó откры́та.	kák naščót aḅédə aḷék ↓ stalóvəjə davnó atkri̊tə ↓	How about dinner, Oleg? The dining hall's been open for a long time.[1]
О. 2	Хорошó. Идём обéдать. Я́ ужé гóлоден.	xəraš̋ő ↓ iḍőm aḅédəṭ ↓ já užé gőlədin ↓	Fine. Let's go eat dinner. I'm already hungry.
Л. 3	Интерéсно, чтó сегóдня на обéд. Ты́ смотрéл?	inṭiŗésnə ↓ štó şivódņə nəaḅét ↓ tí smatŗél ↑	I wonder what's for dinner today. Did you look?
О. 4	Дá. Кáк всегдá, «Щи́ да кáша — пи́ща нáша». Былá ры́ба, но бóльше нéт.	dắ ↓ kák fşigdắ ↓ ščí də kắšə | ṛíščə nắšə ↓ bilá ri̊bə ↓ no bóḷši ņét ↓	Yes. Same as always, "Schi and kasha is our diet."[2] There was fish, but it's all gone.
Л. 5	Вóт досáда! Дáже идти́ тудá не хóчется.	vót dasắdə ↓ dắži iṭṭí tudá | ņixŏčitcə ↓	How annoying! I don't even feel like going there.

NOTES   [1] **Столóвая** is a feminine adjective which functions as a noun. It is derived from **столóвая кóмната** *table room*. **Столóвая** is used here as *dining hall*, but it also means [*second class*] *restaurant* as well as dining room.

[2] «**Щи́ да кáша — пи́ща нáша**» is a colloquial expression illustrating the humble food that comprises the Russian rural diet. **Щи́** is a soup made of sauerkraut or cabbage. **Кáша** is cooked cereal, which may be served at any meal and eaten with butter, salt, or gravy; or with milk and sugar. **Бóрщ** is a vegetable soup, primarily made of beets.

пообе́дать   [pɐɐb̥éd̥ət̢]   to eat dinner, have dinner
Вы́ уже́ пообе́дали?   Have you had dinner already?
ребя́та   [r̢ib̢atə]   children, kids, fellows, guys
Приве́т, ребя́та!   Hi, fellows!
Приве́т, ребя́та! Вы́ уже́ пообе́дали?   Hi, fellows! Have you had dinner already?

ещё   [jiščó]   yet, still; else, some more, another
Не́т ещё.   Not yet.

опя́ть   [ɐp̢át̢]   again
в столо́вой   [fstalóvəj]   at (or in) the dining hall
В столо́вой опя́ть щи́ и ка́ша.   At the dining hall it's schi and kasha again.

селёдка   [s̢il̢ótkə]   herring
А я́ купи́л селёдку.   But I bought herring.
как ра́з   [kakrás]   just, it just happens
А я́ как ра́з купи́л селёдку.   Well, it just happens I bought herring.
А я́ как ра́з купи́л селёдку. Хоти́те?   Well, it just happens I bought herring. Want some?

друго́е де́ло   [drugójə d̢élə]   another matter, a different thing
Э́то друго́е де́ло!   That's different!
Селёдка — э́то друго́е де́ло!   Herring! That's different!

у на́с е́сть   [unás jés̢t̢]   we have (lit. by us there is)
хле́б   [x̢l̢ép]   bread
Хле́б у на́с е́сть.   We have bread.
огурцы́   [agurcí]   cucumbers
Огурцы́ то́же.   Cucumbers too.
Хле́б у на́с е́сть. Огурцы́ то́же.   We have bread. Cucumbers too.

же   [ži]   (unstressed emphatic particle)
Где́ же они́?   Where are they?
шка́ф   [škáf]   cupboard, wardrobe, dresser
в шкафу́   [fškafú]   in the cupboard
Где́ же они́? В шкафу́?   Where are they, in the cupboard?

окно́   [aknó]   window
на окне́   [nəakn̢é]   on the window [ledge]
Не́т, на окне́.   No, on the window [ledge].

наре́жь!   [nar̢éš]   slice!
Наре́жь огурцы́!   Slice the cucumbers!
Оле́г, наре́жь огурцы́!   Oleg, slice the cucumbers!

я́щик   [jáščik]   drawer, box [wooden]
в я́щике   [vjáščik̢i]   in the drawer
Но́ж в я́щике.   The knife's in the drawer.
сто́л   [stól]   desk, table
в столе́   [fstal̢é]   in the desk, in the table
Но́ж в столе́, в я́щике.   The knife's in the desk drawer.

вѝжу [γɨ́žu]	I see
не вѝжу [n̦iγɨ́žu]	I don't see
Не вѝжу.	I don't see [it].

вѝлка [γɨ́lkə]	fork
вѝлки [γɨ́lk̦i]	forks
Ту́т то́лько вѝлки.	There are just forks here.
ло́жка [lóškə]	spoon
ло́жки [lóšk̦i]	spoons
то́лько [tól̦kə]	only, just
Ту́т то́лько вѝлки и ло́жки.	There are just forks and spoons here.

| на столе́ [nəstal̦é] | on the table, on the desk. |
| **Во́т о́н, на столе́.** | Here it is, on the desk. |

| смотре́ть в окно́ | to look out the window, look in the window |
| О́н смотре́л в окно́. | He was looking out (or in) the window. |

Вы́ уже́ пообе́дали?

Have you had dinner already?

К. — Кири́лл   О. — Оле́г   Л. — Ле́в

К.	1	Приве́т, ребя́та! Вы́ уже́ пообе́дали?	pr̦iγ̦ét ↑ r̦ib̦átə ↓ vɨ užé pəab̦édal̦i ↓	Hi, fellows! Have you had dinner already?
О.	2	Не́т ещё. В столо́вой опя́ть щи и ка́ша.	n̦ét jiščó ↓ fstalóvəj ap̦áț ščí i kašə ↓	Not yet. At the dining hall it's schi and kasha again.
К.	3	А я́ как ра́з купи́л селёдку. Хоти́те?	a já kakrás | kup̦íl șil̦ótku ↓ xațíți ↑	Well it just so happens I bought herring. Want some?
Л.	4	Селёдка — это друго́е де́ло.	șil̦ótkə ↓ étə drugójə d̦élə ↓	Herring![1] That's different!
О.	5	Хле́б у на́с е́сть. Огурцы́ то́же.	xl̦ép unás jéșț ↓ agurcɨ́ tóži ↓	We have bread. Cucumbers too.
К.	6	Где́ же они́? В шкафу́?	gd̦éži an̦í ↓ fškafǘ ↑	Where are they, in the cupboard?[2]
О.	7	Не́т, на окне́.	n̦ét ↓ nəakn̦é ↓	No, on the window [ledge].

Л. 8 Олég,
нарéжь огурцы́.
Нóж в столé,
в я́щике.

alék ↓
naŗéš agurcĭ ↓
nóš fstaļé |
vjáščiḳi ↓

Oleg, slice the cucumbers. The knife is in the desk drawer.[3]

О. 9 Не ви́жу.
Ту́т тóлько ви́лки
и лóжки.

ņiɣĭžu ↑
tút tóḷkə ɣĭlḳi |
i lóšḳi ↓

I don't see it. There are just forks and spoons here.

К. 10 Вóт óн,
на столé.

vót ón ↓
nəstaļé ↓

Here it is, on the desk.

NOTES

[1] Herring is a very common food in the Russian diet; it is served not only as an appetizer, but as a main course as well.

[2] Each room in a university dormitory has its **шкáф,** which may serve both as a cupboard and as a wardrobe. (Built-in closets are not to be found in the Soviet Union, nor are they generally found elsewhere in Europe.) Each floor in the dormitory has a kitchen where students can prepare tea, snacks, or light meals.

[3] **Я́щик** is used here as *drawer*, but it also means *box*. It differs from **корóбка,** which designates a small box or one made of cardboard, in that it is usually larger and made of wood. Note also that **стóл** means both *table* and *desk;* the latter comes from **пи́сьменный стóл** *writing table*.

Basic sentence patterns

1. Интерéсно, чтó сегóдня на обéд?
   — Щи́ и кáша.
   — Бóрщ и кáша.
   — Селёдка.
   — Ры́ба.
   — Бóрщ и ры́ба.

   Wonder what's for dinner today?
   Schi and kasha.
   Borsch and kasha.
   Herring.
   Fish.
   Borsch and fish.

2. Óн недáвно пи́л чáй.
   Онá _____ пилá ___.
   Они́ _____ пи́ли ___.
   Óн недáвно пи́л кóфе.
   Онá _____ пилá ___.
   Они́ _____ пи́ли ___.
   Óн недáвно пи́л молокó.
   Онá _____ пилá ___.
   Они́ _____ пи́ли ___.

   He drank tea awhile ago.
   She drank _____.
   They drank _____.
   He drank coffee awhile ago.
   She drank _____.
   They drank _____.
   He drank milk awhile ago.
   She drank _____.
   They drank _____.

3. Столóвая откры́та?
   Лаборатóрия откры́та?
   Пóчта откры́та?
   Корóбка откры́та?

   Is the dining hall open?
   _____ laboratory open?
   _____ post office open?
   _____ box open?

Двéрь откры́та?	Is the door open?
Завóд откры́т?	_____ plant open?
Клýб откры́т?	_____ club open?
Я́щик откры́т?	_____ drawer open?
Горсовéт откры́т?	_____ gorsovet open?
Портфéль откры́т?	_____ briefcase open?
Собрáние откры́то?	_____ meeting open?
Окнó откры́то?	_____ window open?
Общежи́тие откры́то?	_____ dormitory open?

4. Вы́ ужé гóлодны?

— Дá, я ужé гóлоден.	Are you already hungry?
— Дá, я ужé голоднá.	Yes, I'm already hungry.
— Дá, мы́ ужé гóлодны.	Yes, _____.
— Нéт, я ещё не гóлоден.	Yes, we're already hungry.
— Нéт, я ещё не голоднá.	No, I'm not hungry yet.
— Нéт, мы́ ещё не гóлодны.	No, _____.
	No, we're not hungry yet.

5. Вы́ ужé пообéдали?

— Дá, я ужé пообéдал.	Have you already had dinner?
— Дá, я ужé пообéдала.	Yes, I've already had dinner.
— Дá, мы́ ужé пообéдали.	Yes, _____.
— Ещё нéт.	Yes, we've already had dinner.
Вы́ ужé обéдали?	Not yet.
— Нéт, я ещё не обéдал.	Have you already had dinner?
— Нéт, я ещё не обéдала.	No, I haven't had dinner yet.
— Нéт, мы́ ещё не обéдали.[1]	No, _____.
	No, we _____.

6. У нáс éсть хлéб.

_____ бóрщ.	We have bread.
_____ ры́ба.	_____ borsch.
_____ кáша.	_____ fish.
_____ щи́.	_____ kasha.
_____ огурцы́.	_____ schi.
_____ чáй.	_____ cucumbers.
_____ кóфе.	_____ tea.
_____ молокó.	_____ coffee.
	_____ milk.

7. Гдé же нóж?

— На столé.	Where's the knife?
— В я́щике.	On the table.
— На окнé.	In the drawer.
— В столé, в я́щике.	On the window sill.
— В портфéле.	In the desk (or table) drawer.
— В корóбке.	In the briefcase.
— В шкафý.	In the cardboard box.
	In the cupboard.

---

[1] In both the question and answer, either the imperfective **обéдал** or the perfective **пообéдал** may be used. The difference in meaning is slight, with **пообéдал** focusing on the completion of the activity: _Have you already finished eating dinner?_ Note, however, that in the negative answers, only **обéдал** is used.

Pronunciation practice: hard versus soft consonants

A.   [t] vs. [ţ]   Usual Cyrillic spelling т; also ть, д, or дь.

Note the pronunciation of hard [t] in the following:

[napóčtu]	на по́чту	to the post office
[stuḑént]	студе́нт	student

and compare it with soft [ţ]:

[sp̦išiţi]	спеши́те	you're hurrying
[pasláţ]	посла́ть	to send, mail

The formation of Russian hard [t] differs from that of English *t* in that the tip of the tongue closes off the air stream by making contact against the back surface of the upper teeth, whereas English *t* is formed by stopping the air stream farther back, on the ridge of the gums behind the teeth. Soft Russian [ţ], on the other hand, is formed by a closure of the front part of the blade of the tongue (not the tip) against the ridge of the gums and has the effect on the ear of being followed by a y-like glide. In addition, neither Russian hard [t] nor soft [ţ] (nor any other Russian consonant, for that matter) ever has the puff of breath that usually accompanies English *t*.

> Sound Drill: Practice the Russian paired examples illustrating hard [t] and soft [ţ], imitating your instructor (or the tape) as accurately as you can. Be sure to avoid the puff of breath that often accompanies the English *t*.

B.   [d] vs. [ḑ]   Usual Cyrillic spelling д; sometimes дь, т, or ть.

Note the pronunciation of hard [d] in the following:

[davnó]	давно́	for a long time
[zdaróvi]	здоро́вы	healthy
[kudá]	куда́	where to
[idú]	иду́	I'm going

and compare it with soft [ḑ]:

[ɣíḑil]	ви́дел	saw
[ḑilá]	дела́	affairs
[nəzavóḑi]	на заво́де	at the plant
[iḑót]	идёт	is going

Russian hard [d] is made with the tongue in the same position as Russian hard [t] and [n], that is, well forward of the position for making the corresponding English sounds and with the tongue touching the teeth. Russian soft [ḍ] is made with the tongue in the same position as for Russian [ṭ] and [ṇ].

> Sound Drill: Practice the Russian paired examples illustrating hard [d] and soft [ḍ], imitating your instructor (or the tape) as accurately as you can.

C.   [n] vs. [ṇ]   Usual Cyrillic spelling **н**; sometimes **нь**.

Note the pronunciation of hard [n] in the following:

[nǝurók]	на урóк	to the lesson
[napóčtu]	на пóчту	to the post office
[nú]	нý	well

and compare it with soft [ṇ]:

[ṇínǝ]	Нúна	Nina
[dǝsyidáṇjǝ]	до свидáния	good-bye
[fpalṇé]	вполнé	fully, completely
[ḍéṇ]	дéнь	day

Russian hard [n] is formed, like Russian hard [t], by closing off the air stream with the tip of the tongue which strikes the back surface of the upper teeth. (Be careful not to make an English *n*, where the air stream is closed farther back on the gums above the upper teeth!)

Russian soft [ṇ] is formed like Russian soft [ṭ], that is, with the front part of the upper surface of the tongue against the ridge of the gums above the upper teeth and with the tip of the tongue touching the teeth. It has the effect of being followed by a y-like glide and sounds something like English *ny* in such words as ca*ny*on and o*ni*on; however, the y-like glide in Russian must *never* be separated and made a separate consonant sound as it is in English.

> Sound Drill: Practice the Russian examples illustrating hard [n] and soft [ṇ], imitating your instructor (or the tape) as accurately as you can. Notice particularly that before [k] and [g], Russian [n] does not take on the *ng* sound that occurs in such English words as *bank* and *finger*.

Grammatical gender of nouns

All Russian nouns belong to one of three genders: masculine, feminine, or neuter. Besides distinctions based on natural gender, such as we find in English, Russian assigns *all* nouns to one of the three categories.

MASCULINE		FEMININE		NEUTER	
студе́нт	student	студе́нтка	student	письмо́	letter
клу́б	club	жена́	wife	окно́	window
уро́к	lesson	по́чта	post office	пла́тье	dress
ча́й	tea	ры́ба	fish	собра́ние	meeting
го́род	city	пра́вда	truth	общежи́тие	dormitory
учи́тель	teacher	лаборато́рия	laboratory		

It is essential for the student of Russian to know the gender of each noun he encounters. This is important because such words as adjectives and past tense verbs vary their form in agreement with the gender of the noun they accompany.

EXAMPLE

MASCULINE SUBJECT	Мо́й портфе́ль бы́л та́м.	My briefcase was there.
FEMININE SUBJECT	Моя́ жена́ была́ та́м.	My wife was there.
NEUTER SUBJECT	Моё письмо́ бы́ло та́м.	My letter was there.

The gender of most nouns can be predicted from the written nominative singular form. Nouns whose final letter in the nominative singular is a hard consonant, **ч**, **щ**, or **й** (i.e., with a zero ending), are masculine. Similarly, most nouns ending in **–а** or **–я** are feminine, and nouns ending in **–о**, **–ё**, or **–е** are neuter.

MASCULINE		FEMININE		NEUTER	
му́ж	husband	сестра́	sister	у́тро	morning
обе́д	dinner	зима́	winter	перо́	pen
сто́л	table	коро́бка	box (cardboard)	де́ло	business
но́ж	knife	шко́ла	school	мо́ре	sea
Ива́н	Ivan	Ири́на	Irina	по́ле	field
клю́ч	key	Росси́я	Russia	житьё	existence
бо́рщ	borsch	Га́ля	Galya	бельё	linen
ча́й	tea	семья́	family		

Nouns ending in **–а** or **–я** are masculine, however, if they refer to a male person: **дя́дя** *uncle*, **де́душка** *grandfather*, **Ва́ня** *Vanya* (*Johnny*), **Ми́ша** *Misha* (*Mike*), **Стёпа** *Styopa* (*Steve*), **Гри́ша** *Grisha* (*Greg*), **Ва́ся** *Vasya*. Most of these are nicknames.

Nouns whose gender can*not* be ascertained from the written form alone are those whose nominative singular ends in the soft sign **–ь**. Most of these nouns are feminine, but many are masculine. They will be identified as m (masculine) or f (feminine) in the glossaries, for example, **о́сень** (f) *fall*, **о́чередь** (f) *line*, **две́рь** (f) *door*, **портфе́ль** (m) *briefcase*, **де́нь** (m) *day*; otherwise the gender of nouns will not ordinarily be indicated.

Verbal aspects

Compared with the highly complex system of tenses in English, the Russian verb is structurally very simple. English makes considerable use of such auxiliary verbs as *do*, *have*, *be*, and *will* in forming its many compound tenses. Russian uses only a single compound tense used to form one kind of future; otherwise, past, present, and future in Russian verbs are expressed by simple, one-word verb forms.

To illustrate the economy of forms in the Russian system, compare the following:

RUSSIAN	ENGLISH
рабо́тал	worked, was working, did work, used to work, have worked, had worked, had been working

Similarly, all of the following English verbal concepts *can* be expressed in Russian by the simple present verb **рабо́таю**: [I] work, [I] am working, [I] do work, [I] have been working, [I] have worked.

Despite its structural simplicity, however, the Russian verb possesses an added dimension called "aspect," which enables it to make refinements comparable to the English. The system of "aspects" involves two contrasting categories: *imperfective aspect* versus *perfective aspect*. The aspect a Russian speaker uses depends on the way he views the action.

Broadly speaking, the *imperfective aspect* focuses on the activity as a process, without regard to its terminating point in time. The *perfective aspect*, on the other hand, focuses on the activity as a completed (or to be completed) action marked off in time, often emphasizing the result rather than the process. Compare the use of the two aspects in the past tense of the verbs **покупа́ть** and **купи́ть**:

IMPERFECTIVE	Я покупа́ла пода́рок.	I was buying a present.
PERFECTIVE	Что́ же вы́ купи́ли?	And what did you buy?

Note also the differences between the following:

IMPERFECTIVE	Мы́ неда́вно пи́ли ча́й.	We *drank* (or *were drinking*) tea not long ago.
PERFECTIVE	Мы́ уже́ вы́пили ча́й.	We already *drank* (or *finished drinking*) the tea.
IMPERFECTIVE	Она́ смотре́ла в окно́.	She *was looking* out the window.
PERFECTIVE	Она́ посмотре́ла в окно́.	She *took a look* out the window.
IMPERFECTIVE	Что́ вы́ де́лали?	What *did* you *do*? Or What *were* you *doing*?
PERFECTIVE	Что́ вы́ сде́лали?	What *did* you *do*? Or What *did* you get *done*? Or What *have* you *done*?

Imperfective and perfective verbs often differ structurally only in that one is prefixed and the other not. Both imperfective and perfective verbs may be used in the past and future. In the present, only imperfective verbs are used.

	PAST	PRESENT	FUTURE
IMPERFECTIVE	я смотре́л *I was looking* *I looked*	я смотрю́ *I'm looking* *I look*	я бу́ду смотре́ть *I'll be looking* *I'll look*
PERFECTIVE	я посмотре́л *I took a look*		я посмотрю́ *I'll take a look*

Note that it is almost always the perfective verb that is prefixed:

IMPERFECTIVE	PERFECTIVE	IMPERFECTIVE	PERFECTIVE
пи́ть	вы́пить	смотре́ть	посмотре́ть
де́лать	сде́лать	идти́	пойти́

STRUCTURE AND DRILLS

Replacement of nouns by third person pronouns: óн, она́, оно́, and они́

MODELS

Где́ Кири́лл? — Во́т о́н.	Where's Kirill? Here he is.
Где́ портфе́ль? — Во́т о́н.	Where's the briefcase? Here it is.
Где́ Ири́на? — Во́т она́.	Where's Irina? Here she is.
Где́ коро́бка? — Во́т она́.	Where's the box? Here it is.
Где́ общежи́тие? — Во́т оно́.	Where's the dormitory? Here it is.
Где́ письмо́? — Во́т оно́.	Where's the letter? Here it is.
Где́ Кири́лл и Ири́на? — Во́т они́.	Where are Kirill and Irina? Here they are.
Где́ огурцы́? — Во́т они́.	Where are the cucumbers? Here they are.

■ REPETITION DRILL

Repeat the above models after your instructor (or the tape) until you can answer the questions automatically according to the pattern.

■ QUESTION-ANSWER DRILLS

1. *Where's the student?*
   He's here.
   т: Где́ студе́нт?
   s: **Óн ту́т.**
   т: Где́ студе́нтка?
   s: **Она́ ту́т.**
   (Ни́на, Цара́пкин, Евге́ний, Ми́ла, жена́, му́ж, Оле́г, Óля, Ле́в)

2. *Where's the briefcase?*
   It's there.
   т: Где́ портфе́ль?
   s: **Óн та́м.**
   т: Где́ по́чта?
   s: **Она́ та́м.**
   (письмо́, собра́ние, клу́б, лаборато́рия, общежи́тие, селёдка, две́рь, коро́бка, о́чередь, ча́й, окно́, ло́жка, ви́лка, я́щик, пода́рок)

3. *Where's the knife, on the table?*
   Yes, it's on the table.
   т: Где́ но́ж, на столе́?
   s: **Да́, о́н на столе́.**
   т: Где́ ча́й, на столе́?
   s: **Да́, о́н на столе́.**
   (бо́рщ, портфе́ль, коро́бка, селёдка, ло́жки, ви́лки, огурцы́, письмо́, ча́й, материа́л, молоко́, обе́д, хле́б, ры́ба)

4. *Is the knife there?*
   Yes, it's there.
   т: Но́ж та́м?
   s: **Да́, о́н та́м.**
   т: Ры́ба та́м?
   s: **Да́, она́ та́м.**
   (письмо́, огурцы́, ча́й, собра́ние, сто́л, авто́бус, конце́рт, пода́рок, портфе́ль, ры́ба, пла́тье, шка́ф)

DISCUSSION

The masculine pronoun **о́н** substitutes for masculine nouns such as **сто́л** *table*, **Ва́ня** *Vanya*, **уро́к** *lesson*, and **де́нь** *day*.

The feminine pronoun **она́** substitutes for feminine nouns such as **жена́** *wife*, **селёдка** *herring*, **лаборато́рия** *laboratory*, and **о́чередь** *line* or *turn*.

The neuter pronoun **онó** substitutes for neuter nouns such as **письмó** *letter*, **окнó** *window*, **ýтро** *morning*, and **плáтье** *dress*.

Óн and **онá** mean *he* and *she* respectively when referring to person and *it* when referring to things. **Онó** means only *it*, since one does not use **онó** in referring to persons.[1]

Interrogatives ктó and чтó

MODELS

Ктó тáм бы́л?	Who was there?
— Тáм былá Ни́на.	Nina was there.
— Тáм бы́л Ивáн.	Ivan was there.
— Тáм бы́ли Ни́на и Ивáн.	Nina and Ivan were there.
Чтó бы́ло на столé?	What was on the table?
— На столé бы́л подáрок.	There was a present on the table.
— На столé былá ры́ба.	There was a fish on the table.
— На столé бы́ло письмó.	There was a letter on the table.
— На столé бы́ли огурцы́.	There were cucumbers on the table.

■ **REPETITION DRILL**

Repeat the above models after your instructor (or the tape) until the verb agreement becomes automatic. (Note that in the question **бы́л** is used with **ктó** and **бы́ло** with **чтó**.)

■ **CUED QUESTION-ANSWER DRILLS**

The following drills should be performed as simple repetition drills until the student(s) can answer automatically. (During the repetition stage the teacher may ask for both group and individual responses.)

1. (*Mila*) *Who was there?*
   Mila was there.
   т: (Ми́ла) Ктó тáм бы́л?
   s: **Тáм былá Ми́ла.**
   т: (Хитрóв) Ктó тáм бы́л?
   s: **Тáм бы́л Хитрóв.**
   (мýж, женá, Ни́на, Лéв, Евгéний, Семён, Олéг и Óля, Ни́на и Ивáн. студéнт и студéнтка)

2. (*a table*) *What was there?*
   There was a table there.
   т: (стóл) Чтó тáм бы́ло?
   s: **Тáм бы́л стóл.**
   т: (ры́ба) Чтó тáм бы́ло?
   s: **Тáм былá ры́ба.**
   (письмó, урóк, собрáние, концéрт, подáрок, бóрщ, плáтье, корóбка, огурцы́, чáй, хлéб, ви́лки и лóжки)

---

[1] The Russian pronouns **óн, онá,** and **онó** are used only in reference to a specific masculine, feminine, or neuter noun. They are never used to translate the empty English introductory *it* in such sentences as: *It's late.* The *it* of such sentences is simply omitted in Russian.

EXAMPLES Ужé пóздно.   It's already late.
Тáм бы́ло интерéсно? Was it interesting there?
Ещё рáно.   It's still early.

3. (*Nina*) *Who was standing there?*
             Nina was standing there.

т: (Ни́на) Кто́ та́м стоя́л?
s: **Та́м стоя́ла Ни́на.**
т: (Ле́в и Ми́ла) Кто́ та́м стоя́л?
s: **Та́м стоя́ли Ле́в и Ми́ла.**
    (студе́нт, студе́нтка, Оле́г, О́ля, Ца-
    ра́пкин, Хитро́в, студе́нт и студе́нтка)

DISCUSSION

In terms of grammatical agreement, **кто́** *who* is treated as masculine singular even though the person asking the question may know that the referent will be a female person or more than one person. Similarly, **что́** is treated as neuter singular. Note that **что́** *what* is pronounced [štó].

Introductory э́то

MODELS

Что́ э́то?   What's that?
— Э́то письмо́.   It's a letter.
А э́то что́?   And what's this?
— Э́то пода́рок О́ле.   It's a present for Olya.
Э́то ты́, Кири́лл?   Is that you, Kirill?
— Не́т, э́то я́, Ле́в.   No, it's me, Lev.
Э́то друго́е де́ло.   That's different.
Что́ э́то, огурцы́?   What are those, cucumbers?

■ CUED QUESTION-ANSWER DRILLS

The item to be substituted is to be given first, followed by the question and then the student answer.

1. (*a letter*) *What's that?*
                 It's a letter.
    т: (письмо́) Что́ э́то?
    s: **Э́то письмо́.**
    т: (я́щик)   Что́ э́то?
    s: **Э́то я́щик.**
    (сто́л, ры́ба, ка́ша, селёдка, две́рь,
    окно́, портфе́ль, ча́й, ко́фе, авто́бус,
    но́ж)

2. (*Evgeny*) *Who's there?*
               It's me, Evgeny.
    т: (Евге́ний) Кто́ та́м?
    s: **Э́то я́, Евге́ний.**
    т: (Ни́на)   Кто́ та́м?
    s: **Э́то я́, Ни́на.**
    (Кири́лл, Ле́в, Семён, Цара́пкин, Ми́ла,
    Хитро́в, Кири́лл, О́льга, Оле́г, Семён
    Фили́ппович)

DISCUSSION

The introductory word **э́то** usually indicates something not previously described or specified, but about which some statement is to be made. It can be translated as *this*, *that*, *these*, *those*, and sometimes (particularly in a rejoinder) *it*.

The irregular present tense of хотéть

Я́ хочу́ пойти́ на концéрт.	I want to go to the concert.
Ты́ хо́чешь _____ .	You want _____ .
Óн хо́чет _____ .	He wants _____ .
Мы́ хоти́м _____ .	We want _____ .
Вы́ хоти́те _____ .	You want _____ .
Они́ хотя́т _____ .	They want _____ .

■ REPETITION DRILL

Repeat the model after your instructor (or the tape) until you can reproduce all forms accurately.

■ REPETITION-SUBSTITUTION DRILL

She wants to go to the concert.
т: Она́ хо́чет пойти́ на концéрт.
s: **Она́ хо́чет пойти́ на концéрт.**
  (Кири́лл, ты́, я́, Ни́на, мы́, они́, вы́, Олéг
  и Cáша)

■ QUESTION-ANSWER DRILL

Don't you want to go there?
No, I don't.
т: Вы́ не хоти́те идти́ туда́?
s: **Нéт, не хочу́.**
т: Óн не хо́чет идти́ туда́?
s: **Нéт, не хо́чет.**
  (ты́, Cáша, Евгéний, они́, Ми́ла, вы́, Ни́на
  и Олéг)

DISCUSSION

    The verb **хотéть** has an irregular present tense. It follows a first conjugation pattern in the singular and a second conjugation pattern in the plural. Note that the final stem consonant is **ч** in the singular and **т** in the plural, and that the stress is on the endings except for the second and third persons singular.

SINGULAR	PLURAL
хочу́	хоти́м
хо́чешь	хоти́те
хо́чет	хотя́т

The past tense

MASCULINE SUBJECT	Óн **бы́л** в гóроде.	He was in town.
	Я́ давнó вáс не **ви́дел**.	I haven't seen you in a long time.
	Ты́ **купи́л** селёдку?	Did you buy herring?
	Сегóдня мýж нé **был** на слýжбе.	My husband wasn't at work today.
FEMININE SUBJECT	Онá давнó вáс не **ви́дела**.	She hasn't seen you in a long time.
	Ни́на, ты́ **былá** в гóроде?	Nina, were you in town?
	Дá, я́ **покупáла** плáтье.	Yes, I was buying a dress.
	Я́ дóлго **стоя́ла** в óчереди.	I stood in line for a long time.
NEUTER SUBJECT	Вчерá **бы́ло** собрáние.	There was a meeting yesterday.
	Письмó **бы́ло** на столé.	The letter was on the table.
	Молокó **стоя́ло** на окнé.	The milk was standing on the window sill.
PLURAL SUBJECT	А гдé вы́ **бы́ли**?	And where have you been?
	Они́ **стоя́ли** в óчереди.	They were standing in line.
	Чтó вы́ **дéлали**?	What have you been doing?
	Мы́ недáвно **пи́ли** чáй.	We drank tea awhile ago.
	Лóжки **бы́ли** на столé.	The spoons were on the table.

■ REPETITION DRILL

Repeat the above models, observing the basic pattern. The past tense is regularly signaled by the suffix –л, usually added to a vowel-ending stem. The endings that follow are gender-number endings, with zero for masculine, –a for feminine, –o for neuter, and –и for plural. Note that the past tense forms always have a hard л in the singular, but a soft л in the plural: пи́л [p̣íl] versus пи́ли [p̣íḷi], стоя́л [stajál] versus стоя́ли [stajáḷi].

■ REPETITION-SUBSTITUTION DRILLS

1. *We drank tea not long ago.*
   т: Мы́ недáвно пи́ли чáй.
   s: **Мы́ недáвно пи́ли чáй.**
   (мýж, они́, Евгéний, Ни́на, Óля, вы́, студéнт и студéнтка, женá)

2. *Ivan was hurrying to the meeting.*
   т: Ивáн спеши́л на собрáние.
   s: **Ивáн спеши́л на собрáние.**
   (ты́, Ни́на, мýж, вы́, женá, онá, я́, мы́, мýж и женá, они́, óн, онá)

3. *He hasn't seen you in a long time.*
   т: Óн давнó вáс не ви́дел.
   s: **Óн давнó вáс не ви́дел.**
   (мы́, мýж, женá, Óля, Гáля, мы́, они́, Царáпкин)

■ TRANSFORMATION DRILLS

1. *The borsch is on the table.*
   The borsch was on the table.
   т: Бóрщ на столé.
   s: **Бóрщ бы́л на столé.**

   т: Плáтье на столé.
   s: **Плáтье бы́ло на столé.**
   (нóж, корóбка, письмó, подáрок, лóжка, лóжки, кáша, чáй, обéд, щи́, хлéб)

2. *The herring is in the cupboard.*
   The herring was in the cupboard.
   т: Селёдка в шкафу́.
   s: **Селёдка была́ в шкафу́.**

т: Материа́л в шкафу́.
s: **Материа́л бы́л в шкафу́.**
(огурцы́, ры́ба, ка́ша, ча́й, ви́лки, ло́жки, хле́б, портфе́ль, письмо́, коро́бка)

■ QUESTION-ANSWER DRILLS

1. *Where was Evgeny?*
   He was at the meeting.
   т: Где́ бы́л Евге́ний?
   s: **О́н бы́л на собра́нии.**
   т: Где́ была́ Ни́на?
   s: **Она́ была́ на собра́нии.**
   (О́ля, Кири́лл, студе́нтка, жена́, Ле́в и Оле́г, студе́нт и студе́нтка)

3. *Where's Olya, downtown?*
   No, but she was downtown.
   т: Где́ О́ля, в го́роде?
   s: **Не́т, но она́ была́ в го́роде.**
   т: Где́ Евге́ний, в го́роде?
   s: **Не́т, но о́н бы́л в го́роде.**
   (Цара́пкин, Кири́лл Па́влович, о́н, они́, она́)

2. *What was she doing?*
   She was standing in line.
   т: Что́ она́ де́лала?
   s: **Она́ стоя́ла в о́череди.**
   т: Что́ о́н де́лал?
   s: **О́н стоя́л в о́череди.**
   Что́ они́ де́лали?
   Что́ вы́ де́лали, Семён?
   Что́ вы́ де́лали, Ми́ла?
   Что́ ты́ де́лал, Са́ша?
   Что́ ты́ де́лала, Ни́на?

■ TRANSFORMATION DRILL

Where was Olya standing?
Where was she standing?
т: Где́ стоя́ла О́ля?
s: **Где́ она́ стоя́ла?**[1]
т: Где́ стоя́л Евге́ний?
s: **Где́ о́н стоя́л?**
Где́ стоя́ли Кири́лл и Семён?
(Ни́на, Ле́в, Ми́ла, му́ж и жена́)

■ QUESTION-ANSWER DRILLS

1. *What did you buy, Oleg?*
   I bought bread and herring.
   т: Что́ вы́ купи́ли, Оле́г?
   s: **Я́ купи́л хле́б и селёдку.**
   т: Что́ вы́ купи́ли, О́ля?
   s: **Я́ купи́ла хле́б и селёдку.**
   Что́ вы́ купи́ли, ребя́та?
   Что́ купи́л Ле́в?
   Что́ купи́ла О́ля?
   Что́ купи́ла жена́?
   Что́ купи́л му́ж?

2. *What were you doing, Olya?*
   I was buying a briefcase.
   т: Что́ вы́ де́лали, О́ля?
   s: **Я́ покупа́ла портфе́ль.**
   т: Что́ вы́ де́лали, Ле́в?
   s: **Я́ покупа́л портфе́ль.**
   (Ми́ла, Кири́лл, Ни́на, Семён, Са́ша)

---

[1] In где́ questions of this type the pronoun must *precede* the verb: Где́ **она́ стоя́ла?** A noun, however, may appear either before or after the verb: Где́ Ольга стоя́ла? (*Or* Где́ стоя́ла О́льга?)

The past tense of Russian verbs is expressed by the past tense suffix –л plus the appropriate gender or number ending to agree with the subject.

With most verbs the past tense suffix is added to a form of the stem ending in a vowel: бы́–л, ду́ма–л, покупа́–л, ви́де–л, стоя́–л, говори́–л, and so forth.

Stress. The stress is usually the same in all four forms of past tense, but may shift to the ending in the feminine form, particularly with the shorter verbs. Compare был, бы́ло, бы́ли with была́ (f); also пил, пи́ло, пи́ли with пила́ (f). In the combinations не́ был, не́ было, and не́ были, the stress shifts from the verb to the negative particle не. Note, however, that it remains on the verb in the feminine form не была́.

REFERENCE LIST OF PAST TENSE FORMS				
Infinitive	*Masculine*	*Feminine*	*Neuter*	*Plural*
бы́ть be	был	был–а́	бы́л–о	бы́л–и
пи́ть drink	пил	пил–а́	пи́л–о	пи́л–и
зна́ть know	знал	зна́л–а	зна́л–о	зна́л–и
посла́ть send	посла́л	посла́л–а	посла́л–о	посла́л–и
де́лать do	де́лал	де́лал–а	де́лал–о	де́лал–и
доста́ть get	доста́л	доста́л–а	доста́л–о	доста́л–и
слы́шать hear	слы́шал	слы́шал–а	слы́шал–о	слы́шал–и
рабо́тать work	рабо́тал	рабо́тал–а	рабо́тал–о	рабо́тал–и
обе́дать dine	обе́дал	обе́дал–а	обе́дал–о	обе́дал–и
пообе́дать dine	пообе́дал	пообе́дал–а	пообе́дал–о	пообе́дал–и
покупа́ть buy	покупа́л	покупа́л–а	покупа́л–о	покупа́л–и
купи́ть buy	купи́л	купи́л–а	купи́л–о	купи́л–и
спеши́ть hurry	спеши́л	спеши́л–а	спеши́л–о	спеши́л–и
ви́деть see	ви́дел	ви́дел–а	ви́дел–о	ви́дел–и
смотре́ть look	смотре́л	смотре́л–а	смотре́л–о	смотре́л–и
посмотре́ть look	посмотре́л	посмотре́л–а	посмотре́л–о	посмотре́л–и
хоте́ть want	хоте́л	хоте́л–а	хоте́л–о	хоте́л–и

ЧТЕ́НИЕ И ПИСЬМО́ READING AND WRITING

А, а   А вы куда? Как дела на заводе?

Б, б   Было собрание. Рыбы больше нет. Вы были больны.

В, в   Давно вас не видел. Вы здоровы?

Г, г   Говорят, обед готов. Где огурцы?

Д, д, д Да. До свидания. Где вы достали?
На заводе.

Е, е Привет жене! Очень интересно.
Есть хочется.

Ё, ё Вот идёт Семён. Всё утро там
был.

Ж, ж Жена на службе. Можно войти?
Пожалуйста. Скажите, где нож?

З, з, з Здравствуйте! Вы здоровы?
Пожалуйста, заходите.

И, и Извините, Иван Иванович!
Спасибо, Ирина.

Й, й Это мой чай. Красивый материал.
Читайте! Нью Йорк.

К, к Коля, кто там? Как дела?
Куда идёт Кирилл?

Л, л Лев и Кирилл были на службе.
Люба купила платье.

М, м Мы там были. Там мой материал.
Семён в ГУМе.

Н, н Нет. Ну, ничего, Нина. Где Ирина
Ивановна?

О, о Он идёт домой. Вот мой автобус.
Вполне здоров. Обед готов.

П, п Пожалуйста! Это платье. Куда
вы спешите?

Р, р, р	Красивый материал. Говорят, Ирина в городе.
С, с	Семён всю зиму не был на службе. Где стол? Можно посмотреть? До свидания.
Т, т	Ты тут? Вот идёт автобус. Что ты!
У, у	У нас есть огурцы. Я спешу. Я иду на почту.
Ф, ф	Семён Филиппович на службе. Где Африка? Софья Филипповна там. Портфель тут.
Х, х	Хорошо. Заходите. Хотите посмотреть?
Ц, ц	Огурцы на столе. Где концерт? Царапкин там.
Ч, ч	Что вы! Чай на столе. Очень красивый. Как насчёт обеда? Иван Иванович стоял в очереди.
Ш, ш	Куда ты спешишь? Хорошо. Каша хорошая. Шура спешит на концерт.
Щ, щ	Борщ ещё не готов. Нож в ящике. Где Хрущёв? Щи на столе.
ъ	Кто это съел? Ты съел огурцы?
ы	Где вы были?

ь   Вот очередь. Нарежь огурцы Где портфель ? Ты теперь работаешь ?

Э, э   Это ты, Коля ? Нет, это я, Нина. Это ужасно !

Ю, ю   Юрий всю зиму был болен. Я работаю на почте.

Я, я   Я иду домой. До свидания. Говорят, Коля опять болен. Он стоял в очереди. Где Ялта ?

PREPARATION FOR CONVERSATION

Пе́рвый де́нь в университе́те

пе́рвый де́нь	the first day
Пе́рвый де́нь в университе́те.	The first day at the university.
де́вять	nine
почти́	almost
Уже́ почти́ де́вять.	It's almost nine already.
пора́	time, it's time
Пора́ идти́.	It's time to be going.
гото́в (m), гото́ва (f)	ready
Но я́ ещё не гото́ва.	But I'm not ready yet.
ру́чка	pen, penholder
моя́ ру́чка	my pen
[я] зна́ю	I know
Не зна́ю, где́ моя́ ру́чка.	I don't know where my pen is.
по́лка	shelf, bookcase
на по́лке	on the shelf, on the bookcase
во́н та́м	over there, over yonder
А во́н та́м, на по́лке, не она́?	But over there on the shelf, isn't [that] it?
тетра́дь (f)	notebook
э́ти тетра́ди	these notebooks, those notebooks
все́ э́ти тетра́ди	all those notebooks
тебе́	for you, to you
заче́м	why, what for, for what purpose
заче́м тебе́	why do you need
И заче́м тебе́ все́ э́ти тетра́ди?	And why do you need all those notebooks?
пра́вда	truth; it's the truth, that's right
Да́, пра́вда.	Yes, you're right.
кни́га	book
кни́ги	books
взя́ть (pfv)	to take

◀ **Ле́кция по хи́мии в МГУ.**

[я] возьму́	I'll take
Я возьму́ то́лько кни́ги.	I'll take just the books.
одну́ тетра́дь	one notebook
Возьму́ то́лько кни́ги и одну́ тетра́дь.	I'll take just the books and one notebook.
возьми́	take!
каранда́ш	pencil
И каранда́ш возьми́.	And take a pencil.
И ещё каранда́ш возьми́.	And take a pencil too.
пошли́	let's go! we're off!
Ну́, пошли́!	Well, let's go!
всё	all, everything (*here* all set)
Ну́ всё, пошли́!	Well, all set, let's go!
Во́т и университе́т!	Here's the university!
ре́ктор	the chancellor, the president (of the university)
о́н бу́дет говори́ть	he'll speak
Где́ бу́дет говори́ть ре́ктор?	Where will the chancellor speak?
зда́ние [zdáɲjə]	building
большо́е зда́ние	the large building
ты́ ви́дишь	you see
Ты́ ви́дишь большо́е зда́ние?	Do you see the large building?
· Во́н та́м. Ви́дишь большо́е зда́ние?	Over there. Do you see the large building?
библиоте́ка	library
про́тив библиоте́ки	opposite the library
Во́н та́м. Ви́дишь большо́е зда́ние про́тив библиоте́ки?	Over there. Do you see the large building opposite the library?
Да́, ви́жу.	Yes, I see.
тогда́	then, in that case
пока́	so long
Ну́, тогда́ пока́.	Well, so long then.

SUPPLEMENT

перо́	pen point, pen
Где́ перо́?	Where's a pen? *or* Where's a pen point?
че́й (m)	whose
Че́й э́то каранда́ш?	Whose pencil is this?
— Мо́й.	Mine.
чья́ (f)	whose
Чья́ э́то кни́га?	Whose book is this?
— Моя́.	Mine.
чьё (n)	whose
Чьё э́то письмо́?	Whose letter is this?
— Моё.	Mine.
за́л	hall (room within a building)
Во́т за́л, где́ бу́дет говори́ть ре́ктор.	Here's the hall where the chancellor will speak.

Пе́рвый де́нь в университе́те

Н. — Никола́й (Ко́ля), бра́т
Г. — Гали́на (Га́ля), сестра́

Н.	1	Га́ля,	gắļə ↓
		уже́ почти́ де́вять.	užé pačți ḑếɣiț ↓
		Пора́ идти́.	pará ițțí ↓
Г.	2	Но я́ ещё не гото́ва.	no já jiščó ņigatŏvə ↓
		Не зна́ю,	ņiznắju |
		где́ моя́ ру́чка.[1]	gḑé majá rűčkə ↓
Н.	3	А во́н та́м,	a vón tắm |
		на по́лке,	napőlķi ↓
		не она́?	ņianắ ↑
		И заче́м тебе́	i začếm țiḇé |
		всё э́ти тетра́ди?	fşé éți țitrắḑi ↓
Г.	4	Да́, пра́вда.	dắ ↓ prắvdə ↓
		Возьму́ то́лько кни́ги	vaẓmú tóļkə kņigi |
		и одну́ тетра́дь.	i adnú țitrắț ↓
Н.	5	И ещё каранда́ш возьми́.	i jiščó kərandắš vaẓmí ↓
Г.	6	Ну́ всё.	nú fşő ↓
		Пошли́![2]	pašļí ↓

* * *

Н.	7	Во́т и университе́т!	vót i uņiɣirşițět ↓
Г.	8	Где́ бу́дет говори́ть ре́ктор?[3]	gḑé búḑit gəvaṛíț ṛěktər ↓
Н.	9	Во́н та́м.	vón tắm ↓
		Ви́дишь большо́е зда́ние	ɣíḑiš baļšójə zdáņjə |
		про́тив библиоте́ки?	próțif ḃibļiațěķi ↓
Г.	10	Да́, ви́жу.	dắ ↓ ɣížu ↓
Н.	11	Ну́, тогда́ пока́.	nú tagdá pakắ ↓

NOTES

[1] Of the two words for *pen*, **ру́чка** is more commonly used in the Soviet Union now than **перо́.** More specifically, **ру́чка** means *penholder* and **перо́** *pen point.* Notice that these terms all refer to the old-fashioned type of pen used with an inkwell. *Fountain pen* is **авторучка.**

[2] **Пошли́** *let's go* is actually the plural past tense form of **пойти́** *to go, to set off* used as a special imperative in highly colloquial style. Compare it with the English expression *we're off.*

[3] **Ре́ктор** is comparable to our *university* or *college president* or *chancellor.* At the beginning of each academic year freshmen assemble in a large hall to hear an address given by him.

америка́нский	American (adj only)
америка́нский студе́нт	an American student
Óн америка́нский студе́нт.	He's an American student.
твóй пéрвый дéнь	your first day
пройти́ (pfv I)	to pass, go by
прошёл	passed, went [by]
Ка́к прошёл твóй пéрвый дéнь?	How did your first day go?
ничегó	all right (*lit.* nothing)
Ничегó.	All right.
оди́н (m)	one, a
америка́нец	American
оди́н америка́нец	an American
Та́м бы́л оди́н америка́нец.	There was an American there.
лéкция	lecture, class (at university level)
на лéкции	at the lecture, in class
у на́с на лéкции	at our lecture, in our class
У на́с на лéкции бы́л оди́н америка́нец.	There was an American at our lecture.
ты́ зна́ешь	you know
Зна́ешь, у на́с на лéкции бы́л оди́н америка́нец.	You know, there was an American at our lecture.
óн стои́т	he's standing, he stands
Óн та́м стои́т.	He's standing over there.
тóт, та́, тó; тé	that (over there, yon); that person, that one
вóн тóт	that person over there, the one over there
Вóн тóт, что та́м стои́т?	That fellow standing over there?
мóжет бы́ть [móž(id)bíţ]	maybe, perhaps
Мóжет бы́ть, вóн тóт, что та́м стои́т?	That fellow standing over there perhaps?
Та́к э́то Фили́пп Гра́нт.	Why that's Philip Grant.
егó	him; his
Ты́ егó зна́ешь?	Do you know him?
познакóмиться [pəznakóṃitcə]	to become acquainted, meet, be introduced
Интерéсно познакóмиться.	[It'd be] interesting to meet [him].
Ты́ егó зна́ешь? Интерéсно познакóмиться.	Do you know him? [It'd be] interesting to meet [him].
Э́то моя́ сестра́.	This is my sister.
Привéт, Фили́пп. Э́то моя́ сестра́ Га́ля.	Hi Philip. This is my sister Galya.
бра́т	brother
Э́то мóй бра́т Кóля.	This is my brother, Kolya.
сейча́с[1]	now, just now, right away
Я́ ва́с сейча́с ви́дел.	I saw you just now.

---

[1] This word may be pronounced either [şijčás] or [şičás].

ка́жется	it seems
Я ва́с, ка́жется, сейча́с ви́дел.	It seems I saw you just now.
аудито́рия	auditorium, lecture room, classroom
в аудито́рии	in the auditorium
в то́й аудито́рии	in that auditorium, in the auditorium there
Я ва́с, ка́жется, сейча́с ви́дел в то́й аудито́рии.	It seems I saw you just now in the auditorium there.
Да́, я та́м была́.	Yes, I was there.
по-ру́сски	Russian
вы́ говори́те	you speak
Вы́ говори́те по-ру́сски.	You speak Russian.
А вы́ хорошо́ говори́те по-ру́сски.	You speak Russian well, by the way.
вы́ ду́маете	you think
мне́ ка́жется	it seems to me
Вы́ ду́маете? А мне́ ка́жется — не о́чень.	You think so? It seems to me I don't [speak it] very [well].
что́ вы́ (что́ вы́ говори́те)!	you're not serious! what do you mean (*lit.* what are you saying)!
Ну́ что́ вы́! Вполне́ хорошо́.	Why what do you mean! [You speak] quite well.
вы́ учи́ли	you studied
ру́сский язы́к	Russian, language Russian
Где́ вы́ учи́ли ру́сский язы́к?	Where did you study Russian?
шко́ла	school (below university level)
в шко́ле	in school
Где́ вы́ учи́ли ру́сский язы́к, в шко́ле?	Where did you study Russian, in school?
Не́т, в университе́те.	No, at the university.

SUPPLEMENT

Аме́рика	America
О́н учи́л ру́сский язы́к в Аме́рике.	He studied Russian in America.
америка́нка	[an] American (f)
Кто́ она́, америка́нка?	What is she, an American?
я говорю́	I speak
Я́ говорю́ по-ру́сски.	I speak Russian.
Я́ говорю́ по-англи́йски.	I speak English.
Я́ не говорю́ по-англи́йски.	I don't speak English.
непло́хо	not badly, not too badly
Вы́ непло́хо говори́те по-ру́сски.	You don't speak Russian too badly.

Америка́нский студе́нт

Н. — Никола́й (Ко́ля)
Г. — Гали́на (Га́ля)
Ф. Г. — Фили́пп Гра́нт (америка́нец)

Н.	1	Ка́к прошёл тво́й пе́рвый де́нь, Га́ля?	kák prašól tvój p̦érvij d̦é̞n̦ ↓ gǎ̞l̦ə ↓
Г.	2	Ничего́. Зна́ешь, у на́с на ле́кции бы́л оди́н америка́нец.[1]	n̦ičivó ↓ znǎ̞jiš ↓ unás nal̦ěkciji | bíl ad̦ín am̦iŗikǎ̞n̦ic ↓
Н.	3	Мо́жет бы́ть, во́н то́т, что та́м стои́т? Та́к э́то Фили́пп Гра́нт.	móž(íd)bíţ vón tǒt ↓ štə tám stajít ↑ tək étə f̦il̦íp grǎ̞nt ↓
Г.	4	Ты́ его́ зна́ешь? Интере́сно познако́миться.	tí jivó znǎ̞jiš ↑ inţiŗésnə pəznakő̞m̦itcə ↓
Н.	5	Приве́т, Фили́пп! Э́то моя́ сестра́ Га́ля.	pŗiɣét f̦il̦íp ↓ étə majá șistrá gǎ̞l̦ə ↓
Ф. Г.	6	Здра́вствуйте![2] Я́ ва́с, ка́жется, сейча́с ви́дел в то́й аудито́рии.	zdrǎ̞stujţi ↓ já vás kážitcə șičás ɣíd̦il | ftój aud̦itő̞ŗiji ↓
Г.	7	Да́, я́ та́м была́. А вы́ хорошо́ говори́те по-ру́сски.	dǎ̞ ↓ já tám bɨlǎ̞ ↓ a ví xərašó gəvaŗíţi parǔ̞sk̦i ↓
Ф. Г.	8	Вы́ ду́маете? А мне́ ка́жется — не о́чень.	ví dǔ̞məjiţi ↓ a mn̦é kážitcə n̦iő̞čin̦ ↓
Н.	9	Ну́, что́ вы́! Вполне́ хорошо́.	nú štő̞ ví ↓ fpaln̦ě xərašó ↓
Г.	10	Где́ вы́ учи́ли ру́сский язы́к, в шко́ле?[3]	gd̦é vɨ učíl̦i rúsk̦ij jizǐk ↓ fškő̞l̦i ↑
Ф. Г.	11	Не́т, в университе́те.	n̦ět ↓ vun̦iɣirşiţéţi ↓

NOTES

[1] The nouns **америка́нец** and **америка́нка** refer to an American male and female respectively. The adjective **америка́нский** can never be used alone to refer to the person. Thus **америка́нский студе́нт** or **америка́нская студе́нтка** is used for *an American student*, but only **америка́нец** or **америка́нка** for *an American*. Notice that none of these words is capitalized in Russian.

² When introduced, Russians usually say simply **здра́вствуйте** *hello*. With older people or distinguished individuals, however, one should use the more polite forms corresponding to our *Very pleased to meet you:* **О́чень прия́тно** (*or* **О́чень прия́тно познако́миться [с ва́ми]**).

³ **Ру́сский язы́к** is used for *Russian* here, but the adverbial form **по-ру́сски** is used with such verbs as **говори́ть** *to speak*, **чита́ть** *to read*, and **писа́ть** *to write*.

Compare	Вы́ зна́ете **ру́сский язы́к?**	Do you know Russian?
	Где́ вы́ учи́ли **ру́сский язы́к?**	Where did you study Russian?
with	Вы́ говори́те **по-ру́сски?**	Do you speak Russian?
	Вы́ чита́ете **по-ру́сски?**	Do you read Russian?

Basic sentence patterns

1. Э́то мо́й пе́рвый де́нь в университе́те. It's my first day at the university.
   —————————— в шко́ле. —————————— in school.
   —————————— в лаборато́рии. —————————— in the laboratory.
   —————————— в общежи́тии. —————————— in the dormitory.
   —————————— на заво́де. —————————— at the plant.
   —————————— на слу́жбе. —————————— on the job.

2. Пора́ идти́, Ко́ля. Ты́ уже́ гото́в? Time to be going, Kolya. Are you ready yet?
   — Да́, гото́в. Yes, I am.
   — Не́т ещё. Not yet.
   — Да́, я́ уже́ гото́в. Yes, I'm ready.
   — Не́т, я́ ещё не гото́в. No, I'm not ready yet.

3. Пора́ идти́, Га́ля. Ты́ уже́ гото́ва? Time to be going, Galya. Are you ready yet?
   — Да́, гото́ва. Yes, I am.
   — Не́т ещё. Not yet.
   — Да́, я́ уже́ гото́ва. Yes, I'm ready.
   — Не́т, я́ ещё не гото́ва. No, I'm not ready yet.

4. Пора́ идти́, ребя́та. Вы́ уже́ гото́вы? Time to be going, fellows. Are you ready yet?
   — Да́, мы́ гото́вы. Yes, we are.
   — Не́т ещё. Not yet.
   — Да́, мы́ уже́ гото́вы. Yes, we're ready.
   — Не́т, мы́ ещё не гото́вы. No, we're not ready yet.

5. Уже́ пора́ идти́ на ле́кцию? Is it already time to go to the lecture?
   — Да́, уже́ пора́. Yes, it's already time.
   — Да́, давно́ пора́. Yes, it's long since time.
   — Да́, уже́ де́вять. Yes, it's already nine.
   — Да́, почти́ де́вять. Yes, it's almost nine.
   — Да́, пошли́. Yes, let's go.
   — Не́т, ещё ра́но. No, it's early still.

6. Идём в университе́т. Let's go to the university.
   ——— в библиоте́ку. ——— to the library.
   ——— в аудито́рию. ——— to the auditorium.

Идём в клу́б.	Let's go to the club.
_____ в общежи́тие.	_____ to the dormitory.
_____ в лаборато́рию.	_____ to the laboratory.
_____ в го́род.	_____ to town.

7. Я спешу́ на рабо́ту.　　　　　　I'm hurrying to work.
　_____ на по́чту.　　　　　_____ to the post office.
　_____ на конце́рт.　　　　_____ to the concert.
　_____ на ле́кцию.　　　　_____ to the lecture.
　_____ на собра́ние.　　　_____ to the meeting.

8. Э́то моя́ сестра́ Га́ля.　　　　This is my sister Galya.
　____ мо́й бра́т Ко́ля.　　　　_____ my brother Kolya.
　____ моя́ жена́.　　　　　　_____ my wife.
　____ мо́й му́ж.　　　　　　_____ my husband.

9. Я ва́с ви́дел на ле́кции.　　　I saw you at the lecture.
　_____ на собра́нии.　_____ at the meeting.
　_____ на конце́рте.　_____ at the concert.
　_____ на заво́де.　　_____ at the plant.
　_____ в го́роде.　　_____ downtown.
　_____ в ГУ́Ме.　　　_____ in GUM.

10. Он тепе́рь в университе́те.　He's at the university now.
　_____ в клу́бе.　　　____ at the club _____.
　_____ в общежи́тии.　____ in the dormitory ____.
　_____ в аудито́рии.　____ in the auditorium ____.
　_____ в библиоте́ке.　____ at the library _____.

11. Вы́ не говори́те по-ру́сски?　You don't speak Russian, do you?
　Вы́ непло́хо говори́те по-ру́сски.　You don't speak Russian [too] badly.
　___ хорошо́ _____.　You speak Russian well.
　___ всегда́ _____.　You always speak Russian.
　___ то́же _____.　You also speak Russian.
　___ опя́ть _____.　You're speaking Russian again.
　___ о́чень хорошо́ _____.　You speak Russian very well.
　___ вполне́ хорошо́ _____.　You speak Russian quite well.

12. Вы́ говори́те по-англи́йски?　Do you speak English?
　— Да́, говорю́.　　　　　Yes, I do.
　— Да́, я говорю́ по-англи́йски.　Yes, I speak English.
　— Да́, но не о́чень хорошо́.　Yes, but not very well.
　— Не́т, не говорю́.　　　No, I don't.
　— Не́т, я не говорю́ по-англи́йски.　No, I don't speak English.

13. Вы́ понима́ете по-англи́йски?　Do you understand English?
　— Да́, понима́ю.　　　　Yes, I do.
　— Да́, я понима́ю по-англи́йски.　Yes, I understand English.
　— Не́т, не понима́ю.　　No, I don't.
　— Не́т, я не понима́ю по-англи́йски.　No, I don't understand English.

14. Вы́ купи́ли селёдку?　　　Did you buy herring?
　_____ ры́бу?　　　　_____ fish?
　_____ кни́гу?　　　　_____ a book?
　_____ тетра́дь?　　　_____ a notebook?

_____ хлéб?	_____ bread?
_____ чáй?	_____ tea?
_____ кóфе?	_____ coffee?
_____ молокó?	_____ milk?
_____ огурцы́?	_____ cucumbers?
_____ тетрáди?	_____ notebooks?

Pronunciation practice: hard versus soft consonants

A.   [s] vs. [ş]   Usual Cyrillic spelling **c**; sometimes **сь**, **з**, or **зь**.

Note the pronunciation of hard [s] in the following:

[vás]	вác	you
[aftóbus]	автóбус	bus

and compare it with soft [ş]:

[şim̧ón]	Семён	Simon
[fşú]	всю́	all
[p̧işmó]	письмó	letter

Russian hard [s] is fairly similar to English *s*. Soft [ş] is made by bringing the front part of the blade of the tongue toward the upper gum ridge. It has the effect of being followed by a y-like glide.

> Sound Drill: Practice the Russian paired examples illustrating hard [s] and soft [ş], imitating your instructor (or the tape) as accurately as you can.

B.   [z] vs. [ẓ]   Usual Cyrillic spelling **з**; sometimes **зь**, **с**, or **сь**.

Note the pronunciation of hard [z] in the following:

[zdrástujţi]	здрáвствуйте	hello
[zdaróvi]	здорóвы	healthy
[nəzavóḑi]	на завóде	at the plant

and compare it with soft [ẓ]:

[ẓímu]	зи́му	winter
[ẓínə]	Зи́на	Zina

Russian [z] and [ẓ] are made with the vocal organs in the same position as for Russian [s] and [ş], but, in addition, they are voiced.

> Sound Drill: Practice the Russian paired examples illustrating hard [z] and soft [ẓ], imitating your instructor (or the tape) as accurately as you can.

C.   [r] vs. [ṛ]   Usual Cyrillic spelling **р**; sometimes **рь**.

Note the pronunciation of hard [r] in the following:

[zdrástujṭi]	здра́вствуйте	hello
[nəurók]	на уро́к	to the lesson
[zdaróvi]	здоро́вы	healthy
[xərašó]	хорошо́	good, well

and compare it with soft [ṛ]:

[ḳiṛíl]	Кири́лл	Kirill
[gəvaṛát]	говоря́т	they say
[ṭiṛéṛ]	тепе́рь	now

Russian hard [r] is unlike any variety of American English *r*. It is something like the "rolled" Scottish *r* and practically identical with the *r* of Spanish, Italian, modern Greek, Serbo-Croatian, or Polish. In pronouncing Russian [r], the tongue is trilled or vibrated, making one or more taps against the ridge of the gums behind the upper teeth. (American children sometimes make such a trill in imitating the sound of a machine gun or an airplane engine.) Soft [ṛ] is formed similarly, but the middle surface of the tongue is arched higher giving the effect of a y-like glide.[1]

> Sound Drill: Practice the Russian paired examples illustrating hard [r] and soft [ṛ], imitating your instructor (or the tape) as accurately as you can.

Intonation practice

Introductory remarks

Within any major segment of speech some syllables are spoken at a higher relative pitch level than others. We designate these as 1 low, 2 middle, 3 high, and 4 extra-high, with the extra-high level occurring much less frequently than the other three.

These levels are indicated graphically by a line which we call the *intonation contour*, drawn above the major segment through the primary and secondary stress points and ending in an arrow. An upward stroke indicates a slight rise in the voice (typical of certain kinds of questions), and a downward stroke indicates a falling of the voice. The primary stress point is indicated by a small circle and the secondary stress points by small black dots on the intonation contour directly above the stressed syllables.

EXAMPLE

Ни́на была́ в ГУ́Ме.

---

[1] One hears something like the Russian [r] in certain imitations of upper-class British speech, for example, in the pronunciation of *terribly* when the r sounds almost like a *d*.

Intonation drills

A. *Statements with falling contours.* In contours of this type the high peak occurs in the first part of the segment, dropping gradually thereafter and making the sharpest drop on or immediately before the syllable with primary stress. The basic range is from 2 or 3 down to 1, although the starting point may be an upward rise from level 2 to level 3. These countours are typical of neutral statements, exclamations, and commands.

Imitate the teacher or tape as accurately as you can.

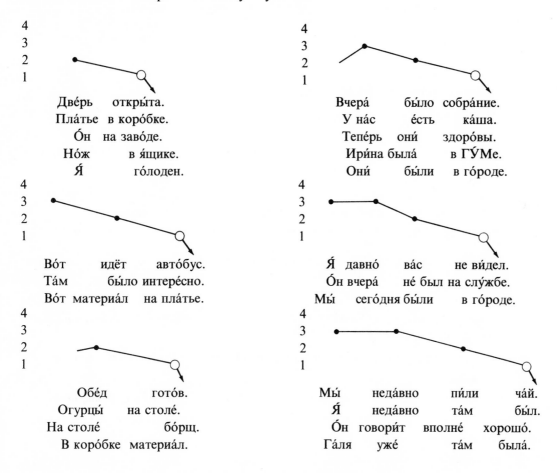

Двéрь	откры́та.	
Плáтье	в корóбке.	
Óн	на завóде.	
Нóж	в я́щике.	
Я́	гóлоден.	

Вчерá	бы́ло	собрáние.
У нáс	éсть	кáша.
Тепéрь	они́	здорóвы.
Ири́на былá		в ГУ́Ме.
Они́	бы́ли	в гóроде.

Вóт	идёт	автóбус.
Тáм	бы́ло интерéсно.	
Вóт материáл	на плáтье.	

Я́ давнó	вáс	не ви́дел.
Óн вчерá	нé был на слу́жбе.	
Мы́	сегóдня бы́ли	в гóроде.

Обéд	готóв.
Огурцы́	на столé.
На столé	бóрщ.
В корóбке	материáл.

Мы́	недáвно	пи́ли	чáй.
Я́	недáвно	тáм	бы́л.
Óн говори́т	вполнé	хорошó.
Гáля	ужé	тáм	былá.

B. *Questions with falling contours.* The contour is similar to that of statements, but the range is wider, starting with level 4 and dropping gradually thereafter to level 2. The primary stress may be either on the question word itself or on the last stressed syllable. This contour is typical of questions beginning with a question word. Note that the voice does not *rise* at the end as it often does in English.

Imitate your teacher or the tape as accurately as you can.

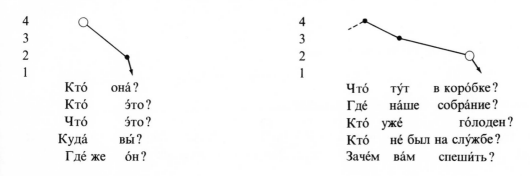

Ктó	онá?
Ктó	э́то?
Чтó	э́то?
Кудá	вы́?
Гдé же	óн?

Чтó	ту́т	в корóбке?
Гдé	нáше	собрáние?
Ктó	ужé	гóлоден?
Ктó	нé был на слу́жбе?	
Зачéм	вáм	спеши́ть?

Где   нож?
Где огурцы?
Где   Кирилл?

Куда́ вы́   идёте?
Где   вы́   бы́ли?
Кто́   вас   ви́дел?
Что́   вы́   де́лали?
Где   они́   стоя́ли?
Что́   вы́   ви́дели?
Что́   бы́ло в коро́бке?

The four noun declensions in Russian:
сто́л–, окно́–, жена́–, and две́рь-class nouns

According to the patterning of their case endings, Russian nouns may be divided into four basic types. We shall use a model noun to represent each basic type.

1. **сто́л**–class	2. **окно́**–class	3. **жена́**–class	4. **две́рь**–class

1. **Сто́л**-class nouns are masculine. Their nominative singular ends in a consonant letter (including **–й**) or **–ь**.

> EXAMPLES
>
> авто́бус, приве́т, уро́к, Кири́лл, Семён, му́ж, клу́б, университе́т, бо́рщ, ча́й, де́нь, портфе́ль.

2. **Окно́**-class nouns are neuter. Their nominative singular ends in the letter **–о**, **–е**, or **–ё**.

> EXAMPLES
>
> письмо́, у́тро, де́ло, пла́тье, собра́ние, пе́ние *singing*, общежи́тие, бельё *linen*.

3. **Жена́**-class nouns are chiefly feminine; a few that refer to males are masculine. Their nominative singular ends in the letter **–а** or **–я**.

> EXAMPLES
>
> слу́жба, ры́ба, селёдка, лаборато́рия, коро́бка, пра́вда, Ни́на, Ми́ла, Га́ля, Ко́ля *Kolya*, Ми́ша *Misha*, дя́дя *uncle*.

4. **Две́рь**-class nouns are feminine. Their nominative singular always ends in the letter **–ь**.

> EXAMPLES
>
> две́рь, о́сень, о́чередь, тетра́дь.

■ EXERCISE

Arrange four columns with the following heads:

1. **сто́л**   2. **окно́**   3. **жена́**   4. **две́рь**

Put each of these nouns in its proper column:
телефо́н, убо́рщица, де́ло, о́чередь, пла́тье, шко́ла, ле́кция, собра́ние, ча́й, окно́, язы́к, клю́ч, исто́рия, каранда́ш, ка́рта, о́сень, фи́льм, геро́й, неде́ля, перо́, свида́ние, учи́тельница, пе́ние, у́гол, мо́ре, тетра́дь, молоко́, результа́т, слу́жба, Лёв, ка́ша, огуре́ц, де́нь, портфе́ль, Ко́ля.

STRUCTURE AND DRILLS

The accusative singular of nouns ending in –a and –я

MODELS

Я купи́л селёдку.	I bought herring.
_____ ры́бу.	_____ fish.
_____ ру́чку.	_____ a pen.
_____ ви́лку.	_____ a fork.
_____ ло́жку.	_____ a spoon.
_____ по́лку.	_____ a bookcase.
_____ кни́гу.	_____ a book.

Я ви́жу Ни́ну.	I see Nina.
_____ Ми́лу.	_____ Mila.
_____ студе́нтку.	_____ the coed.
_____ сестру́.	_____ my sister.
_____ жену́.	_____ my wife.
_____ О́лю.	_____ Olya.
_____ Ко́лю.	_____ Kolya.
_____ Са́шу.	_____ Sasha.

Я иду́ в лаборато́рию.	I'm going to the laboratory.
_____ в аудито́рию.	_____ to the lecture hall.
_____ в библиоте́ку.	_____ to the library.
_____ в шко́лу.	_____ to school.
_____ на по́чту.	_____ to the post office.
_____ на слу́жбу.	_____ to work.
_____ на ле́кцию.	_____ to the lecture.

■ REPETITION DRILLS

Repeat the above models, noting that when nouns ending in –a or –я in the nominative singular serve as the direct object or the object of a preposition after a motion verb, the endings –a and –я are replaced by –y and –ю respectively.

■ RESPONSE DRILLS

1. *Where's the vodka?*
   Did you buy vodka?
   т: Где́ во́дка?
   s: **Вы купи́ли во́дку?**
   т: Где́ ры́ба?
   s: **Вы купи́ли ры́бу?**
   (кни́га, ви́лка, ло́жка, по́лка, селёдка, ру́чка)

3. *The school's open.*
   I'm going to school.
   т: Шко́ла откры́та.
   s: **Я иду́ в шко́лу.**

2. *There's the post office.*
   Yes, I see the post office.
   т: Та́м по́чта.
   s: **Да́, я́ ви́жу по́чту.**
   т: Та́м лаборато́рия.
   s: **Да́, я́ ви́жу лаборато́рию.**
   (коро́бка, ры́ба, ка́ша, аудито́рия, ло́жка, ви́лка, Ни́на, О́ля)

   т: Аудито́рия откры́та.
   s: **Я иду́ в аудито́рию.**
   (лаборато́рия, библиоте́ка, шко́ла, аудито́рия)

4. *Nina was at the lecture.*
   Did you see Nina?
   т: Ни́на была́ на ле́кции.
   s: **Вы́ ви́дели Ни́ну?**

т: Ко́ля бы́л на ле́кции.
s: **Вы́ ви́дели Ко́лю?**
   (сестра́, Ми́ла, О́ля, Га́ля, Са́ша,
   студе́нтка Ни́на)

■ CUED QUESTION-ANSWER DRILL

(*a lecture*)	*Where are you going?*
	To a lecture.
т: (ле́кция)	Куда́ вы́ идёте?
s:	**На ле́кцию.**
т: (библиоте́ка)	Куда́ вы́ идёте?
s:	**В библиоте́ку.**

   (слу́жба, по́чта, шко́ла, аудито́рия,
   лаборато́рия, ле́кция)

DISCUSSION

NOMINATIVE SINGULAR	ACCUSATIVE SINGULAR
–а and –я	–у and –ю
жена́	жену́
ры́ба	ры́бу
селёдка	селёдку
Га́ля	Га́лю
О́ля	О́лю
Ко́ля	Ко́лю

The direct object of a verb or the object of a preposition accompanying a motion verb is in the accusative case. **Жена́**-class nouns replace –**а** and –**я** of the nominative singular with –**у** and –**ю** respectively in the accusative singular. Note that while most of these nouns are feminine, some are masculine: **Та́м бы́л Ко́ля** *Kolya was there*; **Я́ ви́дел Ко́лю** *I saw Kolya.*

Inanimate **сто́л**- and **окно́**-class nouns have accusatives which are like their nominatives both in the singular and the plural:

Я́ ви́жу сто́л.	I see the table.
_____ столы́.	____ the tables.
_____ окно́.	____ the window.
_____ о́кна.	____ the windows.
_____ огуре́ц.	____ the cucumber.
_____ огурцы́.	____ the cucumbers.

All **две́рь**-class nouns (animate and inanimate) have singular accusatives like their nominative singular. (In the plural, the accusative is like the nominative only if the noun is inanimate.)

Я́ ви́жу две́рь.	I see the door.
_____ две́ри.	____ the doors.
_____ Любо́вь Петро́вну.	____ Lyubov Petrovna.

The second conjugation verb говори́ть

PAST	говори́л, говори́ла, говори́ло, говори́ли
PRESENT	говорю́, говори́шь, говори́т, говори́м, говори́те, говоря́т

■ SUBSTITUTION DRILLS

1. *You talked for a long time.*
   т: Вы́ до́лго говори́ли.
   s: **Вы́ до́лго говори́ли.**
   (о́н, она́, они́, ты́, мы́, вы́, я́)

2. *He speaks Russian.*
   т: О́н говори́т по-ру́сски.
   s: **О́н говори́т по-ру́сски.**
   (они́, вы́, я́, мы́, ты́, она́, мы́, о́н)

■ QUESTION-ANSWER DRILLS

1. *Do you speak Russian?*
   Yes, I do.
   т: Вы́ говори́те по-ру́сски?
   s: **Да́, говорю́.**
   т: Она́ говори́т по-ру́сски?
   s: **Да́, говори́т.**
   (ты́, они́, Фили́пп, вы́, америка́нец, Гра́нт)

2. *How do I speak Russian?*
   You don't speak Russian [too] badly.
   т: Ка́к я́ говорю́ по-ру́сски?
   s: **Вы́ непло́хо говори́те по-ру́сски.**
   т: Ка́к они́ говоря́т по-ру́сски?
   s: **Они́ непло́хо говоря́т по-ру́сски.**
   (о́н, мы́, ты́, она́, вы́, я́, Фили́пп, америка́нец Гра́нт)

3. *Does she speak English?*
   No, she doesn't.
   т: Она́ говори́т по-англи́йски?
   s: **Не́т, не говори́т.**
   т: Ты́ говори́шь по-англи́йски?
   s: **Не́т, не говорю́.**
   (Ко́ля, вы́, бра́т, они́, сестра́, ты́)

■ CUED QUESTION-ANSWER DRILLS

1. (*Tsarapkin*) *Who's speaking?*
   It's Tsarapkin speaking.
   т: (Цара́пкин) Кто́ говори́т?
   s: **Говори́т Цара́пкин.**
   т: (Ни́на) Кто́ говори́т?
   s: **Говори́т Ни́на.**
   (Кири́лл Па́влович, ре́ктор, Ни́на, Евге́ний, Ле́в)

2. (*the chancellor*) *Who spoke?*
   The chancellor spoke.
   т: (ре́ктор) Кто́ говори́л?
   s: **Говори́л ре́ктор.**
   т: (его́ жена́) Кто́ говори́л?
   s: **Говори́ла его́ жена́.**
   (америка́нец Гра́нт, Хитро́в, Никола́й, Ми́ла, Евге́ний, Ни́на, Га́ля)

DISCUSSION

The second conjugation verb говори́ть, unlike спеши́ть, has its stem ending in a soft consonant. The spelling ending of the first person singular of говори́ть is –ю, and that of the third person plural is –ят: говорю́, говоря́т. Since спеши́ть has its stem ending in a hard consonant, the first person singular has the ending –у and the third person plural has the ending –ат: спешу́, спеша́т. The stress pattern is the same in both verbs. The endings for the other persons are written the same for both verbs: –и́шь, –и́т, –и́м, –и́те. Note from the transcription following that р is soft throughout in говори́ть, and that ш is hard throughout in спеши́ть. (It is only a convention of the spelling system that и and not ы is written after hard consonant ш.)

говор–ю́	[gəvaṛ–ú	**спеш–у́**	[sp̧iš–ú
–и́шь	–íš	–и́шь	–íš
–и́т	–ít	–и́т	–ít
–и́м	–ím	–и́м	–ím
–и́те	–íţi	–и́те	–íţi
–я́т	–át]	–а́т	–át]

Possessive modifiers

MODELS

NONCHANGING FORMS

Э́то **его́** сто́л.	This is his table.
Э́то **её** сто́л.	This is her table.
Э́то **их** сто́л.	This is their table.
Э́то **его́** по́лка.	This is his bookshelf.
Э́то **её** по́лка.	This is her bookshelf.
Э́то **их** по́лка.	This is their bookshelf.
Э́то **его́** письмо́.	This is his letter.
Э́то **её** письмо́.	This is her letter.
Э́то **их** письмо́.	This is their letter.

CHANGING FORMS

Че́й э́то портфе́ль?	Whose briefcase is this?
— Э́то **мо́й** портфе́ль.	It's my briefcase.
— Э́то **тво́й** портфе́ль.	It's your briefcase.
Чья́ э́то кни́га?	Whose book is this?
— Э́то **моя́** кни́га.	It's my book.
— Э́то **твоя́** кни́га.	It's your book.
Чьё э́то письмо́?	Whose letter is this?
— Э́то **моё** письмо́.	It's my letter.
— Э́то **твоё** письмо́.	It's your letter.
Че́й э́то сто́л?	Whose table is this?
— Э́то **на́ш** сто́л.	It's our table.
— Э́то **ва́ш** сто́л.	It's your table.
Чья́ э́то по́лка?	Whose shelf is this?
— Э́то **на́ша** по́лка.	It's our shelf.
— Э́то **ва́ша** по́лка.	It's your shelf.
Чьё э́то общежи́тие?	Whose dormitory is this?
— Э́то **на́ше** общежи́тие.	It's our dormitory.
— Э́то **ва́ше** общежи́тие.	It's your dormitory.

Repeat the above models observing the pattern. Note that there are two types of modifiers:

1. Those that do not change their form to agree with the word they modify: **его́, её, их.**

2. Those that change their form according to the word they modify: **чей, чья, мо́й, моя́, на́ш, ва́ш, тво́й.**

Observe also that **тво́й, твоя́,** and **твоё** relate to **ты́,** while **ва́ш, ва́ша,** and **ва́ше** relate to **вы́.**

■ QUESTION-ANSWER DRILLS

1. *Where's my briefcase?*
   Your briefcase is on the table.
   т: Где́ мо́й портфе́ль?
   s: **Ва́ш портфе́ль на столе́.**
   т: Где́ мо́й материа́л?
   s: **Ва́ш материа́л на столе́.**
   (я́щик, бо́рщ, каранда́ш, ча́й, но́ж)

2. *Where's our dinner?*
   Your dinner is there.
   т: Где́ на́ш обе́д?
   s: **Ва́ш обе́д та́м.**
   т: Где́ на́ш бо́рщ?
   s: **Ва́ш бо́рщ та́м.**
   (ча́й, заво́д, шка́ф, сто́л, хле́б)

3. *Where's my sister?*
   Your sister's here.
   т: Где́ моя́ сестра́?
   s: **Ва́ша сестра́ ту́т.**
   т: Где́ моя́ кни́га?
   s: **Ва́ша кни́га ту́т.**
   (две́рь, жена́, ру́чка, шко́ла, тетра́дь, коро́бка, аудито́рия)

4. *Where's our school?*
   Our school is there.
   т: Где́ на́ша шко́ла?
   s: **На́ша шко́ла та́м.**
   т: Где́ на́ша кни́га?
   s: **На́ша кни́га та́м.**
   (по́лка, две́рь, столо́вая)

5. *Where's my husband?*
   Your husband is there.
   т: Где́ мо́й му́ж?
   s: **Тво́й му́ж та́м.**
   т: Где́ мо́й сто́л?
   s: **Тво́й сто́л та́м.**
   (пода́рок, я́щик, бра́т, портфе́ль, шка́ф)

6. *Where's your material?*
   My material is there.
   т: Где́ тво́й материа́л?
   s: **Мо́й материа́л та́м.**
   т: Где́ тво́й сто́л?
   s: **Мо́й сто́л та́м.**
   (каранда́ш, бо́рщ, му́ж, обе́д)

■ SUBSTITUTION DRILL

Whose pencil is that?
т: Че́й э́то каранда́ш?
s: **Че́й э́то каранда́ш?**
т: _____(перо́)?
s: **Чьё э́то перо́?**

(материа́л, пла́тье, ры́ба, я́щик, бо́рщ, две́рь, окно́, письмо́, но́ж, коро́бка, портфе́ль, сто́л, по́лка)

■ QUESTION-ANSWER DRILLS

1. *Whose letter is that?*
   That's my letter.
   т: Чьё э́то письмо́?
   s: **Э́то моё письмо́.**
   т: Чья́ э́то кни́га?
   s: **Э́то моя́ кни́га.**
   (портфе́ль, две́рь, окно́, но́ж, я́щик, коро́бка, сто́л, пла́тье)

2. *Whose pen is that, yours?*
   Yes, that's my pen.
   т: Чьё э́то перо́, ва́ше?
   s: **Да́, э́то моё перо́.**
   т: Че́й э́то портфе́ль, ва́ш?
   s: **Да́, э́то мо́й портфе́ль.**
   (кни́га, две́рь, я́щик, тетра́дь, окно́, каранда́ш, по́лка)

3. *Whose dress is that, yours?*
   Yes, it's my dress.
   т: Чьё э́то пла́тье, твоё?
   s: **Да́, э́то моё пла́тье.**
   т: Чья́ э́то ка́ша, твоя́?
   s: **Да́, э́то моя́ ка́ша.**
   (но́ж, сто́л, обе́д, ры́ба, костю́м, ча́й, коро́бка)

4. *Is that your pencil?*
   No, it's his pencil.
   т: Э́то ва́ш каранда́ш?
   s: **Не́т, э́то его́ каранда́ш.**
   т: Э́то ва́ше перо́?
   s: **Не́т, э́то его́ перо́.**
   (портфе́ль, сто́л, две́рь, ча́й, кни́га, письмо́, жена́, но́ж, сестра́, окно́, материа́л)

5. *Is that your dress?*
   No, that's her dress.
   т: Э́то твоё пла́тье?
   s: **Не́т, э́то её пла́тье.**
   т: Э́то тво́й му́ж?
   s: **Не́т, э́то её му́ж.**
   (твоя́ тетра́дь, перо́, ча́й, письмо́, сестра́, окно́, материа́л)

6. *Is this our bread?*
   No, that's their bread.
   т: Э́то на́ш хле́б?
   s: **Не́т, э́то и́х хле́б.**
   т: Э́то на́ша селёдка?
   s: **Не́т э́то и́х селёдка.**
   (сто́л, ча́й, кни́га, окно́, материа́л, но́ж, коро́бка, обе́д, по́лка, пи́ща)

■ PROGRESSIVE SUBSTITUTION DRILLS

1. *This is my briefcase.*
   Э́то мо́й портфе́ль.
   ———— (кни́га).
   ———— (письмо́).
   — (твоё) ————.
   ———— (тетра́дь).
   ———— (каранда́ш).
   — (ва́ш) ————.
   ———— (по́чта).
   ———— (общежи́тие).

   This is my briefcase.
   Э́то мо́й портфе́ль.
   Э́то моя́ кни́га.
   Э́то моё письмо́.
   Э́то твоё письмо́.
   Э́то твоя́ тетра́дь.
   Э́то тво́й каранда́ш.
   Э́то ва́ш каранда́ш.
   Э́то ва́ша по́чта.
   Э́то ва́ше общежи́тие.

2. *This is our dormitory.*
   Э́то на́ше общежи́тие.
   ———— (по́лка).
   ———— (пода́рок).
   — (мо́й) ————.
   ———— (сестра́).
   ———— (окно́).
   — (твоё) ——.
   ———— (коро́бка).
   ———— (материа́л).
   — (ва́ш) ————.
   ———— (шко́ла).
   ———— (общежи́тие).
   — (на́ше) ————.
   ———— (пи́ща).
   ———— (сто́л).

   This is our dormitory.
   Э́то на́ше общежи́тие.
   Э́то на́ша по́лка.
   Э́то на́ш пода́рок.
   Э́то мо́й пода́рок.
   Э́то моя́ сестра́.
   Э́то моё окно́.
   Э́то твоё окно́.
   Э́то твоя́ коро́бка.
   Э́то тво́й материа́л.
   Э́то ва́ш материа́л.
   Э́то ва́ша шко́ла.
   Э́то ва́ше общежи́тие.
   Э́то на́ше общежи́тие.
   Э́то на́ша пи́ща.
   Э́то на́ш сто́л.

3. *Here's our chancellor.*

т: Во́т на́ш ре́ктор.

s: **Во́т на́ш ре́ктор.**

т: _____ (общежи́тие).

s: **Во́т на́ше общежи́тие.**

___ (ва́ше) _____.

Во́т ва́ше общежи́тие.

_____ (авто́бус).

_____ (уро́к).

_____ (ле́кция).

Во́т на́ше письмо́.

___ (моё) _____.

_____ (перо́).

_____ (портфе́ль).

___ (твой) _____.

_____ (письмо́).

_____ (кни́га).

_____ (каранда́ш).

_____ (пла́тье).

DISCUSSION

There are two types of *possessive modifiers* in Russian:

1. Those that do *not* change their form to agree with the word they accompany.

его́	his, its
её	her, hers, its
и́х	their, theirs

Note that **его́** is pronounced [jivó].

EXAMPLES

его́ портфе́ль	его́ сестра́	его́ письмо́	его́ тетра́ди
её портфе́ль	её сестра́	её письмо́	её тетра́ди
и́х портфе́ль	и́х сестра́	и́х письмо́	и́х тетра́ди

2. Those with grammatical endings which change to agree in gender, number, and case with the word they accompany:

MASCULINE	FEMININE	NEUTER	
чей	чья́	чьё	whose
мо́й	моя́	моё	my, mine
твой	твоя́	твоё	your, yours
на́ш	на́ша	на́ше	our, ours
ва́ш	ва́ша	ва́ше	your, yours

Note that **твой, твоя́,** and **твоё** refer to **ты́,** while **ва́ш, ва́ша,** and **ва́ше** refer to **вы́.**

EXAMPLES

чей каранда́ш
whose pencil

чья́ сестра́
whose sister

чьё письмо́
whose letter

мо́й каранда́ш
my pencil

моя́ сестра́
my sister

моё письмо́
my letter

ва́ш каранда́ш
your pencil

ва́ша сестра́
your sister

ва́ше письмо́
your letter

The perfective future of the first conjugation verbs пойти and взять

Я́ пойду́ на конце́рт.	I'll go to a concert.
Ты́ пойдёшь _____.	You'll go _____.
О́н пойдёт _____.	He'll go _____.
Мы́ пойдём _____.	We'll go _____.
Вы́ пойдёте _____.	You'll go _____.
Они́ пойду́т _____.	They'll go _____.

■ REPETITION DRILL

Repeat the model after your instructor (or the tape) until you can reproduce all the forms accurately. Note that the endings are exactly like the present tense endings of the imperfective verb идти́, but that the meaning is future.

■ SUBSTITUTION DRILLS

1. *I'm going to go to a dinner.*
   т: Я́ пойду́ на обе́д.
   s: **Я́ пойду́ на обе́д.**
   т: (Они́) _____.
   s: **Они́ пойду́т на обе́д.**
   (она́, ты́, вы́, мы́, Са́ша, Ко́ля и Га́ля, я́)

2. *I'll go to the library tomorrow.*
   т: Я́ пойду́ в библиоте́ку за́втра.
   s: **Я́ пойду́ в библиоте́ку за́втра.**
   т: (О́н)_____.
   s: **О́н пойдёт в библиоте́ку за́втра.**
   (мы́, бра́т, сестра́, ты́, вы́, они́, бра́т и сестра́, я́)

■ TRANSFORMATION DRILL

I'm going to the dormitory.
I'll go to the dormitory.
т: Я́ иду́ в общежи́тие.
s: **Я́ пойду́ в общежи́тие.**

т: Ты́ идёшь в общежи́тие.
s: **Ты́ пойдёшь в общежи́тие.**
(мы́, Никола́й, Га́ля, они́, вы́, о́н)

■ QUESTION-ANSWER DRILL

Are you going to the club today?
No, I'll go there tomorrow.
т: Вы́ идёте в клу́б сего́дня?
s: **Не́т, я́ пойду́ туда́ за́втра.**

т: Они́ иду́т в клу́б сего́дня?
s: **Не́т, они́ пойду́т туда́ за́втра.**
(Евге́ний, ты́, мы́, она́, сестра́, Ни́на, Цара́пкин)

Я́ возьму́ то́лько кни́ги.	I'll just take books.
Ты́ возьмёшь _____.	You'll ____ take ____.
О́н возьмёт _____.	He'll ____ take ____.
Мы́ возьмём _____.	We'll ____ take ____.
Вы́ возьмёте _____.	You'll ____ take ____.
Они́ возьму́т _____.	They'll ____ take ____.

■ REPETITION DRILL

Repeat the model after your instructor (or the tape) until you can reproduce all the forms accurately. The pattern of endings is the same as for the present tense of **идти** and the perfective future of **пойти**. Note that since **взять** is a perfective verb, the meaning of the forms is future.

■ SUBSTITUTION DRILLS

1. *They'll take these notebooks.*
   т: Они́ возьму́т э́ти тетра́ди.
   s: **Они́ возьму́т э́ти тетра́ди.**
   т: (Я)_____.
   s: **Я возьму́ э́ти тетра́ди.**
   (Га́ля, ты́, вы́, мы́, сестра́, Оле́г и Кири́лл, ты́, я́)

2. *I'll take these books.*
   т: Я́ возьму́ э́ти кни́ги.
   s: **Я́ возьму́ э́ти кни́ги.**
   т: (Она́)_____.
   s: **Она́ возьмёт э́ти кни́ги.**
   (Кири́лл, ты́, мы́, они́, бра́т, О́ля, Са́ша и Ко́ля, я́, вы́)

■ CUED QUESTION-ANSWER DRILL

(*I*) *Who'll take these notebooks?*
        I will.
т: (я) Кто́ возьмёт э́ти тетра́ди?
s: **Я́ возьму́.**
т: (он) Кто́ возьмёт э́ти тетра́ди?
s: **О́н возьмёт.**
(они́, мы́, вы́, ты́, Са́ша, Ни́на, бра́т)

DISCUSSION

The perfective verb **пойти** is the aspect pair of the imperfective verb **идти**. Both **пойти** and **взять** *to take* are first conjugation perfective verbs which take the same set of endings in their perfective future as **идти** does in the present.

SINGULAR	пойд–у́	I'll go	возьм–у́	I'll take
	–ёшь	you'll go	–ёшь	you'll take
	–ёт	he (she)'ll go	–ёт	he (she)'ll take
PLURAL	–ём	we'll go	–ём	we'll take
	–ёте	you'll go	–ёте	you'll take
	–у́т	they'll go	–у́т	they'll take

For convenience, we may call such endings as these "present-future" endings. Although they are the same for both imperfective and perfective verbs, they have different meanings, depending on the aspect of the verb. When the verb is imperfective, the endings signalize the present tense; when the verb is perfective, the endings signalize the future. It is important to note that the perfective future has in it the particular limitations inherent in the perfective aspect. It describes a future action in terms of its realization, completion, or result; thus it contrasts with the imperfective, which focuses on either the process itself or its repetition.

The second conjugation verb ви́деть

MODELS

MODELS

Ни́на ви́дела О́лю в ГУ́Ме.   Nina saw Olya in GUM.
Лёв ви́дел_____.   Lev saw _____.
Мы́ ви́дели _____.   We saw _____.

Иногда́ я́ ви́жу Ко́лю в клу́бе.   Sometimes I see Kolya at the club.
_____ ты́ ви́дишь _____.   _____ you see _____.
_____ о́н ви́дит _____.   _____ he sees _____.
_____ мы́ ви́дим _____.   _____ we see _____.
_____ вы́ ви́дите _____.   _____ you see _____.
_____ они́ ви́дят _____.   _____ they see _____.

■ REPETITION DRILL

Repeat the given models, noting that in the first person singular, present tense, **ж** replaces the final stem consonant **д**, which occurs in all other forms.

■ SUBSTITUTION DRILLS

1. *I often see Nina in town.*
   т: Я́ ча́сто ви́жу Ни́ну в го́роде.
   s: **Я́ ча́сто ви́жу Ни́ну в го́роде.**
   т: (Мы́)_____.
   s: **Мы́ ча́сто ви́дим Ни́ну в го́роде.**
   (Никола́й, ты́, я́, вы́, моя́ сестра́, они́, мо́й бра́т)

2. *He often used to see Nina in town.*
   т: О́н ча́сто ви́дел Ни́ну в го́роде.
   s: **О́н ча́сто ви́дел Ни́ну в го́роде.**
   т: (Вы́)_____.
   s: **Вы́ ча́сто ви́дели Ни́ну в го́роде.**
   (моя́ сестра́, Га́ля, мо́й бра́т, мы́, они́, на́ша учи́тельница)

■ TRANSFORMATION DRILLS

1. *I rarely saw Galya there.*
   I rarely see Galya there.
   т: Я́ ре́дко та́м ви́дел Га́лю.
   s: **Я́ ре́дко та́м ви́жу Га́лю.**
   т: Они́ ре́дко та́м ви́дели Га́лю.
   s: **Они́ ре́дко та́м ви́дят Га́лю.**
   (о́н, мы́, вы́, я́, сестра́, ты́, они́, мы́, я́)

2. *We sometimes see Nina there.*
   We sometimes saw Nina there.
   т: Мы́ иногда́ та́м ви́дим Ни́ну.
   s: **Мы́ иногда́ та́м ви́дели Ни́ну.**
   т: Никола́й иногда́ та́м ви́дит Ни́ну.
   s: **Никола́й иногда́ та́м ви́дел Ни́ну.**
   (я́, ты́, вы́, они́, сестра́, бра́т, мы́)

■ QUESTION-ANSWER DRILL

Do you see the knife?
No, I don't.
т: Ты́ ви́дишь но́ж?
s: **Не́т, не ви́жу.**
т: Вы́ ви́дите но́ж?
s: **Не́т, не ви́жу.**
(они́, о́н, она́, ты́, вы́)

DISCUSSION

The verb **ви́деть** differs from the other second conjugation verbs already discussed (**спеши́ть** and **говори́ть**) in that there is an alternation of stem consonants in the first person singular of the present tense. In **ви́деть,** the **д** is automatically replaced by **ж** in the first person singular and the ending is **–у.** Compare the three patterns of second conjugation verbs:

	спеши́ть *to hurry*	говори́ть *to speak*	ви́деть *to see*
PRESENT STEM	спеш–	говор–	ви́д–
	спеш–у́ –и́шь –и́т –и́м –и́те –а́т	говор–ю́ –и́шь –и́т –и́м –и́те –я́т	ви́ж–у ви́д–ишь –ит –им –ите –ят
PAST STEM	спеши́–	говори́–	ви́де–
	спеши́–л –ла –ло –ли	говори́–л –ла –ло –ли	ви́де–л –ла –ло –ли

Second person imperatives: familiar versus plural-polite forms

MODELS

Скажи́, где́ ты́ вчера́ бы́л?　　　　Say, where were you yesterday?
Скажи́те, где́ вы́ вчера́ бы́ли?　　　Say, ＿＿＿＿＿＿＿＿＿＿?

Извини́, я́ спешу́ на авто́бус.　　　Excuse me, I'm hurrying to catch a bus.
Извини́те, я́ спешу́ на авто́бус.　　Excuse me, ＿＿＿＿＿＿＿＿.

Заходи́. Давно́ тебя́ не ви́дел.　　　Come in, I haven't seen you in a long time.
Заходи́те. Давно́ ва́с не ви́дел.　　Come in, ＿＿＿＿＿＿＿＿＿.

Наре́жь, пожа́луйста, огурцы́.　　　Please slice the cucumbers.
Наре́жьте, пожа́луйста, огурцы́.　　＿＿＿ slice ＿＿＿＿＿.

Возьми́ э́ти кни́ги.　　　　　　　　Take these books.
Возьми́те э́ти кни́ги.　　　　　　　Take ＿＿＿＿＿.

Здра́вствуй, Оле́г!　　　　　　　　Hello, Oleg!
Здра́вствуйте, ребя́та!　　　　　　Hello, fellows!

■ REPETITION DRILL

Repeat the given models, noting that the plural-polite imperative is exactly like the familiar imperative except for the addition of the unstressed suffix **–те.**[1]

---

[1] At this stage the student is not expected to form the imperative; rather, he should recognize those which he encounters and either add or delete the formal-plural suffix **–те.** Thus, given the familiar imperative **чита́й!** *read!* he will be expected to know that the formal-plural is **чита́йте!**

1. *Slice the bread!*

   т: Наре́жь хле́б!

   s: Наре́жьте хле́б!

   т: Заходи́, пожа́луйста!

   s: Заходи́те, пожа́луйста!

   Скажи́, вчера́ бы́ло собра́ние?

   Возьми́ то́лько одну́ тетра́дь!

   Здра́вствуй, Ле́в!

   Извини́, во́т мо́й авто́бус!

   Не говори́!

   Посмотри́!

   Поступа́й в университе́т!

   Чита́й!

   Повтори́!

   Не спеши́!

2. *Look, here comes Nina.*

   т: Смотри́те, во́т идёт Ни́на.

   s: Смотри́, во́т идёт Ни́на.

   т: Возьми́те э́ти кни́ги.

   s: Возьми́ э́ти кни́ги.

   Заходи́те, две́рь не заперта́.

   Наре́жьте хле́б и огурцы́.

   Извини́те, я́ спешу́ на уро́к.

   Не говори́те!

   Посмотри́те!

   Поступа́йте в университе́т!

   Чита́йте по-ру́сски!

DISCUSSION

Imperatives call primarily for action rather than a verbal response. The most common type is the second person imperative.

EXAMPLES

Пожа́луйста, заходи́те!	Come in, please!
Извини́те. Во́т идёт мо́й авто́бус.	Excuse me. Here comes my bus.
Смотри́, во́т идёт Смирно́в.	Look, there goes Smirnov.
Наре́жь огурцы́.	Cut the cucumbers.
Скажи́те, вчера́ бы́ло собра́ние?	Tell me, was there a meeting yesterday?

The familiar imperative (used in addressing **ты́**) differs structurally from the formal-plural imperative (used in addressing **вы́**) only in that the unstressed suffix –те is added in the latter form.

FAMILIAR	FORMAL-PLURAL	
наре́жь	наре́жьте	cut!
смотри́	смотри́те	look!
спроси́	спроси́те	ask!
отве́ть	отве́тьте	answer!
повтори́	повтори́те	repeat!
измени́	измени́те	change!
замени́	замени́те	substitute!
здра́вствуй	здра́вствуйте	hello (*lit.* be healthy)!

– Здра́вствуйте, Оле́г Фили́ппович! Здра́вствуйте, Лев Па́влович! – Куда́ вы так спеши́те? На ле́кцию? – Нет, на по́чту. А вы куда́? – Я иду́ домо́й. – Скажи́те, вчера́ бы́ло собра́ние? – Да. И бы́ло о́чень интере́сно. – Извини́те. Вот идёт мой авто́бус. Всего́ хоро́шего! – До свида́ния! Приве́т жене́!

– Здра́вствуйте, Кири́лл Па́влович! – А, Семён Фили́ппович! Давно́ вас не ви́дел. Говоря́т, вы бы́ли больны́? – Да. Всю зи́му не́ был на слу́жбе. – А тепе́рь вы здоро́вы? – Вполне́. – А как жена́, здоро́ва? – Спаси́бо, здоро́ва.

– Ни́на! Обе́д гото́в? Что ты! Мы неда́вно пи́ли чай. – Да, но я уже́ го́лоден. У нас есть ры́ба? – Нет. Ры́бы бо́льше нет. – А борщ у нас есть? – Да. И ка́ша то́же. Наре́жь огурцы́. Они́ на столе́. – Хорошо́. А где нож? – Он в столе́, в я́щике.

PREPARATION FOR CONVERSATION   **Я́ забы́л сво́й портфе́ль**

свой портфе́ль	my briefcase
забы́ть (pfv I)	to forget, leave (inadvertently)
Я́ забы́л сво́й портфе́ль.	I forgot my briefcase.
телефо́н (телефо́ны)	telephone (telephones)
звони́ть (II)[1]	to ring, to phone
звони́т телефо́н	the phone is ringing.
Ма́ша (variant of Мари́я)	Masha
Ма́ша, звони́т телефо́н.	Masha, the phone is ringing.
к телефо́ну	to (or toward) the telephone
подойти́ (pfv I)	to approach, go up to
Подойди́ к телефо́ну!	Go to the phone!
Подойди́, пожа́луйста, к телефо́ну!	Go answer the phone, please!
алло́ [aḷó]	hello
слу́шать (I)	to listen
Алло́! Я́ слу́шаю.	Hello! (*Lit.* Hello! I'm listening.)
попроси́ть (pfv II)	to ask, request
Попроси́те Ива́на Никола́евича к телефо́ну!	Ask Ivan Nikolaevich [to come] to the phone!
Попроси́те, пожа́луйста, Ива́на Никола́евича к телефо́ну!	Please ask Ivan Nikolaevich to come to the phone!
Кто́ говори́т?	Who's speaking? *or* Who's calling?
Сейча́с. А кто́ говори́т?	Right away. And who's calling?
Ку́рочкин.	Kurochkin.
у телефо́на	on the phone, on the line (*lit.* at the phone)
Я́ у телефо́на, Бори́с Миха́йлович.	Hello (*lit.* I'm on the line), Boris Mikhailovich.
де́ло (дела́)	thing(s), matter(s)
в чём	in what
В чём де́ло?	What's the matter?

---

[1] The symbols (I) and (II) stand for the first and second conjugations. Henceforth verb aspect will be indicated only for perfective verbs. Thus, (I) means that the verb is imperfective and first conjugation; (pfv I) means that the verb is perfective and first conjugation.

◀ **Уличный продавец пилава в Ташкенте.**

у вáс   at your place; you have

ли   whether, if (question particle)

не забы́л ли я   didn't I forget, whether or not I forgot

Не забы́л ли я у вáс свóй портфéль?   Didn't I leave my briefcase at your place?

узнáть (pfv II)   to find out, learn, recognize

Я хотéл узнáть, не забы́л ли я у вáс свóй портфéль.   I wanted to find out whether or not I left my briefcase at your place.

минýтку   just a minute

нигдé   nowhere, not . . . anywhere

Минýтку. Нéт, нигдé не ви́жу.   Just a minute. No, I don't see it anywhere.

остáвить (pfv II)   to leave

Мóжет бы́ть вы́ в университéте остáвили?   Maybe you left it at the university?

подýмать (pfv I)   to think, think a bit

о, об, обо (*plus* prepositional case)   about, of, on (concerning)

об э́том   about that, of that

Кáк я об э́том не подýмал!   How is it I didn't think of that!

тудá   there, to that place

войти́ тудá   to get in (*lit.* to enter there)

смóчь (pfv I)   to be able, can

я смогý   I'll be able

Но я́ не смогý тудá войти́.   But I won't be able to get in.

двéри (pl of двéрь)   doors, door, doorway

Двéри ужé зáперты.   The doors are already locked.

убóрщица (убóрщицы)   cleaning woman (cleaning women)

А убóрщица?   How about the cleaning woman?

откры́ть (pfv I)   to open

мóчь (I)   to be able, can

онá мóжет   she can

А убóрщица? Онá мóжет откры́ть.   How about the cleaning woman? She can open [the doors].

клю́ч (ключи́)   key(s)

у неё éсть   [uɳijó jéşt̢]   she has

У неё éсть ключи́.   She has the keys.

о нéй   about her

Конéчно. Я о нéй забы́л.   Of course. I forgot about her.

совсéм   completely, altogether

Конéчно. Я о нéй совсéм забы́л.   Of course. I forgot all about her.

SUPPLEMENT

вахтёр (вахтёры)   custodian(s) (compare Fr. *concierge*)

Гдé вахтёр? Óн мóжет откры́ть двéри.   Where's the custodian? He can open the door[s].

звонóк (звонки́)   bell(s), doorbell(s)

Чтó э́то, звонóк?   What's that, the bell?

позвони́ть (pfv II)   to phone, call on the phone

Онá позвони́ла домóй.   She telephoned home.

Я забы́л сво́й портфе́ль

И.Н. — Ива́н Никола́евич (профе́ссор Орло́в)
М.И. — Мари́я Ива́новна Орло́ва (Ма́ша, его́ жена́)
Б.М. — Бори́с Миха́йлович (профе́ссор Ку́рочкин)

И. Н.	1	Ма́ша, звони́т телефо́н! Подойди́, пожа́луйста.	mắšə ↓ zvaṇít ṭiḷifốn ↓ pədajḍí pažáləstə ↓
М. И.	2	Алло́! Я слу́шаю![1]	aḷố ↑ já slűšəju ↓
Б. М.	3	Попроси́те, пожа́луйста, Ива́на Никола́евича к телефо́ну.	pəpraṣíṭi pažáləstə | ivánə ṇikaláičə kṭiḷifónu ↓
М. И.	4	Сейча́с. А кто́ говори́т?	ṣičás ↓ a któ gəvaṛít ↓
Б. М.	5	Ку́рочкин.	kűrəčḳin ↓
И. Н.	6	Я у телефо́на, Бори́с Миха́йлович. В чём де́ло?	já uṭiḷifốnə | baṛis ṃixálič ↓ fčóm ḍế́lə ↓
Б. М.	7	Я хоте́л узна́ть, не забы́л ли я у ва́с сво́й портфе́ль.[2]	já xaṭél uznắṭ | ṇizabĭl ḷi já uvás | svój partfḗḷ ↓
И. Н.	8	Мину́тку. Не́т, нигде́ не ви́жу.[3] Мо́жет быть, вы́ в университе́те оста́вили.	ṃinűtku ↓ ṇḗt ↓ ṇigḍé ṇiɣĭžu ↓ móž(id)bíṭ | ví vuṇiɣirṣiṭḗṭi astáɣiḷi ↓
Б. М.	9	Ка́к я об э́том не поду́мал! Но я не смогу́ туда́ войти́. Две́ри уже́ за́перты.[4]	kắk já abétəm ṇipadúməl ↓ no já ṇismagú tudá vajṭĭ ↑ dɣéṛi užé zắpirti ↓
И. Н.	10	А убо́рщица? Она́ мо́жет откры́ть, у неё́ е́сть ключи́.	a ubőrščicə ↓ aṇá móžit atkríṭ ↓ uṇijó jéṣṭ kḷučĭ ↓ ·
Б. М.	11	Коне́чно! Я о не́й совсе́м забы́л.	kaṇḗšnə ↓ já aṇéj safṣém zabĭl ↓

NOTES

[1] Russians answer the telephone in various ways, corresponding to our *hello:*
Я у телефо́на.
Алло́! *or* Алло́, я слу́шаю.
Да́? *or* Да́, я слу́шаю.
[Я] слу́шаю.

Despite its spelling, **алло́** is pronounced with a single л, usually soft: [aḷó].

² The possessive modifier **свой** is equivalent to **мой** in this sentence. **Свой** means *one's own* and can refer to any person. It is not used to modify the subject of a sentence, but refers *back to the subject for its meaning*:

Я забыл **свой** портфель.	I forgot *my* briefcase.
Ты забыл **свой** портфель.	You forgot *your* briefcase.
Она забыла **свой** портфель.	She forgot *her* briefcase.

³ Note that **нигде** *nowhere* is used in a double negative construction in Russian. This is true of all such negative constructions: **никогда**, **ничего**, **никуда**, and so forth.

Я его **нигде не** вижу.	I don't see it (*or* him) anywhere.
Вы **никогда не** говорите по-русски.	You never speak Russian.
Я **ничего** об этом **не** знаю.	I don't know anything about it.
Я **никуда не** иду.	I'm not going anywhere.

⁴ Russians often use the plural form **двери** to mean a *single door* as well as more than one door. In the meaning *doorway*, the plural is used:

Он стоял в **дверях**.	He stood in the *doorway*.

PREPARATION FOR CONVERSATION

Студенты писали о народах СССР

народы СССР	the peoples of the U.S.S.R.
о народах СССР	about the peoples of the U.S.S.R.
писать (I)	to write
Студенты писали о народах СССР.	The students wrote about the peoples of the U.S.S.R.
результат (результаты)	result(s)
неплохой	not half bad, pretty good
неплохие результаты	pretty good results
по-моему	in my opinion, I think
По-моему, результаты неплохие.	In my opinion the results are pretty good.
Вы о чём это? (*full form* Вы о чём это говорите?)	What's that you're talking about?
экзамен (экзамены)	examination(s)
Вы о чём это? Об экзаменах?	What are you talking about? The examinations?
работа (работы)	work(s), paper(s) (written)
о работах студентов	about the students' papers
Нет, о работах студентов.	No, about the students' papers.
Они писали о народах СССР.	They wrote about the peoples of the U.S.S.R.
вот как!	really! you don't say! is that so!
Где их работы?	Where are their papers?
Вот как! Где их работы?	Is that so! Where are their papers?

стул (стулья)
здесь
Вот здесь, на стуле.

агá [ahá]
Агá, вижу!

якут (якуты)
этот (m), эта (f), это (n)
Эта работа о якутах.
украинец (украинцы)
эти работы
Эти работы об украинцах.
Эта работа о якутах, эти об украинцах.

написать (pfv I)
А о чём написал Козлов?

грузин (грузины)
Козлов написал о грузинах.
отлично
О грузинах. И отлично написал.

молодец (молодцы)
Он молодец!

Рад это слышать!

доволен, довольна, –о, –ы
профессор (профессорá)
Всé профессорá довóльны.
им
Всé профессорá им довóльны.
Всé нáши профессорá им довóльны.

рýсские
о рýсских
А вóт рабóта о рýсских.

Петрóва
Это Петрóва написáла.

мнóго
о нéй
Дá? Я о нéй ужé мнóго слышал.

лýчшие студéнты
Онá и Козлóв — лýчшие студéнты.
факультéт (факультéты)
на факультéте
на этом факультéте
Онá и Козлóв — лýчшие студéнты на этом факультéте.

chair(s)
here
Right here on the chair.

aha! ahhh!
Aha, I see!

Yakut(s)
this, that
This paper is on the Yakuts.
Ukrainian(s)
these papers
These papers are on the Ukrainians.
This paper is on the Yakuts, and these are on the Ukrainians.

to write
And what did Kozlov write about?

Georgian(s)
Kozlov wrote about the Georgians.
excellently
About the Georgians. And he wrote excellently.
one who does an outstanding job
He's terrific!

Glad to hear it.

pleased, satisfied
professor(s)
All the professors are pleased.
by him, with him
All the professors are pleased with him.
All our professors are pleased with him.

the Russians
on the Russians, about the Russians
And here's a paper on the Russians.

Miss Petrov
Miss Petrov wrote that.

much, a lot, a good deal
about her
Yes? I've already heard a good deal about her.

the best students
She and Kozlov are the best students.
department(s)
in the department
in this department
She and Kozlov are the best students in this department.

сочинéние

composition

Мы́ писа́ли сочинéние.

We were writing a composition.

учи́тель (учителя́)

teacher(s) (below university level)

Óн ва́ш учи́тель?

Is he your teacher?

учи́тельница (учи́тельницы)

female teacher(s) (below university level)

Она́ ва́ша учи́тельница?

Is she your teacher?

гру́ппа (гру́ппы)

group(s), section(s)

в гру́ппе

in the group, in the section

Они́ лу́чшие студéнты в э́той гру́ппе.

They're the best students in this group.

Студéнты писа́ли о наро́дах СССР

И. Н. — Ива́н Никола́евич
Б. М. — Бори́с Миха́йлович

Б. М.	1	По-мо́ему, результа́ты неплохи́е.	pamője̋jimu | r̨izul̨ta̋ti n̨iplax̨i̋ji↓
И. Н.	2	Вы́ о чём э́то? Об экза́менах?	ví ačőm étə ↓ abɨgza̋m̨inəx ↓
Б. М.	3	Нéт, о рабо́тах студéнтов. Они́ писа́ли о наро́дах СССР.[1]	n̨ét ↓ arabótəx stuđéntəf ↓ an̨i p̨isáļi anaródəx ésésésér̨ ↓
И. Н.	4	Во́т ка́к! Гдé и́х рабо́ты?	võt kák ↓ gđé íx rabőti ↓
Б. М.	5	Во́т здéсь, на сту́ле.	vód zđéş ↓ nastűļi˙↓
И. Н.	6	Ага́, ви́жу. Э́та рабо́та о яку́тах, э́ти об украи́нцах. А о чём написа́л Козло́в?	ahã́ ↓ y̨ížu ↓ étə rabótə ajikűtəx | éţi abukraíncəx ↓ a ačőm nəp̨isál kazlőf ↑
Б. М.	7	О грузи́нах. И отли́чно написа́л! Óн молодéц![2]	agruz̨ĭnəx ↓ i atļĭčnə nəp̨isál ↓ ón məlađéc ↓
И. Н.	8	Ра́д э́то слы́шать. Ка́жется, всé на́ши профессора́ и́м дово́льны.[3]	rắt étə slíšəţ ↓ ka̋žitcə | fşé náši prəf̨isará im davóļni ↓

Б. М.   9 А во́т рабо́та о ру́сских.   a vót rabótə arúsķix ↓
            Э́то Петро́ва написа́ла.[4]   étə ṗitrṓvə nəṗisálə ↓

И. Н. 10 Да́?   dắ ↑
            Я́ о не́й уже́ мно́го слы́шал. já aṇéj užé mnṓgə slíšəl ↓
            Она́ и Козло́в —   aná i kazlṓf ↑
            лу́чшие студе́нты   lúcšiji stuḑḗnti |
            на э́том факульте́те.[5]   naétəm fəkuļţḗţi ↓

NOTES   [1] In the abbreviation **СССР** *U.S.S.R.*, the letters stand for **Сою́з Сове́тских Социалисти́ческих Респу́блик** *Union of Soviet Socialist Republics*. Unlike **ГУМ**, **СССР** is not declined:

Compare **в ГУМе** *in GUM* with **в СССР** *in the U.S.S.R.*

[2] The noun **молоде́ц** is a term of praise that can be applied to anyone who does a good job or comes through successfully. It is often used when we would say: *nice going! fine! good boy! good girl!* i.e., as an exclamation of approval.

[3] **Профе́ссор** is grammatically masculine, but may refer to a woman as well as a man:

Она́ на́ш профе́ссор.   She's our professor.

Compare it with the masculine noun **учи́тель**, which has a corresponding feminine equivalent **учи́тельница**. Note, however, that the masculine plural **учителя́** can refer to a mixed group of teachers, but that the feminine plural **учи́тельницы** refers only to women teachers.

[4] **Петро́ва** is the feminine form of **Петро́в** and may mean Miss or Mrs. Petrov, depending upon the context. It is not considered impolite to refer to a man or woman simply by using the last name; for example, **Во́т идёт Цара́пкина** means *Here comes Miss (or Mrs.) Tsarapkin*. In addressing the person, however, either the first name and patronymic or the nickname is usual. **Господи́н** and **госпожа́** are used by Russians only when referring to foreigners or by emigré Russians.

[5] **Факульте́т** does *not* mean *faculty* in the American sense, but corresponds to the branches of the university we call *schools*, *divisions*, or *departments*. For example, **филологи́ческий факульте́т** (**филфа́к** for short) means *department of languages and literatures*, and **медици́нский факульте́т** *school of medicine*.

Basic sentence patterns

1. Где огурцы́?
   ⎯ и́х рабо́ты?
   ⎯ ключи́?
   ⎯ ви́лки?
   ⎯ ло́жки?
   ⎯ кни́ги?
   ⎯ тетра́ди?

   Where are the cucumbers?
   _____ their papers?
   _____ the keys?
   _____ the forks?
   _____ the spoons?
   _____ the books?
   _____ the notebooks?

2. Где студе́нты?
   ⎯ учи́тельницы?
   ⎯ учителя́?
   ⎯ профессора́?

   Where are the students?
   _____ the women teachers?
   _____ the teachers?
   _____ the professors?

3. Во́т ключи́.
   ⎯ тетра́ди.
   ⎯ кни́ги.
   ⎯ ви́лки.
   ⎯ ло́жки.
   ⎯ огурцы́.
   ⎯ и́х рабо́ты.

   Here are the keys.
   _____ the notebooks.
   _____ the books.
   _____ the forks.
   _____ the spoons.
   _____ the cucumbers.
   _____ their papers.

4. Где пи́сьма?
   — Во́т зде́сь, на сту́ле.
   _____ на окне́.
   _____ на столе́.
   _____ на по́лке.

   Where are the letters?
   Here on the chair.
   ⎯ on the window sill.
   ⎯ on the desk (or table).
   ⎯ on the shelf.

5. Где пи́сьма?
   — Во́т зде́сь, в я́щике.
   _____ в портфе́ле.
   _____ в кни́ге.
   _____ в тетра́ди.
   _____ в коро́бке.

   Where are the letters?
   Here in the drawer.
   ⎯ in the briefcase.
   ⎯ in the book.
   ⎯ in the notebook.
   ⎯ in the box.

6. Я́ о не́й мно́го слы́шал.
   ⎯ нём _____.
   ⎯ ни́х _____.
   ⎯ ва́с _____.

   I've heard a lot about her.
   _____ him.
   _____ them.
   _____ you.

7. О ко́м ты́ говори́шь?
   — О вахтёре.
   — О Кири́лле.
   — О Цара́пкине.
   — О Ни́не.
   — О Ко́ле.
   — О Га́ле.
   — О Са́ше.

   Whom are you talking about?
   About the custodian.
   About Kirill.
   About Tsarapkin.
   About Nina.
   About Kolya.
   About Galya.
   About Sasha.

8. О ко́м они́ говоря́т?   Whom are they talking about?
   — О профе́ссоре.   About the professor.
   — Об Ива́не.   About Ivan.
   — Об убо́рщице.   About the cleaning lady.
   — Об учи́теле.   About the teacher.
   — Об О́ле.   About Olya.
   — Об америка́нке.   About the American [woman].
   — Об америка́нце.   About the American [man].

9. О́н говори́л о Евге́нии.   He was talking about Evgeny.
   _____ о Мари́и.   _____ about Maria.
   _____ о тетра́ди.   _____ about the notebook.
   _____ о лаборато́рии.   _____ about the laboratory.
   _____ о собра́нии.   _____ about the meeting.
   _____ о сочине́нии.   _____ about the composition.
   _____ о две́ри.   _____ about the door.
   _____ о ле́кции.   _____ about the lecture.
   _____ об общежи́тии.   _____ about the dormitory.
   _____ об о́сени.   _____ about autumn.
   _____ об о́череди.   _____ about the line.

10. О чём вы́ говори́те?   What are you talking about?
    — О клу́бе.   About the club.
    — О заво́де.   About the plant.
    — О борще́.   About the borsch.
    — О конце́рте.   About the concert.
    — О портфе́ле.   About the briefcase.
    — О шка́фе.   About the cupboard.
    — О ча́е.   About tea.
    — О селёдке.   About herring.

11. О чём ты́ говори́шь?   What are you talking about?
    — О шко́ле.   About school.
    — О письме́.   About a letter.
    — О молоке́.   About the milk.
    — Об университе́те.   About the university.
    — Об экза́мене.   About the exam.
    — Об авто́бусе.   About the bus.
    — Об обе́де.   About dinner.
    — Об окне́.   About the window.

12. О чём писа́ли студе́нты?   What did the students write about?
    — Они́ писа́ли о наро́дах СССР.   They wrote about the peoples of the U.S.S.R.
    _____ о яку́тах.   _____ about the Yakuts.
    _____ о грузи́нах.   _____ about the Georgians.
    _____ об украи́нцах.   _____ about the Ukrainians.
    _____ об америка́нцах.   _____ about the Americans.
    _____ об америка́нках.   _____ about American women.

Pronunciation practice: hard versus soft consonants

A.   [p] vs. [p̯]   Usual Cyrillic spelling **п**; also **пь, б,** or **бь**.

Note the pronunciation of hard [p] in the following:

[napóčtu]	на по́чту	to the post office
[pažálǝstǝ]	пожа́луйста	please

and compare it with soft [p̯]:

[sp̯išiţi]	спеши́те	you're hurrying
[p̯érvij]	пе́рвый	first

These are labial consonants, formed (like the English *p*) by completely closing the lips. Soft [p̯] has the effect of a y-like glide following it.

> Sound Drill: Practice the Russian paired examples illustrating hard [p] and soft [p̯], imitating your instructor (or the tape) as accurately as you can. Be sure to avoid the puff of breath that often accompanies the English *p*. Note that before [i̵], a w-like off-glide is often heard after hard [p].

B.   [b] vs. [b̯]   Usual Cyrillic spelling **б**; also **бь, п,** or **пь**.

Note the pronunciation of hard [b] in the following:

[bróşiţ]	бро́сить	to drop
[aftóbus]	авто́бус	bus
[spaşíbǝ]	спаси́бо	thank you

and compare it with soft [b̯]:

[nǝab̯ét]	на обе́д	for dinner
[fklúb̯i]	в клу́бе	at the club
[naslúžb̯i]	на слу́жбе	at work

Russian [b], like the corresponding English sound, is made by completely closing the lips. The soft [b̯] will usually have the effect of a y-like glide following it.

> Sound Drill: Practice the Russian paired examples illustrating hard [b] and soft [b̯], imitating your instructor (or the tape) as accurately as you can. Note that before [i̵], a w-like off-glide is often heard after hard [b].

C. [m] vs. [m̦] Usual Cyrillic spelling **м**; sometimes **мь**.

Note the pronunciation of hard [m] in the following:

[z̦ímu]	зúму	winter
[mój]	мóй	my
[p̦iṣmó]	письмó	letter

and compare it with soft [m̦]:

[ṣim̦ón]	Семён	Semyon
[m̦ílə]	Мúла	Mila

Russian [m], like Russian [b] and [p] and the corresponding sounds in English, is made with a complete closure of the lips. The soft [m̦] usually has the effect of a y-like glide following it.

Sound Drill: Practice the Russian paired examples illustrating hard [m] and soft [m̦], imitating your instructor (or the tape) as accurately as you can. Note that before [ɨ], a w-like off-glide is often heard after hard [m].

Intonation practice: part I—questions without question words

Questions with a rising contour. This contour is characteristic of questions without question words; these sentences usually present an alternative which can be answered "yes" or "no." In such questions the final word carries the major stress. The pitch begins at about level 2 and rises to a peak on the major stress. It is either sustained or, in unstressed final syllables, it may drop.

Practice the following drills, imitating the tape or the instructor.

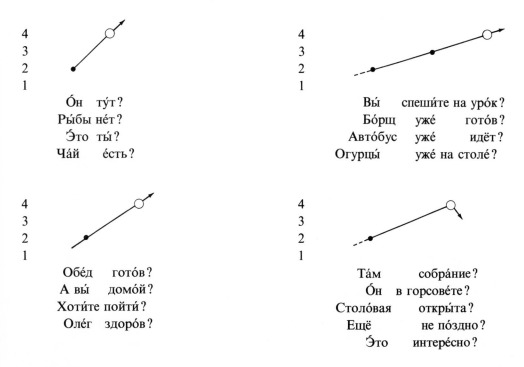

4		4	
3		3	
2		2	
1		1	

Óн тýт?
Рúбы нéт?
Э́то тú?
Чáй éсть?

Вú спешúте на урóк?
Бóрщ ужé готóв?
Автóбус ужé идёт?
Огурцú ужé на столé?

Обéд готóв?
А вú домóй?
Хотúте пойтú?
Олéг здорóв?

Тáм собрáние?
Óн в горсовéте?
Столóвая открúта?
Ещё не пóздно?
Э́то интерéсно?

Вы́	уже́	идёте?
Она́	рабо́тает в шко́ле?	
Две́ри	ещё	не за́перты?
Э́то	ту́т	в коро́бке?
Вы́	идёте	на по́чту?

Ты́	об э́том	поду́мал?
Вы́	уже́	пообе́дали?
Они́	говоря́т	об экза́менах?
Э́то	рабо́ты	студе́нтов?
Ты́	его́	зна́ешь?

■ TRANSFORMATION DRILL

Pronounce the following questions as statements.

О́н	идёт?
Э́то	ча́й?
Они́	ту́т?
Огурцы́	на столе́?

О́н	идёт.
Э́то	ча́й.
Они́	ту́т.
Огурцы́	на столе́.

■ TRANSFORMATION DRILL

Pronounce the following statements as questions.

О́н	идёт	домо́й.
Ры́бы	бо́льше	не́т.
Авто́бус	уже́	идёт.
Вчера́	бы́л	бо́рщ.
Обе́д	уже́	гото́в.

О́н	идёт	домо́й?
Ры́бы	бо́льше	не́т?
Авто́бус	уже́	идёт?
Вчера́	бы́л	бо́рщ?
Обе́д	уже́	гото́в?

STRUCTURE AND DRILLS

The nominative plural of nouns

MODELS

Ка́к дела́?	How are *things*?
У на́с е́сть **огурцы́.**	We have *cucumbers*.
Ту́т то́лько **ви́лки** и **ло́жки.**	Here are only *forks* and *spoons*.
Где́ её **тетра́ди** и **кни́ги?**	Where are her *notebooks* and *books*?

Две́ри уже́ за́перты.	The *doors* are already locked.
У него́ есть **ключи́.**	He has *keys.*
Результа́ты неплохи́е.	The *results* aren't bad.
Где́ их **рабо́ты?**	Where are their *papers?*
О чём писа́ли **студе́нты?**	What did the *students* write about?
Где́ **учителя́?**	Where are the *teachers?*
Все́ **профессора́** им дово́льны.	All the *professors* are pleased with him.
Все́ **зда́ния** бы́ли за́перты.	All the *buildings* were locked.

NOMINATIVE PLURAL: TABLE OF BASIC NOUN ENDINGS		
жена́-class nouns and most **сто́л**-class nouns	**окно́**-class nouns and some **сто́л**-class nouns	**две́рь**-class nouns
HARD STEMS **—ы**	**—а**	
SOFT STEMS **—и**	**—я**	**—и**

Notes

1. The ending –и occurs instead of –ы in the hard stem **сто́л**- and **жена́**-class nouns whose final consonant is ж, ш, к, г, or х: **ножи́, карандаши́, америка́нки, кни́ги, ло́жки.**

2. Some **сто́л**-class nouns take the nominative plural ending –а or –я, which is practically always stressed: **профессора́, учителя́, города́.**

3. Many nouns have a different place of stress in the plural than they have in the singular. Compare **жена́** with **жёны**, **окно́** with **о́кна**, **письмо́** with **пи́сьма**, **го́род** with **города́**, and **сестра́** with **сёстры.**

4. Some **стол**-class nouns have an inserted vowel in the nominative singular which does not appear elsewhere in the declension. Compare the singular **де́нь** with the plural **дни́**, **звоно́к** with **звонки́,** and **пода́рок** with **пода́рки.** Most nouns ending in –ец in the nominative singular have this feature. Compare **америка́нец** with **америка́нцы, украи́нец** with **украи́нцы,** and **огуре́ц** with **огурцы́.**

5. A few **сто́л**- and **окно́**-class nouns have their stems softened and expanded in the plural by the addition of [j]. The nominative plural of such nouns is written with –ь *plus* я (–ья). Compare **перо́** with **пе́рья, бра́т** with **бра́тья,** and **сту́л** with **сту́лья.** In the plural of **му́ж,** the soft sign is written but the ж is not pronounced soft: **мужья́** [mužjá].

■ STRUCTURE REPLACEMENT DRILLS

Nominative singular to nominative plural.

1. *Where was the bus?*
   Where were the buses?
   т: Где́ бы́л авто́бус?
   s: **Где́ бы́ли авто́бусы?**
   т: Где́ была́ шко́ла?
   s: **Где́ бы́ли шко́лы?**
   (завод, стол, материал, телефон, университет, концерт, экзамен, работа, группа)

2. *There was a book on the shelf.*
   There were books on the shelf.
   т: На по́лке была́ кни́га.
   s: **На по́лке бы́ли кни́ги.**
   т: На по́лке бы́л я́щик.
   s: **На по́лке бы́ли я́щики.**
   (коробка, тетрадь, вилка, портфель, ключ)

3. *Where's the key?*
   Where are the keys?
   т: Где ключ?
   s: **Где ключи?**
   т: **Где ключи?**
   s: **Где ложки?**
   (дверь, полка, ручка, портфель, очередь)

4. *Orlov was here.*
   The Orlovs were here.
   т: Орлов был здесь.
   s: **Орловы были здесь.**
   т: Курочкин был здесь.
   s: **Курочкины были здесь.**
   (Царапкин, американка, Хитров, уборщица, студент, студентка, учительница)

■ MIXED STRUCTURE REPLACEMENT DRILLS

Nominative plural to nominative singular and vice versa.

1. *The windows are there.*
   The window is there.
   т: Окна там.
   s: **Окно там.**
   т: Окно там.
   s: **Окна там.**
   (города, город, профессор, профессора)

2. *The knives were in the drawer.*
   The knife was in the drawer.
   т: Ножи были в ящике.
   s: **Нож был в ящике.**
   т: Карандаш был в ящике.
   s: **Карандаши были в ящике.**
   (нож, карандаши, ножи, карандаш)

■ MIXED STRUCTURE REPLACEMENT DRILL

Nominative singular to nominative plural and vice versa.

Where was the bell?
Where were the bells?
т: Где был звонок?
s: **Где были звонки?**
т: Где были украинцы?
s: **Где был украинец?**
(огурец, звонки, американец, украинец, огурцы, подарок)

■ MIXED STRUCTURE REPLACEMENT DRILLS

Nominative plural to nominative singular and vice versa.

1. *The chairs are here.*
   The chair is here.
   т: Стулья здесь.
   s: **Стул здесь.**
   т: Брат здесь.
   s: **Братья здесь.**
   (перья, мужья, братья, муж, перо, стул)

2. *Where's the chair?*
   Where are the chairs?
   т: Где стул?
   s: **Где стулья?**
   т: Где братья?
   s: **Где брат?**
   (муж, перья, стулья, брат, мужья)

■ STRUCTURE REPLACEMENT DRILLS

1. *The students have already found out about it.*
   The student has already found out about it.
   т: Студе́нты уже́ узна́ли об э́том.
   s: **Студе́нт уже́ узна́л об э́том.**
   т: Убо́рщицы уже́ узна́ли об э́том.
   s: **Убо́рщица уже́ узна́ла об э́том.**
   (учи́тельницы, жёны, мужья́, бра́тья, сёстры, учителя́, профессора́, америка́нки, америка́нцы)

2. *The student already found out about it.*
   The students already found out about it.
   т: Студе́нт уже́ узна́л об э́том.
   s: **Студе́нты уже́ узна́ли об э́том.**
   т: Жена́ уже́ узна́ла об э́том.
   s: **Жёны уже́ узна́ли об э́том.**
   (муж, брат, сестра́, учи́тель, убо́рщица, профе́ссор, украи́нец, америка́нка)

3. *You don't know where the knife is, do you?*
   You don't know where the knives are, do you?
   т: Ты́ не зна́ешь, где́ но́ж?
   s: **Ты́ не зна́ешь, где́ ножи́?**
   т: Ты́ не зна́ешь, где́ каранда́ш?
   s: **Ты́ не зна́ешь, где́ карандаши́?**
   (портфель, книга, ключ, тетрадь, вилка, платье, сочинение, подарок, стул)

■ QUESTION-ANSWER DRILLS

1. *Was Professor Orlov there?*
   All the professors were there.
   т: Профе́ссор Орло́в бы́л та́м?
   s: **Всё профессора́ бы́ли та́м.**
   т: Студе́нт Козло́в бы́л та́м?
   s: **Всё студе́нты бы́ли та́м.**
   Студе́нтка Петро́ва была́ та́м?
   На́ш грузи́н бы́л та́м?
   На́ш украи́нец бы́л та́м?
   На́ш яку́т бы́л та́м?
   На́ша гру́ппа была́ та́м?
   Ва́ш учи́тель бы́л та́м?

2. *He's a student, but who are they?*
   They're students too.
   т: О́н студе́нт, а кто́ они́?
   s: **Они́ то́же студе́нты.**
   т: Она́ учи́тельница, а кто́ они́?
   s: **Они́ то́же учи́тельницы.**
   О́н профе́ссор, а кто́ они́?
   Она́ убо́рщица, а кто́ они́?
   О́н учи́тель, а кто́ они́?
   О́н украи́нец, а кто́ они́?
   О́н грузи́н, а кто́ они́?
   О́н яку́т, а кто́ они́?
   Она́ америка́нка, а кто́ они́?
   О́н америка́нец, а кто́ они́?

■ MIXED STRUCTURE REPLACEMENT DRILLS

Nominative plural to nominative singular and vice versa.

1. *You don't know where the pens are, do you?*
   You don't know where the pen is, do you?
   т: Ты́ не зна́ешь, где́ ру́чки?
   s: **Ты́ не зна́ешь, где́ ру́чка?**
   т: Ты́ не зна́ешь, где́ пла́тья?
   s: **Ты́ не зна́ешь, где́ пла́тье?**
   (сочинения, собрания, стулья, учителя, шкафы, перья, тетради)

2. *Is there a chair there?*
   Are there any chairs there?
   т: Та́м е́сть сту́л?
   s: **Та́м е́сть сту́лья?**
   т: Та́м е́сть перо́?
   s: **Та́м е́сть пе́рья?**
   (коро́бка, шка́ф, окно́, огуре́ц, ло́жка, я́щик)

NOUNS: TABLE OF NOMINATIVE PLURAL ENDINGS			
сто́л-class	**окно́**-class	**жена́**-class	**две́рь**-class
–ы or **–и** (in most instances)	**–а** or **–я**	**–ы** or **–и**	only **–и**
–а́ or **–я́** (in some instances)			

1. All **две́рь**-class nouns spell their nominative plural ending with **–и** (usually unstressed), which replaces **–ь** of the nominative singular: **две́рь, две́ри; о́чередь, о́череди; тетра́дь, тетра́ди.**

2. Most **окно́**-class nouns spell their nominative plural ending with **–а** (replacing nominative singular **–о**) or **–я** (replacing nominative singular **–е** or **–ё**): **окно́, о́кна; де́ло, дела́; собра́ние, собра́ния; пла́тье, пла́тья.**

3. Some **сто́л**-class nouns spell their nominative plural ending with **–а** or **–я**, which is almost always stressed: **профе́ссор, профессора́; го́род, города́; учи́тель, учителя́; кра́й, края́** *regions*. Note that the plural ending **–я** replaces **–ь** and **–й** of the nominative singular in the spelling of these forms.

4. All **жена́**-class nouns and most **сто́л**-class nouns spell their nominative plural ending with **–ы** or **–и: жена́, жёны; сто́л, столы́; авто́бус, авто́бусы; сестра́, сёстры; клю́ч, ключи́.** Note that nouns ending in **–я, –й,** or **–ь** in the nominative singular replace these letters with **–и** in the nominative plural: **исто́рия, исто́рии** *history*; **ча́й, чаи́; портфе́ль, портфе́ли.**

Hard stem **жена́-** and **сто́л**-class nouns take the ending **–и** instead of **–ы** if their stem ends in **к, г, х, ш,** or **ж: уро́к, уро́ки; кни́га, кни́ги; но́ж, ножи́; каранда́ш, карандаши́; коро́бка, коро́бки.** Note that **к, г,** and **х** are then pronounced soft before **–и.**

Inserted vowels and alternation of stems

As compared with endings, which regularly change, stems are relatively stable. However, some stems show a regular pattern of alternation, with a vowel occurring in certain forms and not in others. In the examples below, note that the nominative singular contains the inserted vowel **o** or **e** as its next to last letter, while the nominative plural occurs without the inserted vowel.

NOMINATIVE SINGULAR	NOMINATIVE PLURAL	BASIC STEM
америка́нец	америка́нцы	**америка́нц–**
молоде́ц	молодцы́	**молодц–**
украи́нец	украи́нцы	**украи́нц–**
звоно́к	звонки́	**звонк–**
огуре́ц	огурцы́	**огурц–**

The vowel is inserted between the last two stem consonants and serves not only to break the cluster, but also, frequently, to carry the stress. Such inserted "cluster-breaking" vowels typically occur in case forms with a zero ending, i.e., in the nominative singular of **стóл**-class nouns and in the genitive plural of **женá**- and **окнó**-class nouns.

Expanded stems in the plural

Although singular and plural stems are usually the same, some nouns have a plural stem that differs in certain respects. For example, some **окнó**- and **стóл**-class nouns with a singular stem ending in a hard consonant, soften this consonant (if it can be softened) and add a [j] for the plural stem. Note that in the Cyrillic writing system, the [j] is expressed by means of **ь** followed by the soft-series vowel letter **я** for the nominative plural.

NOMINATIVE SINGULAR		NOMINATIVE PLURAL	
брáт	[brát]	брáтья	[brátjə]
перó	[p̦iró]	пéрья	[p̦ér̦jə]
мýж	[múš]	мужья́	[mužjá]
стýл	[stúl]	стýлья	[stúl̦jə]

The nominative plural of possessive modifiers

MODELS

Чьи́ э́то ключи́? — *Whose* keys are these?
Мои́ ключи́ в портфéле. — *My* keys are in the briefcase.
Э́то твои́ тетрáди. — Those are *your* notebooks.
Всé нáши профессорá и́м довóльны. — All *our* professors are pleased with him.
Гдé вáши кни́ги? — Where are *your* books?
Гдé и́х рабóты? — Where are *their* papers (*lit.* works)?

■ STRUCTURE REPLACEMENT DRILLS

1. *Is that your key?*
   Are those your keys?
   т: Э́то вáш ключ?
   s: **Э́то вáши ключи́?**
   т: Э́то вáше сочинéние?
   s: **Э́то вáши сочинéния?**
   (платье, окно, портфель, коробка, дверь, карандаш, нож, тетрадь, стол)

2. *Whose book is that?*
   Whose books are those?
   т: Чья́ э́то кни́га?
   s: **Чьи́ э́то кни́ги?**
   т: Чьё э́то перó?
   s: **Чьи́ э́то пéрья?**
   (стол, работа, сочинение, огурец, материал, нож, карандаш, полка, портфель, ключ)

■ QUESTION-ANSWER DRILL

Whose pens are these?
These are our pens.
т: Чьи́ э́то пе́рья?
s: **Э́то на́ши пе́рья.**

т: Чьи́ э́то карандаши́?
s: **Э́то на́ши карандаши́.**
(кни́ги, тетра́ди, сочине́ния, рабо́ты, материа́лы, коро́бки, я́щики, ножи́)

■ MIXED STRUCTURE REPLACEMENT DRILL

Singular to plural and vice versa.

Where is your brother?
Where are your brothers?
т: Где́ твой брат?
s: **Где́ твои́ бра́тья?**

т: Где́ твои́ сёстры?
s: **Где́ твоя́ сестра́?**
(ру́чка, портфе́ли, по́лка, экза́мены, стол, учителя́, дверь, ключи́, ножи́, каранда́ш, тетра́дь)

■ QUESTION-ANSWER DRILLS

1. *Are those his keys?*
   No, those are my keys.
   т: Э́то его́ ключи́?
   s: **Нет, э́то мои́ ключи́.**
   т: Э́то его́ огурцы́?
   s: **Нет, э́то мои́ огурцы́.**
   (портфе́ль, портфе́ли, коро́бка, кни́ги, рабо́та, пе́рья, нож, студе́нты, перо́)

2. *Whose notebooks are these?*
   Yours.
   т: Чьи́ э́то тетра́ди?
   s: **Твои́.**
   т: Чья́ э́то кни́га?
   s: **Твоя́.**
   (стол, сочине́ние, шкафы́, коро́бки, рабо́та, перо́, пе́рья, нож, карандаши́)

■ RESPONSE DRILLS

1. *Here's my sister.*
   These are her books.
   т: Во́т моя́ сестра́.
   s: **Э́то её кни́ги.**
   т: Во́т мо́й брат.
   s: **Э́то его́ кни́ги.**
   (мои́ студе́нты, мои́ сёстры, моя́ учи́тельница, мо́й муж, мои́ бра́тья, мо́й профе́ссор, мои́ профессора́)

2. *This is my pencil.*
   And whose is this?
   т: Э́то мо́й каранда́ш.
   s: **А э́то чей?**
   т: Э́то мои́ тетра́ди.
   s: **А э́то чьи́?**
   (окно́, ножи́, ключи́, сочине́ние, чай, по́лка, кни́ги, портфе́ль, хлеб, ру́чка)

■ PROGRESSIVE SUBSTITUTION DRILL

1. *Where is your brother?*
   т: Где́ ваш брат?
   s: **Где́ ваш брат?**
   т: _____ (бра́тья)?
   s: **Где́ ва́ши бра́тья?**
   т: _____ (сёстры)?
   s: **Где́ ва́ши сёстры?**
   ____ (твоя́) ____?
   _____ (муж)?
   _____ (учи́тельница)?

   Где́ твоя́ учи́тельница?
   _____ (о́кна)?
   ____ (на́ше) ____?
   _____ (авто́бус)?
   _____ (ключи́)?

2. *This is my briefcase.*

т: Э́то мо́й портфе́ль.

s: **Э́то мо́й портфе́ль.**

т: ___ (его́) _____ .

s: **Э́то его́ портфе́ль.**

т: _____ (каранда́ш).

s: **Э́то его́ каранда́ш.**

_____ (перо́).

___ (мой) _____ .

Э́то мой пе́рья.

_____ (коро́бка).

___ (его́) _____ .

_____ (коро́бки).

_____ (учи́тель).

___ (и́х) _____ .

_____ (учителя́).

___ (её) _____ .

DISCUSSION

All possessive modifiers of the changing type have nominative plurals that end in **-и**.

whose чьи́	*my, mine* мои́	*your, yours* твои́	*our, ours* на́ши	*your, yours* ва́ши

The third person possessives, **его́**, **её**, and **и́х**, never change their form and thus have no special forms for the plural.

Где́ её рабо́ты?	Where are her papers?
Где́ его́ рабо́ты?	Where are his papers?
Где́ и́х рабо́ты?	Where are their papers?

The prepositional case: singular and plural endings of nouns

MODELS

Где́ вы́ учи́ли ру́сский язы́к, **в шко́ле**?	Where did you study Russian, *in school?*
— Не́т, **в университе́те**.	No, *at the university.*
Я́ ва́с ви́дел **на ле́кции**.	I saw you *at the lecture.*
Я́ ва́с ви́дел **в аудито́рии**.	I saw you *in the auditorium.*
Во́т но́ж, **на столе́**.	Here's the knife *on the table.*
Она́ была́ **в го́роде**.	She was *in town.*
Э́то твои́ кни́ги **на по́лке**?	Are these your books *on the shelf?*
О́н и Петро́ва — лу́чшие студе́нты **в э́той гру́ппе**.	He and Miss Petrov are the best students *in this group.*
Во́т и́х рабо́ты, зде́сь **на сту́ле**.	Here are their papers *on the chair.*
Вы́ до́лго стоя́ли **в о́череди**?	Did you stand *in line* long?
О ко́м вы́ ду́маете?	*Whom* are you thinking *about?*
— **О Мари́и**.	*About Maria.*
— **Об Ива́не**.	*About Ivan.*
— **О Льве́**.	*About Lev.*
Студе́нты писа́ли **о наро́дах** СССР.	The students wrote *about the peoples of the* U.S.S.R.
Козло́в писа́л **о грузи́нах**.	Kozlov wrote *about the Georgians.*

PREPOSITIONAL CASE: TABLE OF NOUN ENDINGS		
	most **стóл-**, **окнó-**, and **женá**-class nouns **–е**	**двéрь**-class nouns and all nouns ending in **–ий**, **–ия**, and **–ие** in the nominative singular **–и**
SINGULAR	на столé в шкóле об окнé об учи́теле о плáтье	в óчереди о Евгéнии на лéкции об общежи́тии в здáнии
PLURAL	HARD STEMS **–ах** SOFT STEMS **–ях**	**–ях**
	на столáх в шкóлах об óкнах об учителя́х	в очередя́х в дверя́х на лéкциях об общежи́тиях в здáниях

Note: The prepositional case is always used with a preposition, usually one of the following:

в (*or* **во**)	in, at
на	on, at
о (*or* **об**, *or* **обо**)	about, concerning, on, of

The alternate form of **в** is **во**, used before certain consonant clusters: **во всём** *in everything*, **во Фрáнции** *in France*.

Alternate forms of **о** are **об** and **обо**. **Об** is used before words beginning with **а, о, у, э**, and **и**: **об э́том, об украи́нцах**. **Обо** occurs only in a few fixed phrases, such as **обо мнé** *about me* and **обо всём** *about everything*.

■ REPETITION DRILL

Repeat the models given above until you are familiar with the endings of the prepositional case.

■ CUED SUBSTITUTION DRILLS

1.   (*Lev*)   *She was talking about Lev.*
 т: (Лёв) Онá говори́ла о Львé.
 s: **Онá говори́ла о Львé.**
 т: (брáт) (Онá) _____ .
 s: **Онá говори́ла о брáте.**
        (сестра, муж, профессор, Галя, город, книга, карандаш, нож, дело, полка, чай)

2.   (*Ivan*)   *We were thinking about Ivan.*
 т: (Ивáн) Мы́ дýмали об Ивáне.
 s: **Мы́ дýмали об Ивáне.**
 т: (обéд) (Мы́) _____ .
 s: **Мы́ дýмали об обéде.**
        (урок, учитель, университет, Орлов, экзамен, учительница, общежитие, осень)

■ CUED QUESTION-ANSWER DRILLS

Cue should be given before the question is asked.

1. (*Kirill*) *Who are you thinking about?*
   About Kirill.
   т: (Кири́лл) О ко́м вы́ ду́маете?
   s: **О Кири́лле.**
   т: (Ко́ля) О ко́м вы́ ду́маете?
   s: **О Ко́ле.**
   (Га́ля, Козло́в, Семён, Мари́я, Ма́ша, Ни́на, Евге́ний, Цара́пкин, Бори́с, Ку-рочкин, Никола́й)

2. (*Ivan*) *Whom are you talking about?*
   About Ivan.
   т: (Ива́н) О ко́м ты́ говори́шь?
   s: **Об Ива́не.**
   (Оля, учитель, учительница, Орлов, американка, уборщица)

3. (*Professor Orlov*) *Whom is he asking about?*
   About Professor Orlov.
   т: (профе́ссор Орло́в) О ко́м о́н спра́шивает?
   s: **О профе́ссоре Орло́ве.**
   (Иван, Нина, Коля, американка, Мария, учитель, учительница, Олег, Николай)

■ QUESTION-ANSWER DRILLS

1. *Have you forgotten about Lev?*
   No, I haven't forgotten about Lev.
   т: Ты́ забы́л о Льве́?
   s: **Не́т, я́ не забы́л о Льве́.**
   т: Ты́ забы́л о звонке́?
   s: **Не́т, я́ не забы́л о звонке́.**
   (об америка́нце, об украи́нце, о Льве́, о звонке́, о пода́рке, об америка́нце)

2. *Were you thinking about Lev?*
   Yes, I was thinking about Lev.
   т: Ты́ ду́мал о Льве́?
   s: **Да́, я́ ду́мал о Льве́.**
   т: Ты́ ду́мал об учи́теле?
   s: **Да́, я́ ду́мал об учи́теле.**
   (о профессоре Орлове, о сестре, о Гале, о брате, о Коле, об Иване Петровиче, об Ирине Петровне)

■ STRUCTURE REPLACEMENT DRILLS

1. *She forgot about the students.*
   She forgot about the student.
   т: Она́ забы́ла о студе́нтах.
   s: **Она́ забы́ла о студе́нте.**
   т: Она́ забы́ла о профессора́х.
   s: **Она́ забы́ла о профе́ссоре.**
   (о братьях, о сёстрах, о книгах, о школах, о лекциях, о перьях, о платьях, о работах)

2. *Ivan didn't write about the schools.*
   Ivan didn't write about the school.
   т: Ива́н не писа́л о шко́лах.
   s: **Ива́н не писа́л о шко́ле.**
   т: Ива́н не писа́л о профессора́х.
   s: **Ива́н не писа́л о профе́ссоре.**
   (об учителях, о братьях, о книгах, об уроках, об университетах, о городах, об очередях, о грузинах)

3. *Do you want to find out about the exam?*
   Do you want to find out about the exams?
   т: Вы́ хоти́те узна́ть об экза́мене?
   s: **Вы́ хоти́те узна́ть об экза́менах?**
   т: Вы́ хоти́те узна́ть об уро́ке?
   s: **Вы́ хоти́те узна́ть об уро́ках?**
   (об автобусе, об обеде, об учителе, о лекции, о собрании)

4. *What have you heard about her brother?*
   What have you heard about her brothers?
   т: Что́ вы́ слы́шали о её бра́те?
   s: **Что́ вы́ слы́шали о её бра́тьях?**
   т: Что́ вы́ слы́шали о её сестре́?
   s: **Что́ вы́ слы́шали о её сёстрах?**
   (о его профессоре, о его учителе, о её учительнице, о его сочинении, о её работе)

The sisters forgot about the brothers.
The brothers forgot about the sisters.

т: Сёстры забы́ли о бра́тьях.
s: **Бра́тья забы́ли о сёстрах.**
т: Профессора́ забы́ли о студе́нтах.
s: **Студе́нты забы́ли о профессора́х.**
Мужья́ забы́ли о жёнах.
Студе́нты забы́ли об учителя́х.
Убо́рщицы забы́ли о профессора́х.
Грузи́ны забы́ли о яку́тах.
Украи́нцы забы́ли о грузи́нах.
Учителя́ забы́ли об учи́тельницах.

The book is in the drawer.
The books are in the drawers.

т: Кни́га в я́щике.
s: **Кни́ги в я́щиках.**
т: Ру́чка на столе́.
s: **Ру́чки на стола́х.**
Клю́ч в портфе́ле.
Пода́рок в коро́бке.
Студе́нт на ле́кции.
Сестра́ на экза́мене.
Студе́нты в аудито́рии.
Учи́тель в библиоте́ке.

| (*The meetings*) | *What did they write about?* |
| | *About the meetings.* |

т: (собра́ния)   О чём они́ писа́ли?
s: **О собра́ниях.**
т: (наро́ды СССР) О чём они́ писа́ли?
s: **О наро́дах СССР.**

(кни́ги, его работы, языки, лекции,
экзамены, американцы, учителя́,
города СССР)

DISTRIBUTION OF ENDINGS IN THE PREPOSITIONAL CASE

1. *Singular:* –е and –и

a. Most **сто́л-, окно́-,** and **жена́**-class nouns take –е as their ending in the prepositional singular: **на столе́, об окне́, о жене́, о ры́бе, в го́роде, о пла́тье, о Га́ле, об Ива́не, о Льве́.**[1]

Hard consonants are regularly replaced by their soft counterparts before –е in the prepositional singular. Compare **сто́л** [stól] with **на столе́** [nəstaļé] and **окно́** [aknó] with **в окне́** [vakņé]. **Ж, ш,** and **ц** remain hard in this position since they have no soft counterparts: **убо́рщица** [uborščicə], **об убо́рщице** [abubórščici].

b. All **две́рь**-class nouns and those nouns with a nominative singular ending in **–ий, –ия,** or **–ие** spell their prepositional singular ending with **–и: о две́ри, в о́череди, об о́сени, о собра́нии, о пе́нии, об Евге́нии, о зда́нии.**

2. *Plural:* –ах and –ях

a. Nouns whose stems end in a hard consonant or **ч** or **щ** spell their prepositional plural ending **–ах: о ключа́х, о ща́х, о стола́х, о жёнах, о кни́гах, о по́лках, о профессора́х, об украи́нцах, о пи́сьмах.**

b. All others take the ending **–ях** in the prepositional plural: **о дверя́х, о портфе́лях, об учителя́х, о пла́тьях, о бра́тьях, о пе́рьях, о собра́ниях, о сочине́ниях.**

Note that **–ь** is written in the prepositional plural only if it is also written in the nominative plural: Compare **о мужья́х** (nom pl **мужья́**) with **об очередя́х** (nom pl **о́череди**).

---

[1] Note that the name **Лёв** *Lev* has the inserted vowel **е** in the nominative singular only. In the other forms, **ь** must be inserted to preserve the softness of the **л: о Льве́.**

Prepositions в and на with the prepositional case

MODELS

Где ваш брат?	Where's your brother?
— На работе.	At work.
— На обеде.	At a dinner.
— На концерте.	At a concert.
— На почте.	At the post office.
— На экзамене.	At an exam.
— На уроке.	At a lesson.
— На собрании.	At a meeting.
— На лекции.	At a lecture.
— На заводе.	At the plant.
— На службе.	At work.
Где ваша сестра?	Where's your sister?
— В университете.	At the university.
— В школе.	At school.
— В лаборатории.	At the laboratory.
— В библиотеке.	At the library.
— В ГУМе.	At GUM.
— В городе.	Downtown *or* In town.
— В аудитории.	In the auditorium.
— В клубе.	At the club.
— В общежитии.	In the dormitory.
— В горсовете.	At the gorsovet.

■ REPETITION DRILL

Repeat the models given, noting that with certain nouns only **на** can be used, with others only **в**.

■ STRUCTURE REPLACEMENT DRILL

They're now at the exams.
They're now at the exam.
т: Они теперь на экзаменах.
s: **Они теперь на экзамене.**

т: Они теперь на лекциях.
s: **Они теперь на лекции.**
(на собраниях, на заводах, на уроках, в библиотеках, в аудиториях, в общежитиях, в лабораториях, в школах, в клубах)

■ CUED QUESTION-ANSWER DRILLS

1. (*singing lesson*) *Where were you?*
   At a singing lesson.
   т: (урок пения) Где вы были?
   s: **На уроке пения.**
   т: (работа) Где вы были?
   s: **На работе.**
   (обед, завод, почта, экзамен, концерт, собрание, служба, лекция)

2. (*laboratory*) *Just where is she?*
   At the laboratory.
   т: (лаборатория) Где же она?
   s: **В лаборатории.**
   т: (город) Где же она?
   s: **В городе.**
   (ГУМ, школа, клуб, аудитория, библиотека, университет, общежитие)

3. (work) *Where is he now?*
At work.

т: (рабо́та) Где́ о́н тепе́рь?
s: **На рабо́те.**
т: (шко́ла) Где́ о́н тепе́рь?
s: **В шко́ле.**

(университет, почта, экзамен, лаборатория, собрание, завод, концерт, город, урок, обед, лекция)

4. (meetings) *Where did they hear about it?*
At the meetings.

т: (собра́ния) Где́ они́ об э́том слы́шали?
s: **На собра́ниях.**
т: (экза́мены) Где́ они́ об э́том слы́шали?
s: **На экза́менах.**

(заводы, города, уроки, школы, библиотеки, университеты, лаборатории)

■ RESPONSE DRILL

There's the school.
Kolya's in school.

т: Во́т шко́ла.
s: **Ко́ля в шко́ле.**
т: Во́т заво́д.
s: **Ко́ля на заво́де.**

(почта, клуб, аудитория, университет, ГУМ, лаборатория, библиотека, школа, общежитие)

■ CUED QUESTION-ANSWER DRILL

(plant) *Where's Ivan?*
At the plant.

т: (завод) Где́ Ива́н?
s: **На заво́де.**
т: (школа) Где́ Ни́на?
s: **В шко́ле.**

(университет) Где́ ре́ктор?
(работа) Где́ Са́ша?

(лекция) Где́ студе́нты?
(город) Где́ Ле́в?
(аудитория) Где́ Кири́лл?
(экзамен) Где́ профе́ссор Орло́в?
(лаборатория) Где́ Ми́ла?
(концерт) Где́ тво́й бра́т?
(обед) Где́ твоя́ сестра́?
(общежитие) Где́ студе́нтки?

■ PROGRESSIVE SUBSTITUTION DRILLS

1. *Irina Ivanovna was in town.*
   т: Ири́на Ива́новна была́ в го́роде.
   s: **Ири́на Ива́новна была́ в го́роде.**
   т: (Ва́ша сестра́)_____.
   s: **Ва́ша сестра́ была́ в го́роде.**
   _____ (по́чте).
   ___ (бра́т) _____.
   _____ (собра́нии).
   (Его́) _____.
   ___ (учителя́) _____.
   _____ (экза́менах).
   ___ (студе́нты) _____.
   (На́ши) _____.
   _____ (экза́мене).
   ___ (профессора́) _____.
   _____ (университе́те).

2. *My brother is downtown.*
   т: Мо́й бра́т в го́роде.
   s: Мо́й бра́т в го́роде.
   т: ___ (сестра́) _____.
   s: **Моя́ сестра́ в го́роде.**
   _____ (шко́ле).
   ___ (бра́тья) _____.
   _____ (заво́де).
   (Её) _____.
   _____ (ле́кциях).
   _____ (ГУ́Ме).
   ___ (му́ж) _____.
   (Тво́й) _____.
   _____ (общежи́тии).

English *in* (i.e., *in the interior*) is usually rendered by Russian **в** and English *on* (*on the surface*) by Russian **на**.

в столе́	in the desk (*or* table)
на столе́	on the desk (*or* table)
в кни́ге	in the book
на кни́ге	on the book

However, the English concept *at* may be rendered by either **на** or **в**, especially if the place described is viewed in terms of its function or the activity carried on there. In such instances, the choice between **на** or **в** is not dictated by the idea of position "inside" or "outside," but is fixed for a particular noun and must be memorized by the student as a set phrase. As a general rule, **в** is more commonly used if the place is a building or enclosure, and **на** is used if the place is described in terms of the activity carried on there.

1. **на**

на собра́нии, на собра́ниях	at a meeting, at meetings
на экза́мене, на экза́менах	at the exam, at exams
на заво́де, на заво́дах	at the plant, at plants
на уро́ке, на уро́ках	at the lesson, at lessons
на ле́кции, на ле́кциях	at the lecture, at lectures
на по́чте	at the post office
на слу́жбе	at work, on the job
на рабо́те	at work
на обе́де	at a dinner

2. **в**

в клу́бе, в клу́бах	at the club, at (*or* in) clubs
в библиоте́ке, в библиоте́ках	at (*or* in) the library, at (*or* in) libraries
в шко́ле, в шко́лах	at (*or* in) school, in schools
в университе́те, в университе́тах	at the university, at universities
в ГУ́Ме	at (*or* in) GUM

The personal pronouns and interrogatives кто́, что́ in the prepositional case

MODELS

О чём они́ писа́ли?	*What* did they write about?
О ко́м вы́ говори́те?	*Whom* are you talking about?
Она́ говори́ла обо **мне́**.	She was talking about *me*.
_____ о **тебе́**.	_____ about *you*.
_____ о **ва́с**.	_____ about *you*.
_____ о **на́с**.	_____ about *us*.
Я́ о **нём** мно́го слы́шал.	I've heard a lot about *him*.
_ о **не́й** _____.	_____ about *her*.
_ о **ни́х** _____.	_____ about *them*.

■ REPETITION DRILL

Practice the models until you are familiar with all the forms.

1. *Were you thinking about Nina?*
   Yes, I was thinking about her.
   т: Вы́ ду́мали о Ни́не?
   s: Да́, я́ ду́мал о не́й.
   т: Вы́ ду́мали о Ко́ле?
   s: Да́, я́ ду́мал о нём.
      (об учи́тельнице, о Га́ле,
      об Ива́не, о его́ сестре́,
      о её бра́те)

2. *Who was he writing about, me?*
   Yes, about you.
   т: О ко́м о́н писа́л, обо мне́?
   s: Да́, о тебе́.
   т: О ко́м о́н писа́л, о тебе́?
   s: Да́, обо мне́.
      (о ва́с, о ни́х, о нём, о не́й,
      о на́с, о тебе́)

■ RESPONSE DRILLS

1. *She was thinking about me.*
   About whom?
   т: Она́ ду́мала обо мне́.
   s: О ко́м?
   т: Она́ ду́мала об уро́ке.
   s: О чём?
      (о шко́ле, о Га́ле, о тебе́,
      о на́с, об экза́менах, об учи́теле,
      о собра́нии, о сестре́)

2. *Oh, you're here!*
   We were just talking about you.
   т: А́, вы́ зде́сь!
   s: Мы́ как ра́з говори́ли о ва́с.
   т: А́, ты́ зде́сь!
   s: Мы́ как ра́з говори́ли о тебе́.
      (он, они́, она́, Ко́ля, Ни́на,
      Га́ля)

■ CUED QUESTION-ANSWER DRILL

   (You) *Whom was he asking about?*
         About you.
   т: (вы́) О ко́м о́н спра́шивал?
   s: **О ва́с.**
   т: (ты́) О ко́м о́н спра́шивал?
   s: **О тебе́.**
      (я, она́, мы, вы, он, они́)

■ QUESTION-ANSWER DRILL

Who is he?
I haven't heard of him.
т: Кто́ о́н?
s: Я́ о нём не слы́шал.

т: Кто́ вы́?
s: Я́ о ва́с не слы́шал.
   (они́, ты, она́, он,
   вы, она́)

■ RESPONSE DRILLS

1. *I've heard a lot about American women.*
   What have you heard about them?
   т: Я́ мно́го слы́шал об америка́нках.
   s: Что́ вы́ о ни́х слы́шали?
   т: Я́ мно́го слы́шал о ва́с.
   s: Что́ вы́ обо мне́ слы́шали?
      (о его́ сестре́, о его́ учителя́х, о её
      бра́те, об украи́нцах, о его́ учи́теле, об
      америка́нцах, о её профе́ссоре, о её
      му́же, о его́ жене́)

2. *She's terrific.*
   The professors speak highly of her.
   т: Она́ молоде́ц.
   s: Профессора́ о не́й хорошо́ говоря́т.
   т: Вы́ молоде́ц.
   s: Профессора́ о ва́с хорошо́ говоря́т.
      (он, мы, вы все, они́, ты, я)

■ PROGRESSIVE SUBSTITUTION DRILL

I didn't think about that.

T: Я об э́том не поду́мал.

S: **Я об э́том не поду́мал.**

(Он) _____.

____ (о не́й) _____.

(Вы) _____.

____ (обо мне́) _____.

_____ (не слы́шали).

____ (о на́с) _____.

(Они́) _____.

Они́ о на́с не слы́шали.

____ (о тебе́) _____.

_____ (не писа́ли).

(Она́) _____.

____ (о ва́с) _____.

_____ (не забы́ла).

(Мы) _____.

____ (о ни́х) _____.

(Он) _____.

____ (об э́том) _____.

_____ (не поду́мал).

Remarks on stress shift in nouns

A change in the position of the stress occurs frequently in the Russian declension of nouns, but it follows fairly regular patterns. The most typical of these patterns are given below.

1. Stress shift from stem in the singular to endings in the plural.

NOM SG	PREP SG	NOM PL	PREP PL
го́род	в го́роде	города́	в города́х
де́ло	о де́ле	дела́	о дела́х
му́ж	о му́же	мужья́	о мужья́х
учи́тель	об учи́теле	учителя́	об учителя́х
профе́ссор	о профе́ссоре	профессора́	о профессора́х
шка́ф	о шка́фе	шкафы́	о шкафа́х

2. Stress shift from endings in the singular to stem in the plural:

NOM SG	PREP SG	NOM PL	PREP PL
жена́	о жене́	жёны	о жёнах
сестра́	о сестре́	сёстры	о сёстрах
зима́	о зиме́	зи́мы	о зи́мах
окно́	на окне́	о́кна	на о́кнах
перо́	о пере́	пе́рья	о пе́рьях
письмо́	о письме́	пи́сьма	о пи́сьмах

3. Stress shift from stem in the nominative singular to endings in all the singular and plural forms where a vowel ending exists.

NOM SG	PREP SG	NOM PL	PREP PL
сто́л	на столе́	столы́	на стола́х
звоно́к	о звонке́	звонки́	о звонка́х
каранда́ш	о карандаше́	карандаши́	о карандаша́х
клю́ч	о ключе́	ключи́	о ключа́х
но́ж	о ноже́	ножи́	о ножа́х
огуре́ц	об огурце́	огурцы́	об огурца́х
язы́к	о языке́	языки́	о языка́х

The third group of nouns actually have their stress consistently on the endings, where there actually are endings. Where the ending is zero (as in the nominative singular) the stress is of necessity on the stem, usually on the last syllable.

— Мы недавно пили чай, но я опять голоден. — Уже можно обедать, обед на столе. У нас сегодня борщ, каша, рыба и огурцы.

Иван Николаевич всю зиму не был на службе. Он был болен. Его жена, Мария Ивановна, тоже была больна. Теперь Иван Николаевич и Мария Ивановна здоровы.

Нина Ивановна вчера была в городе. Она покупала материал на костюм. Она долго стояла в очереди и купила очень красивый материал.

— Кто там? — Это я. — Мария Ивановна? — Да. — Здравствуйте, заходите пожалуйста! Рада вас видеть. — Знаете, я была в городе. Покупала материал на костюм. Хотите посмотреть? — Конечно. — Правда красивый? — Очень. Где вы купили? — В ГУМе.

— Как идёт работа на заводе? — Хорошо. А как ваши дела? — Тоже хорошо, спасибо. — Ну, до свидания! — Всего хорошего!

— Семён, нарежь, пожалуйста, огурцы!
— Хорошо. А где они? — Там, на окне.
— А где нож, в шкафу? — Нет в столе,
в ящике.

— Олёг, ты слы́шал? Говоря́т, Ни́на больна́.
— Нет, она́ здоро́ва. Смотри́, во́т она́ идёт.
— Ни́на, куда́ вы́ идёте?
— А́, здра́вствуйте. Я́ иду́ в э́то зда́ние. Та́м сейча́с бу́дет говори́ть ре́ктор.
— Пошли́ и мы́, Олёг. Это интере́сно.

Сего́дня у на́с на ле́кции бы́л оди́н америка́нец. О́н учи́л ру́сский язы́к в университе́те в Аме́рике и вполне́ хорошо́ говори́т по-ру́сски. Интере́сно с ни́м познако́миться. Но ка́к? Мо́жет быть за́втра о́н бу́дет в столо́вой.

— Хоти́те пойти́ на конце́рт, Ми́ла?
— С удово́льствием. Кста́ти, э́то беспла́тно?
— Да́. Ну, пока́. Я́ сейча́с спешу́ на собра́ние в клу́б.
— До свида́ния.

PREPARATION FOR CONVERSATION	**Где́ мо́й слова́рь?**

слова́рь (словари́) (m) — dictionary (dictionaries)
Где́ мо́й слова́рь? — Where's my dictionary?
у тебя́ — you have; at your place.
У тебя́ мо́й слова́рь? — Do you have my dictionary?
Влади́мир, у тебя́ мо́й слова́рь? — Vladimir, do you have my dictionary?

у меня́ — I have; at my place
Не́т, не у меня́. — No, I don't.

о́н у Семёнова — Semyonov has it
ра́зве — really; are you sure!
Ра́зве о́н не у Семёнова? — Are you sure Semyonov doesn't have it?

у него́   [uɲivó] — he has; at his place
у него́ не́т — he doesn't have it
Не́т, у него́ не́т. — No, he doesn't have it.
спра́шивать (I) — to ask, inquire
    (pfv спроси́ть)
то́лько что   [tóḷkəštə] — just, just now
Я́ то́лько что спра́шивал. — I just asked.
Не́т, у него́ не́т. Я́ то́лько что — No, he doesn't have it. I just asked.
спра́шивал.

о́н у Козло́ва — Kozlov has it
Тогда́, мо́жет бы́ть, о́н — Then maybe Kozlov has it?
у Козло́ва?

заня́тия (pl) — studies, classes
на заня́тиях — at classes
Козло́ва не́ было. — Kozlov was absent (*or* missing).
Козло́ва сего́дня не́ было — Kozlov didn't attend his classes
на заня́тиях. — today.

Мо́жет бы́ть, ты́ оста́вил сво́й — Maybe you left your dictionary at
слова́рь в библиоте́ке? — the library?

Я́ та́м не́ был. — I haven't been there.

◀ **Прода́жа кни́г на Не́вском проспе́кте в Ленингра́де.**   **139**

пошёл, пошла́, пошло́, пошли́   went
   (irreg past of пойти́)
Я́ пошёл домо́й.   I went home.
   после заня́тий   after classes
По́сле заня́тий я́ пошёл домо́й.   After classes I went home.
   сра́зу   immediately, right away, at once
Сра́зу по́сле заня́тий я́ пошёл домой.   Right after classes I went home.

   како́й-то слова́рь   a dictionary, some sort of dictionary
В столо́вой я́ ви́дел како́й-то слова́рь.   I saw a dictionary in the dining hall.
   у на́с в столо́вой   in our dining hall
У на́с в столо́вой я́ ви́дел како́й-то слова́рь.   I saw a dictionary in our dining hall.
   подожда́ть (pfv I)   to wait (a limited amount of time)
Подожди́, у на́с в столо́вой я́ ви́дел како́й-то слова́рь.   Wait a second, I saw a dictionary in our dining hall.

   наве́рно   probably, likely
Э́то, наве́рно, мо́й слова́рь.   It's probably my dictionary.
   посмотрю́   I'll take a look
Э́то, наве́рно, мо́й. Пойду́ посмотрю́.   It's probably mine. I'll go take a look.

   магази́н   store
   до́лжен, должна́, должно́, должны́   must, have to, got to (*lit.* obliged, obligated)
Я́ до́лжен пойти́ в магази́н.   I've got to go to the store.
   ко́е-что́   [kójə štó]   a thing or two, a couple of things
А́ я́ до́лжен пойти́ в магази́н ко́е-что́ купи́ть.   And I've got to go to the store to buy a couple of things.

SUPPLEMENT

   исто́рия   history
У меня́ тепе́рь исто́рия.   I have history now.
   литерату́ра   literature
У меня́ тепе́рь литерату́ра.   I have literature now.
   геогра́фия   geography
У меня́ тепе́рь геогра́фия.   I have geography now.
   матема́тика   mathematics
У меня́ тепе́рь матема́тика.   I have mathematics now.
   фи́зика   physics
У меня́ тепе́рь фи́зика.   I have physics now.
   хи́мия   chemistry
У меня́ тепе́рь хи́мия.   I have chemistry now.

Где́ мо́й слова́рь?

Н. — Никола́й   В. — Влади́мир

Н. 1 Влади́мир,
у тебя́ мо́й слова́рь?

vlaḑímir ↓
uţiḅá mój slavár̗ ↓

В. 2 Не́т,
не у меня́.
А ра́зве о́н не у Семёнова?[1]

ņĕt ↓
ņiuṃiņá ↓
a rázɣi ón ņiuşiṃőnəvə ↓

Н. 3 Не́т,
у него́ не́т.
Я́ то́лько что спра́шивал.

ņĕt ↓
uņivó ņĕt ↓
já tólkəštə spráši̯vəl ↓

В. 4 Тогда́, мо́жет бы́ть,
о́н у Козло́ва?

tagdá móžidbíţ
ón ukazlővə ↓

Н. 5 Козло́ва сего́дня
не́ было на заня́тиях.[2]

kazlóvə şivódņə
ņébilə nəzaņáţijəx ↓

В. 6 Мо́жет бы́ть,
ты́ оста́вил сво́й слова́рь
в библиоте́ке?

móžidbíţ
tɨ astáɣil svój slavár̗
vḅibḷiaţĕ̗ḳi ↓

Н. 7 Я́ та́м не́ был.[3]
Сра́зу по́сле заня́тий
пошёл домо́й.

já tám ņĕbɨl ↓
srázu pósḷi zaņáţij
pašól damőj ↓

В. 8 Подожди́,
у на́с в столо́вой
я́ ви́дел како́й-то
слова́рь.

pədaždḯ ↓
unás fstalővəj |
já ɣíḑil kakójtə slavár̗ ↓

Н. 9 Э́то, наве́рно, мо́й.
Пойду́ посмотрю́.

étə naɣérnə mőj ↓
pajdú pəsmatr̗ű ↓

В. 10 А я́ до́лжен пойти́ в магази́н
ко́е-что́ купи́ть.[4]

a já dólžin pajţí vməgazḯn ↑
kójə štó kuṟíţ ↓

NOTES   [1] **Ра́зве** is a word used to express surprise or incredulity, such as: *you don't mean to say! it isn't possible! really!* and so forth.

[2] Note the use of the plural **заня́тия** to mean *class*. This is the usual word for classes or studies at the university. **Ле́кция** may also be used to refer to university classes, but it is more often used in its literal sense (*lecture*) to describe an event outside class, such as a talk by a visiting lecturer. Compare also **уро́к** (literally *lesson*), used both to mean any kind of *private lesson* and *class* at the pre-university level.

Студе́нты тепе́рь на заня́тиях.	The students are in classes now.
Я́ иду́ на ле́кцию.	I'm going to a lecture.
Ученики́ на уро́ках.	The pupils are in class (*lit.* at their lessons).

³ Contrast **Я та́м не́ был** *I haven't been there* with **Козло́ва сего́дня не́ было на заня́тиях** *Kozlov wasn't at his classes today*. In the second example, a neuter verb and a genitive case subject are used to emphasize Kozlov's absence, i.e., to point out that he was missing.

⁴ **До́лжен** is a short-form adjective used together with the infinitive to mean *must*, *has* (or *have*) *to*. Its literal meaning is *obliged* or *obligated*.

PREPARATION FOR CONVERSATION   **В магази́не**

ка́рта	map
Евро́па	Europe
ка́рты Евро́пы	maps of Europe
у ва́с е́сть	you have
У ва́с е́сть ка́рты Евро́пы?	Do you have maps of Europe?
продавщи́ца	saleslady
ожида́ть (I)	to expect
Не́т, но мы́ ожида́ем за́втра.	No, but we're expecting them tomorrow.
неде́ля (неде́ли)	week(s)
на сле́дующей неде́ле	next week
Не́т, но мы́ ожида́ем на сле́дующей неде́ле.	No, but we're expecting them next week.
на э́той неде́ле	this week
Не́т, но мы́ ожида́ем на э́той неде́ле.	No, but we're expecting them this week.
Кита́й	China
ка́рта Кита́я	a map of China
У ва́с е́сть ка́рта Кита́я?	Do you have a map of China?
У ва́с не́т ка́рты Кита́я?	Don't you have a map of China?
А ка́рты Кита́я у ва́с не́т?	And you don't have a map of China?
то́же	too, also; either
А ка́рты Кита́я у ва́с то́же не́т?	And you don't have a map of China either?
е́сть	there is, there are
У на́с е́сть ка́рта Кита́я.	We do have a map of China.
пожа́луйста	please, you're welcome
во́т пожа́луйста	here you are
Во́т, пожа́луйста.	Here you are.
и	also, too
мне́ нужна́ ка́рта	I need a map
Но мне́ нужна́ и ка́рта Евро́пы.	But I need a map of Europe, too.
всё-таки	nevertheless, still, just the same
Но мне́ всё-таки нужна́ и ка́рта Евро́пы.	But just the same I need a map of Europe, too.
кио́ск	stand, newsstand
спроси́ть (pfv II) (ipfv спра́шивать)	to ask, inquire
А вы́ спроси́те в кио́ске.	Ask at the newsstand.
у́гол (gen sg угла́)	corner

на углу́	on the corner
А вы́ спроси́те в кио́ске на углу́.	Ask at the newsstand on the corner.
та́м то́же не́т	[it's] not there either
Я́ уже́ та́м бы́л. Та́м то́же не́т.	I've already been there. They don't have it there either.
а́тлас	atlas
Ка́к насчёт а́тласа?	How about an atlas?
Ка́к тогда́ насчёт а́тласа?	How about an atlas then?
дорого́й	expensive, dear
А́тлас, наве́рно, о́чень дорого́й?	An atlas is probably very expensive, isn't it?
Не́т, не о́чень.	No, not very.
принести́ (pfv I)	to bring
я́ принесу́	I'll bring
Не́т, не о́чень. Сейча́с принесу́.	No, not very. I'll bring one right away.

SUPPLEMENT

у неё е́сть	she has
У неё е́сть а́тлас?	Does she have an atlas?
у ни́х е́сть	they have
У ни́х е́сть а́тлас?	Do they have an atlas?
кусо́к (gen sg куска́)	piece
Хоти́те ещё кусо́к хле́ба?	Want another piece of bread?
стака́н	glass
Хоти́те ещё стака́н молока́?	Want another glass of milk?
ча́шка	cup
Хоти́те ещё ча́шку ко́фе?	Want another cup of coffee?

В магази́не

В. — Влади́мир
П. — Продавщи́ца

В.	1	У ва́с е́сть	uvás jéşţ
		ка́рты Евро́пы?	kárti jivrópi ↓
П.	2	Не́т,	ņét ↓
		но мы́ ожида́ем	no mí ažɨdájim |
		на сле́дующей неде́ле.	naşļédujuščij ņiḑéļi ↓
В.	3	А ка́рты Кита́я	akárti ķitájə ↓
		у ва́с то́же не́т?[1]	uvás tóži ņét ↓
П.	4	Не́т, е́сть.[2]	ņét↓ jéşţ↓
		Во́т, пожа́луйста.[3]	vót↓ pažáləstə↓

В.	5 Хорошо́. Но мне́ всё-таки нужна́ и ка́рта Евро́пы.	xərašő ↓ no mn̦é fṣőtək̦i nužná | i kártə jivrőp̦i ↓
П.	6 А вы́ спроси́те в кио́ске на углу́.[4]	a ví spraṣíṭi fk̦iósk̦i nəuglű ↓
В.	7 Я́ уже́ та́м бы́л. Та́м то́же не́т.	já užé tám bĭl ↓ tám tőži n̦ét ↓
П.	8 Ка́к тогда́ насчёт а́тласа?	kák tagdá naščót ắtləsə ↓
В.	9 А́тлас, наве́рно, о́чень дорого́й?	átlas nay̆érnə óči̦n̦ dəragőj ↓
П.	10 Не́т, не о́чень. Сейча́с принесу́.	n̦ḗt ↓ n̦iőči̦n̦ ↓ ṣičás pr̦in̦isű ↓

NOTES

[1] Note that **то́же** means *too* or *also* in affirmative sentences, but *neither* or *not . . . either* in negative ones:

Compare	Жена́ то́же рабо́тает в горсове́те.	My wife works at the gorsovet, too.
with	Ка́рты Кита́я у ва́с то́же не́т?	You don't have a map of China either?
	Я́ то́же его́ не зна́ю.	Neither do I know him *or* I don't know him either.

[2] In answering negative questions, Russians *usually* begin their answer with **не́т** regardless of whether the answer is affirmative or negative:

А ка́рты Кита́я у ва́с то́же не́т?	And you don't have a map of China either?
— Не́т, е́сть.	Yes, we do.
Ты́ та́м не́ был?	Weren't you there?
— Не́т, бы́л.	Yes, I was.
— Не́т, не́ был.	No, I wasn't.

[3] **Пожа́луйста** is a polite word used in various situations:

Пожа́луйста, заходи́те.	Come in, please.
Во́т, пожа́луйста.	Here you are.
Пожа́луйста.	You first (at a door or entrance).
Спаси́бо. — Пожа́луйста.	Thank you. You're welcome.

[4] A few **сто́л**-nouns like **шка́ф** and **у́гол** have a second prepositional case ending in stressed –у́, which occurs only when they are used with prepositions **на** and **в**.

Compare	Кио́ск на углу́.	The newsstand is *on the corner.*
with	Я́ говорю́ об угле́.	I'm talking *about the corner.*
Compare	Огурцы́ в шкафу́.	The cucumbers are *in the cupboard.*
with	Я́ говорю́ о шка́фе.	I'm talking *about the cupboard.*

Basic sentence patterns

1. У вác есть словáрь?
   — Дá, есть.
   — Дá, у меня́ есть словáрь.
   У тебя́ есть словáрь?
   — Дá, есть.
   — Дá, у меня́ есть словáрь.
   У негó есть словáрь?
   — Дá, есть.
   — Дá, у негó есть словáрь.
   У неё есть словáрь?
   — Дá, есть.
   — Дá, у неё есть словáрь.
   У нác есть словáрь?
   — Дá, есть.
   — Дá, у нác есть словáрь.
   У ни́х есть словáрь?
   — Дá, есть.
   — Дá, у ни́х есть словáрь.

   Do you have a dictionary?
   Yes, I do.
   Yes, I have a dictionary.
   Do you have a dictionary?
   Yes, I do.
   Yes, I have a dictionary.
   Does he have a dictionary?
   Yes, he does.
   Yes, he has a dictionary.
   Does she have a dictionary?
   Yes, she does.
   Yes, she has a dictionary.
   Do we have a dictionary?
   Yes, we do.
   Yes, we have a dictionary.
   Do they have a dictionary?
   Yes, they do.
   Yes, they have a dictionary.

2. У вác есть словáрь?
   — Нéт, у меня́ нéт словаря́.
   У тебя́ есть словáрь?
   — Нéт, у меня́ нéт словаря́.
   У негó есть словáрь?
   — Нéт, у негó нéт словаря́.
   У неё есть словáрь?
   — Нéт, у неё нéт словаря́.
   У нác есть словáрь?
   — Нéт, у нác нéт словаря́.
   У ни́х есть словáрь?
   — Нéт, у ни́х нéт словаря́.

   Do you have a dictionary?
   No, I don't have a dictionary.
   Do you have a dictionary?
   No, I don't have a dictionary.
   Does he have a dictionary?
   No, he doesn't have a dictionary.
   Does she have a dictionary?
   No, she doesn't have a dictionary.
   Do we have a dictionary?
   No, we don't have a dictionary.
   Do they have a dictionary?
   No, they don't have a dictionary.

3. У вác есть портфéль?
   — Дá, у меня́ есть портфéль.
   — Нéт, у меня́ нéт портфéля.

   Do you have a briefcase?
   Yes, I have a briefcase.
   No, I don't have a briefcase.

4. У вác есть рýчка?
   — Дá, у меня́ есть рýчка.
   — Нéт, у меня́ нéт рýчки.

   Do you have a pen?
   Yes, I have a pen.
   No, I don't have a pen.

5. У вác есть молокó?
   — Дá, у нác есть молокó.
   — Нéт, у нác нéт молокá.

   Do you have milk?
   Yes, we have milk.
   No, we don't have any milk.

6. Чтó у вác тепéрь?
   — У меня́ тепéрь литератýра.
   _____ рýсский язы́к.
   _____ геогрáфия.
   _____ истóрия.
   _____ математика.
   _____ фи́зика.
   _____ хи́мия.

   What do you have now?
   I have literature now.
   _____ Russian _____.
   _____ geography _____.
   _____ history _____.
   _____ mathematics _____.
   _____ physics _____.
   _____ chemistry _____.

7. Козло́ва сего́дня не́т.
   Влади́мира _____.
   Евге́ния _____.
   Кири́лла _____.
   Семёна _____.
   Льва́ _____.
   Оле́га _____.
   Никола́я _____.

   Kozlov is absent today.
   Vladimir _____.
   Evgeny _____.
   Kirill _____.
   Semyon _____.
   Lev _____.
   Oleg _____.
   Nikolay _____.

8. Ко́ли вчера́ не́ было на заня́тиях.
   Га́ли _____.
   Ни́ны _____.
   Ми́лы _____.
   Мари́и _____.
   Ма́ши _____.
   О́ли _____.

   Kolya was absent from classes yesterday.
   Galya _____.
   Nina _____.
   Mila _____.
   Maria _____.
   Masha _____.
   Olya _____.

9. Его́ там не́ было?
   — Не́т, не́ было.
   — Не́т, о́н та́м бы́л.
   Её та́м не́ было?
   — Не́т, не́ было.
   — Не́т, она́ та́м была́.
   И́х та́м не́ было?
   — Не́т, не́ было.
   — Не́т, они́ та́м бы́ли.

   Wasn't he there?
   No, he wasn't.
   Yes, he was there.
   Wasn't she there?
   No, she wasn't.
   Yes, she was there.
   Weren't they there?
   No, they weren't.
   Yes, they were there.

10. Че́й э́то портфе́ль?
    — Влади́мира.
    — Семёнова.
    — Оле́га.
    — Семёна.
    — Профе́ссора Орло́ва.
    — Бра́та.
    — Хитро́ва.
    — Цара́пкина.
    — Учи́теля.
    — Никола́я.
    — Евге́ния.

    Whose briefcase is that?
    Vladimir's.
    Semyonov's.
    Oleg's.
    Semyon's.
    Professor Orlov's.
    My brother's.
    Khitrov's.
    Tsarapkin's.
    The teacher's.
    Nikolay's.
    Evgeny's.

11. Чьи́ э́то ключи́?
    — Убо́рщицы.
    — Продавщи́цы.
    — Сестры́.
    — Жены́.
    — Мари́и.
    — Учи́тельницы.
    — Ни́ны Петро́вны.

    Whose keys are these?
    The cleaning lady's.
    The saleslady's.
    My sister's.
    My wife's.
    Maria's.
    The teacher's (f).
    Nina Petrovna's.

12. Это де́ло Ни́ны.   That's Nina's business.

_____ О́ли.	_____ Olya's _____.
_____ Га́ли.	_____ Galya's _____.
_____ Ко́ли.	_____ Kolya's _____.
_____ Са́ши.	_____ Sasha's _____.
_____ продавщи́цы.	_____ the saleslady's ____.
_____ убо́рщицы.	_____ the cleaning lady's ____.
_____ вахтёра.	_____ the custodian's ____.
_____ Козло́ва.	_____ Kozlov's _____.
_____ ре́ктора.	_____ the chancellor's ____.
_____ Льва́.	_____ Lev's _____.

Pronunciation practice:
hard versus soft consonants

A.   [v] vs. [ɣ]   Usual Cyrillic spelling **в**; sometimes **г** or **вь**.

Note the pronunciation of hard [v] in the following:

[ivа́n]	Ива́н	Ivan
[ví]	вы́	you

and compare it with soft [ɣ]:

[dəsɣidа́ŋjə]	до свида́ния	good-bye
[ɣíḑil]	ви́дел	saw

Russian [v], like the corresponding English sound, is made by bringing the upper teeth close to the lower lip. Before [o] (and especially [ɨ]) there is often the auditory effect of a w-like off-glide. Soft [ɣ], on the other hand, has the auditory effect of being followed by a y-like off-glide.

> Sound Drill: Practice the Russian paired examples illustrating hard [v] and soft [ɣ], imitating your instructor (or the tape) as accurately as you can.

B.   [f] vs. [f̦]   Usual Cyrillic spelling **ф**; also **в**; sometimes **вь** or **фь**.

Note the pronunciation of hard [f] in the following:

[ţiļifón]	телефóн	telephone
[áfŗikə]	Áфрика	Africa
[fpalŋé]	вполнé	completely

and compare it with soft [f̦]:

[fiļíp]	Филúпп	Philip
[praf̦ésər]	профéссор	professor
[partf̦éļ]	портфéль	briefcase

Russian [f], like the corresponding English sound, is made by bringing the upper teeth close to the lower lip. Soft [f̦] has the effect of a y-like glide following it.

> Sound Drill: Practice the Russian paired examples illustrating hard [f] and soft [f̦], imitating your instructor (or the tape) as accurately as you can. Note that before [o] (and especially [i]), a w-like off-glide is often heard after hard [f].

C.   [l] vs. [ļ]   Usual Cyrillic spelling **л**; sometimes **ль**.

Note the pronunciation of hard [l] in the following:

[ɣíḍil]	вúдел	saw
[ŋébil]	нé был	wasn't
[ḍilá]	делá	affairs
[fpalŋé]	вполнé	completely

and compare it with soft [ļ]:

[ļéf]	Лéв	Lev
[baļní]	больнú	sick
[partf̦éļ]	портфéль	briefcase
[učíţiļ]	учúтель	teacher

Russian hard [l] is made with the tip of the tongue against the back of the upper teeth and with the middle of the tongue lowered or hollowed out. English has a somewhat similar *l* in words like ba*ll*, bu*ll*, and who*l*e. In Russian the tongue muscles are tenser and the tongue hollower.

Russian soft [ļ] is formed with the front part of the blade of the tongue (not the tip) in contact with the ridge of the gums behind the upper teeth. Soft [ļ] has somewhat the effect of being followed by a y-like glide as in English mi*lli*on.

> Sound Drill: Practice the Russian paired examples illustrating hard [l] and soft [ļ], imitating your instructor (or the tape) as accurately as you can.

Intonation practice: part II—questions without question words

Questions with a rising-falling contour. This contour is typical of questions where the major stress is not on the last word. The pitch rises to a high peak at level 4 on the major stress and then drops to a point somewhere between levels 1 and 2.

Practice the following drills, imitating the tape or the instructor.

```
Вы́   говори́те   по-ру́сски?
Э́то      ты́,      О́ля?
Вчера́      бы́ло собра́ние?
Он   давно́      бо́лен?
```

```
Вы́   слы́шали   об э́том?
Она́   мо́жет   пойти́?
Вы́   до́лго      рабо́тали?
Вы хоти́те      ко́фе?
```

■ **TRANSFORMATION DRILL**

Pronounce the following statements as questions.

```
Он      не́ был   на экза́мене.
Она́   доста́ла      огурцы́.
У на́с      е́сть      ко́фе.
Э́то      ва́ша      кни́га.
```

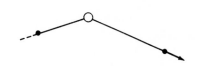

```
Он      не́ был   на экза́мене?
Она́   доста́ла      огурцы́?
У на́с      е́сть      ко́фе?
Э́то      ва́ша      кни́га?
```

■ **TRANSFORMATION DRILL**

Pronounce the following questions as statements.

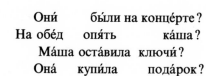

```
Они́      бы́ли на конце́рте?
На обе́д   опя́ть      ка́ша?
Ма́ша оста́вила ключи́?
Она́   купи́ла      пода́рок?
```

```
Они́      бы́ли на конце́рте.
На обе́д   опя́ть      ка́ша.
Ма́ша оста́вила   ключи́.
Она́   купи́ла      пода́рок.
```

STRUCTURE AND DRILLS

To have in Russian: affirmative y constructions in the present tense

MODELS

У вáс éсть карандáш?	Do you have a pencil?
— Дá, éсть.	Yes, I do.
— Дá, у меня́ éсть карандáш.	Yes, I have a pencil.
У вáс éсть кни́га?	Do you have a book?
— Дá, éсть.	Yes, I do.
— Дá, у меня́ éсть кни́га.	Yes, I have a book.
У вáс éсть перó?	Do you have a pen [point]?
— Дá, éсть.	Yes, I do.
— Дá, у меня́ éсть перó.	Yes, I have a pen [point].
У вáс éсть тетрáди?	Do you have notebooks?
— Дá, éсть.	Yes, I do.
— Дá, у меня́ éсть тетрáди.	Yes, I have notebooks.
У тебя́ мóй карандáш?	Do you have my pencil?
— Дá, у меня́.	Yes, I do.
— Дá, óн у меня́.	Yes, I have it.
У тебя́ моя́ кни́га?	Do you have my book?
— Дá, у меня́.	Yes, I do.
— Дá, онá у меня́.	Yes, I have it.
У тебя́ моё перó?	Do you have my pen [point]?
— Дá, у меня́.	Yes, I do.
— Дá, онó у меня́.	Yes, I have it.
У тебя́ мои́ тетрáди?	Do you have my notebooks?
— Дá, у меня́.	Yes, I do.
— Дá, они́ у меня́.	Yes, I have them.
У вáс сегóдня экзáмен?	Do you have an exam today?
— Дá, у нáс сегóдня экзáмен.	Yes, we have an exam today.
У вáс сегóдня лéкция?	Do you have a lecture today?
— Дá, у нáс сегóдня лéкция.	Yes, we have a lecture today.
У вáс сегóдня собрáние?	Do you have a meeting today?
— Дá, у нáс сегóдня собрáние.	Yes, we have a meeting today.
У вáс сегóдня экзáмены?	Do you have examinations today?
— Дá, у нáс сегóдня экзáмены.	Yes, we have examinations today.

■ REPETITION DRILL

Repeat the models after your instructor or the tape until you are familiar with the patterns.

■ REPETITION-SUBSTITUTION DRILL

We do have cucumbers.

т: У нáс éсть огурцы́.

s: **У нáс éсть огурцы́.**

    (борщ, кáша, чáй, кóфе, селёдка, мо-
локó, ры́ба, телефóн, ключи́, словáрь)

1. *Do you have a pencil?*
   Yes, I do.
   т: У тебя́ есть каранда́ш?
   s: **Да́, есть.**
   т: У тебя́ есть кни́га?
   s: **Да́, есть.**
   (ручка, нож, тетрадь, атлас, портфель, молоко, борщ, селёдка)

2. *Do you have fish?*
   Yes, we have fish.
   т: У ва́с есть ры́ба?
   s: **Да́, у на́с есть ры́ба.**
   т: У ва́с есть огурцы́?
   s: **Да́, у на́с есть огурцы́.**
   (столы, атлас, карта Европы, карандаши, книги, тетради, материал на платье)

3. *Do you have a pencil?*
   Yes, I have a pencil.
   т: У тебя́ есть каранда́ш?
   s: **Да́, у меня́ есть каранда́ш.**
   т: У тебя́ есть ру́чка?
   s: **Да́, у меня́ есть ру́чка.**
   (книга, тетрадь, полка, портфель, коробка, тетради, нож)

4. *Do we have fish?*
   Yes, we do.
   т: У на́с есть ры́ба?
   s: **Да́, есть.**
   т: У на́с есть ключи́?
   s: **Да́, есть.**
   (карта Европы, вилки, ложки, карта Китая, книги, карандаши, перья)

■ QUESTION-ANSWER DRILLS

1. *Do you have my keys?*
   Yes, I do.
   т: Мои́ ключи́ у тебя́?
   s: **Да́, у меня́.**
   т: Мои́ ключи́ у Козло́ва?
   s: **Да́, у него́.**
   (у неё, у них, у вас, у него, у тебя, у Владимира, у Нины)

2. *Do you have my notebook?*
   Yes, I have it.
   т: У тебя́ моя́ тетра́дь?
   s: **Да́, она́ у меня́.**
   т: У тебя́ мо́й а́тлас?
   s: **Да́, о́н у меня́.**
   (моя ручка, моя карта Китая, мой нож, мои письма, моё письмо, моя ложка, моё сочинение, мой карандаш)

   т: Что́ у тебя́ тепе́рь, хи́мия?
   s: **Да́, у меня́ тепе́рь хи́мия.**
   (экзамен, собрание, урок пения, история, математика, литература, физика, география)

3. *What do you have now, history?*
   Yes, I have history now.
   т: Что́ у тебя́ тепе́рь, исто́рия?
   s: **Да́, у меня́ тепе́рь исто́рия.**

DISCUSSION

The concept *to have* is most commonly expressed in Russian by means of the preposition **у** plus the genitive case form of the noun or pronoun to indicate the possessor. The thing had or possessed is in the nominative case and is the grammatical subject of the Russian sentence.

У ва́с есть кни́га?	Do you have a book? (*Lit.* By you is a book?)
— У меня́ есть кни́га.	I have a book.
У на́с есть ры́ба.	We have fish *or* We do have fish.
У ва́с есть огурцы́?	Do you have cucumbers?
— Да́, есть.	Yes, we do.
У Влади́мира есть портфе́ль.	Vladimir has a briefcase.

Есть is required in those constructions where the speaker wishes to establish or affirm the presence or existence of the subject under discussion. If it is used in the question it must be repeated in the answer. It is omitted when some other part of the sentence is focused on.

Чтó у тебя́ тепéрь, рýсский язы́к?	*What* do you have now, *Russian?*
— Нéт, у меня́ тепéрь истóрия.	No, I have *history* now.
У вáс мóй словáрь?	Do *you* have my dictionary?
У вáс мóй словáрь?	Do you have *my* dictionary?
У вáс словáрь?	Is it a *dictionary* you have?

To have had in Russian: affirmative y constructions in the past tense

MODELS

У вáс бы́л экзáмен?	Did you have an exam?
_____ урóк?	_____ a lesson?
_____ урóк пéния?	_____ a singing lesson?
_____ англи́йский язы́к?	_____ English?
_____ рýсский язы́к?	_____ Russian?
У вáс былá лéкция?	Did you have a lecture?
_____ истóрия?	_____ history?
_____ матемáтика?	_____ mathematics?
_____ геогрáфия?	_____ geography?
_____ литератýра?	_____ literature?
У вáс бы́ло собрáние?	Did you have a meeting?
_____ сочинéние?	_____ a composition?
_____ пéние?	_____ singing?
У вáс бы́ли экзáмены?	Did you have exams?
_____ урóки?	_____ lessons?
_____ собрáния?	_____ meetings?
_____ лéкции?	_____ lectures?
_____ заня́тия?	_____ classes?

■ REPETITION DRILL

Repeat the above models, noting that for the past tense the appropriate form of бы́л, былá, бы́ло, or бы́ли must be used to agree with the noun denoting the thing had or possessed.

■ QUESTION-ANSWER DRILLS

1. *Did you already have an exam?*
   Yes, we did.
   т: У вáс ужé бы́л экзáмен?
   s: Дá, бы́л.
   т: У вáс ужé бы́ло собрáние?
   s: Дá, бы́ло.
   (лекция, урок пения, география, экзамены, физика, математика, химия)

2. *Did you have exams yesterday?*
   Yes, we did have exams yesterday.
   т: У вáс вчерá бы́ли экзáмены?
   s: Дá, у нáс вчерá бы́ли экзáмены.
   т: У вáс вчерá бы́л урóк?
   s: Дá, у нáс вчерá бы́л урóк.
   (собрание, уроки, лекция, история, литература, экзамен, русский язык, занятия)

1. *I have a box.*
   I had a box.
   т: У меня́ есть коро́бка.
   s: **У меня́ была́ коро́бка.**
   т: У меня́ есть портфе́ль.
   s: **У меня́ бы́л портфе́ль.**
   (каранда́ш, по́лка, перо́, ру́чка, тетра́ди, нож, ножи́, ключ, ключи́)

2. *We're having a meeting today.*
   We had a meeting today.
   т: У на́с сего́дня собра́ние.
   s: **У на́с сего́дня бы́ло собра́ние.**
   т: У на́с сего́дня пе́ние.
   s: **У на́с сего́дня бы́ло пе́ние.**
   (ру́сский язы́к, экза́мен, экза́мены, сочине́ние, уро́к, ры́ба, борщ, ка́ша)

1. *We had an exam, did you?*
   So did we.
   т: У на́с бы́л экза́мен, а у ва́с?
   s: **У на́с то́же бы́л.**
   т: У на́с была́ ле́кция, а у ва́с?
   s: **У на́с то́же была́.**
   (экза́мены, сочине́ние, ру́сский язы́к, пе́ние, исто́рия, геогра́фия, собра́ние, заня́тия)

2. *Did you already have singing?*
   Yes, I did.
   т: У тебя́ уже́ бы́ло пе́ние?
   s: **Да́, бы́ло.**
   т: У тебя́ уже́ была́ матема́тика?
   s: **Да́, была́.**
   (пе́ние, уро́ки, исто́рия, фи́зика, хи́мия, сочине́ние)

(*a meeting*) *What did you have yesterday?*
            We had a meeting.
т: (собра́ние) Что́ у ва́с вчера́ бы́ло?
s: **У на́с бы́ло собра́ние.**
т: (экза́мены) Что́ у ва́с вчера́ бы́ло?
s: **У на́с бы́ли экза́мены.**
(ру́сский язы́к, заня́тия в лаборато́рии, сочине́ние, пе́ние, ле́кция. рабо́та в лаборато́рии)

DISCUSSION

To express the concept *to have* in the past tense in an affirmative sentence, Russian uses the appropriate form af **бы́л, была́, бы́ло,** or **бы́ли** to agree with the grammatical subject, i.e., the thing *had.*

У на́с бы́л бо́рщ.	*We had borsch.*
_____ была́ ры́ба.	_____ *fish.*
_____ бы́ло собра́ние.	_____ *a meeting.*
_____ бы́ли экза́мены.	_____ *exams.*

The most typical affirmative response to questions using this construction is a short answer containing the confirming **да́** plus the appropriate verb form.

У тебя́ бы́л экза́мен?	*Did you have an exam?*
—Да́, бы́л.	*Yes, I did.*

The genitive singular of nouns

Это ключи́ профе́ссора.	These are the professor's keys.
_____ вахтёра.	_____ the custodian's ____.
_____ ре́ктора.	_____ the chancellor's ____.
_____ бра́та.	_____ Brother's ____.
_____ Влади́мира.	_____ Vladimir's ____.
_____ Никола́я.	_____ Nikolay's ____.
_____ учи́теля.	_____ the teacher's ____.

Где́ ключи́ сестры́?	Where are Sister's keys?
_____ учи́тельницы?	_____ the teacher's ____?
_____ продавщи́цы?	_____ the saleslady's ____?
_____ убо́рщицы?	_____ the cleaning lady's ____?
_____ америка́нки?	_____ the American woman's ____?
_____ Мари́и?	_____ Maria's ____?

Спроси́ насчёт письма́.	Ask about the letter.
_____ окна́.	_____ the window.
_____ молока́.	_____ the milk.
_____ пе́ния.	_____ the singing.
_____ сочине́ния.	_____ the composition.
_____ общежи́тия.	_____ the dormitory.
_____ собра́ния.	_____ the meeting.

TABLE OF GENITIVE SINGULAR ENDINGS				
сто́л- and **окно́**-class nouns		**жена́**-class nouns		**две́рь**-class nouns
–а	or –я	–ы	or –и	–и
стола́	Никола́я	жены́	Га́ли	две́ри
телефо́на	ча́я	ка́рты	Ко́ли	о́череди
звонка́	учи́теля	сестры́	Мари́и	о́сени
студе́нта	пла́тья	Евро́пы	исто́рии	тетра́ди
де́ла	собра́ния	Ни́ны	ка́ши	
окна́	сочине́ния		кни́ги	
пера́			коро́бки	
письма́			студе́нтки	

Notes

1. **Сто́л**–class nouns ending in **–ь** and **–й** and **окно́**–class nouns ending in **–е** or **–ё** in the nominative singular take **–я** in the genitive singular. All other **сто́л**– and **окно́**–class nouns take **–а** in the genitive singular. **Окно́**–class nouns have the same ending as in the nominative plural, but the stress may differ. Compare **пи́сьма** (nominative plural) with **письма́** (genitive singular) and **дела́** (nominative plural) with **де́ла** (genitive singular).

2. **Жена́**– and **две́рь**–class nouns have the same ending in the genitive singular as in the nominative plural. But note that with **жена́**-class nouns, the stress may differ. Compare **жёны** (nominative plural) with **жены́** (genitive singular) and **сёстры** (nominative plural) with **сестры́** (genitive singular).

■ REPETITION DRILL

Repeat the above models after your instructor or the tape until you are familiar with the pattern of genitive singular endings.

■ CUED QUESTION-ANSWER DRILL

    (*Kurochkin*) *Whose briefcase is that?*
              Kurochkin's.
т: (Ку́рочкин) Че́й э́то портфе́ль?
s: **Ку́рочкина.**
т: (Влади́мир) Че́й э́то портфе́ль?
s: **Влади́мира.**
(Ни́на, Козло́в, Никола́й, учи́тель, америка́нец, Орло́в, америка́нка, Ива́н, Мари́я)

■ INTEGRATION DRILLS

1. *This is a book. This is a student.*
   This is a student's book.
   т: Э́то кни́га. Э́то студе́нт.
   s: **Э́то кни́га студе́нта.**
   т: Э́то каранда́ш. Э́то Орло́в.
   s: **Э́то каранда́ш Орло́ва.**
   Э́то тетра́дь. Э́то Влади́мир.
   Э́то портфе́ль. Э́то профе́ссор.
   Э́то рабо́та. Э́то грузи́н.
   Э́то студе́нты. Э́то профе́ссор Орло́в.
   Э́то сочине́ние. Э́то Козло́в.

2. *This is a dictionary. This is the teacher.*
   This is the teacher's dictionary.
   т: Э́то слова́рь. Э́то учи́тель.
   s: **Э́то слова́рь учи́теля.**
   т: Э́то ка́рта. Э́то Кита́й.
   s: **Э́то ка́рта Кита́я.**
   Э́то ключи́. Э́то Никола́й.
   Э́то результа́ты. Э́то собра́ние.
   Э́то ка́рта. Э́то Евро́па.
   Э́то а́тлас. Э́то Евге́ний.
   Э́то учи́тель. Э́то шко́ла.
   Э́то ру́чка. Э́то америка́нец.
   Э́то кни́га. Э́то продавщи́ца.
   Э́то стака́н. Э́то молоко́.

3. *Here's a briefcase. Here's a teacher.*
   Here's a teacher's briefcase.
   т: Во́т портфе́ль. Во́т учи́тельница.
   s: **Во́т портфе́ль учи́тельницы.**
   т: Во́т убо́рщица. Во́т шко́ла.
   s: **Во́т убо́рщица шко́лы.**
   Во́т ка́рта. Во́т Евро́па.
   Во́т две́рь. Во́т аудито́рия.
   Во́т учи́тель. Во́т гру́ппа.
   Во́т окно́. Во́т америка́нка.
   Во́т кни́га. Во́т продавщи́ца.
   Во́т пла́тье. Во́т Ни́на.
   Во́т ви́лка. Во́т Ми́ла.
   Во́т ча́шка. Во́т ча́й.

4. *This is a dictionary. This is a professor.*
   This is the professor's dictionary.
   т: Э́то слова́рь. Э́то профе́ссор.
   s: **Э́то слова́рь профе́ссора.**
   т: Э́то портфе́ль. Э́то Ко́ля.
   s: **Э́то портфе́ль Ко́ли.**
   Э́то сто́л. Э́то Мари́я.
   Э́то рабо́та. Э́то Га́ля.
   Э́то обе́д. Э́то Ко́ля.
   Э́то о́кна. Э́то библиоте́ка.
   Э́то пла́тье. Э́то продавщи́ца.
   Э́то слова́рь. Э́то Га́ля.
   Э́то две́ри. Э́то ГУ́М.

5. *Here's the library. Here's the university.*
   Here's the university library.

   т: Во́т библиоте́ка. Во́т университе́т.

   s: **Во́т библиоте́ка университе́та.**

   т: Во́т кни́га. Во́т учи́тель.

   s: **Во́т кни́га учи́теля.**

   Во́т портфе́ль. Во́т профе́ссор Ку́рочкин.

   Во́т ка́рта. Во́т зда́ние.

   Во́т кни́ги. Во́т Никола́й.

   Во́т сочине́ние. Во́т Евге́ний.

   Во́т студе́нты. Во́т профе́ссор Орло́в.

   Во́т материа́лы. Во́т собра́ние.

   Во́т ча́шка. Во́т ко́фе.

6. *The teacher is here. But where is her husband?*
   Where's the teacher's husband?

   т: Учи́тельница ту́т. А где́ её му́ж?

   s: **Где́ му́ж учи́тельницы?**

   т: Профе́ссор Орло́в ту́т. А где́ его́ студе́нты?

   s: **Где́ студе́нты профе́ссора Орло́ва?**

   Влади́мир ту́т. А где́ его́ сестра́?

   Козло́в ту́т. А где́ его́ бра́т?

   Учи́тель Хитро́в ту́т. А где́ его́ жена́?

   Никола́й ту́т. А где́ его́ бра́т?

   Ни́на ту́т. А где́ её му́ж?

   Мари́я ту́т. А где́ её учи́тель?

DISCUSSION

Unlike the prepositional case, the genitive is used both with and without a preposition. Used without a preposition, it indicates a relationship of possession or descriptive limitation.

му́ж сестры́	sister's husband
кни́га Ива́на	Ivan's book, a book of Ivan's
ру́чка Мари́и	Maria's pen, a pen of Maria's
ка́рта Евро́пы	a map of Europe
наро́д Кита́я	the people of China
учи́тель пе́ния	a singing teacher, a teacher of singing
уро́к геогра́фии	a geography lesson
стака́н молока́	a glass of milk

Note that, unlike the English possessive, the Russian genitive normally *follows* the noun indicating what is possessed or described.

The genitive of кто́, что́, and the personal pronouns

MODELS

У ва́с е́сть слова́рь?	Do *you* have a dictionary?
У тебя́ е́сть слова́рь?	Do *you* have a dictionary?
У кого́ мо́й а́тлас?	*Who* has my atlas?
— У меня́.	*I* do.
— У него́.	*He* does.
— У неё.	*She* does.
— У на́с.	*We* do.
— У ни́х.	*They* do.
Насчёт чего́ они́ спра́шивали?	*What* was it they were asking about?

NOM	я́	ты́	о́н оно́	она́	мы́	вы́	они́	кто́	что́
GEN	меня́	тебя́	его́ (него́)	её (неё)	на́с	ва́с	и́х (ни́х)	кого́	чего́

The alternate third person pronouns, **него́, неё,** and **них,** are used only when the personal pronouns are preceded by a preposition: **у него́, у неё,** and **у них.** Note that г in **его́, него́, кого́,** and **чего́** is pronounced [v]: [jivó], [ɲivó], [kavó], and [čivó].

■ REPETITION DRILL

Repeat the above models after your instructor or the tape.

■ QUESTION-ANSWER DRILLS

1. *Where is he, at the university?*
   Yes, he has exams today.
   т: Где́ о́н, в университе́те?
   s: **Да́, у него́ сего́дня экза́мены.**
   т: Где́ она́, в университе́те?
   s: **Да́, у неё сего́дня экза́мены.**
   (они, Кирилл, Галя, студенты)

2. *And where are you going, to a lecture?*
   Yes, I have history now.
   т: А вы́ куда́, на ле́кцию?
   s: **Да́, у меня́ сейча́с исто́рия.**
   т: А они́ куда́, на ле́кцию?
   s: **Да́, у ни́х сейча́с исто́рия.**
   (Ирина, ты, ваш студент, твоя сестра,
   Коля, твои братья, Ирина и Галя)

3. *What does Galya have now?*
   She has history now.
   т: Что́ у Га́ли тепе́рь?
   s: **У неё тепе́рь исто́рия.**
   т: Что́ у тебя́ тепе́рь?
   s: **У меня́ тепе́рь исто́рия.**
   (у них, у Коли, у нас, у Козлова, у вас)

■ CUED QUESTION-ANSWER DRILLS

1. (*We*) *Who has Russian now?*
   We do.
   т: (мы́) У кого́ тепе́рь ру́сский язы́к?
   s: **У на́с.**
   т: (они́) У кого́ тепе́рь ру́сский язы́к?
   s: **У ни́х.**
   (вы, она, я, он, они, ты, мы, они, он)

2. (*They*) *Who has my dictionary?*
   They have your dictionary.
   т: (они́) У кого́ мо́й слова́рь?
   s: **У ни́х.**
   т: (о́н) У кого́ мо́й слова́рь?
   s: **У него́.**
   (она, вы, он, я, мы, они)

■ STRUCTURE REPLACEMENT DRILLS

1. *Vladimir has the key.*
   He has the key.
   т: Клю́ч у Влади́мира.
   s: **Клю́ч у него́.**
   т: Клю́ч у сестры́.
   s: **Клю́ч у неё.**
   (у студента, у жены, у Коли и Гали,
   у брата, у Козлова и Семёнова, у
   Николая, у Марии)

2. *My sister has an atlas.*
   She has an atlas.
   т: У сестры́ е́сть а́тлас.
   s: **У неё е́сть а́тлас.**
   т: У Никола́я е́сть а́тлас.
   s: **У него́ е́сть а́тлас.**
   (у Коли и Гали, у Любови, у студента,
   у Семёна, у Семёнова, у Козлова и
   Семёнова, у Владимира)

1. *Is Galya at classes?*
   No, she has a meeting now.
   т: Га́ля на заня́тиях?
   s: **Не́т, у неё сейча́с собра́ние.**
   т: Ива́н на заня́тиях?
   s: **Не́т, у него́ сейча́с собра́ние.**
   (Ни́на, её сестра, Никола́й, они, Ирина,
   Лев, Семёнов, студент, Любовь, Коля,
   Борис, Мария)

2. *Do you have Russian now?*
   No, I have singing.
   т: У ва́с тепе́рь ру́сский язы́к?
   s: **Не́т, у меня́ тепе́рь пе́ние.**
   т: У Ири́ны тепе́рь ру́сский язы́к?
   s: **Не́т, у неё тепе́рь пе́ние.**
   (у меня, у нас, у Владимира, у них)

The genitive case in не́т constructions

MODELS

Кого́ здесь не́т?	Who isn't here? *or* Who's missing?
— Здесь не́т Козло́ва.	Kozlov isn't here.
_____ Никола́я.	Nikolay _____.
_____ Ко́ли.	Kolya _____.
_____ Ни́ны.	Nina _____.
_____ Мари́и.	Maria _____.

О́н здесь?	Is he here?
— Не́т, его́ не́т.	No, he isn't.
Она́ здесь?	Is she here?
— Не́т, её не́т.	No, she isn't.

Борща́ бо́льше не́т.	There's no more borsch.
Хле́ба _____.	_____ bread.
Ча́я _____.	_____ tea.
Молока́ _____.	_____ milk.
Ры́бы _____.	_____ fish.
Ка́ши _____.	_____ kasha.
Селёдки _____.	_____ herring.

У ва́с не́т карандаша́?	You don't have a pencil, do you?
_____ а́тласа?	_____ an atlas _____?
_____ словаря́?	_____ a dictionary ___?
_____ пера́?	_____ a pen _____?
_____ молока́?	_____ milk _____?
_____ ка́рты Евро́пы?	_____ a map of Europe _____?
_____ тетра́ди?	_____ a notebook _____?
_____ кни́ги?	_____ a book _____?

■ REPETITION DRILL

Repeat the above models after your instructor (or the tape), noting that the subject of sentences using не́т is always in the genitive case in Russian.

These drills should first be performed as simple repetition drills, then repeated as structure replacement drills.

1. *The map is on the table.*
   There isn't any map on the table!
   т: Ка́рта на столе́.
   s: **Ка́рты не́т на столе́!**
   т: Ры́ба на столе́.
   s: **Ры́бы не́т на столе́!**
   (нож, каша, письмо, коробка, чай, перо, портфель, сочинение, вилка, словарь)

2. *Professor Orlov is here.*
   Professor Orlov isn't here.
   т: Профе́ссор Орло́в здесь.
   s: **Профе́ссора Орло́ва здесь не́т.**
   т: О́н здесь.
   s: **Его́ здесь не́т.**
   (уборщица, она, брат, Мария, он, Маша, она, украинец, он, Коля, он, Николай)

3. *Do you have a map of China?*
   You don't have a map of China, do you?
   т: У ва́с е́сть ка́рта Кита́я?
   s: **У ва́с не́т ка́рты Кита́я?**
   т: У ва́с е́сть но́ж?
   s: **У ва́с не́т ножа́?**
   (ключ, атлас, ручка, тетрадь, карта Америки, шкаф, коробка, перо, словарь)

■ CUED QUESTION-ANSWER DRILLS

1. (*Kozlov*) *Who's not here yet?*
   Kozlov.
   т: (Козло́в) Кого́ ещё не́т?
   s: **Не́т Козло́ва.**
   т: (Ни́на) Кого́ ещё не́т?
   s: **Не́т Ни́ны.**
   (Влади́мир, учи́тельница, Никола́й, профе́ссор Орло́в, Ива́н, му́ж Мари́и, учи́тель, убо́рщица, бра́т Ни́ны)

2. (*phone*) *What's missing here?*
   There's no phone here.
   т: (телефо́н) Чего́ здесь не́т?
   s: **Здесь не́т телефо́на.**
   т: (молоко́) Чего́ здесь не́т?
   s: **Здесь не́т молока́.**
   (полка, стул, атлас, словарь, звонок, ключ, нож, хлеб, стол)

■ QUESTION-ANSWER DRILL

1. *Where's the fish?*
   There isn't any fish left.
   т: Где́ ры́ба?
   s: **Ры́бы бо́льше не́т.**
   т: Где́ ча́й?
   s: **Ча́я бо́льше не́т.**
   (каша, борщ, селёдка, молоко, хлеб)

2. *Is Kozlov here?*
   No, Kozlov isn't here.
   т: Козло́в здесь?
   s: **Не́т, Козло́ва здесь не́т.**
   т: Ку́рочкин здесь?
   s: **Не́т, Ку́рочкина здесь не́т.**
   (Нина, Коля, ректор, вахтёр, профессор Орлов, Олег, Мария, Николай, Кирилл)

3. *Do you have a map of Europe?*
   No, I don't have a map of Europe.
   т: У вáс éсть кáрта Еврóпы?
   s: **Нéт, у меня́ нéт кáрты Еврóпы.**
   т: У вáс éсть áтлас?
   s: **Нéт, у меня́ нéт áтласа.**
   (словарь, клю́ч, перо́, портфéль, телефóн, тетрáдь, сестрá, брат)

4. *Is Kozlov here?*
   Kozlov is absent (or missing) today.
   т: Козлóв здéсь?
   s: **Козлóва сегóдня нéт.**
   т: Николáй здéсь?
   s: **Николáя сегóдня нéт.**
   (Кóля, Владимир, Ивáн, Óля, Хитров,
   Мария, Борис, Нина, Курóчкин)

5. *Is there a library there?*
   No, there's no library there.
   т: Тáм éсть библиотéка?
   s: **Нéт, тáм нéт библиотéки.**
   т: Тáм éсть пóчта?
   s: **Нéт, тáм нéт пóчты.**
   (завóд, университéт, общежитие, зал,
   шкóла, телефóн, магазин, аудитóрия,
   клуб, киóск, лаборатóрия)

DISCUSSION

Нéт means both *no* (as the opposite of **дá**) and *there is* (or *are*) *no* or *there isn't* (or *aren't*) *any.* Historically it comes from a combination of **не** plus **éсть.**

When **нéт** is used in constructions with the genitive it focuses on the lack or absence of the subject. It differs from constructions using the nominative plus **не,** where the focus is not on the absence but on some other element of the sentence.

| *Compare* | **Егó** здéсь **нéт.** | He's not here (i.e., he's missing *or* absent). |
| *with* | **Óн не** здéсь, а в гóроде. | He's not here; he's in town. |

The genitive case in past tense нé было constructions

MODELS

Когó тáм **нé было?**	*Who wasn't* there (i.e., who was missing)?
— Тáм нé было Козлóва.	Kozlov wasn't there.
_____ Николáя.	Nikolay _____.
_____ Кóли.	Kolya _____.
_____ Марúи.	Maria _____.
_____ Нины.	Nina _____.
_____ Óли.	Olya _____.

Егó тáм нé было?	Wasn't he there?
— Нéт, нé было.	No, he wasn't.
Её тáм нé было?	Wasn't she there?
— Нéт, нé было.	No, she wasn't.

Чегó тáм нé было?	What was missing? *or* What wasn't there?
— Тáм нé было борщá.	There wasn't any borsch.
_____ чáя.	_____ tea.
_____ хлéба.	_____ bread.
_____ молокá.	_____ milk.

— Та́м не́ было ры́бы.	There wasn't any fish.
_____ ка́ши.	_____ kasha.
_____ селёдки.	_____ herring.
У меня́ не́ было карандаша́.	I didn't have a pencil.
_____ а́тласа.	_____ an atlas.
_____ словаря́.	_____ a dictionary.
_____ портфе́ля.	_____ a briefcase.
_____ пера́.	_____ a pen.
_____ сочине́ния.	_____ a composition.
_____ ка́рты Евро́пы.	_____ a map of Europe.
_____ тетра́ди.	_____ a notebook.
_____ кни́ги.	_____ a book.

REPETITION DRILL

Repeat the above models after your instructor (or the tape), noting that for the past tense **не́ было** corresponds to **не́т** of the present and that here too the subject is in the genitive case. **Не́ было** is pronounced with a single stress which falls on **не́**: [n̡ébi̯lə].

■ REPETITION-STRUCTURE REPLACEMENT DRILLS

1. *There's no fish.*
   There was no fish.
   т: Ры́бы не́т.
   s: **Ры́бы не́ было.**
   т: Авто́буса не́т.
   s: **Авто́буса не́ было.**
   (материала, очереди, портфеля, словаря, карты Китая, коробки, работы, борща, собрания)

2. *We don't have [any] work.*
   We didn't have [any] work.
   т: У на́с не́т рабо́ты.
   s: **У на́с не́ было рабо́ты.**
   т: У на́с не́т клу́ба.
   s: **У на́с не́ было клу́ба.**
   (собрания, учителя, карты СССР, телефона, библиотеки, аудитории, экзамена, урока, лекции)

■ QUESTION-ANSWER DRILLS

1. *Was the custodian there?*
   No, he wasn't.
   т: Вахтёр та́м бы́л?
   s: **Не́т, его́ не́ было.**
   т: Его́ жена́ та́м была́?
   s: **Не́т, её не́ было.**
   (Коля и Галя, ваш муж, её брат, она, он, они, продавщица, наш студент)

2. *Did you have a meeting?*
   No, we didn't have a meeting.
   т: У ва́с бы́ло собра́ние?
   s: **Не́т, у на́с не́ было собра́ния.**
   т: У ва́с бы́л уро́к пе́ния?
   s: **Не́т, у на́с не́ было уро́ка пе́ния.**
   (работа, лекция, история, экзамен, ключ, атлас, сочинение)

3. *Was there borsch?*
   No, there wasn't.
   т: Бо́рщ бы́л?
   s: **Не́т, не́ было.**
   т: Ры́ба была́?
   s: **Не́т, не́ было.**
   (экзамен, каша, борщ, селёдка, кофе, обед, урок пения, хлеб, очередь, звонок, собрание)

Kozlov wasn't there.
Who wasn't there?
T: Козло́ва та́м не́ было.
S: **Кого́ та́м не́ было?**
T: А́тласа та́м не́ было.
S: **Чего́ та́м не́ было?**

(очереди, Коли, портфеля, Николая, киоска, Владимира, карты Китая, Ни́ны)

■ STRUCTURE REPLACEMENT DRILLS

1. *There was fish on the table.*
   There wasn't any fish on the table.
   T: На столе́ была́ ры́ба.
   S: **На столе́ не́ было ры́бы.**
   T: На столе́ бы́л обе́д.
   S: **На столе́ не́ было обе́да.**

   (чай, каша, молоко, подарок, сочинение, селёдка, хлеб, словарь, ручка,
   атлас, платье)

3. *I had a dictionary.*
   I didn't have a dictionary.
   T: У меня́ бы́л слова́рь.
   S: **У меня́ не́ было словаря́.**
   T: У меня́ была́ кни́га.
   S: **У меня́ не́ было кни́ги.**

   (урок, пение, география, лекция, экзамен, история, урок физики, литература)

2. *We had a meeting yesterday.*
   We didn't have a meeting yesterday.
   T: У на́с вчера́ бы́ло собра́ние.
   S: **У на́с вчера́ не́ было собра́ния.**
   T: У на́с вчера́ бы́л экза́мен.
   S: **У на́с вчера́ не́ было экза́мена.**

   (химия, математика, концерт, физика,
   урок пения, лекция, история)

■ PROGRESSIVE SUBSTITUTION DRILLS

1. *I have a pencil.*
   T: У меня́ е́сть каранда́ш.
   S: **У меня́ е́сть каранда́ш.**
   T: _____ (не́т) _____.
   S: **У меня́ не́т карандаша́.**
   _____ (е́сть) _____.
   _____ (не́ было) ____.
   _____ (е́сть) _____.
   (У тебя́) _____.
   _____ (тетрадь).
   _____ (не́т) _____.
   _____ (е́сть) _____.
   _____ (не́ было) ____.
   _____ (е́сть) _____.

2. *He has a briefcase.*

т: У него́ е́сть портфе́ль.
s: **У него́ е́сть портфе́ль.**
т: _____ (не́т) _____.
s: **У него́ не́т портфе́ля.**
_____ (не́ было) _____.
_____ (не́т) _____.
_____ (е́сть) _____.
_____ (не́ было) _____.
_____ (е́сть) _____.
(У неё) _____.
_____ (ка́рта).

У неё е́сть ка́рта.
_____ (не́т) _____.
_____ (е́сть) _____.
_____ (не́ было) _____.
_____ (е́сть) _____.
(Та́м) _____.
_____ (две́рь).
_____ (не́т) _____.
_____ (е́сть) _____.
_____ (не́ было) _____.
_____ (е́сть) _____.

DISCUSSION

Не́т of the present tense is replaced in the past tense by **не́ было** in constructions focusing on the absence of a thing or person. The noun or pronoun indicating the missing thing or person is in the genitive case.

However, the nominative may be used for the subject (together with **не** plus **бы́л, была́, бы́ло,** or **бы́ли**) if the focus is not on the absence itself, but on some other element of the sentence.

Compare	Ни́на давно́ не была́ в клу́бе.	Nina hasn't been at the club in a long time.
with	Ни́ны не́ было в клу́бе.	Nina wasn't at the club.
Compare	Ива́н бы́л не на ле́кциях, а на собра́нии.	Ivan wasn't at lectures; he was at the meeting.
with	Ива́на не́ было на собра́нии.	Ivan wasn't at the meeting.

ЧТЕ́НИЕ И ПИСЬМО́

Вчера я забыл в университете свой портфель. А в портфеле были ключи. Я думал, что наша уборщица может открыть двери, но она тоже забыла ключи. Я - профессор, но уборщица! Как она забыла?!

- Кто там? Мария Петровна? - Нет, это Нина Ивановна. - А, давно вас не видела. Заходите, пожалуйста! - Спасибо. А где ваша сестра? На службе? - Нет, она в городе.

– Ты куда? – В общежитие, а ты? Я тоже. Ты не знаешь, вчера было собрание? – Да, было, но я там не был. – А где ты был? – На концерте.

– Оля, ты готова? – Нет ещё. Где моя ручка? – Вот она. Смотри, уже почти девять! Пора идти! – Ну, хорошо, хорошо, я уже готова. До свидания, мама!

– Здравствуйте, Иван Иванович! – А, Мария Петровна! Здравствуйте! – Как ваша жена? Всё ещё больна? – Нет, уже здорова. Вчера была на службе. – Рада это слышать. Ну, пока! Я спешу на автобус.

– Нина, о чём вы думаете? – Об экзамене. – Зачем о нём думать? Он уже прошёл. – Да, но я, кажется, не очень хорошо написала. – Нет, я слышал, что вы отлично написали. – Вот как! Я очень рада.

– Алло! Коля? Нет, это Лев. – Здравствуйте, Лев! Ну, как Коля? Здоров? – Да, он уже вполне здоров. – Я очень рад это слышать. Он где теперь? – Кажется, в библиотеке. – Кстати, у вас вчера был экзамен? – Да. Мы писали о народах СССР. – Это интересно. Вы уже знаете результаты? – Нет ещё.

— Кто у телефона? — Иван Иванович Орлов. — А, здравствуйте, Иван Иванович. Как прошёл экзамен? — Очень хорошо. Студенты отлично написали. — Рад это слышать. Я вижу, что наши студенты молодцы.

— О ком вы говорите, о Гранте? — Нет, о Козлове. Он опять отлично написал. — Я слышал, что он молодец. — Да. Знаете о чём он написал? — Нет, не знаю. О чём? — О грузинах и их истории. — Вот как! Это интересно. Могу ли я посмотреть? — Конечно. Вот его работа.

— Дверь открыта? — Нет. — А где твой ключ? — В портфеле. — А портфель где? — В университете. — Ну хорошо, тогда возьми мой ключ. — Спасибо.

— У меня завтра экзамен. Где мой словарь? — На столе. — Его тут нет. — Тогда, может быть, он на полке. — Не вижу. А, вот он, на стуле.

PREPARATION FOR CONVERSATION   Замо́лвите за меня́ слове́чко!

за меня́	for me, in my behalf
слове́чко (var of сло́во)	word
замо́лвить слове́чко	to put in a good word
Замо́лвите за меня́ слове́чко!	Put in a good word for me!
с *or* со (*plus* gen)	from, off, since
с рабо́ты	from work
Вы́ с рабо́ты идёте?	Are you coming from work?
Здра́вствуйте, Ни́на! С рабо́ты идёте?	Hello, Nina! Are you coming from work?
Не́т, я́ в горсове́те была́.	No, I've been to the gorsovet.
ко́мната	room
Не́т, я́ в горсове́те была́, насчёт ко́мнаты.	No, I've been to the gorsovet about a room.
како́й	what, which
Како́й ко́мнаты?	What room?
В чём де́ло?	What's the matter?
заявле́ние	application
заявле́ние на ко́мнату	application for a room
пода́ть (pfv irreg)	to give, serve, submit
пода́ть заявле́ние	to submit an application
Я́ подала́ заявле́ние на ко́мнату.	I submitted an application for a room.
жда́ть (ipfv I)	to wait
на́до	it's necessary, one has to
На́до та́к до́лго жда́ть.	You have to wait so long.
Я́ подала́ заявле́ние на ко́мнату, но на́до та́к до́лго жда́ть.	I submitted an application for a room, but you have to wait so long.
во́т что́!	so that's it!
А́х, во́т что́!	Oh, so that's it!
дру́г (nom pl друзья́)	friend
хоро́ший дру́г	good friend

Та́м рабо́тает мо́й хоро́ший дру́г Алексе́ев.

ведь [yiţ] (unstressed)

Зна́ете, ведь та́м рабо́тает мо́й хоро́ший дру́г Алексе́ев.

Что́ вы́ говори́те!

Ива́н Ива́нович, замо́лвите за меня́ слове́чко!

ми́лый

Ива́н Ива́нович, ми́лый, замо́лвите за меня́ слове́чко!

предложи́ть (pfv II)
ва́м

Я хоте́л ва́м э́то предложи́ть.

как ра́з

Я как ра́з хоте́л ва́м э́то предложи́ть.

большо́е спаси́бо

Большо́е ва́м спаси́бо!

что́ та́м!

Ну́ что́ та́м!

ста́рый
ста́рые друзья́

Мы́ ведь ста́рые друзья́.

My good friend Alexeev works there.

after all, the thing is, as a matter of fact,

You know, as a matter of fact, my good friend Alexeev works there.

You don't say!

Ivan Ivanovich, put in a good word for me!

kind, dear, nice

My dear Ivan Ivanovich, put in a good word for me!

to suggest, propose
to you, for you

I wanted to suggest that to you.

just, the very thing

That's the very thing I wanted to suggest to you.

thanks very much, thanks a lot

Thank you very much!

what for!

Whatever for!

old
old friends

We're old friends after all.

SUPPLEMENT

сло́во (pl слова́)

Э́то ру́сское сло́во?

рестора́н

Вы́ идёте в рестора́н?

теа́тр
Большо́й теа́тр

Вы́ идёте в Большо́й теа́тр?

кварти́ра

У ва́с е́сть кварти́ра?

до́м

Э́то ва́ш до́м?

па́рк

Куда́ вы́ идёте? — В па́рк.

word

Is that a Russian word?

restaurant

Are you going to a restaurant?

theater
the Bolshoi Theater

Are you going to the Bolshoi Theater?

apartment

Do you have an apartment?

house, building

Is that your house? or Is that the building where you live?

park

Where are you going? To the park.

Замо́лвите за меня́ слове́чко!

И.И. — Ива́н Ива́нович
Н. — Ни́на

И. И.	1	Здра́вствуйте, Ни́на!	zdrắstujţi ņínə ↓
		С рабо́ты идёте?	srabŏti iḍóţi ↓
Н.	2	Не́т,	ņḗt ↓
		я́ в горсове́те была́,	já vgorsaɣḗţi bilá ↓
		насчёт ко́мнаты.	naščót kŏmnəti ↓
И. И.	3	Како́й ко́мнаты?	kakŏj kómnəti ↓
		В чём де́ло?	fčóm ḍélə ↓
Н.	4	Я́ подала́ заявле́ние	já pədalá zəjivļéņjə
		на ко́мнату,	nakŏmnətu ↓
		но́ на́до та́к до́лго	nó nádə tắg dólgə
		жда́ть!¹	ždáţ ↓
И. И.	5	А́х, во́т что!	áx vŏt štó ↓
		Зна́ете,	znắjiţi ↓
		ведь та́м рабо́тает	ɣiţ tám rabótəjit
		мо́й хоро́ший дру́г Алексе́ев.	mój xaróšij drúk aḷikşḗjif ↓
Н.	6	Что́ вы́ говори́те!	štó ví gəvaŗíţi ↓
		Ива́н Ива́нович,	iván iváṇich ↓
		ми́лый,	ṃĩlij ↓
		замо́лвите за меня́ слове́чко!	zamŏlɣiţi zəṃiņá slaɣéčkə ↓
И. И.	7	Я́ как ра́з хоте́л	já kak rás xaţél
		ва́м э́то предложи́ть.	vám étə pŗidlažĩţ ↓
Н.	8	Большо́е ва́м спаси́бо!	baḷšŏjə vám spaşíbə ↓
И. И.	9	Ну́ что́ та́м!	nú štŏ tám ↓
		Мы́ ведь ста́рые друзья́!	mí ɣiţ stáriji druʐjá ↓

NOTES

¹ In order to obtain a room in a government-owned house, it is necessary to apply to the regional soviet or, in this instance, to the *city council* горсове́т. Waiting lists are very long since housing is one of the major problems in the large cities of the U.S.S.R.

PREPARATION FOR CONVERSATION   **В горсове́те**

секрета́рь (m)	secretary
О́н на́ш секрета́рь.	He's our secretary.
Она́ на́ш секрета́рь.	She's our secretary.
у себя́	in one's room, in one's office

товáрищ	comrade, friend, colleague
Товáрищ Алексéев у себя́?	Is comrade Alexeev in?
Скажи́те, товáрищ Алексéев у себя́?	Tell [me], is comrade Alexeev in?
Москвá	Moscow
Нéт, óн сейчáс в Москвé.	No, he's in Moscow at the moment.
А Вóлков здéсь?	Well, is Volkov here?
проходи́ть (II) (pfv пройти́)	to pass, go by
Дá, проходи́те пожáлуйста!	Yes, go on in, please!
Á, привéт! Давнó тебя́ не ви́дел!	Hi! I haven't seen you in a long time!
кáк живёшь [káɡ žɨɣóš]	how are you? how's it going?
Здрáвствуй, кáк живёшь?	Hello, how are you?
Ничегó.	All right.
прóсьба [prózbə]	request, favor
мáленькая	small, little
У меня́ мáленькая прóсьба.	I have a small favor [to ask].
получи́ть (pfv II)	to obtain, receive, get
дéвушка	young lady, girl (in late teens)
однá дéвушка	a certain young lady
Тýт однá дéвушка кóмнаты получи́ть не мóжет.	There's a certain young lady who can't get a room.
никáк	in no way, by no means, not in any way
Тýт однá дéвушка никáк кóмнаты получи́ть не мóжет.	There's a certain young lady who simply can't get a room.
Дá? Ктó онá? Гдé рабóтает?	Is that so? Who is she? Where does she work?
студéнтка–заóчница	correspondence-school student
фáбрика	factory
Онá студéнтка-заóчница, рабóтает на фáбрике.	She's a correspondence-school student and works at a factory.
Агá, на фáбрике. Э́то хорошó.	Ahhh, at a factory. That's good.
сдéлать (pfv I)	to do, get done
чтó-нибудь	something, anything
Мы́ чтó-нибудь сдéлаем.	We'll do something [about it].
Вóт спаси́бо!	Well, thanks.

SUPPLEMENT

жи́ть (ipfv I)	to live
Гдé вы́ живёте?	Where do you live?
— Я́ живý прóтив пáрка.	I live across from the park.
откýда	from where
Откýда вы́ идёте? — С рабóты.	Where are you coming from? From work.
из *or* изо (*plus* gen)	from, out of
Откýда вы́ идёте? — Из гóрода.	Where are you coming from? From town.
от *or* ото (*plus* gen)	from

Я получи́л письмо́ от бра́та.	I received a letter from my brother.
до *(plus* gen)	up to, until, before
Óн звони́л до рабо́ты.	He called (*or* telephoned) before work.
о́коло *(plus* gen)	near, by, about
Я живу́ о́коло па́рка.	I live near the park.
без *or* безо *(plus* gen)	without
Я без бра́та не пойду́.	I won't go without my brother.
для *(plus* gen)	for
Вы́ э́то сде́лаете для меня́?	Will you do that for me?

В горсове́те

И.И. — Ива́н Ива́нович
С. — Секрета́рь (Ири́на Петро́вна)
В. — Во́лков (Пётр Ники́тич)

И.И.	1	Здра́вствуйте,	zdrắstujţi |
		Ири́на Петро́вна!	iŗínə ŗitrŏ̃vnə ↓
		Скажи́те,	skaži̇̌ţi ↓
		това́рищ Алексе́ев у себя́?[1]	taváŗišč aļikşéjif uşiḅắ ↑
С.	2	Нéт,	ŋĕ̃t ↓
		óн сейча́с в Москве́.	ón şičás vmaskɣĕ̃ ↓
И.И.	3	А Во́лков здéсь?	a vólkəv zḍĕ̃ş ↑
С.	4	Дá,	dắ ↓
		проходи́те, пожа́луйста!	prəxaḍíţi pažáləstə ↓
И.И.	5	Á,	ắ ↓
		приве́т, Во́лков!	pŗiɣĕ̃t vólkəf ↓
		Давно́ тебя́ не ви́дел.	davnŏ̃ ţiḅá ŋiɣíḍil ↓
В.	6	Здра́вствуй,	zdrắstuj ↓
		ка́к живёшь?	kág žiɣŏ̃š ↓
И.И.	7	Ничего́.	ŋičivŏ̃ ↓
		У меня́ ма́ленькая про́сьба.	uṃiŋá máļiŋkəjə prŏ̃ʑbə ↓
		Ту́т одна́ де́вушка	tút adná ḍĕ̃vuškə |
		ко́мнаты получи́ть не мо́жет.	kŏ̃mnəti pəlučíţ ŋimóžit ↓
В.	8	Дá?	dắ ↑
		Кто́ она́?	ktŏ̃ aná ↓
		Где́ рабо́тает?	gḍé rabŏ̃təjit ↓

И.И.	9	Она́ студе́нтка-зао́чница, рабо́тает на фа́брике.	aná stuḍéntkə zaóčṇicə ↓ rabótəjit nafãbṛiḳi ↓
В.	10	Ага́, на фа́брике. Э́то хорошо́. Мы́ что́-нибудь сде́лаем.²	ahã̌ ↓ nafãbṛiḳi ↓ étə xərašő ↓ mí štóṇibuḍ zḍéləjim ↓
И.И.	11	Во́т спаси́бо.	võt spaşíbə ↓

NOTES

¹ Here **това́рищ** means *comrade* in the political sense, i.e., a party member. It is very common in official situations, however, for Soviet citizens to use the word (especially in the plural) without any necessary implication that persons so addressed are party members. A foreigner should never use **това́рищ** in addressing a Soviet citizen.

Това́рищ is also used in the nonpolitical sense, meaning *comrade* or *friend*, but it implies a more casual relationship than **дру́г** *friend*. One may have many **това́рищи,** but few **друзья́.**

Both **дру́г** and **това́рищ,** like **профе́ссор** and **секрета́рь,** are grammatically masculine, but may refer to both men and women:

Óн мо́й хоро́ший дру́г.	He's my good friend.
Она́ мо́й хоро́ший дру́г.	She's my good friend.
Това́рищ Петро́в бы́л здесь.	Comrade Petrov was here.
Това́рищ Петро́ва была́ здесь.	Comrade Petrov (f) was here.

² Students who work at factories and take correspondence courses have a priority in obtaining lodgings. The Soviet **студе́нт-зао́чник** or **студе́нтка-зао́чница** differs somewhat from the American correspondence-school student in that the latter does his entire work through correspondence. The Soviet correspondence-school student must meet at least once or twice a year for laboratory sessions, summary lectures, consultations on future work, and examinations.

Basic sentence patterns

1. Вы́ идёте с рабо́ты?
   — Не́т, с конце́рта.
   — Не́т, с обе́да.
   — Не́т, с экза́мена.
   — Не́т, с уро́ка пе́ния.
   — Не́т, с собра́ния.
   — Не́т, с по́чты.
   — Не́т, с ле́кции.

Are you coming from work?
No, from a concert.
No, from a dinner.
No, from an exam.
No, from a singing lesson.
No, from a meeting.
No, from the post office.
No, from a lecture.

2. Вы́ идёте из клу́ба?
   — Не́т, из рестора́на.
   — Не́т, из теа́тра.
   — Не́т, из па́рка.
   — Не́т, из университе́та.

Are you coming from the club?
No, from the restaurant.
No, from the theater.
No, from the park.
No, from the university.

— Нét, из ГУ́Ма.

— Нét, из горсовéта.

— Нét, из общежи́тия.

— Нét, из библиотéки.

— Нét, из лаборатóрии.

No, from GUM.

No, from the gorsovet.

No, from the dormitory.

No, from the library.

No, from the laboratory.

3. Я́ егó ви́дел до урóка.

_____ концéрта.

_____ обéда.

_____ чáя.

_____ экзáмена.

_____ собрáния.

_____ лéкции.

_____ рабóты.

_____ слýжбы.

I saw him before the lesson.

_____ the concert.

_____ dinner (*or* noon).[1]

_____ tea.[2]

_____ the exam.

_____ the meeting.

_____ the lecture.

_____ work.

_____ work.

4. Пóсле урóка óн пошёл домóй.

_____ концéрта _____.

_____ собрáния _____.

_____ чáя _____.

_____ экзáмена _____.

After the lesson he went home.

_____ the concert _____.

_____ the meeting _____.

_____ the tea _____.

_____ the exam _____.

5. Срáзу пóсле обéда мы́ пошли́ домóй.

_____ собрáния _____.

_____ лéкции _____.

_____ рабóты _____.

_____ шкóлы _____.

Right after the dinner we went home.

_____ the meeting _____.

_____ the lecture _____.

_____ work _____.

_____ school _____.

6. Э́то для вáс.

_____ тебя́.

_____ нáс.

_____ негó.

_____ неё.

_____ ни́х.

This is for you.

_____ you.

_____ us.

_____ him.

_____ her.

_____ them.

7. Мы́ э́то сдéлаем для Ивáна.

_____ Ни́ны.

_____ профéссора Орлóва.

_____ учи́теля.

_____ учи́тельницы.

We'll do it for Ivan.

_____ Nina.

_____ Professor Orlov.

_____ the teacher.

_____ the teacher.

8. Они́ без вáс не пойдýт.

_____ нáс _____.

_____ тебя́ _____.

_____ меня́ _____.

_____ негó _____.

They won't go without you.

_____ us.

_____ you.

_____ me.

_____ him.

9. Мы́ без неё не пойдём.

_____ Ивáна _____.

_____ Ири́ны _____.

_____ Кóли _____.

We won't go without her.

_____ Ivan.

_____ Irina.

_____ Kolya.

---

[1] **Обéд** is frequently used in the sense *noon*. Thus **до обéда** may mean both *before dinner* and *before noon*. Similarly, **пóсле обéда** means both *after dinner* and *afternoon*, as well as *in the afternoon*.

[2] **Чáй** is often used to refer to breakfast or morning tea.

10. Где вы́ бы́ли?	Where have you been?
— У профе́ссора Орло́ва.	To see Professor Orlov.
— У дру́га.	To see a friend.
— У Ива́на.	To see Ivan.
— У Петра́.	To see Pyotr.
11. Где вы́ обе́дали?	Where did you eat dinner?
— У Никола́я.	At Nikolay's.
— У бра́та.	At my brother's.
— У сестры́.	At my sister's.
— У Ни́ны.	At Nina's.
— У Га́ли.	At Galya's.
— У Мари́и Ива́новны.	At Maria Ivanovna's.
12. Отку́да вы́?	Where are you from?
— Из Ленингра́да.	From Leningrad.
— Из Кита́я.	From China.
— Из Москвы́.	From Moscow.
— Из Евро́пы.	From Europe.
— Из Аме́рики.	From America.
— Из СССР.	From the U.S.S.R.
13. Отку́да вы́ идёте?	Where are you coming from?
— Из ГУ́Ма.	From GUM.
— Из го́рода.	From town.
— Из магази́на на углу́.	From the store on the corner.
— Из библиоте́ки.	From the library.
— С рабо́ты.	From work.
— С по́чты.	From the post office.
— С фа́брики.	From the factory.
— С заво́да.	From the plant.
14. Отку́да вы́ э́то получи́ли?	Where did you get that?
— Из клу́ба.	From the club.
— Из библиоте́ки.	From the library.
— Из лаборато́рии.	From the laboratory.
— С фа́брики.	From the factory.
— С заво́да.	From the plant.
15. От кого́ вы́ э́то получи́ли?	From whom did you get that?
— От профе́ссора Орло́ва.	From Professor Orlov.
— От америка́нца.	From an American.
— От Влади́мира.	From Vladimir.
— От Петра́.	From Pyotr.
— От Евге́ния.	From Evgeny.
16. От кого́ вы́ э́то слы́шали?	From whom did you hear that?
— От секретаря́.	From the secretary.
— От учи́теля.	From the teacher.
— От сестры́.	From my sister.
— От Ири́ны.	From Irina.
— От Мари́и Ива́новны.	From Maria Ivanovna.

17. Где́ ва́ш до́м?
— О́коло па́рка.
— О́коло университе́та.
— О́коло теа́тра.
— О́коло рестора́на.
— О́коло общежи́тия.
— О́коло по́чты.
— О́коло фа́брики.
— О́коло шко́лы.
— О́коло библиоте́ки.

Where's your house?
Near the park.
Near the university.
Near the theater.
Near the restaurant.
Near the dormitory.
Near the post office.
Near the factory.
Near the school.
Near the library.

18. Где́ библиоте́ка? — Про́тив теа́тра.
Где́ общежи́тие? — Про́тив па́рка.
Где́ кио́ск? — Про́тив рестора́на.

Где́ теа́тр? — Про́тив университе́та.

Где́ рестора́н? — Про́тив ГУ́Ма.
Где́ клу́б? — Про́тив библиоте́ки.
Где́ ва́ш до́м? — Про́тив шко́лы.
Где́ магази́н? — Про́тив по́чты.
Где́ большо́й за́л? — Про́тив лаборато́рии.
Где́ шко́ла? — Про́тив фа́брики.
Где́ лаборато́рия? — Про́тив аудито́рии.

Where's the library? Across from the theater.
Where's the dorm? Across from the park.
Where's the newsstand? Across from the restaurant.
Where's the theater? Across from the university.
Where's the restaurant? Across from GUM.
Where's the club? Across from the library.
Where's your house? Across from the school.
Where's the store? Across from the post office.
Where's the large hall? Across from the laboratory.
Where's the school? Across from the factory.
Where's the laboratory? Across from the auditorium.

19. Вы́ спра́шивали насчёт обе́да?
_____ борща́?
_____ ча́я?
_____ молока́?
_____ ры́бы?
_____ ка́ши?
_____ селёдки?
_____ во́дки?

Did you ask about dinner?
_____ borsch?
_____ tea?
_____ milk?
_____ fish?
_____ kasha?
_____ herring?
_____ vodka?

20. А ка́к насчёт собра́ния?
_____ сочине́ния?
_____ ка́рты?
_____ литерату́ры?
_____ геогра́фии?
_____ а́тласа?
_____ портфе́ля?

And how about the meeting?
_____ the composition?
_____ a map?
_____ literature?
_____ geography?
_____ an atlas?
_____ a briefcase?

21. Вы́ насчёт уро́ка?
_____ экза́мена?
_____ собра́ния?
_____ ко́мнаты?
_____ кварти́ры?
_____ рабо́ты?

Are you here about the lesson?
_____ the exam?
_____ the meeting?
_____ the room?
_____ the apartment?
_____ the work?

Pronunciation practice: hard consonants [k], [g], and [x] and their soft counterparts [ķ], [ğ], and [x̧].

Hard consonants [k], [g], and [x] are regularly replaced by their soft counterparts [ķ], [ğ], and [x̧] before vowels [e] and [i].

A. Hard [k] and soft counterpart [ķ]
    Usual Cyrillic spelling к; sometimes г.

    Note the pronunciation of hard [k] in the following:

[maskvá]	Москвá	Moscow
[kudá]	кудá	where (to)
[urók]	урóк	lesson
[skaží]	скажú	tell me

    and compare it with soft [ķ]:

[γílķi]	вúлки	forks
[fkarópķi]	в корóбке	in the box
[uróķi]	урóки	lessons
[ņiķítə]	Никúта	Nikita
[carápķin]	Царáпкин	Tsarapkin

    Russian hard [k] is made in much the same way as English *k* except that there is not the slight h-like puff of breath typical of the English *k*.

> Sound Drill: Practice the Russian examples illustrating hard [k] and soft [ķ], imitating your instructor (or the tape) as accurately as you can. Notice that hard [k] occurs before [o], [a], [u], and [ə], whereas soft [k] occurs before [e] and [i]. At the end of a word, only hard [k] occurs—never soft [ķ].

B. Hard [g] and soft counterpart [ğ]
    Usual Cyrillic spelling г; sometimes к.

    Note the pronunciation of hard [g] in the following:

[gəvaŗát]	говоря́т	they say
[vgúṃi]	в ГУ́Ме	at GUM

    and compare it with soft [ğ]:

[jivgéņij]	Евгéний	Evgeny
[ğít]	гид	guide

    Russian hard [g] and soft [ğ] are made with the vocal organs in the same position as for hard [k] and soft [ķ], but they are voiced.

> Sound Drill: Practice the Russian examples illustrating hard [g] and soft [g̣], imitating your instructor (or the tape) as accurately as you can. Notice that hard [g] occurs before [o], [a], [u], and [ə], whereas soft [g̣] occurs before [e] and [i].

C. Hard [x] and soft counterpart [x̣]
Usual Cyrillic spelling **x**; rarely **г**.

Note the pronunciation of hard [x] in the following:

[xərašó]	хорошо́	good
[zəxaḍíṭi]	заходи́те	come in

and compare it with soft [x̣]:

[x̣itróf]	Хитро́в	Khitrov
[sx̣émə]	схе́ма	scheme

The sound [x] does not occur in English (though it does appear in German a*ch*, Ba*ch*, and Bu*ch*, or in Spanish mu*j*er and hi*j*o). It is formed in the same part of the mouth as [k] and [g]; but, instead of completely closing off the air stream, the back of the tongue merely approaches the back part of the roof of the mouth so that the air stream vibrates in the constricted passage thus produced. The soft counterpart [x̣] is produced slightly further forward in the mouth.

> Sound Drill: Practice the Russian examples illustrating hard [x] and soft [x̣], imitating your instructor (or the tape) as accurately as you can. Notice that hard [x] occurs before [o], [a], [u], and [ə], whereas soft [x̣] occurs before [e] and [i]. At the end of a word, only hard [x] occurs—never soft [x̣].

Intonation practice: emphatic statements with rising-falling intonation curve

Emphatic statements with rising-falling contours are those in which the major stress is not in the final position, but is shifted forward to a medial position in the sentences. The intonation contour is similar to that of questions without question words which have their major stress in the medial position, except that the entire contour is on a lower level and the drop after the major stress is sharper.

EMPHATIC INTONATION

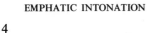

Óн не́ был на слу́жбе!
Они́ бы́ли на заво́де.
Она́ доста́ла материа́л.
У на́с е́сть ча́й.

QUESTION INTONATION

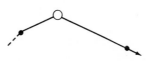

Óн не́ был на слу́жбе?
Они́ бы́ли на заво́де?
Она́ доста́ла материа́л?
У на́с е́сть ча́й?

A. Listen to the tape and practice the intonation in the following emphatic statements.

Она́	**купи́ла**	материа́л!
Ива́н	**опя́ть**	ту́т!
Вчера́	**бы́ло**	собра́ние!
Мари́я	**не была́**	в ГУ́Ме!
Оле́г	**давно́**	бо́лен!

B. Now practice these same sentences as questions. Remember that the rising-falling contour is neutral for questions and does not imply any special emphasis.

Она́	купи́ла материа́л?
Ива́н	опя́ть ту́т?
Вчера́	бы́ло собра́ние?
Мари́я не была́	в ГУ́Ме?
Оле́г	давно́ бо́лен?

C. Using the same basic sentences, practice them as neutral statements now. Note that here the intonation curve has a falling contour and that the primary stress is on the last stressed syllable.

Она́	купи́ла матери́ал.
Ива́н	опя́ть ту́т.
Вчера́	бы́ло собра́ние.
Мари́я не была́	в ГУ́Ме.
Оле́г	давно́ бо́лен.

D. Practice the following set of longer statements with neutral intonation. Again the contour is falling and the primary stress is on the last stressed syllable of the utterance.

Бори́с	мо́жет	э́то принести́.
Никола́й	бы́л	вчера́ в библиоте́ке.
Она́	смо́жет	откры́ть две́ри.
Оле́г	хоте́л	принести́ слова́рь.
Козло́в	бы́л	вчера́ на заня́тиях.
Она́	пойдёт	за́втра в клу́б.

E. Practice the same sentences, changing them to emphatic statements with a rising-falling contour and with the primary stress shifted to the second element.

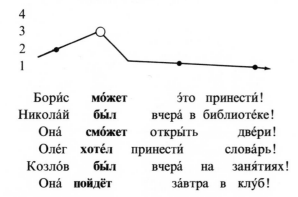

Бори́с	**мо́жет**	э́то принести́!
Никола́й	**бы́л**	вчера́ в библиоте́ке!
Она́	**смо́жет**	откры́ть две́ри!
Оле́г	**хоте́л**	принести́ слова́рь!
Козло́в	**бы́л**	вчера́ на заня́тиях!
Она́	**пойдёт**	за́втра в клу́б!

F. Now practice the same sentences, changing them to *questions*. Again the contour is rising-falling and the primary stress is on the second element. Note the sharper peak and drop that is typical of the question, as contrasted with the emphatic statements.

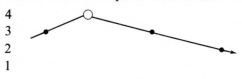

Бори́с	мо́жет	э́то принести́?
Никола́й	бы́л	вчера́ в библиоте́ке?
Она́	смо́жет	откры́ть две́ри?
Оле́г	хоте́л	принести́ слова́рь?
Козло́в	бы́л	вчера́ на заня́тиях?
Она́	пойдёт	за́втра в клу́б?

STRUCTURE AND DRILLS

The preposition у: further uses with the genitive case

MODELS

Она́ стоя́ла у две́ри.	She was standing at (*or* by) the door.
_____ у окна́.	_____ at (*or* by) the window.
_____ у стола́.	_____ at (*or* by) the table.
_____ у шка́фа.	_____ at (*or* by) the cupboard.
_____ у телефо́на.	_____ at (*or* by) the phone.
Я был у бра́та.	I was at my brother's place.
_____ у Оле́га.	_____ at Oleg's place.
_____ у Петра́.	_____ at Pyotr's _____.
_____ у профе́ссора Орло́ва.	_____ at Professor Orlov's _____.
_____ у дру́га.	_____ at a friend's _____.
_____ у Льва́.	_____ at Lev's _____.
_____ у Никола́я.	_____ at Nikolay's _____.
_____ у сестры́.	_____ at my sister's _____.
_____ у Мари́и Ива́новны.	_____ at Maria Ivanovna's _____
_____ у Га́ли.	_____ at Galya's _____.
_____ у Ко́ли.	_____ at Kolya's _____.
Он э́то доста́л у Козло́ва.	He got it from Kozlov.
_____ у учи́теля.	_____ from the teacher.
_____ у секретаря́.	_____ from the secretary.
_____ у Ири́ны.	_____ from Irina.
_____ у Мари́и.	_____ from Maria.
_____ у Га́ли.	_____ from Galya.
_____ у Коли.	_____ from Kolya.
У кого́ вы э́то узна́ли?	From whom did you find that out?
— У профе́ссора Орло́ва.	From Professor Orlov.
— У бра́та.	From my brother.
— У му́жа.	From my husband.
— У Петра́.	From Pyotr.
— У Евге́ния.	From Evgeny.
— У секретаря́.	From the secretary.
— У това́рища Алексе́ева.	From comrade Alexeev.
— У сестры́.	From my sister.
— У О́ли.	From Olya.
— У убо́рщицы.	From the cleaning woman.
— У жены́.	From my wife.
У кого́ вы спра́шивали?	Whom did you ask? *Or* Of whom did you inquire?
— У Кири́лла.	Kirill.
— У Влади́мира.	Vladimir.
— У Цара́пкина.	Tsarapkin.
— У Во́лкова.	Volkov.
— У Семёна Фили́пповича.	Semyon Filippovich.

— У учи́теля.	The teacher.
— У Никола́я.	Nikolay.
— У Ми́лы.	Mila.
— У Ма́ши.	Masha.
— У Мари́и Петро́вны.	Maria Petrovna.
— У продавщи́цы.	The saleslady.

Ка́к у ва́с прошёл экза́мен?	How did your exam go?
____ у Оле́га _____ ?	_____ Oleg's _____ ?
____ у него́ _____ ?	_____ his _____ ?
____ у Ни́ны _____ ?	_____ Nina's _____ ?
____ у неё _____ ?	_____ her _____ ?
____ у ни́х _____ ?	_____ their _____ ?
____ у Никола́я _____ ?	_____ Nikolay's __ ?

■ REPETITION-DRILL

Repeat the above models after your instructor or the tape until you are familiar with the various **y** constructions illustrated.

■ CUED SUBSTITUTION DRILLS

1. (window) *There was a girl standing at the window.*
    т: (окно́)   У окна́ стоя́ла де́вушка.
    s: **У окна́ стоя́ла де́вушка.**
    т: (две́рь)   (У) _____.
    s: **У две́ри стоя́ла де́вушка.**
    (полка, стол, шкаф, карта, телефон, окно, дверь)

2. (brother) *Yesterday he visited his brother.*
    т: (бра́т)   Вчера́ о́н бы́л у бра́та.
    s: **Вчера́ о́н бы́л у бра́та.**
    т: (сестра́) (Вчера́) _____.
    s: **Вчера́ о́н бы́л у сестры́.**
    (друг, Николай, Коля, Ирина, Мила, Мария Ивановна, учитель, товарищ Волков)

3. (Pyotr) *Have you already asked (or inquired of) Pyotr?*
    т: (Пётр)   Вы́ уже́ спра́шивали у Петра́?
    s: **Вы́ уже́ спра́шивали у Петра́?**
    т: (О́льга) (Вы́) _____?
    s: **Вы́ уже́ спра́шивали у О́льги?**
    (она, Владимир, они, Нина, Коля, он, Курочкин, Иван Иванович)

4. (you) *He left the briefcase at your place.*
    т: (вы́)   О́н забы́л у ва́с портфе́ль.
    s: **О́н забы́л у ва́с портфе́ль.**
    т: (они́) (О́н) _____.
    s: **О́н забы́л у ни́х портфе́ль.**
    (она, я, ты, Иван, Нина, её муж, Борис, Ирина)

■ SUBJECT REVERSAL DRILLS

1. *They're at Professor Orlov's.*
   Professor Orlov is at their place.
   т: Они́ у профе́ссора Орло́ва.
   s: **Профе́ссор Орло́в у ни́х.**
   т: Я́ у бра́та.
   s: **Бра́т у меня́.**
   Мы́ у Льва́ Ники́тича.
   О́н у Га́ли.
   Они́ у сестры́.
   Она́ у учи́теля.
   Я́ у сестры́.

2. *Kozlov was visiting Pyotr.*
   Pyotr was visiting Kozlov.
   т: Козло́в бы́л у Петра́.
   s: **Пётр бы́л у Козло́ва.**
   т: Козло́в бы́л у Льва́ Ники́тича.
   s: **Ле́в Ники́тич бы́л у Козло́ва.**
   Ко́ля бы́л у Га́ли.
   Бра́т бы́л у сестры́.
   Учи́тель бы́л у учи́тельницы.
   Мари́я была́ у профе́ссора.

1. *Did Irina get that?*
   Yes, and I [got it] from Irina.
   т: Это Ирина достала?
   s: **Да, а я у Ирины.**
   т: Это учитель достал?
   s: **Да, а я у учителя.**
   (брат, Козлов, учительница, ректор,
   Иван, её муж, продавщица, секретарь,
   Лев Никитич)

2. *Did Pyotr find that out?*
   Yes, and I [found out] from Pyotr.
   т: Это Пётр узнал?
   s: **Да, а я у Петра.**
   т: Это Николай узнал?
   s: **Да, а я у Николая.**
   (Мария, Владимир, её сестра, Семёнов,
   его жена, Коля, профессор Петров, Лев
   Никитич)

■ CUED QUESTION-ANSWER DRILL

   (teacher)   *Whom did you ask?*
                    The teacher.
   т: (учитель)   У кого вы спрашивали?
   s: **У учителя.**
   т: (учительница) У кого вы спрашивали?
   s: **У учительницы.**
   (американец, её муж, уборщица, Коля,
   профессор Петров, Ирина, Галя, Лев
   Никитич)

■ RESPONSE DRILL

Kolya's coming.
Wonder how his exam went.
т: Коля идёт.
s: **Интересно, как у него прошёл экзамен?**
т: Мария идёт.
s: **Интересно, как у неё прошёл экзамен?**
(Николай, Ирина и Оля, Галя, Иван
Иванович, Маша)

■ CUED QUESTION-ANSWER DRILLS

1. (Kolya) *Where's the briefcase?*
            On Kolya's desk.
   т: (Коля) Где портфель?
   s: **У Коли на столе.**
   т: (они) Где портфель?
   s: **У них на столе.**
   (я, ты, она, мы, вы, он, Галя, Николай,
   учительница, учитель)

2. (window) *Where was Nina standing?*
             At the window.
   т: (окно)   Где стояла Нина?
   s: **У окна.**
   т: (телефон) Где стояла Нина?
   s: **У телефона.**
   (дверь, шкаф, карта, полка, стол, окно)

DISCUSSION

The preposition **у** is always followed by the genitive case. Besides its use in *to have* constructions (e.g., **у меня есть**), it has several other functions.

1. In a purely spatial sense with inanimate nouns, it indicates close proximity.

   Он стоял **у окна.**   He was standing at (*or* by) the window.
   Подожди **у двери.**   Wait at (*or* by) the door.

2. With nouns and pronouns referring to people, it designates a place in terms of the person located there. Thus it functions like the French *chez* and may be translated *at the house* (or *office* or *place*) *of.* Forms of the verb **быть** plus **у** often correspond to the English concept *to visit*.

   Я оставил **у вас** портфель.   I left the briefcase at your place.
   Она была **у брата.**   She was at her brother's *or* She was visiting her
                                     brother.

3. Used with nouns and pronouns referring to people, and in conjunction with such verbs as **узна́ть, спра́шивать,** and **доста́ть, у** indicates the source of a thing.

У кого́ вы́ э́то доста́ли?	*From whom* did you get that?
— У Ири́ны.	*From Irina.*
У кого́ ты́ э́то узна́л?	*From whom* did you find that out?
— У Ко́ли.	*From Kolya.*
У кого́ вы́ спра́шивали?	*Whom* did you ask? or *Of whom* did you inquire?
— У секретаря́.	*The secretary.*

4. The use of **у** plus the genitive form of a noun or pronoun sometimes substitutes for a possessive modifier, especially if there is no real possession involved.

Ка́к прошёл **у тебя́** уро́к?	How did *your* lesson go?
Кто́ **у ва́с** учи́тель?	Who's *your* teacher?

Prepositions meaning *from:* из, с, and от

MODELS

О́н идёт из па́рка.	He's coming from the park.
_____ из теа́тра.	_____ from the theater.
_____ из рестора́на.	_____ from the restaurant.
_____ из университе́та.	_____ from the university.
_____ из общежи́тия.	_____ from the dormitory.
_____ из библиоте́ки.	_____ from the library.
_____ из лаборато́рии.	_____ from the laboratory.
_____ из шко́лы.	_____ from the school.
Она́ идёт с конце́рта.	She's coming from the concert.
_____ с уро́ка.	_____ from a lesson.
_____ с заво́да.	_____ from the plant.
_____ с обе́да.	_____ from dinner.
_____ с собра́ния.	_____ from the meeting.
_____ с фа́брики.	_____ from the factory.
_____ с рабо́ты.	_____ from work.
_____ со слу́жбы.	_____ from work.
_____ с ле́кции.	_____ from the lecture.
_____ с по́чты.	_____ from the post office.
О́н получи́л письмо́ от бра́та.	He received a letter from his brother.
_____ от дру́га.	_____ from a friend.
_____ от Никола́я.	_____ from Nikolay.
_____ от сестры́.	_____ from his sister.
_____ от жены́.	_____ from his wife.
_____ от О́ли.	_____ from Olya.
_____ от Мари́и.	_____ from Maria.

Óн получи́л от неё письмо́ из Москвы́.	He got a letter from her from Moscow.	
_____ от него́ _____.	_____ from him _____.	
_____ от ни́х _____.	_____ from them _____.	
_____ от меня́ _____.	_____ from me _____.	
_____ от на́с _____.	_____ from us _____.	
_____ от ва́с _____.	_____ from you _____.	
_____ от тебя́ _____.	_____ from you _____.	

■ REPETITION DRILL

Repeat the above models, noting that the preposition **из** *from* is the directional opposite of the preposition **в** *to*, and that the preposition **с** *from* is the directional opposite of the preposition **на** *to*.

■ STRUCTURE REPLACEMENT DRILLS

1. *He's going to the park.*
   He's coming from the park.
   т: Óн идёт в па́рк.
   s: **Óн идёт из па́рка.**
   т: Óн идёт в рестора́н.
   s: **Óн идёт из рестора́на.**
   (в библиоте́ку, в общежи́тие, в теа́тр, в горсове́т, в клу́б, в шко́лу, в университе́т, в аудито́рию, в магази́н)

2. *They're going to the concert.*
   They're coming from the concert.
   т: Они́ иду́т на конце́рт.
   s: **Они́ иду́т с конце́рта.**
   т: Они́ иду́т на слу́жбу.
   s: **Они́ иду́т со слу́жбы.**
   (на уро́к, на по́чту, на собра́ние, на обе́д, на фа́брику, на экза́мен, на рабо́ту, на ле́кцию)

■ RESPONSE DRILL

Vladimir was in Moscow recently.
Did you get a letter from Vladimir?
т: Влади́мир неда́вно бы́л в Москве́.
s: **Вы́ получи́ли от Влади́мира письмо́?**
т: Ири́на неда́вно была́ в Москве́.
s: **Вы́ получи́ли от Ири́ны письмо́?**
(Кири́лл, он, она́, они́, я, мы, Са́ша, Ни́на, она́)

■ STRUCTURE REPLACEMENT DRILLS

1. *She sent a letter to Moscow.*
   She received a letter from Moscow.
   т: Она́ посла́ла письмо́ в Москву́.
   s: **Она́ получи́ла письмо́ из Москвы́.**
   т: Она́ посла́ла письмо́ в Ленингра́д.
   s: **Она́ получи́ла письмо́ из Ленингра́да.**
   Она́ посла́ла письмо́ в Аме́рику.
   Она́ посла́ла письмо́ в Кита́й.
   Она́ посла́ла письмо́ в Евро́пу.
   Она́ посла́ла письмо́ в СССР.

2. *They were at the concert.*
   They're coming from the concert.
   т: Они́ бы́ли на конце́рте.
   s: **Они́ иду́т с конце́рта.**
   т: Они́ бы́ли в па́рке.
   s: **Они́ иду́т из па́рка.**
   (в библиоте́ке, на фа́брике, на по́чте, в магази́не, на ле́кции, на экза́мене, в рестора́не, в теа́тре, на собра́нии, в общежи́тии)

1. *I was at my brother's place.*
   I heard it from my brother.

   т: Я́ бы́л у бра́та.

   s: **Я́ э́то слы́шал от бра́та.**

   т: Я́ бы́л у сестры́.

   s: **Я́ э́то слы́шал от сестры́.**

   (у дру́га, у Ни́ны, у профе́ссора Орло́ва,
   у Са́ши, у ре́ктора, у него́, у неё, у них)

2. *The spoons are in the drawer.*
   Take the spoons from the drawer.

   т: Ло́жки в я́щике.

   s: **Возьми́ ло́жки из я́щика.**

   т: Ло́жки на столе́.

   s: **Возьми́ ло́жки со стола́.**

   (в шкафу́, на шкафу́, в коро́бке, на
   сту́ле, на по́лке, в портфе́ле, в я́щике)

■ CUED QUESTION-ANSWER DRILL

(*Moscow*)	*Where did he phone from?*
	From Moscow.

т: (Москва́)   Отку́да о́н звони́л?

s: **Из Москвы́.**

т: (Ленингра́д) Отку́да о́н звони́л?

s: **Из Ленингра́да.**

(магази́н на углу́, ГУМ, горсове́т,
университе́т, общежи́тие, го́род, школа, библиоте́ка)

■ STRUCTURE REPLACEMENT DRILL

He was at the plant.
He phoned from the plant.

т: О́н бы́л на заво́де.

s: **О́н звони́л с заво́да.**

т: О́н бы́л на слу́жбе.

s: **О́н звони́л со слу́жбы.**

(на по́чте, на рабо́те, на фа́брике,
на слу́жбе)

■ RESPONSE DRILL

My friend is in Moscow.
I received a letter from Moscow.

т: Мо́й дру́г в Москве́.

s: **Я́ получи́л письмо́ из Москвы́.**

т: Мо́й дру́г в Ленингра́де.

s: **Я́ получи́л письмо́ из Ленингра́да.**

(в Кита́е, в Москве́, в Евро́пе,
в Аме́рике, в СССР)

DISCUSSION

All three prepositions, **из**, **с**, and **от**, mean *from*, but each is limited in its sphere of usage: nouns or pronouns referring to people require **от**, but for places and things **из** and **с** are generally used. **Из** is used with inanimate nouns which take the preposition **в**, whereas **с** is used with nouns which take **на**.

Она́ идёт **в го́род**.	She's going *to town*.
Она́ идёт **из го́рода**.	She's coming *from town*.
Она́ идёт **на ле́кцию**.	She's going *to the lecture*.
Она́ идёт **с ле́кции**.	She's coming *from the lecture*.

Notes

1. The preposition **с** has a variant form **со**, used before certain consonant clusters:

Она́ идёт **со слу́жбы**.	She's coming *from* work.
Возьми́ каранда́ш **со стола́**!	Take the pencil *from* the table!

2. The prepositions **из** and **от** also have variants **изо** and **ото,** but these occur far less frequently, for example:

изо дня́ в де́нь	day in, day out
де́нь **ото** дня́	from day to day

3. All prepositions are pronounced as a unit with the word that follows. Prepositions **от** and **из,** like most short prepositions, are normally pronounced without a stress: **от него́** [atɲivó], **из го́рода** [izgórədə]. When preposition **с** precedes a word beginning with another **с,** it is pronounced without a break as a long [s]: **с собра́ния** [ssabráɲjə].

Other prepositions requiring the genitive case

MODELS

Я его́ ви́дел по́сле уро́ка.	I saw him after the lesson.
_____ конце́рта.	_____ the concert.
_____ экза́мена.	_____ the exam.
_____ обе́да.	_____ dinner.
_____ собра́ния.	_____ the meeting.
_____ ле́кции.	_____ the lecture.
_____ рабо́ты.	_____ work.
_____ шко́лы.	_____ school.

Я хочу́ э́то сде́лать до уро́ка.	I want to get it done before the lesson.
_____ до конце́рта.	_____ before the concert.
_____ до экза́мена.	_____ before the exam.
_____ до собра́ния.	_____ before the meeting.
_____ до ле́кции.	_____ before the lecture.

Для кого́ э́то?	Who is this for?
— Для меня́.	For me.
— Для тебя́.	For you.
— Для него́.	For him.
— Для неё.	For her.
— Для ни́х.	For them.
— Для ва́с.	For you.
— Для на́с.	For us.
— Для профе́ссора.	For the professor.
— Для учи́тельницы.	For the teacher.

Где́ о́н живёт?	Where does he live?
— О́н живёт про́тив па́рка.	He lives opposite the park.
_____ теа́тра.	_____ the theater.
_____ рестора́на.	_____ the restaurant.
_____ общежи́тия.	_____ the dormitory.
_____ по́чты.	_____ the post office.
_____ шко́лы.	_____ the school.
_____ фа́брики.	_____ the factory.
_____ библиоте́ки.	_____ the library.

Где они живут?	Where do they live?
— Они живут около парка.	They live near the park.
_____ театра.	_____ the theater.
_____ ресторана.	_____ the restaurant.
_____ завода.	_____ the plant.
_____ общежития.	_____ the dormitory.
_____ почты.	_____ the post office.
_____ школы.	_____ the school.
_____ фабрики.	_____ the factory.
_____ библиотеки.	_____ the library.

Как насчёт хлеба?	How about bread?
_____ борща?	_____ borsch?
_____ чая?	_____ tea?
_____ молока?	_____ milk?
_____ рыбы?	_____ fish?
_____ каши?	_____ kasha?
_____ селёдки?	_____ herring?

■ REPETITION DRILL

Repeat the given models, noting that all six prepositions (**после, до, для, против, около,** and **насчёт**) require the genitive form of the noun or pronoun following.

■ QUESTION-ANSWER DRILLS

1. *When did you see her, after the concert?*
   No, before the concert.
   т: Когда вы её видели, после концерта?
   s: **Нет, до концерта.**
   т: Когда вы её видели, после лекции?
   s: **Нет, до лекции.**
   (после работы, после собрания, после школы, после урока, после обеда, после службы)

2. *Where did she wait for him, at the club?*
   No, opposite the club.
   т: Где она его ждала, в клубе?
   s: **Нет, против клуба.**
   т: Где она его ждала, в библиотеке?
   s: **Нет, против библиотеки.**
   (на фабрике, в общежитии, на заводе, на почте, в ресторане, в аудитории, в лаборатории, в клубе)

3. *Where did you wait, in the restaurant?*
   No, on the corner near the restaurant.
   т: Где вы ждали, в ресторане?
   s: **Нет, на углу около ресторана.**
   т: Где вы ждали, в библиотеке?
   s: **Нет, на углу около библиотеки.**
   (на почте, в парке, на фабрике, в горсовете, на заводе, в школе)

4. *Do you live near the park?*
   Just opposite the park.
   т: Вы живёте около парка?
   s: **Как раз против парка.**
   т: Вы живёте около школы?
   s: **Как раз против школы.**
   (около завода, около клуба, около горсовета, около библиотеки, около ресторана, около общежития, около театра)

5. *When did he call, before the meeting?*
   No, after the meeting.
   т: Когда он звонил, до собрания?
   s: **Нет, после собрания.**

   т: Когда он звонил, до обеда?
   s: **Нет, после обеда.**
   (до лекции, до работы, до концерта, до урока, до клуба, до службы, до школы)

■ RESPONSE DRILLS

1. *Where is he?*
We won't go without him.
т: Где́ же о́н?
s: **Мы́ без него́ не пойдём.**
т: Где́ же Ири́на?
s: **Мы́ без Ири́ны не пойдём.**
(они́, Кири́лл, она́, Са́ша, Оле́г)

2. *He isn't here yet.*
I won't go without him.
т: Его́ ещё не́т.
s: **Я́ без него́ не пойду́.**
т: Га́ли ещё не́т.
s: **Я́ без Га́ли не пойду́.**
(Бори́са, Ни́ны, её, и́х, секретаря́, его́)

3. *Where is he?*
We bought this for him.
т: Где́ о́н?
s: **Мы́ э́то купи́ли для него́.**
т: Где́ Ни́на?
s: **Мы́ э́то купи́ли для Ни́ны.**
(она́, Кири́лл, Евге́ний, Алексе́ев, они́, Мари́я Ива́новна)

4. *You can buy fish here.*
How about fish?
т: Зде́сь мо́жно купи́ть ры́бу.
s: **Ка́к насчёт ры́бы?**
т: Зде́сь мо́жно купи́ть хле́б.
s: **Ка́к насчёт хле́ба?**
(селёдку, молоко́, ча́й, слова́рь, а́тлас, ка́рту, ру́чку, сто́л)

■ SUBJECT REVERSAL DRILLS

1. *The theater's over there, opposite the post office.*
The post office is over there, opposite the theater.
т: Теа́тр во́н та́м, проти́в по́чты.
s: **По́чта во́н та́м, про́тив теа́тра.**
т: Лаборато́рия во́н та́м, проти́в аудито́рии.
s: **Аудито́рия во́н та́м, про́тив лаборато́рии.**
Библиоте́ка во́н та́м, против рестора́на.
Общежи́тие во́н та́м, против шко́лы.
Шко́ла во́н та́м, против заво́да.
Па́рк во́н та́м, против фа́брики.
Магази́н во́н та́м, против теа́тра.

3. *He won't go without me.*
I won't go without him.
т: О́н без меня́ не пойдёт.
s: **Я́ без него́ не пойду́.**
т: Они́ без неё не пойду́т.
s: **Она́ без ни́х не пойдёт.**

2. *He did it for us.*
We did it for him.
т: О́н э́то сде́лал для на́с.
s: **Мы́ э́то сде́лали для него́.**
т: Она́ э́то сде́лала для ва́с.
s: **Вы́ э́то сде́лали для неё.**
Я́ э́то сде́лал для тебя́.
Они́ э́то сде́лали для него́.
Мы́ э́то сде́лали для неё.
Ко́ля э́то сде́лал для Га́ли.
Сестра́ э́то сде́лала для бра́та.
Бори́с э́то сде́лал для Ива́на.

Мы́ без тебя́ не пойдём.
Она́ без ни́х не пойдёт.
Вы́ без на́с не пойдёте.
Я́ без него́ не пойду́.

DISCUSSION

Unlike most of the shorter prepositions, which are ordinarily pronounced with no stress, the prepositions **о́коло**, **про́тив**, **по́сле**, and **насчёт** are pronounced with stress. Although weaker than the stress of the word following, they serve to maintain the [o] vowel quality, which in the unstressed prepositions **до** and **от** is reduced to [a] or [ə].

Note, however, that if the speaker wishes to point up a contrast, even the shorter prepositions may be pronounced with a stress:

Вы́ та́м бы́ли **по́сле** конце́рта?
— Не́т, **до́** конце́рта.

Were you there *after* the concert?
No, *before* the concert.

Verbs with infinitives ending in –чь: мóчь and смóчь

MODELS

IMPERFECTIVE PRESENT

Я могу́ откры́ть окно́.	I can open the window.
Ты мóжешь _____.	You can _____.
Óн мóжет _____.	He can _____.
Мы́ мóжем _____.	We can _____.
Вы́ мóжете _____.	You can _____.
Они́ мóгут _____.	They can _____.

IMPERFECTIVE PAST

Óн не мóг откры́ть двéри.	He couldn't open the door.
Онá не моглá _____.	She couldn't _____.
Они́ не могли́ _____.	They couldn't _____.

PERFECTIVE FUTURE

Я не смогу́ пойти́ на собрáние.	I won't be able to go to the meeting.
Ты́ не смóжешь _____.	You won't be able _____.
Óн не смóжет _____.	He won't be able _____.
Мы́ не смóжем _____.	We won't be able _____.
Вы́ не смóжете _____.	You won't be able _____.
Они́ не смóгут _____.	They won't be able _____.

PERFECTIVE PAST

Óн не смóг пойти́ в клу́б.	He was unable to go to the club.
Онá не смоглá _____.	She was unable _____.
Они́ не смогли́ _____.	They were unable _____.

■ **REPETITION DRILL**

Repeat the above models, observing particularly the replacement of the stem consonant г by ж in the second and third persons singular and in the first and second persons plural. Note also the pattern of stress shift in both past and non-past forms.

■ **SUBSTITUTION DRILLS**

1. *I can't write without a pencil.*
   т: Я́ не могу́ писáть без карандашá.
   s: **Я́ не могу́ писáть без карандашá.**
   (она, мы, вы, ты, они, он)

2. *I won't be able to get into the building without a key.*
   т: Без ключá я не смогу́ войти́ в здáние.
   s: **Без ключá я́ не смóгу войти́ в здáние.**
   (ты, мы, вы, он, я, она, они)

3. *My husband couldn't get any coffee.*
   т: Му́ж не смóг достáть кóфе.
   s: **Му́ж не смог достáть кóфе.**
   (девушки, он, Саша, она, жена, Пётр Иванович, студентки, вы)

4. *She couldn't attend classes.*
   т: Онá не моглá бы́ть на заня́тиях.
   s: **Онá не моглá бы́ть на заня́тиях.**
   (они, мы, вы, Нина, Ирина, Козлов, Коля, Владимир, студенты)

Were you at the concert, Nina?
No, I couldn't go.

т: Ни́на, вы́ бы́ли на конце́рте?

s: **Не́т, я́ не смогла́ пойти́.**

т: Са́ша, ты́ бы́л на конце́рте?

s: **Не́т, я́ не смо́г пойти́.**

Óля, ты́ была́ на конце́рте?
Пётр Ива́нович бы́л на конце́рте?
Ири́на Петро́вна была́ на конце́рте?
Они́ бы́ли на конце́рте?

■ RESPONSE DRILLS

1. *I'm not busy now.*
   I'll be able to go to the club.

   т: Я́ тепе́рь не за́нят.

   s: **Я́ смогу́ пойти́ в клу́б.**

   т: Ты́ тепе́рь не за́нят.

   s: **Ты́ смо́жешь пойти́ в клу́б.**

   (они, вы, Оля, мы, Саша, девушки)

2. *I'm busy now.*
   I can't go to the club.

   т: Я́ тепе́рь за́нят.

   s: **Я́ не могу́ пойти́ в клу́б.**

   т: Ты́ тепе́рь за́нят.

   s: **Ты́ не мо́жешь пойти́ в клу́б.**

   (они, вы, Оля, мы, Саша, девушки)

3. *I don't have a pencil.*
   I can't write.

   т: У меня́ не́т карандаша́.

   s: **Я́ не могу́ писа́ть.**

   т: У ва́с не́т карандаша́.

   s: **Вы́ не мо́жете писа́ть.**

   (у неё, у них, у тебя, у него, у меня,
   у них)

4. *My sister was sick.*
   She couldn't work.

   т: Моя́ сестра́ была́ больна́.

   s: **Она́ не могла́ рабо́тать.**

   т: Мо́й му́ж бы́л бо́лен.

   s: **О́н не мо́г рабо́тать.**

   (жена и сестра, мой брат, мои сёстры,
   вахтёр, уборщица)

5. *She doesn't have a room.*
   She simply can't get a room.

   т: У неё не́т ко́мнаты.

   s: **Она́ ника́к не мо́жет получи́ть ко́мнату.**

   т: У меня́ не́т ко́мнаты.

   s: **Я́ ника́к не могу́ получи́ть ко́мнату.**

   (у нас, у них, у тебя, у вас, у Нины,
   у меня)

DISCUSSION

Only a small number of Russian verbs have infinitives ending in **–чь**. All belong to the first conjugation, and all have basic stems ending in **г** or **к**. So far we have encountered only **мо́чь** (imperfective) and **смо́чь** (perfective) *can, to be able.*

In the present-future of **мо́чь** and **смо́чь**, the basic **г** of the stem is replaced by **ж** in the second and third persons singular and in the first and second persons plural.

Compare	я́ могу́	я́ смогу́
	они́ мо́гут	они́ смо́гут
with	ты́ мо́жешь	ты́ смо́жешь
	о́н мо́жет	о́н смо́жет
	мы́ мо́жем	мы́ смо́жем
	вы́ мо́жете	вы́ смо́жете.

Note that the stress is on the ending only in the first person singular: **могу́, смогу́**; otherwise it falls on the **o** of the stem: e.g., **мо́жешь, смо́жешь**, and so forth.

In the past tense, the suffix л does not appear in the masculine form, but does appear elsewhere.

я (ты, он) мóг   я (ты, он) смóг
я (ты, онá) моглá   я (ты, онá) смоглá
онó моглó   онó смоглó
мы́ (вы́, они́) моглú   мы́ (вы́, они́) смоглú

Note that in the past tense the stress is on the ending, where there is an ending vowel.

Further past tense drills

MODELS

Вы уже знали об этом?	Did you already know about it?
— Нет, не знал.	No, I didn't know.
— Нет, не знала.	No, _____.
Вы уже послали письмо?	Have you already sent the letter?
— Да, уже послал.	Yes, I already sent it.
— Да, уже послала.	Yes, _____.
Где вы работали?	Where did you work?
— Я работал на фабрике.	I worked in a factory.
— Я работала на фабрике.	I _____.
Вы уже пообедали?	Have you already had dinner?
— Нет, я ещё не обедал.	No, I haven't yet.
— Нет, я ещё не обедала.	No, _____.
Вы уже посмотрели её комнату?	Have you already looked at her room?
— Нет, я ещё не смотрел.	No, I haven't yet.
— Нет, я ещё не смотрела.	No, _____.
Вы слушали лекции в университете?	Did you attend lectures at the university?
— Да, слушал.	Yes, I did.
— Да, слушала.	Yes, ____.
Вы уже спросили его?	Have you already asked him?
— Нет, я ещё не спрашивал.	No, I haven't yet.
— Нет, я ещё не спрашивала.	No, _____.
Вы уже написали письмо?	Have you already written the letter?
— Нет, я ещё не написал.	No, I haven't yet written it.
— Нет, я ещё не написала.	No, _____.

■ REPETITION DRILL

Repeat the above models, noting that often (but not always) a past imperfective verb is used in a negative answer to a question using a perfective verb.

■ SUBSTITUTION DRILLS

1. *Grant studied Russian at the university.*
   т: Грáнт учи́л рýсский язы́к в универ-
   сите́те.
   s: **Грáнт учи́л рýсский язы́к в универ-
   сите́те.**
   (вы, мы, Саша, она, студентки, студенты, Кирилл, девушки, Нина)

2. *He was asking where this building was.*
   т: Óн спрáшивал, гдé э́то здáние.
   s: **Óн спрáшивал, гдé э́то здáние.**
   (она, мы, Владимир, Орлов, Маша,
   они)

3. *Orlov left your dictionary at my place.*
   т: Орло́в оста́вил ваш слова́рь у меня́.
   s: **Орло́в оста́вил ваш слова́рь у меня́.**
   (они, учитель, девушки, Оля, Саша)

4. *I wrote a letter home yesterday.*
   т: Я́ вчера́ написа́л письмо́ домо́й.
   s: **Я́ вчера́ написа́л письмо́ домо́й.**
   (мы, Евгений, Маша, девушки, Лев, Борис, они)

5. *I waited for you for a long time.*
   т: Я́ до́лго ва́с жда́л.
   s: **Я́ до́лго ва́с жда́л.**
   (мы, он, она, они, Саша, Владимир, девушки)

6. *I already submitted an application for a room.*[1]
   т: Я́ уже́ по́дал заявле́ние на ко́мнату.[1]
   s: **Я́ уже́ по́дал заявле́ние на ко́мнату.**
   (Борис, Нина, они, он, вы, мой друг, мы)

7. *She took the atlas from the library.*
   т: Она́ взяла́ а́тлас из библиоте́ки.
   s: **Она́ взяла́ а́тлас из библиоте́ки.**
   (мы, он, Нина, Кирилл, они)

8. *I wanted to suggest that to you.*
   т: Я́ хоте́л ва́м э́то предложи́ть.
   s: **Я́ хоте́л ва́м э́то предложи́ть.**
   (Орлов, учительница, профессора, мы, Иван Иванович, мой друг, мои друзья)

■ STRUCTURE REPLACEMENT DRILLS

1. *She wanted to write a composition.*
   She wrote a composition.
   т: Она́ хоте́ла написа́ть сочине́ние.
   s: **Она́ написа́ла сочине́ние.**
   т: Она́ хоте́ла купи́ть пла́тье.
   s: **Она́ купи́ла пла́тье.**
   (узнать результаты, откры́ть окно́, достать материал, посмотреть его работу, пить чай)

2. *He forgot to open the window.*
   He opened the window.
   т: О́н забы́л откры́ть окно́.
   s: **О́н откры́л окно́.**
   т: О́н забы́л написа́ть сочине́ние.
   s: **О́н написа́л сочине́ние.**
   (спросить у Олега, оставить у неё подарок, послать письмо, взять словарь, купить хлеб, достать материал)

3. *They can buy the present.*
   They bought the present.
   т: Они́ мо́гут купи́ть пода́рок.
   s: **Они́ купи́ли пода́рок.**
   т: Они́ мо́гут спроси́ть у Влади́мира.
   s: **Они́ спроси́ли у Влади́мира.**
   (замолвить словечко, получить книги из Москвы, э́то сделать, послать письмо)

■ QUESTION-ANSWER DRILLS

1. *Don't you want to see the room, Nina?*
   I already did.
   т: Ни́на, ты́ не хо́чешь посмотре́ть ко́мнату?
   s: **Я́ уже́ посмотре́ла.**
   т: Ко́ля, ты́ не хо́чешь посмотре́ть ко́мнату?
   s: **Я́ уже́ посмотре́л.**

   Са́ша, ты́ не хо́чешь пообе́дать в столо́вой?
   О́льга, ты́ не хо́чешь пообе́дать в столо́вой?
   Семён, ты́ не хо́чешь купи́ть ка́рту Кита́я?
   О́ля, ты́ не хо́чешь купи́ть ка́рту Кита́я?

---

[1] The masculine and plural forms have two possible stresses: **по́дал** (*or* **пода́л**) and **по́дали** (*or* **пода́ли**). The feminine has stress on the last syllable only: **подала́.**

2. *Nina, have you already had dinner?*
No, I haven't yet had dinner.

т: Ни́на, ты́ уже́ пообе́дала?

s: **Не́т, ещё не обе́дала.**

т: Ко́ля, ты́ уже́ пообе́дал?

s: **Не́т, ещё не обе́дал.**

Ири́на, ты́ уже́ спроси́ла об э́том?

Семён, ты́ уже́ спроси́л об э́том?

О́ля, ты́ уже́ посмотре́ла его́ рабо́ту?

Бори́с, ты́ уже́ посмотре́л его́ рабо́ту?

Ми́ла, ты́ уже́ поду́мала об э́том?

Влади́мир, ты́ уже́ поду́мал об э́том?

ЧТЕ́НИЕ И ПИСЬМО́

Вчера́ мы обе́дали в рестора́не о́коло па́рка. Бы́ли мои́ друзья́, Бори́с и его́ жена́ Ми́ла. По́сле обе́да мы пи́ли ча́й. Они́ спра́шивали меня́ о заня́тиях в университе́те. Я́ спра́шивал Ми́лу о рабо́те в лаборато́рии. По́сле ча́я мы пошли́ домо́й.

Все́ студе́нты говоря́т об экза́менах. Они́ писа́ли о наро́дах С С С Р. Результа́ты, ка́жется, неплохи́е. Но все́, коне́чно, хотя́т зна́ть, кто написа́л лу́чше. „Об э́том ра́но спра́шивать," – говоря́т профессора́ Орло́в и Куро́чкин.

В магази́не на углу́ не́т ка́рт Евро́пы. Их ожида́ют на сле́дующей неде́ле. Но е́сть ка́рты С С С Р и Кита́я. На по́лке я́ ви́жу большо́й а́тлас. Мо́жет бы́ть, он не о́чень дорого́й, но я́ не хочу́ его́ покупа́ть сейча́с.

– Во́т на сту́ле како́й-то а́тлас. Ты́ не зна́ешь, че́й он? – Мо́жет бы́ть Козло́ва? – У него́ не́т а́тласа. – Тогда́, наве́рно, э́то Семёнова. – Да́, мо́жет бы́ть.

- Привет, Саша! Где ты достал тетради? - В магазине на углу. - Вот как! А я вчера там был и не видел. - Но сегодня уже есть. - А карты? - Кажется, тоже есть.

- Владимир, ты куда? - В город. - Ты думаешь, магазины уже открыты? - Конечно. Сейчас уже девять часов. - Ну, тогда я тоже пойду. Ведь сегодня день рождения Ирины. - Я не забыл. Я хочу для неё кое-что купить.

— Мне нужна "История СССР." У вас есть? — Нет, ожидаем на следующей неделе. — А как насчёт "Истории Китая"? "История Китая" у нас есть. Вот она. — А скажите, карта Европы у вас тоже есть? — Да, сейчас принесу.

— Где Пётр Иванович? Ты не знаешь? — Кажется, сразу после обеда он пошёл домой. — Разве он забыл, что у нас сейчас экзамен? — Наверно забыл.

— Маша, обед готов? — Ещё нет. — А я уже голоден. — Подожди, пожалуйста, минутку. Каша ещё не готова. — А что ещё на обед? — Борщ и рыба.

— Оля, я вижу, ты была в ГУМе? — Да, только что была. — Ты не забыла купить ручку? — Вот, досада! Забыла. — А что это в коробке? — Подарок для тебя. Видишь, об этом я не забыла.

— Вот селёдка. И хлеб есть, и огурцы. — Но где у тебя ножи и вилки? — Кажется, в ящике. — В ящике нет. В шкафу тоже не вижу. — Тогда посмотри на полке. — Да, вот они. И хлеб тоже здесь.

PREPARATION FOR CONVERSATION

В суббо́ту бу́дут та́нцы

суббо́та [subótə]   Saturday
в суббо́ту [fsubótu]   on Saturday
бу́дут (fut of бы́ть)   will be
та́нцы (sg та́нец)   dance, dancing, dances
В суббо́ту бу́дут та́нцы.   There'll be a dance on Saturday.
до́ма   at home
сиде́ть (II)   to be sitting, to sit
я́ сижу́, они́ сидя́т   I sit, they sit
вре́мя (n)   time
ве́сь (m), вся́ (f), всё (n)   all
Ты́ всё вре́мя сиди́шь до́ма.   You sit at home all the time.
Зи́на, ты́ всё вре́мя сиди́шь до́ма.   Zina, you sit at home all the time.

пойдём (imperative)   let's go!
Пойдём в клу́б!   Let's go to the club!
Пойдём в суббо́ту в клу́б!   Let's go to the club on Saturday!

Та́м всегда́ та́к ску́чно!   It's always so boring there!
Не́т, спаси́бо. Та́м всегда́ та́к ску́чно!   No, thanks. It's always so boring there!

ра́з   occasion, time
на э́тот ра́з   this time, on this occasion
Да́, но́ на э́тот ра́з бу́дут та́нцы.   Yes, but this time there'll be dancing.

Та́нцы? Э́то друго́е де́ло!   Dancing? That's a different story!
танцева́ть (I)   to dance
я́ танцу́ю, они́ танцу́ют   I dance, they dance
люби́ть (II)   to love, like
я́ люблю́, они́ лю́бят   I love, I like; they love, they like
Я́ люблю́ танцева́ть.   I love to dance.
Та́нцы? Э́то друго́е де́ло! Танцева́ть я́ люблю́.   Dancing? That's different! I love to dance.

◀ В Ленингра́дской опере.

вме́сте	together
всё вме́сте	all together
Пойдём всё вме́сте!	Let's all go together!
Пойдём всё вме́сте: я, ты, Влади́мир и Оле́г.	Let's all go together: you and I, Vladimir and Oleg!
Ты́ Оле́га зна́ешь?	Do you know Oleg?
Немно́го.	Slightly (*lit.* a little).
Я́ его́ немно́го зна́ю.	I know him slightly.
ку́рс	class (year), course
на одно́м ку́рсе	in the same class
Мы́ на одно́м ку́рсе.	We're in the same class.
знако́м	acquainted, familiar
ма́ло	little, too little, very little, few
Мы́ ма́ло знако́мы.	We're barely acquainted.
Мы́ на одно́м ку́рсе, но ма́ло знако́мы.	We're in the same class, but we're barely acquainted.
па́рень (m) (pl па́рни)	lad, boy, fellow
Воло́дя говори́т, что о́н хоро́ший па́рень.	Volodya says he's a nice boy.
това́рищ по ко́мнате	roommate
Они́ това́рищи по ко́мнате.	They're roommates.
увиде́ть (pfv II)	to see, catch sight of
я́ уви́жу, они́ уви́дят	I'll see, they'll see
Уви́дим.	We'll see.
зна́чит	it means; so, then
так зна́чит	so then, well then
Так зна́чит, в суббо́ту?	So, on Saturday, then?
Уви́дим. Так зна́чит, в суббо́ту?	We'll see. So, on Saturday, then?
ско́лько (*plus* gen)	how much, how many
во ско́лько	at what time
Во ско́лько?	At what time?
В де́вять.	At nine.
ве́чер (pl вечера́)	evening(s)
ве́чером	in the evening
сего́дня ве́чером	this evening
Что́ ты де́лаешь сего́дня ве́чером?	What are you doing this evening?
фи́льм	film, picture, movie
война́	war
ми́р	peace; world
Я́ иду́ на фи́льм «Война́ и ми́р».	I'm going to the movie *War and Peace*.
Говоря́т, хоро́ший.	They say it's good.

с ни́м	with him
Вы́ с ни́м знако́мы?	Are you acquainted with him?
с ней	with her
Вы́ с ней знако́мы?	Are you acquainted with her?
с ни́ми	with them
Вы́ с ни́ми знако́мы?	Are you acquainted with them?
познако́мить (pfv II)	to introduce, acquaint
я познако́млю, они́ познако́мят	I'll introduce, they'll introduce
Я́ ва́с познако́млю с ней.	I'll introduce you to her.
сюда́	here, over [here], this way, in this direction
О́н идёт сюда́.	He's coming over [here].
назва́ть (pfv I)	to name
назову́, назову́т	I'll name, they'll name
Назови́те дни́ неде́ли!	Name the days of the week!
понеде́льник*	Monday
вто́рник	Tuesday
среда́	Wednesday
четве́рг	Thursday
пя́тница	Friday
суббо́та [subótə]	Saturday
воскресе́нье	Sunday

В суббо́ту бу́дут та́нцы

Ка́тя	1	Зи́на,	ʐínə ↓
		ты́ всё вре́мя сиди́шь до́ма.	tí fʂó vrémə ʂiḑíš dốmə ↓
		Пойдём в суббо́ту в клу́б.	pajḑóm fsubótu fklúp ↓
Зи́на	2	Не́т, спаси́бо.	ņét ↓ spaʂíbə ↓
		Та́м всегда́ та́к ску́чно!	tám fʂigdá ták skűšnə ↓
Ка́тя	3	Да́,	dắ ↓
		но́ на э́тот ра́з	nó naétət rás |
		бу́дут та́нцы.¹	búdut tắnci ↓
Зи́на	4	Та́нцы?	tắnci ↑
		Э́то друго́е де́ло!	étə drugốjə ḑélə ↓
		Танцева́ть я́ люблю́.	tənciváţ já ļubļű ↓
Ка́тя	5	Пойдём всё вме́сте:	pajḑóm fʂé vṃḗʂţi ↓
		я́,	jắ |
		ты́,	tí |
		Влади́мир	vlaḑíṃir |
		и Оле́г.²	i aļḗk ↓
		Ты́ Оле́га зна́ешь?	tí aļégə znắjiš ↑

---

* Note that Russians consider Monday the first day of the week and Sunday the last. This is reflected in the names: **вто́рник** (from **второ́й** *second*), **четве́рг** (from **четвёртый** *fourth*), and **пя́тница** (from **пя́тый** *fifth*).

Зи́на	6	Немно́го.	ņimnṓgə ↓
		Мы́ на одно́м ку́рсе,	mí nəadnóm kűŗşi ↓
		но ма́ло знако́мы.[3]	no málə znakṓmi ↓
Ка́тя	7	Воло́дя говори́т,	valódə gəvaŗít ǀ
		что о́н хоро́ший па́рень.[4, 5]	štə ón xaróšij páŗiņ ↓
		Они́ това́рищи по ко́мнате.	aņí taváŗišči pakṓmnəţi ↓
Зи́на	8	Уви́дим.	uɣḯḑim ↓
		Так зна́чит, в суббо́ту?	tagznáčit fsubṓtu ↓
		Во ско́лько?	vaskṓḷkə ↓
Ка́тя	9	В де́вять.	vḑéɣiţ ↓
		А что́ ты́ де́лаешь	a štó tí ḑéləjiš ǀ
		сего́дня ве́чером?	şivódņə ɣéčirəm ↓
Зи́на	10	Я́ иду́ на фи́льм «Война́ и ми́р».	já idú naſíḷm vajná i ḿir ↓
		Говоря́т, хоро́ший.	gəvaŗát xaróšij ↓

NOTES

[1] **Та́нцы** is ordinarily used in the plural unless a specific type of dance is referred to:

Compare	Пойдём на та́нцы.	Let's go to the dance.
with	Не́т, э́то не ру́сский та́нец.	No, that's not a Russian dance.

[2] In Russian it is correct and not at all impolite to start with oneself in referring to a group:

Пойдём все́ вме́сте: я́, ты́, Влади́мир и Оле́г.

Russians do not put a comma after the next to the last item in a series if the conjunction **и** precedes the last item. If the **и** is omitted, then the comma must be used: **я́, ты́, Влади́мир, Оле́г.**

[3] In the expression **на одно́м ку́рсе,** the noun **ку́рс** is used to mean *class year* (comparable to such terms as *freshman* or *sophomore*). **Ку́рс** can also mean *course*, as in **ку́рс исто́рии** *history course*.

[4] **Воло́дя** is a nickname for **Влади́мир.** Similarly, **Ка́тя** is short for **Екатери́на,** and **Зи́на** for **Зинаи́да.**

[5] The word **па́рень** *boy*, *lad*, or *fellow* was formerly restricted to a country or working-class boy. Since World War II its usage has been extended to refer to any young man.

PREPARATION FOR CONVERSATION   **Оле́г ду́мает пойти́ в кино́**

кино́ (n indeclinable)	[ķinó]	movies, cinema
в кино́	[fķinó]	to the movies, at the movies
Оле́г ду́мает пойти́ в кино́.		Oleg is thinking of going to the movies.

читáть (I)
я читáю, они́ читáют
Что́ ты́ читáешь?
Что́ ты́ читáешь, исто́рию?

to read
I read, they read
What are you reading?
What are you reading, history?

«Евге́ний Оне́гин»
Я читáю «Евге́ния Оне́гина».

Eugene Onegin
I'm reading *Eugene Onegin*.

стихи́
Во́т ка́к, стихи́!

verses, poetry
You don't say! Poetry!

Я читáю «Войну́ и ми́р».
А я сейчáс читáю «Войну́ и ми́р».

I'm reading *War and Peace*.
Well, I'm reading *War and Peace* now.

ромáн
э́тот ромáн
Я люблю́ э́тот ромáн.

novel
that novel, this novel
I love that novel.

его́ (acc of о́н, оно́)
мно́го рáз
Я мно́го рáз читáл его́.

it, him
many times
I've read it many times.

идёт фи́льм
В кино́ идёт америкáнский
фи́льм.
Кстáти, в кино́ идёт америкáнский
фи́льм.
Кстáти, знáешь, в кино́ идёт
америкáнский фи́льм.
**Кстáти, знáешь, в кино́ идёт
америкáнский фи́льм «Войнá и ми́р».**

a film is playing (*or* showing)
There's an American film showing at the
movies.
Incidentally, there's an American film showing
at the movies.
Incidentally, you know, there's an American
film showing at the movies.
Incidentally, you know the American film
War and Peace is showing at the movies.

Я о́чень хочу́ его́ посмотре́ть.
**Дá, знáю. Я о́чень хочу́ его́
посмотре́ть.**

I want very much to see it.
Yes, I know. I want very much to see it.

когдá
Ты́ когдá дýмаешь пойти́?

when
When is it you're thinking of going?

послезáвтра [posļizáftrə]
и́ли
Зáвтра и́ли послезáвтра.

the day after tomorrow
or
Tomorrow or the day after.

почему́
А почему́ ты́ спрáшиваешь?

why
Why do you ask?

зáвтра ве́чером
Зи́на идёт зáвтра ве́чером.
**Я слы́шал, что́ Зи́на идёт
зáвтра ве́чером.**

tomorrow evening, tomorrow night
Zina's going tomorrow evening.
I heard Zina was going tomorrow evening.

Я то́же пойду́ зáвтра.
Дá? Тогдá я то́же пойду́ зáвтра.

I'll go tomorrow, too.
Really? Then I'll go tomorrow, too.

счита́ть (I) [ščitáţ]	to count, consider
счита́ю, счита́ют [ščitáju, ščitájut]	I count, they count
от одного́ до десяти́	from one to ten
Счита́йте от одного́ до десяти́!	Count from one to ten!
оди́н	one
два́	two
три́	three
четы́ре	four
пя́ть	five
ше́сть	six
се́мь	seven
во́семь	eight
де́вять	nine
де́сять	ten
час	hour, o'clock, one o'clock
Во ско́лько вы́ пое́дете?	At what time will you go?
— В ча́с.	At one [o'clock].
— В два́.	At two.
— В три́.	At three.
— В четы́ре.	At four.
— В пя́ть.	At five.
— В ше́сть.	At six.
— В се́мь.	At seven.
— В во́семь.	At eight.
— В де́вять.	At nine.
— В де́сять.	At ten.

Оле́г ду́мает пойти́ в кино́

В. — Влади́мир   О. — Оле́г

В. 1 Здра́вствуй, Оле́г!
Что́ ты́ чита́ешь?
Исто́рию?

zdrăstuj aļék ↓
štó tí čitájiš ↓
istőŗiju ↑

О. 2 Не́т,
«Евге́ния Оне́гина».[1]

ņĕt ↓
jivgéņijə aņĕginə ↓

В. 3 Во́т ка́к,
стихи́!
А я́ сейча́с чита́ю
«Войну́ и ми́р».

vőt kák ↑
sţixĭ ↓
a jă şičás čitáju |
vajnú i ɱĭr ↓

О. 4 Я́ люблю́ э́тот рома́н.
Мно́го ра́з чита́л его́.

já ļubļũ étət ramán ↓
mnógə răs čitál jivó ↓

B. 5 Кстáти, знáешь,
в кинó идёт
америкáнский фи́льм
«Войнá и ми́р».

kstáţi znǎjiš ↓
fķinó idót |
amiŗikánsķij fĭļm
vajná i mĭr

O. 6 Дá,
знáю.
Я óчень хочý егó посмотрéть.

dǎ ↓
znǎju ↓
já óčiŋ xačú jivó pəsmatŗéţ ↓

B. 7 Ты́ когдá дýмаешь пойти́?

tí kagdǎ dúmajiš pajţí ↓

O. 8 Зáвтра
и́ли послезáвтра.
А почемý ты́ спрáшиваешь?

zǎftrə ↓
íļi posļizǎftrə ↓
a pəčimú tí sprǎšivəjiš ↓

B. 9 Я́ слы́шал,
что Зи́на идёт
зáвтра вéчером.

já slĭšəl |
štə ẑínə idót |
zǎftrə yéčirəm ↓

O. 10 Дá?
Тогдá я́ тóже пойдý зáвтра.

dǎ ↑
tagdá já tóži pajdú zǎftrə ↓

NOTES

[1] «**Евгéний Онéгин**» is Alexander Pushkin's (1799-1837) famous novel in verse, written during the 1820's. Note that titles of books, movies, plays, and so forth are declined in Russian unless preceded by the nouns *book*, *movie*, *play*, and so forth.

Compare	Я читáю «Войнý и ми́р».	I'm reading *War and Peace*.
with	Я читáю ромáн «Войнá и ми́р».	I'm reading the novel *War and Peace*.

Basic sentence patterns

1. Ты́ знáешь Олéга?	Do you know Oleg?
_____ Евгéния?	_____ Evgeny?
_____ Кири́лла?	_____ Kirill?
_____ Царáпкина?	_____ Tsarapkin?
_____ Алексéева?	_____ Alexeev?
_____ Львá?	_____ Lev?
_____ секретаря́?	_____ the secretary?
_____ Сáшу?	_____ Sasha?
_____ Кóлю?	_____ Kolya?
_____ Володю?	_____ Volodya?
_____ Гáлю?	_____ Galya?
_____ Ни́ну?	_____ Nina?
_____ Мари́ю?	_____ Maria?
_____ Ири́ну Петрóвну?	_____ Irina Petrovna?

2. Вы́ егó знáете?	Do you know him?
___ её ____?	_____ her?
___ и́х ____?	_____ them?
___ меня́ ___?	_____ me?
___ нáс ___?	_____ us?

3. Попроси́те Ива́на Никола́евича к
телефо́ну.

_____ Бори́са Миха́йловича _____.
_____ Влади́мира _____.
_____ профе́ссора Орло́ва _____.
_____ Евге́ния _____.
_____ секретаря́ _____.
_____ учи́теля Смирно́ва _____.
_____ Ко́лю _____.
_____ Воло́дю _____.
_____ Са́шу _____.
_____ Мари́ю _____.
_____ Ни́ну _____.
_____ Га́лю _____.
_____ Ири́ну Петро́вну _____.

Ask Ivan Nikolaevich to come to the phone.

___ Boris Mikhailovich _____.
___ Vladimir _____.
___ Professor Orlov _____.
___ Evgeny _____.
___ the secretary _____.
___ Teacher Smirnov _____.
___ Kolya _____.
___ Volodya _____.
___ Sasha _____.
___ Maria _____.
___ Nina _____.
___ Galya _____.
___ Irina Petrovna _____.

4. Что́ вы́ чита́ете?
— Рома́н.
— Стихи́.
— «Евге́ния Оне́гина».
— «Бори́са Годуно́ва».
— «До́ктора Жива́го».
— «Войну́ и ми́р».
— «А́нну Каре́нину».
— Исто́рию.
— Геогра́фию.

What are you reading?
A novel.
Poetry.
Eugene Onegin.
Boris Godunov.
Doctor Zhivago.
War and Peace.
Anna Karenina.
History.
Geography.

5. Я́ люблю́ ча́й.
_____ бо́рщ.
_____ хле́б.
_____ молоко́.
_____ огурцы́.
_____ щи́.
_____ ка́шу.
_____ ры́бу.
_____ селёдку.

I'm very fond of tea.
_____ borsch.
_____ bread.
_____ milk.
_____ cucumbers.
_____ schi.
_____ kasha.
_____ fish.
_____ herring.

6. На сле́дующей неде́ле я́ бу́ду в Москве́.
_____ ты́ бу́дешь _____.
_____ о́н бу́дет _____.
_____ мы́ бу́дем _____.
_____ вы́ бу́дете _____.
_____ они́ бу́дут _____.

Next week I'll be in Moscow.
_____ you'll be _____.
_____ he'll be _____.
_____ we'll be _____.
_____ you'll be _____.
_____ they'll be _____.

7. Я́ бу́ду чита́ть «Евге́ния Оне́гина».
Ты́ бу́дешь _____.
О́н бу́дет _____.
Мы́ бу́дем _____.
Вы́ бу́дете _____.
Они́ бу́дут _____.

I'll be reading *Eugene Onegin.*
You'll be _____.
He'll be _____.
We'll be _____.
You'll be _____.
They'll be _____.

8. Я люблю́ танцева́ть.
   Ты лю́бишь _____.
   Она́ лю́бит _____.
   Мы́ лю́бим _____.
   Вы́ лю́бите _____.
   Они́ лю́бят _____.

I love to dance.
You love ____.
She loves ____.
We love ____.
You love ____.
They love ____.

9. Я́ всё вре́мя сижу́ до́ма.
   Ты́ _____ сиди́шь __.
   О́н _____ сиди́т ____.
   Мы́ _____ сиди́м ____.
   Вы́ _____ сиди́те ____.
   Они́ _____ сидя́т ____.

I sit (or stay) home all the time.
You sit (or stay) _____.
He sits (or stays) _____.
We sit (or stay) _____.
You sit (or stay) _____.
They sit (or stay) _____.

10. Я его́ уви́жу сего́дня ве́чером.
    Ты́ _ уви́дишь _____.
    Она́ _ уви́дит _____.
    Мы́ _ уви́дим _____.
    Вы́ _ уви́дите _____.
    Они́ _ уви́дят _____.

I'll see him this evening.
You'll see _____.
She'll see _____.
We'll see _____.
You'll see _____.
They'll see _____.

11. Я всегда́ её ви́жу в теа́тре.
    Ты́ _____ ви́дишь _____.
    О́н _____ ви́дит _____.
    Мы́ _____ ви́дим _____.
    Вы́ _____ ви́дите _____.
    Они́ _____ ви́дят _____.

I always see her at the theater.
You __ see _____.
He ____ sees _____.
We ____ see _____.
You ____ see _____.
They __ see _____.

12. Я за́втра куплю́ молоко́.
    Ты́ _____ ку́пишь _____.
    Она́ _____ ку́пит _____.
    Мы́ _____ ку́пим _____.
    Вы́ _____ ку́пите _____.
    Они́ _____ ку́пят _____.

I'll buy milk tomorrow.
You'll buy _____.
She'll buy _____.
We'll buy _____.
You'll buy _____.
They'll buy _____.

13. Я оста́влю портфе́ль в клу́бе.
    Ты́ оста́вишь _____.
    О́н оста́вит _____.
    Мы́ оста́вим _____.
    Вы́ оста́вите _____.
    Они́ оста́вят _____.

I'll leave the briefcase at the club.
You'll leave _____.
He'll leave _____.
We'll leave _____.
You'll leave _____.
They'll leave _____.

14. Я спрошу́ об э́том у Льва́.
    Ты́ спро́сишь _____.
    О́н спро́сит _____.
    Мы́ спро́сим _____.
    Вы́ спро́сите _____.
    Они́ спро́сят _____.

I'll ask Lev about it.
You'll ask _____.
He'll ask _____.
We'll ask _____.
You'll ask_____.
They'll ask _____.

15. Како́й сего́дня де́нь?
    — Сего́дня воскресе́нье.
    _____ понеде́льник.
    _____ вто́рник.
    _____ среда́.

What day is today?
Today is Sunday.
_____ Monday.
_____ Tuesday.
_____ Wednesday.

— Сего́дня четве́рг.	Today is Thursday.
_____ пя́тница.	_____ Friday.
_____ суббо́та.	_____ Saturday.

16. Пойдём в воскресе́нье в клу́б. — Let's go to the club on Sunday.

_____ в понеде́льник _____.	_____ on Monday.
_____ во вто́рник _____.	_____ on Tuesday.
_____ в сре́ду _____.	_____ on Wednesday.
_____ в четве́рг _____.	_____ on Thursday.
_____ в пя́тницу _____.	_____ on Friday.
_____ в суббо́ту _____.	_____ on Saturday.

17. Она́ ве́сь де́нь сиде́ла до́ма. — She stayed home all day.

___ ве́сь ве́чер _____.	_____ all evening.
___ всё у́тро _____.	_____ all morning.
___ всё ле́то _____.	_____ all summer.
___ всю зи́му _____.	_____ all winter.
___ всю неде́лю _____.	_____ all week.
___ всё вре́мя _____.	_____ all the time.

Pronunciation practice: unpaired consonants [š], [ž], [c], [č], [šč], and [j]

Some consonants occur without soft or hard counterparts. Three consonants are always pronounced hard: [š], [ž], and [c]. Three are always pronounced soft: [č], [šč], and [j].

A. Hard consonant [š]
Usual Cyrillic spelling **ш**; also **ж, шь,** or **жь.**

Note the pronunciation of hard [š] in the following:

[ví sp̦išíți]	вы́ спеши́те	you're hurrying
[já slíšəl]	я́ слы́шал	I heard
[xərašó]	хорошо́	good

The Russian consonant [š] is always hard. It differs from the corresponding English sound (usually spelled *sh* in words like *sh*op, cru*sh*, and bu*sh*) in that the tip of the tongue is curled slightly up and back, and the sound is made farther back in the mouth.

> Sound Drill: Practice the Russian examples illustrating [š], imitating your instructor (or the tape) as accurately as you can. Remember that even when Cyrillic **e, и,** and **ь** are written after **ш**, they are still pronounced hard.

B. Hard consonant [ž]
Usual Cyrillic spelling ж; sometimes жь.

Note the pronunciation of hard [ž] in the following:

[žiná]	жена́	wife
[naslúžb̦i]	на слу́жбе	at work

Russian [ž] is a hard consonant formed with the tongue in the same position as for [š], but it is pronounced voiced. It is similar to the English *s* in leisure and pleasure, except that the Russian sound is made with the tip of the tongue curled up and back and is produced farther back in the mouth. (Russian [ž] is articulated in approximately the same position in the mouth as American English *r*.)

> Sound Drill: Practice the Russian examples illustrating [ž], imitating your instructor (or the tape) as accurately as you can. Remember that even when Cyrillic **e**, **ё**, and **и** are written after **ж**, they are still pronounced hard.

C. Hard consonant [c]
Usual Cyrillic spelling **ц**.

Note the pronunciation of hard [c] in the following:

[kancért]	конц́рт	concert
[agurcí]	огурцы́	cucumbers
[aț̦éc]	от́ц	father

The Russian sound [c] is like the *ts* in English ca*ts*, and in the foreign-derived words *ts*etse and *ts*ar. The tip of the tongue touches the gum ridge behind the upper teeth. It is always pronounced hard.

> Sound Drill: Practice the Russian examples illustrating [c], imitating your instructor (or the tape) as accurately as you can. Remember that even when Cyrillic **e** and **и** are written after **ц**, they are still pronounced hard.

D. Soft consonant [č]
Usual Cyrillic spelling **ч**; sometimes **чь**.

Note the pronunciation of soft [č] in the following:

[čáj]	ча́й	tea
[napóčtu]	на по́чту	to the post office
[fčirá]	вчера́	yesterday
[óčiņ]	о́чень	very

Russian [č] is formed much like English *ch* in *ch*eap or *ch*in, but without the puff of breath which occurs with English *ch* in the above words.

> Sound Drill: Practice the Russian examples illustrating [č], as well as the paired sets contrasting [č] and soft [ț], imitating your instructor (or the tape) as accurately as you can. Remember that even when Cyrillic **a**, **o**, and **y** are written after **ц**, they are still pronounced soft.

E. Soft consonant [šč]

Usual Cyrillic spelling щ; sometimes щь or сч (rarely ждь).

Note the pronunciation of soft [šč] in the following:

[ščí]	щи́	schi
[bóršč]	бо́рщ	borsch
[naščót]	насчёт	with regard to
[jáščik]	я́щик	drawer, box
[p̦íščə]	пи́ща	food, fare

The Russian sound represented by [šč] is pronounced either as a long soft [š] or as a soft [š] followed by a [č], also soft. It sounds something like the *sch* in English mi*sch*ief, pronounced rapidly with *sh* instead of *s*. The sound [šč] is considered soft in the Russian sound system and has no hard counterpart.

> Sound Drill: Practice the Russian examples illustrating long soft [šč], imitating your instructor (or the tape) as accurately as you can. Remember that even when Cyrillic **a** and **y** are written after **щ**, they are still pronounced soft.

F. Soft consonant [j][1]

Note the pronunciation of soft [j] in the following:

[já]	я	I
[mój]	мо́й	my
[dəsyidáɲjə]	до свида́ния	good-bye
[angínəj]	ангѝной	with a sore throat

Russian [j] is pronounced much like the English *y* in *y*ou and bo*y*, except that the Russian sound is made with the tongue much tenser and more elevated, particularly after a vowel. Russian [j] is considered a soft consonant and has no hard counterpart.

> Sound Drill: Practice the Russian examples illustrating [j], imitating your instructor (or the tape) as accurately as you can.

Intonation practice: review of falling intonation contours

Reread the discussion on intonation contours in Lesson 6.

A. Review of statements with falling contours.

О́н здесь.	He's here.
Алексе́ев у себя́.	Alexeev's in.
Она́ на собра́нии.	She's at a meeting.
Влади́мир у телефо́на.	Vladimir's on the phone.

---

[1] In the Cyrillic writing system, the consonant sound [j] is ordinarily expressed by the separate letter **й** after a vowel only when there is no vowel immediately following, i.e., at the end of a word or just before another consonant: **мо́й** [mój], **тро́йка** [trójkə]. It is most often expressed through use of the soft-series vowel letters, particularly at the beginning of a word or between vowels: **я** [já], **мою́** [majú].

Ви́лки в шкафу́.	The forks are in the cupboard.
Она́ в магази́не.	She's at the store.
А́тлас дорого́й.	The atlas is expensive.
О́н в Москве́.	He's in Moscow.
Пойду́ посмотрю́.	I'll go take a look.
Во́т рестора́н.	Here's the restaurant.
Вчера́ бы́л конце́рт.	Yesterday there was a concert.
У на́с е́сть бо́рщ.	We have borsch.
Тепе́рь она́ больна́.	She's sick now.
Вахтёр стоя́л у две́ри.	The custodian stood at the door.
Мы́ уже́ обе́дали.	We've already had dinner.
О́н сейча́с в Москве́.	He's in Moscow now.
У меня́ ма́ленькая про́сьба.	I have a small favor to ask.
Она́ рабо́тает на фа́брике.	She works at a factory.
Я́ иду́ с рабо́ты.	I'm coming from work.
Замо́лвите за меня́ слове́чко.	Put in a good word for me.
Большо́е ва́м спаси́бо.	Thanks very much.
Мы́ ведь ста́рые друзья́.	We're old friends, after all.
Я́ давно́ ва́с не ви́дел.	I haven't seen you in a long time.
Она́ опя́ть купи́ла пла́тье.	She has bought a dress again.
О́н вполне́ тепе́рь здоро́в.	He's completely well now.
Мы́ неда́вно пи́ли ча́й.	We drank tea awhile ago.
Ни́на до́лго стоя́ла в о́череди.	Nina stood in line a long time.
На́до та́к до́лго жда́ть.	One has to wait so long.
Ведь та́м рабо́тает Алексе́ев.	Alexeev works there, after all.

B. Review of questions with falling contours (question-word questions).

Кто́ та́м?	Who's there?
Кто́ спра́шивает?	Who's calling?
Где́ вахтёр?	Where's the custodian?
Где́ кио́ск?	Where's a newsstand?
Что́ э́то?	What's that?
Куда́ идёшь?	Where are you going?
Заче́м спеши́ть?	What's the hurry?
Ка́к Ни́на?	How's Nina?
Где́ она́ была́?	Where was she?
Кто́ та́м стоя́л?	Who was standing there?
Что́ э́то в шкафу́?	What's that in the cupboard?
У кого́ вы́ бы́ли?	Whom did you go to see?
Что́ вы́ де́лали?	What were you doing?
Кто́ э́то говори́т?	Who's that talking?
Куда́ они́ спеша́т?	Where are they hurrying to?
Отку́да вы́ идёте?	Where are you coming from?
Заче́м тебе́ спеши́ть?	What's your hurry?
О ко́м он спра́шивал?	Who was he asking about?
Что́ сего́дня на обе́д?	What's for dinner today?
О чём написа́л Козло́в?	What did Kozlov write about?
Куда́ вы́ та́к спеши́те?	Where are you going in such a hurry?
Что́ вы́ тепе́рь де́лаете?	What are you doing now?

Что́ э́то та́м в углу́?	What's that in the corner there?
Где́ ты́ э́то доста́ла?	Where did you get that?
Ка́к тепе́рь насчёт обе́да?	How about dinner now?
Отку́да вы́ э́то получи́ли?	Where did you get that?
У кого́ вы́ э́то узна́ли?	From whom did you learn that?
Заче́м тебе́ э́ти тетра́ди?	What do you need these notebooks for?
Где́ стои́т на́ш ре́ктор?	Where's our chancellor standing?
Ка́к прошёл тво́й уро́к?	How did your lesson go?
Ка́к тогда́ насчёт а́тласа?	How about an atlas then?

STRUCTURE AND DRILLS

The accusative of кто́, что́, and the personal pronouns

MODELS

Что́ вы́ та́м ви́дели?	What did you see there?
Кого́ вы́ та́м ви́дели?	Whom did you see there?
Все́ профессора́ меня́ зна́ют.	All the professors know me.
_____ тебя́ _____.	_____ you.
_____ его́ _____.	_____ him.
_____ её _____.	_____ her.
_____ на́с _____.	_____ us.
_____ ва́с _____.	_____ you.
_____ и́х _____.	_____ them.
Спроси́те его́, ка́к пройти́ в ГУ́М.	Ask him how to get to GUM.
_____ её _____.	___ her _____.
_____ и́х _____.	___ them _____.
Не смотри́ на него́!	Don't look at him (or it)!
_____ на неё!	_____ her (or it)!
_____ на ни́х!	_____ them!
Замо́лвите за меня́ слове́чко!	Put in a good word for me!
_____ за него́ _____!	_____ for him!
_____ за неё _____!	_____ for her!
_____ за на́с _____!	_____ for us!
_____ за ни́х _____!	_____ for them!

■ REPETITION DRILL

Repeat the above models, noting that the accusative is like the genitive for all personal pronouns and кто́, but that что́ has an accusative like the nominative. Note also that after prepositions the third person pronouns are него́, неё, and ни́х; otherwise they are его́, её, and и́х.

■ STRUCTURE REPLACEMENT DRILL

Ask Ivan Nikolaevich [to come] to the phone.
Ask him [to come] to the phone.
т: Попроси́те Ива́на Никола́евича к телефо́ну.
s: **Попроси́те его́ к телефо́ну.**

т: Попроси́те Га́лю к телефо́ну.
s: **Попроси́те её к телефо́ну.**
(вахтёра, Воло́дю, Ни́ну, Мари́ю Петро́вну, Евге́ния, Ка́тю, Зи́ну, Петра́, Никола́я)

Where's your dictionary?
I left it at home.
т: Где́ ваш слова́рь?
s: **Я его́ забы́л до́ма.**
т: Где́ ва́ша ка́рта?
s: **Я её забы́л до́ма.**

(ва́ше перо́, ваш нож, ва́ша кни́га, ва́ши
тетра́дки, ва́ши словари́, ва́ша рабо́та,
ваш а́тлас, ваш портфе́ль, ва́ше со-
чине́ние, ва́ши ключи́)

■ RESPONSE DRILLS

1. *Ah, there you are!*
We've been expecting you for a long time.
т: А, во́т вы!
s: **Мы́ ва́с давно́ ожида́ем.**
т: А, во́т ты!
s: **Мы́ тебя́ давно́ ожида́ем.**
(она́, они́, Ко́ля, убо́рщица, учи́тель
Семёнов, Ни́на, Ольга Петро́вна, Лев
Ники́тич)

2. *Here's the dress material.*
Where did you get it?
т: Во́т материа́л на пла́тье.
s: **Где́ вы́ его́ доста́ли?**
т: Во́т ка́рта Кита́я.
s: **Где́ вы́ её доста́ли?**
(а́тлас Аме́рики, ка́рты Евро́пы, каран-
да́ш, огурцы́, ры́ба, кни́ги, портфе́ль,
тетра́ди, слова́рь)

3. *Kozlov was there.*
I saw him.
т: Козло́в та́м бы́л.
s: **Я его́ ви́дел.**
т: Она́ та́м была́.
s: **Я её ви́дел.**
(ты, он, вы, они́, Никола́й, твои́ сёстры,
Ка́тя, профе́ссор Орло́в, твои́ бра́тья)

4. *Zina isn't ready yet.*
Wait for her.
т: Зи́на ещё не гото́ва.
s: **Подожди́ её.**
т: Я́ ещё не гото́в.
s: **Подожди́ меня́.**
(мы, Оле́г и Зи́на, бра́т, она́, сестра́,
они́, твоя́ жена́, он, твой муж)

5. *He's here.*
Do you know him?
т: О́н ту́т.
s: **Ты́ его́ зна́ешь?**
т: Она́ ту́т.
s: **Ты́ её зна́ешь?**
(Ири́на, Ко́ля, Козло́в, мой бра́т, моя́
сестра́, мои́ бра́тья, мои́ сёстры)

6. *He's not here yet.*
We're expecting him.
т: Его́ ещё не́т.
s: **Мы́ его́ ожида́ем.**
т: Учи́тельницы ещё не́т.
s: **Мы́ её ожида́ем.**
(их, Ко́ли, Никола́я, продавщи́цы, его́,
профе́ссора, Семёнова и его́ жены́)

7. *There's Zina over there.*
Ask her.
т: Во́н та́м Зи́на.
s: **Спроси́те её.**
т: Во́н та́м Воло́дя.
s: **Спроси́те его́.**
(Ири́на Петро́вна, убо́рщицы, мой
бра́т, моя́ сестра́, учителя́, учительница, Оле́г, студе́нты)

8. *We saw the factory.*
What did you see?
т: Мы́ ви́дели заво́д.
s: **Что́ вы́ ви́дели?**
т: Мы́ ви́дели Зи́ну.
s: **Кого́ вы́ ви́дели?**
(а́тлас, ка́рты, Воло́дю, фи́льм, ва́шу
сестру́, её бра́та, библиоте́ку, учителя́,
результа́ты экза́мена, Мари́ю, ком-
на́ту)

DISCUSSION

The accusative of personal pronouns and **кто́** has the same form as the genitive. The accusative
of **что́**, however, is like the nominative.

NOM	я́	ты́	о́н, оно́	она́	мы́	вы́	они́	кто́	что́
ACC	меня́	тебя́	его́ (него́)	её (неё)	на́с	ва́с	и́х (ни́х)	кого́	что́

The alternate forms, **него́**, **неё**, and **ни́х**, are used only with prepositions: **Посмотри́ на него́!** *Look at him!* **Замо́лвите за неё слове́чко!** *Put in a good word for her!*

The accusative singular of nouns

MODELS

Кого́ вы́ та́м ви́дели?	Whom did you see there?
— Бори́са.	Boris.
— Влади́мира.	Vladimir.
— Профе́ссора Орло́ва.	Professor Orlov.
— Евге́ния.	Evgeny.
— Никола́я.	Nikolay.
— Ко́лю.	Kolya.
— Воло́дю.	Volodya.
— Са́шу.	Sasha.
— Ири́ну.	Irina.
— Мари́ю.	Maria.
— Любо́вь.	Lyubov.

Что́ вы́ купи́ли?	What did you buy?
— Хле́б.	Bread.
— Ча́й.	Tea.
— Молоко́.	Milk.
— Ка́рту Кита́я.	A map of China.
— Ры́бу.	Fish.
— Селёдку.	Herring.
— Тетра́дь.	A notebook.

Куда́ о́н пошёл?	Where did he go?
— На уро́к.	To class.
— На конце́рт.	To a concert.
— В клу́б.	To the club.
— В па́рк.	To the park.
— На собра́ние.	To a meeting.
— В общежи́тие.	To the dormitory.
— На фа́брику.	To the factory.
— В шко́лу.	To school.
— В библиоте́ку.	To the library.
— В лаборато́рию.	To the laboratory.
— На ле́кцию.	To the lecture (*or* class).

Когда́ вы́ бу́дете до́ма.	When will you be home?
— В воскресе́нье.	On Sunday.
— В понеде́льник.	On Monday.

— Во вто́рник.	On Tuesday.
— В сре́ду.	On Wednesday.
— В четве́рг.	On Thursday.
— В пя́тницу.	On Friday.
— В суббо́ту.	On Saturday.

Я бу́ду у ни́х ве́сь де́нь.	I'll be at their place all day.
_____ ве́сь ве́чер.	_____ all evening.
_____ всё у́тро.	_____ all morning.
_____ всё ле́то.	_____ all summer.
_____ всю зи́му.	_____ all winter.
_____ всю весну́.	_____ all spring.
_____ всю о́сень.	_____ all autumn.
_____ всю неде́лю.	_____ all week.

■ REPETITION DRILL

Repeat the given models, noting that the accusative singular is like the nominative singular except for:
1. Animate **сто́л**-nouns, which use the genitive singular endings.
2. **Жена́**-nouns, which have the endings **–у** and **–ю** in the accusative singular.

■ CUED SUBSTITUTION DRILL

(Oleg)	*Do you know Oleg?*
т: (Оле́г)	Вы́ зна́ете Оле́га?
s:	**Вы́ зна́ете Оле́га?**
т: (профе́ссор Орло́в) (Вы́)	_____ ?
s:	**Вы́ зна́ете профе́с-сора Орло́ва?**

(Никола́й, учи́тель, Семёнов, его́ сестра́, америка́нец Грант, Са́ша, студе́нт Козло́в, Евге́ний, его́ това́рищ, секрета́рь)

■ RESPONSE DRILLS

1. *We have no bread.*
   I bought bread today.
   т: У на́с не́т хле́ба.
   s: **Я сего́дня купи́л хле́б.**
   т: У на́с не́т ча́я.
   s: **Я сего́дня купи́л ча́й.**
   (нет рыбы, нет молока, нет кофе, нет селёдки, нет атласа, нет словаря, нет карты Европы)

2. *There's Professor Orlov over there.*
   I know Professor Orlov.
   т: Во́н та́м профе́ссор Орло́в.
   s: **Я зна́ю профе́ссора Орло́ва.**
   т: Во́н та́м Любо́вь Петро́вна.
   s: **Я зна́ю Любо́вь Петро́вну.**
   (Володя, Курочкин, Борис Михайлович, Ирина Ивановна, Коля, его секретарь)

■ QUESTION-ANSWER DRILLS

1. *Where's the key?*
   I left the key on the table.
   т: Где́ клю́ч?
   s: **Клю́ч я́ оста́вил на столе́.**
   т: Где́ кни́га?
   s: **Кни́гу я́ оста́вил на столе́.**
   (молоко, тетрадь, ручка, словарь, письмо, коробка, материал)

2. *Was the exam on Monday?*
   No, on Tuesday.
   т: Экза́мен бы́л в понеде́льник?
   s: **Не́т, во вто́рник.**
   т: Экза́мен бы́л во вто́рник?
   s: **Не́т, в сре́ду.**
   (в среду, в четверг, в пятницу)

1. *Where's the park?*
   I want to go to the park.
   т: Где па́рк?
   s: **Я хочу́ пойти́ в па́рк.**
   т: Где общежи́тие?
   s: **Я хочу́ пойти́ в общежи́тие.**
   (ГУМ, шко́ла, фа́брика, клуб, большо́й
   зал, библиоте́ка)

2. *Maybe Katya heard about that.*
   Ask Katya.
   т: Мо́жет бы́ть Ка́тя слы́шала об э́том.
   s: **Спроси́те Ка́тю.**
   т: Мо́жет бы́ть Лев слы́шал об э́том.
   s: **Спроси́те Льва́.**
   (Любо́вь Петро́вна, Евге́ний, профе́ссор
   Курочкин, Пётр Ива́нович, его́
   това́рищ по ко́мнате, Оля, учи́тель
   Семёнов)

3. *Nina and Katya were there.*
   I saw only Katya.
   т: Та́м бы́ли Ни́на и Ка́тя.
   s: **Я ви́дел то́лько Ка́тю.**
   т: Та́м бы́ли Орло́в и Ку́рочкин.
   s: **Я ви́дел то́лько Ку́рочкина.**
   (Воло́дя и Оле́г, брат и сестра́, Оля и
   Никола́й, студе́нт и студе́нтка,
   убо́рщица и вахтёр, муж и жена́)

4. *Over there is the university.*
   I've already seen the university.
   т: Во́н та́м университе́т.
   s: **Я уже́ ви́дел университе́т.**
   т: Во́н та́м общежи́тие.
   s: **Я уже́ ви́дел общежи́тие.**
   (по́чта, лаборато́рия, дверь, зда́ние
   библиоте́ки, её ко́мната, их аудито́рия,
   магази́н)

DISCUSSION

Only **жена́**-nouns and animate **сто́л**-nouns have accusatives which differ from the nominative. Animate **сто́л**-nouns have accusatives exactly like their genitives. **Жена́**-nouns have accusatives ending in –**у** (for nominatives ending in –**а**) and –**ю** (for nominatives ending in –**я**).

NOUN ENDINGS IN THE ACCUSATIVE SINGULAR				
сто́л-nouns		**окно́**-nouns	**жена́**-nouns	**дверь**-nouns
Inanimate (same as nominative)	Animate (same as genitive)	(same as nominative)	–у and –ю	(same as nominative)
сто́л	Козло́ва	окно́	жену́	две́рь
портфе́ль	му́жа	де́ло	сестру́	о́чередь
каранда́ш	украи́нца	у́тро	Зи́ну	Любо́вь
ГУ́М	яку́та	перо́	убо́рщицу	о́сень
та́нец	профе́ссора	собра́ние	Ко́лю	тетра́дь
фи́льм	студе́нта	сочине́ние	Га́лю	
Кита́й	бра́та	пла́тье	неде́лю	
у́гол	Льва́	пе́ние	Ка́тю	
а́тлас	Кири́лла		Воло́дю	
	Евге́ния		исто́рию	
	па́рня			

A few **жена́**-nouns with the stress on the ending in the nominative singular shift the stress back to the stem in the accusative singular. Compare **зима́** with **зи́му** *winter*, **среда́** with **сре́ду** *Wednesday*, and **доска́** with **до́ску** *board*.

Summary remarks. The accusative functions primarily to indicate the goal of a verbal action, i.e., the direct object of a transitive verb. Used in conjunction with such prepositions as **в** and **на**, it indicates the goal to which the action is directed.

The accusative is also frequently used in expressions of time, where it may occur either with or without a preposition, for example, **в суббо́ту**, **на э́тот раз**, **всю зи́му.** When used without a preposition, it indicates the complete span of time encompassed by the activity.

Second conjugation verbs with a stem consonant change in the first person singular present-future

Вы́ давно́ здесь сиди́те?	Have you been sitting here long?
— Да́, всё у́тро сижу́ здесь.	Yes, I've been sitting here all morning.
Вы́ за́втра уви́дите Ни́ну?	Will you see Nina tomorrow?
— Да́, уви́жу.	Yes, I will.
Попроси́те его́ к телефо́ну.	Ask him to the phone.
— Хорошо́, сейча́с попрошу́.	O.K., I'll do it right away.
Спроси́те Ку́рочкина об э́том.	Ask Kurochkin about that.
— Я́ за́втра его́ спрошу́.	I'll ask him tomorrow.
Что́ вы́ ку́пите в ГУ́Ме?	What are you going to buy at GUM?
— Я́ куплю́ пода́рок Ни́не.	I'll buy a present for Nina.
Вы́ лю́бите ча́й?	Do you like tea?
— Да́, о́чень люблю́.	Yes, I'm very fond of it.
Где́ вы́ оста́вите клю́ч?	Where will you leave the key?
— Я́ оста́влю его́ в я́щике.	I'll leave it in the drawer.
Вы́ меня́ познако́мите?	Will you introduce me?
— Да́, познако́млю.	Yes, I will.

■ REPETITION DRILL

Repeat the above models, noting that there are two types of change which may take place in the first person singular of second conjugation verbs:

1. Replacement of the final stem consonant by an automatic alternate (compare **ты́ ви́дишь, о́н ви́дит** with **я́ ви́жу**).

2. The addition of a soft **л** (compare **ты́ лю́бишь, о́н лю́бит** with **я́ люблю́**).

■ SUBSTITUTION DRILLS

1. *You sit home all the time.*
   т: Ты́ всё вре́мя сиди́шь до́ма.
   s: **Ты́ всё вре́мя сиди́шь до́ма.**
   (она, мы, вы, они, Катя, я, моя жена, ваши братья)

2. *Zina loves to dance.*
   т: Зи́на лю́бит танцева́ть.
   s: **Зи́на лю́бит танцева́ть.**
   (мы все, наши студентки, я, вы, ты, эта девушка, Петр и Мила, я)

3. *I'll leave the key with Pyotr.*
   т: Я́ оста́влю клю́ч у Петра́.
   s: **Я́ оста́влю клю́ч у Петра́.**
   (она, ты, мы, вы, я, они)

4. *I sometimes see Zina at the movies.*
   т: Я́ иногда́ ви́жу Зи́ну в кино́.
   s: **Я́ иногда́ ви́жу Зи́ну в кино́.**
   (Олег, ты, они, вы, я, мои друзья, мы, мой товарищ по комнате)

5. *When shall I see you again?*

   T: Когда́ я́ опя́ть ва́с уви́жу?

   S: **Когда́ я́ опя́ть ва́с уви́жу?**

   (он, мы, Воло́дя, я, эти америка́нцы, они́)

6. *I'll ask him for the key.*

   T: Я́ попрошу́ у него́ клю́ч.

   S: **Я́ попрошу́ у него́ клю́ч.**

   (ты, они́, мы, вы, я, Ива́н, она́, на́ши студе́нты)

7. *I'll ask them about that.*

   T: Я́ спрошу́ и́х об э́том.

   S: **Я́ спрошу́ и́х об э́том.**

   (мы, вы, Ка́тя, де́вушки, ты, он, я, студе́нтки)

8. *We'll buy bread tomorrow.*

   T: Мы́ за́втра ку́пим хле́б.

   S: **Мы́ за́втра ку́пим хле́б.**

   (я, ты, вы, она́, я, они́, он, я, мы, вы, ты, я)

9. *I'll introduce him to her.*

   T: Я́ его́ познако́млю с не́й.

   S: **Я́ его́ познако́млю с не́й.**

   (они́, мы, Ка́тя, я, ты, вы, Оле́г, де́вушки, Воло́дя)

■ STRUCTURE REPLACEMENT DRILLS

1. *Whom did you ask about this?*
   Whom will you ask about this?

   T: Кого́ ты́ спроси́л об э́том?

   S: **Кого́ ты́ спро́сишь об э́том?**

   T: Кого́ вы́ спроси́ли об э́том?

   S: **Кого́ вы́ спро́сите об э́том?**

   (мы, они́, я, она́, он)

2. *I left the dictionary on his desk.*
   I'll leave the dictionary on his desk.

   T: Я́ оста́вил слова́рь у него́ на столе́.

   S: **Я́ оста́влю слова́рь у него́ на столе́.**

   T: Она́ оста́вила слова́рь у него́ на столе́.

   S: **Она́ оста́вит слова́рь у него́ на столе́.**

   (мы, они́, Ка́тя, вы, Евге́ний, ты, я, студе́нт, америка́нец)

3. *She bought suit material.*
   She'll buy suit material.

   T: Она́ купи́ла материа́л на костю́м.

   S: **Она́ ку́пит материа́л на костю́м.**

   T: Я́ купи́л материа́л на костю́м.

   S: **Я́ куплю́ материа́л на костю́м.**

   (Воло́дя, они́, вы, сестра́, я, Козло́в)

4. *Zina used to sit home all the time.*
   Zina sits at home all the time.

   T: Зи́на всё вре́мя сиде́ла до́ма.

   S: **Зи́на всё вре́мя сиди́т до́ма.**

   T: Вы́ всё вре́мя сиде́ли до́ма.

   S: **Вы́ всё вре́мя сиди́те до́ма.**

   (я, она́, эти студе́нты, ты, они́, мы, он)

5. *She loved you.*
   She loves you.

   T: Она́ ва́с люби́ла.

   S: **Она́ ва́с лю́бит.**

   T: О́н ва́с люби́л.

   S: **О́н ва́с лю́бит.**

   (мой бра́т, я, они́, мы, этот америка́нец)

6. *They often used to see Oleg.*
   They often see Oleg.

   T: Они́ ча́сто ви́дели Оле́га.

   S: **Они́ ча́сто ви́дят Оле́га.**

   T: Я́ ча́сто ви́дел Оле́га.

   S: **Я́ ча́сто ви́жу Оле́га.**

   (он, студе́нтка, Зи́на, мы, на́ши де́вушки, вы, ты, я)

DISCUSSION

Second conjugation verbs undergo a stem change in the first person singular present-future if their stem ends in д, т, с, з, б, п, в, ф, or м.

1. Dentals д, т, с, and з are automatically replaced by their palatal alternates ж, ч, ш, and ж respectively, and the first person singular ending is spelled –у.

2. Labials б, п, в, ф, and м add a soft л before the first person singular ending –ю.

		GROUP 1		GROUP 2			
INFINITIVE		**ви́деть** *to see* (ipfv)	**спроси́ть** *to ask* (pfv)	**люби́ть** *to love* (ipfv)	**купи́ть** *to buy* (pfv)	**оста́вить** *to leave* (pfv)	**познако́мить** *to introduce* (pfv)
SG	1	ви́жу	спрошу́	люблю́	куплю́	оста́влю	познако́млю
	2	ви́дишь	спро́сишь	лю́бишь	ку́пишь	оста́вишь	познако́мишь
	3	ви́дит	спро́сит	лю́бит	ку́пит	оста́вит	познако́мит
PL	1	ви́дим	спро́сим	лю́бим	ку́пим	оста́вим	познако́мим
	2	ви́дите	спро́сите	лю́бите	ку́пите	оста́вите	познако́мите
	3	ви́дят	спро́сят	лю́бят	ку́пят	оста́вят	познако́мят

Note that the change in stem occurs only in the first person singular.

If the stress is on the last syllable of the infinitive, it will fall on the ending of the first person singular, but will often shift back one syllable in all other forms of the present-future. Compare **спроси́ть, спрошу́** with **спро́сишь, спро́сит, спро́сим, спро́сите, спро́сят.** If the stress of the infinitive falls on a syllable other than the last, it will remain on that same syllable in all forms, for example, **оста́вить, оста́влю, оста́вишь, оста́вит, оста́вим, оста́вите, оста́вят.**

In the past tense, the stress is consistently on the same syllable as in the infinitive, for example, **ви́деть, ви́дел, ви́дела, ви́дело, ви́дели; люби́ть, люби́л, люби́ла, люби́ло, люби́ли.**

The future of бы́ть
and the formation of the imperfective future

MODELS

Я́ бу́ду та́м в суббо́ту.
Ты́ бу́дешь _____.
О́н бу́дет _____.
Мы́ бу́дем _____.
Вы́ бу́дете _____.
Они́ бу́дут _____.

I'll be there on Saturday.
You'll be _____.
He'll be _____.
We'll be _____.
You'll be _____.
They'll be _____.

Что́ вы́ бу́дете де́лать?
— Мы́ бу́дем рабо́тать.

What will you be doing?
We'll be working.

Что́ ты́ бу́дешь де́лать?
— Я́ бу́ду чита́ть.

What will you be doing?
I'll be reading *or* I'll read.

Что́ Оле́г бу́дет де́лать?
— О́н бу́дет писа́ть пи́сьма.

What will Oleg be doing?
He'll be writing letters.

Что́ они́ бу́дут де́лать?
— Они́ бу́дут танцева́ть.

What will they be doing?
They'll be dancing.

Что́ мы́ бу́дем де́лать?
— Мы́ бу́дем пи́ть ча́й.

What shall we do?
We'll drink tea.

■ REPETITION DRILL

Repeat the given models, noting that the future of **бы́ть** may be used alone (in the sense of *will* or *shall be*) or in combination with imperfective infinitives to form the imperfective future. Remember that the future forms of **бы́ть** can never be combined with perfective infinitives.

■ QUESTION-ANSWER DRILLS

1. *Will you be home this evening?*
   No, I won't.
   т: Вы́ бу́дете до́ма сего́дня ве́чером?
   s: **Не́т, не бу́ду.**
   т: Оле́г бу́дет до́ма сего́дня ве́чером?
   s: **Не́т, не бу́дет.**
     (они, ты, твой брат, ваша сестра)

2. *Will you be working tomorrow?*
   Yes, I will.
   т: Ты́ бу́дешь рабо́тать за́втра?
   s: **Да́, бу́ду.**
   т: Секрета́рь бу́дет рабо́тать за́втра?
   s: **Да́, бу́дет.**
     (эта студентка, вы, мы, ваши
     товарищи, вахтёр)

3. *What are you going to do, drink tea?*
   Yes, we're going to drink tea.
   т: Что́ бы́ бу́дете де́лать, пи́ть ча́й?
   s: **Да́, мы́ бу́дем пи́ть ча́й.**
   т: Что́ вы́ бу́дете де́лать, танцева́ть?
   s: **Да́, мы́ бу́дем танцева́ть.**
     (писать сочинение, читать стихи,
     говорить с ними, ждать секретаря,
     слушать лекции, обедать в ресторане)

■ STRUCTURE REPLACEMENT DRILLS

1. *I didn't ask about that.*
   I won't ask about that.
   т: Я́ об э́том не спра́шивал.
   s: **Я́ об э́том не бу́ду спра́шивать.**
   т: Она́ об э́том не спра́шивала.
   s: **Она́ об э́том не бу́дет спра́шивать.**
     (ты, мы, он, вы, они, учительница,
     профессора, украинец, студенты)

2. *I didn't think about that.*
   I won't think about that.
   т: Я́ об э́том не ду́мал.
   s: **Я́ об э́том не бу́ду ду́мать.**
   т: Вы́ об э́том не ду́мали.
   s: **Вы́ об э́том не бу́дете ду́мать.**
     (они, мы, ты, я, жена, мои товарищи)

3. *We drank tea.*
   We'll drink tea.
   т: Мы́ пи́ли ча́й.
   s: **Мы́ бу́дем пи́ть ча́й.**
   т: Ты́ пи́л ча́й.
   s: **Ты́ бу́дешь пи́ть ча́й.**
     (они, вы, она, он, я, муж и жена, моя
     сестра, мой товарищ, студенты, этот
     парень)

■ QUESTION-ANSWER DRILLS

1. *Who'll be there? Volodya?*
   Yes, Volodya will be there.
   т: Кто́ та́м бу́дет? Воло́дя?
   s: **Да́, та́м бу́дет Воло́дя.**
   т: Кто́ та́м бу́дет? Студе́нты?
   s: **Да́, та́м бу́дут студе́нты.**
   (Мари́я, ваш брат, учителя́, твои́
   това́рищи, продавщи́цы, Зи́на)

2. *What will you be doing?*
   I'll be reading.
   т: Что́ вы́ бу́дете де́лать?
   s: **Я́ бу́ду чита́ть.**
   т: Что́ он бу́дет де́лать?
   s: **О́н бу́дет чита́ть.**
   (они́, мы, ты, она́, твой това́рищ,
   студе́нты, твоя́ сестра́)

3. *Will you drink tea?*
   No, I won't.
   т: Ты́ бу́дешь пи́ть ча́й?
   s: **Не́т, не бу́ду.**
   т: Она́ бу́дет пи́ть ча́й?
   s: **Не́т, не бу́дет.**
   (мы, они́, он, вы, твой това́рищ, э́ти
   па́рни, учи́тельницы)

4. *Will you be dancing?*
   Yes, I will.
   т: Вы́ бу́дете танцева́ть?
   s: **Да́, бу́ду.**
   т: Она́ бу́дет танцева́ть?
   s: **Да́, бу́дет.**
   (ты, мы, студе́нты, твой това́рищ,
   украи́нцы, твоя́ сестра́, грузи́ны, э́тот
   па́рень)

■ STRUCTURE REPLACEMENT DRILLS

1. *I'm reading War and Peace.*
   I'll be reading War and Peace.
   т: Я́ чита́ю «Войну́ и ми́р».
   s: **Я́ бу́ду чита́ть «Войну́ и ми́р».**
   т: О́н чита́ет «Войну́ и ми́р».
   s: **О́н бу́дет чита́ть «Войну́ и ми́р».**
   (они́, мы, ты, она́, студе́нты, вы, мой
   това́рищ)

2. *What were you doing?*
   What will you be doing?
   т: Что́ вы́ де́лали?
   s: **Что́ вы́ бу́дете де́лать?**
   т: Что́ вы́ писа́ли?
   s: **Что́ вы́ бу́дете писа́ть.**
   (чита́ли, покупа́ли, пи́ли, спра́шивали)

3. *We're sitting by the window.*
   We'll be sitting by the window.
   т: Мы́ сиди́м у окна́.
   s: **Мы́ бу́дем сиде́ть у окна́.**
   т: Я́ сижу́ у окна́.
   s: **Я́ бу́ду сиде́ть у окна́.**
   (они́, Козло́в, Ка́тя, ты, вы, студентки, он)

4. *Zina's at the dance.*
   Zina will be at the dance.
   т: Зи́на на та́нцах.
   s: **Зи́на бу́дет на та́нцах.**
   т: Они́ на та́нцах.
   s: **Они́ бу́дут на та́нцах.**
   (на́ши па́рни, я, мы, Воло́дя и его́
   това́рищ)

5. *He was at the library.*
   He'll be at the library.
   т: О́н бы́л в библиоте́ке.
   s: **О́н бу́дет в библиоте́ке.**
   т: Вы́ бы́ли в библиоте́ке.
   s: **Вы́ бу́дете в библиоте́ке.**
   (все профессора́, э́та студе́нтка, я, э́тот
   студе́нт, мы, они́)

As in the past tense, the imperfective and perfective aspects are sharply contrasted in the future. The imperfective future is used to describe future activity not specifically marked off in time, or activity expected to occur more than once in the future. Thus the focus is on the activity as a process or recurring phenomenon. This type of future is formed by means of the future of **быть** plus the imperfective infinitive.

The perfective future, on the other hand, describes future activity of a more concrete, realizable nature. It focuses on the completion or accomplishment of the activity, and it concerns itself more with the result than the process. It is a simple form, structurally like the present tense and employing the same personal endings as the present tense.

EXAMPLES

IPFV FUT	Я́ бу́ду ду́мать об э́том.	I'll be thinking about it.
PFV FUT	Я́ поду́маю об э́том.	I'll think about it *or* I'll think it over.
IPFV FUT	Мы́ что́-нибудь бу́дем де́лать.	We'll [be] do[ing] something.
PFV FUT	Мы́ что́-нибудь сде́лаем.	We'll do something *or* We'll get something done.
IPFV FUT	Они́ бу́дут мно́го спра́шивать.	They'll ask a lot of questions.
PFV FUT	Они́ спро́сят об э́том.	They'll ask about that.

In short, the imperfective aspect emphasizes the "doing," whereas the perfective emphasizes "getting the thing done."

Куда́ and где́: directional versus locational concepts

Куда́ вы́ спеши́те?	Where are you hurrying to?
— **Домо́й**.	Home.
Где́ вы́ бы́ли ве́сь де́нь?	Where have you been all day?
— **До́ма**.	At home.
Куда́ она́ идёт?	Where's she going?
— Она́ идёт **на по́чту**.	She's on her way to the post office.
Где́ она́?	Where is she?
— Она́ **на по́чте**.	She's at the post office now.
Пойдём **в клу́б**.	Let's go to the club.
В клу́бе бу́дут та́нцы.	There'll be dancing at the club.
Я́ не хочу́ идти́ **туда́**.	I don't want to go there.
Кто́ **та́м** бу́дет?	Who'll be there?
Иди́ **сюда́**.	Come here.
О́н **зде́сь**.	He's here.

■ REPETITION DRILL

Repeat the given models, noting that the distinction between "directional" and "locational" concepts in Russian is observed both in the adverbs and in the case system.

■ CUED QUESTION-ANSWER DRILL

    (*park*)   *Where's she going?*
                      To the park.

т: (па́рк)   Куда́ она́ идёт?
s: **В па́рк.**
т: (па́рк)   Где́ она́ была́?
s: **В парке.**
    (магази́н)   Куда́ вы́ идёте?
    (магази́н)   Где́ вы́ доста́ли костю́м?
    (лаборато́рия) Куда́ вы́ спеши́те?
    (лаборато́рия) Где́ она́ рабо́тает?
    (заво́д)   Куда́ о́н пошёл?
    (заво́д)   Где́ ва́ш му́ж?
    (по́чта)   Куда́ пошёл Ива́н?
    (по́чта)   Где́ о́н тепе́рь?
    (библиоте́ка) Куда́ она́ спеши́ла?
    (библиоте́ка) Где́ она́ тепе́рь?

■ RESPONSE DRILL

He was at the club.
Where?
т: О́н бы́л в клу́бе.
s: **Где́?**
т: О́н спеши́л на обе́д.
s: **Куда́?**
    Я́ ду́маю пойти́ в кино́.
    Они́ бу́дут танцева́ть в клу́бе.
    Я́ забы́л слова́рь в столо́вой.
    Они́ иду́т домо́й.

    Я́ пойду́ в магази́н.
    Мы́ спеши́ли на рабо́ту.
    Я́ оста́вил сво́й портфе́ль до́ма.
    Пойдём в библиоте́ку.
    Вы́ спроси́те в магази́не на углу́.
    О́н забы́л ключи́ на заво́де.
    Я́ спеши́л на по́чту.
    Мы́ идём на та́нцы.
    Студе́нты сейча́с на экза́менах.

■ STRUCTURE REPLACEMENT DRILLS

1. *He's here.*
   He's coming this way (or *here*).
   т: О́н зде́сь.
   s: **О́н идёт сюда́.**
   т: О́н на рабо́те.
   s: **О́н идёт на рабо́ту.**
      (он в библиотеке, на концерте, здесь,
      там, дома)

2. *I'm at work.*
   I'm on my way to work.
   т: Я́ на рабо́те.
   s: **Я́ иду́ на рабо́ту.**
   т: Я́ на уро́ке.
   s: **Я́ иду́ на уро́к.**
      (на заводе, на почте, на лекции, на
      собрании, на службе, на экзамене, на
      обеде)

3. *He's going to town.*
   He's been in town.
   т: О́н идёт в го́род.
   s: **О́н бы́л в го́роде.**
   т: О́н идёт в магази́н.
   s: **О́н бы́л в магази́не.**
      (в ГУМ, в школу, в библиотеку, в
      университет, в кино, в клуб, в обще-
      житие)

1. *He's already been downtown.*
   I'm going downtown now.
   т: Óн ужé бы́л в гóроде.
   s: **Тепéрь я́ иду́ в гóрод.**
   т: Óн ужé бы́л на рабóте.
   s: **Тепéрь я́ иду́ на рабóту.**
   (в библиотеке, на заводе, на уроке, в школе, на экзамене, в общежитии, в ГУМе, на собрании)

2. *I forgot my briefcase at the library.*
   I'm going to the library.
   т: Я забы́л портфéль в библиотéке.
   s: **Я́ иду́ в библиотéку.**
   т: Я забы́л портфéль в университéте.
   s: **Я́ иду́ в университéт.**
   (в школе, в ГУМе, в магазине, в обще-житии, дома, в горсовете)

3. *It's time to go to school.*
   Well, here we are at school already.
   т: Порá идти́ в шкóлу.
   s: **Ну́ во́т, мы́ ужé в шкóле.**

   т: Порá идти́ на рабóту.
   s: **Ну́ во́т, мы́ ужé на рабóте.**
   (в библиотеку, в университет, в ма-газин, на службу, на почту)

■ QUESTION-ANSWER DRILL

Was he at home?
Yes, but where were you?
т: Óн бы́л дóма?
s: **Дá, а гдé вы́ бы́ли?**
т: Óн спеши́л на обéд?
s: **Дá, а кудá вы́ спеши́ли?**
Óн бы́л в кинó?

Óн спеши́л в кинó?
Óн э́то слы́шал в шкóле?
Óн пошёл в шкóлу?
Óн э́то читáл в библиотéке?
Óн спеши́л в библиотéку?
Óн бы́л в пáрке?
Óн пошёл в пáрк?

DISCUSSION

The distinction between *where to* and *where at* is observed both in the adverbs (кудá versus гдé; домóй versus дóма) and in the case system. For example, prepositions **в** and **на** must be followed by the accusative if destination is involved and by the prepositional if only location is involved.

1. **Кудá** question with destinational (*where to*) adverb or *accusative case* in the answer:

Кудá вы́ идёте?	Where are you going [to]?
— Домóй.	Home[ward].
— В клýб.	To the club.
— На пóчту.	To the post office.
— В шкóлу.	To school.
— На слýжбу.	To work.

2. **Гдé** question with locational (*where at*) adverb or *prepositional case* in the answer:

Гдé вы́ бы́ли?	Where were you?
— Дóма.	At home.
— В клýбе.	At the club.
— На пóчте.	At the post office.
— В шкóле.	At school.
— На слýжбе.	At work.

KEY QUESTION WORD	TYPE OF VERB	TYPE OF ADVERB	CASE REQUIRED AFTER в AND на
куда́	*destinational* e.g. идти́, пойти́, спеши́ть	*destinational* домо́й, туда́, сюда́	*accusative* на по́чту, в шко́лу
где́	*locational* e.g. бы́ть, жи́ть, сиде́ть, рабо́тать	*locational* до́ма, та́м, здесь	*prepositional* на по́чте, в шко́ле

ЧТÉНИЕ И ПИСЬМÓ

— Вы не зна́ете, фильм „Война и мир" уже идёт? — Да. Я его видел. — А где он идёт? В городе? — Нет, здесь, в кино на углу. — Ах, здесь! Тогда я пойду сегодня вечером.

— Почему ты не был на лекции? — Я был болен. А о чём говорил профессор? — О романе „Война и мир". Ты читал этот роман? — Конечно, читал. А когда у нас будет экзамен? — На следующей неделе.

— Катя, хотите завтра вечером пойти в клуб? — Нет, не хочется. В клубе очень скучно. — Что вы! Там будут танцы. — Я не люблю танцевать. — Как тогда насчёт кино? Сегодня идёт фильм „Борис Годунов." — А, это интересно. — Так пойдём? — Хорошо.

— Завтра мы идём на „Евгения Онегина." — Это американский фильм? — Нет, русский. Говорят, хороший. — А вы не знаете, этот фильм будет долго идти? — Кажется, всю неделю. — Тогда я пойду в субботу.

— Галя, ты всё время сидишь дома. Пойдём завтра в театр. — Не могу. Я и Володя идём завтра вечером на танцы. — Ты и Володя? А я и не знала, что вы знакомы. — Мы уже давно знакомы.

— Ты был сегодня в общежитии? — Нет ещё. Сразу после занятий пошёл в кино. — Да? А что там идёт? — Американский фильм „Война и мир". — Вот как! Хороший? — Да. У нас такие фильмы редко видишь.

— Зина, вы знакомы? Это мой товарищ Олег. — Конечно, знакомы. Мы на одном курсе. — Вот как? Я не знала. — Да, знакомы и вечером идём вместе в кино.

— Вы не знаете, столовая уже открыта? — Да, и я уже пообедал. — А что было сегодня на обед? Наверно, как всегда, щи? — Да, щи и, конечно, каша. Была рыба, но больше нет. — Вот досада! Даже идти не хочется.

— Зина, почему ты всё время сидишь дома? — А куда здесь можно пойти? — В клуб, в кино. — В клубе скучно. — Нет, не всегда, в пятницу будут танцы. — А это дрогое дело. Танцевать я люблю.

— Кирилл, кто это? — Это Филипп, студент из Америки. — Ты знаком с ним? — Да, мы часто обедаем вместе в столовой. — Он хороший парень? — Да, очень. Хочешь, я тебя познакомлю с ним? — Конечно. Буду очень рад.

— Назовите дни недели. — Дни недели: понедельник, вторник, среда, четверг, пятница, суббота, воскресенье. — Какой сегодня день? — Сегодня среда. — Какой день был вчера? — Вчера был вторник. — А какой день будет завтра? — Завтра будет четверг. — А послезавтра? — Послезавтра будет пятница.

Я хочу пойти в кино. Я спросила, что идёт в кино и узнала, что идёт «Война и мир». Я уже видела этот фильм. Может быть пойти в клуб? Там, наверно, будут танцы.

Вчера на лекции профессор Орлов очень интересно говорил о народах С.С.С.Р.: о якутах и грузинах. На следующей неделе он будет говорить об украинцах. Олег уже слышал его много раз, а я только один раз.

У Козлова и его товарища в четверг экзамены. Они всё утро сидели в библиотеке. Сейчас они идут в ресторан. После обеда они опять пойдут в библиотеку.

Я спросил товарища, где можно достать американский словарь Вебстера. Он не знал. Мы спросили в библиотеке, но там такого словаря не было. Тогда мы спросили в магазине на углу, но там тоже не было, и продавщица не знала, где его можно купить.

Николай и Галя весь день сидели в библиотеке. Они были очень голодны. Они хотели пообедать в столовой, но там был только борщ и каша. Тогда Николай и Галя пошли в ресторан.

PREPARATION FOR CONVERSATION   **В кино́**

до́брый	kind, good
До́брый ве́чер.	Good evening.
До́брый ве́чер, Зи́на.	Good evening, Zina.
Вы́ что́ ту́т де́лаете?	What are you doing here?
Оле́г! Вы́ что́ ту́т де́лаете?	Oleg! What are you doing here?
карти́на (gen pl карти́н)	picture
э́та карти́на	this (*or* that *or* the) picture
Я́ хочу́ посмотре́ть э́ту карти́ну.	I want to see this picture.
Я́ то́же хочу́ посмотре́ть э́ту карти́ну.	I, too, want to see the picture.
да во́т [dəvót]	well, why
Да во́т то́же хочу́ посмотре́ть э́ту карти́ну.	Why, I want to see the picture, too.
Во́т ка́к!	Is that so!
ходи́ть (II)	to go, attend
хожу́, хо́дят	I go, they go
Вы́ никогда́ не хо́дите в кино́.	You never go to the movies.
А я́ ду́мала, что вы́ никогда́ не хо́дите в кино́.	But I thought you never went to the movies.
Ка́к ви́дите, хожу́.	As you see, I do.
встре́тить (pfv II)	to meet, encounter
встре́чу, встре́тят	I'll meet, they'll meet
Я́ ва́с встре́тил.	I met you.
уда́ча	luck, good luck
во́т уда́ча	what luck, what a lucky break
И во́т уда́ча — ва́с встре́тил.	And what a lucky break—I've met you.
ка́ждый	each, every
Вы́ меня́ ви́дите ка́ждый де́нь.	You see me every day.
Почему́ уда́ча? Вы́ меня́ ви́дите ка́ждый де́нь.	Why is it a lucky break? You see me every day.
Да́, но на заня́тиях.	Yes, but in class.

◀ **Памятник Пушкину на Пушкинском сквере и кино «Россия».**

поговори́ть (pfv II)	to talk (a bit), have a talk
поговорю́, поговоря́т	I'll have a talk, they'll have a talk
не поговори́шь	one can't talk, you can't talk (*lit.* you won't talk)
Та́м не поговори́шь.	You can't talk there.
Да́, но на заня́тиях. Та́м не поговори́шь.	Yes, but [only] in class. You can't [really] talk there.
А о чём же вы́ хоти́те поговори́ть?	And what is it you want to talk about?
мно́гое	many things, lots of things
О мно́гом.	About a lot of things.
себя́	oneself (refl pron)
о себе́	about oneself
о ва́с, о себе́	about you, about myself
наприме́р	for example
Наприме́р о ва́с, о себе́.	For example, about you, about myself.
успе́ть (pfv I)	to succeed, manage, make it
успе́ю, успе́ют	I'll manage, they'll manage
Не успе́ем.	We won't succeed *or* We won't be able to.
вре́мени не́т	there's no time
Не успе́ем, вре́мени не́т.	We won't be able to [because] there isn't time.
открыва́ть (I)	to open
открыва́ю, открыва́ют	I'm opening, they're opening
Уже́ две́ри открыва́ют.	They're opening the doors already.
Не успе́ем, вре́мени не́т. Уже́ две́ри открыва́ют.	We won't be able to [because] there isn't time. They're opening the doors already.

SUPPLEMENT

опа́здывать (I)	to come late, to be late
опа́здываю, опа́здывают	I come late, they come late
Вы́ всегда́ опа́здываете.	You always come late.
опозда́ть (pfv I)	to be late
опозда́ю, опозда́ют	I'll be late, they'll be late
я́ опозда́л(а)	I'm late, I was late
Извини́те, что я опозда́л(а).	Excuse me for being late.
но́чь (f)	night
но́чью	at night
споко́йный	quiet, calm, serene
Споко́йной но́чи![1]	Good night!
игра́ть в (*plus* acc)	to play (a game)
Вы́ игра́ете в ка́рты?	Do you play cards?
Вы́ игра́ете в те́ннис? [ftéṇis]	Do you play tennis?
Вы́ игра́ете в футбо́л? [fſudból]	Do you play soccer?
Вы́ игра́ете в бейсбо́л? [vbejzból]	Do you play baseball?
Вы́ игра́ете в хоккей? [fxaḳéj]	Do you play hockey?
весна́	spring
Вы́ бу́дете та́м всю́ весну́?	Will you be there all spring?
весно́й	in spring

---

[1] **Споко́йной но́чи,** like **всего́ хоро́шего,** is in the genitive case. This is usual with farewells and wishes for happiness.

Весно́й мы́ ча́сто игра́ем в те́ннис.	In spring we often play tennis.
ле́то	summer
Вы́ бу́дете та́м всё ле́то?	Will you be there all summer?
ле́том	in summer
Ле́том мы́ ча́сто игра́ем в бейсбо́л.	In summer we often play baseball.
зимо́й	in winter
Зимо́й мы́ ча́сто игра́ем в хокке́й.	In winter we often play hockey.
о́сенью	in autumn
О́сенью мы́ ча́сто игра́ем в футбол.	In autumn we often play soccer.
ско́ро	soon
В магази́не ско́ро бу́дут ка́рты.	They'll soon have maps in the store.

В кино́

Оле́г 1 До́брый ве́чер, Зи́на!

Зи́на 2 Оле́г! Вы́ что́ ту́т де́лаете?

Оле́г 3 Да во́т то́же хочу́ посмотре́ть э́ту карти́ну.

Зи́на 4 Во́т ка́к! А я ду́мала, что вы́ никогда́ не хо́дите в кино́.[1,2]

Оле́г 5 Ка́к ви́дите, хожу́. И во́т уда́ча — ва́с встре́тил.

Зи́на 6 Почему́ уда́ча? Вы́ меня́ ви́дите ка́ждый де́нь.

Оле́г 7 Да́, но на заня́тиях. Та́м не поговори́шь.

Зи́на 8 А о чём же вы́ хоти́те поговори́ть?

Оле́г 9 О мно́гом. Наприме́р о ва́с, о себе́.[3]

Зи́на 10 Не успе́ем, вре́мени не́т. Уже́ две́ри открыва́ют.[4]

NOTES

[1] Note that in a subordinate clause, Russians use the present tense if the present tense is really meant. Compare the English, *I thought you never went to the movies*, where a past tense verb *went* is required because it is preceded by a past tense verb *thought* in the main clause. The Russian past tense is only used to describe events in the past that no longer occur in the present. **Я́ ду́мала, что вы́ никогда́ не ходи́ли в кино́** would mean *I thought you never used to go* (or *had gone*) *to the movies.*

Activities begun in the past and continuing in the present require the present tense in Russian. For example:

Вы́ давно́ зде́сь живёте?	Have you been living here long?
Я́ зде́сь рабо́таю с о́сени.	I've been working here since fall.

[2] **Ходи́ть** differs from **идти́** in that it describes the activity of going in general terms, *to go* or *to attend*, whereas **идти́** is more specific and means *to be going* or *to be on one's way*

Compare	Я́ хожу́ на собра́ния.	I go to the meetings (I attend meetings).
with	Я́ иду́ на собра́ние.	I'm going to a meeting (I'm on my way to a meeting).

With such adverbs as **ча́сто, ре́дко, никогда́,** and **иногда́,** the verb **ходи́ть** is normally used: **Вы ча́сто хо́дите в па́рк?** *Do you often go to the park?*

³ Note that the reflexive personal pronoun **себе́** (rather than **мне**) must be used here since the subject of the sentence and the object of the preposition **о** are the same:

> **Я не хочу́ говори́ть о себе́.**   I don't want to talk about *myself.*

The single form **себе́** can refer to any of the personal pronouns:

Она́ ду́мает то́лько о себе́.	She thinks only of *herself.*
Они́ ду́мают то́лько о себе́.	They think only of *themselves.*
Вы ду́маете то́лько о себе́.	You think only of *yourself* (or *yourselves*).

Себе́ has no nominative form. It is usually cited in the accusative-genitive form **себя́.**

⁴ If one is late to a motion-picture performance, he will not be allowed to enter while the picture is being shown; nor is it customary to leave before the picture is over. If this were done at a play, it would be considered *uncultured* **некульту́рно.**

PREPARATION FOR CONVERSATION   **По́сле кино́**

ну́ ка́к?

понра́виться (pfv II)¹

well, how about it?

to like (*lit.* to appeal to)

Ну́ ка́к? Понра́вилось?

Well, how about it? Did you like it?

тако́й

Я таки́х карти́н ещё не ви́дела.

such, so, like that

I haven't seen any pictures like that before.

О́чень. Я таки́х карти́н ещё не ви́дела.

Very much. I haven't seen any pictures like that before.

Я то́же.

Neither have I *or* Same here.

Толсто́й (gen sg Толсто́го)

понима́ние

Толстой

understanding

Я не ожида́л тако́го понима́ния Толсто́го.

Я не ожида́л от америка́нцев тако́го понима́ния Толсто́го.

I didn't expect such understanding of Tolstoy.

I didn't expect such understanding of Tolstoy from the Americans.

игра́ть (I)

Кто́ игра́л Ната́шу?

и́мя (gen *and* prep sg и́мени, nom *and* acc pl имена́, gen pl имён)

to play

Who played Natasha?

name, first name

Я забы́ла и́мя.

А кто́ игра́л Ната́шу? Я забы́ла и́мя.

I forgot the name *or* I've forgotten the name.

But who played Natasha? I forgot the name.

---

¹ The verb **понра́виться** is a reflexive verb which is typically used in constructions requiring the dative case. The form **понра́вилось** is neuter past tense, and it may be literally translated as *it appealed* or *it made a favorable impression.*

помнить (II)
помню, помнят
Я то́же и́мени не по́мню.

to remember
I remember, they remember
I don't remember her name either.

вы́говорить (pfv II)
вы́говорю, вы́говорят
не вы́говоришь

to pronounce, say
I'll pronounce, they'll pronounce
one can't pronounce, you can't pronounce
(*lit.* you won't pronounce)

У ни́х имена́ — не вы́говоришь.

They have names you can't pronounce.

Америка́нцы не мо́гут вы́говорить ру́сских имён.

Americans can't pronounce Russian names.

А америка́нцы, наве́рно, ру́сских имён не мо́гут вы́говорить.

Americans probably can't pronounce Russian names either.

Наве́рно.

Probably.

Вы́ ча́сто хо́дите в кино́ и́ли в клу́б?

Do you often go to the movies or to the club?

Скажи́те, вы́ ча́сто хо́дите в кино́ и́ли в клу́б?

Tell me, do you often go to the movies or to the club?

В кино́ — ча́сто, а в клу́б — не́т.

To the movies, often; but to the club, no.

на та́нцы
ра́зве что [rázɣištə]
Ра́зве что на та́нцы.

to dances, to a dance
unless maybe
Unless maybe to a dance.

Так вы́ лю́бите танцева́ть?

Then you like to dance?

Хоти́те пойти́ в суббо́ту?

Do you want to go Saturday?

С удово́льствием.

I'd be glad to *or* I'd love to.

договори́ться (pfv II)
договори́лись
Зна́чит, договори́лись.

to agree, come to an understanding
we've agreed, it's agreed, it's a date
Then it's a date.

SUPPLEMENT

фами́лия
Ка́к ва́ша фами́лия?
— Моя́ фами́лия Петро́в.
Ка́к ва́ше и́мя?
— Моё и́мя Пётр.
и́мя и о́тчество
Ка́к ва́ше и́мя и о́тчество?[1]
—Моё и́мя и о́тчество Пётр Ива́нович.

last name, family name
What's your last name?
My last name is Petrov.
What's your first name?
My first name is Pyotr.
first name and patronymic
What are your first name and patronymic?
My first name and patronymic are
Pyotr Ivanovich.

зва́ть (I)
зову́, зову́т
Ка́к ва́с зову́т?

to call
I call, they call
What's your name? (*Lit.* What do they call you?)

— Меня́ зову́т Бори́с Петро́вич Орло́в.

My name is Boris Petrovich Orlov.

---

[1] Russians usually omit the conjunction и in speech.

После кино́

Оле́г   1   Ну́ ка́к? Понра́вилось?[1]

Зи́на   2   О́чень. Я таки́х карти́н ещё не ви́дела.

Оле́г   3   Я то́же. Не ожида́л от америка́нцев тако́го понима́ния Толсто́го.[2]

Зи́на   4   Да́. А кто́ игра́л Ната́шу? Я забы́ла и́мя.[3,4]

Оле́г   5   Я то́же и́мени не по́мню. У ни́х имена́ — не вы́говоришь.[5]

Зи́на   6   А америка́нцы, наве́рно, ру́сских имён не мо́гут вы́говорить.[6]

Оле́г   7   Наве́рно. Скажи́те, вы́ ча́сто хо́дите в кино́ и́ли в клу́б?

Зи́на   8   В кино́ — ча́сто, а в клу́б — не́т. Ра́зве что на та́нцы.

Оле́г   9   Так вы́ лю́бите танцева́ть? Хоти́те пойти́ в суббо́ту?

Зи́на   10   С удово́льствием.

Оле́г   11   Зна́чит, договори́лись.

NOTES

[1] The verb **нра́виться** (perfective **понра́виться**) is the usual word for *to like* and expresses a milder appreciation than **люби́ть,** which means both *to like* and *to love*. In connection with something experienced for the first time, **нра́виться, понра́виться** must be used: **Ну́, понра́вилось?** *Well, did you like it?* **Люби́ть** describes a stronger, more deep-seated emotion or attitude: **Я люблю́ танцева́ть** *I'm very fond of dancing*. In the sense of *to love*, only **люби́ть** can be used.

[2] **Ле́в Толсто́й** (1828-1910) is one of the major figures in Russian literature. His long novel **«Война́ и ми́р»** *War and Peace* was written in the early 1860's. Notice that **Толсто́й** is adjectival in its declension, e.g., **Толсто́го** (gen sg).

[3] The noun **и́мя,** like **вре́мя** and a handful of other Russian nouns with the nominative ending in **–мя,** is neuter. **И́мя** usually applies to the first name, but is sometimes used in reference to both first and last names, especially when speaking of prominent personalities. In asking a person's name, the adverb **ка́к** is used:

Ка́к ва́ше и́мя?	What's your first name?
Ка́к ва́ше и́мя и о́тчество?	What are your first name and patronymic?
Ка́к ва́ша фами́лия?	What's your last name?
Ка́к его́ зову́т?	What's his name?

[4] Note that Russians use the perfective past of certain verbs when, in corresponding situations, the present tense is more common in English:

Я забы́л её и́мя.	I forget her name *or* I've forgotten. . . .
Я опозда́л. Извини́те.	I'm late (*lit.* I came late). Excuse me.
Я уста́л.	I'm tired *or* I've become tired.

[5] The second person singular perfective future without the pronoun **ты́** is often used in negative constructions in Russian to make a general or impersonal statement. In English this is normally expressed by *you can't* or *one can't*:

На ле́кциях не поговори́шь.   You can't talk at lectures.
У ни́х имена́ — не вы́говоришь.   They have names you can't pronounce.

⁶ **Ру́сский** is the only name for a nationality that can serve as both adjective and noun in Russian:

Óн ру́сский, а не америка́нец.   He's a Russian, not an American.
Óн хорошо́ зна́ет ру́сский язы́к.   He knows the Russian language well.

Compare **америка́нец** *an American* with **америка́нский** *American* in the following sentences:

Óн америка́нец.   He's an American.
Óн америка́нский студе́нт.   He's an American student.

Remember that none of the words referring to nationalities is capitalized in Russian: **ру́сский, америка́нский, америка́нец, англи́йский.** Only the names of countries are capitalized: **Сове́тский Сою́з** *Soviet Union*, **Аме́рика, А́нглия, Росси́я.**

Basic sentence patterns

1. Та́м мно́го профессоро́в.   There are a lot of professors there.
      столо́в.   _____ tables _____.
      авто́бусов.   _____ buses _____.
      кио́сков.   _____ newsstands ____.
      магази́нов.   _____ stores _____.
      клу́бов.   _____ clubs _____.
      заво́дов.   _____ plants _____.
      а́тласов.   _____ atlases _____.

2. У на́с не́т карандаше́й.   We don't have any pencils.
      ноже́й.   _____ knives.
      ключе́й.   _____ keys.
      ще́й.   _____ schi.
      словаре́й.   _____ dictionaries.
      тетра́дей.   _____ notebooks.

3. Зде́сь не́т карти́н.   There are no pictures here.
      кни́г.   _____ books ____.
      ка́рт.   _____ maps ____.
      шко́л.   _____ schools ____.
      библиоте́к.   _____ libraries ____.
      учи́тельниц.   _____ teachers ____.
      фа́брик.   _____ factories ____.

4. Та́м не́ было коро́бок.   There weren't any boxes there.
      по́лок.   _____ shelves _____.
      досо́к.   _____ blackboards ____.
      ви́лок.   _____ forks _____.
      ло́жек.   _____ spoons _____.
      ча́шек.   _____ cups _____.

Та́м не́ было ру́чек.   There weren't any pens there.

_____ о́кон.   _____ windows _____.

_____ пи́сем.   _____ letters _____.

5. У ни́х не́ было ле́кций.   They didn't have any lectures.

   _____ аудито́рий.   _____ auditoriums.

   _____ лаборато́рий.   _____ laboratories.

   _____ заня́тий.   _____ classes.

   _____ собра́ний.   _____ meetings.

   _____ общежи́тий.   _____ dormitories.

   _____ сочине́ний.   _____ compositions.

   _____ заявле́ний.   _____ applications.

6. Вы́ купи́ли костю́м?   Did you buy a suit?

— Не́т, я́ не купи́л костю́ма.   No, I didn't buy a suit.

Вы́ купи́ли пода́рок?   Did you buy a present?

— Не́т, я́ не купи́л пода́рка. No, I didn't buy a present.

Вы́ купи́ли ча́й?   Did you buy tea?

— Не́т, я́ не купи́л ча́я.   No, I didn't buy tea.

Вы́ купи́ли селёдку?   Did you buy herring?

— Не́т, я́ не купи́л селёдки. No, I didn't buy herring.

Вы́ купи́ли ка́рту?   Did you buy a map?

— Не́т, я́ не купи́л ка́рты.   No, I didn't buy a map.

Вы́ купи́ли тетра́дь?   Did you buy a notebook?

— Не́т, я́ не купи́л тетра́ди. No, I didn't buy a notebook.

Вы́ купи́ли молоко́?   Did you buy milk?

— Не́т, я́ не купи́л молока́. No, I didn't buy milk.

7. Вы́ доста́ли шкафы́?   Did you get the cupboards?

— Не́т, я́ не доста́л шкафо́в. No, I didn't get the cupboards.

Вы́ доста́ли а́тласы?   Did you get the atlases?

— Не́т, я́ не доста́л а́тласов. No, I didn't get the atlases.

Вы́ доста́ли кни́ги?   Did you get the books?

— Не́т, я́ не доста́л кни́г.   No, I didn't get the books.

Вы́ доста́ли карти́ны?   Did you get the pictures?

— Не́т, я́ не доста́л карти́н. No, I didn't get the pictures.

Вы́ доста́ли коро́бки?   Did you get the boxes?

— Не́т, я́ не доста́л коро́бок. No, I didn't get the boxes.

Вы́ доста́ли портфе́ли?   Did you get the briefcases?

— Не́т, я́ не доста́л портфе́лей. No, I didn't get the briefcases.

Вы́ доста́ли словари́?   Did you get the dictionaries?

— Не́т, я́ не доста́л словаре́й. No, I didn't get the dictionaries.

Вы́ доста́ли тетра́ди?   Did you get the notebooks?

— Не́т, я́ не доста́л тетра́дей. No, I didn't get the notebooks.

8. Я́ не ви́жу ножа́.   I don't see any knife.

_____ портфе́ля.   _____ briefcase.

_____ словаря́.   _____ dictionary.

_____ а́тласа.   _____ atlas.

_____ письма́.   _____ letter.

9. Я не покупа́л хле́ба.   I didn't buy any bread.
_____ молока́.   _____ milk.
_____ ры́бы.   _____ fish.
_____ бума́ги.   _____ paper.
_____ материа́ла.   _____ material.
_____ ча́я.   _____ tea.

10. Я́ жду́ профе́ссора Орло́ва.   I'm waiting for Professor Orlov.
Ты́ ждёшь _____.   You're waiting for_____.
О́н ждёт _____.   He's waiting for _____.
Мы́ ждём _____.   We're waiting for _____.
Вы́ ждёте _____.   You're waiting for _____.
Они́ ждут _____.   They're waiting for _____.

11. Я́ его́ подожду́.   I'll wait for him.
Ты́ ____ подождёшь.   You'll wait ____.
Она́ ____ подождёт.   She'll wait ____.
Мы́ ____ подождём.   We'll wait ____.
Вы́ ____ подождёте.   You'll wait ____.
Они́ ____ подожду́т.   They'll wait____.

12. Я́ принесу́ по́чту.   I'll bring [in] the mail.[1]
Ты́ принесёшь _____.   You'll bring [in] ____.
О́н принесёт _____.   He'll bring [in] ____.
Мы́ принесём _____.   We'll bring [in] ____.
Вы́ принесёте _____.   You'll bring [in] ____.
Они́ принесу́т _____.   They'll bring [in] ____.

13. Я́ не успе́ю написа́ть пи́сьма.   I won't have time to write letters.
Ты́ не успе́ешь _____.   You won't have time _____.
О́н не успе́ет _____.   He won't have time _____.
Мы́ не успе́ем _____.   We won't have time _____.
Вы́ не успе́ете _____.   You won't have time _____.
Они́ не успе́ют _____.   They won't have time _____.

14. Я́ открыва́ю о́кна ка́ждый де́нь.   I open the windows every day.
Ты́ открыва́ешь _____.   You open _____.
Она́ открыва́ет _____.   She opens _____.
Мы́ открыва́ем _____.   We open _____.
Вы́ открыва́ете _____.   You open _____.
Они́ открыва́ют _____.   They open _____.

15. Ка́к ва́ше и́мя?   What's your first name?
— Моё и́мя Никола́й.   My first name is Nikolay.
_____ Гали́на.   _____ Galina.
_____ Мари́я.   _____ Maria.

16. Ка́к ва́ша фами́лия?   What's your last name?
— Моя́ фами́лия Петро́в.   My last name is Petrov.
_____ Петро́ва.   _____ Petrova.
_____ Орло́в.   _____ Orlov.

---

[1] Notice that **по́чта** means *mail* as well as *post office*.

— Моя́ фами́лия Орло́ва.	My last name is Orlova.
_____ Ку́рочкин.	_____ Kurochkin.
_____ Ку́рочкина.	_____ Kurochkina.

17. Ка́к ва́ше и́мя и о́тчество?
— Моё и́мя и о́тчество Пётр Ники́тич.

_____ Влади́мир Ива́нович.
_____ Зинаи́да Петро́вна.
_____ Ири́на Миха́йловна.

What are your first name and patronymic?
My first name and patronymic are Pyotr
Nikitich.
_____ Vladimir Ivanovich.
_____ Zinaida Petrovna.
_____ Irina Mikhailovna.

18. До́брое у́тро, Зи́на!
До́брый де́нь, Зи́на!
До́брый ве́чер, Зи́на!
Споко́йной но́чи, Зи́на!

Good morning, Zina!
Good afternoon, Zina!
Good evening, Zina!
Good night, Zina!

19. Зимо́й мы́ ча́сто игра́ем в ка́рты.
Весно́й _____ .
О́сенью мы́ ре́дко игра́ем в ка́рты.
Ле́том _____ .

In winter we often play cards.
In spring _____ .
In autumn we rarely play cards.
In summer _____ .

Pronunciation practice: double consonants

In English double consonants are heard only at a boundary between two words. Written double consonant *letters* within the word (as in *Bill*, *hammer*) are pronounced as single consonants.

Compare   **Will Lee go?**   *with*   **Will 'e go?**
           Ann names.   **Ann Ames.**
           Kiss Sal.   **Kiss Al.**

In Russian, however, double consonants are heard not only across word boundaries, but also within words.

Compare   [attáɲi] от Та́ни   *with*   [atáɲi] от А́ни
           from Tanya   from Anya

           [ánnə] А́нна   [ivánə] Ива́на
           Anna   of Ivan

Double consonants occur in Russian mainly at the point where a prefix or preposition joins the rest of the word, but they may also occur at other places within a word (e.g., [ánnə]).

Note, however, that not every *written* sequence of two identical letters necessarily indicates a double consonant in pronunciation. Russians tend to pronounce many double letter sequences with a single consonant, especially in foreign-derived words. Thus, **профе́ссор** and **суббо́та** contain only single consonants in pronunciation. Usage varies in this respect. Many Russians pronounce **гру́ппа** with a single [p], though orthographic handbooks prescribe [pp]. In rapid speech double consonants often tend to be replaced by single consonants.

> Sound Drill: Practice the Russian examples illustrating the contrast between double and single consonants, imitating your instructor (or the tape) as accurately as you can. Be sure to pronounce the double consonants as *long* consonants, without a break in the middle.

Intonation practice:
review of rising and rising-falling contours

Reread the discussion on rising and rising-falling intonation contours in Lessons 7, 8, and 9.

A. Review of questions with rising contours (questions without a question word).

Óн здéсь?	Is he here?
Вóлков у себя́?	Is Volkov in?
Она́ в гóроде?	Is she in town?
Влади́мир на рабóте?	Is Vladimir at work?
Лóжки в я́щике?	Are the spoons in the drawer?
А́тлас дорогóй?	Is the atlas expensive?
Они́ на собра́нии?	Are they at a meeting?
Она́ студéнтка?	Is she a student?
Вы́ друзья́?	Are you friends?

Автóбус ужé идёт?	Is the bus coming already?
Та́м бы́ло интерéсно?	Was it interesting there?
Ты́ идёшь домóй?	Are you going home?
Óн пошёл в магази́н?	Did he go to the store?
Вы́ бы́ли больны́?	Were you sick?
Вы́ рабóтаете в горсовéте?	Do you work at the gorsovet?
У тебя́ тепéрь истóрия?	Do you have history now?
Бóрщ ужé готóв?	Is the borsch ready yet?
Лóжки ужé на столé?	Are the spoons already on the table?
Вы́ ужé пообéдали?	Have you already eaten dinner?
Ты́ егó зна́ешь?	Do you know him?
Вы́ спеши́те на автóбус?	Are you hurrying to the bus?
Това́рищ Алексéев у себя́?	Is comrade Alexeev in?
Óн сейча́с в Москвé?	Is he in Moscow now?
Они́ егó зна́ют?	Do they know him?
Вы́ о нéй слы́шали?	Have you heard about her?
Она́ сейча́с рабóтает?	Is she working now?

B. Review of questions with rising-falling contours (questions without question words).

Она́ купи́ла материа́л?	Did she buy the material?
Ири́на опя́ть больна́?	Is Irina sick again?
У ни́х éсть кóмната?	Do they have a room?
Они́ бы́ли на заня́тиях?	Did they attend classes?
Она́ доста́ла слова́рь?	Did she get hold of the dictionary?
Студéнты узна́ли об э́том?	Did the students find out about it?
Олéг давнó бóлен?	Has Oleg been ill long?
У ва́с сегóдня экза́мены?	Are your exams today?
Са́ша бы́л в шкóле?	Was Sasha in school?

Она́ уже́ купи́ла слова́рь?	Has she already bought the dictionary?
Ольга Петро́вна опя́ть больна́?	Is Olga Petrovna sick again?
Мари́я Ива́новна была́ в ГУ́Ме?	Was Maria Ivanovna at GUM?
У Ива́на Ива́новича есть ко́мната?	Does Ivan Ivanovich have a room?
Вы́ вчера́ слу́шали конце́рт?	Did you listen to the concert yesterday?
Ле́в уже́ получи́л письмо́?	Has Lev already received the letter?
Оле́г уже́ давно́ бо́лен?	Has Oleg been ill a long time now?
Студе́нты уже́ узна́ли об э́том?	Did the students already find out about it?
Она́ уже́ подала́ заявле́ние?	Has she already submitted an application?

C. Review of emphatic statements with rising-falling contours.

Оле́г **давно́** здоро́в!	Oleg has *long* since recovered!
Ми́ла **опя́ть** здесь!	Mila is here *again*!
У неё **есть** ко́мната!	She *does* have a room!
Жена́ **всегда́** до́ма!	My wife's *always* home!
Они́ **не хотя́т** обе́дать!	They *don't want* to eat dinner!
Она́ уже́ **доста́ла** материа́л!	She already *got* the material!
Ни́на уже́ **подала́** заявле́ние!	Nina already *has* submitted her application!
Оле́г уже́ **получи́л** письмо́!	Oleg's already *received* the letter!
Вы́ о не́й **опя́ть** забы́ли!	You forgot about her *again*!
У ни́х уже́ **есть** ко́мната!	They already *have* a room.
Това́рищ Алексе́ев **опя́ть** не обе́дал!	Comrade Alexeev didn't have his dinner *again*!
Библиоте́ка **давно́** заперта́!	The library has *long* since been closed!
Мы́ уже́ **спра́шивали** у него́!	We already *asked* him!
Я́ уже́ **написа́л** письмо́!	I already *wrote* the letter!

■ TRANSFORMATION DRILLS

Change the following emphatic statements (with rising-falling contours) to questions (with rising-falling contours on a higher pitch level).

Ми́ла опя́ть здесь!	Ми́ла опя́ть здесь?
Они́ бы́ли в Москве́!	Они́ бы́ли в Москве́?
У неё есть ко́мната!	У неё есть ко́мната?
Ка́тя купи́ла материа́л!	Ка́тя купи́ла материа́л?
Зи́на всегда́ до́ма!	Зи́на всегда́ до́ма?
Ни́на уже́ подала́ заявле́ние!	Ни́на уже́ подала́ заявле́ние?
Бра́т уже́ посла́л письмо́!	Бра́т уже́ посла́л письмо́?
Това́рищ Во́лков опя́ть бо́лен!	Това́рищ Во́лков опя́ть бо́лен?
О́кна у ни́х всегда́ за́перты!	О́кна у ни́х всегда́ за́перты?
Сестра́ уже́ получи́ла письмо́!	Сестра́ уже́ получи́ла письмо́?
Ты́ возьмёшь э́ти кни́ги!	Ты́ возьмёшь э́ти кни́ги?

STRUCTURE AND DRILLS

The present-future of first conjugation verbs patterned like рабо́тать and идти́

FIRST CONJUGATION PRESENT-FUTURE ENDINGS		EXAMPLES	
		идти́ (ipfv) *to be going*	рабо́тать (ipfv) *to work*
SINGULAR 1	–у or –ю	иду́	рабо́таю
2	–ешь (–ёшь)	идёшь	рабо́таешь
3	–ет (–ёт)	идёт	рабо́тает
PLURAL 1	–ем (–ём)	идём	рабо́таем
2	–ете (–ёте)	идёте	рабо́таете
3	–ут or –ют	иду́т	рабо́тают

Note that the second person singular ending is conventionally spelled with a final –ь even though ш is always pronounced hard.

MODELS

1. *First conjugation verbs which pattern like* рабо́тать *in the present-future:*

Что́ вы́ де́лаете?	What are you doing?
— Я́ ничего́ не де́лаю.	I'm not doing anything.
Вы́ его́ зна́ете?	Do you know him?
— Да́, зна́ю.	Yes, I do.
О чём вы́ ду́маете?	What are you thinking about?
— Я́ ду́маю об экза́менах.	I'm thinking about the exams.
Вы́ понима́ете, о чём о́н говори́т?	Do you understand what he's talking about?
— Не́т, не понима́ю.	No, I don't.
Когда́ вы́ э́то сде́лаете?	When will you do this?
— Я́ э́то сде́лаю за́втра.	I'll get it done tomorrow.
Что́ вы́ покупа́ете?	What are you buying?
— Я́ покупа́ю материа́л на костю́м.	I'm buying material for a suit.
Когда́ вы́ узна́ете об э́том?	When will you find out about it?
— Я́ узна́ю послеза́втра.	I'll find out the day after tomorrow.
Что́ вы́ чита́ете?	What are you reading?
— Я́ чита́ю стихи́.	I'm reading poetry.
Где́ вы́ сего́дня обе́даете?	Where are you eating dinner today?
— Я́ обе́даю в столо́вой.	I'm eating dinner in the dining hall.
Вы́ не успе́ете на авто́бус.	You won't make the bus on time.
— Не́т, успе́ю.	Yes, I will.
Кого́ вы́ ожида́ете?	Whom are you expecting?
— Я́ ожида́ю дру́га из Москвы́.	I'm expecting a friend from Moscow.

Вы́ **игра́ете** в те́ннис?	Do you play tennis?
— Да́, **игра́ю.**	Yes, I do.
Вы́ не **опозда́ете** на конце́рт?	Won't you be late for the concert?
— Не́т, не **опозда́ю.**	No, I won't be late.
Вы́ ча́сто **опа́здываете** на рабо́ту?	Are you often late to work?
— Не́т, я никогда́ не **опа́здываю.**	No, I'm never late.

2. *First conjugation verbs which pattern like* **идти́** *in the present-future:*

Вы́ **пойдёте** за́втра в теа́тр?	Will you be going to the theater tomorrow?
— Не́т, я **пойду́** послеза́втра.	No, I'll go the day after.
Вы́ **зайдёте** в библиоте́ку?	Will you drop in at the library?
— Да́, я **зайду́** туда́ по́сле заня́тий.	Yes, I'll drop by there after classes.
Кого́ вы́ **ждёте?**	Whom are you waiting for?
— Я́ **жду́** Оле́га.	I'm waiting for Oleg.
Вы́ **войдёте** в до́м?	Are you going to go into the house?
— Не́т, не **войду́.**	No, I'm not.
Вы́ меня́ здесь **подождёте?**	Will you wait for me here?
— Да́, **подожду́.**	Yes, I will.
Вы́ **принесёте** сво́й слова́рь?	Will you bring your dictionary?
— Да́, **принесу́.**	Yes, I will.
Вы́ **возьмёте** э́ти кни́ги?	Will you take these books?
— Да́, **возьму́.**	Yes, I will.
Где́ вы́ **живёте?**	Where do you live?
— Я́ **живу́** про́тив па́рка.	I live across from the park.

■ REPETITION DRILL

Repeat the given models, noting the two types of verb patterns.

■ SUBSTITUTION DRILLS[1]

1. *I don't know.*
   Я́ не зна́ю.
   Вы́ не зна́ете.
     (мы, ты, Мила, студенты, вы, я, вахтёр)

2. *She's rarely late to work.*
   Она́ ре́дко опа́здывает на рабо́ту.
   Вы́ ре́дко опа́здываете на рабо́ту.
     (ты, мы, они, я, Мила, вы, ты)

3. *Won't you be late to the concert?*
   Ты́ не опозда́ешь на конце́рт?
   Вы́ не опозда́ете на конце́рт?
     (мы, она, они, ты, я, ваш брат, ваши
     друзья)

4. *You won't make it to the bus on time.*
   Вы́ не успе́ете на авто́бус.
   Он не успе́ет на авто́бус.
     (я, они, ты, она, мы, Галя, вы, Пётр)

5. *In the afternoon we play cards.*
   По́сле обе́да **мы́** игра́ем в ка́рты.
   По́сле обе́да **они́** игра́ют в ка́рты.
     (я, вы, её друзья, ты, студенты, моя
     сестра, мы)

---

[1] Henceforth the drills will appear without the labels *T* (for teacher) and *S* (for student). In Substitution Drills, the word to be replaced will be indicated by boldface type in the models; in all other drills, the student's response appears in boldface.

■ QUESTION-ANSWER DRILLS

1. *What's Oleg doing?*
   He's reading a letter.
   Что́ Оле́г де́лает?
   О́н чита́ет письмо́.
   Что́ ты́ де́лаешь?
   Я́ чита́ю письмо́.
   (студенты, учительница, учителя́,
   продавщица, ты, они, вы, секретарь,
   студентки)

2. *When will you go home?*
   I'm already on my way.
   Когда́ ты́ пойдёшь домо́й?
   Я́ уже́ иду́.
   Когда́ о́н пойдёт домо́й?
   О́н уже́ идёт.
   (они, вы, она, студенты, продавщица,
   эти девушки, уборщица)

3. *Where is your application?*
   I'll bring it right away.
   Гдé твоё заявле́ние?
   Я́ сейча́с принесу́.
   Гдé её заявле́ние?
   Она́ сейча́с принесёт.
   (ваше, их, его, её, их, твоё)

■ STRUCTURE REPLACEMENT DRILLS

1. *I waited a little.*
   I'll wait a little.
   Я́ немно́го подожда́л.
   Я́ немно́го подожду́.
   Она́ немно́го подождала́.
   Она́ немно́го подождёт.
   (мы, он, ты, они, вы, профессор,
   студенты, сестра, учителя́)

2. *What were you buying?*
   What are you buying?
   Что́ ты́ покупа́л?
   Что́ ты́ покупа́ешь?
   Что́ она́ покупа́ла?
   Что́ она́ покупа́ет?
   (вы, он, они, мы, учитель, профессора́,
   учительница)

3. *I'm on my way to a lecture.*
   I'll go to a lecture.
   Я́ иду́ на ле́кцию.
   Я́ пойду́ на ле́кцию.
   О́н идёт на ле́кцию.
   О́н пойдёт на ле́кцию.
   (мы, она, ты, они, вы, я и мой товарищ,
   учитель)

■ SUBSTITUTION DRILLS

1. *I'll bring coffee right away.*
   Я́ сейча́с принесу́ ко́фе.
   Жена́ сейча́с принесёт ко́фе.
   (брат, они, мы, Нина и Катя)

2. *I'll wait for him on the corner.*
   Я́ подожду́ его́ на углу́.
   Мы́ подождём его́ на углу́.
   (мой брат, ребята, ты, я,
   она, Владимир, вы, мы)

■ RESPONSE DRILLS

1. *I have to buy a couple of things.*
   I'll drop in this store.
   Я́ до́лжен ко́е-что́ купи́ть.
   Я́ зайду́ в э́тот магази́н.

   Она́ должна́ ко́е-что́ купи́ть.
   Она́ зайдёт в э́тот магази́н.
   (мы должны, они должны, он должен,
   я должна)

2. *I live near the park.*

 Do you live near the park too?

 Я живу́ о́коло па́рка.

 Ты́ то́же живёшь о́коло па́рка?

 Я покупа́ю материа́л.

 Ты́ то́же покупа́ешь материа́л?

 Я де́лаю уро́ки.

 Я ду́маю о заня́тиях.

 Я жду́ дру́га.

 Я чита́ю «Войну́ и ми́р».

 Я игра́ю в те́ннис.

 Я рабо́таю на фа́брике.

3. *We'll think about it.*

 Will you think about it too?

 Мы́ поду́маем об э́том.

 Вы́ то́же поду́маете об э́том?

 Мы́ подождём на углу́.

 Вы́ то́же подождёте на углу́?

 Мы́ принесём пода́рки.

 Мы́ пойдём в кино́.

 Мы́ возьмём тетра́ди.

 Мы́ войдём в ко́мнату.

 Мы́ зайдём в библиоте́ку.

DISCUSSION

According to the pattern of their present-future endings, most first conjugation verbs drilled and discussed so far fall into two groups:

1. Those like **идти́**, with the written present-future stem ending in a consonant, to which the stressed endings –у́, –ёшь, –ёт, –ём, –ёте, –у́т are added: жд-у́, жд-ёшь, жд-ёт, жд-ём, жд-ёте, жд-у́т. The stem consonant is hard before the endings of the first person singular and the third person plural, but is soft before the other endings. Compare [ždú], [ždút] with [žḍóš], [žḍót], [žḍóm], [žḍóṭi]. Other verbs which pattern similarly are пойти́, войти́, подойти́, подожда́ть, принести́, взя́ть, жи́ть.

Note that in contrast with the present-future, the infinitive-past tense stem of the verbs in this group may be considerably different. Compare жи́ть, жи́л with живу́, живёшь; and взя́ть, взя́л with возьму́, возьмёшь.

2. Those like **рабо́тать**, with the written present-future stem ending in a vowel, to which the unstressed endings –ю, –ешь, –ет, –ем, –ете, –ют are added: чита́-ю, чита́-ешь, чита́-ет, чита́-ем, чита́-ете, чита́-ют.[1] Other verbs which pattern similarly are ду́мать, поду́мать, зна́ть, узна́ть, де́лать, сде́лать, покупа́ть, обе́дать, пообе́дать, понима́ть, слу́шать, спра́шивать, ожида́ть.

The genitive plural of nouns

The endings of the genitive plural present more complications than those of any other case. For this reason only the most basic ones will be treated in this lesson.

MODELS

Та́м бы́ло мно́го студе́нтов.	There were lots of students there.
_____ профессоро́в.	_____ professors ___.
_____ столо́в.	_____ tables _____.
_____ кио́сков.	_____ newsstands __.
_____ а́тласов.	_____ atlases _____.
_____ пода́рков.	_____ presents _____.

[1] In structural terms, the present-future stem of such verbs actually ends in the consonant *sound* [j], which, as we know, is not written with an independent symbol when it occurs between vowels. The soft-series vowel letters of the endings thus contain not only the ending, but also the final consonant of the present-future stem, e.g., [čitáj-, čitáj–u, čitáj–ut]. The imperative of verbs of this type is the one form in which the [j] of the stem is represented by a separate letter in Cyrillic (–й), e.g., чита́й! чита́йте! спра́шивай! спра́шивайте!

У нáс нéт ножéй.	We don't have any knives.
_____ карандашéй.	_____ pencils.
_____ ключéй.	_____ keys.
_____ товáрищей.	_____ friends.
_____ портфéлей.	_____ briefcases.
_____ словарéй.	_____ dictionaries.

Тáм мáло дверéй.	There are few doors there.
_____ очередéй.	_____ lines _____.
_____ тетрáдей.	_____ notebooks _____.

Тáк мнóго дéл!	So many things to do!
_____ слóв!	_____ words!
_____ книг!	_____ books!
_____ картúн!	_____ pictures!
_____ кóмнат!	_____ rooms!

Тáм мнóго óкон.	There are lots of windows there.
_____ пúсем.	_____ letters _____.

У меня́ нéт вúлок.	I don't have any forks.
_____ пóлок.	_____ shelves.
_____ лóжек.	_____ spoons.
_____ рýчек.	_____ pens.
_____ сестёр.	_____ sisters.

У нáс нé было лéкций.	We didn't have any lectures.
_____ лаборатóрий.	_____ laboratories.
_____ аудитóрий.	_____ auditoriums.
_____ собрáний.	_____ meetings.
_____ общежúтий.	_____ dormitories.
_____ заня́тий.	_____ classes.

TYPICAL ENDINGS FOR NOUNS IN THE GENITIVE PLURAL			
(Endings are based on the plural stem)			
стóл-nouns	**окнó-nouns**	**женá-nouns**	**двéрь-nouns**
HARD STEMS –ов SOFT STEMS –ей	(zero) –й	(zero) –й or –ь	–ей
столóв студéнтов áтласов урóков профессорóв	дéл слóв óкон пúсем	жён кнúг дéвушек сестёр корóбок	
ключéй товáрищей ножéй карандашéй портфéлей словарéй	собрáний сочинéний общежúтий заявлéний заня́тий здáний	лéкций истóрий лаборатóрий аудитóрий недéль	тетрáдей очередéй дверéй ночéй

Notes

1. Most **стол**-nouns ending in a hard consonant take the ending **–ов** in the genitive plural. Those ending in **ж, ш,** or a soft consonant other than **й,** take the ending **–ей.**

2. All **дверь**-nouns take the ending **–ей** in the genitive plural.

3. Most **окно-** and **жена**-nouns have a zero ending in the genitive plural. In structural terms this usually makes their genitive plural form identical with their plural stem: **жён, книг, картин, дел, имён.** The stem may be slightly modified, however, in two ways:

    a. A vowel may be inserted between the last two consonants of the stem as in **окон** (stem **окн–**), **студенток** (stem **студентк–**), **девушек** (stem **девушк–**), and **сестёр** (stem **сестр–**).

    b. If the stem ends in the sound [j], orthographic conventions require that it be written **й**: **собраний** (stem [sabráņij–]), **лекций** (stem [ļékcij–]). If the stem ends in a soft consonant other than [j], **ч,** or **щ,** the symbol **ь** must be written to indicate the basic softness of the stem final consonant: **недель** (stem [ņiḑéļ–]).

■ CUED SUBSTITUTION DRILLS

1. (*atlases*)   *And how about the atlases?*
(атласы) А ка́к насчёт а́тласов?
(столы́) **А ка́к насчёт столо́в?**
(романы, экзамены, стихи, ящики, уроки, фильмы, шкафы, костюмы)

2. (*pencils*)   *The students have no pencils.*
(карандаши́) У студе́нтов не́т карандаше́й.
(ножи́)   **У студе́нтов не́т ноже́й.**
(ключи, словари, портфели, тетради, карандаши, ножи)

■ CUED QUESTION-ANSWER DRILL

(*teachers*) *From whom did she hear it?*
     From the teachers.
(учителя́) От кого́ она́ э́то слы́шала?
    От учителе́й.
(продавщи́цы) От кого́ она́ э́то слы́шала?
    От продавщи́ц.

(их жёны, его сёстры, уборщицы, заочницы, профессора, студенты, учительницы, учителя, студентки, американки)

■ QUESTION-ANSWER DRILLS

1. *Where are the keys?*
There are no keys here.
Где́ ключи́?
Зде́сь не́т ключе́й.
Где́ ножи́?
Зде́сь не́т ноже́й.
   (карандаши, сочинения, книги, словари, тетради, письма, вилки, ложки)

2. *Were there any maps there?*
No, there weren't any maps there.
Та́м бы́ли ка́рты?
Не́т, та́м ка́рт не́ было.
Та́м бы́ли тетра́ди?
Не́т, та́м тетра́дей не́ было.
   (полки, коробки, девушки, книги, картины, вилки, ложки, окна, письма)

3. *Do you have any pencils?*
No, we don't have any pencils.
Карандаши́ у ва́с е́сть?
Не́т, карандаше́й у на́с не́т.
А́тласы у ва́с е́сть?
Не́т, а́тласов у на́с не́т.
   (тетради, полки, романы, стихи, словари, портфели, шкафы, костюмы)

The teachers were at our house.
We were at the teachers'.
Учителя́ бы́ли у на́с.
Мы́ бы́ли у учителе́й.
Студе́нты бы́ли у на́с.
Мы́ бы́ли у студе́нтов.
    (профессора́, его́ сёстры, убо́рщицы, их
    жёны, продавщи́цы, студе́нтки, учи́тель-
    ницы, америка́нки, секретари́)

■ INTEGRATION DRILL

These are dresses. These are sisters.
These are the sisters' dresses.
Э́то пла́тья.   Э́то сёстры.
Э́то пла́тья сестёр.
Э́то портфе́ли.   Э́то профессора́.
Э́то портфе́ли профессоро́в.
Э́то тетра́ди.   Э́то студе́нты.
Э́то кни́ги.   Э́то учителя́.
Э́то ко́мнаты.   Э́то продавщи́цы.
Э́то ключи́.   Э́то убо́рщицы.
Э́то карандаши́. Э́то учи́тельницы.

■ STRUCTURE REPLACEMENT DRILLS

We don't have a dormitory.
We don't have any dormitories.
У на́с не́т общежи́тия.
У на́с не́т общежи́тий.
У на́с не́т собра́ния.
У на́с не́т собра́ний.
    (ле́кции, уро́ка, авто́буса, заня́тий, сто-
    ла́, учи́теля, ка́рты, сочине́ния, ко́мнаты,
    ключа́, шка́фа, ру́чки)

■ STRUCTURE REPLACEMENT DRILL

Here are the bookcases.
There are a lot of bookcases here.
Во́т по́лки.
Зде́сь мно́го по́лок.
Во́т магази́ны.
Зде́сь мно́го магази́нов.
    (ножи́, заво́ды, карандаши́, зда́ния,
    о́кна, рестора́ны, телефо́ны, две́ри,
    общежи́тия, ко́мнаты)

The accusative plural of nouns

MODELS

Мы́ должны́ купи́ть а́тласы.	We have to buy atlases.
_____ портфе́ли.	_____ briefcases.
_____ тетра́ди.	_____ notebooks.
_____ карандаши́.	_____ pencils.
_____ ло́жки.	_____ spoons.
_____ ви́лки.	_____ forks.
_____ пе́рья.	_____ pen points.
_____ сту́лья.	_____ chairs.
_____ пла́тья.	_____ dresses.

Вы́ ви́дели и́х студе́нтов?	Did you see their students?
_____ профессоро́в?	_____ professors?
_____ това́рищей?	_____ friends?
_____ учителе́й?	_____ teachers?
_____ студе́нток?	_____ girl students?
_____ сестёр?	_____ sisters?

■ REPETITION DRILL

Repeat the given models, noting that where the direct object is inanimate, the accusative form is like the nominative, but where the direct object is animate, the accusative form is like the genitive.

1. *Where are your keys?*
   We forgot the keys.
   Где́ ва́ши ключи́?
   Мы́ забы́ли ключи́.
   Где́ ва́ши кни́ги?
   Мы́ забы́ли кни́ги.
   (карандаши, тетради, словари, карты, атласы, портфели)

2. *Where are the students?*
   We saw the students at the club.
   Где́ студе́нты?
   Мы́ ви́дели студе́нтов в клу́бе.
   Где́ студе́нтки?
   Мы́ ви́дели студе́нток в клу́бе.
   (учителя́, профессора́, её сёстры, девушки, его товарищи, американки, секретари́, якуты)

■ RESPONSE DRILLS

1. *Here are cucumbers for you.*
   Where did you get such cucumbers?
   Во́т, пожа́луйста, огурцы́.
   Где́ вы́ доста́ли таки́е огурцы́?
   Во́т, пожа́луйста, пе́рья.
   Где́ вы́ доста́ли таки́е пе́рья?
   (ручки, карандаши, стулья, чашки, ложки, вилки, ножи)

2. *Look, there go the students!*
   I see students every day.
   Посмотри́, та́м иду́т студе́нты.
   Я́ ви́жу студе́нтов ка́ждый де́нь.
   Посмотри́, та́м иду́т продавщи́цы.
   Я́ ви́жу продавщи́ц ка́ждый де́нь.
   (учителя, её сёстры, их жёны, учительницы, девушки, секретари, студентки)

3. *Here are his compositions.*
   I've already read his compositions.
   Во́т его́ сочине́ния.
   Я́ уже́ чита́л его́ сочине́ния.
   Во́т его́ стихи́.
   Я́ уже́ чита́л его́ стихи́.
   (работы, книги, романы, заявления, письма)

4. *The shelves are ready.*
   Want to take a look at the shelves?
   По́лки гото́вы.
   Хоти́те посмотре́ть по́лки?
   О́кна гото́вы.
   Хоти́те посмотре́ть о́кна?
   (двери, столы, стулья, ящики, общежития, дома, комнаты, квартиры)

■ STRUCTURE REPLACEMENT DRILL

1. *Ask the teacher.*
   Ask the teachers.
   Спроси́те учи́теля.
   Спроси́те учителе́й.
   Спроси́те его́ сестру́.
   Спроси́те его́ сестёр.
   (продавщицу, профессора, студентку, учительницу, вахтёра, американку)

2. *Where did you see the factory?*
   Where did you see the factories?
   Где́ вы́ ви́дели фа́брику?
   Где́ вы́ ви́дели фа́брики?
   Где́ вы́ ви́дели студе́нта?
   Где́ вы́ ви́дели студе́нтов?
   (автобус, очередь, картину, студентку, девушку, профессора, его сестру, его товарища, лабораторию, ручку, вахтёра)

3. *I just met my sister.*
   I just met my sisters.
   Я́ то́лько что встре́тил сестру́.
   Я́ то́лько что встре́тил сестёр.
   Я́ то́лько что встре́тил това́рища.
   Я́ то́лько что встре́тил това́рищей.
   (учительницу, учителя, профессора, студентку, секретаря)

SUMMARY OF NOUN ENDINGS IN THE ACCUSATIVE CASE

1. *Singular*
   a. Inanimate **стóл**-nouns and all **окнó-** and **двéрь**-nouns have accusative singular forms exactly like the nominative singular: стóл, чáй, окнó, плáтье, двéрь, Любóвь, мáть *mother*.
   b. Animate **стóл**-nouns borrow the genitive singular endings (**–a, –я**) for the accusative singular: товáрища, Владúмира, студéнта, Николáя, учúтеля, пáрня.
   c. Only **женá**-nouns have endings in the accusative singular distinct from those of the nominative or genitive singular (**–у, –ю**); these are used for *both* animate and inanimate nouns: женý, кнúгу, сестрý, Гáлю, истóрию, Кóлю, лéкцию.

2. *Plural*
   a. *All* inanimate nouns have accusative plural forms exactly like the nominative plural: столы́, словарú, кнúги, лéкции, óкна, сочинéния, двéри.
   b. *All* animate nouns have accusative plural forms exactly like the genitive plural: студéнтов, учителéй, жён, профессорóв, сестёр, товáрищей, матерéй *mothers*.

The genitive case with не бýдет constructions

MODELS

Зáвтра не бýдет урóка.	There won't be a lesson tomorrow.
_____ урóков.	_____ any lessons _____.
_____ лéкции.	_____ a lecture _____.
_____ лéкций.	_____ any lectures _____.
_____ собрáния.	_____ a meeting _____.
_____ собрáний.	_____ any meetings _____.

■ REPETITION DRILL

Repeat the given models, noting that the genitive is required in future **не бýдет** constructions.

■ STRUCTURE REPLACEMENT DRILLS

We had no classes yesterday.
We won't have any classes tomorrow.
Вчерá у нáс нé было урóков.
Зáвтра у нáс не бýдет урóков.

Вчерá у нáс нé было лéкции.
Зáвтра у нáс не бýдет лéкции.
(собрания, занятий, урока, экзамена, экзаменов, собраний)

■ QUESTION-ANSWER DRILLS

1. *Will there be bread in the store?*
   No, there won't be any bread.
   В магазúне бýдет хлéб?
   Нéт, хлéба не бýдет.
   В магазúне бýдет молокó?
   Нéт, молокá не бýдет.
   (селёдка, чай, рыба, ножи, тетради)

2. *But will Zina be there?*
   No, Zina won't be there.
   А Зúна тáм бýдет?
   Нéт, Зúны тáм не бýдет.
   А Олéг тáм бýдет?
   Нéт, Олéга тáм не бýдет.
   (их жёны, её брат, профессора, Козлов, Алексеев, учителя, вахтёр, девушки, секретарь, его товарищи, студентки)

Just as **нéт** and **нé было** are accompanied by the genitive in the present and past, so, too, **не бýдет** is accompanied by the genitive in the future to indicate a missing thing or person.

Compare the affirmative and negative sentences below, noting that the nominative subject in the affirmative examples is replaced by the genitive in the corresponding negative examples and that the negative **не бýдет** (like **нé было** of the past tense) is a fixed form.

AFFIRMATION	NEGATIVE
У нáс зáвтра бýдет лéкция. *We'll have a lecture tomorrow.*	У нáс зáвтра не бýдет лéкции. *We won't have a lecture tomorrow.*
У нúх зáвтра бýдут урóки. *They'll have classes tomorrow.*	У нúх зáвтра не бýдет урóков. *They won't have classes tomorrow.*

The genitive case for the direct object of negated verbs

MODELS

Я не хочý молокá.   I don't want any milk.
_____ чáя.   _____ tea.
_____ борщá.   _____ borsch.
_____ ры́бы.   _____ fish.
_____ селёдки.   _____ herring.

Мы́ такúх картúн ещё не вúдели.   We haven't seen pictures like that before.
_____ фúльмов _____.   _____ films _____.
_____ портфéлей _____.   _____ briefcases _____.
_____ домóв _____.   _____ houses _____.
_____ теáтров _____.   _____ theaters _____.
_____ квартúр _____.   _____ apartments _____.
_____ аудитóрий _____.   _____ auditoriums _____.
_____ библиотéк _____.   _____ libraries _____.
_____ общежúтий _____.   _____ dormitories _____.
_____ здáний _____.   _____ buildings _____.

Мы́ ещё не знáем всéх студéнтов.   We don't know all the students yet.
_____ дéвушек.   _____ girls _____.
_____ вахтёров.   _____ custodians _____.
_____ учителéй.   _____ teachers _____.
_____ студéнток.   _____ coeds _____.
_____ секретарéй.   _____ secretaries _____.
_____ слóв.   _____ words _____.

■ REPETITION DRILL

Repeat the given models, noting that after negated verbs the direct object is in the genitive case.

■ STRUCTURE REPLACEMENT DRILL

1. *I like novels.*
   I don't like novels.
   Я люблю́ рома́ны.
   Я не люблю́ рома́нов.
   Я люблю́ хи́мию.
   Я не люблю́ хи́мии.
   (стихи, осень, весну, зиму, географию, физику, литературу)

2. *Why is she opening the door?*
   Why doesn't she open the door?
   Почему́ она́ открыва́ет две́рь?
   Почему́ она́ не открыва́ет две́ри?
   Почему́ она́ открыва́ет окно́?
   Почему́ она́ не открыва́ет окна́?
   (о́кна, ящик, коробки, книгу, атлас, двери, тетрадь, тетради)

■ QUESTION-ANSWER DRILLS

1. *Did he get the books?*
   No, he didn't get the books.
   О́н доста́л кни́ги?
   Не́т, он не доста́л кни́г.
   О́н доста́л ключи́?
   Не́т, он не доста́л ключе́й.
   (тетрадь, словари, костюм, тетради, вилки, ножи, ложки, коробки, карандаши)

3. *Did you see his dictionary?*
   No, I didn't see his dictionary.
   Вы́ ви́дели его́ слова́рь?
   Не́т, я его́ словаря́ не ви́дел.

2. *Did you buy the suit?*
   No, I didn't buy the suit.
   Ты́ купи́ла костю́м?
   Не́т, я не купи́ла костю́ма.
   Ты́ купи́ла материа́л?
   Не́т, я не купи́ла материа́ла.
   (атлас, портфель, платье, ручку, чай, карандаш, карту)

   Вы́ ви́дели его́ тетра́дь?
   Не́т, я его́ тетра́ди не ви́дел.
   (книги, комнату, роман, портфель, квартиру, картину, картины)

■ RESPONSE DRILL

She probably forgot his name.
No, she didn't forget his name.
Она́, наве́рно, забы́ла его́ и́мя.
Не́т, она́ не забы́ла его́ и́мени.
Она́, наве́рно, забы́ла ключи́.
Не́т, она́ не забы́ла ключе́й.
(перо, ручку, подарок, ключ, его день рождения, его фамилию, его отчество)

DISCUSSION

Although, according to strict grammatical rules, the direct object of negated verbs should be in the genitive case, there are some exceptions. The most common of these are:

1. In informal spoken Russian the accusative singular of **жена́**-nouns is often used instead of the expected genitive:

Я́ не чита́л э́ту кни́гу (*or* Я́ не чита́л э́той кни́ги) *I haven't read this book.*

2. If the negated verb is followed by an infinitive, the accusative is often used instead of the expected genitive:

Я́ не могу́ откры́ть окно́ (*or* Я́ не могу́ откры́ть окна́) *I can't open the window.*

Demonstrative э́тот in the nominative, accusative, genitive, and prepositional cases

	SINGULAR			PLURAL
	Masculine	*Neuter*	*Feminine*	
NOM	э́тот	э́то	э́та	э́ти
ACC	*inanimate* э́тот *animate* э́того [étəvə]	э́то	э́ту	*inanimate* э́ти *animate* э́тих
GEN	э́того [étəvə]		э́той	э́тих
PREP	(об) э́том		э́той	э́тих

MODELS

Э́тот слова́рь не мой. This dictionary isn't mine.
Э́то письмо́ не моё. This letter _____.
Э́та кни́га не моя́. This book _____.
Э́та тетра́дь не моя́. This notebook _____.
Э́ти тетра́ди не мои. These notebooks aren't mine.

Вы ви́дите э́того студе́нта? Do you see that student?
_____ э́ту студе́нтку? _____ that coed?
_____ э́тих студе́нтов? _____ those students?
_____ э́тих студе́нток? _____ those coeds?

Возьми́ э́тот рома́н! Take this novel!
_____ э́ту кни́гу! ____ this book!
_____ э́то письмо́! ____ this letter!
_____ э́ту тетра́дь! ____ this notebook!
_____ э́ти стихи́! ____ these verses!

Я не ви́дел э́того рома́на. I haven't seen this novel.
_____ э́той кни́ги. _____ this book.
_____ э́того письма́. _____ this letter.
_____ э́той тетра́ди. _____ this notebook.
_____ э́тих стихо́в. _____ these verses.

Я не слы́шал об э́том рома́не. I haven't heard about this novel.
_____ э́той кни́ге. _____ this book.
_____ э́том де́ле. _____ this affair.
_____ э́той про́сьбе. _____ this request.
_____ э́тих стиха́х. _____ these verses.

■ REPETITION DRILL

Repeat the given models, noting particularly that genitive endings are used for the animate masculine accusative in the singular and for all animate accusatives in the plural.

■ RESPONSE DRILLS

1. *Whose key is this?*
   This one here?
   Чéй э́то клю́ч?
   Вóт э́тот?
   Чьй э́то стихи́?
   Вóт э́ти?
   (окно, словарь, дверь, книги, комната, работа, роман, портфель, сочинение, нож)

3. *I'll see you on Friday.*
   This Friday?
   Я́ вáс уви́жу в пя́тницу.
   В э́ту пя́тницу?

2. *Here's our room.*
   No, this room isn't ours.
   Вóт нáша кóмната.
   Нéт, э́та кóмната не нáша.
   Вóт нáша двéрь.
   Нéт, э́та двéрь не нáша.
   (ключ, окно, автобус, карандаши, ножи, словарь)

   Я́ вáс уви́жу в четвéрг.
   В э́тот четвéрг?
   (в субботу, в понедельник, в среду, в воскресенье, во вторник)

■ STRUCTURE REPLACEMENT DRILLS

1. *This is my table.*
   This table is mine.
   Э́то мóй стóл.
   Э́тот стóл мóй.
   Э́то моя́ кóмната.
   Э́та кóмната моя́.
   (мой портфель, мои книги, моя карта, моё перо, мои ключи, моё сочинение, моя дверь)

2. *This is my table.*
   My table is this one here.
   Э́то мóй стóл.
   Мóй стóл вóт э́тот.
   Э́то моя́ кóмната.
   Моя́ кóмната вóт э́та.
   (мой портфель, мои книги, моя карта, мои ключи, моё окно, моя дверь)

■ TRANSFORMATION DRILLS

1. *These dictionaries are [available] in the library.*
   This dictionary is [available] in the library.
   Э́ти словари́ éсть в библиотéке.
   Э́тот словáрь éсть в библиотéке.
   Э́ти ромáны éсть в библиотéке.
   Э́тот ромáн éсть в библиотéке.
   (книги, карты, атласы, письма, словари, сочинения, романы)

3. *Have you already seen these pictures?*
   Have you already seen this picture?
   Вы́ ужé ви́дели э́ти карти́ны?
   Вы́ ужé ви́дели э́ту карти́ну?

2. *What did you find out from these students?*
   What did you find out from this student?
   Что́ ты́ узнáл от э́тих студéнтов?
   Что́ ты́ узнáл от э́того студéнта?
   Что́ ты́ узнáл от э́тих профессорóв?
   Что́ ты́ узнáл от э́того профéссора?
   (учителей, уборщиц, парней, учительниц, девушек, студенток)

   Вы́ ужé ви́дели э́тих америкáнцев?
   Вы́ ужé ви́дели э́того америкáнца?
   (эти шкафы, эти сочинения, этих девушек, эти работы, этих студентов, этих студенток)

■ EXPANSION DRILL

We were talking about the lecture.
We were talking about this (or that) lecture.
Мы́ говори́ли о лéкции.
Мы́ говори́ли об э́той лéкции.

Мы́ говори́ли об áтласе.
Мы́ говори́ли об э́том áтласе.
(об уроках, о карте, о клубе, о собрании, о концерте, о курсах, о фильмах, о картинах)

It is important to note the difference between the unchanging introductory э́то (see Lesson 5) and the declinable demonstrative э́тот, э́та, э́то, э́ти. Note the following, which are complete sentences; the voice drops at the end of each:

Э́то ко́мната.	This is a room.
Э́то перо́.	This is a pen.

Compare them with the following, which are not sentences; in speech the voice level is sustained:

э́та ко́мната	this room
э́то перо́	this pen

Whereas unchanging э́то is independent of the other elements in the sentence, the demonstrative э́тот must agree in number, gender, and case with its noun referent. Note the following:

Э́то бы́л не мо́й слова́рь.	It wasn't my dictionary.
Э́тот слова́рь бы́л не мо́й.	That dictionary wasn't mine.

In the first case э́то is independent; бы́л and мо́й are masculine to agree with слова́рь. In the second case э́тот, бы́л, and мо́й are all masculine to agree with слова́рь.

ЧТЕ́НИЕ И ПИСЬМО́

Катя любит танцевать. В субботу она и Олег пойдут вместе в клуб, там будут танцы. После танцев они хотят посмотреть американский фильм. Олег уже его видел, а Катя нет.

Зина была в магазине. Там она встретила Катю. Катя купила материал на костюм. Материал был красивый, но дорогой. Завтра девушки опять пойдут в магазин, но уже вместе.

Владимир и Зина на одном курсе. Они часто после лекций ходят вместе в ресторан. Сегодня после обеда они идут *в клуб. Там будут танцы народов СССР.*

— Можно войти? — Конечно, заходите! Вы же знаете, наша дверь никогда не заперта. — Я хотел спросить насчёт концерта. Когда он будет? — В девять. И, знаете, это бесплатно. — Вот хорошо! Я не знал.

Га́ля всё вре́мя сиди́т до́ма. В клу́бе всегда́ то́лько та́нцы, а танцева́ть она́ не лю́бит. В кино́ она́ то́же не хо́дит. Она́ давно́ ви́дела все́ э́ти фи́льмы. Говоря́т, что ско́ро бу́дет идти́ америка́нский фи́льм. Э́то друго́е де́ло. Тогда́ Га́ля не бу́дет сиде́ть до́ма. Она́ пойдёт посмотре́ть э́тот фи́льм.

Оле́г чита́ет «Евге́ния Оне́гина», а Влади́мир «Войну́ и ми́р». Оле́г то́же чита́л «Войну́ и ми́р», и да́же мно́го ра́з. Он говори́т, что о́чень лю́бит э́тот рома́н.

Воло́дя и Оле́г — това́рищи по ко́мнате. Ка́тя и Зи́на то́же живу́т вме́сте. Зи́на и Оле́г на одно́м ку́рсе, но ма́ло знако́мы: то́лько «здра́вствуйте» и «до свида́ния». Но в суббо́ту они́ ду́мают всё вме́сте пойти́ на та́нцы.

— Куда́ вы́ спеши́те, Га́ля?
— В библиоте́ку. Я́ всегда́ хожу́ туда́ по́сле ле́кций.
— Почему́ же я́ ва́с никогда́ та́м не ви́дел?
— Не зна́ю. Я чита́ю в э́той библиоте́ке ка́ждый де́нь.
— И я то́же. Где́ вы́ лю́бите сиде́ть?
— Я́ сижу́ всегда́ у окна́.
— Тепе́рь бу́ду зна́ть.

— Куда́ вы́ идёте та́к по́здно?
— Я́ спешу́ в общежи́тие. Та́м бу́дут все́ на́ши ребя́та.
— А что́ вы́ бу́дете та́м де́лать?
— Игра́ть в ка́рты.
— Но́чью?
— Да́, та́м мо́жно игра́ть то́лько но́чью.

PREPARATION FOR CONVERSATION   **Мы́ попу́тчики**

попу́тчик   [papúččik]

Мы́ попу́тчики.

проводни́к, –а́; –и́, –о́в[1]

биле́т

Ва́ш биле́т.

граждани́н, –а; гра́ждане,
   гра́ждан[1]

Ва́ш биле́т, граждани́н.

ме́сто, –а; места́, ме́ст

Ме́сто во́семь зде́сь.

ваго́н

мя́гкий

мя́гкий ваго́н

Мя́гкий ваго́н, ме́сто во́семь зде́сь.

Спаси́бо. О́, кого́ я ви́жу?!

е́хать (unidirectional I), е́ду, е́дут

И вы́ е́дете?

Га́ля! И вы́ е́дете?

Да́. Здра́вствуйте.

иска́ть (I), ищу́, и́щут

Во́т ищу́ своё ме́сто. Проводни́к!

ве́рхний, –яя, –ее

Ва́ше ме́сто ве́рхнее.

ни́жний, –яя, –ее

проси́ть (II), прошу́, про́сят

traveling companion, fellow traveler

We're traveling companions.

conductor, guide

ticket

Your ticket.

citizen

Your ticket, sir.

place, seat, berth; position, job, space,
   room

Berth eight is here.

railroad car

soft

soft car, first-class car

First-class car, berth eight is here.

Thank you. Oh, who's that I see?

to be going (by vehicle)

Are you going, too?

Galya! Are you going, too?

Yes. Hello.

to look for, seek

I'm just looking for my seat. Conductor!

upper

Your berth is the upper.

lower

to request, ask for

---

[1] Nouns with shifting stress or other unpredictable features in the declension are given in four forms: nominative singular genitive singular, nominative plural, and genitive plural.

Я проси́ла ни́жнее.	I asked for a lower.
ка́сса	ticket window, box office, cash register
А я в ка́ссе проси́ла ни́жнее.	But I asked for a lower at the ticket window.
спа́ть (II), сплю, спя́т	to sleep
неудо́бно	[it's] uncomfortable, [it's] inconvenient
наверху́	upstairs, on top, in the upper
Наверху́ спа́ть неудо́бно.	It's uncomfortable sleeping in an upper.
оши́бка	mistake, error
Э́то, наве́рно, оши́бка.	It's probably a mistake.
купе́ (indeclinable n) [kupé]	compartment, sleeping compartment
У меня́ то́же ме́сто в э́том купе́.	I also have a berth in this compartment.
Подожди́те! Э́то, наве́рно, оши́бка.	Wait a minute! It's probably a mistake.
У меня́ то́же ме́сто в э́том купе́.	I have a berth in this compartment, too.
удивля́ться (I)	to be surprised
Не удивля́йтесь!	Don't be surprised!
е́здить (multidirectional II), е́зжу, е́здят	to go (by vehicle), ride, travel
в одно́м купе́	in one compartment
Они́ е́здят в одно́м купе́.	They travel in the same compartment.
же́нщина	woman
мужчи́на [muščínə]	man
Же́нщины и мужчи́ны е́здят в одно́м купе́.	Women and men travel in the same sleeping compartment.
у нас	in our country, in our society (*lit.* by us)
У нас же́нщины и мужчи́ны е́здят в одно́м купе́.	In our country women and men travel in the same sleeping compartment.
Что́ вы говори́те!	You don't say!
пое́хать (pfv I), пое́ду, пое́дут	to go (by vehicle), ride, travel
Мы́ в одно́м купе́ пое́дем.	We'll travel in the same compartment.
с ва́ми	with you
мы́ с ва́ми	you and I
Мы́ с ва́ми в одно́м купе́ пое́дем?	Will you and I travel in the same compartment?
Так зна́чит, мы́ с ва́ми в одно́м купе́ пое́дем?	Then you mean you and I will travel in the same compartment?
Да́. А вы́ куда́ е́дете?	Yes. And where is it you're going?
В Москву́, а вы́?	To Moscow. And you?
Я́ то́же.	So am I.
Во́т мы́ и попу́тчики.	Well, so we're traveling companions.

SUPPLEMENT

сто́ить (II), сто́ит, сто́ят	to cost, be (in price)
Ско́лько сто́ит биле́т в Москву́?	How much is a ticket to Moscow?
жёсткий ваго́н	hard car, second-class car
в жёстком ваго́не	in (*or* on) the second-class car

У меня́ ме́сто в жёстком ваго́не.	I have a seat in the second-class car.
в мя́гком ваго́не	in (*or* on) the first-class car
У меня́ ме́сто в мя́гком ваго́не.	I have a seat in the first-class car.
по́езд, –а; поезда́, –о́в	train
на по́езде	on the train, by train
Вы́ е́дете на по́езде?	Are you going on the train?
внизу́	downstairs, below
Где́ ва́ша ко́мната, наверху́ и́ли внизу́?	Where's your room, upstairs or downstairs?
плати́ть (II), плачу́, пла́тят	to pay
Плати́те в ка́ссе!	Pay at the ticket window!
заплати́ть (pfv II)	to pay
Вы́ уже́ заплати́ли?	Did you already pay?
плати́ть (*or* заплати́ть) за (*plus* acc)	to pay for
Ско́лько вы́ заплати́ли за биле́ты?	How much did you pay for the tickets?
ста́нция	station
на ста́нции	at the station
на ста́нцию	to the station
По́езд стои́т на ста́нции.	The train is in the station.

Мы́ попу́тчики

Гр. — Фили́пп Гра́нт, америка́нец
Г. — Га́ля
П. — Проводни́к [1]

П. 1 Ва́ш биле́т, граждани́н.[2] Мя́гкий ваго́н,[3] ме́сто во́семь зде́сь.

Гр. 2 Спаси́бо. О́, кого́ я́ ви́жу?! Га́ля! И вы́ е́дете?

Г. 3 Да́. Здра́вствуйте. Во́т ищу́ своё ме́сто. Проводни́к!

П. 4 Ва́ше ме́сто ве́рхнее.

Г. 5 А я́ в ка́ссе проси́ла ни́жнее. Наверху́ спа́ть неудо́бно.

Гр. 6 Подожди́те! Э́то, наве́рно, оши́бка! У меня́ то́же ме́сто в э́том купе́.

Г. 7 Не удивля́йтесь. У на́с же́нщины и мужчи́ны е́здят в одно́м купе́.[4]

Гр. 8 Что́ вы́ говори́те! Так зна́чит, мы́ с ва́ми в одно́м купе́ пое́дем?

Г. 9 Да́. А куда́ вы́ е́дете?

Гр. 10 В Москву́, а вы́?

Г. 11 Я́ то́же. Во́т мы́ и попу́тчики.

NOTES
[1] The **проводни́к** on Russian trains is the man in charge of an individual car. He differs from an American conductor in that the latter is responsible for several cars or the whole train. Thus job is something between that of a conductor and a porter. **Проводни́к** also means *guide*.

² Like all nouns ending in **–анин**, **граждани́н** loses **–ин** in the plural, and has the special nominative plural ending **–е**: **гра́ждане**. The stem thus ends in soft [ņ] in the nominative plural, but in hard [n] elsewhere in the plural: **мно́го гра́ждан, о гра́жданах.**

Although the American student or tourist in the Soviet Union may hear the word **граждани́н** used by train and streetcar conductors, bus drivers, and policemen, he should not use it himself in addressing Soviet citizens. Under no circumstances should he use **господи́н** or **госпожа́**. The best way to get the attention of a stranger is by saying **извини́те, прости́те**, or **скажи́те, пожа́луйста**. Although the student probably will not use the terms himself, he may hear himself addressed as **молодо́й челове́к** or, in the case of a girl, **де́вушка**.

³ The so-called *soft car* **мя́гкий ваго́н** consists of first-class compartments with soft seats; each compartment accommodating four persons. Compartments in the *hard car* **жёсткий ваго́н** have hard seats; each compartment seats six persons and sleeps four. In selling tickets, no attempt is made to separate men from women in sleeping cars, and the American tourist may be surprised to find he is sharing a sleeping car on a Russian train with one or more persons of the opposite sex.

⁴ The verbs **е́здить** and **е́хать** describe going by vehicle or some means other than on foot. **Е́здить** is used for the general (multidirectional) activity and **е́хать** for the specific (unidirectional) activity. In this respect they parallel **ходи́ть** and **идти́** exactly.

Compare	Мы́ ча́сто е́здим в Ки́ев.	We often go to Kiev.
	Мы́ ча́сто хо́дим в па́рк.	We often go to the park.
with	Мы́ е́дем в Ки́ев.	We're on our way to Kiev.
	Мы́ идём в па́рк.	We're on our way to the park.

PREPARATION FOR CONVERSATION   **В Москве́**

шофёр	driver (of car)
администра́тор	clerk, administrator
носи́льщик	porter
Носи́льщик!	Porter!
бага́ж	luggage, baggage
получи́ть (pfv II), получу́, полу́чат	to receive, get,
Получи́те мо́й бага́ж, пожа́луйста.	Get my luggage, please.
квита́нция	receipt, claim check
Во́т квита́нция.	Here's the claim check.
Носи́льщик! Получи́те мо́й бага́ж, пожа́луйста. Во́т квита́нция.	Porter! Get my luggage, please. Here's the claim check.
Сейча́с. А где́ вы́ бу́дете жда́ть?	Right away. Where will you wait?
ожида́ние	waiting, wait, expectation
за́л ожида́ния	waiting room
В за́ле ожида́ния.	In the waiting room.
ве́щь (f) (gen pl веще́й)	thing
Во́т ва́ши ве́щи.	Here are your things.
копе́йка (gen pl копе́ек)	kopeck
три́дцать [tŗítcəţ]	thirty
Три́дцать копе́ек, пожа́луйста.	Thirty kopecks, please.

Вóт вáши вéщи. Три́дцать копéек, пожáлуйста.	Here are your things. Thirty kopecks, please.
такси́ (indecl n)	taxi
Такси́!	Taxi!
багáжник	baggage compartment, luggage carrier, trunk
положи́ть (pfv II), положу́, полóжат	to put
Я положу́ вáши вéщи в багáжник.	I'll put your things in the baggage compartment.
разреши́ть (pfv II), разрешу́, разрешáт	to permit, allow
Я положу́ вáши вéщи в багáжник, разреши́те?	I'll put your things in the baggage compartment, O.K.?
вáм куда́?	where do you want to go?
Вáм куда́?	Where to?
гости́ница	hotel
В гости́ницу «Украи́на».	To the Hotel Ukraine.
прие́хать (pfv I), прие́ду, прие́дут	to arrive (by vehicle)
прие́хали	[we've] arrived, here we are
с вáс	from you; you owe
рубль, рубля́; –и́, –éй (m)	ruble
Прие́хали. С вáс рубль.	Here we are. That'll be one ruble.
Моя́ фами́лия Грáнт.	My name is Grant.
нóмер, –а; номерá, – óв	hotel room, number, issue
небольшóй	small
заказáть (pfv I), закажу́, закáжут	to order, make a reservation
Я заказáл небольшóй нóмер.	I ordered a small room.
лю́кс	deluxe class
Я заказáл небольшóй нóмер лю́кс.	I ordered a small room, deluxe class.
для одногó	a single, for one
Я заказáл небольшóй нóмер лю́кс для одногó.	I ordered a small single room, deluxe class.
этáж, –á; –и́, –éй	story, floor
на пя́том этажé	on the fifth floor
Вáш нóмер на пя́том этажé.	Your room is on the fifth floor.
удóбство	convenience, comfort
Всé удóбства.	[It has] all the conveniences.
вáнная	bathroom
убóрная	toilet, lavatory
водá	water
горя́чая водá	hot water
Всé удóбства: вáнная, убóрная, горя́чая водá.	All the conveniences: bath, lavatory, hot water.
напрáво	on the right, to the right
ли́фт	elevator
Ли́фт напрáво.	The elevator is to the right.
прекрáсно	excellent, fine
Прекрáсно.	Fine.

пешко́м	on foot
Я́ пойду́ пешко́м.	I'll go on foot.
нале́во	on the left, to the left
Где́ ли́фт?	Where's the elevator?
— Нале́во.	To the left.
пря́мо	straight, straight ahead, directly
Иди́те пря́мо.	Go straight ahead.
вокза́л [vagzál][1]	station, terminal
на вокза́л	to the station
на вокза́ле	in (or at) the station
Мы́ до́лго сиде́ли на вокза́ле.	We sat in the station a long time.
поезжа́й! поезжа́йте!	drive! go (by vehicle)!
Поезжа́йте в гости́ницу «Украи́на»!	Drive to the Hotel Ukraine!
Я́ е́ду в Ки́ев.	I'm going to Kiev.
Я́ е́ду в Ташке́нт.	I'm going to Tashkent.
Я́ е́ду в Ха́рьков.	I'm going to Kharkov.
Я́ е́ду во Владивосто́к.	I'm going to Vladivostok.
Я́ е́ду в Я́лту.	I'm going to Yalta.
Я́ е́ду в Оде́ссу.	I'm going to Odessa.
удо́бный (adv удо́бно)	convenient, comfortable
У ни́х удо́бная кварти́ра.	They have a comfortable apartment.

В Москве́

Гр. — Гра́нт
Нос. — Носи́льщик
Шоф. — Шофёр
Адм. — Администра́тор

Гр.　1 Носи́льщик! Получи́те мо́й бага́ж, пожа́луйста. Во́т квита́нция.

Нос.　2 Сейча́с. А где́ вы́ бу́дете жда́ть?

Гр.　3 В за́ле ожида́ния.

Нос.　4 Во́т ва́ши ве́щи. Три́дцать копе́ек, пожа́луйста. Такси́![1]

Шоф.　5 Я́ положу́ ва́ши ве́щи в бага́жник, разреши́те? Ва́м куда́?

Гр.　6 В гости́ницу «Украи́на».

Шоф.　7 Прие́хали. С ва́с ру́бль.

---

[1] Compare вокза́л with ста́нция. Вокза́л is a railway terminal or station building, whereas ста́нция can refer to any station. Notice that both require the preposition на:

Он встре́тил жену́ на авто́бусной ста́нции.	He met his wife at the bus station.
Он встре́тил жену́ на вокза́ле.	He met his wife at the railway station.

Гр.   8 Моя́ фами́лия Гра́нт. Я́ заказа́л небольшо́й но́мер лю́кс для одного́.[2]

Адм.   9 Да́, ваш но́мер на пя́том этаже́. Всё удо́бства: ва́нная, убо́рная, горя́чая вода́. Лифт напра́во.

Гр.   10 Прекра́сно.

NOTES   [1] Russians seldom check their luggage or use the help of porters. Tipping is officially forbidden in the Soviet Union, but most foreigners are expected to tip hotel servants, waiters, and check-room attendants.

[2] Only **лю́кс** guarantees hot water. At most hotels one gets only cold water, has no private bath, and has to share toilet facilities with other guests on the same floor. This is typical not only in the Soviet Union, but common in European countries as well.

Basic sentence patterns

1. Куда́ вы́ е́дете?
   — В Москву́.
   — Я́ е́ду в Москву́
   — В Ленингра́д.
   — Мы́ е́дем в Ленингра́д.
   — Зна́чит мы́ попу́тчики.
   — Я́ то́же е́ду в Ленингра́д.
   — Мы́ пое́дем в одно́м купе́.

   Where are you going?
   To Moscow.
   I'm going to Moscow.
   To Leningrad.
   We're going to Leningrad.
   Then we're traveling companions.
   I'm on my way to Leningrad, too.
   We'll ride in the same compartment.

2. Ва́ше ме́сто ве́рхнее и́ли ни́жнее?
   — Ве́рхнее.
   — Ни́жнее.
   — Ни́жнее лу́чше, чем ве́рхнее.
   — Неудо́бно спа́ть наверху́.
   — Я́ в ка́ссе проси́л ни́жнее.

   Do you have an upper or a lower?
   An upper.
   A lower.
   The lower is better than the upper.
   It's uncomfortable sleeping in an upper.
   I asked for a lower at the ticket window.

3. Гдé вы́ бу́дете жда́ть?
   — В за́ле ожида́ния.
   — На углу́.
   — О́коло кио́ска.
   — В гости́нице.
   — На ста́нции.
   — На вокза́ле.

   Where will you be waiting?
   In the waiting room.
   On the corner.
   Near the newsstand.
   At the hotel.
   At the station.
   At the station (or railway terminal).

4. Я́ положу́ ва́ши ве́щи на сто́л.
   _____ на э́тот сту́л.
   _____ на по́лку.
   _____ в ко́мнату.

   I'll put your things on the table.
   _____ on this chair.
   _____ on the bookcase.
   _____ in the room.

Я положу́ ва́ши ве́щи в коро́бку.	I'll put your things in the box.
_____ в шка́ф.	_____ in the dresser.
_____ в портфе́ль.	_____ in the briefcase.
_____ в я́щик.	_____ in the drawer.

5. Носи́льщик поло́жит ва́ши ве́щи в бага́жник. The porter will put your things in the luggage compartment.

_____ в такси́.	_____ in the taxi.
_____ в авто́бус.	_____ in the bus.
_____ в у́гол.	_____ in the corner.

6.
Во́т ва́ша квита́нция.	Here's your receipt (*or* claim check).
____ ва́ш биле́т.	_____ your ticket.
____ ва́ша ва́нная.	_____ your bathroom.
____ ва́ш бага́ж.	_____ your luggage.
____ ва́ше ме́сто.	_____ your seat (*or* berth).
____ ва́ше купе́.	_____ your compartment.
____ ва́ши ве́щи.	Here are your things.

7.
Э́то на́ш по́езд.	This is our train.
____ на́ша гости́ница.	_____ our hotel.
____ на́ша ста́нция.	_____ our station.
____ на́ш но́мер.	_____ our [hotel] room.
____ на́ша ко́мната.	_____ our room.

8.
Я ищу́ своё ме́сто.	I'm looking for my seat (*or* berth).
_____ сво́й но́мер.	_____ my [hotel] room.
_____ своё купе́.	_____ my compartment.
_____ такси́.	_____ a taxi.

9.
Мы́ и́щем кио́ск.	We're looking for a newsstand.
_____ проводника́.	_____ the conductor.
_____ шофёра.	_____ a taxi driver.
_____ администра́тора.	_____ the clerk in charge.
_____ носи́льщика.	_____ a porter.
_____ вахтёра.	_____ the custodian.

10.
Где́ ли́фт?	Where's the elevator?
— Напра́во.	To the right.
— Иди́те напра́во.	Go to the right.
— Нале́во.	To the left.
— Иди́те нале́во.	Go to the left.
— Иди́те пря́мо.	Go straight ahead.

11.
Куда́ вы́ е́дете?	Where are you going?
— В Ленингра́д.	To Leningrad.
— В Москву́.	To Moscow.
— В Ки́ев.	To Kiev.
— В Оде́ссу.	To Odessa.
— В Аме́рику.	To America.
— В СССР.	To the U.S.S.R.

12.
Ва́м куда́?	Where to?
— В гости́ницу «Украи́на».	To the Hotel Ukraine.
— На ста́нцию.	To the station.

— На вокза́л.	To the railway terminal.
— В университе́т.	To the university.
— На по́чту.	To the post office.
— В Большо́й теа́тр.	To the Bolshoi Theater.
— В ГУ́М.	To GUM.

13. Ско́лько сто́ит биле́т в Москву́?   How much is a ticket to Moscow?
    _____ в Ленингра́д?   _____ to Leningrad?
    _____ в Ки́ев?   _____ to Kiev?
    _____ в Оде́ссу?   _____ to Odessa?

14. Я́ е́ду то́лько до Москвы́.   I'm only going as far as Moscow.
    _____ до Ленингра́да.   _____ as far as Leningrad.
    _____ до Ки́ева.   _____ as far as Kiev.
    _____ до Ха́рькова.   _____ as far as Kharkov.
    _____ до Ташке́нта.   _____ as far as Tashkent.
    _____ до Владивосто́ка.   _____ as far as Vladivostok.
    _____ до Я́лты.   _____ as far as Yalta.
    _____ до Оде́ссы.   _____ as far as Odessa.

15. Вы́ ча́сто е́здите в Москву́?   Do you often go to Moscow?
    _____ в Ленингра́д?   _____ to Leningrad?
    _____ в Ки́ев?   _____ to Kiev?
    _____ в Я́лту?   _____ to Yalta?
    _____ в Оде́ссу?   _____ to Odessa?
    _____ во Владивосто́к?   _____ to Vladivostok?

16. Ско́лько э́то сто́ит?   How much does this cost?
    — Оди́н ру́бль.   One ruble.
    — Два́ рубля́.   Two rubles.
    — Три́ рубля́.   Three rubles.
    — Четы́ре рубля́.   Four rubles.
    — Пя́ть рубле́й.   Five rubles.
    — Ше́сть рубле́й.   Six rubles.
    — Се́мь рубле́й.   Seven rubles.
    — Во́семь рубле́й.   Eight rubles.
    — Де́вять рубле́й.   Nine rubles.
    — Де́сять рубле́й.   Ten rubles.

17. Ско́лько с меня́?   How much do I owe?
    — Одна́ копе́йка.   One kopeck.
    — Две́ копе́йки.   Two kopecks.
    — Три́ копе́йки.   Three kopecks.
    — Четы́ре копе́йки.   Four kopecks.
    — Пя́ть копе́ек.   Five kopecks.

18. С ва́с ше́сть копе́ек.   You owe six kopecks.
    _____ се́мь копе́ек.   _____ seven kopecks.
    _____ во́семь копе́ек.   _____ eight kopecks.
    _____ де́вять копе́ек.   _____ nine kopecks.
    _____ де́сять копе́ек.   _____ ten kopecks.

Pronunciation practice: special consonant clusters

A. Hard [čš] (spelled чш, дш, or тш).

[lúčšij] лу́чший
better

[mláčšij] мла́дший
younger

[xúčšij] ху́дший
worse

[páčšij] па́дший
fallen

[prašéčšij] проше́дший
gone

[zablúčšij] заблу́дший
gone astray

[zaɣáčšij] завя́дший
wilted

[cɣéčšij] цве́тший
bloomed

B. Long soft [čč] (spelled тч or дч).

[papúččik] попу́тчик
traveling companion

[ščóččik] счётчик
meter

[zdáččik] сда́тчик
lessor

[şíččik] си́тчик
kind of cotton

[aččót] отчёт
account, report

[óččij] о́тчий
father's

[buféččik] буфе́тчик
lunch counter attendant

[gażéččik] газе́тчик
newsboy

[raķéččik] раке́тчик
rocket technician

[baļéččik] бале́тчик
ballet dancer

[razɣéččik] разве́дчик
scout

[zavóččik] заво́дчик
factory owner

[kabáččik] каба́тчик
innkeeper

[ɣiččiná] ветчина́
ham

C. Hard [dž]. This combination occurs when a prefix ending in д or т combines with a root which begins with the voiced consonant ж. It also occurs in foreign-derived words.

[ṛidžák] пиджа́к
jacket

[džás] джа́з
jazz

[džút] джу́т
jute

[džém] дже́м
jam

[padžéč] подже́чь
to set fire to

[pədžigáṭiļ] поджига́тель
inciter

[padžárij] поджа́рый
thin, haggard

[adžiḷíšč] от жили́щ
from the dwellings

[ódžil] о́тжил
his time has passed

[adžéč] отже́чь
anneal; glass, metal

[ódžik] о́тжиг
annealing

[ażirbajdžán] Азербайджа́н
Azerbaidzhan (S.S.R.)

D. Hard [tc]. This combination occurs very frequently, especially in the infinitive and third person singular and plural of verbs with the reflexive particle –ся. It is spelled тс, тьс, дс, тц, or дц.

[dvátcət] два́дцать
twenty

[tṛítcət] три́дцать
thirty

[kanátci] кана́дцы
Canadians

[ṭiḇétci] тибе́тцы
Tibetans

[mítcə] мы́ться
to wash
[mójitcə] мо́ется
he washes
[mójutcə] мо́ются
they wash
[atcá] отца́
of father

[inarótci] иноро́дцы
foreigners
[ḷiṇingrátci] ленингра́дцы
people of Leningrad
[brátci] бра́тцы
brothers

STRUCTURE AND DRILLS

Two-stem first conjugation verbs

Many verbs of the first conjugation show a marked difference between the stem used to form the infinitive and past tense and that used to form the present-future. Verbs such as these we call "two-stem" verbs.

STEM взя–	STEM возьм–
INFINITIVE взя́ть PAST взя́л, взяла́, взя́ли	FUTURE возьму́, возьмёшь, возьмёт

In order to manipulate the various forms of the Russian verb, it is essential to recognize certain broad rules of compatibility vis-à-vis stems and endings.

1. Infinitive and past tense endings begin with consonants (т and л) and, in almost all verbs, are added to a form of the stem ending in a vowel: жи́–ть, жи́–л.
2. Present-future endings begin with vowels and are added to a form of the stem ending in a consonant: жив–у́, жив–ёшь, жив–у́т.[1]

MODELS

Other two-stem verbs already encountered by the student in some of their forms.

посла́ть (pfv) *to send*
    Я́ уже́ посла́л письмо́.
    I already sent the letter.
сказа́ть (pfv) *to say, tell*
    Что́ вы́ сказа́ли?
    What did you say?
заказа́ть (pfv) *to order*
    Она́ заказа́ла биле́ты.
    She ordered the tickets.
иска́ть (ipfv) *to look for*
    Вы́ меня́ иска́ли?
    Were you looking for me?
наре́зать (pfv) *to slice*
    Оле́г уже́ наре́зал хле́б.
    Oleg already sliced the bread.

пошлю́, пошлёшь, пошлю́т
    Я́ за́втра пошлю́ письмо́.
    I'll send the letter tomorrow.
скажу́, ска́жешь, ска́жут
    О́н ничего́ не ска́жет.
    He won't say anything.
закажу́, зака́жешь, зака́жут
    Она́ зака́жет биле́ты.
    She'll order the tickets.
ищу́, и́щешь, и́щут
    Вы́ и́щете рабо́ту?
    Are you looking for work?
наре́жу, наре́жешь, наре́жут
    Оле́г наре́жет хле́б.
    Oleg will slice the bread.

---

[1] In [j]–stem verbs, the present-future stem ends in the consonant *sound* [j].

писа́ть (ipfv) *to write*
Мы́ писа́ли пи́сьма.
We were writing letters.

пишу́, пи́шешь, пи́шут
Мы́ пи́шем пи́сьма.
We're writing letters.

написа́ть (pfv) *to write*
Вы́ написа́ли домо́й?
Have you written home?

напишу́, напи́шешь, напи́шут
Не́т, я за́втра напишу́.
No, I'll write tomorrow.

жи́ть (ipfv) *to live*
Вы́ до́лго та́м жи́ли?
Did you live there long?

живу́, живёшь, живу́т
Вы́ давно́ здесь живёте?
Have you lived here long?

доста́ть (pfv) *to get*
Вы́ доста́ли биле́ты?
Did you get the tickets?

доста́ну, доста́нешь, доста́нут
О́н доста́нет биле́ты.
He'll get the tickets.

откры́ть (pfv) *to open*
Вахтёр откры́л две́рь.
The custodian opened the door.

откро́ю, откро́ешь, откро́ют
Вахтёр откро́ет две́рь.
The custodian will open the door.

закры́ть (pfv) *to close*
Вы́ уже́ закры́ли о́кна?
Did you already close the windows?

закро́ю, закро́ешь, закро́ют
Не́т, я сейча́с закро́ю.
No, I'll do it now.

бы́ть *to be*
Где́ вы́ бы́ли?
Where were you?

бу́ду, бу́дешь, бу́дут
Где́ вы́ бу́дете после обе́да?
Where will you be this afternoon?

забы́ть (pfv) *to forget*
Она́ забы́ла о собра́нии.
She forgot about the meeting.

забу́ду, забу́дешь, забу́дут
Вы́ не забу́дете на́с?
You won't forget us, will you?

пи́ть (ipfv) *to drink*
Вы́ уже́ пи́ли ча́й?
Have you had tea already?

пью, пьёшь, пью́т
Вы́ пьёте ко́фе?
Do you drink coffee?

танцева́ть (ipfv) *to dance*
Вы́ мно́го танцева́ли?
Did you dance much?

танцу́ю, танцу́ешь, танцу́ют
Вы́ танцу́ете?
Do you dance?

е́хать (ipfv) *to be going*
Мы́ е́хали в Ташке́нт.
We were on our way to Tashkent.

е́ду, е́дешь, е́дут
Мы́ е́дем в Ташке́нт.
We're on our way to Tashkent.

прие́хать (pfv) *to arrive*
Они́ уже́ прие́хали.
They've already arrived.

прие́ду, прие́дешь, прие́дут
Они́ прие́дут в четве́рг.
They'll arrive on Thursday.

■ SUBSTITUTION DRILLS

1. *I'm writing a letter*
   Я́ пишу́ письмо́.
   Они́ пи́шут письмо́.
   (мы, вы, ты, он, она, я, они)

2. *I'll write the letter.*
   Я́ напишу́ письмо́.
   Она́ напи́шет письмо́.
   (мы, они, ты, Евгений, я, вы, они)

3. *The custodian will open the doors.*
   Вахтёр откро́ет две́ри.
   Я́ откро́ю две́ри.
   (проводник, мы, они, ты, вы,
   носильщики, шофёр)

4. *I'm looking for a hotel.*
   Я́ ищу́ гости́ницу.
   Она́ и́щет гости́ницу.
   (мы, ты, Зина, они, вы, Филипп)

5. *I don't drink coffee.*

Я́ не пью́ ко́фе.

Мы́ не пьём ко́фе.

    (они, вы, Наташа, ты, муж, жена)

6. *They'll order the tickets.*

Они́ зака́жут биле́ты.

Я́ закажу́ биле́ты.

    (Ирина, ты, вы, Козлов, они, я)

■ STRUCTURE REPLACEMENT DRILLS

1. *Do you dance much?*

  Did you dance much?

Вы́ мно́го танцу́ете?

Вы́ мно́го танцева́ли?

О́н мно́го танцу́ет?

О́н мно́го танцева́л?

    (она, они, он, Галя)

2. *He forgot the keys.*

  He'll forget the keys.

О́н забы́л ключи́.

О́н забу́дет ключи́.

Ты́ забы́л ключи́.

Ты́ забу́дешь ключи́.

    (я, мы, вы, она)

3. *We lived in Kiev.*

  We live in Kiev.

Мы́ жи́ли в Ки́еве.

Мы́ живём в Ки́еве.

Я́ жи́л в Ки́еве.

Я́ живу́ в Ки́еве.

    (вы, они, Зина, я, мы)

4. *He was looking for you.*

  He's been looking for you.

О́н ва́с иска́л.

О́н ва́с и́щет.

Я́ ва́с иска́л.

Я́ ва́с ищу́.

    (они, мы, она, Алексеев, я)

5. *Oleg will get the tickets.*

  Oleg got the tickets.

Оле́г доста́нет биле́ты.

Оле́г доста́л биле́ты.

Я́ доста́ну биле́ты.

Я́ доста́л биле́ты.

    (мы, они, вы, Наташа, ты, Волков)

■ QUESTION-ANSWER DRILLS

1. *Have you already sent the letter?*

  No, I'll send it tomorrow.

Вы́ уже́ посла́ли письмо́?

Не́т, я́ за́втра пошлю́.

Она́ уже́ посла́ла письмо́?

Не́т, она́ за́втра пошлёт.

    (Олег, ты, они, мы, Зина, вы)

2. *Have they already arrived?*

  No, they'll arrive today.

Они́ уже́ прие́хали?

Не́т, они́ прие́дут сего́дня.

Ва́ш дру́г уже́ прие́хал?

Не́т, о́н прие́дет сего́дня.

    (ваши друзья, твоя сестра, украинцы)

■ MIXED STRUCTURE REPLACEMENT DRILL

Past tense to present-future and vice versa.

1. *He didn't say a thing.*

  He won't say a thing.

О́н ничего́ не сказа́л.

О́н ничего́ не ска́жет.

Вы́ ничего́ не ска́жете.

Вы́ ничего́ не сказа́ли.

Она́ ничего́ не сказа́ла.

Мы́ ничего́ не ска́жем.

Они́ ничего́ не сказа́ли.

Я́ ничего́ не скажу́.

Ты́ ничего́ не сказа́л.

2. *I'll slice the bread.*

  I've sliced the bread.

Я́ наре́жу хле́б.

Я́ наре́зал хле́б.

Ты́ наре́зал хле́б.

Ты́ наре́жешь хле́б.

Мы́ наре́жем хле́б.

Оле́г наре́зал хле́б.

Они́ наре́жут хле́б.

Вы́ наре́зали хле́б.

О́льга наре́жет хле́б.

Я́ наре́зал хле́б.

3. *They closed the windows.*
   They'll close the windows.
   Они́ закры́ли о́кна.
   Они́ закро́ют о́кна.
   Мы́ закро́ем о́кна.
   Мы́ закры́ли о́кна.

Я́ закры́л о́кна.
Ка́тя закры́ла о́кна.
Проводники́ закры́ли о́кна.
Вы́ закро́ете о́кна.

Genitive plural noun endings: special problems

1. **Сто́л**-nouns with stems ending in the always-hard consonant **ц** take the ending **–ов** only if the stress falls on the ending: **огурцо́в**. If the stress falls on the stem, the ending is spelled **–ев**: **америка́нцев, украи́нцев, та́нцев**. Remember that this is merely a spelling convention and that **ц** is always *pronounced* hard: [aṃiṛikáncif, ukrajíncif, agurcóf].

2. Particular problems arise in forming the genitive plural of certain **сто́л–** and **окно́**-nouns with stems ending in the consonant sound [j].

   a. **Сто́л**-nouns ending in **й** in the nominative singular take the genitive plural ending **–ев** (stressed: **–ёв**).

NOM SG		NOM PL	GEN PL
геро́й	hero	геро́и	геро́ев
ча́й	tea	чаи́	чаёв

   b. Most **сто́л–** and **окно́**-nouns which terminate in *unstressed* **–ья** in the nominative plural take the ending **–ев** (retaining the preceding **–ь**). Most are nouns with only their plural stems ending in [j].

NOM PL		GEN PL
бра́тья	brothers	бра́тьев
сту́лья	chairs	сту́льев
пе́рья	pen points	пе́рьев
пла́тья	dresses	пла́тьев

   c. Those **сто́л**-nouns whose nominative plural terminates in *stressed* **–ья** have a zero-ending genitive plural with **е** inserted before the final **–й**. Here **–й** is not an ending, strictly speaking, but the Cyrillic way of representing the stem consonant [j] after the inserted vowel.

NOM PL			GEN PL	
мужья́	[mužjá]	husbands	муже́й	[mužéj]
друзья́	[druẓjá]	friends	друзе́й	[druẓéj]
сыновья́	[sinaɣjá]	sons	сынове́й	[sinaɣéj]

3. A few **сто́л**-nouns have zero-ending genitive plural forms which are identical with their nominative singular forms.

NOM SG		GEN PL	
оди́н ра́з	one time	мно́го ра́з	many times
оди́н солда́т	one soldier	мно́го солда́т	many soldiers
оди́н грузи́н	one Georgian	мно́го грузи́н	many Georgians

4. A few other nouns, such as **ребя́та** and **господа́** (plural of **господи́н**), have a zero ending in the genitive plural.

NOM PL		GEN PL
ребя́та	guys, fellows, kids	ребя́т
господа́	gentlemen, ladies and gentlemen	госпо́д

5. **Стол**-nouns ending in **–анин** or **–янин** in the nominative singular lose the suffix **–ин** in the plural and have a zero ending in the genitive plural.

NOM SG		NOM PL	GEN PL
граждани́н	citizen	гра́ждане	гра́ждан
англича́нин	Englishman	англича́не	англича́н
египтя́нин	Egyptian	египтя́не	египтя́н

■ RESPONSE DRILL

I don't see any chairs.
Where are the chairs?
Я́ не ви́жу сту́льев.
Где́ сту́лья?
Я́ не ви́жу америка́нцев.
Где́ америка́нцы?
(украинцев, грузин, ребят, платьев, перьев, её братьев, их мужей, его друзей, огурцов)

■ CUED QUESTION-ANSWER DRILL

(Georgians) Whom did you ask?
The Georgians.
(грузи́ны) У кого́ вы́ спра́шивали?
У грузи́н.
(мужья́) У кого́ вы́ спра́шивали?
У муже́й.
(друзья, братья, ребята, девушки, украинцы, американцы, парни, учителя́)

■ QUESTION-ANSWER DRILLS

1. *Don't you have any dresses?*
We do. The dresses are over there.
Не́т ли у ва́с пла́тьев?
Е́сть. Пла́тья во́н та́м.
Не́т ли у ва́с сту́льев?
Е́сть. Сту́лья во́н та́м.
(огурцов, перьев, ножей, словарей, карандашей, стульев, атласов, столов)

2. *Where are the dresses?*
I don't see any dresses.
Где́ пла́тья?
Я́ не ви́жу пла́тьев.
Где́ америка́нцы?
Я́ не ви́жу америка́нцев.
(стулья, перья, их мужья, его друзья, грузины, ребята, огурцы, её братья, украинцы)

3. *Can one get chairs there?*
No, there are no chairs there.
Та́м мо́жно доста́ть сту́лья?
Не́т, та́м не́т сту́льев.
Та́м мо́жно доста́ть пе́рья?
Не́т, у ни́х не́т пе́рьев.
(платья, огурцы, стулья, перья)

4. *Do they have dictionaries?*
No, they don't have any dictionaries.
У ни́х е́сть словари́?
Не́т, у ни́х не́т словаре́й.
У ни́х е́сть пе́рья?
Не́т, у ни́х не́т пе́рьев.
(стулья, платья, братья, портфели, ножи, карандаши, друзья, огурцы)

■ SUBJECT REVERSAL DRILL

Their brothers were at our place.
We were at their brothers' place.

Их бра́тья бы́ли у на́с.

Мы́ бы́ли у и́х бра́тьев.

Их мужья́ бы́ли у на́с.

Мы́ бы́ли у и́х муже́й.

(их друзья́, грузи́ны, ребя́та, американцы, украи́нцы, их жёны, их сёстры)

■ TRANSLATION DRILL

1. There are no pens here. 2. There are no chairs in the dormitory. 3. There are no Americans in the dormitory. 4. There are no Ukrainians in the dormitory. 5. There are no Georgians in the dormitory. 6. There are no dresses at GUM. 7. He has no brothers. 8. He has no friends. 9. The fellows have lots of time. 10. The husbands have no time. 11. I've read *War and Peace* many times. 12. We were at [our] friends'. 13. We were at our brothers' (places).

The use of the genitive after numbers

MODELS

С ва́с два́ рубля́.

_____ три́ _____.

_____ четы́ре_____.

Э́то сто́ит две́ копе́йки.

_____ три́ _____.

_____ четы́ре _____.

Биле́т сто́ит пя́ть рубле́й.

_____ ше́сть _____.

_____ се́мь _____.

_____ во́семь _____.

_____ де́вять _____.

_____ де́сять _____.

Я́ заплати́л пя́ть копе́ек.

_____ ше́сть _____.

_____ се́мь _____.

_____ во́семь _____.

_____ де́вять _____.

_____ де́сять _____.

You owe two rubles.

_____ three _____.

_____ four _____.

This costs two kopecks.

_____ three _____.

_____ four _____.

A ticket costs five rubles.

_____ six _____.

_____ seven _____.

_____ eight _____.

_____ nine _____.

_____ ten _____.

I paid five kopecks.

_____ six _____.

_____ seven _____.

_____ eight _____.

_____ nine _____.

_____ ten _____.

■ REPETITION DRILL

Repeat the given models, noting that the genitive singular is required after **два́, две́, три́,** and **четы́ре**; and the genitive plural for **пя́ть** on up. Note also that **две́** replaces **два́** with all feminine nouns. Compare **две́ сестры́, две́ тетра́ди** with **два́ рубля́, два́ сло́ва.**

Response with consecutive numbers (one to ten).

1. *How much does this cost?*
   One ruble.
   Ско́лько э́то сто́ит?
   Оди́н ру́бль.
   Ско́лько э́то сто́ит?
   Два́ рубля́.

2. *How much do I owe?*
   One kopeck.
   Ско́лько с меня́?
   Одна́ копе́йка.
   Ско́лько с меня́?
   Две́ копе́йки.

3. *How many notebooks do you have?*
   I have one notebook.
   Ско́лько у ва́с тетра́дей?
   У меня́ одна́ тетра́дь.
   Ско́лько у ва́с кни́г?
   У меня́ две́ кни́ги.
   (бра́тьев, словаре́й, ру́чек, комнат, ка-
   рандаше́й, пе́рьев, ви́лок, ло́жек)

4. *How much did you pay for it?*
   One ruble, two kopecks.[1]
   Ско́лько вы́ заплати́ли за э́то?
   Оди́н ру́бль две́ копе́йки.
   Ско́лько вы́ заплати́ли за э́то?
   Два́ рубля́ три́ копе́йки.

5. *How many days will you be in Moscow?*
   Only two days.
   Ско́лько дне́й вы́ бу́дете в Москве́?
   То́лько два́ дня́.
   Ско́лько дне́й вы́ бу́дете в Москве́?
   То́лько три́ дня́.

6. *How many weeks will you be in the U.S.S.R.?*
   Two weeks.
   Ско́лько неде́ль вы́ бу́дете в СССР?
   Две́ неде́ли.
   Ско́лько неде́ль вы́ бу́дете в СССР?
   Три́ неде́ли.

DISCUSSION

The number *one* differs from the other numbers in that it is treated as a modifier with separate forms for each gender: **оди́н ру́бль, одна́ копе́йка, одно́ сло́во.**

The other numbers when used in nominative and accusative constructions are accompanied by the genitive case: *genitive singular* for 2, 3, 4; and *genitive plural* for 5 and up. There is a special feminine form for two: **две́;** masculine and neuter nouns require **два́.** It is important to remember that compounds such as 21, 22, 31, 32, 101, and 102 require the noun form to agree with the last element of the compound only: **три́дцать оди́н ру́бль** *31 rubles,* **три́дцать две́ копе́йки** *32 kopecks,* **три́дцать три́ студе́нта** *33 students.*

Unidirectional versus multidirectional verbs of motion

MODELS

UNIDIRECTIONAL

Я́ иду́ в па́рк.	I'm going to the park.	(*on foot*)
Я́ е́ду в Москву́.	I'm going to Moscow.	(*by vehicle*)
Я́ шёл в па́рк.	I was on my way to the park.	(*on foot*)
Я́ е́хал в Москву́.	I was on my way to Moscow.	(*by vehicle*)

[1] Continue up to nine rubles, ten kopecks.

Я́ ча́сто хожу́ в па́рк.	I often go to the park.	(on foot)
Я́ ча́сто е́зжу в Москву́.	I often go to Moscow.	(by vehicle)
Я́ ча́сто ходи́л в па́рк.	I often went to the park.	(on foot)
Я́ ча́сто е́здил в Москву́.	I often went to Moscow.	(by vehicle)

UNIDIRECTIONAL		
INFINITIVE	**идти́** *to be going* (on foot)	**е́хать** *to be going* (by vehicle)
PRESENT	иду́, идёшь, идёт, идём, идёте, иду́т	е́ду, е́дешь, е́дет, е́дем, е́дете, е́дут
PAST	шёл, шла́, шло́, шли́	е́хал, –а, –о, –и
MULTIDIRECTIONAL		
INFINITIVE	**ходи́ть** *to go* (on foot)	**е́здить** *to go* (by vehicle)
PRESENT	хожу́, хо́дишь, хо́дит, хо́дим, хо́дите, хо́дят	е́зжу, е́здишь, е́здит, е́здим, е́здите, е́здят
PAST	ходи́л, –а, –о, –и	е́здил, –а, –о, –и

■ REPETITION DRILL

Repeat the given models, noting that **идти́** and **е́хать** describe motion in process or intended motion. Contrast them with **ходи́ть** and **е́здить**, which describe repeated motion, i.e., motion in more than one direction. In addition, remember that **идти́** and **ходи́ть** ordinarily indicate going on foot, while **е́хать** and **е́здить** indicate going by means of some vehicle.

■ SUBSTITUTION DRILLS

1. *She often goes to concerts.*
   Она́ ча́сто хо́дит на конце́рты.
   Студе́нты ча́сто хо́дят на конце́рты.
   (мы, я, ты, вы, они, Наташа, студентки)

2. *She's on her way to a concert.*
   Она́ идёт на конце́рт.
   Ты́ идёшь на конце́рт.
   (мы, я, они, Кирилл, вы)

3. *I often go to Kiev.*
   Я́ ча́сто е́зжу в Ки́ев.
   Они́ ча́сто е́здят в Ки́ев.
   (администратор, мы, ты, вы, эта женщина, я, они)

4. *Zina and Philip are on their way to Moscow.*
   Зи́на и Фили́пп е́дут в Москву́.
   Вы́ е́дете в Москву́.
   (я, мы, ты, она, наши студентки, Волков, вы, они)

■ STRUCTURE REPLACEMENT DRILLS

1. *I'm on my way to school.*
   I go to school.
   Я́ иду́ в шко́лу.
   Я́ хожу́ в шко́лу.
   Мы́ идём в шко́лу.
   Мы́ хо́дим в шко́лу.
   (Наташа, они, ты, я, вы, мой брат, мы все)

2. *I'm on my way to Leningrad.*
   I often go to Leningrad.
   Я́ е́ду в Ленингра́д.
   Я́ ча́сто е́зжу в Ленингра́д.
   Они́ е́дут в Ленингра́д.
   Они́ ча́сто е́здят в Ленингра́д.
   (мы, ты, товарищ Волков, проводник, вы, я, они)

3. *Were you on your way to the park?*
Did you go to the park?
Вы шли в па́рк?
Вы ходи́ли в па́рк?
Ты шёл в па́рк?
Ты ходи́л в па́рк?

(она шла, они шли, ты шла, Олег шёл)

4. *Were you on your way to Kiev?*
Did you go to Kiev?
Вы е́хали в Ки́ев?
Вы е́здили в Ки́ев?
Она́ е́хала в Ки́ев?
Она́ е́здила в Ки́ев?

(ты ехал, они ехали, Волков ехал,
студентки ехали, ты ехала)

■ RESPONSE DRILLS

1. *We saw you on the bus.*
Were you on your way downtown?
Мы тебя́ ви́дели в авто́бусе.
Ты е́хал в го́род?
Мы ва́с ви́дели в авто́бусе.
Вы е́хали в го́род?

(её, его, тебя, вас, их)

2. *I saw you yesterday near the park.*
Were you on your way to the park?
Вчера́ я ва́с ви́дел о́коло па́рка.
Вы шли в па́рк?
Вчера́ я его́ ви́дел о́коло па́рка.
О́н шёл в па́рк?

(их, её, тебя, вас, его)

■ QUESTION-ANSWER DRILLS

1. *Where were you on Saturday morning?*
I went to the library.
Где́ ты бы́л в суббо́ту у́тром?
Я ходи́л в библиоте́ку.
Где́ она́ была́ в суббо́ту у́тром?
Она́ ходи́ла в библиоте́ку.
Где́ вы́, Ка́тя, бы́ли в суббо́ту у́тром?
Где́ вы́, Оле́г, бы́ли в суббо́ту у́тром?
Где́ ты́, Ири́на, была́ в суббо́ту у́тром?
Где́ они́ бы́ли в суббо́ту у́тром?
Где́ о́н бы́л в суббо́ту у́тром?
Где́ вы́ бы́ли в суббо́ту у́тром?

2. *Where were you last week?*
I went to Kharkov.
Где́ ты бы́л на про́шлой неде́ле?
Я е́здил в Ха́рьков.
Где́ ты была́ на про́шлой неде́ле?
Я е́здила в Ха́рьков.
Где́ вы́, Оле́г, бы́ли на про́шлой неде́ле?
Где́ вы́, Зи́на, бы́ли на про́шлой неде́ле?
Где́ они́ бы́ли на про́шлой неде́ле?
Где́ о́н бы́л на про́шлой неде́ле?
Где́ она́ была́ на про́шлой неде́ле?

3. *Do you walk to work?*
No, I go by bus.
Вы хо́дите на́ рабо́ту пешко́м?
Не́т, я е́зжу на авто́бусе.
Они́ хо́дят на рабо́ту пешко́м?
Не́т, они́ е́здят на авто́бусе.

(она, ты, ваш брат, ваша сестра, они,
вы)

4. *Are you going to the theater by cab?*
No, we're going on foot.
Вы е́дете в теа́тр на такси́?
Не́т, мы́ идём пешко́м.
Ты е́дешь в теа́тр на такси́?
Не́т, я иду́ пешко́м.

(она, они, Евгений, мы, ты, Катя)

DISCUSSION

Most non-prefixed, motion verbs have an added feature not found in other verbs: a double set of imperfectives used to distinguish between *unidirectional* motion and *multidirectional* motion.

The *unidirectional* imperfectives describe a single, one-way trip to a specific destination. It may refer to an action that is (or was) in process or to one intended in the near future.

Я сейча́с иду́ в па́рк.   I'm on my way to the park now.
За́втра я иду́ в кино́.   I'm going to the movies tomorrow.
Я е́ду в Москву́.   I'm on my way to Moscow.
За́втра я е́ду в Москву́.   I'm going to Moscow tomorrow.

The *multidirectional* imperfectives describe movement in more than one direction or unspecified as to destination. This may include one or more round trips, or movement in several directions.

Я не люблю́ ходи́ть.	I don't like to walk.
Я ходи́л в па́рк.	I went to the park (and returned).
Я е́здил в Ки́ев.	I went to Kiev (and returned).
Я ча́сто е́зжу в Ки́ев.	I often go to Kiev.

In addition to the distinction between *unidirectional* and *multidirectional* movement, Russian also distinguishes between movement under one's own power (**идти́, ходи́ть**) and movement by means of some conveyance (**е́хать, е́здить**).

While the verbs **е́хать** and **е́здить** are limited to the description of a person's travel by conveyance, the movement of the conveyance itself is usually described by means of **идти́** or **ходи́ть**.

Compare	Во́т идёт авто́бус.	Here comes the bus.
	Э́тот по́езд идёт в Ки́ев.	This train goes to Kiev.
	Поезда́ сего́дня не хо́дят.	Trains aren't running today.
with	Я е́ду в Ки́ев.	I'm going to Kiev.
	Мы́ е́здили на по́езде.	We went on the train.

The verb **идти́** is also used in many idioms.

В кино́ идёт хоро́ший фи́льм.	There's a good picture showing at the movies.
Идёт до́ждь. (Шёл до́ждь.)	It's raining. (It was raining.)
Идёт снег. (Шёл снег.)	It's snowing. (It was snowing.)
Э́тот костю́м ва́м идёт.	That suit becomes you.

The verbs **ходи́ть** and **е́здить** have perfectives which are very rarely used: **походи́ть** *to do a bit of walking* and **пое́здить** *to do a bit of riding*. The most frequently used perfectives are formed from **идти́** and **е́хать**: **пойти́** and **пое́хать**. These perfectives describe the accomplishment of setting out for one's destination with nothing said about the return.

О́н пошёл в магази́н.	He went to the store *or* He set off for the store.
О́н пое́хал в Москву́.	He went to Moscow *or* He set off for Moscow.

Now note the use of the imperfective past of **ходи́ть** and **е́здить**, which in similar situations, tell us that the person went and returned.

О́н ходи́л в магази́н.	He went to the store (and is already back).
О́н е́здил в Москву́.	He went to Moscow (and is already back).

Long-form adjectives: nominative singular and plural

MODELS

Э́то краси́вый костю́м.	That's a lovely suit.
_____ го́род.	_____ city.
Э́то краси́вое окно́.	That's a lovely window.
_____ общежи́тие.	_____ dormitory.
Э́то краси́вая карти́на.	That's a lovely picture.
_____ ко́мната.	_____ room.
Э́то краси́вые ве́щи.	Those are lovely things.
_____ дома́.	_____ houses.

Этот а́тлас ста́рый. | This atlas is old.
_____ дорого́й. | _____ expensive.
_____ хоро́ший. | _____ good.
Это пла́тье ста́рое. | This dress is old.
_____ дорого́е. | _____ expensive.
_____ хоро́шее. | _____ good.
Эта кни́га ста́рая. | This book is old.
_____ дорога́я. | _____ expensive.
_____ хоро́шая. | _____ good.
Эти кни́ги ста́рые. | These books are old.
_____ дороги́е. | _____ expensive.
_____ хоро́шие. | _____ good.

Како́й большо́й до́м! | What a large house!
_____ хоро́ший _____! | _____ nice _____!
Како́е большо́е зда́ние! | What a large building!
_____ хоро́шее _____! | _____ nice _____!
Кака́я больша́я кварти́ра! | What a large apartment!
_____ хоро́шая _____! | _____ nice _____!
Каки́е больши́е карти́ны! | What large pictures!
_____ хоро́шие _____! | ____ nice _____!

Где́ большо́й за́л? | Where's the large hall?
___ больша́я аудито́рия? | _____ the large auditorium?
___ большо́е общежи́тие? | _____ the large dormitory?
___ больши́е рестора́ны? | Where are the large restaurants?

Это второ́й уро́к. | This is the second lesson.
___ втора́я ле́кция. | _____ the second lecture.
___ второ́е собра́ние. | _____ the second meeting.

У меня́ ста́рый слова́рь. | I have an old dictionary.
_____ ста́рая тетра́дь. | _____ an old notebook.
_____ ста́рое пла́тье. | _____ an old dress.
Мы́ ста́рые друзья́. | We're old friends.

Бо́рщ горя́чий. | The borsch is hot.
_____ хоро́ший. | _____ good.
Вода́ горя́чая. | The water is hot.
_____ хоро́шая. | _____ good.
Молоко́ горя́чее. | The milk is hot.
_____ хоро́шее. | _____ good.
Щи́ горя́чие. | The schi is hot.
___ хоро́шие. | _____ good.

Ни́жний эта́ж за́нят. | The lower floor is occupied.
Ни́жняя кварти́ра занята́. | The lower apartment is occupied.
Ни́жнее ме́сто за́нято. | The lower berth is occupied.
Ни́жние этажи́ за́няты. | The lower floors are occupied.

■ REPETITION DRILL

Repeat the given models, noting the pattern of adjective endings. Observe that the stress may be consistently on the endings (as in большо́й, –о́е, –а́я, –и́е) or on the stem (as in хоро́ший, –ее, –ая, –ие), but that there is no shifting of stress within the various forms of a particular adjective. Soft-stem adjectives always have their stress on the stem.

■ EXPANSION DRILLS

1. *Where are the factories?*
   Where are the large factories?
   Где́ фа́брики?
   Где́ больши́е фа́брики?
   Где́ магази́н?
   Где́ большо́й магази́н?

   (теа́тр, слова́рь, лаборато́рия,
   общежи́тие, окно́, о́чередь, ста́нция,
   но́ж, шка́ф, кино́, па́рк, фа́брика, я́щик,
   рестора́н, библиоте́ка)

2. *Here are the boys.*
   Here are the Russian boys.
   Во́т па́рни.
   Во́т ру́сские па́рни.
   Во́т де́вушка.
   Во́т ру́сская де́вушка.

   (учителя́, слова́рь, ка́рта, фи́льм, рома́н,
   кни́ги, фа́брика)

■ QUESTION-ANSWER DRILL

Is the room large or small?
Small.
Ко́мната больша́я и́ли ма́ленькая?
Ма́ленькая.
Ва́ше ме́сто ве́рхнее и́ли ни́жнее?
Ни́жнее.
Огурцы́ хоро́шие и́ли плохи́е?

Ва́ш ваго́н жёсткий и́ли мя́гкий?
Кварти́ра ма́ленькая и́ли больша́я?
Фи́льм интере́сный и́ли ску́чный?
Ко́мнаты ма́ленькие и́ли больши́е?
Ста́нция больша́я и́ли ма́ленькая?

■ STRUCTURE REPLACEMENT DRILLS

1. *Here's the large auditorium.*
   Here's the small auditorium.
   Во́т больша́я аудито́рия.
   Во́т ма́ленькая аудито́рия.
   Во́т ску́чные кни́ги.
   Во́т интере́сные кни́ги.
   Во́т ве́рхнее ме́сто.
   Во́т плохи́е студе́нты.
   Во́т ма́ленькая ста́нция.
   Во́т хоро́ший студе́нт.
   Во́т мя́гкий ваго́н.
   Во́т ни́жнее ме́сто.
   Во́т жёсткий ваго́н.

3. *You're a good friend.*
   You're good friends.
   Вы́ хоро́ший дру́г.
   Вы́ хоро́шие друзья́.
   Вы́ ста́рый дру́г.
   Вы́ ста́рые друзья́.
   Э́то ма́ленькая ко́мната.
   Э́то ма́ленькое окно́.

2. *The atlases are expensive.*
   The atlas is expensive.
   А́тласы дороги́е.
   А́тлас дорого́й.
   Кни́ги интере́сные.
   Кни́га интере́сная.
   Портфе́ли хоро́шие.
   Общежи́тия больши́е.
   Пла́тья краси́вые.
   Словари́ дороги́е.
   Пе́рья плохи́е.
   Ко́мнаты ма́ленькие.
   Сту́лья удо́бные.

   Во́т мя́гкий ваго́н.
   Во́т жёсткий ваго́н.
   У на́с больша́я аудито́рия.
   У на́с хоро́шая аудито́рия.
   Результа́т неплохо́й.
   Ка́рта небольша́я.
   До́м небольшо́й.

Russian adjectives follow a fairly simple pattern of endings in the spoken language. Because of the peculiarities of the spelling system, however, they appear complicated in writing. For convenience we group them according to their last stem consonant as hard stems, soft stems, and mixed stems.

1. *Hard stems* are those with stems ending in any *hard* consonant except ш, ж, к, г, or х: **больно́й, краси́вый, ста́рый.**
2. *Soft stems* are those with stems ending in soft н: **ни́жний, ве́рхний.**
3. *Mixed stems* are those with stems ending in к, г, х, ш, ж, ч, and щ: **жёсткий, друго́й, большо́й, горя́чий.**

<table>
<tr><td colspan="6" align="center">ADJECTIVE ENDINGS IN THE NOMINATIVE SINGULAR AND PLURAL</td></tr>
<tr><td colspan="2" rowspan="2"></td><td colspan="3" align="center">SINGULAR</td><td rowspan="2">PLURAL</td></tr>
<tr><td align="center">*Masculine*</td><td align="center">*Neuter*</td><td align="center">*Feminine*</td></tr>
<tr><td>HARD STEMS</td><td></td><td align="center">–о́й (–ый)
второ́й
краси́вый</td><td align="center">–ое
второ́е
краси́вое</td><td align="center">–ая
втора́я
краси́вая</td><td align="center">–ые
вторы́е
краси́вые</td></tr>
<tr><td>SOFT STEMS</td><td></td><td align="center">–ий
ни́жний</td><td align="center">–ее
ни́жнее</td><td align="center">–яя
ни́жняя</td><td align="center">–ие
ни́жние</td></tr>
<tr><td rowspan="2">MIXED STEMS</td><td>1. Stems ending in к, г, х</td><td align="center">–о́й (–ий)
друго́и
ма́ленький</td><td align="center">–ое
друго́е
ма́ленькое</td><td align="center">–ая
друга́я
ма́ленькая</td><td align="center">–ие
други́е
ма́ленькие</td></tr>
<tr><td>2. Stems ending in ш, ж, ч, щ</td><td align="center">–о́й (–ий)
большо́й
горя́чий</td><td align="center">–о́е (–ее)
большо́е
горя́чее</td><td align="center">–ая
больша́я
горя́чая</td><td align="center">–ие
больши́е
горя́чие</td></tr>
</table>

Mixed stems ending in к, г, and х follow the same basic pattern of endings as hard stems, except that, instead of –ый (m) and –ые (pl), the endings are –ий and –ие respectively; the preceding к, г, or х is automatically softened. Compare **краси́вый, краси́вые** with **ма́ленький, ма́ленькие.**

Hard stems have the masculine ending –о́й if stressed, but –ый if unstressed. Compare **второ́й, молодо́й** with **ста́рый, краси́вый.**

Mixed stems ending in ш and ж have the masculine and neuter endings –о́й and –о́е if stressed, but –ий and –ее if unstressed. Compare **большо́й, большо́е** with **хоро́ший, хоро́шее.**

Note that some adjectives function as nouns and that some surnames are adjectival in form: **столо́вая** (for **столо́вая ко́мната**), **ва́нная** (for **ва́нная ко́мната**), **Толсто́й, Достое́вский**. The surname for Miss or Mrs. Tolstoy is **Толста́я** and for Miss or Mrs. Dostoevsky, **Достое́вская**. In the plural the Tolstoys are **Толсты́е** and the Dostoevskys **Достое́вские**.

— Доброе утро! — Здравствуйте! Куда вы едете? — В Москву. А вы куда? — Я тоже еду в Москву! — Вот, хорошо! Значит, мы попутчики.

— Здравствуй, Саша! Как живёшь? — Ничего, спасибо. — Это ваше общежитие? — Да. Моя комната на пятом этаже. — Ты живёшь один? — Нет, у меня есть два товарища по комнате: Володя Орлов и Олег Семёнов. Ты их знаешь? — Конечно, уже давно. Они очень хорошие ребята.

— Привет, Филипп! Что вы здесь делаете? — Жду Царапкина. — Это ваш товарищ по комнате? — Да, мы с осени живём вместе. — Я знаю Наташу Царапкину. Это его сестра? — Да. А вот и он идёт. Хотите познакомиться? — Да, конечно.

— Моя́ фами́лия Гра́нт. А ка́к ва́ша фами́лия?
— О́сипов. Я́ из Ленингра́да. А вы́ отку́да?
— Я́ из Аме́рики. То́лько прие́хал сего́дня.
— Во́т ка́к! О́чень ра́д с ва́ми познако́миться. Где́ ва́ша ко́мната?
— Во́т зде́сь, напра́во.
— Та́к мы́ това́рищи по ко́мнате! Во́т уда́ча: я́ как ра́з учу́ англи́йский язы́к.
— О, вы́ говори́те по-англи́йски?
— Немно́го.

— Скажи́те, вы́ пойдёте сего́дня в библиоте́ку?
— Да́, по́сле обе́да.

— Пожáлуйста, возьмúте для меня́ «Войнý и мúр».

— Хорошó. Но вы́, кáжется, недáвно читáли э́тот ромáн?

— Дá, нó такúе вéщи нáдо читáть мнóго рáз.

— Носúльщик, возьмúте, пожáлуйста, мóй багáж.

— Сейчáс. Вы́ хотúте поéхать на таксú?

— Дá, я́ óчень спешý.

— Вóн тáм таксú. Таксú! Положúть вéщи в багáжник?

— Дá, пожáлуйста. Вóт, возьмúте 10 копéек.

— Спасúбо.

— Вы́ чáсто хóдите в кинó?

— Хожý, но не чáсто. Иногдá в суббóту.

— Хотúте пойтú зáвтра вéчером?

— А чтó идёт?

— «Войнá и мúр».

— Э́то, кáжется, америкáнский фúльм?

— Дá, и, говоря́т, хорóший.

— Пойдём. Интерéсно посмотрéть.

— Я́ éду во Владивостóк. Кáжется, мы́ попýтчики?

— Дá, но тóлько до Москвы́. Я́ éду в Москвý.

— Скóлько врéмени éхать до Москвы́?

— Шéсть часóв. А скóлько от Москвы́ до Владивостóка?

— Сéмь днéй, кáжется.

— Тáк дóлго? Когдá же вы́ приéдете?

— Сегóдня понедéльник. Знáчит я́ приéду во Владивостóк на слéдующей недéле, во втóрник úли в срéду.

— Таксú!

— Вáм кудá?

— В гостúницу «Украúна». Тóлько я́ óчень спешý.

— Э́то пя́ть минýт, не бóльше.

— Ну вóт, мы́ ужé éдем пя́ть минýт. Ещё далекó?

— Нéт, сейчáс. Вóн, вúдите, налéво большóй дóм? Э́то и éсть гостúница «Украúна».

— Прекрáсно. Скóлько с меня́?

— Двáдцать копéек.

— Пожáлуйста.

— Вы́ говорúте, что заказáли здéсь нóмер?

— Дá, я́ заказáл небольшóй нóмер для одногó.

— Кáк вáша фамúлия?

— Грáнт. Филúпп Грáнт.

— Вы́ америкáнец?

— Дá. Я́ студéнт Москóвского университéта.

— А, знáчит вы́ не дóлго у нáс бýдете.

— Нéт, тóлько двá дня́.

PREPARATION FOR CONVERSATION

Читáйте «Вечéрнюю Москвý»

вечéрний, –яя; –ее, –ие

Читáйте «Вечéрнюю Москвý».

    газéта

    посовéтовать (pfv I), посовéтую,
      –ешь, –ют

Какýю газéту вы́ мнé посовéтуете читáть?

    извéстие

    «Извéстия» (pl)

    «Прáвда»

**Нѝна, какýю газéту вы́ мнé посовéтуете
читáть — «Прáвду», «Извéстия»?**

Нéт, читáйте «Вечéрнюю Москвý».

    объявлéние

    театрáльный

Тáм театрáльные объявлéния.

    происшéствие

Тáм театрáльные объявлéния,
   происшéствия.

    тóт же, тá же, тó же, тé же

    вездé

    нóвость (f)

Нóвости вездé тé же.

**Тáм театрáльные объявлéния, происшéствия,
а нóвости вездé тé же.**

    чáстный [čásnij]

    чáстные объявлéния

У вáс нéт чáстных объявлéний.

    продавáть (I), продаю́, –ёшь, –ют

---

evening

Read the *Evening Moscow.*

    newspaper

    to advise

What paper would you advise me to read?

    news, news report

    Izvestia (name of newspaper)

    Pravda (name of newspaper)

Nina, which newspaper would you advise me
to read, *Pravda* [or] *Izvestia?*

No, read the *Evening Moscow.*

    notice, announcement, declaration

    theater, theatrical

It has theater notices.

    happening, occurrence, accident, event,
      incident

It has theater notices and [local] events.

    the same

    everywhere

    news, novelty

The news is the same in all of them (*lit.* everywhere).

It has theater notices and local events, and the
news is the same in all of them.

    private, personal

    want ads, private ads

You don't have want ads.

    to sell

◄ Читáльный зáл в одном из Домов культýры.

люд́и, людéй

Ка́к же лю́ди продаю́т свои́ ве́щи?

А скажи́те, во́т у ва́с не́т ча́стных
  объявле́ний, ка́к же лю́ди продаю́т
  свои́ ве́щи?

подéржанный [paɟéržənij]

Подéржанные ве́щи?

комиссио́нные магази́ны

В комиссио́нных магази́нах.
толку́чка
В комиссио́нных и́ли на толку́чках.

знако́мые (acc, gen, *and* prep pl
  знако́мых)
че́рез (*plus* acc)[1]
Че́рез знако́мых.
просто́й (adv про́сто)
В комиссио́нных, на толку́чке, и́ли
  про́сто че́рез знако́мых.

А́х, во́т оно́ что́!

рекла́ма
У ва́с ма́ло рекла́м.
заме́тить (pfv II), заме́чу, заме́тишь, –ят
Я заме́тил, что у ва́с ма́ло рекла́м.
ме́жду про́чим
Ме́жду про́чим, я заме́тил, что у
  ва́с ма́ло рекла́м.

журна́л
У ва́с ма́ло рекла́м, да́же в жур-
на́лах.
«Огонёк» (gen sg «Огонька́»)

У ва́с ма́ло рекла́м, да́же в журна́лах,
  наприме́р в «Огоньке́».

о́черк
США́ (*full form* Соединённые Шта́ты
  Аме́рики) [eššeá] or [ššá]
Вы́ чита́ли о́черк о США́?
после́дний, –яя, –ее, –ие
в после́днем но́мере
В после́днем но́мере бы́л о́черк
  о США́, вы́ чита́ли?

people

Just how do people sell their things?

Tell me, since you don't have want ads, how
  do people sell their things?

secondhand

Secondhand things?

commission stores (state-managed
  secondhand stores)
In commission stores.
flea market, secondhand market
In commission stores or at the flea
  market.
acquaintances, friends

through, across, by way of, in
Through friends.
simple, simply
In commission stores, at the flea market,
  or simply through friends.

Oh, so that's it!

advertisement, advertising
You have so few advertisements.
to notice
I've noticed you have very few advertisements.
by the way, while we're on the subject
By the way, I've noticed you have very
  few ads.

magazine, journal
You have very few ads, even in
  magazines.
Ogonyok (name of Soviet
  magazine—*lit.* small light)
You have so few ads, even in magazines,
  for example, in *Ogonyok*.

sketch, essay, feature story
the U.S.A.

Did you read the feature story on the U.S.A?
last, latest
in the last issue
In the last issue there was a feature story on
  the U.S.A. Did you read it?

---

[1] The preposition **че́рез** is pronounced either with a weak stress on the first syllable or without stress altogether. It has
the meaning *in* only in time expressions: **че́рез ча́с** *in an hour.*

Чита́л. А во́т вы́ на́ш журна́л
«Аме́рика» зна́ете?

   тру́дно (adj тру́дный)
Да́, но его́ тру́дно доста́ть.

   ни
   в како́м кио́ске ни спро́сишь
   отве́т
   распро́дан, –а, –о, –ы
В како́м кио́ске ни спро́сишь, всегда́
   оди́н отве́т: «Распро́даны».

   стра́нно (adj стра́нный)
Стра́нно.

   посо́льство
   достава́ть (I), достаю́, –ёшь, –ю́т
Я́ могу́ достава́ть и́х в на́шем посо́льстве.
Слу́шайте, я́ могу́ достава́ть и́х в
   на́шем посо́льстве.

Во́т хорошо́!

   бра́ть (I), беру́, –ёшь, –у́т (pfv взя́ть)
Я́ тогда́ бу́ду бра́ть у ва́с.

SUPPLEMENT

   сове́товать (I), сове́тую, –ешь, –ют
Что́ вы́ мне́ сове́туете?
   прочита́ть (pfv)
Вы́ уже́ прочита́ли газе́ту?
   лёгкий [ḷóxḳij]
   легко́ [ḷixkó]
Не та́к легко́ доста́ть журна́л «Аме́рика».

   челове́к (pl лю́ди)
О́н хоро́ший челове́к.
Она́ хоро́ший челове́к.
   ра́дио (indecl n)
Послу́шаем ра́дио.
   но́вый
Что́ но́вого?
   молодо́й
Вы́ зна́ете э́того молодо́го челове́ка?
   у́лица
Во́т по́чта через у́лицу.

I did. But do you know our
   magazine *America*?

   hard, difficult
Yes, but it's hard to get hold of it.

   not (negative particle), no matter
   no matter at which newsstand you ask
   answer
   sold out
No matter at what newsstand you ask, it's
   always the same answer: "They're sold out."

   strange
That's strange.

   embassy
   to get, get hold of
I can get them at our embassy.
Listen, I can get them at our
   embassy.

Good!

   to take, get, borrow
Then I'll get them from you.

   to advise
What would you advise me?
   to read (through), to finish reading
Have you finished reading the newspaper?
   easy, light
   easy, easily
It's not so easy to get hold of the magazine
   America.
   person, human being, man
He's a nice person.
She's a nice person.
   radio
Let's listen to the radio.
   new
What's new?
   young
Do you know this young man?
   street
There's the post office across the street.

Читайте «Вечёрнюю Москву́»

Ф. — Фили́пп   Н. — Ни́на

Ф. 1 Ни́на, каку́ю газе́ту вы́ мне́ посове́туете чита́ть — «Пра́вду», «Изве́стия»?[1]

Н. 2 Не́т, чита́йте «Вечёрнюю Москву́»: та́м театра́льные объявле́ния, происше́ствия, а но́вости везде́ те́ же.[2]

Ф. 3 Хорошо́. А скажи́те, во́т у ва́с не́т ча́стных объявле́ний, ка́к же лю́ди продаю́т свои́ ве́щи?

Н. 4 Поде́ржанные? В комиссио́нных, на толку́чке, и́ли про́сто че́рез знако́мых.[3]

Ф. 5 А́х, во́т оно́ что́! Ме́жду про́чим, я́ заме́тил, что у ва́с ма́ло рекла́м.[4] Да́же в журна́лах, наприме́р в «Огоньке́».[5]

Н. 6 Да́. Так вы́ уже́ знако́мы с «Огонько́м»? Кста́ти, в после́днем но́мере бы́л о́черк о США́, вы́ чита́ли?[6]

Ф. 7 Чита́л. А во́т вы́ на́ш журна́л «Аме́рика» зна́ете?[7]

Н. 8 Да́, но его́ тру́дно доста́ть. В како́м кио́ске ни спро́сишь, всегда́ оди́н отве́т: «Распро́даны».

Ф. 9 Стра́нно. Слу́шайте, я́ могу́ достава́ть и́х в на́шем посо́льстве.

Н. 10 Во́т хорошо́! Я́ тогда́ бу́ду бра́ть у ва́с.

NOTES

[1] «Пра́вда» *Pravda* (*Truth*) and «Изве́стия» *Izvestia* (*News*) are the two largest Soviet newspapers; the first is the official party newspaper and the second is the official government newspaper. Each issue is usually made up of four pages, limited to national and international items of political significance. Note that «Изве́стия» is plural: **Я́ э́то чита́л в «Изве́стиях».**

[2] «Вечёрняя Москва́» used to be the only paper in the Soviet Union that published local news items, including accidents. There is also a comparable newspaper in Leningrad called «Вечёрний Ленингра́д».

[3] **Толку́чки** are establishments where practically any secondhand item can be bought or sold. They are frowned on by the government and are frequently closed down or moved to the outskirts of town— to discourage people from patronizing them. **Комиссио́нные магази́ны** are government-supported secondhand stores where people may buy and sell used things. A seller must wait to receive his money until the item has actually been sold.

[4] The Soviet government is now doing a little more advertising of commodities than it did before World War II, using radio, posters, and occasionally even neon signs. Announcements on radio and television tell what goods have come into the state stores. In addition, bulletin boards have been installed in display windows; on these boards, individuals can post announcements of things for sale.

[5] «Огонёк» is a popular weekly illustrated magazine whose contents range from articles on national and international themes to fiction, verse, art reproductions, and crossword puzzles.

⁶ **США** (**Соединённые Шта́ты Аме́рики**) is pronounced [eššeá] by some people and [šša] by others. Some speakers say **об США** [abeššeá] and others **о США** [aššá]. Like **СССР** this abbreviation is not declined: **в США, в СССР.** The basic rule for abbreviations is that they are not declined unless they contain a medial vowel: compare **об СССР** with **о ГУ́Ме.**

⁷ «**Аме́рика**» is an illustrated magazine with articles on life in the U.S.; it is printed in Russian and distributed in the Soviet Union by the U.S. Department of State. Soviet officials allow only a limited number to be sold, often returning large quantities to the American embassy, supposedly unsold. A very limited number of newsstands in the large cities are allowed to sell «**Аме́рика**», and, when the word gets around that a new issue has arrived, friends of the clerks who distribute and sell it usually buy up the few available copies. Secondhand copies sell readily in used-book stores.

PREPARATION FOR CONVERSATION   **Послу́шаем пласти́нки**

пласти́нка	phonograph record
послу́шать (pfv I) (*like* слу́шать)	to listen [to]
Послу́шаем пласти́нки.	Let's listen to records.
подру́га	girl friend (of a girl)
Вы ещё не ви́дели мои́х подру́г.	You haven't seen my girl friends yet.
зайти́ (pfv I), зайду́, –ёшь, –у́т (past зашёл, зашла́, –о́, –и́)	to drop in, stop by, call on
Зайдём в общежи́тие.	Let's drop in at the dormitory.
Хоти́те, зайдём в общежи́тие, познако́млю?	Want to drop in at the dormitory and I'll introduce you?
С больши́м удово́льствием.	With great pleasure *or* I'd like to very much.
про́пуск (pl –а́, –о́в)	pass, entry permit
да́ть (pfv irreg) (past да́л, –а́, –о́, –и; fut да́м, да́шь, да́ст, дади́м, дади́те, даду́т)	to give, let
А мне́ даду́т про́пуск?	But will they give me a pass?
Коне́чно.	Of course.
му́зыка	music
ча́ю (special gen)	[some] tea
вы́пить (pfv I), вы́пью, вы́пьешь, –ют	to drink, to finish drinking
Вы́пьем ча́ю, му́зыку послу́шаем.	We'll drink some tea and listen to music.
прои́грыватель (m)	record player
У на́с е́сть прои́грыватель.	We have a record player.
уголо́к (var of у́гол)	corner
кра́сный	red
кра́сный уголо́к	recreation room

У нас в красном уголке есть проигрыватель.

In our recreation room there's a record player.

Прекрасно.
    песня (gen pl песен)
    народный

Fine.
    song
    folk, popular

Там, наверно, есть русские народные песни?

There probably are Russian folk songs there?

    певец (gen *and* acc sg певца; nom pl певцы, gen *and* acc pl певцов)

    певица
    исполнение
    в исполнении

    singer (m)

    singer (f)
    performance
    performed by

Да, много, и в исполнении лучших певцов и певиц.

Yes, lots, and performed by the best men and women singers.

Я люблю ваши народные песни.
    чёрный
    очи (*poetic for* глаза)

I'm fond of your folk songs.
    black, dark
    eyes

Я так люблю ваши народные песни, например «Очи чёрные».

I'm so fond of your folk songs, for example, "Dark Eyes."

    романс
Да это старый романс.
    петь (I), пою, поёшь, поют
    уже не
    который

    love song (semi classical)
Why, that's an old love song.
    to sing
    no longer
    which, what, that

Да это старый романс, который уже не поют.

Why, that's an old love song that's no longer sung.

    неужели?

Неужели?

    really? you don't say?

Really?

    услышать (pfv II) (*like* слышать)
    мелодия

    to hear
    melody, tune

У нас в Америке эту мелодию часто можно услышать.

In America that tune may often be heard.

Да ну?

No kidding?

    джаз
Мы любим ваш джаз.
А мы любим ваш джаз, только пластинки трудно доставать.

    jazz, popular music
We love your jazz.
By the way, we love your jazz, but it's hard to get records.

Я принесу, у меня их много.

I'll bring some; I have a lot of them.

SUPPLEMENT

    приносить (II), приношу, приносишь, —ят

    to bring

Он часто приносит пластинки.
    белый
    синий

He often brings records.
    white
    dark blue

голубо́й	light blue
зелёный	green
жёлтый	yellow
цве́т, –а (nom pl цвета́)	color
како́го цве́та	what color, of what color

Како́го цве́та ва́ш костю́м? — What color is your suit?
— Си́него (*or* си́ний). — Dark blue.

вку́сный (adv вку́сно) — tasty, good (tasting), delicious
Хоти́те ча́шку вку́сного ко́фе? — Want a cup of good coffee?

глаз, –а; глаза́, глаз — eye
У неё си́ние глаза́. — She has dark blue eyes.

Послу́шаем пласти́нки

Н. — Ни́на   Ф. — Фили́пп

Н. 1 Фили́пп, вы́ ещё не ви́дели мои́х подру́г. Хоти́те, зайдём в общежи́тие, познако́млю?

Ф. 2 С больши́м удово́льствием. А мне́ даду́т про́пуск?[1]

Н. 3 Коне́чно. Вы́пьем ча́ю, му́зыку послу́шаем. У на́с в кра́сном уголке́ е́сть прои́грыватель.[2]

Ф. 4 Прекра́сно. Та́м, наве́рно, е́сть ру́сские наро́дные пе́сни?

Н. 5 Да́, мно́го, и в исполне́нии лу́чших певцо́в и певи́ц.

Ф. 6 Я́ та́к люблю́ ва́ши наро́дные пе́сни, наприме́р «О́чи чёрные».

Н. 7 «О́чи чёрные»? Да э́то ста́рый рома́нс, кото́рый уже́ не пою́т.[3]

Ф. 8 Неуже́ли? А у на́с в Аме́рике э́ту мело́дию ча́сто мо́жно услы́шать.

Н. 9 Да ну́? А мы́ лю́бим ва́ш джа́з, то́лько пласти́нки тру́дно достава́ть.[4]

Ф. 10 Я́ принесу́, у меня́ и́х мно́го.

NOTES

[1] One's *pass* or *entry permit* про́пуск must be shown to the custodian on entering or moving out of a dormitory. Another pass is needed to enter a university library. Also, foreign students must request a special permit for traveling outside the city; this permit must be shown when checking into a hotel.

[2] Кра́сный уголо́к *little red corner* refers to the recreation room in dormitories, factories, schools, universities, and clubs throughout the U.S.S.R. Each recreation room has a portrait of Lenin and sometimes one of Marx, Khrushchev, and others, and the rooms are frequently painted red. Кра́сный originally meant *beautiful*, and in Orthodox tradition the кра́сный у́гол was the right-hand corner of the room where icons or holy pictures were hung.

Basic sentence patterns

1. Како́го цве́та ва́ше пла́тье?   What color is your dress?
   — Зелёного.   Green.
   — Жёлтого.   Yellow.
   — Бе́лого.   White.
   — Чёрного.   Black.
   — Кра́сного.   Red.
   — Голубо́го.   Light blue.
   — Си́него.   Dark blue.

2. Каку́ю газе́ту вы́ чита́ете?   What newspaper are you reading?
   _____ кни́гу _____?   ____ book _____?
   Како́й журна́л _____?   What magazine _____?
   _____ рома́н _____?   ____ novel _____?
   Како́е письмо́ _____?   What letter _____?
   _____ объявле́ние _____?   ____ notice _____?
   Каки́е стихи́ _____?   What verses _____?
   _____ уро́ки _____?   ____ lessons _____?

3. О чём вы́ говори́те?   What are you talking about?
   — О на́шем клу́бе.   About our club.
   _____ факульте́те.   _____ department.
   _____ о́черке.   _____ essay.
   _____ посо́льстве.   _____ embassy.

4. О чём она́ узна́ла?   What did she find out about?
   — О твое́й ко́мнате.   About your room.
   _____ кварти́ре.   _____ apartment.
   _____ уда́че.   _____ success (*or* good luck).
   _____ оши́бке.   _____ mistake.
   _____ гру́ппе.   _____ group.

5. Не забу́дь о на́ших экза́менах.   Don't forget about our exams.
   _____ ле́кциях.   _____ lectures.
   _____ пласти́нках.   _____ records.
   _____ про́игрывателях.   _____ record players.
   _____ ра́дио.   _____ radios.
   _____ пропуска́х.   _____ passes.
   _____ веща́х.   _____ things.
   _____ квита́нциях.   _____ receipts.

6. В "Правде" нет театра́льных объявле́ний.   There aren't any theater ads in *Pravda*.

_____ ча́стных _____.   _____ private _____.

В "Изве́стиях" нет интере́сных объявле́ний.   There aren't any interesting ads in *Izvestia*.

_____ таки́х _____.   _____ such _____.

7. Они́ прие́дут в сле́дующую пя́тницу.   They'll arrive next Friday.

_____ суббо́ту.   _____ Saturday.

_____ сре́ду.   _____ Wednesday.

Я прие́ду в сле́дующий вто́рник.   I'll arrive next Tuesday.

_____ четве́рг.   _____ Thursday.

_____ понеде́льник.   _____ Monday.

Мы прие́дем в сле́дующее воскресе́нье.   We'll arrive next Sunday.

8. Я таки́х карти́н ещё не ви́дел.   I've never seen pictures like that before.

_____ люде́й _____.   _____ people _____.

_____ рекла́м _____.   _____ advertisements _____.

_____ фа́брик _____.   _____ factories _____.

_____ кио́сков _____.   _____ newsstands _____.

_____ та́нцев _____.   _____ dances _____.

9. Я ищу́ небольшо́й я́щик.   I'm looking for a small box.

_____ шка́ф.   _____ cupboard.

_____ сто́л.   _____ table.

_____ небольшу́ю по́лку.   _____ a small shelf.

_____ ко́мнату.   _____ room.

_____ гости́ницу.   _____ hotel.

_____ небольши́е коро́бки.   _____ some small boxes.

_____ стака́ны.   _____ glasses.

_____ ло́жки.   _____ spoons.

10. Мы бы́ли в большо́й аудито́рии.   We were in a large lecture hall.

_____ кварти́ре.   _____ apartment.

_____ ко́мнате.   _____ room.

_____ в большо́м го́роде.   _____ in a large town.

_____ общежи́тии.   _____ dormitory.

_____ за́ле.   _____ hall.

_____ рестора́не.   _____ restaurant.

_____ зда́нии.   _____ building.

11. Здесь нет друго́го проводника́?   Isn't there another conductor here?

_____ носи́льщика?   _____ porter _____?

_____ друго́й продавщи́цы?   _____ saleslady _____?

_____ учи́тельницы?   _____ teacher (f) ____?

12. Вы ско́ро встре́тите други́х профессоро́в.   You'll soon meet other professors.

_____ люде́й.   _____ people.

_____ секретаре́й.   _____ secretaries.

_____ шофёров.   _____ drivers.

_____ америка́нцев.   _____ Americans.

_____ украи́нцев.   _____ Ukrainians.

_____ ру́сских.   _____ Russians.

13. Мо́жно чита́ть? — Хорошо́, чита́йте!
_____ писа́ть? _____ пиши́те!
_____ говори́ть? _____ говори́те!
_____ спроси́ть? _____ спроси́те!
_____ игра́ть? _____ игра́йте!
_____ рабо́тать? _____ рабо́тайте!
_____ слу́шать? _____ слу́шайте!
_____ пи́ть? _____ пе́йте!
_____ пе́ть? _____ по́йте!
_____ откры́ть окно́? _____ откро́йте!
_____ закры́ть две́рь? _____ закро́йте!

Is it all right to read? O.K. go ahead!
_____ write? _____!
_____ talk? _____!
_____ ask? _____!
_____ play? _____!
_____ work? _____!
_____ listen? _____!
_____ drink? _____!
_____ sing? _____!
_____ open the window? _____!
_____ close the door? _____!

14. Вы́ не ви́дели моего́ бра́та?
_____ дру́га?
_____ на́шего шофёра?
_____ проводника́?
_____ мои́х бра́тьев?
_____ друзе́й?
_____ на́ших профессоро́в?
_____ това́рищей?

You didn't see my brother?
_____ friend?
_____ our driver?
_____ guide (or conductor)?
_____ my brothers?
_____ friends?
_____ our professors?
_____ friends (or comrades)?

15. О́н бы́л у мое́й сестры́.
_____ подру́ги.
_____ на́шей учи́тельницы.
_____ америка́нки.

He was at my sister's place.
_____ girl friend's _____.
_____ our teacher's _____.
_____ American woman's _____.

16. Вы́ стоя́ли о́коло своего́ ваго́на.
_____ до́ма.
_____ багажа́.
_____ общежи́тия.
_____ свое́й две́ри.
_____ гости́ницы.
_____ лаборато́рии.
_____ свои́х карти́н.
_____ ка́рт.

You were standing near your coach.
_____ house.
_____ baggage.
_____ dormitory.
_____ your door.
_____ hotel.
_____ laboratory.
_____ your pictures.
_____ maps.

17. Я́ не сплю́.
О́н не спи́т.
Мы́ не спи́м.
Они́ не спя́т.
Ты́ не спи́шь.
Вы́ не спи́те.

I'm not asleep.
He's not asleep.
We're not asleep.
They're not asleep.
You're not asleep.
You're not asleep.

18. О́н ничего́ не заме́тит.
Она́ _____ не заме́тит.
Вы́ _____ не заме́тите.
Мы́ _____ не заме́тим.
Я́ _____ не заме́чу.
Ты́ _____ не заме́тишь.

He won't notice a thing.
She won't notice _____.
You won't notice _____.
We won't notice _____.
I won't notice _____.
You won't notice _____.

19. Я́ ва́с с не́й познако́млю.
О́н _____ познако́мит.
Они́ _____ познако́мят.
Мы́ _____ познако́мим.

I'll introduce you to her.
He'll introduce _____.
They'll introduce _____.
We'll introduce _____.

Вы́ меня́ с не́й познако́мите?
Ты́ _____ познако́мишь?

Will you introduce me to her?
Will you introduce _____?

20. Вы́ услы́шите одного́ из лу́чших певцо́в.
Ты́ услы́шишь _____.
О́н услы́шит _____.
Мы́ услы́шим _____.
Я услы́шу _____.
Они́ услы́шат _____.

You'll hear one of the best singers.
You'll hear _____.
He'll hear _____.
We'll hear _____.
I'll hear _____.
They'll hear _____.

21. Я сейча́с получу́ ва́ши ве́щи.
О́н ____ полу́чит _____.
Они́ ____ полу́чат _____.
Мы́ ____ полу́чим _____.
Вы́ ____ полу́чите _____.
Ты́ ____ полу́чишь_____.

I'll get your things right away.
He'll get _____.
They'll get _____.
We'll get _____.
You'll get _____.
You'll get _____.

22. О́н поло́жит ва́ш бага́ж в такси́.
Я положу́ _____.
Мы́ поло́жим _____.
Они́ поло́жат _____.
Шофёр поло́жит _____.

He'll put your baggage in the taxi.
I'll put _____.
We'll put _____.
They'll put _____.
The driver will put _____.

23. Я за́втра посмотрю́ э́ту карти́ну.
Мы́ ____ посмо́трим _____.
Зи́на ____ посмо́трит _____.
Вы́ ____ посмо́трите _____.
Они́ ____ посмо́трят _____.
Ты́ ____ посмо́тришь _____.

I'll see the picture tomorrow.
We'll see _____.
Zina will see _____.
You'll see _____.
They'll see _____.
You'll see _____.

24. Мы́ с не́й поговори́м об э́том.
Я _____ поговорю́ _____.
Вы́ _____ поговори́те _____.
Ты́ _____ поговори́шь _____.
О́н _____ поговори́т _____.
Они́ _____ поговоря́т _____.

We'll have a talk with her about it.
I'll have _____.
You'll have _____.
You'll have _____.
He'll have _____.
They'll have _____.

Pronunciation practice: initial clusters with [r] or [r̡]

A. Clusters with [r] or [r̡] in second position in the cluster.

[brák] бра́к
marriage
[brát] бра́т
brother
[právdə] пра́вда
truth
[prózbə] про́сьба
request
[vrún] вру́н
liar
[vráč] вра́ч
physician

[srók] сро́к
date, term
[gráf] гра́ф
count
[grús] гру́з
load
[kráj] кра́й
edge
[br̡ét] бре́д
delirium
[br̡ivnó] бревно́
log

[tr̡í] три́
three
[tr̡ét̡ij] тре́тий
third
[zr̡én̡ijə] зре́ние
sight
[sr̡idá] среда́
Wednesday
[fsr̡édu] в сре́ду
on Wednesday
[gr̡éx] гре́х
sin

[francús] француз Frenchman	[pṛiɣét] привéт greetings	[gṛáṣ] грязь dirt
[drúk] дру́г friend	[pṛámə] пря́мо straight	[kṛéslə] крéсло armchair
[drámə] дра́ма drama	[vṛéṃə] врéмя time	[kriłó] крылó wing
[trúdnə] тру́дно difficult	[vṛát] в ря́д into line	[xrám] хра́м temple
[trójkə] тро́йка troika	[fṛigát] фрегáт frigate	[kṛík] кри́к shout
[zračók] зрачóк pupil of eye	[dṛévṇij] дрéвний ancient	[xṛén] хрéн horseradish
[srázu] сра́зу immediately	[dṛimáṭ] дремáть to doze	

B. Clusters with [r] in first position in the cluster.

[rtút] рту́ть quicksilver	[rvánij] рва́ный torn	[rvát] рва́ть to tear	[rtá] ртá of a mouth

STRUCTURE AND DRILLS

The formation of the second person imperative

MODELS

Пожáлуйста, заходи́.	Come in, please.
Пожáлуйста, заходи́те.	Come in, please.
Смотри́, вóт идёт Ни́на.	Look, there goes (or here comes) Nina.
Смотри́те, вóт идёт Ни́на.	Look, there goes (or here comes) Nina.
Подожди́!	Wait a bit!
Подожди́те!	Wait a bit!
Пóй грóмче!	Sing louder!
Пóйте грóмче!	Sing louder!
Нарéжь огурцы́!	Cut the cucumbers!
Нарéжьте огурцы́!	Cut the cucumbers!
Напиши́ э́то!	Write it!
Напиши́те э́то!	Write it!
Не пиши́!	Don't write!
Не пиши́те!	Don't write!
Открóй окнó!	Open the window!
Открóйте окнó!	Open the window!
Не открывáй окнá!	Don't open the window!
Не открывáйте окнá!	Don't open the window!
Танцу́й!	Dance!
Танцу́йте!	Dance!
Не пéй!	Don't drink!
Не пéйте!	Don't drink!
Иди́ домóй!	Go home!
Иди́те домóй!	Go home!

Second person imperatives are based on the present-future stem, which can best be found by dropping the endings –ут, –ют, –ат, and –ят from the third person plural.

The familiar-singular imperative ends in –и, –й, or –ь; the plural-polite imperative is formed by adding unstressed –те to the basic familiar-singular form. Of the three variants, only –и is a true ending; –й and –ь are properly part of the stem itself: –й is written to show that the stem ends in the consonant sound [j], and –ь is written to show that the final stem consonant is soft.

1. *Imperatives in –й.* Most verbs with an imperative in –й have a vowel preceding the written ending of the present-future. Their true stems, however, end in [j], spelled й in the imperative.

THIRD PERSON PLURAL		IMPERATIVE	
дýма–ют	[dúmaj–ut]	дýмай	дýмайте
читá–ют	[čitáj–ut]	читáй	читáйте
танцý–ют	[tancúj–ut]	танцýй	танцýйте
сто–я́т	[staj–át]	стóй	стóйте
по–ю́т	[paj–út]	пóй	пóйте
удивля́–ются	[ud̦ivl̦áj–utcə]	удивля́йся	удивля́йтесь

Imperatives based on the stem [p̦j–] *drink* have an inserted vowel: пéй! вы́пей!

2. *Imperatives in –ь and –и.* The position of stress in the first person singular present-future plays a key role in determining whether the imperative wil be in –и or –ь.

a. If the first person singular ending is *stressed*, a stressed –и́ is added to the third plural stem.

THIRD PERSON PLURAL	FIRST PERSON SINGULAR	IMPERATIVE	
лю́б–ят	люблю́	люби́	люби́те
пойд–ýт	пойдý	пойди́	пойди́те
спрóс–ят	спрошý	спроси́	спроси́те
пи́ш–ут	пишý	пиши́	пиши́те

b. If the first person singular ending is *unstressed*, the imperative is spelled with –ь, which is a sign that the preceding consonant is pronounced soft (if possible).

THIRD PERSON PLURAL	FIRST PERSON SINGULAR	IMPERATIVE	
достáн–ут	достáну	достáнь	достáньте
забýд–ут	забýду	забýдь	забýдьте
остáв–ят	остáвлю	остáвь	остáвьте
встрéт–ят	встрéчу	встрéть	встрéтьте
нарéж–ут	нарéжу	нарéжь	нарéжьте

However, if the stem ends in a cluster of consonants, an unstressed –и is added: помн-ят, помню; the imperative is помни. An unstressed –и may also occur in imperatives from perfective verbs which have the stressed prefix вы–: вы́говорят, вы́говорю; the imperative is вы́говори (like говори́ except for the stress).

Note on aspect: Although imperatives from both aspects may be used in affirmative commands, only imperfective imperatives are ordinarily used in negative commands.

Спроси́ его́!	Ask him!	Не спра́шивай его́!	Don't ask him!
Купи́ а́тлас!	Buy the atlas!	Не покупа́й а́тласа!	Don't buy an atlas!
Напиши́ мне́!	Write to me!	Не пиши́ мне́!	Don't write to me!
Откро́йте окно́!	Open the window!	Не открыва́йте окна́!	Don't open the window!

■ STRUCTURE REPLACEMENT DRILL

Read verses!
Чита́й стихи́!
Чита́йте стихи́!
По́й гро́мче!
По́йте гро́мче!
Купи́ а́тлас!
Бу́дь до́ма!

Спроси́ его́!
Оста́вь клю́ч!
Подожди́ меня́!
Доста́нь ка́рту!
Напиши́ письмо́!
Узна́й об э́том!

■ STRUCTURE REPLACEMENT DRILLS

1. *I'll do it.*
   Do it!
   Я сде́лаю э́то.
   Сде́лай э́то!
   Я стою́ на углу́.
   Сто́й на углу́!
   Я узна́ю об э́том.
   Я игра́ю в те́ннис.
   Я поду́маю об э́том.
   Я чита́ю стихи́.

2. *I'll open the door.*
   Open the door!
   Я откро́ю две́рь.
   Откро́й две́рь!
   Я пью́ ча́й.
   Пе́й ча́й!
   Я всегда́ покупа́ю в э́том магази́не.
   Я де́лаю уро́ки.
   Я танцу́ю.
   Я игра́ю в хокке́й.

3. *I'll bring the tea.*
   Bring the tea!
   Я принесу́ ча́й.
   Принеси́ ча́й!
   Я спрошу́ профе́ссора Орло́ва.
   Спроси́ профе́ссора Орло́ва!
   Я куплю́ а́тлас.
   Я посмотрю́ в окно́.
   Я подожду́ на углу́.
   Я напишу́ сочине́ние.
   Я возьму́ э́ту кни́гу.
   Я позвоню́ в клу́б.
   Я пойду́ на по́чту.

1. *I'm drinking tea.*
   You drink too!
   Я пью ча́й.
   И ты́ пе́й!
   Я откро́ю окно́.
   И ты́ откро́й!
   Я чита́ю стихи́.
   Я поду́маю об э́том.
   Я не ду́маю об экза́мене.
   Я не покупа́ю таки́х веще́й.
   Я стою́ в о́череди.
   Я спра́шиваю, когда́ не зна́ю.

2. *Why don't you listen?*
   Listen!
   Почему́ вы́ не слу́шаете?
   Слу́шайте!
   Почему́ ты́ не чита́ешь?
   Чита́й!
   Почему́ вы́ не захо́дите?
   Почему́ ты́ не пи́шешь?
   Почему́ вы́ не спра́шиваете?
   Почему́ ты́ не пьёшь?
   Почему́ вы́ не говори́те?
   Почему́ ты́ не идёшь?
   Почему́ вы́ не ду́маете?
   Почему́ ты́ не поёшь?
   Почему́ вы́ не поёте?

3. *You walk so much.*
   Don't walk so much!
   Ты́ та́к мно́го хо́дишь.
   Не ходи́ та́к мно́го!
   Вы́ та́к мно́го хо́дите.
   Не ходи́те та́к мно́го!
   Ты́ та́к мно́го пи́шешь.
   Вы́ та́к мно́го пи́шете.
   Ты́ та́к мно́го говори́шь.
   Вы́ та́к мно́го говори́те.

4. *Are you dancing again?*
   Don't do any more dancing!
   Ты́ опя́ть танцу́ешь?
   Не танцу́й бо́льше!
   Вы́ опя́ть танцу́ете?
   Не танцу́йте бо́льше!
   Ты́ опя́ть пьёшь?
   Вы́ опя́ть пьёте?
   Ты́ опя́ть спра́шиваешь?
   Вы́ опя́ть спра́шиваете?
   Ты́ опя́ть поёшь?
   Вы́ опя́ть поёте?

■ STRUCTURE REPLACEMENT DRILLS

1. *Are you going to leave the dictionary at home?*
   Leave the dictionary at home!
   Ты́ оста́вишь слова́рь до́ма?
   Оста́вь слова́рь до́ма!
   Ты́ наре́жешь огурцы́?
   Наре́жь огурцы́!
   Ты́ доста́нешь а́тлас?
   Ты́ встре́тишь меня́ на углу́?
   Ты́ забу́дешь её?
   Ты́ бу́дешь гото́в?

2. *Are you going to open the window?*
   Open the window!
   Вы́ откро́ете окно́?
   Откро́йте окно́!
   Ты́ ку́пишь пла́тье?
   Купи́ пла́тье!
   Ты́ пойдёшь в магази́н?
   Вы́ напи́шете письмо́?
   Ты́ поду́маешь об э́том?
   Вы́ принесёте а́тлас?
   Ты́ подождёшь бра́та?
   Вы́ пойдёте на конце́рт?

3. *Are you going to meet us on the corner?*
   Meet us on the corner!
   Вы́ встре́тите на́с на углу́?
   Встре́тьте на́с на углу́!
   Ты́ ска́жешь твоё и́мя?

   Скажи́ твоё и́мя!
   Вы́ доста́нете ключи́?
   Ты́ посмо́тришь э́тот фи́льм?
   Вы́ ку́пите молоко́?
   Вы́ забу́дете об э́том?

May I bring the tea?
Fine, bring it!
Мóжно принести́ ча́й?
Хорошó, принеси́те!
Мóжно написа́ть об э́том?
Хорошó, напиши́те!

Мóжно подожда́ть ва́с?
Мóжно наре́зать огурцы́?
Мóжно поду́мать немнóго?
Мóжно посмотре́ть э́тот фи́льм?

■ STRUCTURE REPLACEMENT DRILLS

1. *Open the window!*
   Don't open the window!
   Открóйте окнó!
   Не открыва́йте окна́!
   Купи́те ча́й!
   Не покупа́йте ча́я!
   Посмотри́те в окнó!
   Сде́лайте э́то!
   Спроси́те об э́том!
   Поду́майте об э́том!

2. *Buy a dictionary!*
   Don't buy a dictionary!
   Купи́ слова́рь!
   Не покупа́й словаря́!
   Посмотри́ в кни́гу!
   Не смотри́ в кни́гу!
   Напиши́ сочине́ние!
   Открóй две́рь!
   Спроси́ егó!
   Поду́май о зиме́!

■ RESPONSE DRILLS

1. *We're playing cards.*
   You play, too!
   Мы́ игра́ем в ка́рты.
   И вы́ игра́йте!
   Мы́ не ду́маем об э́том.
   И вы́ не ду́майте!
   Мы́ чита́ем рома́ны.
   Мы́ бу́дем та́м.
   Мы́ танцу́ем ка́ждый ве́чер.
   Мы́ не пьём.
   Мы́ не поём.

2. *We're reading Tolstoy.*
   You read Tolstoy, too!
   Мы́ чита́ем Толстóго.
   Вы́ тóже чита́йте Толстóго!
   Мы́ покупа́ем в э́том магази́не.
   Вы́ тóже покупа́йте в э́том магази́не!
   Мы́ пи́шем сочине́ние.
   Мы́ поём.
   Мы́ ду́маем об э́том.
   Мы́ бу́дем та́м.
   Мы́ забу́дем об э́том.

SUMMARY OF RULES FOR FORMING THE BASIC **ты́** IMPERATIVE

1. If the present-future stem ends in the sound [j], or (in spelling terms) if the endings of the present-future are immediately preceded by a vowel letter or **ь**, the imperative is spelled with **й**: **покупа́й!** (stem [pəkupáj–], first person singular **покупа́ю**). Note that the stress occasionally shifts back to the stem (compare **стóй! стóйте!** with **стою́**). Verbs like **пи́ть**, with **ь** directly before their present-future endings, have an inserted vowel in their stem: **пéй, вы́пей** (stem [pj–], first person singular **пью́**).

2. If the present-future stem ends in any other consonant (but not a cluster), and if the stem is stressed in the first person singular, the imperative is spelled with –**ь**, as in **забу́дь!** (first person singular **забу́ду**). The –**ь** must be written, even though the consonant is one that cannot be soft, as in **наре́жь!**

3. If the present-future stem ends in a consonant cluster, even though the stress is on the stem in the first person singular present-future, the ending –**и** is added for the imperative, as in **пóмни!** (first person singular **пóмню**).

4. If the present-future stem ends in a consonant and the first person singular ending *is* stressed, the imperative ending is –**й**, as in **говори́!** (first person singular **говорю́**) and **иди́!** (first person singular **иду́**).

5. Perfective verbs with the stressed prefix **вы́–** form their imperative in the same way as the imperative of the verb they derive from, for example, **вы́пей!** (compare **пей!**), **вы́говори!** (compare **говори́!**), **вы́режь!** (compare **ре́жь!** *cut!* **наре́жь!** *slice!*).

The declension of adjectives: nominative, accusative, genitive, and prepositional cases

MODELS

Я купи́л но́вый костю́м.	I bought a new suit.
_____ но́вое ра́дио.	_____ a new radio.
_____ но́вую пласти́нку.	_____ a new record.
_____ но́вые пласти́нки.	_____ some new records.
Я ищу́ хоро́ший портфе́ль.	I'm looking for a good briefcase.
_____ хоро́шее ра́дио.	_____ a good radio.
_____ хоро́шую ко́мнату.	_____ a good room.
_____ хоро́шие пласти́нки.	_____ some good records.
Вы зна́ете э́того молодо́го челове́ка?	Do you know this young man?
_____ э́ту молоду́ю де́вушку?	_____ this young lady?
_____ э́тих молоды́х люде́й?	_____ these young people?
Вы лю́бите Достое́вского?	Are you fond of Dostoevsky?
_____ Толсто́го?	_____ Tolstoy?
_____ ру́сские рома́ны?	_____ Russian novels?
_____ таки́е стихи́?	_____ such verses?
_____ ста́рые рома́нсы?	_____ old love songs?
Я не люблю́ Достое́вского.	I don't like Dostoevsky.
_____ Толсто́го.	_____ Tolstoy.
_____ ру́сских рома́нов.	_____ Russian novels.
_____ таки́х стихо́в.	_____ such verses.
_____ ста́рых рома́нсов.	_____ old love songs.
Хоти́те ча́шку вку́сного ко́фе?	Want a cup of delicious coffee?
_____ хоро́шего ___?	_____ good _____?
_____ горя́чего ___?	_____ hot _____?
У ни́х не́т хоро́шего клу́ба.	They don't have a good club.
_____ общежи́тия.	_____ dormitory.
_____ хоро́шей библиоте́ки.	_____ a good library.
_____ лаборато́рии.	_____ laboratory.
_____ хоро́ших теа́тров.	_____ any good theaters.
_____ па́рков.	_____ parks.
_____ рестора́нов.	_____ restaurants.
Мы́ говори́ли об э́том но́вом зда́нии.	We were talking about that new building.
_____ большо́м ___.	_____ big _____.
_____ об э́том но́вом общежи́тии.	_____ about that new dormitory.
_____ большо́м ___.	_____ large _____.

Мы́ говори́ли об э́той но́вой гости́нице.   We were talking about that new hotel.

_____ большо́й ____.   _____ large ____.

_____ об э́тих но́вых магази́нах.   _____ about these new stores.

_____ больши́х_____.   _____ large ____.

Мы́ говори́м о после́днем но́мере «Пра́вды».   We're speaking of the last issue of *Pravda*.

_____ экза́мене.   _____ exam.

_____ собра́нии.   _____ meeting.

_____ уро́ке.   _____ lesson.

Мы́ говори́м о его́ после́дней кни́ге.   We're talking about his latest book.

_____ рабо́те.   _____ work.

_____ о после́дних новостя́х.   _____ about the latest news.

_____ изве́стиях.   _____ news reports.

	SINGULAR			PLURAL
	Masculine	*Neuter*	*Feminine*	
ACC	*inanimate* / *animate* молодо́й / молодо́го ста́рый / ста́рого си́ний / си́него друго́й / друго́го ру́сский / ру́сского большо́й / большо́го хоро́ший / хоро́шего	молодо́е ста́рое си́нее друго́е ру́сское большо́е хоро́шее	молоду́ю ста́рую си́нюю другу́ю ру́сскую большу́ю хоро́шую	*inanimate* / *animate* молоды́е / молоды́х ста́рые / ста́рых си́ние / си́них други́е / други́х ру́сские / ру́сских больши́е / больши́х хоро́шие / хоро́ших
GEN	молодо́го ста́рого си́него друго́го ру́сского большо́го хоро́шего		молодо́й ста́рой си́ней друго́й	молоды́х ста́рых си́них други́х
PREP	о молодо́м о ста́ром о си́нем о друго́м о ру́сском о большо́м о хоро́шем		ру́сской большо́й хоро́шей	ру́сских больши́х хоро́ших

GENERAL OBSERVATIONS

1. The endings of adjectives modifying masculine and neuter nouns are distinct from each other only in the nominative and accusative singular; in all the other cases, they share the same endings.

2. Only adjectives modifying feminine nouns have endings in the accusative singular which are always distinct from those used in the nominative singular: –ую and –юю (но́вую, другу́ю, большу́ю, после́днюю, ве́рхнюю).

3. Adjectives modifying neuter and *inanimate* masculine nouns have the same endings in the accusative singular as in the nominative singular. Those adjectives modifying *animate* masculine nouns in the accusative singular have the same endings as in the genitive singular. Note that **г** in the endings **–ого** and **–его** is pronounced [v].

4. In the plural, adjectives modifying *inanimate* nouns use nominative plural endings; those modifying *animate* nouns use genitive plural endings.

■ RESPONSE DRILLS

1. *This room is a small one.*
   I asked for a large one.
   Э́тот но́мер ма́ленький.
   Я проси́л большо́й.
   Э́ти ножи́ ма́ленькие.
   Я проси́л больши́е.
   Э́та коро́бка ма́ленькая.
   Э́тот а́тлас ма́ленький.
   Э́та ло́жка ма́ленькая.
   Э́тот шка́ф ма́ленький.
   Э́та по́лка ма́ленькая.
   Э́та ка́рта ма́ленькая.

2. *You didn't happen to see the new record?*
   I'm looking for the new record.
   Вы́ не ви́дели но́вой пласти́нки?
   Я ищу́ но́вую пласти́нку.
   Вы́ не ви́дели голубо́го пла́тья?
   Я ищу́ голубо́е пла́тье.
   (синего костюма, русской газеты, американского журнала, жёлтой тетра́ди, старого портфеля)

■ EXPANSION DRILL

Do you know that girl?
Do you know that lovely girl?
Вы́ зна́ете э́ту де́вушку?
Вы́ зна́ете э́ту краси́вую де́вушку?
Вы́ зна́ете э́того па́рня?
Вы́ зна́ете э́того краси́вого па́рня?
(эту песню, эту женщину, этого студента, это место, эту американку, эту мелодию, этот город)

■ CUED QUESTION-ANSWER DRILL

(*green*)   *What color is this book?*
             Green.
(зелёный)   Како́го цве́та э́та кни́га?
             Зелёного.
(бе́лый)   Како́го цве́та э́та кни́га?
             Бе́лого.
(красный, жёлтый, синий, голубой, чёрный)

■ QUESTION-ANSWER DRILLS

1. *Where's the American singer?*
   The American singer isn't here yet.
   Где́ америка́нский певе́ц?
   Америка́нского певца́ ещё не́т.
   Где́ америка́нская певи́ца?
   Америка́нской певи́цы ещё не́т.
   Где́ но́вый учи́тель?
   Где́ но́вая учи́тельница?
   Где́ ста́рый шофёр?
   Где́ вече́рняя газе́та?
   Где́ после́дний но́мер журна́ла?

2. *Are the new students here?*
   I don't see the new students.
   Но́вые студе́нты здесь?
   Я не ви́жу но́вых студе́нтов.
   Поде́ржанные ве́щи здесь?
   Я не ви́жу поде́ржанных веще́й.
   Вече́рние газе́ты здесь?
   Молоды́е лю́ди здесь?
   Жёлтые ча́шки здесь?
   Но́вые журна́лы здесь?
   Ста́рые пласти́нки здесь?
   Больши́е стака́ны здесь?

■ STRUCTURE REPLACEMENT DRILL

There was a lovely picture there.
There were many lovely pictures there.
Та́м была́ краси́вая карти́на.
Та́м бы́ло мно́го краси́вых карти́н.
Та́м бы́л но́вый до́м.
Та́м бы́ло мно́го но́вых домо́в.
Та́м бы́л небольшо́й шка́ф.

Та́м бы́ло просто́е пла́тье.
Та́м бы́л чёрный костю́м.
Та́м бы́ло но́вое общежи́тие.
Та́м бы́ло интере́сное объявле́ние.
Та́м была́ но́вая рекла́ма.

■ RESPONSE DRILLS

1. *You're a good student.*
   For a good student it isn't difficult.
   Вы́ хоро́ший студе́нт.
   Для́ хоро́шего студе́нта э́то не тру́дно.
   Вы́ хоро́шие студе́нты.
   Для́ хоро́ших студе́нтов э́то не тру́дно.
   Вы́ хоро́шая студе́нтка.
   Вы́ хоро́ший проводни́к.
   Вы́ хоро́ший администра́тор.
   Вы́ хоро́шая учи́тельница.
   Вы́ хоро́ший учи́тель.
   Вы́ хоро́шие учителя́.

2. *These things are expensive.*
   Don't buy expensive things.
   Э́ти ве́щи дороги́е.
   Не покупа́й дороги́х веще́й.
   Э́тот портфе́ль плохо́й.
   Не покупа́й плохо́го портфе́ля.
   Э́ти пласти́нки ста́рые.
   Э́то ра́дио дорого́е.
   Э́тот материа́л жёсткий.
   Э́тот рома́н ску́чный.

■ QUESTION-ANSWER DRILLS

1. *Did he ask about old magazines?*
   No, about new ones.
   О́н спра́шивал о ста́рых журна́лах?
   Не́т, о но́вых.
   О́н спра́шивал о ста́рой пласти́нке?
   Не́т, о но́вой.
   (о ста́ром рома́нсе, о ста́рых пе́снях,
   о ста́рой рабо́те, о ста́ром сочине́нии,
   о ста́ром заявле́нии, о ста́рых та́нцах)

2. *Are you talking about the small lecture hall?*
   No, about the large one.
   Вы́ говори́те о ма́ленькой аудито́рии?
   Не́т, о большо́й.
   Вы́ говори́те о ма́ленькой библиоте́ке?
   Не́т, о большо́й.
   (о ма́леньком шка́фе, о ма́леньком
   общежи́тии, о ма́ленькой лаборато́рии,
   о ма́леньком до́ме, о ма́ленькой
   оши́бке, о ма́леньком за́ле, о малень-
   ком магази́не)

■ RESPONSE DRILLS

1. *Here's the recreation room.*
   They're waiting for us in the recreation room.
   Во́т кра́сный уголо́к.
   Они́ на́с жду́т в кра́сном уголке́.
   Во́т жёсткий ваго́н.
   Они́ на́с жду́т в жёстком ваго́не.
   (но́вое общежи́тие, ста́рая аудито́рия,
   Большо́й теа́тр, америка́нское посоль-
   ство, но́вая кварти́ра)

2. *Have you seen the new building?*
   Everyone's been talking about the new building.
   Вы́ ви́дели но́вое зда́ние?
   Все́ говоря́т о но́вом зда́нии.
   Вы́ ви́дели америка́нских студе́нтов?
   Все́ говоря́т об америка́нских студе́нтах.
   (но́вую гости́ницу, вече́рнюю газе́ту,
   после́дний но́мер «Изве́стий», но́вое
   объявле́ние, но́вое посо́льство, но́вого
   администра́тора, америка́нский фи́льм)

	SINGULAR			PLURAL
	Masculine	*Neuter*	*Feminine*	
	LONG-FORM ADJECTIVE ENDINGS IN NOMINATIVE, ACCUSATIVE, GENITIVE, AND PREPOSITIONAL CASES			
NOM	–о́й, –ый, –ий	–ое, –ее	–ая, –яя	–ые, –ие
ACC	(*inanimate* — nom) (*animate* — gen)		–ую, –юю	(*inanimate* — nom) (*animate* — gen)
GEN	–ого, –его		–ой, –ей	–ых, –их
PREP	–ом, –ем			

Note: The letter г in the endings **–ого** and **–его** is pronounced [v].

REMARKS ON THE DISTRIBUTION OF ENDINGS IN THE GENITIVE AND PREPOSITIONAL CASES

1. *Masculine and neuter endings in the genitive and prepositional singular.*

a. Hard-stem adjectives and mixed stems ending in к, г, and x take **–ого** in the genitive and **–ом** in the prepositional: **но́вого, но́вом**; **друго́го, друго́м**.
b. Soft-stem adjectives take **–его** in the genitive and **–ем** in the prepositional: **после́днего, после́днем**.
c. Mixed stems ending in ш and ж take **–о́го** in the genitive and **–о́м** in the prepositional if the ending is stressed; if it is unstressed they take **–его** and **–ем**. Compare **большо́го, большо́м** with **хоро́шего, хоро́шем**.

2. *Feminine endings in the genitive-prepositional singular (genitive identical with prepositional).*

a. Hard stems and mixed stems ending in к, г, and x take **–ой**: **но́вой, друго́й**.
b. Soft stems take **–ей**: **после́дней**.
c. Mixed stems ending in ш and ж take **–о́й** if the ending is stressed; if it is unstressed they take **–ей**. Compare **большо́й** with **хоро́шей**.

3. *Plural endings in the genitive-prepositional (genitive identical with prepositional).*

a. Hard stems take the ending **–ых** in the genitive-prepositional: **но́вых, молоды́х**.
b. Soft stems and all mixed stems take the ending **–их** in the genitive-prepositional: **после́дних, други́х, больши́х**.

The declension of чей and the possessive modifiers: nominative, accusative, genitive, and prepositional cases

MODELS

Че́й рома́н вы́ чита́ете?	Whose novel are you reading?
Чье́ сочине́ние вы́ чита́ете?	Whose composition are you reading?
Чью́ кни́гу вы́ чита́ете?	Whose book are you reading?
Чьи́ стихи́ вы́ чита́ете?	Whose verses are you reading?

Вы́ зна́ете моего́ бра́та?
_____ на́шего _____?
Вы́ зна́ете мою́ сестру́?
_____ на́шу _____?
Вы́ зна́ете мои́х сестёр?
_____ на́ших _____?

Óн оста́вил свóй словáрь дóма.
_____ свою́ кни́гу _____.
_____ своё сочине́ние _____.
_____ свои́ пи́сьма _____.

Мы́ вчера́ бы́ли у твоего́ бра́та.
_____ у ва́шего _____.
_____ у твое́й сестры́.
_____ у ва́шей _____.
_____ у твои́х друзе́й.
_____ у ва́ших _____.

Вы́ ещё не ви́дели на́шего гóрода.
_____ на́шего общежи́тия.
_____ на́шей кварти́ры.
_____ на́ших карти́н.

Мы́ говори́ли о твоём до́ме.
_____ ва́шем _____.
_____ твоём заявле́нии.
_____ ва́шем _____.
_____ твое́й про́сьбе.
_____ ва́шей _____.
_____ твои́х кни́гах.
_____ ва́ших _____.

Do you know my brother?
_____ our _____?
Do you know my sister?
_____ our _____?
Do you know my sisters?
_____ our _____?

He left his dictionary home.
_____ his book _____.
_____ his composition _____.
_____ his letters _____.

We were at your brother's place yesterday.
_____ at your brother's place _____.
_____ at your sister's place _____.
_____ at your sister's place _____.
_____ at your friends' place _____.
_____ at your friends' place _____.

You still haven't seen our city.
_____ our dormitory.
_____ our apartment.
_____ our pictures.

We were talking about your house.
_____ your _____.
_____ your application.
_____, your _____.
_____ your request.
_____ your _____.
_____ your books.
_____ your_____.

■ REPETITION DRILL

Repeat the above models, observing the pattern of endings.

■ RESPONSE DRILLS

1. *Here comes my brother.*
   Do you know my brother?
   Вóт идёт мóй брáт.
   Вы́ зна́ете моего́ бра́та?
   Вóт идёт моя́ сестра́.
   Вы́ зна́ете мою́ сестру́?
   (мои бра́тья, мои сёстры, мой друг, моя подруга)

2. *Here's your briefcase.*
   You forgot your briefcase again.
   Вóт вáш портфéль.
   Вы́ опя́ть забы́ли свóй портфéль.
   Вóт вáша кни́га.
   Вы́ опя́ть забы́ли свою́ кни́гу.
   (ваше заявление, ваши вещи, ваша газета, ваш журнал, ваши пластинки, ваша квитанция, ваш билет)

3. *Take my notebook.*
   No, thanks, I'll take my own.
   Возьми́ мою́ тетра́дь.
   Нéт, спаси́бо. Я́ возьму́ свою́.
   Возьми́ моё ра́дио.

   Нéт, спаси́бо. Я́ возьму́ своё.
   (мой карандаш, мою ручку, мой словарь, моё перо, мои тетради, мою карту, мои билеты)

300   LESSON 13

1. *Whose mistake was she talking about?*
   About mine.

   О чьéй ошúбке онá говорúла?

   О моéй.

   О чьём письмé онá говорúла?

   О моём.

   (о чьих стихах, о чьём очерке, о чьей
   картине, о чьём сочинении, о чьих
   вещах, о чьих журналах, о чьём билете,
   о чьей просьбе)

2. *Are you reading your own application?*
   No, yours.

   Вы читáете своё заявлéние?

   Нéт, вáше.

   Вы читáете своё сочинéние?

   Нéт, вáше.

   (своё письмо, свои стихи, свою работу,
   свой очерк, свою книгу)

■ EXPANSION DRILL

You haven't seen the city yet.
You haven't seen our city yet.

Вы ещё не вúдели гóрода.

Вы ещё не вúдели нáшего гóрода.

Вы ещё не вúдели квартúры.

Вы ещё не вúдели нáшей квартúры.

(дóма, общежития, картин, комнаты,
вокзала, университета, школы)

■ SUBJECT REVERSAL DRILL

Your brother was at my place yesterday.
I was at your brother's yesterday.

Твóй брáт вчерá бы́л у меня́.

Я́ вчерá бы́л у твоегó брáта.

Твои друзья́ вчерá бы́ли у меня́.

Я́ вчерá бы́л у твои́х друзéй.

(твои сёстры, твой друг, твоя подруга,
твои братья)

■ STRUCTURE REPLACEMENT DRILL

I was reading your novel.
I was talking about your novel.

Я́ читáл вáш ромáн.

Я́ говорúл о вáшем ромáне.

Я́ читáл вáши стихú.

Я́ говорúл о вáших стихáх.

(вашу работу, ваше сочинение, ваш
очерк, вашу книгу, ваше заявление,
ваши работы)

	SINGULAR			PLURAL
	Masculine	*Neuter*	*Feminine*	
NOM	чéй мóй, твóй, свóй нáш, вáш	чьё моё, твоё, своё нáше, вáше	чья́ моя́, твоя́, своя́ нáша, вáша	чьú мои, твои, свои нáши, вáши
ACC	(*like* nom *or* gen)	(*like* nom)	чью́ мою́, твою́, свою́ нáшу, вáшу	(*like* nom *or* gen)
GEN	чьегó моегó, твоегó, своегó нáшего, вáшего		чьéй моéй, твоéй, своéй нáшей, вáшей	чьúх мои́х, твои́х, свои́х нáших, вáших
PREP	(о) чьём (о) моём, твоём, своём (о) нáшем, вáшем			

Possessive adjectives all belong to the soft declension, with endings in the oblique cases (genitive, prepositional, dative, and instrumental) like those of the soft-stem adjectives. Note that, except for **на́ш** and **ва́ш**, which have their stress consistently on the stem, the possessive modifiers all have ending stress.

The reflexive possessive **сво́й**, **своё**, **своя́**, **свои́** *one's own* declines exactly like **мо́й** and **тво́й**. Rarely used in the nominative, it may substitute for **мо́й**, **тво́й**, **на́ш**, or **ва́ш** in those situations where subject and possessor are the same.

Я́ ва́м да́л **мо́й (сво́й)** портфе́ль.	I gave you *my* briefcase.
Мы́ говори́м о **на́шем (своём)** дру́ге.	*We're* talking about *our* friend.
Вы́ мне́ да́ли **ва́шу (свою́)** кни́гу.	*You* gave me *your* book.
Вы́ мне́ да́ли **мою́** кни́гу.	*You* gave me *my* book.

It is only when the subject is in the third person that **сво́й** plays a distinctive role. It differs in meaning from **его́**, **её**, and **и́х**, the unchanging third person possessives.

Compare	О́н забы́л **сво́й** портфе́ль.	He forgot his (own) briefcase.
with	О́н забы́л **его́** портфе́ль.	He forgot his (someone else's) briefcase.
Compare	Зи́на чита́ла **свою́** кни́гу.	Zina was reading her (own) book.
with	Зи́на чита́ла **её** кни́гу.	Zina was reading her (someone else's) book.
Compare	Они́ говори́ли о **свои́х** друзья́х.	They were talking about their (own) friends.
with	Они́ говори́ли об **и́х** друзья́х.	They were talking about their (other's) friends.

Possessive modifiers are often omitted when it is clear from the context that the possessor and the subject are the same: **Я́ бы́л у бра́та** (*or* **у моего́ бра́та**) *I was at my brother's place.*

Review of second conjugation verbs

PRESENT-FUTURE ENDINGS		позвони́ть (pfv) *to phone*	стоя́ть (ipfv) *to stand*	слы́шать (ipfv) *to hear*	проси́ть (ipfv) *to ask*	купи́ть (pfv) *to buy*
SG	1	–ю or –у	позвоню́	стою́	слы́шу	прошу́	куплю́
	2	–ишь	позвони́шь	стои́шь	слы́шишь	про́сишь	ку́пишь
	3	–ит	позвони́т	стои́т	слы́шит	про́сит	ку́пит
PL	1	–им	позвони́м	стои́м	слы́шим	про́сим	ку́пим
	2	–ите	позвони́те	стои́те	слы́шите	про́сите	ку́пите
	3	–ят or –ат	позвоня́т	стоя́т	слы́шат	про́сят	ку́пят

■ SUBSTITUTION DRILLS

1. *You never go to the movies.*
   Вы́ никогда́ не хо́дите в кино́.
   Они́ никогда́ не хо́дят в кино́.
   (мы, я, она, ты, его друзья, мой
   товарищ по комнате, вы)

2. *I hear the bell.*
   Я́ слы́шу звоно́к.
   О́н слы́шит звоно́к.
   (мы, вы, ты, они, Наташа, студенты,
   мы все)

3. *She always asks that the windows be opened.*
   Она́ всегда́ про́сит открыва́ть о́кна.
   Они́ всегда́ про́сят открыва́ть о́кна.
   (я, вы, Зина, мы, ты, учи́тель,
   секрета́рь, учи́тельницы)

4. *I'll phone home tomorrow.*
   За́втра **я́** позвоню́ домо́й.
   За́втра **мы́** позвони́м домо́й.
   (она, вы, они, Олег, мы, я)

5. *Comrade Alexeev often goes to Kiev.*
   Това́рищ Алексе́ев ча́сто е́здит в Ки́ев.
   Э́ти проводники́ ча́сто е́здят в Ки́ев.
   (мы, они, я, вы, ты, эта женщина)

6. *I don't remember her name.*
   Я́ не по́мню её и́мени.
   Ты́ не по́мнишь её и́мени.
   (они, вы, студенты, мы, я)

7. *Volodya talks a lot at meetings.*
   Воло́дя мно́го говори́т на собра́ниях.
   Э́ти студе́нты мно́го говоря́т на
   собра́ниях.
   (ты, вы, я, наш вахтёр, мы все)

■ STRUCTURE REPLACEMENT DRILLS

1. *Irina was looking out the window.*
   Irina is looking out the window.
   Ири́на смотре́ла в окно́.
   Ири́на смо́трит в окно́.
   Вы́ смотре́ли в окно́.
   Вы́ смо́трите в окно́.
   (студенты, я, мы, ты, Коля)

2. *We often used to stand in line.*
   We often stand in line.
   Мы́ ча́сто стоя́ли в о́череди.
   Мы́ ча́сто стои́м в о́череди.
   Я́ ча́сто стоя́л в о́череди.
   Я́ ча́сто стою́ в о́череди.
   (вы, люди, моя сестра, ты, мы, я)

■ QUESTION-ANSWER DRILLS

1. *I'm not asleep yet, how about you fellows?*
   We're not asleep, either.
   Я́ ещё не сплю́, а вы́, ребя́та?
   Мы́ то́же не спи́м.
   Я́ ещё не сплю́, а э́тот па́рень?
   О́н то́же не спи́т.
   Я́ ещё не сплю́, а ты́, Ко́ля?
   Я́ ещё не сплю́, а о́н?
   Я́ ещё не сплю́, а ты́?
   Я́ ещё не сплю́, а вы́, това́рищи?
   Я́ ещё не сплю́, а э́ти лю́ди?
   Я́ ещё не сплю́, а э́тот граждани́н?
   Я́ ещё не сплю́, а на́ши попу́тчики?
   Я́ ещё не сплю́, а вы́, де́вушки?

2. *She pays very little for her room, how about you?*
   I also pay very little.
   Она́ ма́ло пла́тит за ко́мнату, а вы́?
   И я́ ма́ло плачу́.
   Она́ ма́ло пла́тит за ко́мнату,
   а её сестра́?
   И она́ ма́ло пла́тит.
   (а ты; а эта певица; а эти заочницы;
   а этот господин; а эта американка;
   а вы, ребята)

3. *When are you going to see that film?*
   We'll see it tomorrow.
   Когда́ вы́ посмо́трите э́тот фи́льм?
   Мы́ посмо́трим его́ за́втра.
   Когда́ певе́ц посмо́трит э́тот фи́льм?
   О́н посмо́трит его́ за́втра.
   (твои подруги, певица, ты, Володя и
   Пётр, твой товарищ по комнате, ты,
   секретарь, вы, эта девушка)

4. *Will you permit that?*
   Of course we will.
   Вы́ разреши́те э́то?
   Коне́чно, мы́ разреши́м.
   Ребя́та разреша́т э́то?
   Коне́чно, они́ разреша́т.
   (секретарь, их братья, эта американка,
   Оля и Галя, ваша учительница, мой
   брат, его сестра, товарищ Царапкин)

She ought to receive a letter soon.
She'll receive a letter soon.
Она́ ско́ро должна́ получи́ть письмо́.
Она́ ско́ро полу́чит письмо́.
Вы́ ско́ро должны́ получи́ть письмо́.
Вы́ ско́ро полу́чите письмо́.

(бра́тья, америка́нка, ты, учи́тельницы,
я, граждани́н Семёнов, эти америка́нцы,
мы, профе́ссор)

■ STRUCTURE REPLACEMENT DRILL

1. *I met her at the station.*
   I'll meet her at the station.
   Я́ её встре́тил на вокза́ле.
   Я́ её встре́чу на вокза́ле.
   Проводни́к её встре́тил на вокза́ле.
   Проводни́к её встре́тит на вокза́ле.
   (шофёр, эта же́нщина, америка́нские
   певцы́, мы, друзья́, этот мужчи́на)

2. *Do you hear me?*
   Вы́ меня́ слы́шите?
   Ты́ меня́ слы́шишь?
   Вы́ меня́ встре́тите?
   Ты́ меня́ встре́тишь?
   Вы́ меня́ ви́дите?
   Вы́ меня́ извини́те?
   Вы́ меня́ услы́шите?
   Вы́ меня́ по́мните?
   Вы́ меня́ лю́бите?
   Вы́ меня́ познако́мите?

■ SUBJECT REVERSAL DRILLS

1. *I won't [be able to] hear the custodian.*
   The custodian won't [be able to] hear me.
   Я́ не услы́шу вахтёра.
   Вахтёр меня́ не услы́шит.
   Я́ не услы́шу сестёр.
   Сёстры меня́ не услы́шат.
   (секретаря́, тебя́, вас, ребя́т, певи́ц,
   певцо́в, студе́нток, Фили́ппа, де́вушек)

2. *He'll pay for them.*
   They'll pay for him.
   О́н запла́тит за ни́х.
   Они́ запла́тят за него́.
   О́н запла́тит за меня́.
   Я́ заплачу́ за него́.
   (тебя́, Зи́ну, ребя́т, неё, меня́, нас, вас,
   Козло́ва, ни́х, попу́тчиков, этого чело-
   ве́ка)

■ QUESTION-ANSWER DRILLS

1. *Will you study the Russian language?*
   I'm already studying Russian.
   Вы́ бу́дете учи́ть ру́сский язы́к?
   Я́ уже́ учу́ ру́сский язы́к.
   Э́тот студе́нт бу́дет учи́ть ру́сский язы́к?
   О́н уже́ у́чит ру́сский язы́к.
   (америка́нская певи́ца, ты, этот па́рень,
   твоя́ подру́га, америка́нский певе́ц,
   америка́нские певцы́, эта америка́нка,
   эти америка́нцы)

2. *Where will you put the records?*
   I'll put them on the table.
   Куда́ вы́ поло́жите пласти́нки?
   Я́ положу́ и́х на сто́л.
   Куда́ учи́тель поло́жит пласти́нки?
   О́н поло́жит и́х на сто́л.
   (она́, студе́нты, певе́ц, певи́ца,
   убо́рщицы, ты, мы, вы, де́вушки)

DISCUSSION

1. *Comparison between the present-future endings of first and second conjugation verbs.*

Verbs of the second conjugation have the vowels –и– and –я– (*or* –а–) in their present-future endings as compared with –е– (*or* –ё–) and –ю– (*or* –у–) for verbs of the first conjugation.

FIRST CONJUGATION						
зна́ю	зна́ешь	зна́ет	зна́ем	зна́ете	зна́ют	(е and ю)
иду́	идёшь	идёт	идём	идёте	иду́т	(ё and у)
SECOND CONJUGATION						
стою́	стои́шь	стои́т	стои́м	стои́те	стоя́т	(и and я)
слы́шу	слы́шишь	слы́шит	слы́шим	слы́шите	слы́шат	(и and а)

2. Alternation of stems in the present-future of second conjugation verbs.

Alternation of the final stem consonant occurs *only* in the first person singular. There are two types:

TYPE 1 (Stems ending in с, з, т, д, ст)	TYPE 2 (Stems ending in п, б, в, ф, м)
Compare спроси́ть, спро́сят *with* спрошу́ *Compare* ви́деть, ви́дят *with* ви́жу *Compare* встре́тить, встре́тят *with* встре́чу *Compare* заходи́ть, захо́дят *with* захожу́	*Compare* люби́ть, лю́бят *with* люблю́ *Compare* оста́вить, оста́вят *with* оста́влю *Compare* спать, спят *with* сплю́ *Compare* познако́мить, познако́мят *with* познако́млю

3. The present-future stem versus the infinitive-past stem.

In second conjugation verbs the endings of the infinitive and past are consistently added to a form of the stem which ends in a vowel. This vowel is automatically dropped before the endings of the present-future.

INFINITIVE-PAST	PRESENT-FUTURE
смотре́–ть –л, –ла, –ли	**смотр**–ю́, –ишь, –ят
слы́ша–ть –л, –ла, –ли	**слы́ш**–у, –ишь, –ат
говори́–ть –л, –ла, ли	**говор**–ю́, –и́шь, –я́т

4. Stress patterns in the present-future.

The same three basic stress patterns that are found in first conjugation verbs are also found in second conjugation verbs:

a. Stress consistently falls on the ending: говорю́, говори́шь, говори́т, говори́м, говори́те, говоря́т.

b. Stress consistently falls on the stem: встре́чу, встре́тишь, встре́тит, встре́тим, встре́тите, встре́тят.

c. Stress falls on the ending in the first person singular, but shifts back to the stem in all other forms: прошу́, про́сишь, про́сит, про́сим, про́сите, про́сят.

Нина студентка-заочница; она работает на фабрике. Кирилл Павлович слышал, что Нина ищет комнату. Он был в горсовете у Алексеева и говорил о Нине. Алексеев сказал, что Нина не будет долго ждать.

Кирилл Павлович встретил Семёна Филипповича в магазине на углу. Семён Филиппович всю зиму был болен. Теперь он уже почти здоров, но всё ещё не работает. Его жена с осени работает в горсовете. Кирилл Павлович рад это слышать. Хорошо, что она работает.

Филипп Грант ехал в Москву. Он сидел в купе и читал „Вечернюю Москву". Галя тоже ехала в этом купе. Она читала журнал „Огонёк". Там был очерк о США. Галя мало знает об Америке. Она всегда с большим удовольствием читает журнал „Америка", но его трудно доставать: он всегда распродан.

Америка́нские пласти́нки о́чень тру́дно достава́ть. Га́ля купи́ла и́х на толку́чке. Сего́дня её подру́ги пойду́т в кра́сный уголо́к, где́ е́сть прои́грыватель. Они́ бу́дут та́м слу́шать му́зыку и танцева́ть. Га́ля принесёт свои́ но́вые пласти́нки.

— Зна́ешь, Оле́г, я встре́тил сего́дня Ка́тю.

— Где́? В библиоте́ке?

— Не́т, в кра́сном уголке́.

— Интере́сно, она́ ничего́ не спра́шивала обо мне́?

— Не́т, она́, как всегда́, говори́ла то́лько о себе́.

— Пра́вда, она́ ду́мает и говори́т всегда́ то́лько о себе́.

— Она́ и живёт то́лько для себя́.

— Ка́жется, ва́ши ребя́та лю́бят на́шу америка́нскую му́зыку?

— Да́, джа́з мы́ о́чень лю́бим. То́лько пласти́нки доста́ть тру́дно.

— А я́ о́чень люблю́ ва́ши наро́дные мело́дии и уже́ купи́л мно́го пласти́нок.

— Интере́сно, каки́е.

— Хоти́те послу́шать?

— Да́, коне́чно.

— Хорошо́, я́ принесу́ и́х сего́дня ве́чером. Е́сли хоти́те, я́ принесу́ и свои́ америка́нские.

— О, да́, пожа́луйста! Мы́ и́х с удово́льствием послу́шаем.

— Здесь идёт «Война́ и ми́р». Э́то америка́нский фи́льм.

— Зна́ю, но ты́ ви́дишь, Га́ля, кака́я о́чередь у ка́ссы? Мы́ мо́жем пойти́ на друго́й фи́льм.

— Не́т, я́ хочу́ то́лько на э́тот! Я́ так люблю́ э́тот рома́н!

— Ну, хорошо́, пойдём на э́тот.

— Во́т мо́й това́рищ по ко́мнате, Га́ля. Хо́чешь, я́ тебя́ познако́млю?

— Что́ ты́, Оле́г? Я́ ве́дь его́ хорошо́ зна́ю, э́то Никола́й Петро́в. Здра́вствуй, Ко́ля!

— А, Га́ля, приве́т! Что́ ты́ тут у на́с де́лаешь?

— Да во́т хочу́ посмотре́ть ва́ш кра́сный уголо́к. Оле́г говори́т, что́ у ва́с хоро́ший прои́грыватель и но́вые пласти́нки.

— Отли́чно. Сейча́с бу́дем слу́шать му́зыку и танцева́ть.

Ни́на хо́чет чита́ть журна́л «Аме́рика», но она́ не зна́ет, где его́ доста́ть. Когда́ она́ спра́шивает в кио́ске, ей всегда́ отвеча́ют, что о́н распро́дан. Я́ достаю́ э́тот журна́л у знако́мого америка́нца Гра́нта, но я́ не хочу́ ей говори́ть об э́том.

У Зи́ны е́сть хоро́ший прои́грыватель и мно́го пласти́нок. Она́ лю́бит наро́дные пе́сни и ста́рые рома́нсы. Сего́дня к не́й зайдёт Фили́пп. О́н принесёт америка́нские пласти́нки, и они́ бу́дут слу́шать джа́з и танцева́ть.

Во́лков купи́л биле́ты в теа́тр, но Га́ля не мо́жет пойти́, она́ ве́чером рабо́тает. Во́лков говори́т, что тогда́ он то́же не пойдёт. О́н спра́шивает Га́лю, не зна́ет ли она́, кто́ хо́чет пойти́. Она́ отвеча́ет, что её подру́ги хоте́ли пойти́, но не доста́ли биле́тов. Она́ ду́мает, что они́ с удово́льствием ку́пят у Во́лкова э́ти биле́ты.

Пётр зашёл в клу́б послу́шать ле́кцию о ру́сских наро́дных пе́снях, но профе́ссор бы́л бо́лен и, ле́кции не́ было. Тогда́ о́н пошёл в ко́мнату, где стои́т прои́грыватель и мо́жно слу́шать пласти́нки. Там о́н встре́тил Зи́ну, и они́ до́лго вме́сте слу́шали ста́рые ру́сские рома́нсы в хоро́шем исполне́нии.

PREPARATION FOR CONVERSATION   **На та́нцах**

устáть (pfv I), устáну, –ешь, –ут   to be tired (*or* exhausted), to get tired
Я устáла.   I'm tired *or* I'm exhausted.
у́ф!   ooh! ugh!
У́ф, устáла!   Ooh, I'm exhausted!
жáрко (adj жáркий)   hot
Тáк жáрко!   It's so hot!
У́ф, устáла! Тáк жáрко!   Ooh, I'm exhausted! It's so hot!

отдохну́ть (pfv I), отдохну́, –ёшь, –у́т   to rest, have a rest
Отдохнём!   Let's rest! *or* We'll rest!
давáть (I), даю́, –ёшь, –ю́т   to give, let
давáй! –те! (imper)   give! let's!
Давáйте отдохнём!   Let's have a rest!

свобóдный   free, unoccupied, vacant
Вóн тáм свобóдные сту́лья.   Over there are some empty chairs.

впрóчем   then again, but then, however
А впрóчем, гдé Кáтя и Волóдя?   But then again, where are Katya and
          Volodya?

к (*or* ко) (*plus* dat)   toward, to
и́м (*or* ни́м) (dat of они́)   to them, for them
к ни́м   to them, to see them, to their place
Пойдём к ни́м!   Let's go see them! *or* Let's go join them!
мóжет (*full form* мóжет бы́ть)   maybe, perhaps
Мóжет пойдём к ни́м?   Maybe we should join them?

предложи́ть (pfv II), предложу́,   to suggest, propose, offer
    предлóжишь, –ат
чтó-то   something
Я хотéл вáм чтó-то предложи́ть.   I wanted to suggest something to you.

Дá, я слу́шаю.   Yes, I'm listening.

◀ **Студенты играют в шахматы в Красном уголке общежития.**   **309**

перейти (pfv I), перейду, –ёшь, –у́т
перейти на «ты»

Дава́йте перейдём на «ты́».

Мы́ ведь уже́ хоро́шие друзья́.

согла́сен, согла́сна, –о, –ы
Хорошо́, я́ согла́сна.

Во́т и прекра́сно!

вы́пить (pfv I), вы́пью, вы́пьешь,
  вы́пьют
на́до вы́пить
За э́то на́до вы́пить!
хотя́
хотя́ бы
лимона́д
**За э́то на́до вы́пить, хотя́ бы лимона́да.
Хоти́те?**

Не «хоти́те», а «хо́чешь».

забыва́ть (I), забыва́ю, –ешь, –ют
Не забыва́й, что мы́ на «ты́».

**Не «хоти́те», а «хо́чешь». Не забыва́й,
что мы́ на «ты́».**

привы́кнуть (pfv I), привы́кну, –ешь,
  –ут (past привы́к, привы́кла,
  –о, –и)
Я́ ещё не привы́к.
Извини́, я́ ещё не привы́к.

буфе́т
Пойдём в буфе́т.

SUPPLEMENT
двор
  на дворе́
Сего́дня на дворе́ о́чень жа́рко.
  свежо́
На дворе́ свежо́.
  пого́да
Кака́я сего́дня пого́да?
  тепло́ (adj тёплый)
Сего́дня тепло́.
Сего́дня тёплая пого́да.
  хо́лодно (adj холо́дный)
Сего́дня хо́лодно.
Сего́дня холо́дная пого́да.
  отдыха́ть (I), отдыха́ю, –ешь, –ют
Вы́ отдыха́ете?

to go over, go across
to switch to "ты," start using the
  familiar form of address
Let's switch to "ты."

We're already good friends after all.

agreed, agreeable
Fine, I'm willing.

That's wonderful.

to drink, have a drink

it's necessary to drink, we have to drink
We must drink to that!
although
even if only, at least
lemonade
We must drink to that, even if only some
  lemonade. Want to?

Not "вы́," "ты́." (*Lit.* Not "хоти́те," but
  "хо́чешь.")
to forget
Don't forget we're using "ты́."

Not "вы́," "ты́." Don't forget we're using
  "ты́" now.

to get used to, to be used to, to become
  accustomed to

I'm not used to it yet.
Excuse me, I'm not used to it yet.

snack bar, sideboard
Let's go to the snack bar.

yard, backyard, courtyard
outside, outdoors, out; in the yard
It's very hot out today.
cool, chilly
It's cool outdoors *or* It's chilly out.
weather
What's the weather today?
warm
It's warm today.
The weather is warm today.
cold
It's cold today.
The weather is cold today.
to rest, relax, vacation
Are you resting?

предлага́ть (I), предлага́ю, –ешь, –ют	to suggest, propose, offer
Что́ вы́ предлага́ете?	What are you suggesting?
переходи́ть (II) (*like* ходи́ть)	to go across, go over
Здесь мо́жно переходи́ть у́лицу?	Is it all right to cross the street here?
привы́чка	habit
Э́то стра́нная привы́чка.	That's a strange habit.
плохо́й	bad, poor
Э́то плоха́я привы́чка.	That's a bad habit.

На та́нцах

Зи́на 1 У́ф, уста́ла! Та́к жа́рко![1]

Оле́г 2 Дава́йте отдохнём! Во́н та́м свобо́дные сту́лья.

Зи́на 3 Хорошо́! А впро́чем, где́ Ка́тя и Воло́дя? Мо́жет пойдём к ни́м?

Оле́г 4 Пойдём. Зна́ете, Зи́на, я хоте́л ва́м что́-то предложи́ть.

Зи́на 5 Да́, я слу́шаю.

Оле́г 6 Дава́йте перейдём на «ты́». Мы́ ведь уже́ хоро́шие друзья́.

Зи́на 7 Хорошо́, я согла́сна.

Оле́г 8 Во́т и прекра́сно! За э́то на́до вы́пить, хотя́ бы лимона́да.[2] Хоти́те?

Зи́на 9 Не «хоти́те», а «хо́чешь». Не забыва́й, что мы́ на «ты́».

Оле́г 10 Извини́, я ещё не привы́к.[3] Пойдём в буфе́т.[4]

NOTES

[1] Both **жа́ркий** and **горя́чий** mean *hot*, but ordinarily they are not interchangeable. In reference to weather, climate, and room temperature, only **жа́ркий** is used, for example, **Како́й жа́ркий де́нь!** *What a hot day!* **Горя́чий**, on the other hand, must be used in referring to objects or things that are hot, for example, **горя́чая вода́** *hot water*.

[2] Note that the genitive form **лимона́да** is used here. Nouns denoting divisible matter are used in the genitive case to indicate a portion of the whole amount, i.e., *some*. For example, compare **Я́ вы́пил молока́** *I drank some milk* with **Я́ вы́пил молоко́** *I drank up the milk*, i.e., all the milk. The word **лимона́д** is used by some Russians not only for *lemonade*, but for almost any soft drink.

[3] In this conversation we find two more examples of past tense verbs in Russian, both perfective, where present tense constructions are used in English:

У́ф, уста́ла!	Ooh, I'm exhausted!
Я́ ещё не привы́к.	I'm not used to it yet.

[4] As used here, **буфе́т** is a snack bar or food counter with very limited fare, mostly cold. Although Khrushchev prohibited the sale of alcoholic beverages in snack bars, it is sometimes possible to obtain beer there. The word is also used to describe a cupboard or sideboard where dishes, utensils, table linens, snacks, and beverages are kept.

ша́хматы (pl only)
игра́
Игра́ в ша́хматы.
   за столо́м
Ка́жется, э́то Ка́тя и Воло́дя за столо́м.
Зи́на, смотри́: ка́жется, э́то Ка́тя и Воло́дя за столо́м.

   они́ игра́ют в ша́хматы
Да́, в ша́хматы игра́ют.

Пойдём к ни́м.

Я́ не зна́л, что ты́ игра́ешь.
Ка́тя, я́ и не зна́л, что ты́ игра́ешь.

   ещё ка́к (*or* ка́к ещё)!
И ещё ка́к!

   ма́т
   мне́ (dat of я́)
Она́ дала́ мне́ ма́т.
   два́ ра́за
Она́ два́ ра́за дала́ мне́ ма́т.

Да ну́! Э́то я́ до́лжен посмотре́ть.

   сади́ться (II), сажу́сь, сади́шься, –я́тся
   вме́сто (*plus* gen)
Лу́чше ты́, Оле́г, сади́сь вме́сто меня́.

   с меня́ дово́льно
С меня́ уже́ дово́льно.

   сыгра́ть (pfv I), сыгра́ю, –ешь, –ют
   вдвоём
   почему́ бы не сыгра́ть
Почему́ бы ва́м вдвоём не сыгра́ть?
А почему́ бы ва́м, ребя́та, вдвоём не сыгра́ть?

   ва́м бу́дет ску́чно
   боя́ться (II) [bajátcə], бою́сь, бои́шься, –я́тся
Бою́сь, что ва́м бу́дет ску́чно.
   пожа́луй
Пожа́луй. То́лько бою́сь, что ва́м бу́дет ску́чно.
Пожа́луй. То́лько бою́сь, что ва́м, де́вушки, бу́дет ску́чно.

chess, chessboard, chess set
game, play, playing
A game of chess.
   at the table
I guess that's Katya and Volodya at the table.
Look, Zina, I guess that's Katya and Volodya at the table.

   they're playing chess
Yes, they're playing chess.

Let's go join them!

I didn't know you play[ed].
Katya, I didn't even know you play[ed].

   and how!
And how!

   checkmate
   to me, for me
She beat me (*lit.* gave me checkmate).
   two times, twice
She beat me twice.

No kidding! That I've got to see!

   to sit down, take a seat
   instead of, in place of
You'd better sit down in my place, Oleg.

   I've had enough, I've had it
I've already had enough.

   to play, play a game
   two together
   why not play a game
Why don't you two play a game together?
Well, why don't you two boys play a game together?

   you'll be bored
   to be afraid

I'm afraid you'd be bored.
   that's an idea, I wouldn't mind, perhaps
That's an idea. But I'm afraid you'd be bored.

That's an idea. But I'm afraid you girls would be bored.

во́здух	air
све́жий	fresh, cool
на све́жий во́здух	out into fresh air
вы́йти (pfv I), вы́йду, вы́йдешь, –ут	to go out, get off (a vehicle), come out
(past вы́шел, вы́шла, –о, –и)	
Мы́ вы́йдем на све́жий во́здух.	We'll go out into the fresh air.
Мы́ вы́йдем немно́го на све́жий во́здух.	We'll go out for a bit of fresh air.
Хо́чешь, Зи́на?	Want to, Zina?
ла́дно	all right, O.K.
Ла́дно.	O.K.
приходи́ть (II) (*like* ходи́ть)	to come, arrive
на́м (dat pl of мы́)	to us, for us
Приходи́те к на́м.	Come see us *or* Come join us.
ко́нчить (pfv II), ко́нчу, –ишь, –ат	to finish
А вы́ приходи́те к на́м, когда́ ко́нчите.	And you come join us when you've finished.

SUPPLEMENT

конча́ть (I), конча́ю, –ешь, –ют	to finish
Когда́ вы́ конча́ете рабо́ту?	When do you finish working? *or* When are you through working?
и́з дому	from one's house, from home
Ва́м письмо́ и́з дому.	There's a letter for you from home.
выходи́ть (II) (*like* ходи́ть)	to go out, come out, get off (a vehicle)
Он ре́дко выхо́дит и́з дому.	He rarely goes out of the house.
прийти́ (pfv I), приду́, –ёшь, –у́т	to come, arrive
(past пришёл, пришла́, –о́, –и́)	
Когда́ вы́ придёте к на́м?	When will you come to see us?
Ка́жется, ва́ш по́езд пришёл.	It seems your train has arrived.
гуля́ть (I), гуля́ю, –ешь, –ет	to walk (for pleasure), stroll
Вы́ ча́сто гуля́ете в па́рке?	Do you often stroll in the park?
погуля́ть (pfv I) (*like* гуля́ть)	to go for a stroll, go for a walk
Дава́йте погуля́ем.	Let's go for a walk (*or* stroll).

Игра́ в ша́хматы

З. — Зи́на	В. — Влади́мир
О. — Оле́г	К. — Ка́тя

О.   1 Зи́на, смотри́: ка́жется, э́то Ка́тя и Воло́дя за столо́м.

З.   2 Да́, в ша́хматы игра́ют.[1] Пойдём к ни́м.

О.   3 Ка́тя, я́ и не зна́л, что ты́ игра́ешь.

В.   4 И ещё ка́к! Уже́ два́ ра́за дала́ мне́ ма́т.

O. 5 Да ну! Это я до́лжен посмотре́ть.

В. 6 Лу́чше ты́, Оле́г, сади́сь вме́сто меня́. С меня́ уже́ дово́льно.

К. 7 А почему́ бы ва́м, ребя́та, вдвоём не сыгра́ть?

О. 8 Пожа́луй. То́лько бою́сь, что ва́м, де́вушки, бу́дет ску́чно.

К. 9 Не́т, мы́ вы́йдем немно́го на све́жий во́здух. Хо́чешь, Зи́на?

З. 10 Ла́дно. А вы́, ребя́та, приходи́те к на́м, когда́ ко́нчите.[2]

NOTES

[1] Chess has traditionally been a very popular game with Russians of all ages. The Soviet government prides itself on having the best chess players in the world. As a result of winning only second place at an international chess tournament, the government took measures to insure a crop of future champions by introducing a course in chess playing in Russian secondary schools.

[2] Notice that English often uses the present or even the past tense after *when*, whereas Russian more accurately uses the future:

Приходи́те к на́м, **когда́ вы́ ко́нчите.**   Come join us *when you finish* (or *when you've finished*—lit. *when you shall have finished*).

Basic sentence patterns

1. Дава́йте сыгра́ем в ка́рты. Let's play a game of cards.
   _____ в ша́хматы. _____ of chess.
   _____ в футбо́л. _____ of soccer.
   _____ в те́ннис. _____ of tennis.
   _____ в бейсбо́л. _____ of baseball.
   _____ в хокке́й. _____ of hockey.

2. Дава́йте отдохнём. Let's take a break *or* Let's rest a while.
   _____ перейдём на «ты́». _____ switch to "ты́."
   _____ пойдём в кино́. _____ go to the movies.
   _____ вы́пьем за э́то. _____ drink to that *or* Let's drink a toast to that.
   _____ вы́йдем на све́жий во́здух. _____ go get some fresh air.
   _____ сыгра́ем в ша́хматы. _____ have a game of chess.
   _____ пойдём к ни́м. _____ go join the others *or* Let's go see them.
   _____ пойдём в буфе́т. _____ go to the snack bar.

3. Я хоте́л ва́м что́-то предложи́ть. I had something I wanted to suggest to you.
   _____ ей _____. _____ to her.
   _____ им _____. _____ to them.
   _____ ему́ _____. _____ to him.
   О́н хоте́л мне́ что́-то предложи́ть. He had something he wanted to suggest to me.
   _____ на́м _____. _____ to us.

4. Мне́ нужна́ ка́рта Евро́пы.
   Ва́м _____.
   На́м _____.
   Тебе́ _____.
   И́м _____.
   Ему́ _____.
   Е́й _____.

I need a map of Europe.
You _____.
We _____.
You _____.
They _____.
He needs _____.
She _____.

5. Мне́ ну́жен но́вый а́тлас.
   _____ слова́рь.
   _____ секрета́рь.
   Мне́ нужна́ но́вая продавщи́ца.
   _____ ко́мната.
   _____ ру́чка.
   _____ тетра́дь.
   Мне́ ну́жно но́вое ра́дио.
   _____ перо́.
   Мне́ нужны́ но́вые тетра́ди.
   _____ по́лки.
   _____ сту́лья.

I need a new atlas.
_____ dictionary.
_____ secretary.
I need a new saleslady.
_____ room.
_____ pen.
_____ notebook.
I need a new radio.
_____ pen [point].
I need new notebooks.
_____ shelves.
_____ chairs.

6. Мне́ хо́лодно.
   ____ жа́рко.
   ____ ску́чно.
   Ва́м не хо́лодно?
   _____ жа́рко?
   _____ ску́чно?

I'm cold.
____ hot.
____ bored.
Aren't you cold?
_____ hot?
_____ bored?

7. Ка́к на дворе́?
   — На дворе́ хорошо́.
   _____ тепло́.
   _____ хо́лодно.
   _____ жа́рко.
   _____ свежо́.

What's it like outdoors?
It's nice out.
____ warm ___.
____ cold ___.
____ hot ___.
____ chilly ___.

8. . Ка́к сего́дня тепло́!
   _____ хо́лодно!
   _____ жа́рко!
   _____ хорошо́!

How warm it is today!
____ cold _____!
____ hot _____!
____ nice _____!

9. Кака́я сего́дня пого́да?
   — Пого́да сего́дня хоро́шая.
   _____ плоха́я.
   _____ тёплая.
   _____ холо́дная.
   _____ жа́ркая.

What's the weather like today?
The weather's nice today.
_____ bad ____.
_____ warm ___.
_____ cold ___.
_____ hot ____.

10. Ва́м письмо́ и́з дому.
    _____ из Москвы́.
    _____ из Ленингра́да.
    _____ из Евро́пы.
    _____ из Кита́я.
    _____ из Аме́рики.
    _____ из США.

There's a letter for you from home.
_____ from Moscow.
_____ from Leningrad.
_____ from Europe.
_____ from China.
_____ from America.
_____ from the U.S.A.

11. Я́ ва́м звони́л в ча́с.
   — ей _____.
   — ему́ _____.
   О́н мне́ звони́л по́сле обе́да.
   —— на́м _____.
   —— тебе́ _____.

I called you at one.
_____ her _____.
_____ him _____.
He called me after lunch (*or* in the afternoon).
_____ us _____.
_____ you _____.

12. О́н пришёл ко мне́.
   _____ к тебе́.
   _____ к на́м.
   _____ к ва́м.
   _____ к не́й.
   _____ к ни́м.
   О́н пришёл к себе́ домо́й.

He came to see me.
_____ you.
_____ us.
_____ you.
_____ her.
_____ them.
He came back home *or* He's come home.

13. Когда́ вы́ ко́нчите рабо́тать?
   _____ о́н ко́нчит _____?
   _____ они́ ко́нчат _____?
   _____ мы́ ко́нчим _____?
   _____ ты́ ко́нчишь _____?
   _____ я́ ко́нчу _____?

When will you be through working?
_____ will he be _____?
_____ will they be _____?
_____ will we be _____?
_____ will you be _____?
_____ will I be _____?

14. Вы́ уже́ конча́ете обе́дать?
   О́н ___ конча́ет _____?
   Ты́ ___ конча́ешь _____?
   Они́ ___ конча́ют _____?
   Я́ уже́ конча́ю обе́дать.
   Мы́ ___ конча́ем _____.
   Она́ ___ конча́ет _____.

Are you just about finished eating dinner?
Is he _____ finished _____?
Are you _____ finished _____?
Are they _____ finished _____?
I'm just about finished eating dinner.
We're _____ finished _____.
She's _____ finished _____.

15. Она́ даёт уро́ки англи́йского языка́.
   Они́ даю́т _____.
   Мы́ даём _____.
   Я́ даю́ _____.
   Вы́ даёте уро́ки ру́сского языка́?
   О́н даёт _____ ?
   Ты́ даёшь _____ ?

She gives English lessons.
They give _____.
We give _____.
I give _____.
Do you give Russian lessons?
Does he give _____ ?
Do you give _____ ?

16. Они́ ему́ даду́т про́пуск.
   Вы́ ____ дади́те _____.
   Мы́ ____ дади́м _____.
   Ты́ ____ да́шь _____.
   Она́ ____ да́ст _____.
   Я́ _____ да́м _____.

They'll give him a pass.
You'll give _____.
We'll give _____.
You'll give _____.
She'll give _____.
I'll give _____.

17. Я́ ва́м да́м зна́ть.
   О́н ___ да́ст ____.
   Мы́ ___ дади́м ___.
   Они́ ___ даду́т ____.
   Вы́ мне́ дади́те зна́ть?
   Ты́ ___ да́шь _____ ?

I'll let you know.
He'll let _____.
We'll let _____.
They'll let ____.
Will you let me know?
Will you let _____ ?

18. Когда́ ко́нчишь, ты́ немно́го отдохнёшь?   When you finish, will you rest a bit?
        _____ ко́нчите, вы́ _____ отдохнёте?   _____ you finish, will you rest _____?
    Когда́ ко́нчу, я́ немно́го отдохну́.   When I finish, I'll rest a bit.
        _____ ко́нчит, она́ _____ отдохнёт.   _____ she finishes, she'll rest _____.
        _____ ко́нчим, мы́ _____ отдохнём.   _____ we finish, we'll rest _____.
        _____ ко́нчат, они́ _____ отдохну́т.   _____ they finish, they'll rest _____.

19. Ле́том я́ отдыха́ю в Я́лте.   During the summer I vacation in Yalta.
        _____ мы́ отдыха́ем _____.   _____ we vacation _____.
        _____ ты́ отдыха́ешь _____.   _____ you vacation _____.
        _____ они́ отдыха́ют _____.   _____ they vacation _____.
        _____ вы́ отдыха́ете _____.   _____ you vacation _____.
        _____ Хрущёв отдыха́ет _____.   _____ Khrushchev vacations _____.

20. Она́ к нему́ уже́ привы́кла.   She's already used to him.
      _____ к на́м _____.   _____ to us.
      _____ к ни́м _____.   _____ to them.
      _____ к ва́м _____.   _____ to you.
      _____ ко мне́ _____.   _____ to me.
      _____ к тебе́ _____.   _____ to you.

Pronunciation practice: final clusters with [r] or [ṛ]

A. Final clusters with [r] followed by a hard consonant.

[górp] го́рб hump	[čórt] чёрт devil	[fárs] фа́рс farce
[şérp] се́рб Serb	[óčirk] о́черк sketch, outline	[tórs] то́рс torso
[bórt] бо́рт shipboard	[párk] па́рк park	[kúrs] ку́рс course
[márt] ма́рт March	[γérx] ве́рх peak	[tórf] то́рф peat
[spírt] спи́рт alcohol, spirits	[syérx] све́рх above	[ņérf] не́рв nerve
[spórt] спо́рт sport	[mórš] мо́рж walrus	[nórm] но́рм of norms
[tórt] то́рт cake	[márš] ма́рш march	[ḍórn] дёрн turf

B. Final clusters with [ṛ] followed by a soft consonant.

Note: Although the writing system does not indicate it, the **p** preceding a soft consonant is pronounced soft.

[skóṛp̦] ско́рбь grief	[γéṛf] ве́рфь shipyard	[skátiṛṭ] ска́терть tablecloth
[ḟéṛş] фе́рзь queen (in chess)	[sméṛṭ] сме́рть death	[čétγiṛṭ] че́тверть quarter

C. Clusters with [r] in final position.

[ákr] а́кр
acre

[žánr] жа́нр
genre

[ţiátr] теа́тр
theater

[métr] ме́тр
meter

[aşótr] осётр
sturgeon

[ḷítr] ли́тр
liter

[smótr] смо́тр
review

[céntr] це́нтр
center

[ṃiṇístr] мини́стр
minister

[ţígr] ти́гр
tiger

D. Clusters with [ṛ] in final position.

[şinţábṛ] сентя́брь
September

[akţábṛ] октя́брь
October

[najábṛ] ноя́брь
November

[ḍikábṛ] дека́брь
December

[vnútṛ] вну́трь
inside

STRUCTURE AND DRILLS

The dative of кто́, что́, the personal pronouns, and the reflexive personal pronoun себя́

NOM	кто́	что́	я́	ты́	о́н, оно́	она́	мы́	вы́	они́	(no nom)
DAT	кому́	чему́	мне́	тебе́	ему́ (нему́)	ей (ней)	на́м	ва́м	и́м (ни́м)	себе́

Notes

1. The alternate third person forms, **ему́, ней**, and **ни́м**, are used when a preposition precedes the pronoun: **к нему́, к ней**, and **к ни́м**.

2. The dative reflexive personal pronoun **себе́** *to* (or *for*) *oneself* has no nominative. It is used when the subject and indirect object are the same: Я́ купи́л **себе́** пласти́нку. (I bought a record *for myself*.)

MODELS

Я́ хоте́л ва́м что́-то сказа́ть.
_____ ему́ _____.
_____ тебе́ _____.
_____ ей _____.
_____ и́м _____.

I wanted to tell you something.
_____ him _____.
_____ you _____.
_____ her _____.
_____ them _____.

О́н хоте́л мне́ что́-то сказа́ть.
_____ на́м _____.

He wanted to tell me something.
_____ us _____.

Кому́ э́то письмо́? Мне́?

_____? Тебе́?

_____? На́м?

_____? Ва́м?

_____? Ему́?

_____? Е́й?

_____? И́м?

Я́ к ва́м приду́ в суббо́ту.

__ к нему́ _____.

__ к тебе́ _____.

__ к не́й _____.

__ к ни́м _____.

Приходи́те к на́м в суббо́ту.

_____ ко мне́ _____.

Я́ куплю́ ва́м э́ту пласти́нку.

_____ себе́ _____.

_____ тебе́ _____.

_____ ему́ _____.

_____ е́й _____.

_____ и́м _____.

Она́ ку́пит себе́ но́вый портфе́ль.

_____ тебе́ _____.

_____ мне́ _____.

_____ на́м _____.

Who is that letter for? Me?

_____? You?

_____? Us?

_____? You?

_____? Him?

_____? Her?

_____? Them?

I'll come and see you on Saturday.

_____ him _____.

_____ you _____.

_____ her _____.

_____ them _____.

Come and see us on Saturday.

_____ me _____.

I'll buy you this record.

_____ myself _____.

_____ you _____.

_____ him _____.

_____ her _____.

_____ them _____.

She'll buy herself a new briefcase.

_____ you _____.

_____ me _____.

_____ us _____.

■ CUED QUESTION-ANSWER DRILL

(*you*) *To whom did the teacher say that?*
  To you.
(вы́) Кому́ учи́тель э́то сказа́л?
  Ва́м.
(я) Кому́ учи́тель э́то сказа́л?
  Мне́.
(мы, ты, они, он, она)

■ RESPONSE DRILLS

1. *Oh, you're here already!*
   I'll bring you the paper.
   Áх, вы́ уже́ здéсь!
   Я́ принесу́ ва́м газе́ту.
   Áх, она́ уже́ здéсь!
   Я́ принесу́ е́й газе́ту.
   (ты, он, они, Галя, ректор)

2. *I don't know his house number.*
   He doesn't want to tell me.
   Я́ не зна́ю но́мера его́ до́ма.
   Óн мне́ не хо́чет говори́ть.
   Она́ не зна́ет но́мера его́ до́ма.
   Óн е́й не хо́чет говори́ть.
   (мы, профессор Алексеев, ты, вы, ректор, ребята)

3. *I wasn't home.*
   Who came to see me?
   Меня́ не́ было до́ма.
   Кто́ ко мне́ приходи́л?
   Бра́та не́ было до́ма.
   Кто́ к нему́ приходи́л?
   (нас, его, вас, девушек, тебя, певицы,
   их)

5. *He hasn't been to your place yet.*
   He'll come to see you.
   Он у ва́с ещё не́ был.
   Он придёт к ва́м.

4. *She's sick.*
   I'm on my way to see her.
   Она́ больна́.
   Я́ иду́ к не́й.
   Мо́й това́рищ бо́лен.
   Я́ иду́ к нему́.
   (они, жена ректора, ты, секретарь,
   студенты, вы)

   Он у ни́х ещё не́ был.
   Он придёт к ни́м.
   (у нас, у неё, у них, у тебя, у меня, у
   него, у вас, у меня, у нас)

■ SUBJECT REVERSAL DRILL

1. *She bought him a present.*
   He bought her a present.
   Она́ купи́ла ему́ пода́рок.
   О́н купи́л е́й пода́рок.
   Мы́ купи́ли ему́ пода́рок.
   О́н купи́л на́м пода́рок.
   (я купи́л, ты купила, вы купили, они
   купили)

3. *I wrote him a letter.*
   He wrote me a letter.
   Я́ написа́л ему́ письмо́.
   О́н написа́л мне́ письмо́.
   Мы́ написа́ли ему́ письмо́.
   О́н написа́л на́м письмо́.
   (вы написали, ты написал, она на-
   писала, они написали, он написал, я
   написал)

2. *He'll bring her some lemonade.*
   She'll bring him some lemonade.
   О́н принесёт е́й лимона́да.
   Она́ принесёт ему́ лимона́да.
   Я́ принесу́ е́й лимона́да.
   Она́ принесёт мне́ лимона́да.
   (мы принесём, вы принесёте, они при-
   несут, ты принесёшь, он принесёт)

The dative case in impersonal constructions

MODELS

Мне́ та́к жа́рко.	I'm so hot.
На́м _____.	We're____.
Ему́ _____.	He's _____.
Е́й _____.	She's ____.
И́м _____.	They're __.
Ва́м не жа́рко?	Aren't you hot?
Тебе́ _____?	_____ you ___?
Ва́м не бу́дет ску́чно?	Won't you be bored?
Тебе́ _____?	_____ you _____?

Мне́ бу́дет ску́чно.	I'll be bored.
На́м _____.	We'll be ____.
Ему́ _____.	He'll be ____.
Е́й _____.	She'll be ____.
И́м _____.	They'll be ____.
Мне́ бы́ло хо́лодно.	I was cold.
На́м _____.	We were ____.
Ему́ _____.	He was ____.
Е́й _____.	She was ____.
И́м _____.	They were ____.
Тебе́ бы́ло хо́лодно?	Were you cold?
Ва́м _____?	____ you ____?
Мне́ пора́ идти́.	It's time for me to be going.
На́м _____.	_____ us _____.
Заче́м ва́м спеши́ть?	What's your hurry? or Why should you hurry?
____ тебе́ _____?	____ your ____? or _____ you ____?
А мне́ мо́жно посмотре́ть?	May I look? or Is it O.K. for me to look?
_ на́м _____?	____ we ____? or _____ us _____?
Мне́ та́м бы́ло хорошо́.	I was happy there or I felt good there.
Ему́ _____.	He _____ or He _____.
Мне́ хо́чется пи́ть.	I'm thirsty or I feel like having a drink.
На́м _____.	We're ____ or We _____.

■ REPETITION DRILL

Repeat the above models, noting that the person who is involved in each instance is expressed by the dative case in Russian.

■ CUED QUESTION-ANSWER DRILL

(I)   *Who's thirsty?*
        I am.
(я)   Кому́ хо́чется пи́ть?
        Мне́.
(она́)   Кому́ хо́чется пи́ть?
        Е́й.
(вы, ты, он, мы, они, я, она, вы, мы)

■ RESPONSE DRILLS

1. *We'll be dancing.*
   We won't be bored.
   Мы́ бу́дем танцева́ть.
   На́м не бу́дет ску́чно.
   Вы́ бу́дете танцева́ть.
   Ва́м не бу́дет ску́чно.
        (я, он, ты, она, они, он, вы, я)

2. *He went home.*
   He was bored.
   О́н пошёл домо́й.
   Ему́ бы́ло ску́чно.
   Она́ пошла́ домо́й.
   Е́й бы́ло ску́чно.
        (они, ты, вы, мы, я, он, ты, она)

1. *Where are you going?*
   Home. I'm bored here.
   Куда́ ты́ идёшь?
   Домо́й. Мне́ здесь ску́чно.
   Куда́ вы́ идёте?
   Домо́й. На́м здесь ску́чно.

   (он, они, мы, она, ты, вы, он)

2. *Why are you in such a hurry?*
   It's time for me to go home.
   Почему́ ты́ та́к спеши́шь?
   Мне́ пора́ домо́й.
   Почему́ о́н та́к спеши́т?
   Ему́ пора́ домо́й.

   (она, они, вы, ты, он, она, вы)

■ SUBSTITUTION DRILL

He knows that he'll be bored.
О́н зна́ет, что́ ему́ бу́дет ску́чно.
Она́ зна́ет, что́ е́й бу́дет ску́чно.

(мы, вы, я, они, Коля, ты, Галя, все)

■ STRUCTURE REPLACEMENT DRILLS

It's time for us to go.
It was time for us to go.
На́м пора́ идти́.
На́м пора́ бы́ло идти́.
Мне́ пора́ идти́.
Мне́ пора́ бы́ло идти́.

(ей, им, вам, нам, мне, тебе, ему, им, мне)

■ STRUCTURE REPLACEMENT DRILL

He wants to learn the results.
He's curious to know the results.
О́н хо́чет узна́ть результа́ты.
Ему́ интере́сно узна́ть результа́ты.
Мы́ хоти́м узна́ть результа́ты.
На́м интере́сно узна́ть результа́ты.

(они, ты, она, вы, я, мы, он, ты)

■ RESPONSE DRILLS

1. *I was at the flea market.*
   I found it interesting there.
   Я́ бы́л на толку́чке.
   Мне́ та́м бы́ло интере́сно.
   О́н бы́л на толку́чке.
   Ему́ та́м бы́ло интере́сно.

   (мы, она, вы, они, он, я)

2. *We danced for a long time.*
   We're hot.
   Мы́ до́лго танцева́ли.
   На́м жа́рко.
   О́н до́лго танцева́л.
   Ему́ жа́рко.

   (я, они, ты, она, вы, мы, я)

3. *You have time.*
   Why should you hurry?
   У ва́с е́сть вре́мя.
   Заче́м ва́м спеши́ть?
   У тебя́ е́сть вре́мя.
   Заче́м тебе́ спеши́ть?

   (у него, у нас, у них, у неё, у меня, у вас, у тебя, у них)

4. *We want to read.*
   May we read?
   Мы́ хоти́м чита́ть.
   На́м мо́жно чита́ть?
   О́н хо́чет чита́ть.
   Ему́ мо́жно чита́ть?

   (она, я, они, ты, вы, мы, он, я)

DISCUSSION

In impersonal constructions the dative case is used to identify the person affected or involved in the situation. Such dative constructions are especially common in conjunction with infinitives or short-form neuter adjectives ending in –o.

In the past and future, the neuter verb forms **бы́ло** and **бу́дет** are used. They usually precede the infinitive or short-form neuter adjective.

Тебе́ та́м не бу́дет интере́сно.	You won't find it interesting there.
Ему́ пора́ бы́ло идти́.	It was time for him to be going.
Мне́ бы́ло хо́лодно.	I was cold.
На́м бу́дет хо́лодно.	We'll be cold.

The dative personal referent may be omitted for a more general statement.

Жа́рко.	It's hot.
Пора́ идти́.	It's time to be going.
Мо́жно посмотре́ть?	Is it all right to look?
Ка́к интере́сно!	How interesting!

The dative case with ну́жен, нужна́, ну́жно, and нужны́

MODELS

Мне́ ну́жен а́тлас.	I need an atlas.
Мне́ ну́жен бы́л а́тлас.	I needed an atlas.
Мне́ ну́жен бу́дет а́тлас.	I'll need an atlas.
Мне́ нужна́ ка́рта Евро́пы.	I need a map of Europe.
Мне́ нужна́ была́ ка́рта Евро́пы.	I needed a map of Europe.
Мне́ нужна́ бу́дет ка́рта Евро́пы.	I'll need a map of Europe.
Мне́ ну́жно ра́дио.	I need a radio.
Мне́ ну́жно бы́ло ра́дио.	I needed a radio.
Мне́ ну́жно бу́дет ра́дио.	I'll need a radio.
Мне́ нужны́ ключи́.[1]	I need keys.
Мне́ нужны́ бы́ли ключи́.	I needed keys.
Мне́ нужны́ бу́дут ключи́.	I'll need keys.

■ REPETITION DRILL

Repeat the above models, noting the pattern in the present, past, and future.

■ CUED QUESTION-ANSWER DRILLS

1. (*I*)   *Who needs an atlas?*
   I need an atlas.
   (я)   Кому́ ну́жен а́тлас?
   Мне́ ну́жен а́тлас.
   (мы́)   Кому́ ну́жен а́тлас?
   На́м ну́жен а́тлас.
   (она, он, мы, ты, они, я, она, ты)

2. (*chess set*)   *What does he need?*
   He needs a chess set.
   (ша́хматы)   Что́ ему́ ну́жно?
   Ему́ нужны́ ша́хматы.
   (но́ж)   Что́ ему́ ну́жно?
   Ему́ ну́жен но́ж.
   (лимонад, квитанция, пластинки, бумага, журнал, молоко, газета, карандаш, ручка)

3. (*cupboard*)   *What will we need?*
   We'll need a cupboard.
   (шка́ф)   Что́ на́м бу́дет ну́жно?
   На́м бу́дет ну́жен шка́ф.
   (по́лка)   Что́ на́м бу́дет ну́жно?
   На́м бу́дет нужна́ по́лка.
   (ключи, проигрыватель, «Известия», новое место, журнал «Огонёк», «Вечерняя Москва», шахматы)

4. (*secretary*)   *Whom did she need?*
   She needed the (or *a*) *secretary.*
   (секрета́рь)   Кто́ ей бы́л ну́жен?
   Ей бы́л ну́жен секрета́рь.
   (убо́рщица)   Кто́ ей бы́л ну́жен?
   Ей была́ нужна́ убо́рщица.
   (ректор, продавщица, товарищ Волков, учительница, вахтёр, Наташа и Зина, профессор Орлов)

---

[1] Some speakers stress the first syllable of the plural form: ну́жны.

1. *What dictionary does he need?*
   He needs this one.
   Какóй словáрь емý нýжен?
   Емý нýжен вóт э́тот.
   Какóй журнáл емý нýжен?
   Емý нýжен вóт э́тот.
   (полка, роман, перо, книга, стул,
   тетрадь)

2. *Are there any cups here?*
   I need a cup.
   Тýт éсть чáшки?
   Мнé нужнá чáшка.
   Тýт éсть стакáны?
   Мнé нýжен стакáн.
   (ложки, ножи, вилки, карандаши,
   перья, доски, тетради)

■ RESPONSE DRILLS

1. *Here are some pencils.*
   We don't need pencils.
   Вóт карандашú.
   Нáм карандашú не нужнú.
   Вóт пропускá.
   Нáм пропускá не нужнú.
   (словарь, квитанция, ключи, лифт,
   такси, телефон, носильщики, кофе)

2. *Oleg doesn't have an atlas.*
   Does he really need an atlas?
   У Олéга нéт áтласа.
   Рáзве емý нýжен áтлас?
   У Олéга нéт áтласов.
   Рáзве емý нужнú áтласы?
   (нет тетрадей, нет словарей, нет про-
   пуска, нет пера, нет ключей, нет стола,
   нет полки)

3. *Where can one get pencils?*
   She needs pencils.
   Гдé мóжно достáть карандашú?
   Éй нужнú карандашú.
   Гдé мóжно достáть нóж?
   Éй нýжен нóж.
   (перья, материал, коробку, стол,
   тетради, полку, словарь, огурцы)

4. *Where did you get paper?*
   I'll need paper.
   Гдé вú достáли бумáгу?
   Мнé нужнá бýдет бумáга.
   Гдé вú достáли кáрту Еврóпы?
   Мнé нужнá бýдет кáрта Еврóпы.
   (стол, карандаши, полку, пропуск,
   билеты, горячую воду, молоко)

5. *The children got [hold of] some pencils.*
   They needed pencils.
   Ребя́та достáли карандашú.
   Йм нужнú бúли карандашú.
   Ребя́та достáли стýлья.
   Йм нужнú бúли стýлья.
   (стол, полку, книги, словарь, тетради,
   историю Китая, карту Америки)

6. *He had no key.*
   He needed a key.
   У негó нé было ключá.
   Емý нýжен бúл клю́ч.
   У негó нé было прóпуска.
   Емý нýжен бúл прóпуск.
   (рубля, копейки, билета, тетрадей,
   радио, стакана)

DISCUSSION

Нýжен, нужнá, нýжно, and нужнú are the short forms of the long-form adjective нýжный *necessary*. They are used in constructions where the dative indicates the person in need and the nominative indicates the thing needed: Мнé **нужнá** кáрта. (I need a map.—*Lit.* To me a map is necessary.)

In the past tense the appropriate form of **бúл, былá, бúло,** or **бúли** is used in agreement with the short-form adjective and the noun indicating the thing needed.

Емý **нужнá былá** кáрта.	He needed a map.
Емý **нýжен бúл** шофёр.	He needed a driver.
Емý **нужнú бúли** я́щики.	He needed some boxes.

In the future, the appropriate form of **бу́дет** (for singular) or **бу́дут** (for plural) is used with the short-form adjective.

Мне́ **нужна́ бу́дет** ка́рта.	I'll need a map.
Мне́ **нужны́ бу́дут** ка́рты.	I'll need maps.
Мне́ **ну́жно бу́дет** перо́.	I'll need a pen.

The neuter form **ну́жно** is also used in infinitive constructions.

Мне́ **ну́жно** спа́ть.	I need to sleep.
На́м **ну́жно бы́ло** спеши́ть.	We had to hurry.
Ему́ **ну́жно бу́дет** рабо́тать.	He'll need to work.

The imperfective verb дава́ть and its perfective да́ть

	дава́ть (imperfective)	да́ть (perfective)			
PAST	дава́л, дава́ла, дава́ло, дава́ли	да́л не́ дал [n̪édəl]	дала́ не дала́ [n̪idalá]	да́ло не́ дало [n̪édələ]	да́ли не́ дали [n̪édəl̪i]
PRES	даю́, даёшь, даёт, даём, даёте, даю́т				
FUT	бу́ду дава́ть, бу́дешь дава́ть	да́м, да́шь, да́ст, дади́м, дади́те, даду́т			
IMPER	дава́й! дава́йте!	да́й! да́йте!			

MODELS

1. Imperfective verb дава́ть

О́н дава́л уро́ки ру́сского языка́.	He used to give Russian lessons.
Она́ дава́ла _____.	She used to give _____.
Мы́ дава́ли _____.	We used to give _____.
Я́ даю́ уро́ки англи́йского языка́.	I give English lessons.
Ты́ даёшь _____.	You give _____.
О́н даёт _____.	He gives _____.
Мы́ даём _____.	We give _____.
Вы́ даёте _____.	You give _____.
Они́ даю́т _____.	They give _____.
Я́ бу́ду дава́ть уро́ки ру́сского языка́.	I'll be giving Russian lessons.
Ты́ бу́дешь _____.	You'll be giving _____.
О́н бу́дет _____.	He'll be giving _____.
Мы́ бу́дем _____.	We'll be giving _____.
Вы́ бу́дете _____.	You'll be giving _____.
Они́ бу́дут _____.	They'll be giving _____.
Не дава́й и́м так мно́го воды́!	Don't give them so much water!
Не дава́йте _____!	Don't give _____!

2. Perfective verb да́ть

Óн мне́ да́л ключи́.	He gave me the keys.
Óн мне́ не́ дал ключе́й.	He didn't give me the keys.
Она́ мне́ дала́ ключи́.	She gave me the keys.
Она́ мне́ не дала́ ключе́й.	She didn't give me the keys.
Они́ мне́ да́ли ключи́.	They gave me the keys.
Они́ мне́ не́ дали ключе́й.	They didn't give me the keys.

Я́ ему́ да́м пя́ть рубле́й.	I'll give him five rubles.
Ты́ ___ да́шь _____.	You'll give _____.
Она́ ___ да́ст _____.	She'll give _____.
Мы́ ___ дади́м _____.	We'll give _____.
Вы́ ___ дади́те _____.	You'll give _____.
Они́ ___ даду́т _____.	They'll give _____.

Да́й мне́ э́ту кни́гу!	Give me that book!
Да́йте _____!	Give _____!

■ REPETITION DRILL

Repeat the above models, noting that the perfective verb да́ть has an irregular future. Note also that the imperfective verb дава́ть has a present tense based on an alternate form of the stem without –ва–.

■ STRUCTURE REPLACEMENT DRILLS

1. *I'll give [private] lessons.*
   I give [private] lessons.
   Я́ бу́ду дава́ть уро́ки.
   Я́ даю́ уро́ки.
   Óн бу́дет дава́ть уро́ки.
   Óн даёт уро́ки.
   (мои́ това́рищи, моя́ подру́га, мы, э́тот учи́тель, ты, я, э́ти де́вушки, вы, мой друг)

2. *Don't give him the key!*
   Give him the key!
   Не дава́й ему́ ключа́!
   Да́й ему́ клю́ч!
   Не дава́й ей ры́бы!
   Да́й ей ры́бу!
   Не дава́й и́м биле́тов!
   Не дава́й ему́ но́мера телефо́на!
   Не дава́й и́м словаря́!
   Не дава́й ей пропуска́!
   Не дава́й ему́ а́тласа!

3. *I give singing lessons.*
   I used to give singing lessons.
   Я́ даю́ уро́ки пе́ния.
   Я́ дава́л уро́ки пе́ния.
   Мы́ даём уро́ки пе́ния.
   Мы́ дава́ли уро́ки пе́ния.
   (она, они, он, вы, мы)

4. *She gave him ten rubles.*
   She'll give him ten rubles.
   Она́ дала́ ему́ де́сять рубле́й.
   Она́ да́ст ему́ де́сять рубле́й.
   Я́ да́л ему́ де́сять рубле́й.
   Я́ да́м ему́ де́сять рубле́й.
   (я дала́, мы да́ли, они да́ли, вы да́ли, ты дала́, профессор Семёнов да́л, америка́нцы да́ли)

5. *She'll give him the tickets.*
   She gave him the tickets.
   Она́ да́ст ему́ биле́ты.
   Она́ дала́ ему́ биле́ты.

   Я́ да́м ему́ биле́ты.
   Я́ да́л ему́ биле́ты.
   (вахтёрша, мы, Маша, певцы, вы, она, Алексеев)

6. *The teacher let him talk.*
   The teacher didn't let him talk.
   Учи́тель да́л ему́ говори́ть.
   Учи́тель не́ дал ему́ говори́ть.
   Она́ дала́ ему́ говори́ть.
   Она́ не дала́ ему́ говори́ть.

   (Орлов, мы, девушка, учителя, брат,
   сестра, Олег, жена)

7. *I placed an ad in the paper.*
   I'll place an ad in the paper.
   Я да́л объявле́ние в газе́ту.
   Я да́м объявле́ние в газе́ту.
   Мы да́ли объявле́ние в газе́ту.
   Мы дади́м объявле́ние в газе́ту.

   (вы, учитель, ты, этот человек, моя
   подруга, американцы, я, эта женщина,
   мы)

■ QUESTION-ANSWER DRILL

Does Kozlov have the atlas?
No, he gave it to me.
А́тлас у Козло́ва?
Не́т, он да́л его́ мне́.
А́тлас у ни́х?
Не́т, они́ да́ли его́ мне́.

(у Коли, у неё, у Ирины, у него,
у учительницы, у учителей, у Гали)

■ RESPONSE DRILL

He has a dictionary.
He'll give them the dictionary.
У него́ е́сть слова́рь.
Он и́м да́ст слова́рь.
У меня́ е́сть слова́рь.
Я и́м да́м слова́рь.

(у нас, у неё, у тебя, у меня, у вас, у них,
у него, у нас)

DISCUSSION

The perfective verb **да́ть** has an irregular future which must be memorized: **да́м, да́шь, да́ст, дади́м, дади́те, даду́т.** Its imperative is **да́й! да́йте!** Its imperfective counterpart **дава́ть** has a present tense based on the stem [daj–]: **даю́, даёшь, даёт, даём, даёте, даю́т.**

The other forms of **дава́ть**, including the past tense, infinitive, and imperative are based on the longer stem [davá–]: **дава́л, дава́ть, дава́й.** All verbs with infinitives ending in **–ава́ть** follow this same pattern, for example, **продава́ть** *to sell*, **узнава́ть** *to recognize*, **сознава́ть** *to realize*.

Suggestions that include the speaker: part I—perfective verbs

MODELS

Пойдём в суббо́ту в клу́б!
Дава́й пойдём _____!
Дава́йте пойдём _____!

Let's go to the club on Saturday!
Let's go _____!
Let's go _____!

Вы́йдем немно́го на све́жий во́здух!
Дава́й вы́йдем _____!
Дава́йте вы́йдем _____!

Let's go out and get a bit of fresh air!
Let's go out _____!
Let's go out _____!

Зайдём к ни́м!
Дава́й зайдём _____!
Дава́йте зайдём ____!

Let's drop in on them!
Let's drop in _____!
Let's drop in _____!

Отдохнём!
Дава́й отдохнём!
Дава́йте _____!

Let's take a break! *or* Let's rest a bit!
Let's take _____! *or* Let's rest ____!
Let's take _____! *or* Let's rest ____!

Поговори́м об э́том де́ле!   Let's talk a bit about this matter!
Дава́й поговори́м _____!   Let's talk _____!
Дава́йте поговори́м ____!   Let's talk _____!

Сыгра́ем в ша́хматы!   Let's play a game of chess!
Дава́й сыгра́ем ____!   Let's play _____!
Дава́йте сыгра́ем ___!   Let's play _____!

■ REPETITION DRILL

Repeat the above models, noting that either the first person plural perfective verb alone, or the verb combined with **дава́й** (familiar) or **дава́йте** (plural-polite) can be used. **Дава́й(те)** makes the suggestion more tentative and is somewhat comparable to English *How about it?* or *What do you say?*

■ STRUCTURE REPLACEMENT DRILLS

1. *We'll go to the park.*
   Let's go to the park!
   Мы́ пойдём в па́рк.
   Пойдём в па́рк!
   Мы́ подождём о́коло кио́ска.
   Подождём о́коло кио́ска!
   Мы́ забу́дем об этом.
   Мы́ зайдём в буфе́т.
   Мы́ посмо́трим в словаре́.
   Мы́ ку́пим этот материа́л.
   Мы́ оста́вим ему́ ключи́.
   Мы́ пойдём в кино́.

2. *We bought a dictionary.*
   Let's buy a dictionary!
   Мы́ купи́ли слова́рь.
   Ку́пим слова́рь!
   Мы́ поду́мали об этом.
   Поду́маем об э́том!
   Мы́ откры́ли окно́.
   Мы́ сыгра́ли в ша́хматы.
   Мы́ поговори́ли об э́том де́ле.
   Мы́ предложи́ли ему́ рабо́ту.
   Мы́ подожда́ли на углу́.
   Мы́ оста́вили ключи́ на столе́.
   Мы́ вы́пили лимона́да.

3. *Let's buy them a present!*
   Let's buy them a present, how about it?
   Ку́пим и́м пода́рок!
   Дава́й ку́пим и́м пода́рок.
   Поговори́м об э́том!
   Дава́й поговори́м об э́том.
   Пойдём отдохнём!
   Ко́нчим э́ту рабо́ту!
   Принесём сто́л!
   Прочита́ем объявле́ние!
   Зайдём в комиссио́нный магази́н!
   Оста́вим э́тот разгово́р!

4. *I want to go to the theater.*
   How about (us) going to the theater?
   Я́ хочу́ пойти́ в теа́тр.
   Дава́йте пойдём в теа́тр.
   Я́ хочу́ отдохну́ть.
   Дава́йте отдохнём.
   Я́ хочу́ вы́йти на све́жий во́здух.
   Я́ хочу́ спроси́ть об э́том.
   Я́ хочу́ подожда́ть.
   Я́ хочу́ поговори́ть.
   Я́ хочу́ пойти́ на та́нцы.
   Я́ хочу́ зайти́ в э́то зда́ние.

■ QUESTION-ANSWER DRILLS

1. *Well, how about the movies, shall we go?*
   O.K., let's go!
   Ну́, ка́к насчёт кино́, пойдём?
   Ла́дно, пойдём!
   Ну, ка́к насчёт кни́ги, ку́пим?
   Ла́дно, ку́пим!
   Ну, ка́к насчёт обе́да, пообе́даем?

   Ну, ка́к насчёт о́черка, напи́шем?
   Ну, ка́к насчёт ча́я, вы́пьем?
   Ну, ка́к насчёт рабо́ты, ко́нчим?
   Ну, ка́к насчёт пласти́нок, послу́шаем?
   Ну, ка́к насчёт биле́тов, возьмём?
   Ну, ка́к насчёт костю́мов, зака́жем?

2. *Want to go to the club Saturday?*
   O.K., let's go!
   Хоти́те пойти́ в суббо́ту в клуб?
   Хорошо́, дава́йте пойдём!
   Хоти́те немно́го отдохну́ть?
   Хорошо́, дава́йте отдохнём!

Хоти́те с ней поговори́ть?
Хоти́те зайти́ к ни́м?
Хоти́те сыгра́ть в ша́хматы?
Хоти́те замо́лвить за ни́х слове́чко?
Хоти́те посмотре́ть э́тот фи́льм?
Хоти́те войти́ в за́л?

■ RESPONSE DRILLS

1. *Let's take a cab!*
   O.K., let's!
   Дава́йте возьмём такси́.
   Хорошо́, возьмём!
   Дава́йте перейдём на «ты».
   Хорошо́, перейдём!
   Дава́йте напи́шем ему́ письмо́.
   Дава́йте подождём авто́буса.
   Дава́йте отдохнём в па́рке.
   Дава́йте зака́жем биле́ты.
   Дава́йте послу́шаем ру́сские пе́сни.
   Дава́йте пойдём пообе́даем.
   Дава́йте вы́пьем лимона́да.

2. *I have to go to Kiev.*
   Me too. Let's go together!
   Я до́лжен пое́хать в Ки́ев.
   Я то́же. Дава́й пое́дем вме́сте!
   Я до́лжен написа́ть сочине́ние.
   Я то́же. Дава́й напи́шем вме́сте!
   Я до́лжен пойти́ в библиоте́ку.
   Я до́лжен спроси́ть об экза́менах.
   Я до́лжен зайти́ в магази́н.
   Я до́лжен вы́йти на све́жий во́здух.
   Я до́лжен попроси́ть его́ об э́том.
   Я до́лжен подожда́ть това́рища.
   Я до́лжен прочита́ть газе́ту.

3. *I'm going to go to the flea market.*
   Let's go together!
   Я пойду́ на толку́чку.
   Пойдём вме́сте!
   Я закажу́ биле́ты.
   Зака́жем вме́сте!

Я пообе́даю в столо́вой.
Я и́х подожду́.
Я послу́шаю пласти́нки.
Я посмотрю́ журна́л «Аме́рика».
Я погуля́ю в па́рке.
Я зайду́ на по́чту.

DISCUSSION

Most suggestions that include the speaker are expressed using the perfective form of the verb. The basic form is the subjectless first person plural verb.

In informal spoken Russian, however, дава́й or дава́йте often precedes the first person plural form: дава́й for addressing ты́ and дава́йте for addressing вы́. Use of дава́й or дава́йте not only adds an informal tone, but makes the suggestion more tentative and open to discussion. It is somewhat comparable to English suggestions prefaced by: *What [do you] say we . . . ? How about (us) . . . ? Why don't we . . . ?*

Compare	Послу́шаем пласти́нки.	Let's listen to records!
with	Дава́й послу́шаем пласти́нки.	What do you say we listen to records?

The unstressed suffix –те may also be added to the first person plural form of a few verbs, mostly verbs of motion. It makes the suggestion more formal and polite.

Пойдёмте в кино́.	Let's go to the movies! *or* Shall we go to the movies?
Вы́йдемте на све́жий во́здух.	Let's go out for some fresh air! *or* Shall we go out for some fresh air?

The subjectless first person plural of a very few imperfective verbs may also be used in making suggestions: идём, е́дем *let's be on our way! let's go!*

Adverbs and short-form neuter adjectives ending in -o

MODELS

Óн спокóйный человéк.	He's a quiet person.
Óн спокóйно рабóтает.	He works quietly.
Э́то непрáвильный отвéт.	This is an incorrect answer.
Вы́ непрáвильно отвéтили.	You answered incorrectly.
Э́то неудóбные стýлья.	These are uncomfortable chairs.
На ни́х неудóбно сидéть.	It's uncomfortable sitting on them.
Э́то просты́е словá.	These are simple words.
И́х прóсто писáть.	They're simple to write.
Э́то трýдная игрá.	This is a difficult game.
В неё трýдно игрáть.	It's difficult to play it.
Э́то скýчный ромáн.	This is a boring novel.
Егó скýчно читáть.	It's boring reading it.
Э́то дорогáя вéщь.	This is an expensive thing.
Онá дóрого стóит.	It costs a lot (*lit.* dearly).
Э́то лёгкий язы́к.	This is an easy language.
Егó легкó учи́ть.	It's easy to learn.
Óн хорóший студéнт.	He's a good student.
Óн хорошó рабóтает.	He works well.

■ REPETITION DRILL

Repeat the given models, noting that short-form neuter adjectives and adverbs may be formed by dropping the long-form adjective endings and adding –o. Observe that sometimes the stress may differ. Compare **хорóший** with **хорошó**, and **плохóй** with **плóхо**.

■ STRUCTURE REPLACEMENT DRILLS

1. *He lives quietly.*
   He's a quiet person.
   Óн спокóйно живёт.
   Óн спокóйный человéк.
   Óн прóсто живёт.
   Óн простóй человéк.
   (странно, скучно, интересно, свободно)

2. *It was a warm day today.*
   Today was warm.
   Сегóдня бы́л тёплый дéнь.
   Сегóдня бы́ло теплó.
   Сегóдня бы́л хорóший дéнь.
   Сегóдня бы́ло хорошó.
   (холодный, жаркий, отличный, прекрасный, трудный, скучный, плохой)

3. *Tomorrow will be warm.*
   It'll be a warm day tomorrow.
   Зáвтра бýдет теплó.
   Зáвтра бýдет тёплый дéнь.
   Зáвтра бýдет жáрко.
   Зáвтра бýдет жáркий дéнь.
   (холодно, неплохо, хорошо, тепло, жарко)

4. *I have a quiet room.*
   I feel peaceful there.
   У меня́ спокóйная кóмната.
   Мнé тáм спокóйно.
   У меня́ плохáя кóмната.
   Мнé тáм плóхо.
   (хорошая, тёплая, холодная, неудобная, неплохая)

5. He's an excellent secretary.
   He does excellent work. (Lit. He works
      excellently.)
   Óн отли́чный секрета́рь.
   Óн отли́чно рабо́тает.
   Óн хоро́ший секрета́рь.
   Óн хорошо́ рабо́тает.
      (плохо́й, прекра́сный, неплохо́й,
      хоро́ший, отли́чный)

7. That's an interesting business (or affair).
   That's interesting.
   Э́то интере́сное де́ло.
   Э́то интере́сно.
   Э́то плохо́е де́ло.
   Э́то пло́хо.
      (ску́чное, просто́е, лёгкое, тру́дное,
      стра́нное)

6. This is so boring!
   This is such a boring essay!
   Э́то та́к ску́чно!
   Э́то тако́й ску́чный о́черк!
   Э́то та́к интере́сно!
   Э́то тако́й интере́сный о́черк!
      (так хорошо́, так стра́нно, так пло́хо,
      так ску́чно, так интере́сно)

ЧТÉНИЕ И ПИСЬМÓ

В клу́бе бы́ло о́чень жа́рко. Зи́на и Оле́г до́лго танцева́ли, и она́ уста́ла. Оле́г предложи́л ей сту́л, но Зи́на не хоте́ла сиде́ть, она́ хоте́ла вы́йти на све́жий во́здух.

Ко́ля и Воло́дя хорошо́ игра́ют в ша́хматы. Они́ ча́сто хо́дят в клу́б игра́ть, но сего́дня там кино́. Идёт ста́рый фи́льм „Челове́к из рестора́на." Они́ хотя́т его́ посмотре́ть.

Сего́дня они́ не игра́ли в ша́хматы. Ка́тя о́чень уста́ла, ей жа́рко. Она́ хо́чет вы́пить воды́. Влади́мир говори́т, что принесёт ей лимонада. В буфете очередь; ему надо немного подождать. Катя берёт „Огонёк" и читает.

Зина опять забыла, что она и Олег на „ты" и сказала ему: „Дайте мне вашу книгу." Олег просит её не забывать, что они на „ты". Ему, конечно, тоже трудно помнить это, но всё-таки он молодец и не забывает, как Зина.

Вечером Нина и Семён идут в кино, а сейчас им надо отдохнуть. Вот они взяли в библиотеке книги и журналы, сидят и читают. А за столом у окна студент и студентка играют в шахматы. Ей, кажется, скучно, и она часто смотрит в окно. Наверно, студент скоро даст ей мат.

Николай голоден, ему давно пора идти обедать, но надо кончить работу. Ему трудно кончить её. Вчера Галя была здесь, и они вместе работали, а сегодня её нет. Он сделал ошибку, а где — не знает. Теперь он сидит и ищет эту ошибку. Вот досада!

Олег спросил меня о Хитрове, и когда я сказал, что Хитров болен, он позвонил ему. К телефону подошла жена Хитрова и сказала, что он уже вполне здоров и работает. Олег хочет вечером зайти к нему и поговорить о работе.

Нина не ожидала встретить Козлова в клубе. Она не знала, что он часто ходит туда. Ей интересно, что он там делает. Может быть пьёт? Нет, конечно. В клубе не пьют. Там играют в шахматы, слушают музыку, иногда танцуют. Козлов говорит ей, что часто играет в шахматы вон там, за этим столом. Он спрашивает, не хочет ли Зина посмотреть, как он и товарищ будут играть. Но она говорит, что ей будет скучно, она не играет и не понимает этой игры.

— Не хочется сегодня обедать дома.
— А я как раз хотел предложить тебе пойти в ресторан.
— С удовольствием. В какой?
— Здесь на углу есть хороший.
— Я знаю. Я там раз была.
— Так пойдём туда, хорошо?
— Хорошо.

— Хо́чешь, пойдём вме́сте в библиоте́ку?

— А что́ тебе́ та́м ну́жно взя́ть?

— Рома́н «На́ши знако́мые».

— У меня́ есть э́тот рома́н. Хо́чешь, я тебе́ да́м?

— А тебе́ он не ну́жен?

— Не́т, я его́ уже́ чита́л.

— Вы́ уже́ сказа́ли ре́ктору обо мне́?

— Не́т, ещё не говори́л. Я хоте́л предложи́ть ва́м пойти́ к нему́ вме́сте.

— Ва́м ка́жется, что та́к бу́дет лу́чше? Я немно́го бою́сь его́.

— Ну что́ вы́! Он о́чень просто́й и ми́лый челове́к. Пойдёмте!

— Ва́м не ску́чно сиде́ть всё вре́мя до́ма?

— Не́т, я слу́шаю му́зыку.

— Стра́нно, что вы́ лю́бите сиде́ть во́т та́к, слу́шать му́зыку и ничего́ не де́лать. Я та́к не могу́.

— Зна́чит, вы́ не лю́бите му́зыку. Заче́м ва́м тогда́ ва́ш проигрыватель?

— Пра́вда, о́н мне́ не ну́жен. Хоти́те, я ва́м его́ да́м?

— Спаси́бо.

— То́лько о́н о́чень ста́рый.

— Э́то ничего́.

— Га́ля, что́ ты́ ду́маешь о Петро́ве?

— Никола́е и́ли Оле́ге?

— Я его́ и́мени не зна́ю. Ви́дела то́лько два́ ра́за. У него́ си́ние глаза́.

— Зна́чит, э́то Оле́г. Я его́ ви́жу ка́ждый де́нь на ле́кциях.

— Я хоте́ла с ни́м познако́миться.

— Я могу́ тебя́ познако́мить. То́лько бою́сь, что тебе́ бу́дет с ни́м ску́чно. Он всё вре́мя что́-то чита́ет и да́же, ка́жется, пи́шет стихи́.

— Э́то интере́сно. Познако́мь на́с, пожалуйста.

— Хорошо́.

— Интере́сно смотре́ть, ка́к они́ игра́ют, пра́вда?

— Вы́ зна́ете э́ту игру́, во́т ва́м и интере́сно, а я ничего́ не понима́ю, и мне́ ску́чно.

— Тогда́ почему́ бы ва́м не взя́ть журна́л? Во́т после́дний но́мер «Огонька́», хоти́те?

— Спаси́бо, я́ с удово́льствием посмотрю́.

— Та́м, кста́ти, есть о́черк об Аме́рике.

— Смотри́те, во́т проводни́к. Скажи́те ему́.

— Сейча́с. Проводни́к! Я проси́ла в ка́ссе да́ть мне́ ни́жнее ме́сто. Наверху́ мне́ неудо́бно спа́ть.

— Но ва́м да́ли ве́рхнее, и я́ ничего́ не могу́ сде́лать. Мо́жет бы́ть, э́тот граждани́н мо́жет спа́ть наверху́.

— Коне́чно, могу́. Мину́тку, я сейча́с возьму́ свои́ ве́щи. Во́т, пожа́луйста.

— Спаси́бо.

PREPARATION FOR CONVERSATION

Поéдем к нáм на канúкулы

канúкулы, канúкул (pl only)	vacation
на канúкулы	on (*or* for) a vacation, to spend a vacation
Поéдем к нáм на канúкулы.	Let's go to our place on our vacation.
плáн	plan; map (of city)
Какúе у вáс плáны на канúкулы?	What plans do you have for vacation?
покá	for the time being, meanwhile, while
никакóй	not . . . any, none at all
Покá никакúх.	None at all for the time being.
А у вáс какúе плáны?	And what plans do you have?
родúтели, –ей	parents
Мы́ éздим к родúтелям.	We go to see our parents.
колхóз	kolkhoz, collective farm, village
Мы́ éздим к родúтелям в колхóз.	We go to the kolkhoz to see our parents.
мы́ с брáтом	my brother and I
Мы́ с брáтом éздим к родúтелям в колхóз.	My brother and I go to the kolkhoz to see our parents.
обы́чный (adv обы́чно)	usual, usually
Мы́ с брáтом обы́чно éздим к родúтелям в колхóз.	My brother and I usually go to the kolkhoz to see our parents.
отсю́да	from here, hence
километр	kilometer, three-fifths of a mile
пятьдесят [pidˌdisát]	fifty
Это пятьдесят километров отсю́да.	It's fifty kilometers from here.
пригласúть (pfv II), приглашу́, приглáсишь, –ят	to invite
Мы́ ду́мали вáс пригласúть.	We thought of inviting you.
далёкий (adv далекó)	far, far away, distant
Пятьдесят километров — это далекó.	Fifty kilometers is a long way off.
Спасúбо. Но пятьдесят километров — это далекó.	Thanks, but fifty kilometers is a long way off.

◀ **Совхоз в Краснодарском крае.**

разрешéние
Мнé не дадýт разрешéния.

нельзя́
иностра́нец, –нца
Иностра́нцам нельзя́ свобóдно éздить.
по (*plus* dat)

страна́, –ы́; стра́ны, стра́н
Иностра́нцам нельзя́ свобóдно éздить по странé.
Я́ и забы́ла, что иностра́нцам нельзя́ свобóдно éздить по странé.

жа́ль
Да́, óчень жа́ль.

Я́ ва́ших колхóзов ещё не ви́дел.
Я́ ведь ва́ших колхóзов ещё не ви́дел.

сни́мок, –мка
У меня́ éсть мнóго сни́мков.
У меня́ éсть мнóго сни́мков на́шего колхóза.
Послýшайте, у меня́ éсть мнóго сни́мков на́шего колхóза.

показа́ть (pfv I)   (*like* сказа́ть)
Хоти́те, покажý?

Да́, пожа́луйста.

цветнóй
нéкоторый
Ó, нéкоторые да́же цветны́е!

снима́ть (I), снима́ю, –ешь, –ют
са́м, –а́, –ó, са́ми
Вы́ са́ми снима́ли?

аппара́т
Да́, у меня́ нóвый аппара́т.
Зóркий
Да́, у меня́ нóвый аппара́т «Зóркий».

вы́шел, вы́шла, –о, –и
(past tense of вы́йти)
Сни́мки óчень неплóхо вы́шли.

поря́док, –дка
по поря́дку
Дава́йте смотрéть по поря́дку.

permissiom, authorization, permit
They won't give me a permit.

[it's] impossible, one can't, one must not
foreigner
[It's] impossible for foreigners to travel freely.
about, to (different places), in, via, along, around, through, up and down
country
Foreigners can't travel about the country freely.
I forgot that foreigners can't travel about the country freely.

too bad, pity, sorry
Yes, it's really too bad *or* I'm very sorry.

I haven't seen your kolkhozes yet.
After all, I haven't seen your kolkhozes yet.

snapshot, picture
I have a lot of snapshots.
I have a lot of snapshots of our kolkhoz.
Listen, I have a lot of snapshots of our kolkhoz.

to show
I'll show [them to you if] you like (*lit*. You want, I'll show).

Yes, please do.

colored, in color
some, certain
Oh, some are even in color!

to take off, take (a picture)
oneself
Did you take them yourself?

apparatus, camera
Yes, I have a new camera.
Zorky (name of camera)
Yes, I have a new Zorky camera.

The pictures came out very well.

order, arrangement, sequence
in succession, in sequence, one by one
Let's take them one by one.

в поря́дке	in order, all right, O.K.
Всё в поря́дке?	Is everything all right?
бли́зкий (adv бли́зко)	near, close
бли́зко от	close to, near
Вы́ живёте совсе́м бли́зко от на́с.	You live quite close to us.
недалеко́	close, near, not far
Мы́ живём недалеко́ от го́рода.	We live close to (or not far from) town.
приглаша́ть (I)	to invite
Они́ обы́чно приглаша́ют меня́ к себе́ на кани́кулы.	They usually invite me to their place for vacation.
ми́ля, –и; –и, миль	mile
Ско́лько ми́ль отсю́да до вокза́ла?	How many miles is it from here to the station?
отту́да	from there
Ско́лько киломе́тров отту́да до Москвы́?	How many kilometers is it from there to Moscow?

Пое́дем к на́м на кани́кулы

Г. — Га́ля   Ф. — Фили́пп

Г.   1 Фили́пп, каки́е у ва́с пла́ны на кани́кулы?

Ф.   2 Пока́ никаки́х. А у ва́с?

Г.   3 Мы́ с бра́том обы́чно е́здим к роди́телям в колхо́з. Э́то пятьдеся́т киломе́тров отсю́да.[1] Ду́мали ва́с пригласи́ть.

Ф.   4 Спаси́бо, но пятьдеся́т киломе́тров — э́то далеко́. Мне́ не даду́т разреше́ния.[2]

Г.   5 Я́ и забы́ла, что иностра́нцам нельзя́ свобо́дно е́здить по стране́.

Ф.   6 Да́, о́чень жа́ль. Я́ ведь ва́ших колхо́зов ещё не ви́дел.

Г.   7 Послу́шайте, у меня́ есть мно́го сни́мков на́шего колхо́за. Хоти́те, покажу́?

Ф.   8 Да́, пожа́луйста. О́, не́которые да́же цветны́е! Вы́ са́ми снима́ли?

Г.   9 Да́, у меня́ но́вый аппара́т «Зо́ркий».[3]

Ф. 10 Сни́мки о́чень непло́хо вы́шли. Дава́йте смотре́ть по поря́дку.

NOTES   [1] **Колхо́з** is derived from **коллекти́вное хозя́йство** *collective farm*. The word **колхо́з** has almost entirely replaced the old word **дере́вня**, in the sense of *village*. Russian villages usually consist of one long street lined with wooden huts on both sides. Behind each hut is a small garden patch and, as a rule, a small, log bathhouse.

PREPARATION FOR CONVERSATION   Га́ля пока́зывает Фили́ппу сни́мки

пока́зывать (I)	to show
Га́ля пока́зывает Фили́ппу сни́мки.	Galya shows Philip snapshots.
о́бщий, –ая, –ее, –ие	general, over-all, common
ви́д	view, aspect
Во́т о́бщий ви́д.	Here's an over-all view.
по́ле, –я; поля́, –е́й	field
Во́т о́бщий ви́д: ту́т поля́.	Here's an over-all view: over here are the fields.
колхо́зный	kolkhoz, collective farm (adj)
Во́т о́бщий ви́д: ту́т колхо́зные поля́.	Here's an over-all view: over here are the kolkhoz fields.
о́зеро, –а; озёра, озёр	lake
лес, –а; леса́, –о́в	forest, wood(s)
вдали́	in the distance
Ту́т поля́, а вдали́ лес и о́зеро.	Over here are the fields, and in the distance the woods and the lake.
ви́ден, видна́, ви́дно, видны́	visible, can be seen
Вдали́ видны́ лес и о́зеро.	In the distance the woods and the lake can be seen.
Во́т о́бщий ви́д: ту́т поля́, а вдали́ видны́ лес и о́зеро.	Here's an over-all view: over here are fields and in the distance you can see the woods and the lake.
изба́, –ы́; и́збы, изб	village house, hut, cottage, farmhouse
А во́т на́ша изба́.	And here is our house.
деревя́нный	wooden, made of wood
О, деревя́нная?!	Oh, made of wood?
А э́то что́ на у́лице?	And what's that in the street?
коло́дец, –дца	well
Э́то коло́дец.	That's the well.
водопрово́д	running water, plumbing
У на́с не́т водопрово́да.	We don't have running water.

338   LESSON 15

ведро́, –á; вёдра, вёдер
вёдрами
носи́ть (II), ношу́, но́сишь, –ят
На́до во́ду носи́ть вёдрами.

pail, bucket
by (*or* in) pails, in (*or* by) buckets
to carry
We have to carry water in buckets *or* Water
has to be carried in buckets.

представля́ть себе́ (I)
ина́че (*or* и́наче)
Я ина́че представля́л себе́
колхо́з.
**А я, зна́ете, ина́че представля́л
себе́ колхо́з.**

to imagine, envisage, picture
otherwise, differently
I imagined the kolkhoz would be
different.
You know, I imagined the kolkhoz
would be different.

ка́менный
Вы ду́мали, наве́рно, дома́
ка́менные, да́?
электри́чество
**Вы ду́мали, наве́рно: дома́
ка́менные, электри́чество, да́?**

stone, brick
You probably thought the houses would be
brick, didn't you?
electricity, lights
You probably thought the houses would
be brick and [that] there'd be electricity,
didn't you?

стро́ить (II), стро́ю, –ишь, –ят
Тепе́рь стро́ят дома́.
Тепе́рь стро́ят дома́ для
колхо́зников.
Я чита́л в «Огоньке́», каки́е
тепе́рь стро́ят дома́ для
колхо́зников.
**Да́. Я по́мню чита́л в «Огоньке́»,
каки́е тепе́рь стро́ят дома́
для колхо́зников.**

to build, construct
They're building houses now.
They're building houses now for farmers.

I read in *Ogonyok* the kind of houses
they're building now for farmers.

Yes, I remember reading in *Ogonyok* [about]
the kind of houses they're building now
for farmers.

А́, зна́ю.
тури́ст
Таки́е пока́зывают тури́стам.
А́, зна́ю. Таки́е пока́зывают тури́стам.

Oh yes, I know.
tourist
That's the kind they show to tourists.
Oh yes, I know. That's the kind they show
to tourists.

семья́, –и́; се́мьи, семе́й
Во́т ту́т вся на́ша семья́.
Во́т ту́т вся на́ша семья́ за столо́м.
фо́то (indecl n)
**А на э́том фо́то вся на́ша семья́ за
столо́м.**

family
Here is our whole family.
Here is our whole family at the table.
photograph, picture
And in this picture our whole family is at
the table.

висе́ть (II), виси́т, вися́т
ико́на
У ва́с, я ви́жу, ико́ны вися́т.

to be hanging, to hang
icon, holy picture
I see you have icons hanging.

Бо́г, –а
ве́рить (II) (*plus* dat)
ве́рить в (*plus* acc)
Ра́зве вы ве́рите в Бо́га?

Мы с бра́том не ве́рим.

God
to believe, trust
to believe in, have faith in
Do you really believe in God?

My brother and I don't believe.

оте́ц, отца́

мать, ма́тери; ма́тери, –е́й

ве́рующий

Оте́ц и мать у на́с ве́рующие.

father

mother

one who believes, believer

Father and mother are the believers in our family.

це́рковь, це́ркви; –и, –е́й

Оте́ц и мать хо́дят в це́рковь.

church

Father and mother go to church.

У ва́с и це́рковь та́м есть?

Так у ва́с и це́рковь та́м есть?

Do you have a church there?

Then you do have a church there?

село́, –а́; сёла, сёл

сосе́дний, –яя, –ее, –ие

Есть в сосе́днем селе́.

Есть, то́лько не у на́с, а в сосе́днем селе́.

village

neighboring, next

There is one in the next village.

There is one, only [it is] not in ours, but in the neighboring village.

По́сле войны́ откры́ли.

It was opened after the war.

SUPPLEMENT

доро́га

Доро́га не о́чень хоро́шая.

На́ш до́м о́чень бли́зко от доро́ги.

Вы́ зна́ете доро́гу к о́зеру?

по доро́ге

По доро́ге шёл како́й-то челове́к.

По доро́ге домо́й я́ купи́л газе́ту.

на́м по доро́ге

Ка́жется, на́м по доро́ге.

постро́ить (pfv II) (*like* стро́ить)

Здесь ско́ро постро́ят но́вые дома́.

пове́рить (pfv II) (*plus* dat)

Пове́рьте мне́, о́н хоро́ший челове́к.

сосе́д, –а; сосе́ди, –ей[1]

Они́ на́ши сосе́ди.

сосе́дка

На́ша сосе́дка принесла́ на́м э́то.

ве́ра

ве́ра в (*plus* acc)

У него́ не́т ве́ры в себя́.

колхо́зница

Моя́ ма́ть колхо́зница.

road, way, route

The road isn't very good.

Our house is very close to the road.

Do you know the way to the lake?

along the road, on the way

A man was walking along the road.

On my way home I bought a paper.

we're going the same way

Looks like we're going the same way.

to build

They'll soon build new houses here.

to believe

Believe me, he's a good man.

neighbor

They're our neighbors.

neighbor (f)

Our neighbor brought us this.

faith, confidence

faith in, confidence in

He has no faith (*or* confidence) in himself.

collective-farm worker (f)

My mother is a collective-farm worker.

---

[1] Note that the final stem consonant of **сосе́д** *neighbor*, which is hard throughout the singular, becomes soft in the plural. Compare the singular: **сосе́д, сесе́да** [saşét, saşédə] with the plural: **сосе́ди, сосе́дей, о сосе́дях, сосе́дям** [saşédi, saşédij, asaşédəx, saşédəm].

Га́ля пока́зывает Фили́ппу сни́мки

Г. — Га́ля
Ф. — Фили́пп

Г. 1 Во́т о́бщий ви́д: ту́т колхо́зные поля́, а вдали́ видны́ ле́с и о́зеро. А во́т на́ша изба́.

Ф. 2 О́, деревя́нная?! А э́то что́ тако́е на у́лице?

Г. 3 Э́то коло́дец. У на́с нет водопрово́да, на́до во́ду носи́ть вёдрами.[1]

Ф. 4 А я́, зна́ете, ина́че представля́л себе́ колхо́з.

Г. 5 Вы́ ду́мали, наве́рно: дома́ ка́менные, электри́чество, да́?[2]

Ф. 6 Да́. Я́ по́мню чита́л в «Огоньке́», каки́е тепе́рь стро́ят дома́ для колхо́зников.[3]

Г. 7 А́, зна́ю. Таки́е пока́зывают тури́стам. А на э́том фо́то вся́ на́ша семья́ за столо́м.[4]

Ф. 8 У ва́с, я́ ви́жу, ико́ны вися́т. Ра́зве вы́ ве́рите в Бо́га?

Г. 9 Не́т, мы́ с бра́том не ве́рим, но оте́ц и ма́ть у на́с ве́рующие, хо́дят в це́рковь.[5]

Ф. 10 Та́к у ва́с и це́рковь та́м есть?

Г. 11 Е́сть, то́лько не у на́с, а в сосе́днем селе́. По́сле войны́ откры́ли.[6]

NOTES

[1] In Russian cities there was running water (at least cold) even before the Revolution; however, it is still nonexistent in rural areas.

[2] Electric lights are usually not found in rural Russia. Note that the term **ка́менный**, literally *stone*, refers to all nonwooden buildings, i.e., brick, stone, stucco, and so forth.

[3] In some villages, two-family and multi-family houses have been erected under Khrushchev's program to modernize the villages.

[4] Russians usually use the word **фо́то** (short for **фотогра́фия**), rather than **сни́мок**, in reference to snapshots of people.

[5] The noun **це́рковь** (f) *church* has a soft final stem consonant except in certain plural cases where a hard [v] occurs. Compare the nominative plural **це́ркви** [cérkyi] with the prepositional **о церква́х** [acirkváx] and with the dative **церква́м** [cirkvám].

[6] **Село́** is a large village. Characteristically it had a church in pre-Revolution times, but this is not necessarily true today.

Basic sentence patterns

1. Привéт женé!
   _____ сестрé!
   _____ мýжу!
   _____ отцý!
   _____ брáту!
   _____ мáтери!
   _____ родѝтелям!
   _____ друзьям
   _____ брáтьям!
   _____ сёстрам!

   Say hello to your wife.
   _____ sister.
   _____ husband.
   _____ father.
   _____ brother.
   _____ mother.
   _____ parents.
   _____ friends.
   _____ brothers.
   _____ sisters.

2. Покажѝте Филѝппу снѝмки.
   _____ Николáю _____.
   _____ отцý _____.
   _____ сестрé _____.
   _____ мáтери _____.
   _____ родѝтелям _____.
   _____ друзьям _____.
   _____ турѝстам _____.

   Show Philip the snapshots.
   ___ Nikolay _____.
   ___ Father _____.
   ___ Sister _____.
   ___ Mother _____.
   ___ your parents _____.
   ___ your friends _____.
   ___ the tourists _____.

3. На канѝкулы я обы́чно éзжу к родѝтелям.
   _____ к друзьям.
   _____ к брáту.
   _____ к сестрé.

   On my vacation I usually go to see my parents.
   _____ friends.
   _____ brother.
   _____ sister.

   А я éзжу в колхóз.
   _____ в селó.
   _____ в Кѝев.
   _____ в Одéссу.

   And I go to the kolkhoz.
   _____ to the village.
   _____ to Kiev.
   _____ to Odessa.

4. Дáйте эти фóто Грáнту.
   _____ профéссору.
   _____ учѝтелю.
   _____ турѝстам.
   _____ Зѝне.
   _____ учѝтельнице.

   Give these pictures to Grant.
   _____ to the professor.
   _____ to the teacher.
   _____ to the tourists.
   _____ to Zina.
   _____ to the teacher.

5. Мнé не дадýт разрешéния.
   Кóле _____.
   Гáле _____.
   Николáю _____.
   Брáту _____.
   Отцý _____.
   Нáм _____.
   Филѝппу _____.

   They won't give me a pass.
   _____ Kolya _____.
   _____ Galya _____.
   _____ Nikolay _____.
   _____ Brother _____.
   _____ Father _____.
   _____ us _____.
   _____ Philip _____.

6. Мнé нáдо бóльше спáть.
   Зѝне _____.
   Олéгу _____.
   Студéнтам _____.
   Мýжу _____.

   I need more sleep.
   Zina needs _____.
   Oleg needs _____.
   The students need _____.
   My husband needs _____.

Сестре́ на́до бо́льше спа́ть.　　My sister needs more sleep.
Отцу́ _____.　　My father needs _____.
Бра́тьям _____.　　My brothers need _____.

7. Иностра́нцам нельзя́ свобо́дно е́здить　　Foreigners can't travel about freely
　　　　　　　　　по СССР.　　　　　　　　in the U.S.S.R.
_____ по стране́.　　_____ in the country.
_____ по Кита́ю.　　_____ in China.

8. Мы́ ходи́ли по па́рку.　　　　We walked all around the park.
_____ по́ полю.[1]　　　　_____ the field.
_____ по́ лесу.　　　　　_____ the woods.
_____ по колхо́зу.　　　_____ the kolkhoz.
_____ по го́роду.　　　　_____ the city.
_____ по селу́.　　　　　_____ the village.
_____ по вокза́лу.　　　_____ the station.

9. Мне́ его́ жа́ль.　　　　　　　I feel sorry for him.
_____ её _____.　　　　　　　　_____ her.
_____ ва́с _____.　　　　　　　_____ you.
_____ и́х _____.　　　　　　　　_____ them.
_____ тебя́ _____.　　　　　　　_____ you.
Мне́ жа́ль Зи́ну.　　　　　　　_____ Zina.
_____ Ко́лю.　　　　　　　_____ Kolya.
_____ Фили́ппа.　　　　　_____ Philip.
_____ колхо́зников.　　　_____ the collective farmers.

10. У ни́х не́т ве́ры в себя́.　　They have no faith in themselves.
_____ в э́то де́ло.　　_____ in this thing.
_____ в люде́й.　　　_____ in people.
_____ в челове́ка.　　_____ in man.

11. Каки́е у ва́с пла́ны на кани́кулы?　　What are your plans for the vacation?
_____ на за́втра?　　_____ for tomorrow?
_____ на воскресе́нье?　　_____ for Sunday?
_____ на э́ту суббо́ту?　　_____ for this Saturday?
_____ на э́ту неде́лю?　　_____ for this week?
_____ на э́тот ве́чер?　　_____ for this evening?

12. Роди́тели живу́т далеко́ от Москвы́.　　My parents live a long way from Moscow.
_____ недалеко́ от Москвы́.　　_____ not far from Moscow.
_____ бли́зко от Москвы́.　　_____ close to Moscow.
_____ пятьдеся́т киломе́тров　　_____ fifty kilometers from here.
　　　　　　　отсю́да.

_____ далеко́ отсю́да.　　_____ a long way from here.
_____ недалеко́ отсю́да.　　_____ not far away from here.

13. Мы́ прошли́ ми́лю.　　　　We've covered (or walked) a mile.
_____ о́коло ми́ли.　　_____ about a mile.
_____ две́ ми́ли.　　　_____ two miles.
_____ три́ ми́ли.　　　_____ three miles.
_____ пя́ть ми́ль.　　_____ five miles.

---

[1] Note that **по** occasionally takes the stress from the noun: **по́ полю** [pópəļu], **по́ лесу** [póļisu].

Мы́ прошли́ киломе́тр.

_____ о́коло киломе́тра.

_____ два́ киломе́тра.

_____ четы́ре киломе́тра.

_____ пя́ть киломе́тров.

We've covered (or walked) about a kilometer.

_____ about a kilometer.

_____ two kilometers.

_____ four kilometers.

_____ five kilometers.

14. Они́ уже́ прошли́ пя́ть уро́ков.

_____ во́семь _____.

_____ де́сять _____.

They've already covered five lessons.

_____ eight _____.

_____ ten _____.

15. Доро́га идёт к о́зеру.

_____ шла́_____.

Авто́бус идёт в колхо́з.

_____ шёл _____.

_____ пришёл _____.

The road goes to the lake.

_____ went _____.

The bus is going to the kolkhoz.

_____ was going _____.

_____ arrived at _____.

16. Дава́йте игра́ть в ка́рты.

_____ в ша́хматы.

_____ в футбо́л.

_____ в бейсбо́л.

_____ в те́ннис.

_____ в хокке́й.

Let's play cards.

_____ chess.

_____ soccer.

_____ baseball.

_____ tennis.

_____ hockey.

17. Лу́чше не бу́дем игра́ть в ка́рты.

_____ в ша́хматы.

_____ в футбо́л.

_____ в бейсбо́л.

_____ в те́ннис.

_____ в хокке́й.

We'd better not play cards.

_____ chess.

_____ soccer.

_____ baseball.

_____ tennis.

_____ hockey.

18. Та́к не сидя́т.

_____ говоря́т.

_____ танцу́ют.

_____ хо́дят.

_____ игра́ют.

People don't sit like that or That's no way to sit.

_____ talk _____ or _____ to talk.

_____ dance _____ or _____ to dance.

_____ walk _____ or _____ to walk.

_____ play _____ or _____ to play.

19. Две́ри уже́ открыва́ют.

_____ закрыва́ют.

Уже́ выхо́дят из це́ркви.

Пропуско́в бо́льше не даю́т.

Таки́х рома́нов бо́льше не пи́шут.

Его́ стихо́в бо́льше не чита́ют.

They're opening the doors already.

They're closing _____.

People are coming out of church already.

Passes are no longer being given.

They don't write such novels anymore.

People don't read his poetry anymore.

20. Тури́сты обы́чно снима́ют

наши колхо́зы.

_____ на́ши озёра.

_____ на́ши ка́менные дома́.

_____ на́ши и́збы.

_____ на́ши деревя́нные це́ркви.

_____ на́шу деревя́нную це́рковь.

_____ на́ши ру́сские сёла.

_____ на́ших колхо́зников.

_____ на́ших колхо́зниц.

Tourists usually take pictures

of our farms.

_____ of our lakes.

_____ of our stone houses.

_____ of our huts.

_____ of our wooden churches.

_____ of our wooden church.

_____ of our Russian villages.

_____ of our collective farmers.

_____ of our collective-farm women.

21. На э́том фо́то моя́ семья́.

_____ мо́й оте́ц.

_____ мои́ роди́тели.

_____ моя́ ма́ть.

_____ моя́ сосе́дка.

_____ мо́й сосе́д.

_____ мои́ сосе́ди.

_____ на́ши колхо́зники.

My family is in this picture.

My father is _____.

My parents are _____.

My mother is _____.

My neighbor (f) is _____.

My neighbor is _____.

My neighbors are _____.

Our collective farmers are _____.

Pronunciation practice: consonant clusters with [l] or [ļ]

A. Clusters with [l] or [ļ] in second position.

[blánk] бла́нк
blank

[bļískə] бли́зко
close

[bļúdə] блю́до
platter, dish

[vlážnij] вла́жный
humid

[vlásţ] вла́сть
power

[vļésţ] влезть
to crawl into

[kļásţ] кля́сть
to curse

[mlátʃij] мла́дший
younger

[mļétʃnij] мле́чный
milky

[plán] пла́н
plan

[plóxə] пло́хо
it's bad

[plíţ] плы́ть
to be swimming

B. Clusters with [l] or [ļ] in initial position.

[lbá] лба́
of the forehead

[lbí] лбы́
foreheads

[lgáţ] лга́ть
to lie

[lgún] лгу́н
liar

[lʒót] лжёт
he's lying

[lʒí] лжи́
of the lie

[ļvá] Льва́
of Lev

[ļdá] льда́
of ice

[ļdínə] льди́на
ice floe

[ļná] льна́
of flax

[ļsţíţ] льсти́ть
to flatter

[ļʃtʃú] льщу́
I flatter

C. Clusters with [l] or [ļ] in final position.

[pérl] пе́рл
pearl

[smísl] смы́сл
sense

[rúbļ] ру́бль
ruble

[karábļ] кора́бль
ship

[ansámbļ] анса́мбль
ensemble

[ʒurávļ] жура́вль
crane

[spiktákļ] спекта́кль
show

[binókļ] бино́кль
binoculars

[ótrəsļ] о́трасль
branch

[zárəsļ] за́росль
brushwood

[mísļ] мы́сль
thought

[vópļ] во́пль
outcry

D. Clusters with [l] or [ļ] immediately before the final consonant.

[stólp] сто́лб
post

[dólk] до́лг
duty

[póls] по́лз
he crawled

[vólk] во́лк
wolf

[ʃólk] шёлк
silk

[pólk] по́лк
regiment

[ʒólʧ] жёлчь
bile

[váļs] ва́льс
waltz

[púļs] пу́льс
pulse

[áļt] а́льт
alto

[kúļt] ку́льт
cult

[fáļʃ] фа́льшь
falsehood

STRUCTURE AND DRILLS

The dative of nouns: singular and plural

MODELS

Фили́ппу ну́жен про́пуск.   Philip needs a pass.
Влади́миру _____.   Vladimir _____.
Евге́нию _____.   Evgeny_____.
Никола́ю _____.   Nikolay _____.
Ко́ле _____.   Kolya _____.
Ма́ше _____.   Masha _____.
Ири́не _____.   Irina _____.
Мари́и _____.   Maria _____.

Принеси́ отцу́ стака́н воды́.   Bring Father a glass of water.
_____ бра́ту _____.   _____ Brother _____.
_____ америка́нцу _____.   _____ the American (m) _____.
_____ учи́телю _____.   _____ the teacher _____.
_____ секретарю́ _____.   _____ the secretary _____.
_____ учи́тельнице _____.   _____ the teacher _____.
_____ америка́нке _____.   _____ the American (f) _____.
_____ Ни́не _____.   _____ Nina _____.
_____ Мари́и _____.   _____ Maria _____.

Подойди́те к телефо́ну.   Come (or go) to the telephone.
_____ к столу́.   _____ to the table.
_____ к шка́фу.   Come (or go) over to the cupboard.
_____ к окну́.   _____ to the window.
_____ к доске́.   _____ to the blackboard.
_____ к две́ри.   _____ to the door.
_____ к ка́рте.   _____ to the map.

О́н чита́ет ле́кции по му́зыке.   He lectures on music.
_____ по матема́тике.   _____ on mathematics.
_____ по литерату́ре.   _____ on literature.
_____ по фи́зике.   _____ on physics.
_____ по хи́мии.   _____ on chemistry.
_____ по исто́рии.   _____ on history.
_____ по геогра́фии.   _____ on geography.

Позвони́те студе́нтам в понеде́льник.   Call the students on Monday.
_____ студе́нткам _____.   _____ coeds _____.
_____ певца́м _____.   _____ singers _____.
_____ певи́цам _____.   _____ singers (f) _____.
_____ учи́тельницам _____.   _____ teachers _____.
_____ отца́м _____.   _____ fathers _____.
_____ матеря́м _____.   _____ mothers _____.
_____ роди́телям _____.   _____ parents _____.
_____ учителя́м _____.   _____ teachers _____.
_____ секретаря́м _____.   _____ secretaries _____.

По понедéльникам я́ всегдá дóма.	On Mondays I'm always home.
По втóрникам _____.	On Tuesdays _____.
По средáм _____.	On Wednesdays _____.
По четвергáм _____.	On Thursdays _____.
По пя́тницам _____.	On Fridays _____.
По суббóтам _____.	On Saturdays _____.
По воскресéньям _____.	On Sundays _____.

NOUN ENDINGS IN THE DATIVE			
SINGULAR **–у, –ю**		**–е**	**–и**
стóл- and **окнó-**nouns		**женá-**nouns (except **–ия** nouns)	**двéрь-**nouns, **женá-**nouns ending in **–ия**, **и́мя-**nouns
Hard stems and stems ending in **ч** *and* **щ**	*Soft stems*		
–у	**–ю**	**–е**	**–и**
столу́	дню́	женé	двéри
брáту	Николáю	сестрé	мáтери
Козлóву	учи́телю	Натáше	óчереди
телефóну	пáрню	Кóле	истóрии
отцу́	Китáю	Гáле	лéкции
товáрищу	плáтью	дéвушке	Мари́и
ключу́	собрáнию	продавщи́це	и́мени
мéсту			врéмени
окну́			

PLURAL **–ам**	**–ям**
Hard stems and stems ending in **ч** *and* **щ**	*Soft stems*
–ам	**–ям**
утрáм	брáтьям
городáм	деверя́м
гости́ницам	парня́м
дéвушкам	лéкциям
ребя́там	собрáниям
жёнам	учителя́м
сёстрам	очередя́м
óкнам	пéсням
столáм	друзья́м
кáртам	сту́льям
товáрищам	лаборатóриям

Repeat the given models, noting the pattern of endings for nouns in the dative case.

■ CUED QUESTION-ANSWER DRILLS

1. (*Vladimir*)   *Who needs tickets?*
             Vladimir.
(Влади́мир) Кому́ нужны́ биле́ты?
             Влади́миру.
(де́вушки)   Кому́ нужны́ биле́ты?
             Де́вушкам.
(америка́нка, студе́нты, секрета́рь,
Алексе́ев, Ната́ша, её подру́ги,
това́рищ Волко́в)

2. (*Zina*)   *Who are you selling your camera to?*
         To Zina.
(Зи́на)   Кому́ вы́ продаёте ва́ш аппара́т?
        Зи́не.
(Евге́ний) Кому́ вы́ продаёте ва́ш аппара́т?
        Евге́нию.
(профе́ссор Орло́в, Га́ля, америка́нец,
учи́тель, друзья́, това́рищ, Никола́й,
Мари́я)

3. (*friends*) *Who did you call on?*
          Friends.
(друзья́)   К кому́ вы́ заходи́ли?
         К друзья́м.
(роди́тели) К кому́ вы́ заходи́ли?
         К роди́телям.
(профе́ссор Орло́в, америка́нка,
учи́тель, Зи́на, студе́нты, О́ля,
америка́нцы, Гра́нт)

4. (*conveniences*) *What's he accustomed to?*
             Conveniences.
(удо́бства) К чему́ о́н привы́к?
         К удо́бствам.
(джа́з)   К чему́ о́н привы́к?
         К джа́зу.
(Аме́рика, уда́чи, Евро́па, про́сьбы,
рабо́та, Кита́й)

■ RESPONSE DRILLS

1. *Masha's thirsty* or *Masha wants a drink.*
Bring Masha a glass of water.
Ма́ша хо́чет пи́ть.
Принеси́ Ма́ше стака́н воды́.
Оте́ц хо́чет пи́ть.
Принеси́ отцу́ стака́н воды́.
  (сестра́, Оле́г, секрета́рь, певи́ца,
  това́рищ Семёнов, певе́ц, господи́н
  Гра́нт)

2. *Oleg is asking where the lake is.*
Tell Oleg where the lake is.
Оле́г спра́шивает, где́ о́зеро.
Скажи́те Оле́гу, где́ о́зеро.
Учи́тель спра́шивает, где́ о́зеро.
Скажи́те учи́телю, где́ о́зеро.
  (её подру́га, студе́нты, его́ дру́г, его́
  жена́, его́ това́рищ, Га́ля, сёстры)

3. *Doesn't Philip have a permit?*
Give Philip a permit.
У Фили́ппа не́т разреше́ния?
Да́йте Фили́ппу разреше́ние!

У Ко́ли не́т разреше́ния?
Да́йте Ко́ле разреше́ние!
  (америка́нцев, господи́на Гра́нта,
  америка́нки, учителе́й, Козло́ва, Зи́ны)

■ QUESTION-ANSWER DRILLS

1. *Isn't Oleg going to come?*
No, Oleg would be bored there.
Оле́г не придёт?
Не́т, Оле́гу бу́дет та́м ску́чно.
Зи́на не придёт?
Не́т, Зи́не бу́дет та́м ску́чно.
  (студе́нты, её подру́га, и́х друзья́,
  его́ бра́т, Ко́ля, профе́ссор,
  америка́нец, певи́ца)

2. *Does your friend have your camera?*

Yes, I gave it to my friend.

Твóй аппарáт у товáрища?

Дá, я егó дáл товáрищу.

Твóй аппарáт у сестры́?

Дá, я егó дáл сестрé.

   (друзéй, профéссора, её подрýги, товáрища по кóмнате, американца, Зи́ны, брáта)

4. *Is he a professor of music?*

Yes, he lectures on music.

Óн профéссор мýзыки?

Да, óн читáет лéкции по мýзыке.

Óн профéссор математики?

Да, óн читáет лéкции по математике.

3. *Did Nikolay buy an atlas?*

No, Nikolay no longer needs an atlas.

Николáй купи́л áтлас?

Нéт, Николáю áтлас ужé не нýжен.

Зи́на купи́ла áтлас?

Нéт, Зи́не áтлас уже не нýжен.

   (ребя́та, профéссор Курóчкин, отéц, сестра, Фили́пп, учи́тельница)

   (профéссор физики, профéссор хи́мии, профéссор геогрáфии, профéссор литерату́ры, профéссор истории)

■ STRUCTURE REPLACEMENT DRILL

He'll come on Saturday.

He usually comes Saturdays.

Óн придёт в суббóту.

Óн обы́чно прихóдит по суббóтам.

Óн придёт в срéду.

Óн обы́чно прихóдит по средáм.

   (в четвéрг, в воскресéнье, в пя́тницу, во вто́рник, в понедéльник, в суббóту, в срéду)

DISCUSSION: NOUN ENDINGS IN THE DATIVE

Singular

1. Those **стóл-** and **окнó**-nouns taking **–а** in the genitive singular take **–у** in the dative singular; those taking **–я** in the genitive singular take **–ю** in the dative singular.

2. **Женá-** and **двéрь**-nouns have identical forms in the dative singular and the prepositional singular; so, too, do the nouns **и́мя** and **врéмя.**

Plural

Nouns taking **–ах** in the prepositional plural take **–ам** in the dative plural; those taking **–ях** in the prepositional plural take **–ям** in the dative plural.

Stress

1. Stress in the dative singular is the same as that in the genitive and prepositional singular.

NOM SG	GEN SG	PREP SG	DAT SG
стóл	столá	столé	столý
отéц	отцá	отцé	отцý
окнó	окнá	окнé	окнý
женá	жены́	женé	женé
Гáля	Гáли	Гáле	Гáле
двéрь	двéри	двéри	двéри
óчередь	óчереди	óчереди	óчереди
врéмя	врéмени	врéмени	врéмени
мáть	мáтери	мáтери	мáтери

2. Stress in the dative plural is the same as that in the prepositional plural.

NOM PL	GEN PL		PREP PL	DAT PL
слова́	слов		слова́х	слова́м
столы́	столо́в		стола́х	стола́м
отцы́	отцо́в		отца́х	отца́м
о́кна	о́кон *or* око́н		о́кнах	о́кнам
до́ски	досо́к		доска́х	доска́м
жёны	жён		жёнах	жёнам
сёстры	сестёр		сёстрах	сёстрам
па́рни	парне́й		парня́х	парня́м
две́ри	двере́й		двери́х	двери́м
о́череди	очереде́й		очередя́х	очередя́м
времена́	времён		времена́х	времена́м
ма́тери	матере́й		матеря́х	матеря́м
ру́ки	рук		рука́х	рука́м
го́ловы	голо́в		голова́х	голова́м

Dative constructions with на́до

MODELS

Мне́ на́до пойти́ на по́чту.   I need to go to the post office.
Ему́ _____.   He needs _____.
Ей _____.   She needs _____.
Им _____.   They need _____.
Вам _____.   You need _____.
Нам _____.   We need _____.
Тебе́ _____.   You need _____.

Мне́ на́до бы́ло пойти́ в библиоте́ку.   I had to go to the library.
Ему́ _____.   He _____.
Ей _____.   She _____.
Им _____.   They _____.
Вам _____.   You _____.
Нам _____.   We _____.
Тебе́ _____.   You _____.

Мне́ на́до бу́дет е́хать к роди́телям.   I'll have to go to my parents.
Ему́ _____.   He'll have _____ his _____.
Ей _____.   She'll have _____ her _____.
Им _____.   They'll have _____ their _____.
Вам _____.   You'll have _____ your _____.
Нам _____.   We'll have _____ our _____.
Тебе́ _____.   You'll have _____ your _____.

■ REPETITION DRILL

Repeat the given models, noting that на́до is typically used in infinitive constructions together with the dative.

1. *Is Zina going to the collective farm?*
   Yes, she has to go there.
   Зи́на е́дет в колхо́з?
   Да́, е́й на́до туда́ е́хать.
   Оле́г е́дет в колхо́з?
   Да́, ему́ на́до туда́ е́хать.
   (ребя́та, учи́тель, её подру́га, оте́ц, его́
   роди́тели, Га́ля, бра́т)

2. *Did the secretary often go to the village?*
   Yes, he had to go there often.
   Секрета́рь ча́сто е́здил в село́?
   Да́, ему́ ча́сто на́до бы́ло туда́ е́здить.
   Пётр ча́сто е́здил в село́?
   Да́, ему́ ча́сто на́до бы́ло туда́ е́здить.
   (студе́нты, учи́тельница, това́рищ Ца-
   ра́пкин, Ма́ша, оте́ц, её друзья́, сестра́)

■ RESPONSE DRILLS

1. *Is it possible Orlov doesn't know Galya yet?*
   Orlov has got to meet her.
   Ра́зве Орло́в ещё не зна́ет Га́лю?
   Орло́ву на́до с не́й познако́миться.
   Ра́зве Воло́дя ещё не зна́ет Га́лю?
   Воло́де на́до с не́й познако́миться.
   (Са́ша, его́ бра́т, его́ сестра́, де́вушки,
   Зи́на, ребя́та, ты, оте́ц)

2. *Galya heard there was an interesting movie playing.*
   She'll have to see it.
   Га́ля слы́шала, что идёт интере́сный
   фи́льм.
   Е́й на́до бу́дет его́ посмотре́ть.
   Бра́т слы́шал, что идёт интере́сный
   фи́льм.
   Ему́ на́до бу́дет его́ посмотре́ть.
   (ты, сёстры, мы, жена́, профе́ссор, я,
   продавщи́ца, шофёр, студе́нты)

3. *Masha didn't manage (or have time) to order tickets.*
   She has to go and order tickets.
   Ма́ша не успе́ла заказа́ть биле́ты.
   Е́й на́до пойти́ заказа́ть биле́ты.
   Профе́ссор не успе́л заказа́ть биле́ты.
   Ему́ на́до пойти́ заказа́ть биле́ты.
   (оте́ц, вы, бра́тья, ма́ть, мы, подру́ги,
   я, Семён, ты)

4. *Oleg wanted to speak English.*
   He had to study English.
   Оле́г хоте́л говори́ть по-англи́йски.
   Ему́ на́до бы́ло учи́ть англи́йский язы́к.
   Певе́ц хоте́л говори́ть по-англи́йски.
   Ему́ на́до бы́ло учи́ть англи́йский язы́к.
   (де́вушки, её подру́га, его́ това́рищ, их
   друзья́, сестра́, оте́ц, бра́т, студе́нтка)

5. *Kolya's parents are ill.*
   He must go to see his parents.
   Роди́тели Ко́ли больны́.
   Ему́ на́до е́хать к роди́телям.
   Роди́тели Ма́ши больны́.
   Е́й на́до е́хать к роди́телям.
   (Козло́ва, О́ли, вахтёра, Никола́я,
   Мари́и, Воло́ди, шофёра)

6. *I was at the station.*
   I had to buy tickets.
   Я́ бы́л на ста́нции.
   Мне́ на́до бы́ло купи́ть биле́ты.
   Она́ была́ на ста́нции.
   Е́й на́до бы́ло купи́ть биле́ты.
   (он, они́, ты, она́, вы, мы, я)

■ QUESTION-ANSWER DRILL

Why is Kolya in such a hurry?
He has to make it to the post office in time.
Почему́ Ко́ля та́к спеши́т?
Ему́ на́до успе́ть на по́чту.
Почему́ они́ та́к спеша́т?
И́м на́до успе́ть на по́чту.

(вы, твои́ това́рищи, её сестра́, э́ти
де́вушки, э́тот па́рень, твои́ друзья́,
продавщи́ца, ты, Воло́дя)

Ha**до** is an unchanging form used chiefly with infinitives to express an urgent need to perform some activity. The dative which usually accompanies **на́до** focuses on the person for whom the action is necessary. In the past tense **на́до** is followed by **бы́ло**; in the future by **бу́дет.**

Ему́ **на́до бы́ло** пойти́ в го́род.	He had to go downtown.
Ему́ **на́до бу́дет** пойти́ в го́род.	He'll have to go downtown.

In colloquial Russian the infinitive is sometimes omitted. This is especially common with verbs of motion where the destination is mentioned.

Мне́ **на́до** на по́чту.	I need to go to the post office.
Мне́ **на́до бы́ло** на уро́к.	I had to go to class.

The combination **не на́до** is often used as a plea that the addressee *not* do something. Infinitives used with **не на́до** are always imperfective.

Не на́до об э́том говори́ть.	*Don't* talk about that.
Мо́жно откры́ть о́кна?	Is it all right to open the windows?
— Нет, **не на́до** (открыва́ть о́кон).	No, *don't* (open the windows).

Note that **на́до** and the short-form neuter adjective **ну́жно** are often interchangeable in infinitive constructions.

Ему́ **ну́жно бы́ло** спеши́ть.	He had to hurry.
Ему́ **на́до бы́ло** _____.	He had _____.
Мне́ **ну́жно** пойти́ на по́чту.	I've got to go to the post office.
Мне́ **на́до**_____.	I've got_____.

The past tense of the imperfective verb идти́ and its prefixed perfective derivatives

MODELS

Что́ шло́ в кино́?	What was playing at the movies?
— Шёл америка́нский фи́льм.	An American film was playing.
— Шла́ америка́нская карти́на.	An American picture was playing.
— Шли́ америка́нские фи́льмы.	American films were playing.

По́сле ле́кции о́н пошёл домо́й.	After the lecture he went home.
_____ она́ пошла́ _____.	_____ she went ____.
_____ они́ пошли́ _____.	_____ they went ____.

Ка́к прошёл уро́к?	How did the lesson go?
____ прошло́ собра́ние?	____ did the meeting go?
____ прошла́ ле́кция?	____ did the lecture go?
____ прошли́ экза́мены?	____ did the exams go?

О́н вошёл в ко́мнату.	He entered the room.
Она́ вошла́ _____.	She entered _____.
Они́ вошли́ _____.	They entered _____.

Óн на минýтку зашёл в библиотéку.

Онá _____ зашлá _____.

Мы́ _____ зашли́ _____.

Óн пришёл пóсле обéда.

Онá пришлá _____.

Они́ пришли́ _____.

Олéг тóлько что вы́шел.

Зи́на _____ вы́шла.

Дéвушки _____ вы́шли.

He dropped by the library for a minute.

She dropped by _____.

We dropped by _____.

He came after lunch (*or* in the afternoon).

She came _____.

They came _____.

Oleg just stepped out.

Zina __ stepped out.

The girls __ stepped out.

■ REPETITION PRACTICE

Repeat the above models, noting particularly that all perfective verbs derived from идти are patterned alike in the past tense.

■ SUBSTITUTION DRILLS

1. *How did your lesson go?*

   Кáк у вáс прошёл **урóк**?

   Кáк у вáс прошлó **собрáние**?

   (экзáмены, обéд, лéкция, ýтро, врéмя, недéля, суббóта, тáнцы)

2. *Volodya entered the dining hall.*

   Волóдя вошёл в столóвую.

   Они́ вошли́ в столóвую.

   (онá, студéнты, Зи́на и Олéг, учи́тель Семёнов, Натáша, Кáтя и Ни́на)

■ STRUCTURE REPLACEMENT DRILLS

1. *I'm on my way to the station.*

   I was on my way to the station.

   Я́ идý на стáнцию.

   Я́ шёл на стáнцию.

   Óн идёт на стáнцию.

   Óн шёл на стáнцию.

   (они́, вы, онá, егó товáрищ, мы, пáрень, брáтья)

2. *The lesson will go well.*

   The lesson went well.

   Урóк пройдёт хорошó.

   Урóк прошёл хорошó.

   Собрáние пройдёт хорошó.

   Собрáние прошлó хорошó.

   (эта зимá, эта недéля, экзáмены, врéмя, лéкция, вéчер, суббóта, обéд)

3. *He'll stop by the library.*

   He stopped by the library.

   Óн зайдёт в библиотéку.

   Óн зашёл в библиотéку.

   Они́ зайдýт в библиотéку.

   Они́ зашли́ в библиотéку.

   (ты, онá, вы, студéнты, профéссор, учителя́, учи́тельница, твои́ товáрищи)

4. *They'll enter the coach.*

   They entered the coach.

   Они́ войдýт в вагóн.

   Они́ вошли́ в вагóн.

   Мáша войдёт в вагóн.

   Мáша вошлá в вагóн.

   (учи́тельница, её сёстры, её брат, твои́ товáрищи, мы, он, вы, ты, Олéг)

■ STRUCTURE REPLACEMENT DRILLS

1. *I had to stop by the house.*

   I stopped by the house.

   Мнé нáдо бы́ло зайти́ домóй.

   Я́ зашёл домóй.

   Нáм нáдо бы́ло зайти́ домóй.

   Мы́ зашли́ домóй.

   (профéссору, подрýгам, тебé, женé, вам, шофёру, америкáнке)

2. *Katya had to go out of the house.*

   Katya went out of the house.

   Кáте нáдо бы́ло вы́йти и́з дому.

   Кáтя вы́шла и́з дому.

   Отцý нáдо бы́ло вы́йти и́з дому.

   Отéц вы́шел и́з дому.

   (Олéгу, сёстрам, мáтери, вам, учи́телю, нам, дéвушкам, ей)

3. *I didn't want to go over to him.*
I didn't go over to him.
Я не хотéл к немý подойти.
Я к немý не подошёл.

Мы́ не хотéли к немý подойти.
Мы́ к немý не подошли.

(мать, отéц, сестра, брáтья, друг, родители, Кóля, друзья́)

■ QUESTION-ANSWER DRILLS

1. *Where were you hurrying to last night?*
I was on my way to the movies.
Кудá ты́ спешил вчерá вéчером?
Я́ шёл в кинó.
Кудá вáша сестрá спешила вчерá вéчером?
Онá шлá в кинó.

(вы, он, они, твоя учительница, твой товарищ Петров, студенты, этот парень)

2. *Will Kolya go to the post office?*
He has already gone.
Кóля пойдёт на пóчту?
Óн ужé пошёл.
Егó женá пойдёт на пóчту?
Онá ужé пошлá.

(он, их уборщица, твои брáтья, Любовь Петровна, твой товарищ)

■ STRUCTURE REPLACEMENT DRILL

She's walking along the street.
She was walking along the street.
Онá идёт по ýлице.
Онá шлá по ýлице.

Подрýги идýт по ýлице.
Подрýги шли по ýлице.

(мы, продавщица, вы, Володя, сёстры, отéц, мать, Олег)

DISCUSSION

The past tense of **идти** *to be going* is based on an alternate root and has the following forms:

(m)	шёл	(f)	шлá	(n)	шлó	(pl)	шли

All the prefixed perfective derivatives of **идти** have pasts built on these same forms. With the exception of **вы́шел, вы́шла, вы́шло,** and **вы́шли** (from **вы́йти** *to go out*), where the stress is consistently drawn to the prefix **вы́–**, the stress is always on the last syllable of the past tense form.

PAST				INFINITIVE	
пошёл	пошлá	пошлó	пошли	**пойти**	to go
вошёл	вошлá	вошлó	вошли	**войти**	to enter
зашёл	зашлá	зашлó	зашли	**зайти**	to drop in
пришёл	пришлá	пришлó	пришли	**прийти**	to come
прошёл	прошлá	прошлó	прошли	**пройти**	to pass, go, go by, go through
подошёл	подошлá	подошлó	подошли	**подойти**	to go up to, approach
перешёл	перешлá	перешлó	перешли	**перейти**	to go across, cross

Suggestions that include the speaker: part II—imperfective verbs

Дава́йте смотре́ть сни́мки.	Let's look at snapshots!
_____ игра́ть в ка́рты.	____ play cards!
_____ слу́шать пласти́нки.	____ listen to records!
_____ обе́дать в столо́вой.	____ eat dinner in the dining hall!
_____ пи́ть ча́й.	____ drink tea!
_____ рабо́тать вме́сте.	____ work together!
_____ петь пе́сни.	____ sing some songs!
Дава́йте бу́дем смотре́ть сни́мки.	Let's look at snapshots!
_____ игра́ть в ка́рты.	____ play cards!
_____ слу́шать пласти́нки.	____ listen to records!
_____ обе́дать в столо́вой.	____ eat dinner in the dining hall!
_____ пи́ть ча́й.	____ drink tea!
_____ рабо́тать вме́сте.	____ work together!
_____ пе́ть пе́сни.	____ sing some songs!
Дава́йте не бу́дем об э́том говори́ть.	Let's not talk about it!
_____ ходи́ть на его́ ле́кции.	_____ go to his lecture!
_____ обе́дать в столо́вой.	_____ eat dinner in the dining hall!
_____ рабо́тать по суббо́там.	_____ work on Saturdays!
_____ открыва́ть о́кон.	_____ open the windows!
_____ туда́ е́здить.	_____ go there!
Лу́чше не бу́дем сего́дня рабо́тать.	We'd better not work today.
_____ сего́дня танцева́ть.	_____ dance today.
_____ сего́дня спа́ть на дворе́.	_____ sleep outdoors today.
_____ бо́льше туда́ е́здить.	_____ go there anymore.
_____ бо́льше с ни́ми игра́ть.	_____ play with them anymore.
_____ бо́льше об э́том ду́мать.	_____ think about it anymore.

■ REPETITION PRACTICE

Repeat the given models, noting the alternate ways in which suggestions that include the speaker and employ imperfective verbs may be expressed.

■ QUESTION-ANSWER DRILLS

1. *Want to look at snapshots?*
   Fine, let's look at snapshots.
   Хоти́те смотре́ть сни́мки?
   Хорошо́, дава́йте смотре́ть сни́мки.
   Хоти́те пи́ть ча́й?
   Хорошо́, дава́йте пи́ть ча́й.
   (слушать пластинки, читать стихи,
   учить русский язык, работать вечером,
   играть в карты, обедать в столовой,
   петь песни)

2. *Shall we talk about it?*
   No, let's not talk about it
   Мы́ бу́дем говори́ть об э́том?
   Не́т, дава́йте не бу́дем говори́ть об э́том.
   Мы́ бу́дем писа́ть об э́том?
   Не́т, дава́йте не бу́дем писа́ть об э́том.
   (спрашивать об этом, его ждать,
   слушать радио, играть в шахматы,
   ему звонить, стоять в очереди, ему
   отвечать)

3. *Do you want to work today?*
   No, let's not work today.
   Вы́ хоти́те сего́дня рабо́тать?
   Не́т, лу́чше не бу́дем сего́дня рабо́тать.
   Вы́ хоти́те сего́дня игра́ть в ка́рты?
   Не́т, лу́чше не бу́дем сего́дня игра́ть в ка́рты?
   (писать заявление, читать стихи, обедать в столовой, танцевать, спать на дворе, петь романсы)

4. *Shall we read today?*
   No, let's read tomorrow instead.
   Мы́ бу́дем сего́дня чита́ть?
   Не́т, лу́чше бу́дем чита́ть за́втра.
   Мы́ бу́дем сего́дня слушать джа́з?
   Не́т, лу́чше бу́дем слу́шать за́втра.
   (учить слова, писать письмо, играть в шахматы, смотреть снимки, танцевать, искать работу)

■ RESPONSE DRILL

They're playing tennis.
Let's play too!
Они́ игра́ют в те́ннис.
Дава́й то́же игра́ть!

Они́ чита́ют журна́л.
Дава́й то́же чита́ть!
(смотрят снимки, танцуют, обедают, спят, ищут книгу)

DISCUSSION

In affirmative suggestions that include the speaker and use imperfective verbs, **дава́й** (*or* **дава́йте**) may be followed either by the infinitive alone or by **бу́дем** plus the infinitive: Дава́й чита́ть (*or* Дава́й бу́дем чита́ть) *Let's read!*

In negative suggestions employing imperfective verbs, **бу́дем** cannot be omitted. **Лу́чше** is often used instead of **дава́й** (**дава́йте**): Дава́й не бу́дем чита́ть (*or* Лу́чше не бу́дем чита́ть) *Let's not read!*

Impersonal constructions using the subjectless third person plural verb

MODELS

Говоря́т, вчера́ бы́ло собра́ние.
Мне́ говори́ли, что вчера́ бы́ло собра́ние.
Уже́ **открыва́ют** две́ри.
Зде́сь **продаю́т** ры́бу.
Ско́ро **откро́ют** две́ри.
Мне́ **не даду́т** разреше́ния.
Таки́е дома́ **пока́зывают** тури́стам.
Тепе́рь **стро́ят** дома́ для колхо́зников.

They say there was a meeting yesterday.
I was told there was a meeting yesterday.
They're already opening the doors.
Fish is sold here or They sell fish here.
They'll soon open the doors.
They won't give me a pass.
That's the kind of houses they show tourists.
Houses are now being built for the farmers.

■ STRUCTURE REPLACEMENT DRILLS

1. *They sell fish.*
   They sell fish here or *Fish is sold here.*
   Они́ продаю́т ры́бу.
   Зде́сь продаю́т ры́бу.
   Они́ пока́зывают фи́льмы.
   Зде́сь пока́зывают фи́льмы.

Они́ говоря́т по-англи́йски.
Они́ понима́ют по-ру́сски.
Они́ даю́т пропуска́.
Они́ отдыха́ют ле́том.
Они́ продаю́т поде́ржанные ве́щи.

2. *Who told him?*
   Why was he told?
   Кто́ ему́ сказа́л?
   Почему́ ему́ сказа́ли?
   Кто́ ему́ разреши́л?
   Почему́ ему́ разреши́ли?
   (посла́л, да́л, показа́л, прода́л, звони́л,
   написа́л, откры́л, заплати́л,
   предложи́л)

3. *We'll close the doors.*
   They'll soon close the doors or *The doors*
   will soon close.
   Мы́ закро́ем две́ри.
   Ско́ро закро́ют две́ри.
   Мы́ откро́ем две́ри.
   Ско́ро откро́ют две́ри.
   Мы́ напи́шем об э́том в газе́те.
   Мы́ разреши́м е́здить во Владивосто́к.
   Мы́ пока́жем э́ту карти́ну.
   Мы́ откро́ем собра́ние.
   Мы́ принесём обе́д.

4. *The administrator will give us a room.*
   They'll give us a room or *We'll be given a*
   room.
   Администра́тор на́м да́ст но́мер.
   На́м даду́т но́мер.
   Администра́тор на́м откро́ет две́рь.
   На́м откро́ют две́рь.
   Администра́тор на́м позвони́т в ча́с.

Администра́тор на́м пока́жет теа́тр.
Администра́тор на́м об э́том напи́шет.
Администра́тор на́м разреши́т туда́
   пое́хать.
Администра́тор на́м посове́тует куда́
   пойти́.
Администра́тор на́м об э́том ска́жет.

■ RESPONSE DRILL

Who sits like that?
That's no way to sit! or *People don't sit*
   like that!
Кто́ та́к сиди́т?
Та́к не сидя́т!
Кто́ та́к рабо́тает?
Та́к не рабо́тают!
   (пи́шет, чита́ет, игра́ет, стои́т,
   танцу́ет, говори́т)

■ QUESTION-ANSWER DRILL

Will they give you a pass?
They already did.
Тебе́ даду́т про́пуск?
Мне́ уже́ да́ли.
Тебе́ напи́шут об э́том?
Мне́ уже́ написа́ли.
Тебе́ разреша́т измени́ть и́мя?
Тебе́ отве́тят из посо́льства?
Тебе́ позвоня́т с рабо́ты?
Тебе́ пока́жут сни́мки?
Тебе́ ку́пят портфе́ль?

■ STRUCTURE REPLACEMENT DRILLS

1. *I can't sleep.*
   They don't let me sleep.
   Я́ не могу́ спа́ть.
   Мне́ не даю́т спа́ть.
   Я́ не могу́ рабо́тать.
   Мне́ не даю́т рабо́тать.
   (писа́ть, чита́ть, слу́шать, ду́мать,
   игра́ть)

2. *He couldn't speak.*
   They wouldn't let him speak.
   О́н не мо́г говори́ть.
   Ему́ не дава́ли говори́ть.
   О́н не мо́г спроси́ть.
   Ему́ не дава́ли спроси́ть.
   О́н не мо́г отвеча́ть.
   О́н не мо́г откры́ть собра́ние.
   О́н не мо́г слу́шать ра́дио.
   О́н не мо́г отдохну́ть.
   О́н не мо́г ходи́ть в кино́.

The third person plural verb without a subject is used when the action is attributed to an indefinite group. The speaker either does not know the source of the action or finds it convenient not to mention the source, for example, if it is attributed to officials in power. Such constructions may be rendered variously in English, for example, **говоря́т** *they say, people say, it's said.*

Such constructions are often used where English would use the passive voice.

Мне́ говори́ли, что за́втра бу́дет экза́мен.	I was told there'd be an exam tomorrow.
Уже́ открыва́ют две́ри.	The doors are being opened already.
Здесь говоря́т по-ру́сски.	Russian is spoken here.

ЧТЕ́НИЕ И ПИСЬМО́

— Вы уже́ дово́льно хорошо́ говори́те по-ру́сски. Тепе́рь вам ну́жно то́лько бо́льше чита́ть. — Я ка́ждый день чита́ю „Вече́рнюю Москву́". — Э́то хорошо́. Но вам на́до ещё и говори́ть по-ру́сски ка́ждый день. Вот на ва́шем ку́рсе есть ми́лая де́вушка Зи́на. Вы её зна́ете? — Да, но мне с ней о́чень тру́дно говори́ть. Когда́ я с ней говорю́, я всё забыва́ю и то́лько смотрю́ на неё.

Оле́г до́лжен посмотре́ть э́тот фильм. В нём игра́ет его́ сестра́. Она́ мно́го писа́ла ему́ об э́том фи́льме, и ему́ о́чень интере́сно его́ посмотре́ть. Но сего́дня он всё у́тро был на ле́кциях, по́сле ле́кций пошёл к това́рищу, и они́ до́лго вме́сте чита́ли. Нет, сего́дня ему́ бу́дет тру́дно пойти́ в кино́, он уста́л. Лу́чше он пойдёт за́втра.

— Бори́с Миха́йлович, у ва́с нет деревя́нного я́щика?

— Е́сть, а заче́м о́н ва́м?

— Мне́ ну́жно посла́ть роди́телям прои́грыватель.

— А ра́зве у ни́х в колхо́зе е́сть электри́чество?

— Да́, е́сть. Я́ давно́ хоте́л купи́ть и́м прои́грыватель и во́т купи́л. Ду́маю, что э́то бу́дет хоро́ший пода́рок для ни́х.

— Скажи́те, Никола́й, у ва́с в колхо́зе хоро́шие и́збы?

— Да́, о́чень хоро́шие.

— И водопрово́д е́сть?

— Не́т, водопрово́да не́т. Но у на́с мно́го коло́дцев и хоро́шее о́зеро. Да и лю́ди на́ши привы́кли носи́ть во́ду, и́м не тру́дно.

— Мне́ стра́нно э́то слы́шать. У на́с в Аме́рике всё совсе́м ина́че.

— Что́ э́то та́м стро́ят?

— Ка́жется дома́ для колхо́зников.

— О́, ка́менные!

— Да́. В «Огоньке́» неда́вно бы́л об э́том о́черк.

— Ах да́, я́ чита́л, но не зна́л, что э́то об э́том колхо́зе.

— Да́, в э́тих но́вых дома́х, говоря́т, бу́дет электри́чество и да́же водопрово́д.

— Да ну́? И всё удо́бства? Ва́нные, убо́рные?

— Э́того я́ не зна́ю.

— А телефо́н?

— Не ду́маю.

— Зна́ешь, Оле́г, я́ уже́ привы́к зде́сь, в го́роде, к электри́честву и ра́дио, а во́т прие́хал неда́вно в на́ш колхо́з и — ничего́ та́м не́т. Стра́нно да́же, как лю́ди мо́гут жи́ть без э́тих удо́бств!

— А ве́дь ты́ са́м та́к жи́л, когда́ до́ма бы́л.

— Да я́ уже́ и не по́мню об э́том — та́к давно́ э́то бы́ло.

— А во́т ко́нчишь университе́т, мо́жет бы́ть бу́дешь в своём колхо́зе рабо́тать. Опя́ть привы́кнешь.

— Не́т! Я́ в колхо́зе рабо́тать не бу́ду, не хочу́. Впро́чем, когда́ я́ ко́нчу, мо́жет бы́ть та́м уже́ бу́дет электри́чество.

— Га́ля, по́мните, я́ ва́м пока́зывал сни́мки фа́брики, где рабо́тает мо́й оте́ц?

— Да́. Я́ себе́ ина́че представля́ла америка́нские фа́брики.

— Вы́ да́же, ка́жется, не пове́рили мне́, пра́вда?

— Не́т, Фили́пп, я́ ва́м поверила, то́лько я́ уже́ привы́кла ина́че ду́мать об Аме́рике.

— А зна́ете, когда́ я́ сюда́ е́хал, я́ то́же всё себе́ ина́че представля́л.

— Ва́ши студе́нты у́чат англи́йский язы́к?

— Да́, и не́которые уже́ непло́хо говоря́т. Вы́ с ни́ми ра́зве не говори́ли?

— Говори́л, но по-ру́сски. Та́к жа́ль! Я́ не зна́л, что они́ говоря́т по-англи́йски.

— Да́, а я́ как ра́з ду́мал спроси́ть ва́с, господи́н Гра́нт, как они́ говоря́т.

— Я́ за́втра зайду́ к ва́м и поговорю́ с ни́ми.

PREPARATION FOR CONVERSATION

Несча́стный слу́чай

слу́чай   [slúčij]
    case, occasion, incident, event, chance

несча́стный   [ɲiščásnij]
    unhappy, unfortunate

несча́стный слу́чай
    accident, unfortunate incident

Ю́рий Никола́евич, давно́ ва́с не ви́дел!
Yury Nikolaevich, I haven't seen you for a long time!

чтó э́то   [štóetə]
    why, why is it, how come

А что́ э́то вы́ та́к идёте?
But why are you walking like that?

Вы́ ра́зве не слы́шали?
You mean you haven't heard?

нога́ (acc sg но́гу)
    leg, foot

слома́ть (pfv I), слома́ю, –ешь, –ют
    to break

Я́ слома́л себе́ но́гу.
I broke my leg.

упа́сть (pfv I) (fut упаду́, –ёшь, –у́т; past упа́л, –а, –о, –и)
    to fall, fall down

Я́ упа́л и слома́л себе́ но́гу.
I fell and broke my leg.

чу́ть не
    almost, all but, nearly

Я́ чу́ть не слома́л себе́ но́гу.
I almost broke my leg.

Я́ упа́л и чу́ть не слома́л себе́ но́гу.
I fell and almost broke my leg.

Бо́же мо́й!
    good heavens! my goodness! my God!

А́х ты́, Бо́же мо́й!
Oh for heaven's sake!

случи́ться (pfv II)
    to happen

Ка́к же э́то случи́лось?
How in the world did it happen?

предста́вить (pfv II), предста́влю, –вишь, –вят
    to present, introduce

предста́вить себе́
    to imagine

Предста́вьте себе́!
Imagine! *or* Just imagine!

ле́стница   [lésɲicə]
    stairway, stairs, ladder

Предста́вьте себе́! Э́то случи́лось на ле́стнице.
Imagine! It happened on the stairway.

Музе́й в Петродворце́.

вни́з

вни́з по ле́стнице

Я шёл вни́з по ле́стнице.

вдру́г

и вдру́г упа́л

Я шёл вни́з по ле́стнице и вдру́г упа́л.

Предста́вьте себе́, шёл вни́з по на́шей ле́стнице и вдру́г упа́л.

несча́стье   [n̡iščás̡t̡jə]

Во́т несча́стье!

действи́тельно

Во́т, действи́тельно, несча́стье!

глу́пость (f)

Про́сто глу́пость!

шестна́дцать   [šisnátcət̡]

ле́т (gen pl of год *year*)

шестна́дцать ле́т

Шестна́дцать ле́т хожу́ по
   э́той ле́стнице.

осторо́жный, осторо́жно

   (*short form* осторо́жен, –жна,
      –о, –ы)

**Шестна́дцать ле́т хожу́ по э́той
   ле́стнице, всегда́ та́к осторо́жен,
   а ту́т вдру́г упа́л!**

вся́кий

со вся́ким

Э́то со вся́ким мо́жет случи́ться.

обрати́ться (pfv II)   [abrat̡ítcə]

   обращу́сь, обрати́шься, –я́тся

Вы́ к кому́ обрати́лись?

К О́сипову.

вра́ч, –á; –и́, –е́й

Он хоро́ший вра́ч.

несимпати́чный

**Он хоро́ший вра́ч, но челове́к
несимпати́чный.**

безду́шный

како́й-то

Он безду́шный како́й-то.

душа́

Да заче́м ва́м душа́?

специали́ст

Ва́м специали́ст ну́жен.

down, downstairs

down the stairs

I was going down the stairs.

suddenly, all of a sudden

and suddenly fell

I was going down the stairs and suddenly fell.

Imagine! I was going down our stairs and
suddenly fell.

bad luck, misfortune, unhappiness

What an unlucky break!

really, indeed

That was really an unlucky break!

foolishness, stupidity, nonsense

It was plain stupidity!

sixteen

years

sixteen years

I've been walking up and down those
stairs for sixteen years.

careful, carefully

I've been walking up and down those
stairs for sixteen years, always [being] so
careful, and all of a sudden I fall!

anyone, anybody, any

to anybody (*lit.* with anybody)

It can happen to anybody.

to consult, turn to, address

Whom did you consult? *or* What doctor
did you see?

Osipov.

physician, doctor

He's a good physician.

not likable, not nice, not personable

He's a good physician, but not a likable person.

unfeeling, cold, impersonal (*lit.*
without soul, heartless)

a, an; kind of, some kind of

He's kind of cold and unfeeling.

soul, heart, feeling

What's feeling got to do with it?

specialist

You need a specialist.

| прáв, –á, –о, –ы | right |
| **Вы́ прáвы, конéчно.** | You're right, of course. |

дóктор, –а; докторá, –óв	doctor
Я́ не люблю́ ходи́ть к докторáм.	I don't like going to doctors *or* I hate going to doctors.
Кáк я́ не люблю́ ходи́ть к докторáм!	How I hate going to doctors!

SUPPLEMENT

во вся́ком слу́чае	in any case, anyway, in any event
Во вся́ком слу́чае, я́ в Москву́ не поéду.	In any case, I won't go to Moscow.
навéрх	up, upstairs
Пойдём ко мнé навéрх.	Let's go upstairs to my room.
глу́пый	foolish, silly, dumb, stupid
Какáя онá глу́пая!	How foolish she is!
у́мный	wise, intelligent, smart, clever
Онá такáя у́мная!	She's so clever (*or* wise)!
симпати́чный	nice, likable
Óн óчень симпати́чный человéк.	He's a very nice person.
гóд, –а	year
в э́том году́	this year
Рáз в гóд я́ éзжу в Я́лту.	Once a year I go to Yalta.
В э́том году́ я́ тудá не поéду.	This year I won't go there.
мéсяц	month; moon
в э́том мéсяце	this month
Двá рáза в мéсяц мы́ éздили в гóрод.	Twice a month we went to the city.
В э́том мéсяце мы́ тудá не поéдем.	This month we won't go there.

Несчáстный слу́чай

С.П. — Сергéй Пáвлович   Ю.Н. — Ю́рий Николáевич

С.П.   1 Ю́рий Николáевич, давнó вáс не ви́дел! А чтó э́то вы́ тáк идёте?[1]

Ю.Н.   2 Вы́ рáзве не слы́шали? Я́ упáл и чу́ть не сломáл себé нóгу.

С.П.   3 Áх ты, Бóже мóй![2] Кáк же э́то случи́лось?

Ю.Н.   4 Предстáвьте себé, шёл вни́з по нáшей лéстнице и вдру́г упáл.

С.П.   5 Вóт, действи́тельно, несчáстье!

Ю.Н.   6 Прóсто глу́пость! Шестнáдцать лéт хожу́ по э́той лéстнице, всегдá тáк остóрожен, а ту́т вдру́г упáл![3]

С.П.   7 Э́то со вся́ким мóжет случи́ться. Вы́ к кому́ обрати́лись?

Ю.Н.   8 К Óсипову. Óн хорóший врáч, но человéк несимпатúчный. Бездýшный какóй-то.

С.П.   9 Да зачéм вáм душá?[4] Вáм специалúст нýжен.

Ю.Н.   10 Вы́ прáвы, конéчно. Кáк я не люблю́ ходúть к докторáм!

NOTES

[1] **Чтó это**, **чтó** and even **чегó** in a more colloquial style are often substituted for **почемý** *why* in spoken Russian. Stylistically this is something akin to the colloquial English *how come*: **Чтó это вы́ к нáм не захóдите?** *How come you don't drop in to see us?*

[2] **Бóг** *God* is one of the few Russian nouns with a vocative form: **Бóже!** The expression **Бóже мóй!** is a stock phrase with its own special word order. It is not as strong as the English *My God!* but is rather like *Good heavens!* or *My goodness!* In Soviet publications, the word for God is written with a small initial letter.

[3] The form **лéт**, which functions as the genitive plural of **гóд** *year* with numbers and adverbs of quantity, is actually the genitive plural of **лéто** *summer*. Compare **одúн гóд** with **мнóго лéт**, **шестнáдцать лéт**. (Consider the poetic use of English *summers* as, for example, in "She was sixteen *summers* old.") The regular genitive plural form **годóв** is very rarely used. **Гóд** also has alternate forms in the nominative plural: **гóды** and **годá**.

[4] Although **душá** literally means *soul*, it is often best translated as *heart*, in the sense of empathy or sympathetic character. Note that the adjective **бездýшный** is formed from **без** *without* and **душá**.

PREPARATION FOR CONVERSATION   **У дóктора**

чýвствовать себя́ (I)[1]	to feel
чýвствую, чýвствуешь, –ют	
Как вы́ себя́ чýвствуете?	How do you feel?
горáздо	by far, much, considerably
Горáздо лýчше, дóктор.	Much better, doctor.
Я почтú свобóдно хожý.	I have almost no trouble walking. (*Lit.* I walk almost freely.)
Дáже смóг пешкóм к вáм прийтú.	I was even able to come to your office on foot.
сойтú (pfv I) (*like* пойтú)	to go off, get off, come (*or* go) down
ýм, –á	mind, sense
сойтú с умá	to go (*or* be) out of one's mind, to go (*or* be) crazy
Вы́ с умá сошлú?	Are you out of your mind?

---

[1] Forms of **чýвствовать** are simplified in speech. The first **в** should never be pronounced. The second **в** may also be dropped so that in rapid speech **чýвствуете** is usually pronounced [čústujți]. (Compare this with **здрáвствуйте**, which is usually pronounced [zdrástujți] or, in very rapid speech, [zdrásṣți].)

Я вам сказа́л ходи́ть то́лько
по ко́мнате.
   полчаса́
   в де́нь
Ва́м мо́жно ходи́ть то́лько
полчаса́ в де́нь.
   то́

**Я же ва́м сказа́л ходи́ть то́лько
по ко́мнате и то́ не бо́льше,
чём полчаса́ в де́нь.**

   станови́ться (II) [stənaɣítcə]
      становлю́сь, стано́вишься, –ятся
Мне́ стано́вится лу́чше.
   чём ... тём ...
   чём бо́льше, тём лу́чше

Чём бо́льше я хожу́, тём лу́чше
мне́ стано́вится.
   каза́ться (I) (past каза́лось, pres ка́жется)
Мне́ каза́лось, что мне́ стано́вится
лу́чше.

**Извини́те, до́ктор, но мне́ каза́лось, что
чём бо́льше я хожу́, тём лу́чше
мне́ стано́вится.**

   обраща́ться (I) [abrašчáтcə]
      обраща́юсь, обраща́ешься, –ются
Заче́м вы́ ко мне́ обраща́лись?
   вообще́
Заче́м вы́ вообще́ ко мне́ обраща́лись?

   нра́виться (II) [nráɣitcə]
      нра́влюсь, нра́вишься, –ятся
   та́к, ка́к вам нра́вится
   е́сли
**Е́сли вы́ де́лаете та́к, ка́к ва́м
нра́вится, то́ заче́м вы́ тогда́
вообще́ ко мне́ обраща́лись?**

   серди́ться (II) [şirḍítcə]
      сержу́сь, се́рдишься, –ятся
Не серди́тесь, до́ктор.
   то́чный; то́чно
Я́ бу́ду де́лать всё то́чно та́к,
ка́к вы́ ска́жете.
**Не серди́тесь, до́ктор, я́ бу́ду
де́лать всё то́чно та́к, ка́к вы́
ска́жете.**

I told you to walk only about the room.

   half an hour
   per day, a day
You can walk only half an hour a day.

   then

But I told you to walk only about the room
   and then not more than half an hour
   a day.

   to become, get, grow, step

I'm getting better *or* I'm improving.
   the ... the ...
   the more the better

The more I walk, the better I get.

   to seem
It seemed to me I was improving.

Excuse me, doctor, but it seemed to
   me the more I walked, the more
   I improved.

   to consult, turn to, address, go (*or* come) to

Why did you consult me?
   in general, at all
Why did you [bother to] consult me
   at all?
   to like, please, appeal to

   just as you please, exactly as you like
   if
If you do just as you please, then
   why do you bother to consult me
   at all?

   to be angry, to be mad

Don't be angry, doctor.
   exact, precise; exactly, precisely
I'll do everything exactly as you say.

Don't be angry, doctor; I'll do
   everything exactly as you say.

Ну, хорошо́. Покажи́те мне́ ва́шу но́гу. Да́, непло́хо.	Well, all right. Show me your leg. Yes, not bad.
боле́ть (II)	to ache, hurt, pain
У меня́ боли́т нога́.	My leg (*or* foot) hurts.
Она́ у меня́ почти́ совсе́м не боли́т.	It's almost stopped hurting altogether.
масса́ж	massage
де́лать масса́ж	to massage
по утра́м	in the mornings, mornings
На́до де́лать по утра́м масса́ж.	You have to massage it in the mornings.
продолжа́ть (I)	to continue, keep on
Продолжа́йте де́лать по утра́м масса́ж.	Continue massaging it in the mornings.
ма́зь (f)	ointment, salve
реце́пт	prescription, recipe
Я ва́м да́м но́вый реце́пт на ма́зь.	I'll give you a new prescription for ointment.
помога́ть (I) (*plus* dat)	to help
Спаси́бо. Э́та ма́зь мне́ о́чень помога́ет.	Thanks. The ointment really helps me.
Когда́ мне́ прийти́?	When am I to come? *or* When should I come?
Когда́ мне́ прийти́ опя́ть, в сре́ду?	When should I come again, on Wednesday?
коне́ц, конца́; –ы́, –о́в	end
уезжа́ть (I)	to go away, leave (by vehicle)
Не́т, я уезжа́ю в конце́ э́той неде́ли.	No, I'm going away the end of this week.
че́рез пя́ть дне́й	in five days
дне́й че́рез пя́ть	in about five days
Я уезжа́ю дней че́рез пя́ть.	I'm going away in about five days.
верну́ться (pfv I) [yirnútcə]	to come back, return
верну́сь, вернёшься, –у́тся	
Я верну́сь дней че́рез пя́ть.	I'll return in about five days.
ра́ньше	earlier, before
Я верну́сь дней че́рез пя́ть, не ра́ньше.	I'll return in about five days, not before.
Я уезжа́ю в конце́ э́той неде́ли и верну́сь дней че́рез пя́ть, не ра́ньше.	I'm going away the end of this week and will return in about five days, not before.
назна́чить (pfv II)	to set, designate, appoint, assign
назна́чить де́нь	to give an appointment, set a date
Я ва́м назна́чу де́нь.	I'll give you an appointment.
Позвони́те мне́ че́рез неде́лю, и я́ ва́м назна́чу де́нь.	Phone me in a week and I'll give you an appointment.

ху́же

Я́ чу́вствую себя́ гора́здо
ху́же, до́ктор.

рассерди́ться (pfv II)
(*like* серди́ться)

Почему́ о́н та́к на меня́
рассерди́лся?

помо́чь (pfv I) (*like* мо́чь) (*plus* dat)

О́н, наве́рно, ва́м помо́жет.

уе́хать (pfv I)
(*like* е́хать)

Когда́ о́н уе́хал из Москвы́?

Я́ ско́ро уе́ду в Ленингра́д.

нача́ло

О́н уе́хал в нача́ле э́той
неде́ли.

возвраща́ться (I)

Оте́ц возвраща́ется домо́й в ше́сть.

по́зже

Они́ приду́т по́зже.

в конце́ концо́в   [fkancé kancóf]

В конце́ концо́в, о́н получи́л
разреше́ние.

worse

I feel much worse, doctor.

to become angry, get mad

Why did he become so angry with me?

to help

He'll probably help you.

to go away, leave (by vehicle)

When did he leave Moscow?

I'll soon leave for Leningrad.

beginning, start

He went away at the beginning of
the week.

to return, come (*or* go) back

Father returns home at six.

later, later on

They'll come later.

finally, in the end, in the long
run, after all

He finally got a permit.

У до́ктора

О. — О́сипов

Ю.Н. — Ю́рий Никола́евич

О.   1 Здра́вствуйте! Ка́к вы́ себя́ чу́вствуете?

Ю.Н.   2 Гора́здо лу́чше, до́ктор. Я́ почти́ свобо́дно хожу́. Да́же смо́г пешко́м к ва́м
прийти́.

О.   3 Вы́ с ума́ сошли́? Я́ же ва́м сказа́л ходи́ть то́лько по ко́мнате и то́ не бо́льше,
че́м полчаса́ в де́нь.

Ю.Н.   4 Извини́те, до́ктор, но мне́ каза́лось, че́м бо́льше я́ хожу́, те́м лу́чше мне́
стано́вится.

О.   5 Е́сли вы́ де́лаете та́к, ка́к ва́м нра́вится, то заче́м вы́ тогда́ вообще́ ко мне́
обраща́лись?!

Ю.Н.   6 Не сердитесь, доктор, я буду делать всё точно так, как вы скажете.[1]

О.   7 Ну, хорошо. Покажите мне вашу ногу. Да, неплохо.

Ю.Н.   8 Она у меня почти совсём не болит.

О.   9 Хорошо, но продолжайте делать по утрам массаж. Я вам дам новый рецепт на мазь.

Ю.Н. 10 Спасибо. Эта мазь мне очень помогает. Когда мне прийти опять, в среду?

О.   11 Нет, я уезжаю в конце этой недели и вернусь дней через пять, не раньше.[2] Позвоните мне через неделю, и я вам назначу день.

NOTES

[1] Although **врач** and **доктор** can sometimes be used interchangeably, only **доктор** is used as a form of address or with names: **У доктора Осипова**, "**Скажите, доктор . . .**" **Врач** and **доктор** apply to both men and women.

Он (она) хороший врач.	He's (she's) a good doctor.
Это доктор Петрова.	This is Dr. Petrov (f).

General practitioners are mostly women, as are the majority of dentists and oculists in the Soviet Union.

[2] Note the word order in the expression **дней через пять**. The placement of a numeral after the noun which it modifies serves to express approximation. Compare **два часа** *two hours* with **часа два** *about two hours*; **сейчас восемь часов** *it's eight o'clock now* with **сейчас часов восемь** *it's about eight o'clock now*; and **в девять часов** *at nine* with **часов в девять** *around nine*.

Basic sentence patterns

1. Как вам понравился этот врач?   How did you like that doctor?
   _____ понравилась эта мазь?   _____ like that ointment?
   _____ понравилось его пение?   _____ like his singing?
   _____ понравились его родители?   _____ like his parents?

2. Кажется, я ей нравлюсь.   I guess she likes me.
   _____ мы __ нравимся.   _____ likes us.
   _____ он __ нравится.   _____ likes him.
   _____ ты __ нравишься.   _____ likes you.
   _____ они __ нравятся.   _____ likes them.
   _____ вы __ нравитесь.   _____ likes you.

3. Она часто заходила к своей соседке.   She often called on her neighbor.
   _____ к своим соседям.   _____ on her neighbors.
   _____ к своему учителю.   _____ on her teacher.
   _____ к своей сестре.   _____ on her sister.
   _____ к своим знакомым.   _____ on her acquaintances.
   _____ к своему брату.   _____ on her brother.
   _____ к своим подругам.   _____ on her girl friends.

4. Он обрати́лся к хоро́шему врачу́. — He consulted a good physician.
_____ к ру́сскому специали́сту. — _____ the Russian specialist.
_____ к но́вому до́ктору. — _____ the new doctor.
_____ к америка́нскому — _____ the American professor.
               профе́ссору.
_____ к ча́стному врачу́. — _____ a private physician.

5. Мы́ шли́ по краси́вой доро́ге. — We were walking along a lovely road.
_____ ста́рой _____. — _____ an old _____.
_____ но́вой _____. — _____ a new _____.
_____ хоро́шей _____. — _____ a good _____.
_____ прямо́й _____. — _____ a straight _____.
_____ како́й-то _____. — _____ some kind of ___.

6. Покажи́те э́тот фи́льм ва́шим студе́нтам. — Show the film to your students.
_____ свои́м _____. — _____ your _____.
_____ мои́м _____. — _____ my _____.
_____ но́вым _____. — _____ the new _____.
_____ ста́рым _____. — _____ the old _____.
_____ америка́нским ___. — _____ the American _____.
_____ хоро́шим _____. — _____ the good _____.

7. Позвони́те э́той же́нщине. — Give this woman a call.
_____ э́тому челове́ку. — ___ this man _____.
_____ э́тим лю́дям. — ___ these people _____.
_____ э́тому врачу́. — ___ this doctor _____.
_____ э́той де́вушке. — ___ this girl _____.
_____ э́тим молоды́м лю́дям. — ___ these young people _____.

8. Не станови́тесь туда́! — Don't stand (*or* step) there!
Не сади́тесь туда́! — Don't sit (down) there!
Не бо́йтесь! — Don't be afraid!
Не серди́тесь! — Don't be angry!
Не обраща́йтесь к ни́м! — Don't consult them!
Не возвраща́йтесь к ни́м! — Don't go back to them!

9. Я́ удивля́юсь, что вы́ к нему́ обрати́лись. — I'm surprised that you consulted him.
Она́ удивля́ется_____. — She's surprised_____.
Мы́ удивля́емся_____. — We're surprised_____.
Оле́г удивля́ется_____. — Oleg is surprised_____.
Они́ удивля́ются_____. — They're surprised_____.
Ты́ не удивля́ешься, что я́ к нему́ — You're not surprised that I consulted him?
               обрати́лся?
Вы́ не удивля́етесь_____? — You're not surprised_____?

10. Когда́ она́ вернётся? — When will she be back?
_____ты́ вернёшься? — _____ will you be back?
_____вы́ вернётесь? — _____ will you be back?
Я́ верну́сь че́рез неде́лю. — I'll be back in a week.
О́н вернётся_____. — He'll be back_____.
Они́ верну́тся_____. — They'll be back_____.

11. Они́ всегда́ возвраща́ются в ча́с.
    Вы́_____ возвраща́етесь_____.
    Я́_____ возвраща́юсь_____.
    Ты́_____ возвраща́ешься_____.
    Мы́_____ возвраща́емся_____.
    До́ктор____ возвраща́ется_____.

They always return at one.
You_____ return_____.
I_____ return_____.
You_____ return_____.
We _____ return _____.
The doctor _____ returns _____.

12. Вы́ мне́ помо́жете?
    — Да́, я́ ва́м помогу́.
    О́н ва́м помо́жет?
    — Да́, о́н мне́ помо́жет.
    Они́ на́м помо́гут?
    — Да́, они́ на́м помо́гут.
    О́н ва́м помо́г?
    — Да́, помо́г.
    Она́ ва́м помогла́?
    — Да́, помогла́.
    Они́ ва́м помогли́?
    — Да́, помогли́.

Will you help me?
Yes, I'll help you.
Will he help you?
Yes, he'll help me.
Will they help us?
Yes, they'll help us.
Did he help you?
Yes, he did.
Did she help you?
Yes, she did.
Did they help you?
Yes, they did.

13. Когда́ мне́ лу́чше прийти́?
    _____ прие́хать?
    _____ уе́хать?
    _____ зайти́?
    _____ пойти́?
    _____ войти́?
    _____ верну́ться?

When's the best time for me to come?
_____ to arrive?
_____ to leave?
_____ to stop by?
_____ to go?
_____ to go in?
_____ to return?

14. Куда́ мне́ пойти́?
    _____ звони́ть?
    _____ э́то положи́ть?
    _____ пое́хать?
    _____ смотре́ть?
    _____ писа́ть?
    _____ поступа́ть?
    _____ е́хать?

Where am I to (or should I) go?
_____ call?
_____ put this?
_____ drive to?
_____ look?
_____ write?
_____ enroll?
_____ go?

15. Мне́ стано́вится лу́чше.
    _____ ху́же.
    Мне́ станови́лось лу́чше.
    _____ ху́же.
    Стано́вится хо́лодно.
    _____ жа́рко.
    _____ тепло́.
    _____ свежо́
    _____ ску́чно.
    _____ интере́сно.

I'm getting better.
_____ worse.
I was getting better.
_____ worse.
It's getting cold.
_____ hot.
_____ warm.
_____ chilly.
_____ boring.
_____ interesting.

16. Ка́к вы́ себя́ чу́вствуете?
    — Я́ себя́ чу́вствую пло́хо.
    _____ хорошо́.
    _____ лу́чше.
    _____ гора́здо лу́чше.
    _____ ху́же.
    _____ гора́здо ху́же.

How do you feel?
I don't feel well.
I feel fine.
_____ better.
_____ much better.
_____ worse.
_____ much worse.

17. Ка́к по-тво́ему, результа́ты хоро́шие?
    — Да́, по-мо́ему, результа́ты о́чень
      хоро́шие.
    Ка́к по-ва́шему, результа́ты хоро́шие?
    — Да́, по-мо́ему, результа́ты о́чень
      хоро́шие.

What do you think, are the results good?
Yes, in my opinion, the results are very good.

What do you think, are the results good?
Yes, in my opinion, the results are very good.

18. Позвони́те мне́ через неде́лю.
    _____ две́ неде́ли.
    _____ три́ _____.
    _____ четы́ре ___.
    _____ пя́ть неде́ль.
    _____ ше́сть неде́ль.
    _____ ме́сяц.
    _____ два́ ме́сяца.
    _____ ше́сть ме́сяцев.

Call me up in a week.
_____ two weeks.
_____ three _____.
_____ four _____.
_____ five _____.
_____ six _____.
_____ a month.
_____ two months.
_____ six months.

Pronunciation practice: the voicing of ordinarily unvoiced consonants

Contrast the following sets in which к, с, and т are first pronounced voiceless and then are voiced.

A. The letter к pronounced [k]
   [kpáru]   к па́ру
   to the steam
   [któmu]   к то́му
   to the volume

The letter к pronounced [g]
   [gbáru]   к ба́ру
   to the bar
   [gdómu]   к до́му
   to the house

B. The letter с pronounced [s]
   [sp̡ít]   спи́т
   sleeps
   [spór]   спо́р
   argument

The letter с pronounced [z]
   [zb̡ít]   сби́т
   knocked down
   [zbór]   сбо́р
   harvesting

C. The letter т pronounced [t]
   [atšárə]   от ша́ра
   from the sphere
   [atkatát̡]   откача́ть
   to roll off

The letter т pronounced [d]
   [adžárə]   от жа́ра
   from the heat
   [adgadát̡]   отгада́ть
   to guess

STRUCTURE AND DRILLS

Prepositions requiring the dative: к and по

MODELS

Я́ иду́ к до́ктору.
_____ к бра́ту.
_____ к сестре́.
_____ к отцу́.
_____ к ма́тери.
_____ к роди́телям.

I'm on my way to the doctor's.
_____ to my brother's place.
_____ to my sister's place.
_____ to my father's place.
_____ to my mother's place.
_____ to my parents' place.

Подойди́ к телефо́ну.
_____ к столу́.
_____ к окну́.
_____ к доске́.
_____ к ка́рте.
Подойди́ ко мне́.
_____ к на́м.

Go (or come) to the phone.
_____ to the table.
_____ to the window.
_____ to the blackboard.
_____ up to the map.
Come over here to me.
_____ to us.

Э́то на́до сде́лать к обе́ду.
_____ к ве́черу.
_____ ко вто́рнику.
_____ к среде́.
_____ к пя́тнице.
_____ к концу́ ме́сяца.
_____ к нача́лу неде́ли.

This has to be done by noon.
_____ by evening.
_____ by Tuesday.
_____ by Wednesday.
_____ by Friday.
_____ by the end of the month.
_____ by the beginning of the
week.

Вы́ гото́вы к экза́мену?
_____ к уро́ку?
_____ к ле́кции?
_____ к рабо́те?
_____ к экза́менам?
_____ к заня́тиям?
_____ к ле́кциям?
_____ к обе́ду.

Are you prepared (or ready) for the exam?
_____ for the lesson?
_____ for the lecture?
_____ for the work?
_____ for the exams?
_____ for the classes?
_____ for the lectures?
_____ for the dinner?

По вечера́м мы́ гуля́ем в па́рке.
По утра́м _____.
По воскресе́ньям _____.
По суббо́там _____.
По среда́м _____.

In the evenings we stroll in the park.
In the mornings _____.
On Sundays _____.
On Saturdays _____.
On Wednesdays _____.

Не ходи́ по па́рку!
_____ по́ лесу!
_____ по у́лицам!
_____ по́ полю!
_____ по поля́м!
_____ по селу́!
_____ по го́роду!
_____ по доро́ге!
_____ по у́лице!

Don't walk (or wander) around in the park!
_____ in the woods!
_____ in the streets!
_____ in the field!
_____ in the fields!
_____ in the village!
_____ in the city!
_____ in the road!
_____ in the street!

О́н чита́ет ле́кции по ру́сской му́зыке.
_____ по матема́тике.
_____ по исто́рии СССР.
_____ по геогра́фии.
_____ по ру́сской литерату́ре.
_____ по ру́сскому языку́.

He gives lectures on Russian music.
_____ on mathematics.
_____ on the history of the U.S.S.R.
_____ on geography.
_____ on Russian literature.
_____ on the Russian language.

У нáс бы́л экзáмен по рýсскому языкý.   We had an exam on the Russian language.
_____ по фи́зике.   _____ in physics.
_____ по хи́мии.   _____ in chemistry.
_____ по истóрии.   _____ in history.
_____ по геогрáфии.   _____ in geography.
_____ по литератýре.   _____ in literature.

Они́ товáрищи по кýрсу.   They're classmates.
_____ по кóмнате.   _____ roommates.
_____ по шкóле.   _____ schoolmates.
_____ по университéту.   _____ fellow university students.
_____ по рабóте.   _____ co-workers.
_____ по слýжбе.   _____ co-workers.

Онá лю́бит ходи́ть по толкýчкам.   She loves to make the rounds of the flea markets.

_____ по магази́нам.   _____ of the stores.
_____ по ресторáнам.   _____ of the restaurants.

_____ по библиотéкам.   _____ of the libraries.
_____ по докторáм.[1]   _____ of the doctors.

■ REPETITION DRILL

Repeat the given models, noting the various usages of **к** and **по,** both of which require the dative case.

■ STRUCTURE REPLACEMENT DRILLS

1. *On the right was the door.*
   He went over (or *up*) *to the door.*
   Напрáво былá двéрь.
   Óн подошёл к двéри.
   Напрáво бы́л телефóн.
   Óн подошёл к телефóну.
   (окно, стол, лестница, полка, касса, буфет)

2. *On Wednesday we went to the movies.*
   On Wednesdays we used to go to the movies.
   В срéду мы́ ходи́ли в кинó.
   По средáм мы́ ходи́ли в кинó.
   В четвéрг мы́ ходи́ли в кинó.
   По четвергáм мы́ ходи́ли в кинó.
   (в пятницу, в воскресенье, в понедельник, в субботу, во вторник)

3. *I was at my brother's* (*place*).
   I'm going to see my brother.
   Я́ бы́л у брáта.
   Я́ идý к брáту.
   Я́ бы́л у дóктора.
   Я́ идý к дóктору.
   (у врача, у учителя, у Зины, у друга, у американца, у сестры, у Гали, у товарища, у продавщицы, у Наташи)

4. *It'll be ready before noon.*
   It'll be ready by noon.
   Э́то бýдет готóво до обéда.
   Э́то бýдет готóво к обéду.
   Э́то бýдет готóво до четвергá.
   Э́то бýдет готóво к четвергý.
   (до пятницы, до субботы, до понедельника, до среды, до воскресенья, до начала следующей недели, до дня его рождения)

---

[1] Note that there is a slight difference between **ходи́ть к докторáм** and **ходи́ть по докторáм.** The first is neutral, *to go to doctors;* the second means *to go from one doctor to another, to run to different doctors.*

5. *We have a Russian language lesson.*
   We have a lesson on the Russian language.
   У на́с уро́к ру́сского языка́.
   У на́с уро́к по ру́сскому языку́.
   У на́с уро́к исто́рии.
   У на́с уро́к по исто́рии.
   (геогра́фии, хи́мии, фи́зики,
   матема́тики, исто́рии СССР, му́зыки,
   ру́сской литерату́ры)

6. *They entered the hall.*
   They walked (or *wandered*) *about the hall.*
   Они́ вошли́ в за́л.
   Они́ ходи́ли по за́лу.
   Они́ вошли́ в теа́тр.
   Они́ ходи́ли по теа́тру.
   (лаборато́рию, па́рк, ко́мнату, до́м,
   библиоте́ку, вокза́л, магази́н, клу́б,
   горсове́т)

7. *She loves flea markets.*
   She loves to make the rounds of the flea markets.
   Она́ лю́бит толку́чки.
   Она́ лю́бит ходи́ть по толку́чкам.

   Она́ лю́бит магази́ны.
   Она́ лю́бит ходи́ть по магази́нам.
   (библиоте́ки, клу́бы, рестора́ны,
   теа́тры, конце́рты)

■ CUED QUESTION-ANSWER DRILL

(*room*) *Are they acquainted?*
          Yes, they're roommates.
(ко́мната) Они́ знако́мы?
          Да́, они́ това́рищи по ко́мнате.

(ку́рс)   Они́ знако́мы?
          Да́, они́ това́рищи по ку́рсу.
(университе́т, шко́ла, рабо́та, ко́мната,
ку́рс)

DISCUSSION

1. К (Ко)

The preposition **к** always requires the dative. With motion verbs **к** must be used if the destination is a person. In this use it is the destinational opposite of the locational preposition **у**.

Где́ вы́ бы́ли? — У бра́та.	Where were you? At my brother's.
Куда́ вы́ идёте? — К бра́ту.	Where are you going? To my brother's.

When the destination is a place or object, **в** or **на** plus the accusative is used if complete attainment of the goal is implied. However, **к** plus the dative may be used to describe movement toward the goal, i.e., limited attainment of the goal.

Я́ иду́ в па́рк.	I'm going to the park.
Я́ иду́ к па́рку.	I'm walking toward the park.
Иди́те в до́м.	Go into the house.
Иди́те к до́му.	Go up toward the house.

К is also used with time nouns in the sense of *by* or *toward*.

Я́ прие́ду к концу́ ме́сяца.	I'll come toward (*or* by) the end of the month.
К утру́ стано́вится хо́лодно.	Toward morning it gets cold.
Я́ э́то сде́лаю к суббо́те.	I'll get it done by Saturday.
Я́ э́то сде́лаю ко вто́рнику.	I'll get it done by Tuesday.

In conjunction with nouns describing activities, **к** is used in the sense of *for*.

Мы́ ещё не гото́вы к экза́мену.	We're not prepared for the exam yet.
Что́ ты́ купи́л к обе́ду?	What did you buy for dinner?

2. По

По is a preposition used mostly with the dative; it has many meanings, for example, *over*, *along* (the surface of), *to* (various goals), *on*, *in*, *via*, *by*, *according to*, *apiece*, *per person*. Some of these are illustrated below.

по вечера́м, по утра́м	[in the] evenings, [in the] mornings
по среда́м	on Wednesdays
по ра́дио, по телефо́ну	by (*or* over) the radio, by phone
звони́ть по телефо́ну	to call on the phone
по исто́рии, по литерату́ре	on (the subject of) history, literature
по привы́чке, по пла́ну, по оши́бке	by habit, by plan, by mistake
по́ лесу, по́ полю, по го́роду	about the woods, field, city
по доктора́м	to one doctor after another
по магази́нам	to one store after another
по стака́ну, по ча́шке	a glass apiece, a cup apiece

A number of adverbial expressions are formed by prefixing **по.**

по-мо́ему	in my opinion
по-ва́шему	in your opinion
по-ру́сски	in Russian
по-англи́йски	in English

The dative endings of э́тот, че́й, and the possessive pronoun modifiers

THE ENDINGS		
SINGULAR		PLURAL
Masculine and Neuter	*Feminine*	
–ому, –ему	–ой, –ей	–им

MODELS

Кто́ помо́жет э́тому студе́нту?	Who will help this student?
_____ па́рню?	_____ lad?
_____ э́той студе́нтке?	_____ this girl student?
_____ же́нщине?	_____ woman?
_____ э́тим студе́нтам?	_____ these students?
_____ лю́дям?	_____ people?
Позвони́те э́тому врачу́.	Give this (*or* that) physician a call.
_____ до́ктору.	_____ doctor _____.
_____ челове́ку.	_____ man _____.
_____ учи́телю.	_____ teacher _____.
_____ э́той же́нщине.	_____ this (*or* that) woman _____.
_____ де́вушке.	_____ girl _____.
_____ э́тим студе́нткам.	_____ these (*or* those) girl students _____.
_____ де́вушкам.	_____ girls _____.
_____ парня́м.	_____ lads _____.

Пойдём к моему́ дру́гу.	Let's go to my friend's place.
_____ това́рищу.	_____ friend's _____.
_____ бра́ту.	_____ brother's ___.
_____ к мое́й сестре́.	_____ to my sister's _____.
_____ ма́тери.	_____ mother's ____.
_____ подру́ге.	_____ girl friend's _____.
_____ к мои́м роди́телям.	_____ to my parents' ____.
_____ друзья́м.	_____ friends' ___.
_____ това́рищам.	_____ friends' ____.

Приве́т ва́шему му́жу.	Give my regards to your husband.
_____ твоему́ _____.	_____ your _____.
_____ ва́шей жене́.	_____ your wife.
_____ твое́й _____.	_____ your ____.
_____ ва́шим роди́телям.	_____ your parents.
_____ твои́м _____.	_____ your _____.

Мы́ привы́кли к на́шему профе́ссору.	We're used to our professor.
_____ учи́телю.	_____ teacher.
_____ сосе́ду.	_____ neighbor.
_____ к на́шей учи́тельнице.	_____ to our teacher (f).
_____ сосе́дке.	_____ neighbor (f).
_____ к на́шим студе́нтам.	_____ to our students.
_____ профессора́м.	_____ professors.
_____ сосе́дям.	_____ neighbors.
_____ учителя́м.	_____ teachers.

EXPANSION DRILLS

1. *Come over to the window!*
   Come over to this window!
   Подойди́ к окну́!
   Подойди́ к э́тому окну́!
   Подойди́ к по́лке!
   Подойди́ к э́той по́лке!
   (ли́фту, коло́дцу, две́ри, ка́ссе, избе́,
   ка́рте, ваго́ну, буфе́ту)

2. *Give the tourists a pass!*
   Give these tourists a pass!
   Да́йте тури́стам про́пуск!
   Да́йте э́тим тури́стам про́пуск!
   Да́йте певи́це про́пуск!
   Да́йте э́той певи́це про́пуск!
   (иностра́нцу, тури́сту, америка́нке,
   студе́нту, учителя́м, продавщи́це)

3. *Don't walk (or wander) around in the park!*
   Don't walk (or wander) around in this park!
   Не ходи́ по па́рку!
   Не ходи́ по э́тому па́рку!
   Не ходи́ по у́лице!
   Не ходи́ по э́той у́лице!
   (по поля́м, по доро́ге, по го́роду, по
   у́лицам, по́ полю, по́ лесу)

4. *I'm used to the teacher.*
   I'm used to our teacher.
   Я́ привы́к к учи́телю.
   Я́ привы́к к на́шему учи́телю.
   Я́ привы́к к учи́тельнице.
   Я́ привы́к к на́шей учи́тельнице.
   (к сосе́дкам, к сосе́ду, к сосе́дям,
   к профе́ссору, к студе́нтам, к
   америка́нцу)

■ RESPONSE DRILLS

1. *We came up (or went over) to her window.*
   To whose window?
   Мы́ подошли́ к её окну́.
   К чьему́ окну́?

Мы́ подошли́ к её дверя́м.
К чьи́м дверя́м?
(две́ри, сту́лу, столу́, по́лке, шкафу́,
ко́мнате)

2. *She's gone to visit their brother.*
   Whose brother?
   Она́ пое́хала к и́х бра́ту.
   К чьему́ бра́ту?
   Она́ пое́хала к и́х сестре́.
   К чьей сестре́?

(родителям, другу, подруге,
товарищам, отцу, друзьям,
учительнице)

■ EXPANSION DRILLS

1. *He bought his father a present.*
   He bought a present for his (own) father.
   Óн купи́л пода́рок отцу́.
   Óн купи́л пода́рок своему́ отцу́.
   Óн купи́л пода́рок сестре́.
   Óн купи́л пода́рок свое́й сестре́.

   (родителям, другу, подруге, брату,
   товарищу, жене, учителю,
   учительнице)

2. *I went over to the desk.*
   I went over to my desk.
   Я́ подошёл к столу́.
   Я́ подошёл к моему́ столу́.
   Я́ подошёл к окну́.
   Я́ подошёл к моему́ окну́.

   (дверям, шкафу, полкам, лаборатории,
   вагону, школе, общежитию, дому)

■ STRUCTURE REPLACEMENT DRILLS

1. *I returned to my work.*
   We returned to our work.
   Я́ верну́лся к мое́й рабо́те.
   Мы́ верну́лись к на́шей рабо́те.
   Я́ верну́лся к моему́ о́черку.
   Мы́ верну́лись к на́шему о́черку.

   (моим занятиям, моему роману, моей
   книге, моему сочинению, моей просьбе,
   моему плану)

2. *Are you going to see your neighbor?*
   Ты́ пойдёшь к твое́й сосе́дке?
   Вы́ пойдёте к ва́шей сосе́дке?
   Ты́ пойдёшь к твоему́ сосе́ду?
   Вы́ пойдёте к ва́шему сосе́ду?

   (твоему учителю, твоей подруге, твоей
   учительнице, твоим друзьям, твоему
   отцу, твоей сестре, твоим товарищам)

■ STRUCTURE REPLACEMENT DRILL

This student wants to go away.
This student has to go away.
Э́тот студе́нт хо́чет уе́хать.
Э́тому студе́нту на́до уе́хать.
Э́та америка́нка хо́чет уе́хать.
Э́той америка́нке на́до уе́хать.

(этот профессор, эти туристы, этот
доктор, эта девушка, этот иностранец,
эта певица, эти соседи, этот певец)

NOM (m)	э́тот	чей	мо́й	тво́й	сво́й	наш	ваш
(n)	э́то	чьё	моё	твоё	своё	на́ше	ва́ше
DAT	э́тому	чьему́	моему́	твоему́	своему́	на́шему	ва́шему
NOM (f)	э́та	чья́	моя́	твоя́	своя́	на́ша	ва́ша
DAT	э́той	чье́й	мое́й	твое́й	свое́й	на́шей	ва́шей
NOM (pl)	э́ти	чьй	мои́	твои́	свои́	на́ши	ва́ши
DAT	э́тим	чьи́м	мои́м	твои́м	свои́м	на́шим	ва́шим

The dative endings for **чей**, **этот**, and the possessive pronoun modifiers are distributed as follows:

1. The masculine and neuter dative singular ending is **–ему** for all except **этот** and **это**, which take **–ому**. Compare **моему́**, **ва́шему**, **чьему́** with **э́тому**.
2. The feminine dative singular ending is **–ей** for all except **эта**, which takes **–ой**. Compare **мое́й**, **ва́шей**, **чье́й** with **э́той**.
3. The dative plural ending for *all* these modifiers is **–им**: **мои́м**, **ва́шим**, **чьи́м**, **э́тим**.[1]

The dative endings of adjectives: singular and plural

THE ENDINGS		
SINGULAR		PLURAL
Masculine and Neuter	*Feminine*	
–ому, –ему	**–ой, –ей**	**–ым, –им**

MODELS

О́н не привы́к к чёрному хле́бу.	He's not used to black bread.
_____ бе́лому хле́бу.	_____ white bread.
_____ америка́нскому джа́зу.	_____ American jazz.
_____ холо́дному ча́ю.	_____ cold tea.
_____ большо́му го́роду.	_____ the big city.
_____ горя́чему молоку́.	_____ hot milk.
_____ вече́рнему ча́ю.	_____ evening tea.
_____ све́жему во́здуху.	_____ fresh air.
Она́ привы́кла к тако́й рабо́те.	She's used to such work.
_____ ру́сской пи́ще.	_____ Russian food.
_____ но́вой ко́мнате.	_____ the new room.
_____ большо́й кварти́ре.	_____ a big apartment.
_____ горя́чей пи́ще.	_____ hot food.
_____ вече́рней рабо́те.	_____ evening work.
Мы́ привы́кли к краси́вым веща́м.	We're used to beautiful things.
_____ тёплым зи́мам.	_____ warm winters.
_____ таки́м заявле́ниям.	_____ such applications.
_____ таки́м оши́бкам.	_____ such mistakes.
_____ больши́м удо́бствам.	_____ great conveniences.
_____ ма́леньким ко́мнатам.	_____ small rooms.
_____ све́жим огурца́м.	_____ fresh cucumbers.
_____ вече́рним заня́тиям.	_____ evening classes.
_____ тру́дным экза́менам.	_____ difficult exams.

---

[1] Note that in all cases **этот** shows a regular alternation of hard-stem [t] in the singular (**этот, этого, этому, эта, этой**) with soft-stem [t̡] in the plural (**эти, этих, этим**).

Но́вому студе́нту нужна́ ко́мната.	The new student needs a room.
Молодо́му челове́ку _____.	The young man _____.
Америка́нскому тури́сту _____.	The American tourist _____.
Молодо́й де́вушке _____.	The young lady _____.
Но́вой студе́нтке _____.	The new student _____.
Ста́рой же́нщине _____.	The old woman _____.
Но́вым студе́нтам нужны́ ко́мнаты.	The new students need rooms.
Молоды́м лю́дям _____.	The young people _____.
Америка́нским тури́стам _____.	The American tourists _____.

■ REPETITION DRILL

Repeat the given models, noting the pattern of adjective endings in the dative case.

■ STRUCTURE REPLACEMENT DRILLS

1. *This is a new student.*
   Let's help this new student.
   Э́то но́вый студе́нт.
   Помо́жем э́тому но́вому студе́нту.
   Э́то плохо́й студе́нт.
   Помо́жем э́тому плохо́му студе́нту.
      (симпати́чный, хоро́ший, глу́пый, аме-
      рика́нский, неплохо́й, молодо́й, у́мный,
      ру́сский)

2. *A new professor has arrived.*
   The new professor needs a room.
   Прие́хал но́вый профе́ссор.
   Но́вому профе́ссору нужна́ ко́мната.
   Прие́хала но́вая учи́тельница.
   Но́вой учи́тельнице нужна́ ко́мната.
      (но́вые студе́нты, на́ши ста́рые друзья́,
      молодо́й челове́к, наш о́бщий друг,
      америка́нский тури́ст, ру́сские специа-
      ли́сты, англи́йский профе́ссор)

■ STRUCTURE REPLACEMENT DRILLS

He wrote to these beautiful girls.
He wrote to this beautiful girl.
О́н написа́л э́тим краси́вым де́вушкам.
О́н написа́л э́той краси́вой де́вушке.
О́н написа́л э́тим ми́лым де́вушкам.
О́н написа́л э́той ми́лой де́вушке.
   (симпати́чным, ру́сским, интере́сным,
   молоды́м, хоро́шим, краси́вым)

■ CUED QUESTION-ANSWER DRILL

(cold water)	*What's she gotten used to?*
	To cold water.
(холо́дная вода́)	К чему́ она́ привы́кла?
	К холо́дной воде́.
(све́жие огурцы́)	К чему́ она́ привы́кла?
	К све́жим огурца́м.

(горя́чее молоко́, беспла́тные обе́ды,
вку́сные ве́щи, лёгкая уда́ча, така́я
рабо́та, тру́дные экза́мены, краси́вые
ве́щи, све́жая ры́ба, све́жие огурцы́,
све́жий во́здух)

	SINGULAR			PLURAL	
Masculine and Neuter		Feminine			
–ому	–ему	–ой	–ей	–ым	–им
молодо́му	си́нему	молодо́й	си́ней	молоды́м	больши́м
большо́му	вече́рнему	большо́й	вече́рней	но́вым	си́ним
но́вому	све́жему	но́вой	све́жей	ста́рым	вече́рним
ста́рому	хоро́шему	ста́рой	хоро́шей	краси́вым	све́жим
краси́вому		краси́вой			хоро́шим
ру́сскому		ру́сской			ру́сским
друго́му		друго́й			други́м

DISTRIBUTION OF ENDINGS

In the dative singular masculine-neuter, the ending is spelled –ому after hard stems and –ему after soft stems. Compare краси́вому, молодо́му with вече́рнему. Mixed stems take –ому, except where the ending is unstressed and preceded by ш, ж, ч, or щ, in which case it is spelled –ему. Compare друго́му, ру́сскому, большо́му with хоро́шему, све́жему.

In the dative singular feminine, the ending is spelled –ой after hard stems and –ей after soft stems. Compare молодо́й, но́вой with вече́рней. Mixed stems take –ой except where the ending is unstressed and preceded by ш, ж, ч, or щ, in which case it is spelled –ей. Compare друго́й, ру́сской, большо́й with хоро́шей, све́жей. Note that these are the same endings as in the genitive and prepositional singular.

In the dative plural, the endings are spelled –ым for hard stems and –им for soft stems and *all* mixed stems. Compare краси́вым, молоды́м with ру́сским, больши́м, хоро́шим, вече́рним.

Reflexive verbs: part I

MODELS

Я́ верну́сь че́рез неде́лю.	I'll return in a week.
Ты́ вернёшься_____.	You'll return _____.
О́н вернётся _____.	He'll return _____.
Мы́ вернёмся _____.	We'll return _____.
Вы́ вернётесь _____.	You'll return _____.
Они́ верну́тся _____.	They'll return _____.

Оте́ц верну́лся из Москвы́.	Father has returned from Moscow.
Ма́ть верну́лась из го́рода.	Mother has returned from the city.
Роди́тели верну́лись в колхо́з.	Our parents have returned to the kolkhoz.

Я́ сержу́сь на Зи́ну.	I'm mad at Zina.
Ты́ се́рдишься____.	You're _____.
О́н се́рдится _____.	He's _____.
Мы́ се́рдимся _____.	We're _____.
Вы́ се́рдитесь _____.	You're _____.
Они́ се́рдятся _____.	They're _____.

Óн на меня́ рассéрдил **ся**.	He became angry with me.
Она́ _____ рассерди́ла **сь**.	She became angry with_____.
Они́ _____ рассерди́ли**сь**.	They became angry with _____.

Note that the verbs **серди́ться**, **рассерди́ться** are accompanied by **на** plus the accusative to indicate the object of one's anger.

■ REPETITION DRILL

Repeat the given models, observing that reflexive verbs are exactly like nonreflexives structurally except for the addition of the particle **–ся** (after consonants including **й**) or **–сь** (after vowels).

■ SUBSTITUTION DRILL

I usually return at one.
Я обы́чно возвраща́юсь в ча́с.
До́ктор обы́чно возвраща́ется в ча́с.
    (она, мы, они, вы, я, ты, он)

■ STRUCTURE REPLACEMENT DRILLS

1. *It was getting warm.*
   It's getting warm.
   Станови́лось тепло́.
   Стано́вится тепло́.
   Станови́лось свежо́.
   Стано́вится свежо́.
       (жарко, интересно, скучно, трудно, легко)

2. *I'm getting cold.*
   I was getting cold.
   Мне́ стано́вится хо́лодно.
   Мне́ станови́лось хо́лодно.
   Мне́ стано́вится ску́чно.
   Мне́ станови́лось ску́чно.
       (тепло, жарко, холодно, лучше, хуже, интересно, неудобно)

3. *She was angry with him.*
   She's angry with him.
   Она́ на него́ серди́лась.
   Она́ на него́ се́рдится.
   Отéц на него́ серди́лся.
   Отéц на него́ се́рдится.
       (вы, Олег, мать, ты, я, твои родители, сестра, брат)

4. *He became angry with her.*
   He'll become angry with her.
   Óн на неё рассерди́лся.
   Óн на неё рассéрдится.
   Ма́ть на неё рассерди́лась.
   Ма́ть на неё рассéрдится.
       (мои подруги, соседка, отец, мать, вы, мы, я, сосед, профессор)

5. *Sergey returned on Wednesday.*
   Sergey will return on Wednesday.
   Сергéй верну́лся в срéду.
   Сергéй вернётся в срéду.

   Бра́тья верну́лись в срéду.
   Бра́тья верну́тся в срéду.
       (я, все, уборщица, секретарь, мы, туристы, Юра и Олег, вы)

■ RESPONSE DRILL

I'm always well.
I never go to the doctor.
Я́ всегда́ здоро́в.
Я́ никогда́ не обраща́юсь к врачу́.

Ты́ всегда́ здоро́ва.
Ты́ никогда́ не обраща́ешься к врачу́.
    (учителя́, вы, сестра, Николай, Наташа, мы, девушки)

DISTRIBUTION OF THE REFLEXIVE PARTICLE –ся OR –сь				
	SINGULAR			**PLURAL**
PRES-FUT first person –сь second person –ся third person –ся				first person –ся second person –сь third person –ся
PAST (m) –ся	(n) –сь	(f) –сь	(pl) –сь	
IMPER –ся (after consonants [including й]) –сь (after vowels)				

DISCUSSION

Reflexive verbs are those ending in the particle –ся or –сь, with –ся occurring after consonants (including й) and –сь occurring after vowels. Many Russian verbs have both reflexive and non-reflexive forms. Some, like **нра́виться**, are never used without the reflexive particle.

Reflexive verbs cannot have an accusative direct object; from the historical standpoint, the direct object is the attached particle –ся or –сь, which is derived from the reflexive pronoun **себя́.** However, the accusative may be used if preceded by a preposition: **Он рассерди́лся на Ни́ну** *He got mad at Nina.*

Most of the other cases may accompany reflexive verbs, both with and without prepositions, for example:

GEN	Он бои́тся **Ни́ны.**	He's afraid of Nina.
DAT	Он удивля́ется **Ни́не.**	He's amazed at Nina.
DAT	Обрати́сь к **О́сипову**!	Consult Osipov!
INSTR	Хоти́те познако́миться с **ней**?	Want to meet her?

Note on pronunciation: Many Russian speakers do not pronounce the с of –ся or –сь soft, despite its spelling. It should *never* be pronounced soft in the infinitive and third person forms where –ть and –т precede it. In this position it combines in a long, hard, unreleased [c], which we indicate in the transcription by [tc]. Thus, for example, both the infinitive **верну́ться** and the third person plural **верну́тся** are pronounced exactly alike: [γirnútcə].

Reflexive verbs encountered and drilled in this lesson are given below in all their forms.

1. First conjugation

обраща́ться (ipfv) (к + dat) *to turn to, consult, go to*
PAST обраща́лся, обраща́лась, обраща́лось, обраща́лись
PRES обраща́юсь, обраща́ешься, –ется, –емся, –етесь, –ются
IMPER обраща́йся! обраща́йтесь!

возвраща́ться (ipfv) (к + dat) *to return, come back*
PAST возвраща́лся, возвраща́лась, –ось, –ись
PRES возвраща́юсь, возвраща́ешься, –ется, –емся, –етесь, –ются
IMPER возвраща́йся! возвраща́йтесь!

верну́ться (pfv) (imperfective **возвраща́ться**) *to return, come back*
PAST верну́лся, верну́лась, –ось, –ись
FUT верну́сь, вернёшься, –ётся, –ёмся, –ётесь, –у́тся
IMPER верни́сь! верни́тесь!

каза́ться (ipfv) (mostly used impersonally with the dative) *to seem, appear*
PAST каза́лся, каза́лась, –ось, –ись
PRES кажу́сь, ка́жешься, –ется, –емся, –етесь, –утся
IMPER (not used)

2. Second conjugation

обрати́ться (pfv) (imperfective **обраща́ться**) *to turn to, consult, go to*
PAST обрати́лся, обрати́лась, –ось, –ись
FUT обращу́сь, обрати́шься, –йтся, –ймся, –йтесь, –я́тся
IMPER обрати́сь! обрати́тесь!

серди́ться (ipfv) (**на** + acc) *to become angry, to get mad*
PAST серди́лся, серди́лась, –ось, –ись
FUT сержу́сь, се́рдишься, –ится, –имся, –итесь, –ятся
IMPER [не] серди́сь! [не] серди́тесь!

рассерди́ться (pfv) (conjugated like the imperfective **серди́ться**) *to become angry, to get mad*

станови́ться (ipfv) *to stand, get, become*
PAST станови́лся, станови́лась, –ось, –ись
PRES становлю́сь, стано́вишься, –ится, –имся, –итесь, –ятся
IMPER станови́сь! станови́тесь!

случи́ться (pfv) (used only in the third person) *to happen*
PAST случи́лся, случи́лась, –ось, –ись
PRES случи́тся, случа́тся

Нра́виться, понра́виться

MODELS

Что́ вам понра́вилось?	What did you like?
— Мне́ понра́вился «Евге́ний Оне́гин».	I liked *Eugene Onegin*.
— Мне́ понра́вилась «Война́ и мир».	I liked *War and Peace*.
— Мне́ понра́вилось нача́ло э́того фи́льма.	I liked the beginning of the movie.
— Мне́ понра́вились ру́сские пе́сни.	I liked the Russian songs.
Кто́ тебе́ понра́вился?	Whom did you like?
— Мне́ понра́вился Влади́мир.	I liked Vladimir.
— Мне́ понра́вилась Ната́ша.	I liked Natasha.
— Мне́ понра́вились твои́ сёстры.	I liked your sisters.
Как вам понра́вился фи́льм?	How did you like the movie?
— Нам фи́льм о́чень понра́вился.	We really enjoyed the movie.
Как вам понра́вилась карти́на?	How did you like the picture?
— Нам карти́на о́чень понра́вилась.	We really enjoyed the picture.

Как вам понра́вилось её пе́ние?	How did you like her singing?
— На́м её пе́ние о́чень понра́вилось.	We really enjoyed her singing.
Как ва́м понра́вились пласти́нки?	How did you like the records?
— На́м пласти́нки о́чень понра́вились.	We really enjoyed the records.
Тебе́ нра́вится исто́рия?	Do you like history?
— Не́т, мне́ не нра́вится исто́рия.	No, I don't care for history.
Тебе́ нра́вится фи́зика?	Do you like physics?
— Не́т, мне́ не нра́вится фи́зика.	No, I don't care for physics.
Тебе́ нра́вятся его́ стихи́?	Do you like his poetry?
— Не́т, мне́ не нра́вятся его́ стихи́.	No, I don't like his poetry.
Тебе́ нра́вятся э́ти карти́ны?	Do you like these pictures?
— Не́т, мне́ не нра́вятся э́ти карти́ны.	No, I don't like these pictures.
Ей понра́вится э́тот костю́м.	She'll like this suit.
_____ э́тот пода́рок.	_____ this present.
_____ э́та пласти́нка.	_____ this record.
_____ э́та ко́мната.	_____ this room.
_____ э́та у́лица.	_____ this street.
_____ э́то пла́тье.	_____ this dress.
Ей понра́вятся э́ти пе́сни.	She'll like these songs.
_____ э́ти кни́ги.	_____ these books.
_____ э́ти ча́шки.	_____ these cups.
Вы́ мне́ нра́витесь.	I like you.
О́н мне́ нра́вится.	I like him.
Ты́ мне́ нра́вишься.	I like you.
Она́ мне́ нра́вится.	I like her.
Они́ мне́ нра́вятся.	I like them.
Я́ ва́м нра́влюсь?	Do you like me?
Мы́ ва́м нра́вимся?	Do you like us?

■ REPETITION DRILL

Repeat the given models illustrating **нра́виться, понра́виться**. Note that the one who performs the liking is in the dative case and that the object of the liking is in the nominative case in Russian.

■ QUESTION-ANSWER DRILL

What don't you like?
I don't like this camera.
Что́ ва́м не нра́вится?
Мне́ не нра́вится э́тот аппара́т.
Что́ ему́ не нра́вится?
Ему́ не нра́вится э́тот аппара́т.
(ей, тебе, им, ему, вам)

■ STRUCTURE REPLACEMENT DRILLS

1. *We really like that girl.*
   We really liked that girl.
   На́м о́чень нра́вится э́та де́вушка.
   На́м о́чень нра́вилась э́та де́вушка.
   На́м о́чень нра́вится тво́й бра́т.
   На́м о́чень нра́вился тво́й бра́т.

■ STRUCTURE REPLACEMENT DRILL

He loves to sing loudly.
He likes to sing loudly.
О́н лю́бит гро́мко пе́ть.
Ему́ нра́вится гро́мко пе́ть.
Я́ люблю́ гро́мко пе́ть.
Мне́ нра́вится гро́мко пе́ть.
(мы, она, ты, они, я, он, мы)

(ваша сестра, ваш аппарат, эта пластинка, этот очерк, ваш сосед, ваша
соседка)

2. *He'll like this novel.*
He liked this novel.
Ему́ понра́вится э́тот рома́н.
Ему́ понра́вился э́тот рома́н.
Ему́ понра́вится на́ше о́зеро.
Ему́ понра́вилось на́ше о́зеро.

(их кварти́ра, её пе́ние, э́ти певцы́, её исполне́ние, её карти́ны, Оде́сса, Влади-восто́к, Я́лта)

■ RESPONSE DRILLS

1. *She's reading* Doctor Zhivago.
She likes Doctor Zhivago.
Она́ чита́ет «До́ктора Жива́го».
Ей нра́вится «До́ктор Жива́го».
Она́ чита́ет стихи́ Пу́шкина.
Ей нра́вятся стихи́ Пу́шкина.

(рома́н Толсто́го, э́то сочине́ние, о́черк о США, рабо́ты студе́нтов, э́ту кни́гу, рома́ны, «Войну́ и мир», «Евге́ния Оне́гина»)

2. *They brought him kasha.*
He didn't like (or *care for*) *kasha.*
Ему́ принесли́ ка́шу.
Ка́ша ему́ не понра́вилась.
Ему́ принесли́ борщ.
Борщ ему́ не понра́вился.

(чай, атла́сы, ка́рту, портфе́ль, мазь, сту́лья, кни́гу, слова́рь)

■ SUBJECT REVERSAL DRILL

I don't like that doctor.
That doctor doesn't like me.
Э́тот до́ктор мне́ не нра́вится.
Я э́тому до́ктору не нра́влюсь.

Э́та убо́рщица мне́ не нра́вится.
Я э́той убо́рщице не нра́влюсь.

(она́, его́ сестра́, э́та учи́тельница, э́тот профе́ссор, Влади́мир, э́тот учи́тель)

DISCUSSION

The verb **нра́виться** (perfective **понра́виться**) is best translated into English as *to like, enjoy, care for,* but is structurally closer to the English *to appeal to.* Like **ну́жен,** it is used in nominative-dative constructions which appear backward to the English-speaking student: **Вы́ мне́ нра́витесь** *I like you.* (Lit. *You appeal to me*).

As compared with **люби́ть** *to like, love, be fond of,* **нра́виться** expresses a milder attitude on the part of the speaker. **Нра́виться** is more typical of situations describing one's immediate emotional reaction, whereas **люби́ть** describes a more permanent emotional attitude on one's part.

Ва́м нра́вится э́тот рома́н?
— Да́. Я его́ о́чень люблю́. Мно́го ра́з его́ чита́л.

Do you like this novel?
Yes, I'm very fond of it. I've read it many times.

ЧТЕ́НИЕ И ПИСЬМО́

Бы́ло воскресе́нье, и Влади́мир предложи́л Ка́те пое́хать к его́ роди́телям в колхо́з. Ей давно́ хоте́лось с ни́ми познако́миться, посмотре́ть как они живут. Но в это воскресенье Кате надо было много работать. Тогда Владимир спросил насчёт следующего воскресенья. Катя была согласна, и они так и договорились.

Орлов только что пришёл с работы. Он очень устал, но его жена этого не понимает. Она хочет пойти в магазин и купить себе платье. Орлов говорит ей, что он не хочет идти в магазин, что ему это совсем не интересно. Он просит жену не сердиться, но она говорит, что он бездушный человек.

Осипов был болен, но теперь он чувствует себя гораздо лучше. Вчера доктор сказал, что ему уже можно читать, но не больше, чем полчаса в день. Он забыл об этом, и читал сегодня всё утро. Такая глупость! Ведь он всегда осторожен и точно делает всё, что говорит доктор.

— Интере́сно, кто стро́ил э́ту це́рковь?
— Не зна́ю, она́ о́чень ста́рая.
— Тепе́рь таки́х не стро́ят.
— Тепе́рь, по-мо́ему, церкве́й вообще́ не стро́ят.
— Не́т, стро́ят, но ма́ло и не таки́е, коне́чно, как э́та.
— А каки́е же?
— Не зна́ю. Ту́т в сосе́днем селе́, ка́жется, стро́ят. Поезжа́й и посмотри́.

— Зна́ете, в на́ш го́род прие́хал америка́нский вра́ч. Я́ вчера́ с ни́м познако́мился.

— Во́т интере́сно! О́н прие́хал сюда́ жи́ть?

— Не́т, о́н прие́хал посмотре́ть, ка́к рабо́тают на́ши врачи́.

— И что́ ж, ему́ понра́вилось?

— Не зна́ю, мы́ бо́льше говори́ли об Аме́рике, че́м о врача́х.

— Фили́пп, покажи́те мне́ ва́ш аппара́т, пожа́луйста.

— Вы́ ещё не ви́дели америка́нских аппара́тов?

— Не́т. О́н хорошо́ снима́ет?

— Да́, я дово́лен. По́мните, я ва́м пока́зывал цветны́е сни́мки?

— А, по́мню: ви́ды ле́са, о́зера, поле́й.

— Неплохи́е, пра́вда?

— Да́, о́чень хоро́шие. У меня́ таки́е не выхо́дят.

— А како́й у ва́с аппара́т?

— «Зо́ркий».

— Вы́ ча́сто хо́дите пешко́м?

— Не́т, о́чень ре́дко.

— Во́т сра́зу ви́дно, что вы́ америка́нец.

— А почему́ вы́ ду́маете, что америка́нцы ма́ло хо́дят?

— Мне́ та́к говори́ли. И тури́сты из Аме́рики всегда́ то́лько е́здят, никогда́ не хо́дят.

— Ну́, тури́сты — э́то друго́е де́ло. Хотя́ вы́ пра́вы: мы́ лю́бим е́здить.

Оле́г о́чень хоро́ший студе́нт, и това́рищи обраща́ются к нему́, когда́ не понима́ют ле́кций. О́н и́м всегда́ помога́ет. Но сего́дня о́н не по́мнит, о чём говори́л профе́ссор. О́н всё вре́мя смотре́л на Зи́ну и ничего́ не слы́шал. Э́то о́чень стра́нно. Впро́чем, э́то со вся́ким мо́жет случи́ться.

Воло́дя ду́мает, что пора́ идти́ домо́й. Сейча́с уже́ по́здно, о́н уста́л, а за́втра ему́ на́до мно́го рабо́тать. Но Га́ля не хо́чет идти́ домо́й, ей хо́чется ещё погуля́ть. Ей нра́вится э́тот ле́с и о́зеро, во́здух тако́й све́жий. Но что де́лать? Е́сли на́до идти́, то́, коне́чно, она́ пойдёт.

— Ну́ во́т, аппара́т гото́в. Сади́сь, Ка́тя, зде́сь. Я́ хочу́ ви́деть тебя́, э́то о́зеро и на́ш до́м.

— Всё сра́зу?

— Коне́чно.

— А сни́мки бу́дут цветны́е?

— Да́. То́лько сиди́, пожа́луйста, свобо́дно и не ду́май о то́м, что я́ тебя́ снима́ю.

— Хорошо́, я бу́ду ду́мать об экза́менах, и у меня́ бу́дет ску́чный ви́д.

— Не говори́ глу́пости. Ду́май, наприме́р о та́нцах вчера́ в клу́бе.

— И ка́к я та́м упа́ла? Ну́, не серди́сь. Я́ бу́ду ду́мать о тебе́. Хо́чешь?

— Во́т э́то друго́е де́ло. Э́то мне́ нра́вится.

PREPARATION FOR CONVERSATION   **За грибáми**

грúб, –á
за (*plus* instr)
Поéдем в лéс за грибáми.
   найтú (pfv I) (*like* пойтú)
Смотрú, какúе я нашёл грибы́!
   тóчка
   с (*plus* instr)
Смотрú, какúе я нашёл грибы́:
крáсные с бéлыми тóчками.

   вы́бросить (pfv II)
      вы́брошу, вы́бросишь, –ят
Это плохúе, вы́брось!

Вóт досáда!

   растú (I) (pres растý, растёшь, –ýт;
      past рóс, рослá, –ó, –ú)
Úх тýт мнóго растёт!
   ёлка
А úх тýт под ёлками мнóго
растёт.

   рукá, –ú (acc sg рýку); рýки, рýк
   вы́тереть (pfv I) (fut вы́тру, вы́трешь,
      –ут; past вы́тер, вы́терла, –о, –и)
Вы́три рýки.
   платóк, –ткá
Вóт платóк, вы́три рýки.
   подéлать (pfv I) (*like* дéлать)
   чтó ж подéлаешь!
Чтó ж подéлаешь! Вóт платóк,
вы́три рýки.

   чтó-нибудь (gen чегó-нибудь)
А ты́, Тáня, нашлá чтó-нибудь?

mushroom
   for, after (to get); behind, beyond, across
Let's go to the woods after mushrooms.
   to find
Look what mushrooms I found!
   dot, point, period
   with, together with, and
Look what mushrooms I found: red ones
   with white dots!

   to throw out (*or* away), discard

Those are bad; throw them away!

Darn it!

   to grow

There are lots of them growing here!
   fir tree, spruce tree; Christmas tree
There are lots of them growing here under
   the fir trees.

   hand, arm
   to wipe, wipe off, wipe dry

Wipe your hands off.
   handkerchief, kerchief
Here's a handkerchief; wipe your hands off.
   to do
   it can't be helped! what can you do!
It can't be helped! Here's a handkerchief;
   wipe your hands off.

   anything
And how about you, Tanya, have you
   found anything?

◀ **Продажа грибов на ленинградском базаре.**

Да, бе́лые.

Оди́н большо́й и четы́ре ма́леньких.

А во́н то́т гри́б, хоро́ший?

дере́во, –а; дере́вья, –ьев

А во́н то́т гри́б, за де́ревом,
хоро́ший?

не́сколько (*plus* gen)
ещё не́сколько

Да́. А во́н та́м ещё не́сколько.
ли́ст, –а́; ли́стья, ли́стьев
под (*plus* instr)

А во́н та́м под ли́стьями
ещё не́сколько.

Я пойду́ посмотрю́.

трава́
А́й, что́ э́то ту́т в траве́?
ползти́ (I) (pres ползу́, –ёшь, –у́т;
past по́лз, ползла́, –о́, –и́)

А́й, что́ э́то ту́т в траве́ ползёт?

змея́, –й; зме́и, зме́й
Где́? Э́то змея́!

дли́нный
У́х, кака́я дли́нная!

па́лка
би́ть (I), бью́, бьёшь, бью́т
Бе́й её па́лкой!
скоре́е (*or* скоре́й)

Скоре́е! Бе́й её па́лкой!
ка́мень, ка́мня; –и, –е́й (m)
А я́ ка́мнем.
Скоре́е бе́й её па́лкой,
а я́ — ка́мнем.

убива́ть (I), убива́ю, –ешь, –ют
Оста́вьте её, заче́м убива́ть?
де́ти, дете́й
Оста́вьте её, де́ти, заче́м убива́ть?
пу́сть
Пу́сть она́ живёт.
Оста́вьте её, де́ти, заче́м убива́ть?
Пу́сть живёт.

уползти́ (pfv I) (*like* ползти́)
Ну́ во́т, змея́ уползла́.

Yes, white ones.

One big one and four little ones.

How about that mushroom over there;
is it a good one?

tree

How about that mushroom over there
behind the tree; is it a good one?

several, some, a few
a few more, several more, some more

Yes, and over yonder are a few more.
leaf
under, underneath, beneath;
near (a city)

And over yonder under the leaves are
a few more.

I'll go take a look.

grass
Hey, what's this in the grass here?
to be crawling (*or* creeping)

Hey, what's this crawling in the grass here?

snake?
Where? It's a snake!

long
Ooh, how long it is!

stick
to beat, hit, strike
Hit it with a stick!
quick, hurry up (*lit.* sooner,
faster, more quickly)

Quick! Hit it with a stick!
stone, rock
And I'll use a rock. (*Lit.* And I with a rock.)
Quick, hit it with a stick and I'll use
a rock.

to kill
Leave it alone; why kill it?
children
Leave it alone, children; why kill it?
let
Let it live!
Leave it alone, children; why kill it?
Let it live!

to crawl away, creep off
See now, the snake got away.

меша́ть (I)	to disturb, hinder, interfere, butt in; mix, stir
Ты́, ма́ма, всегда́ меша́ешь.	You're always butting in, mamma.
невозмо́жно	impossible
с тобо́й	with you
С тобо́й невозмо́жно ходи́ть в ле́с.	It's impossible going to the woods with you.
С тобо́й про́сто невозмо́жно ходи́ть в ле́с.	It's just impossible going to the woods with you.

SUPPLEMENT

сы́н, –а; сыновья́, сынове́й	son
Ско́лько у ва́с сынове́й?	How many sons do you have?
до́чь, до́чери; –и, –е́й	daughter
Ско́лько у ва́с дочере́й?	How many daughters do you have?
дя́дя, –и; –и, –ей	uncle
Ско́лько у ва́с дя́дей?	How many uncles do you have?
тётя, –и; –и, –ей	aunt
Ско́лько у ва́с тётей?	How many aunts do you have?
де́душка (gen pl де́душек)	grandfather
Где́ живёт ва́ш де́душка?	Where does your grandfather live?
ба́бушка (gen pl ба́бушек)	grandmother
Где́ живёт ва́ша ба́бушка?	Where does your grandmother live?
находи́ть (II) (*like* ходи́ть)	to find
Я́ всегда́ нахожу́ здесь грибы́.	I always find mushrooms here.
находи́ться (II), нахо́дится, нахо́дятся	to be located, to be situated
Где́ нахо́дится ва́ш колхо́з?	Where is your collective farm located?
за́ город [záɡərət]	to the country, out of town, to the suburbs
Пое́дем за́ город.	Let's drive to the country!
за́ городом [záɡərədəm]	out of town, in the country, in the suburbs
Мы́ живём за́ городом.	We live out of town *or* We live in the country.
коро́ткий	short
Я́ напишу́ ему́ коро́ткое письмо́.	I'll write him a short letter.
возмо́жный (adv возмо́жно)	possible
Возмо́жно, что о́н уже́ верну́лся.	It's possible he's already returned.

За гриба́ми

Сы́н 1 Смотри́, каки́е я́ нашёл грибы́: кра́сные с бе́лыми то́чками.

Ма́ть 2 Э́то плохи́е, вы́брось![1]

Сы́н 3 Во́т доса́да! А и́х ту́т под ёлками мно́го растёт!

Ма́ть 4 Что́ ж поде́лаешь! Возьми́ плато́к, вы́три ру́ки.[2,3] А ты́, Та́ня, нашла́ что́-нибудь?

До́чь 5 Да́, бе́лые.[4] Оди́н большо́й и четы́ре ма́леньких.

| Сын | 6 | Ма́ма, а во́н то́т гри́б, за де́ревом, хоро́ший? |

| Ма́ть | 7 | Да́. А во́н та́м под ли́стьями ещё не́сколько. |

| Дочь | 8 | Я́ пойду́ посмотрю́. Ай, что́ э́то ту́т в траве́ ползёт? |

| Сын | 9 | Где́? Э́то змея́! У́х, кака́я дли́нная! Скоре́е бе́й её па́лкой, а я́ — ка́мнем! |

| Ма́ть | 10 | Оста́вьте её, де́ти, заче́м убива́ть?[5] Пу́сть живёт! |

| Сын | 11 | Ну́ во́т, уползла́. Ты́, ма́ма, всегда́ меша́ешь. С тобо́й про́сто невозмо́жно ходи́ть в ле́с. |

NOTES

[1] Russians are great mushroom lovers and usually know how to tell a good mushroom from a bad one. The red ones with the white spots picked by the son are the poisonous **мухомо́ры** *toadstools* (lit. *flykillers*).

[2] After touching poisonous mushrooms one must wash, or at least wipe, one's hands clean.

[3] **Ру́ки** means both *hands* and *arms*; likewise **но́ги** means both *feet* and *legs*.

[4] **Бе́лый гри́б** *edible Boletus* is considered a delicacy by Russians. It has a brown cap which is spongy underneath. The mushroom is called *white* because of the color it acquires when dried; most other species turn dark.

[5] The noun **де́ти** *children* has an archaic singular form **дитя́** *baby, child*. In modern Russian the word used for *baby* or *child* is **ребёнок**; its grammatical plural **ребя́та** is used in the special sense of *kids, guys,* or *fellows*.

PREPARATION FOR CONVERSATION **Пиро́г с гриба́ми**

пиро́г, –а́	pirog (kind of pie)
пиро́г с гриба́ми	pirog filled with mushrooms
Вы́ лю́бите пиро́г с гриба́ми?	Do you like pirog with mushrooms?
стуча́ть (II), стучу́, –и́шь, –а́т	to knock, bang, rap, pound
Та́м, ка́жется, стуча́т.	Someone seems to be knocking.
Алёша! Та́м, ка́жется, стуча́т.	Alyosha, someone seems to be knocking.
Пойди́, пожа́луйста, откро́й.	Please go open the door.
оде́т, –а, –о, –ы	dressed
Я́ не оде́та.	I'm not dressed.
А́, э́то ты́, Лю́ба! Заходи́.	Ah, it's you Lyuba. Come in!
стира́ть (I)	to wash, launder
Ва́ля стира́ет.	Valya's doing the laundry.
Она́ сейча́с придёт.	She'll be right in.
мину́тка (var. of мину́та)	a minute
на мину́тку	for a minute (*or* moment)
Я́ на мину́тку.	I can only stay a moment.
с на́ми	with us, together with us

Я зашла́ пригласи́ть ва́с с на́ми пообе́дать.	I dropped in to invite you to have dinner with us.
Здра́вствуй, ми́лая.	Hello, dear.
Когда́ ты́ верну́лась?	When did you get back?
с детьми́	with the children, and the children
Когда́ ты́ с детьми́ верну́лась?	When did you and the children get back?
наза́д	ago, back
Ча́с наза́д.	An hour ago.
двухчасово́й	two-o'clock (adj), two-hour (adj)
Ча́с наза́д, двухчасовы́м по́ездом.	An hour ago, on the two-o'clock train.
ша́пка	cap
потеря́ть (pfv I), потеря́ю, –ешь, –ют	to lose
Пе́тя потеря́л ша́пку.	Petya lost his cap.
бы (unstressed particle)	would, would have
Мы́ бы ра́ньше верну́лись, но Пе́тя потеря́л ша́пку.	We'd have returned earlier, but Petya lost his cap.
прийти́сь (pfv I) (used with dat)	to have to, to be forced to
На́м придётся иска́ть ша́пку.	We'll have to look for the cap.
На́м пришло́сь иска́ть ша́пку.	We had to look for the cap.
Мы́ бы ра́ньше верну́лись, но Пе́тя потеря́л ша́пку, и на́м пришло́сь её иска́ть.	We'd have returned earlier, but Petya lost his cap and we had to hunt for it.
Ну́ ка́к? Мно́го грибо́в нашли́?	Well, how about it; did you find many mushrooms?
ма́сса	mass, lots, plenty, a great many
Ма́ссу.	Loads.
испе́чь (pfv I) (fut испеку́, испечёшь, испеку́т; past испёк, испекла́, –о́, –и́)	to bake
Я́ уже́ испекла́ пиро́г.	I've already baked a pirog.
свари́ть (pfv II), сварю́, сва́ришь, –ят	to cook (by boiling)
су́п	soup
Я́ уже́ испекла́ пиро́г и свари́ла су́п.	I've already baked a pirog and made soup.
Приходи́те к на́м на обе́д.	Come to our place for dinner.
Большо́е спаси́бо.	Thanks very much.
как то́лько	as soon as
Придём, как то́лько я́ ко́нчу стира́ть.	We'll come just as soon as I finish washing.
оста́ться (pfv I), оста́нусь, –ешься, –утся	to be left, to remain
А тебе́ ещё мно́го оста́лось?	And do you have much left to do?
руба́шка	shirt, slip
ю́бка	skirt
Не́т, одна́ ю́бка и две́ руба́шки.	No, one skirt and two shirts.
Ну́, конча́й скоре́й, и приходи́те.	Well, hurry and finish and come on over!
Бу́дем ва́с жда́ть.	We'll be expecting you.

са́хар	sugar
Вы́ пьёте ча́й с са́харом?	Do you drink your tea with sugar?
лимо́н	lemon
Я́ пью́ ча́й с лимо́ном.	I drink my tea with lemon.
уха́	fish soup, fish chowder
Мы́ о́чень лю́бим уху́.	We like fish chowder very much.
лапша́ (sg only)	noodles
су́п с лапшо́й	noodle soup
Ка́к ва́м нра́вится су́п с лапшо́й?	How do you like the noodle soup?
бульо́н	consommé, bouillon soup, broth
Принеси́те мне́, пожа́луйста, бульо́н.	Bring me consommé, please.
бу́лка	large roll, small loaf of French bread
Купи́те две́ бу́лки.	Buy two loaves of French bread.
бу́лочка	roll
Купи́те, пожа́луйста, бу́лочек.	Please buy some rolls.
Жена́ испекла́ э́ти бу́лочки.	My wife baked these rolls.
пече́нье	cookies
Я́ ва́м куплю́ пече́нья.	I'll buy you some cookies.
то́рт	cake
Како́й вку́сный то́рт!	What a delicious cake!
пе́чь (I) (*like* испе́чь)	to bake
Ва́ша жена́ ча́сто печёт?	Does your wife bake often?
вари́ть (II) (*like* свари́ть)	to cook (by boiling)
Вы́ уже́ ва́рите обе́д?	Are you already cooking dinner?
теря́ть (I) (*like* потеря́ть)	to lose, waste
Не теря́йте на э́то вре́мени.	Don't waste time on that.
тому́ наза́д	ago
Э́то случи́лось го́д тому́ наза́д.	It happened a year ago.
авторучка	fountain pen
Пиши́те авторучкой.	Write with a fountain pen.
ме́л	chalk
Пиши́те ме́лом.	Write with chalk.
недово́лен, –льна, –о, –ы	dissatisfied, displeased
О́н недово́лен результа́тами.	He's dissatisfied with the results.

Пиро́г с гриба́ми

Ва́ля (Валенти́на)
Алёша (Алексе́й, её му́ж)
Лю́ба (Любо́вь, и́х сосе́дка)

Ва́ля   1 Алёша! Та́м, ка́жется, стуча́т. Пойди́, пожа́луйста, откро́й. Я́ не оде́та.

Алёша   2 А́, э́то ты́, Лю́ба. Заходи́, Ва́ля стира́ет, она́ сейча́с придёт.

Люба	3	Я́ на мину́тку. Зашла́ пригласи́ть ва́с с на́ми пообе́дать.
Ва́ля	4	Здра́вствуй, ми́лая. Когда́ ты́ с детьми́ верну́лась?
Люба	5	Ча́с наза́д, двухчасовы́м по́ездом.[1] Мы́ бы ра́ньше верну́лись, но Пе́тя потеря́л ша́пку, и на́м пришло́сь её иска́ть.
Алёша	6	Ну́ ка́к? Мно́го грибо́в нашли́?
Люба	7	Ма́ссу. Я́ уже́ испекла́ пиро́г и свари́ла су́п.[2] Приходи́те к на́м на обе́д.
Ва́ля	8	С больши́м удово́льствием. Придём, как то́лько я́ ко́нчу стира́ть.
Алёша	9	А тебе́ ещё мно́го оста́лось?
Ва́ля	10	Не́т, одна́ ю́бка и две́ руба́шки.
Люба	11	Ну́, конча́й скоре́й, и приходи́те. Бу́дем ва́с жда́ть.

NOTES

[1] It is not uncommon for Russians to take a train to the country, and then go to the forest to pick berries or mushrooms, or just to hike.

[2] **Пиро́г** is a kind of pie, usually rectangular in shape, which contains any of various fillings, for example, meat, cabbage, mushrooms, rice, eggs, carrots, or any combination of these ingredients. The sweet variety with a fruit filling is called **сла́дкий пиро́г** *sweet pie* and usually does not have a crust on top. Small individual ones encased in dough are called **пирожки́** (singular **пирожо́к**) or, if slightly larger, **пироги́**.

Basic sentence patterns

1. Ке́м о́н дово́лен? — With whom is he pleased?
   — Тобо́й. — With you
   — Мно́й. — With me.
   — Ва́ми. — With you.
   — Влади́миром. — With Vladimir.
   — И́м. — With him.
   — Та́ней. — With Tanya.
   — Е́й (е́ю). — With her.
   — Студе́нтами. — With the students.
   — И́ми. — With them.

2. Че́м мне́ писа́ть? — What should I write with?
   — Э́тим карандашо́м. — Use this pencil.
   — Э́той автору́чкой. — Use this fountain pen.

Че́м мне наре́зать хле́б?	What should I cut the bread with?
— Э́тим ножо́м.	Use this knife.
Че́м мне вы́тереть ру́ки?	What should I wipe my hands with?
— Э́тим платко́м.	Use this handkerchief.
Че́м мне меша́ть су́п?	What am I to stir the soup with?
— Э́той ло́жкой.	Use this spoon.

3.
С ке́м оста́нутся де́ти?	With whom are the children going to stay?
— Со мно́й.	With me.
— С ма́терью.	With their mother.
— С роди́телями.	With their parents.
— С отцо́м.	With their father.
— С ба́бушкой.	With their grandmother.
— С дя́дей.	With their uncle.
— С де́душкой.	With their grandfather.
— С тётей.	With their aunt.

4.
Я́ пое́ду вме́сте с Оле́гом.	I'll go along (or together) with Oleg.
_____ с роди́телями.	_____ with my parents.
_____ с детьми́.	_____ with the children.
_____ с э́тими людьми́.	_____ with these people.
_____ с сы́ном.	_____ with my son.
_____ с до́черью.	_____ with my daughter.
_____ с ба́бушкой.	_____ with grandmother.

5.
Пиши́те карандашо́м.	Write with (or in) pencil.
_____ ме́лом.	_____ chalk.
_____ ру́чкой.	_____ pen.
_____ авторучкой.	_____ fountain pen.
_____ перо́м.	_____ pen.
Не стучи́ ножо́м!	Don't rap with your knife!
_____ ло́жкой!	_____ spoon!
_____ ви́лкой!	_____ fork!
Не стучи́те нога́ми!	Don't tap with your feet!
Наре́жь хле́б э́тим ножо́м!	Slice the bread with this knife!
_____ огурцы́_____!	____ the cucumbers_____!
Меша́йте су́п э́той деревя́нной ло́жкой!	Stir the soup with this wooden spoon!

6.
Вы́ пьёте ча́й с лимо́ном?	Do you drink your tea with lemon?
— Не́т, без лимо́на.	No, without lemon.
Вы́ пьёте ча́й с са́харом?	Do you drink your tea with sugar?
— Не́т, без са́хара.	No, without sugar.
Вы́ пьёте ча́й с молоко́м?	Do you drink your tea with milk?
— Не́т, без молока́.	No, without milk.
Вы́ пьёте ча́й с лимо́ном и са́харом?	Do you drink your tea with lemon and sugar?
— Не́т, без ничего́.	No, without anything.

7.
Ба́бушка испекла́ пиро́г с гриба́ми.	Grandmother baked a mushroom pirog.
_____ пиро́г с ры́бой.	_____ a fish pirog.
_____ два́ пирога́.	_____ two pirogs.
_____ не́сколько пирого́в.	_____ several pirogs.

Бабушка испекла булочки.

_____ булку.

_____ булки.

Grandmother baked rolls.

_____ a loaf of white bread.

_____ large rolls.

8. Жена сварила суп.

_____ вкусный суп.

_____ суп с лапшой.

_____ суп с грибами.

_____ бульон.

_____ борщ.

_____ лапшу.

My wife cooked soup.

_____ a delicious soup.

_____ noodle soup.

_____ soup with mushrooms.

_____ consommé.

_____ borsch.

_____ noodles.

9. Зина хочет с тобой познакомиться.
— Со мной?!
Познакомьтесь, это Филипп Грант,
  это Лев Николаевич.
Филипп, познакомься со Львом
  Николаевичем.
— Мы уже знакомы.
Лев Николаевич, познакомьтесь
  с Филиппом Грантом.
— Мы уже вчера познакомились.

Zina wants to meet you.
Me?
I'd like you to meet each other; Philip Grant,
  Lev Nikolaevich.
Philip, meet Lev Nikolaevich.

We're already acquainted.
Lev Nikolaevich, meet Philip Grant.

We already met yesterday.

10. Познакомь меня с Марией.

_____ с Сергеем.

_____ с твоими сыновьями.

_____ дочерьми.

_____ детьми.

Очень приятно с вами познакомиться.

Introduce me to Maria.

_____ Sergey.

_____ your sons.

_____ daughters.

_____ children.

I'm very glad to meet you.

Вы знакомы с моей книгой?

_____ с моим романом?

_____ с моими работами?

Are you familiar with my book?

_____ with my novel?

_____ with my works?

11. Он мне мешает.
Они мне мешают.
Я вам не мешаю?
Вы мне не мешаете.
Ты мне не мешаешь.

He bothers me.
They bother me.
I'm not disturbing you, am I?
You're not disturbing (*or* bothering) me.
You're not disturbing (*or* bothering) me.

12. Вы потеряете много времени.
Он потеряет _____.
Я потеряю _____.
Они потеряют _____.

You'll lose (*or* waste) a lot of time.
He'll lose (*or* waste)_____.
I'll lose (*or* waste)_____.
They'll lose (*or* waste)_____.

Он потерял шапку.
Она потеряла платок.
Они потеряли пять рублей.

He lost his cap.
She lost her [hand]kerchief.
They lost five rubles.

13. Нам придётся пойти в магазин.

_____ работать в субботу.

_____ искать работу.

_____ выбросить эти лимоны.

We'll have to go to the store.

_____ to work on Saturday.

_____ to look for work.

_____ to throw these lemons out.

Нам придётся стира́ть э́ти руба́шки.	We'll have to wash these shirts.
——————— оста́ться ту́т ещё неде́лю.	——————— to stay here another week.
——————— до́лго жда́ть.	——————— to wait a long time.
——————— и́х пригласи́ть.	——————— to invite them.

14. Óн стоя́л за де́ревом.　　　　He stood behind the tree.

——————— до́мом.	——————— the house.
——————— избо́й.	——————— the hut.
——————— кио́ском.	——————— the newsstand.
——————— столо́м.	——————— the table.
——————— две́рью.	——————— the door.
——————— дверьми́.	——————— the doors.

15. Ключи́ под две́рью.　　　　The keys are under the door.

——————— портфе́лем.	——————— the briefcase.
——————— коро́бкой.	——————— the box.
——————— журна́лом.	——————— the magazine.
——————— сни́мками.	——————— the snapshots.
——————— кни́гами.	——————— the books.

16. Гдé нахо́дится ва́ш до́м?　　Where's your house located?

— За́ городом.	Out of town.
— За ле́сом.	Beyond the forest.
— За па́рком.	Across the park.
— За о́зером.	Across the lake.

17. До́чь верну́лась неде́лю тому́ наза́д.　　The daughter returned a week ago.

——————— пя́ть неде́ль тому́ наза́д.	——————— five weeks ago.
——————— ме́сяц тому́ наза́д.	——————— a month ago.
——————— го́д тому́ наза́д.	——————— a year ago.
——————— два́ го́да тому́ наза́д.	——————— two years ago.

18. Мы́ договори́лись на сре́ду.　　We made a date for Wednesday.

——————— за́втра.	——————— tomorrow.
——————— сле́дующий понеде́льник.	——————— next Monday.
——————— сле́дующую пя́тницу.	——————— next Friday.
——————— ча́с.	——————— one.
——————— де́вять часо́в.	——————— nine o'clock.

Pronunciation practice: the unvoicing of ordinarily voiced consonants

The unvoicing of ordinarily voiced consonants in word final position.

A. The letter **б** pronounced [b] or [b̦]

The letter **б** pronounced [p]
The letters **бь** pronounced [p̦]

[x̦ébə] хле́ба	[x̦ép] хле́б
of the bread	bread
[rabí] рабы́	[ráp] ра́б
slaves	slave
[gólub̦i] го́луби	[gólup̦] го́лубь
pigeons	pigeon

B. The letter в pronounced [v] or [ɣ]

    [slévə] слéва
    on the left
    [slívə] слúва
    plum
    [ɣétɣi] вéтви
    branches

The letter в pronounced [f]
The letters вь pronounced [f]

    [léf] лéв
    lion
    [slif] слúв
    of plums
    [ɣétf] вéтвь
    branch

C. The letter г pronounced [g] or [g̦]

    [səpag̦í] сапогú
    high boots
    [vrag̦í] врагú
    enemies
    [kṇígə] кнúга
    book

The letter г pronounced [k]

    [sapók] сапóг
    high boot
    [vrák] врáг
    enemy
    [kṇík] кнúг
    of books

D. The letter д pronounced [d] or [d̦]

    [górədə] гóрода
    of the city
    [gódi̥] гóды
    years
    [m̦éd̦i] мéди
    of copper

The letter д pronounced [t]
The letters дь pronounced [ț]

    [gorət] гóрод
    city
    [gót] гóд
    year
    [m̦éț] мéдь
    copper

E. The letter ж pronounced [ž]

    [naží] ножú
    knives
    [kóži] кóжи
    hides

The letter ж pronounced [š]

    [nóš] нóж
    knife
    [kóš] кóж
    of hides

The unvoicing of ordinarily voiced consonants in a non-final position.

A. The letter б pronounced [b]

    [abd̦iráṭ] обдирáть
    to peel off
    [abžíṭ] обжúть
    to make livable

The letter б pronounced [p]

    [apṭiráṭ] обтирáть
    to wipe off
    [apšíṭ] обшúть
    to saw

B. The letter в pronounced [v]

    [vbáṛi] в бáре
    in a bar
    [vzór] взóр
    glance

The letter в pronounced [f]

    [fpáṛi] в пáре
    in a pair
    [fsór] в сóр
    into rubbish

C. The letter д pronounced [d]

    [pədgarój] под горóй
    at the foot of a mountain
    [padžíṭ] поджúть
    to heal up

The letter д pronounced [t]

    [pətkarój] под корóй
    under bark
    [patšíṭ] подшúть
    to line

Nouns in the instrumental case

The instrumental case without a preposition designates the means by which some action is accomplished. It may specify the tool, instrument, conveyance, agency, or means used to effect the act; or it may indicate the manner in which the act was accomplished.

Наре́жь хлеб **э́тим ножо́м**.	Cut the bread *with this knife*.
Че́м вы́ пи́шете, **карандашо́м**?	What are you writing with, *a pencil*?
Ка́к вы́ прие́хали, **по́ездом**?	How did you come? *By train?*

Several prepositions require the instrumental case, the most common of which is **с (со)** in the meaning *with, in accompaniment with*.

Я́ говори́л с отцо́м.	I was talking with father.
О́н пойдёт с Ко́лей.	He'll go along with Kolya.

Note: The preposition **с** must not be used to translate the English *with* in the sense of *by means of;* the instrumental case form alone expresses the English *with* in such situations: **Пиши́те ру́чкой!** *Write with a pen!*

NOUN ENDINGS IN THE INSTRUMENTAL CASE		
SINGULAR		PLURAL
Masculine and Neuter	*Feminine*	
–ом, –ём, –ем	**–ой, –ёй, –ей, –ью**	**–ами, –ями, –ьми́**

MODELS

Поговори́те с сосе́д**ом**.	Have a talk with your neighbor.
_____ с бра́т**ом**.	_____ your brother.
_____ с отцо́м.	_____ your father.
_____ с секретар**ём**.	_____ your secretary.
_____ с учи́тел**ем**.	_____ your teacher.
_____ с иностра́нц**ем**.	_____ the stranger.
_____ с америка́нц**ем**.	_____ the American.

Я́ нашёл биле́ты под стол**о́м**.	I found the tickets under the table.
_____ под письм**о́м**.	_____ under the letter.
_____ под словар**ём**.	_____ under the dictionary.
_____ под шка́ф**ом**.	_____ under the cupboard.
_____ под портфе́л**ем**.	_____ under the briefcase.
_____ под заявле́ни**ем**.	_____ under the application.
_____ под сочине́ни**ем**.	_____ under the composition.

Она́ верну́лась с газе́т**ой**.	She came back with the paper.
_____ с ры́б**ой**.	_____ with the fish.
_____ с кни́г**ой**.	_____ with the book.
_____ с вод**о́й**.	_____ with the water.
_____ с семь**ёй**.	_____ with her family.
_____ с квита́нци**ей**.	_____ with the receipt.

Она́ уже́ говори́ла с подру́гой.
_____ с сосе́дкой.
_____ с ба́бушкой.
_____ с учи́тельницей.
_____ с продавщи́цей.
_____ с певи́цей.

Она́ до́лго говори́ла с ма́терью.
_____ с до́черью.

Плато́к был под две́рью.
_____ под тетра́дью.
_____ под коро́бкой с ма́зью.

Не стучи́ карандашо́м!
_____ ножо́м!
_____ ме́лом!
_____ ло́жкой!
_____ ви́лкой!
_____ ного́й!
_____ па́лкой!

Я пойду́ за газе́тами.
_____ за огурца́ми.
_____ за бу́лочками.
_____ за лимо́нами.
_____ за кни́гами.
_____ за журна́лами.
_____ за ша́хматами.
_____ за словаря́ми.
_____ за сту́льями.

Я игра́л в ка́рты с това́рищами.
_____ со студе́нтами.
_____ с де́вушками.
_____ со студе́нтками.
_____ с сёстрами.
_____ с друзья́ми.
_____ с роди́телями.
_____ с бра́тьями.
_____ с сыновья́ми.
_____ с учителя́ми.
_____ с дочерьми́.
_____ с детьми́.

Вы дово́льны студе́нтами?
_____ студе́нтками?
_____ профессора́ми?
_____ учителя́ми?
_____ сосе́дями?
_____ секретаря́ми?

She has already talked with her friend.
_____ with her neighbor.
_____ with her grandmother.
_____ with her teacher.
_____ with the saleslady.
_____ with the singer.

She talked for a long time with her mother.
_____ with her daughter.

The handkerchief was under the door.
_____ under the notebook.
_____ under the box with
                                    ointment.

Don't rap with your pencil!
_____ knife!
_____ chalk!
_____ spoon!
_____ fork!
_____ foot!
_____ stick (or cane)!

I'll go get the papers.
_____ the cucumbers.
_____ the rolls.
_____ the lemons.
_____ the books.
_____ the magazines.
_____ the chess set.
_____ the dictionaries.
_____ the chairs.

I was playing cards with friends.
_____ with the students.
_____ with the girls.
_____ with the students.
_____ with my sisters.
_____ with my friends.
_____ with my parents.
_____ with my brothers.
_____ with my sons.
_____ with the teachers.
_____ with my daughters.
_____ with the children.

Are you pleased with the (or your) students?
_____ the (or your) students?
_____ the (or your) professors?
_____ the (or your) teachers?
_____ the (or your) neighbors?
_____ the (or your) secretaries?

Here's chalk.
Write with chalk.
Во́т ме́л.
Пиши́те ме́лом.

Во́т авторучка.
Пиши́те авторучкой.
(каранда́ш, перо́, ру́чка, ме́л, авторучка)

■ CUED SUBSTITUTION DRILLS

1. (*bookshelf*) *He found his cap behind the bookshelf.*
   (по́лка) Óн нашёл ша́пку за **по́лкой.**
   (шка́ф) Óн нашёл ша́пку за **шка́фом.**
   (две́рь, изба́, до́м, буфе́т, це́рковь, де́рево, коро́бка, я́щик)

2. (*sideboard*) *Did you look under the sideboard?*
   (буфе́т) Вы́ иска́ли под **буфе́том?**
   (ли́стья) Вы́ иска́ли под **ли́стьями?**
   (окно́, шка́ф, де́рево, тетра́ди, коро́бка, сту́лья, сто́л)

■ STRUCTURE REPLACEMENT DRILLS

1. *Go with your brother.*
   Go with your brothers.
   Поезжа́й с бра́том!
   Поезжа́й с бра́тьями!
   Поезжа́й с подру́гой!
   Поезжа́й с подру́гами!
   (с америка́нцем, с това́рищем, с пе-
   ви́цей, с америка́нкой, с певцо́м, с тури́-
   стом, с секретарём, с учи́телем, с про-
   во́дником)

2. *I'm acquainted with her uncles.*
   I'm acquainted with her uncle.
   Я́ знако́м с её дя́дями.
   Я́ знако́м с её дя́дей.
   Я́ знако́м с её бра́тьями.
   Я́ знако́м с её бра́том.
   (тётями, подру́гами, друзья́ми, сёстра-
   ми, сосе́дями, учи́тельницами, сосе́д-
   ками, дя́дями)

3. *He returned with the newspapers.*
   He returned with the newspaper.
   Óн верну́лся с газе́тами.
   Óн верну́лся с газе́той.
   Óн верну́лся со словаря́ми.
   Óн верну́лся со словарём.
   (ка́ртами, журна́лами, заявле́ниями,
   сни́мками, па́лками, биле́тами,
   бу́лками, квита́нциями)

4. *I'll stop by for my neighbors.*
   I'll stop by for my neighbor.
   Я́ зайду́ за сосе́дками.
   Я́ зайду́ за сосе́дкой.
   Я́ зайду́ за това́рищами.
   Я́ зайду́ за това́рищем.
   (студе́нтами, америка́нцами, сосе́дями,
   подру́гами, учи́тельницами, друзья́ми,
   певи́цами, доктора́ми)

■ RESPONSE DRILLS

1. *We have no milk.*
   I'll go get the milk.
   У на́с не́т молока́.
   Я́ пойду́ за молоко́м.
   У на́с не́т бу́лочек.
   Я́ пойду́ за бу́лочками.
   (хле́ба, огурцо́в, са́хара, воды́, ча́я,
   бу́лки, пече́нья, ры́бы, лимо́нов)

2. *Grandfather knows the way.*
   Follow Grandfather.
   Де́душка зна́ет доро́гу.
   Иди́ за де́душкой.
   Ю́рий зна́ет доро́гу.
   Иди́ за Ю́рием.
   (его́ оте́ц, его́ де́ти, его́ ба́бушка,
   Евге́ний, его́ дя́дя, его́ роди́тели, его́
   тётя, сосе́д, америка́нец)

1. *Is herring sold here?*
   Yes, this is the line for herring.
   Тут продаю́т селёдку?
   Да́, э́то о́чередь за селёдкой.
   Тут продаю́т лимо́ны?
   Да́, э́то о́чередь за лимо́нами.
   (хлеб, сахар, билеты, рубашки, молоко, лимонад, платки, пластинки, печенье)

2. *Don't you have a fountain pen?*
   I don't like to write with a fountain pen.
   У тебя́ не́т автор́учки?
   Я́ не люблю́ писа́ть автор́учкой.
   У тебя́ не́т карандаша́?
   Я́ не люблю́ писа́ть карандашо́м.
   (нет ручки, нет пера, нет мела, нет авторучки, нет карандаша)

3. *Is Alyosha going too?*
   Yes, Alyosha and I are going together.
   Алёша то́же е́дет?
   Да́, мы́ с Алёшей е́дем вме́сте.
   Тво́й бра́т то́же е́дет?
   Да́, мы́ с бра́том е́дем вме́сте.
   (дети, Люба, твой дядя, Таня, твой отец, твои родители, врач, Сергей, твоя мама)

1. *He has met Zina.*
   Óн познако́мился с Зи́ной.
   Óн познако́мился с Зи́ной.
   ___ (пригласи́л) _____.
   Óн пригласи́л Зи́ну.
   _____ (её де́душку).
   ___ (знако́м с) _____.
   ___ (жда́л) _____.
   _____ (дете́й).
   ___ (игра́л с) _____.
   ___ (иска́л) _____.
   _____ (грибы́).
   ___ (свари́л су́п с) _____.

2. *I saw my uncle.*
   Я уви́дел дя́дю.
   Я́ уви́дел дя́дю.
   ___ (гуля́л с) _____.
   Я́ гуля́л с дя́дей.
   ___ (встре́тил) _____.
   _____ (друзе́й).
   ___ (пое́хал с) _____.
   ___ (пригласи́л) _____.
   _____ (её отца́).
   ___ (познако́мился с) ___.
   ___ (узна́л) _____.
   _____ (Серге́я).
   ___ (рабо́тал с) _____.

DISCUSSION

INSTRUMENTAL SINGULAR OF NOUNS		
стóл- and окнó-nouns stressed –óм, –ём unstressed –ом, –ем	**женá-nouns** –óй, –ёй –ой, –ей	**двéрь-nouns** only –ью (never stressed)
столо́м словарём	жено́й семьёй	две́рью
угло́м учи́телем	зимо́й змеёй	Любо́вью
авто́бусом Никола́ем	сестро́й ле́кцией	о́чередью
ме́лом му́жем	душо́й исто́рией	тетра́дью
ножо́м америка́нцем	пого́дой Ната́шей	ве́щью
карандашо́м па́рнем	по́чтой Воло́дей	ма́терью
ключо́м собра́нием	кни́гой неде́лей	до́черью
перо́м пла́тьем	ша́пкой Мари́ей	
де́лом вре́менем	Зи́ной уда́чей	

1. Hard-stem **стол-** and **окно́-**nouns have the instrumental singular ending **–ом**; soft-stem **стол-** and **окно́-**nouns have the ending **–ём** if stressed, **–ем** if unstressed. Stems ending in **ч, щ, ш, ж,** and **ц** spell their ending **–о́м** if stressed and **–ем** if unstressed. Compare **борщо́м** with **това́рищем**.

2. Hard-stem **жена́-**nouns have the instrumental singular ending **–ой**; soft-stem **жена́-**nouns have the ending **–е́й** if stressed, **–ей** if unstressed. Stems ending in **ч, щ, ш, ж,** and **ц** spell their ending **–о́й** if stressed and **–ей** if unstressed. Compare **душо́й** with **ка́шей**. There are also alternate endings **–ою, –ёю,** and **–ею** which are mostly encountered in literary works: **жено́ю, семьёю,** and **Ната́шею**.

3. All **дверь-**nouns have the instrumental singular ending **–ью**, always unstressed.

4. **Вре́мя-** and **и́мя-**nouns take the unstressed instrumental singular ending **–ем**: **вре́менем** and **и́менем**.

INSTRUMENTAL PLURAL OF NOUNS	
Hard stems and stems ending in **ч** *and* **щ** **–ами**	*Soft stems* **–ями**
стола́ми жёнами о́кнами города́ми доктора́ми сёстрами ножа́ми ключа́ми това́рищами	учителя́ми неде́лями роди́телями сочине́ниями бра́тьями сту́льями зда́ниями

1. Nouns which take **–ах** in the prepositional plural and **–ам** in the dative plural take **–ами** in the instrumental plural. Their stress is identical in all three cases: **стола́х, стола́м, стола́ми; жёнах, жёнам, жёнами.**

2. Nouns which take **–ях** in the prepositional plural and **–ям** in the dative plural take **–ями** in the instrumental plural. Their stress is also identical in all three cases: **учителя́х, учителя́м, учителя́ми; бра́тьях, бра́тьям, бра́тьями.**

3. The nouns **дверь** and **дочь** have an alternate instrumental plural ending **–ьми**: **дверьми́** (or **дверя́ми**), **дочерьми́** (or **дочеря́ми**).

4. The nouns **лю́ди** *people* and **де́ти** *children* have *only* the instrumental plural ending **–ьми**: **людьми́** and **детьми́**.

The instrumental of кто́, что́, the personal pronouns, and the reflexive personal pronoun себя́

NOM	кто́	что́	я́	ты́	(no nom)	о́н, оно́	она́	мы́	вы́	они́
INSTR	ке́м	че́м	мно́й	тобо́й	собо́й	и́м, (ни́м)	ею, (не́й)	на́ми	ва́ми	и́ми, (ни́мн)

Notes

1. Third person alternate forms **ни́м, не́й,** and **ни́ми** occur only with prepositions, for example, **с ни́м, за ни́м, с не́й, за не́й, с ни́ми, за ни́ми.**

2. In addition to **мно́й**, **тобо́й**, **собо́й**, and **не́й**, there are also the alternate instrumental forms **мно́ю**, **тобо́ю**, **собо́ю**, and **не́ю**. These are encountered primarily in literature, especially poetry.

MODELS

Я́ хочу́ с **ни́м** поговори́ть.	I want to have a talk with him.
_____ с **не́й** _____.	_____ with her.
_____ с **ва́ми** _____.	_____ with you.
_____ с **ни́ми** _____.	_____ with them.
_____ с **тобо́й** _____.	_____ with you.
Ре́ктор хо́чет с **на́ми** поговори́ть.	The chancellor wants to have a talk with us.
_____ **со мно́й** _____.	_____ with me.
Возьми́те с **собо́й** каранда́ш и тетра́дь.	Take a pencil and a notebook along (*lit.* with yourself).
С **че́м** вы́ пьёте ча́й?	What do you take in your tea? *or* With what do you drink tea?
— С молоко́м.	Milk.
С **ке́м** вы́ хоти́те говори́ть?	With whom do you want to speak?
— С **ва́ми**.	With you.
Че́м вы́ пи́шете, карандашо́м?	What are you writing with, a pencil?
Ке́м вы́ дово́льны? — **Ва́ми**.	With whom are you pleased? You.
Я́ **собо́й** недово́лен.	I'm dissatisfied with myself.
Ке́м вы́ недово́льны, **мно́й**?	With whom are you dissatisfied, me?
— Не́т, **и́м**.	No, him.
— Не́т, **е́ю**.	No, her.
— Не́т, **собо́й**.	No, myself.

■ CUED QUESTION-ANSWER DRILL

With whom will she go?
With him.

(о́н) С ке́м она́ пойдёт?
    С ни́м.
(я́) С ке́м она́ пойдёт?
    Со мно́й.

(они́, она́, мы́, я́, о́н, вы́, она́, ты́, я́)

■ QUESTION-ANSWER DRILLS

1. *Do you know Oleg?*
   No, I don't know him.
   Ты́ знако́м с Оле́гом?
   Не́т, я́ с ни́м не знако́м.
   Ты́ знако́м с Ва́лей?
   Не́т, я́ с не́й не знако́м.
      (с Ю́рием, с её сосе́дями, с америка́н-
      цем Гра́нтом, с его́ сёстрами, с его́
      ба́бушкой, с его́ де́душкой, с его́ дя́дей,
      с его́ тётей)

2. *Is he pleased with the exams?*
   Yes, he is.
   О́н дово́лен экза́менами?
   Да́, о́н и́ми дово́лен.
   О́н дово́лен тобо́й?
   Да́, о́н мно́й дово́лен.
      (учи́тельницей, шофёром, детьми́,
      мно́й, рабо́той, ва́ми, учи́телем, собо́й,
      на́ми, студе́нтами)

She's displeased with her son.
She's displeased with him.
Она́ сы́ном недово́льна.
Она́ и́м недово́льна.
Она́ сестро́й недово́льна.
Она́ е́ю недово́льна.
   (детьми́, убо́рщицей, вахтёром,
   студе́нтами, учи́телем, до́черью)

I was sitting behind you.
You were sitting behind me.
Я́ сиде́л за ва́ми.
Вы́ сиде́ли за мно́й.
Мы́ сиде́ли за не́й.
Она́ сиде́ла за на́ми.
Вы сиде́ли за не́й.
Он сиде́л за не́й.
Ты сиде́л за не́й.
Они сиде́ли за не́й.
Я сиде́л за не́й.
Мы сиде́ли за не́й.

The instrumental of э́тот, че́й, and the possessive modifiers

SINGULAR		PLURAL
Masculine and Neuter	*Feminine*	
–им	–ой, –ей	–ими

MODELS

Не говори́те с э́тим америка́нцем.
————————— студе́нтом.
————————— тури́стом.
————— с э́той америка́нкой.
————————— студе́нткой.
————— с э́тими студе́нтами.
————————— америка́нцами.
————————— тури́стами.

Don't talk to that American.
————————— student.
————————— tourist.
————————— American woman.
————————— student.
————————— those students.
————————— Americans.
————————— tourists.

С чьи́м дру́гом вы́ танцева́ли?
————— бра́том —————————?
С чье́й до́черью —————————?
————— сестро́й —————————?
С чьи́ми друзья́ми —————?
————— дочерьми́ —————?

Whose friend did you dance with?
————— brother —————————?
————— daughter —————————?
————— sister —————————?
————— friends —————————?
————— daughters —————————?

Де́ти оста́нутся со свои́м отцо́м.
————————— со свое́й ма́терью.
————————— со свои́ми роди́телями.

The children will stay with their father.
————————— with their mother.
————————— with their parents.

Они́ до́лго говори́ли с мои́м бра́том.
————————— с мои́м отцо́м.
————————— с мои́м дя́дей.[1]
————————— с мои́м де́душкой.[1]

They talked with my brother for a long time.
————— with my father —————————.
————— with my uncle —————————.
————— with my grandfather —————————.

---

[1] Note that although **дя́дя** and **де́душка** are **жена́**-class nouns and decline as such, they are still treated as masculine in terms of agreement.

    Мо́й де́душка жи́л в Москве́.   My grandfather lived in Moscow.
    Вы́ говори́ли с мои́м дя́дей?   Did you talk with my uncle?
This is true of all such **жена́**-class nouns referring to males, for example, **мужчи́на, Ко́ля,** and **Воло́дя.**

Они́ до́лго говори́ли с мое́й сестро́й. | They talked with my sister for a long time.
_____ с мое́й ма́терью. | _____ with my mother _____.
_____ с мои́ми роди́телями. | _____ with my parents _____.

Учи́тель не о́чень дово́лен твои́м о́черком. | The teacher isn't very happy with your essay.
_____ твои́м | _____ with your
сочине́нием. | composition.
_____ твое́й рабо́той. | _____ with your work.
_____ твои́ми отве́тами. | _____ with your answers.

За на́шим до́мом растёт мно́го дере́вьев. | There are lots of trees growing behind our house.
За на́шим общежи́тием _____. | _____ behind our
| dormitory.
За на́шей избо́й _____. | _____ behind our hut.
За на́шими дома́ми _____. | _____ behind our houses.

■ REPETITION DRILL

Repeat the given models, noting the pattern of endings in the instrumental case.

■ STRUCTURE REPLACEMENT DRILLS

1. *I'm acquainted with your uncle.*
   Я знако́м с ва́шим дя́дей.
   Я знако́м с твои́м дя́дей.
   Я знако́м с ва́шей тётей.
   Я знако́м с твое́й тётей.
   (роди́телями, сосе́дкой, де́душкой,
   подру́гой, друзья́ми, ма́мой, семьёй)

2. *Alyosha is satisfied with my work.*
   Alyosha is satisfied with your work.
   Алёша дово́лен мое́й рабо́той.
   Алёша дово́лен ва́шей рабо́той.
   Алёша дово́лен мои́м сочине́нием.
   Алёша дово́лен ва́шим сочине́нием.
   (игро́й, о́черком, кни́гой, стиха́ми,
   рома́ном, ку́рсом, ле́кцией)

3. *Did you talk with your father?*
   Вы говори́ли с ва́шим отцо́м?
   Вы говори́ли со свои́м отцо́м?
   Вы говори́ли с ва́шими друзья́ми?
   Вы говори́ли со свои́ми друзья́ми?
   (проводнико́м, сосе́дом, сосе́дями,
   ре́ктором, секретарём, студе́нтами)

4. *We'll go with her uncle.*
   We'll go with our uncle.
   Мы пое́дем с её дя́дей.
   Мы пое́дем с на́шим дя́дей.
   Мы пое́дем с её това́рищами.
   Мы пое́дем с на́шими това́рищами.
   (учи́телем, детьми́, друзья́ми,
   ребя́тами, сы́ном, тётей)

■ EXPANSION DRILLS

1. *The newsstand stood behind the school.*
   The newsstand stood behind this school.
   Кио́ск стоя́л за шко́лой.
   Кио́ск стоя́л за э́той шко́лой.
   Кио́ск стоя́л за рестора́ном.
   Кио́ск стоя́л за э́тим рестора́ном.
   (дере́вьями, до́мом, зда́нием,
   гости́ницей, теа́тром, клу́бом)

2. *The letter is under the newspaper.*
   The letter is under this newspaper.
   Письмо́ под газе́той.
   Письмо́ под э́той газе́той.
   Письмо́ под журна́лом.
   Письмо́ под э́тим журна́лом.
   (ка́ртой, ка́ртами, коро́бкой, кни́гой,
   словарём, заявле́нием, квита́нциями,
   бума́гой)

1. *That fellow bothers me.*
   What am I to do with that fellow?
   Э́тот па́рень мне́ меша́ет.
   Что́ мне́ де́лать с э́тим па́рнем?
   Э́та студе́нтка мне́ меша́ет.
   Что́ мне́ де́лать с э́той студе́нткой?
     (де́ти, сосе́д, де́вушка, лю́ди,
     господи́н, гра́ждане, певи́ца, челове́к)

2. *This soup doesn't taste good.*
   What should be done with this soup?
   Э́тот су́п невку́сный.
   Что́ де́лать с э́тим су́пом?
   Э́та ры́ба невку́сная.
   Что́ де́лать с э́той ры́бой?
     (огурцы́, ка́ша, бульо́н, пече́нье, грибы́,
     уха́, бо́рщ, лапша́)

3. *An accident happened to her son.*
   Whose son?
   С её сы́ном случи́лось несча́стье.
   С чьи́м сы́ном?
   С её тётей случи́лось несча́стье.
   С чье́й тётей?
     (роди́телями, сестро́й, де́душкой, дя́дей,
     ба́бушкой, бра́тьями, отцо́м)

DISCUSSION

э́тот, че́й, AND THE POSSESSIVE MODIFIERS							
NOM (m)	э́тот	че́й	мо́й	тво́й	сво́й	на́ш	ва́ш
(n)	э́то	чьё	моё	твоё	своё	на́ше	ва́ше
INSTR	э́тим	чьи́м	мои́м	твои́м	свои́м	на́шим	ва́шим
NOM (f)	э́та	чья́	моя́	твоя́	своя́	на́ша	ва́ша
INSTR	э́той	чье́й	мое́й	твое́й	свое́й	на́шей	ва́шей
NOM (pl)	э́ти	чьи́	мои́	твои́	свои́	на́ши	ва́ши
INSTR	э́тими	чьи́ми	мои́ми	твои́ми	свои́ми	на́шими	ва́шими

DISTRIBUTION OF ENDINGS

1. The masculine and neuter instrumental singular ending is exactly like that of the dative plural of these forms: –им.

2. The feminine instrumental singular ending is like that of the genitive, dative, and prepositional cases: –ой in э́той and –ей in all the rest.

Alternate endings –ою and –ею may also be encountered in older works of literature and in poetry.

3. The instrumental plural ending is –ими.

Reflexive verbs—part II

MODELS

Я́ ему́ удивля́юсь.	I'm surprised at him.
Она́ —— удивля́ется.	She's surprised ——.
Мы́ —— удивля́емся.	We're surprised ——.

Чему́ ты́ удивля́ешься?	What are you surprised at?
Чему́ они́ удивля́ются?	What are they surprised at?
Чему́ вы́ удивля́етесь?	What are you surprised at?
О́н не удивля́лся на́шим успе́хам.	He wasn't surprised at our success.
Она́ не удивля́лась _____.	She wasn't surprised _____.
Они́ не удивля́лись _____.	They weren't surprised _____.

Note that **удивля́ться** is accompanied by the dative case without a preposition, to express the source of surprise or astonishment.

Я́ бою́сь экза́менов.	I'm afraid of the exams.
Ты́ бои́шься _____.	You're afraid _____.
Она́ бои́тся _____.	She's afraid _____.
Мы́ бои́мся _____.	We're afraid _____.
Вы́ бои́тесь _____.	You're afraid _____.
Они́ боя́тся _____.	They're afraid _____.
О́н боя́лся ма́тери.	He was afraid of his mother.
Она́ боя́лась отца́.	She was afraid of her father.
Они́ боя́лись роди́телей.	They were afraid of their parents.

Note that **боя́ться** is accompanied by the genitive case without a preposition, to express the source of fear.

Мы́ сади́мся обе́дать.	We're sitting down to eat dinner.
Я́ сажу́сь _____.	I'm sitting down _____.
Вы́ сади́тесь _____.	You're sitting down _____.
Она́ сади́тся _____.	She's sitting down _____.
Ты́ сади́шься _____.	You're sitting down _____.
Они́ садя́тся _____.	They're sitting down _____.
О́н уже́ познако́мился с не́й.	He's already been introduced to her.
Ты́ ____ познако́милась _____.	You've ____ been introduced _____.
Мы́ ____ познако́мились _____.	We've _____ been introduced _____.
Я́ познако́млюсь с ни́ми.	I'll make their acquaintance.
Мы́ познако́мимся _____.	We'll make _____ acquaintance.
О́н познако́мится _____.	He'll make _____ acquaintance.
Они́ познако́мятся _____.	They'll make _____ acquaintance.
Когда́ ты́ познако́мишься с ни́ми?	When are you going to meet them?
Когда́ вы́ познако́митесь с ни́ми?	When are you going to meet them?
Познако́мься с мое́й сестро́й.	Meet my sister.
Познако́мьтесь с мои́м бра́том.	Meet my brother.
Не бо́йся!	Don't be afraid!
Не бо́йтесь!	Don't be afraid!
Не удивля́йся!	Don't be surprised!
Не удивля́йтесь!	Don't be surprised!
Не серди́сь!	Don't get mad! *or* Don't be angry!
Не серди́тесь!	Don't get mad! *or* Don't be angry!

What are you afraid of?
We're afraid of the exams.
Чего́ вы́ бои́тесь?
Мы́ бои́мся экза́менов.

Чего́ Зи́на бои́тся?
Зи́на бои́тся экза́менов.

    (ты, студе́нты, э́ти де́вушки, вы, э́тот парень, твоя́ сестра́, твои́ бра́тья)

■ STRUCTURE REPLACEMENT DRILLS

1. *We reached an agreement on this.*
   We'll reach an agreement on this.
   Мы́ договори́лись об э́том.
   Мы́ договори́мся об э́том.
   Они́ договори́лись об э́том.
   Они́ договоря́тся об э́том.
       (ты, они́, вы, я, мы, он, они́)

2. *We don't feel like going to the lake.*
   We didn't feel like going to the lake.
   На́м не хо́чется е́хать на о́зеро.
   На́м не хоте́лось е́хать на о́зеро.
   На́м не хо́чется е́хать в ле́с.
   На́м не хоте́лось е́хать в ле́с.
       (в колхо́з, в село́, в Москву́, на вокза́л)

3. *I stayed home.*
   I'll stay home.
   Я оста́лся до́ма.
   Я оста́нусь до́ма.
   Он оста́лся до́ма.
   Он оста́нется до́ма.
       (мы, де́ти, ты, сы́н, вы, до́чь, сосе́ди, ма́ть)

4. *There'll still be a piece of pirog left.*
   There's still a piece of pirog left.
   Ещё оста́нется кусо́к пирога́.
   Ещё оста́лся кусо́к пирога́.
   Ещё оста́нутся пироги́.
   Ещё оста́лись пироги́.
       (немно́го ка́ши, су́п, грибы́, уха́, молоко́, бульо́н, немно́го борща́, мно́го грибо́в)

5. *I was getting acquainted with the town.*
   I'm getting acquainted with the town.
   Я знако́мился с го́родом.
   Я знако́млюсь с го́родом.

   Он знако́мился с го́родом.
   Он знако́мится с го́родом.
       (мы, сы́н, её до́чери, ты, её роди́тели, бра́т, вы)

■ RESPONSE DRILLS

1. *You've got to meet him.*
   I will.
   Тебе́ на́до с ни́м познако́миться.
   Я познако́млюсь.
   Зи́не на́до с ни́м познако́миться.
   Она́ познако́мится.
       (твои́м роди́телям, вам, её сы́ну, нам, её дочеря́м, ребя́там, мне)

2. *Don't be afraid!*
   I'm not afraid.
   Не бо́йся!
   Я не бою́сь.
   Не серди́сь!
   Я не сержу́сь.
   Не удивля́йся!
   Не сади́сь!
   Не обраща́йся к нему́!
   Не станови́сь в о́чередь!

   Мы́ не сади́мся.
   Не обраща́йтесь к нему́!
   Не бо́йтесь!
   Не станови́тесь туда́!
   Не удивля́йтесь э́тому!

3. *Don't be mad!*
   We're not.
   Не серди́тесь!
   Мы́ не се́рдимся.
   Не сади́тесь!

1. *We'll be eating dinner.*
We're sitting down to eat dinner.
Мы́ бу́дем обе́дать.
Мы́ сади́мся обе́дать.
Сестра́ бу́дет обе́дать.
Она́ сади́тся обе́дать.
(оте́ц и ма́ть, бра́т, тури́сты, я,
убо́рщица, вы, америка́нцы, ты)

3. *You mustn't be afraid of it.*
Don't be afraid of it!
Вы́ не должны́ э́того боя́ться.
Не бо́йтесь э́того!
Вы́ не должны́ к нему́ обраща́ться.
Не обраща́йтесь к нему́!
Вы́ не должны́ э́тому удивля́ться.
Вы́ не должны́ на него́ серди́ться.

2. *It's time for you to sit down and eat dinner.*
Sit down and eat dinner.
Тебе́ пора́ сади́ться обе́дать.
Сади́сь обе́дать.
Тебе́ пора́ с ни́ми познако́миться.
Познако́мься с ни́ми.
Тебе́ пора́ верну́ться домо́й.
Тебе́ пора́ договори́ться об э́том.
Тебе́ пора́ обрати́ться к врачу́.
Тебе́ пора́ сади́ться за сто́л.
Тебе́ пора́ познако́миться с мои́ми
роди́телями.

Вы́ не должны́ с ни́ми знако́миться.
Вы́ не должны́ туда́ возвраща́ться.
Вы́ не должны́ его́ боя́ться.

Reflexive verbs reviewed and drilled in this lesson are given below in all their forms:

1. First conjugation

оста́ться (pvf) *to remain, stay, be left*
PAST   оста́лся, оста́лась, –ось, –ись
FUT   оста́нусь, оста́нешься, –ется, –емся, –етесь, –утся
IMPER   оста́нься! оста́ньтесь!

удивля́ться (ipfv) (+ dat) *to be surprised* (or *amazed*)
PAST   удивля́лся, удивля́лась, –ось, –ись
PRES   удивля́юсь, удивля́ешься, –ется, –емся, –етесь, –ются
IMPER   [не] удивля́йся! [не] удивля́йтесь!

хоте́ться (ipfv) (used impersonally with the dative and the infinitive) *to feel like*
PAST   хоте́лось
PRES   хо́чется
IMPER   (not used)

2. Second conjugation

боя́ться (ipfv) (+ gen) *to fear, to be afraid*
PAST   боя́лся, боя́лась, –ось, –ись
PRES   бою́сь, бои́шься, –и́тся, –и́мся, –и́тесь, –я́тся
IMPER   [не] бо́йся! [не] бо́йтесь!

знако́миться (ipfv) (**с** + instr) *to meet, become acquainted with*
PAST   знако́мился, знако́милась, –ось, –ись
PRES   знако́млюсь, знако́мишься, –ится, –имся, –итесь, –ятся
IMPER   знако́мься! знако́мьтесь!

познако́миться (pfv) (conjugated like imperfective **знако́миться**) *to meet, become acquainted with*

сади́ться (ipfv) *to sit down, take a seat*
PAST   сади́лся, сади́лась, –ось, –ись
PRES   сажу́сь, сади́шься, –и́тся, –и́мся, –и́тесь, –я́тся
IMPER   сади́сь! сади́тесь!

договори́ться (pfv) (с + instr) *to come to an agreement, make a date* (or *appointment*)
PAST   договори́лся, договори́лась, –ось, –ись
FUT   договорю́сь, договори́шься, –и́тся, –и́мся, –и́тесь, –я́тся
IMPER   договори́сь! договори́тесь!

Nouns with declension irregularities:
ма́ть, до́чь, сы́н, де́рево, ли́ст

MODELS

У неё краси́вая до́чь. | She has a beautiful daughter.
_____ краси́вый сы́н. | _____ a handsome son.
У неё краси́вые до́чери. | She has beautiful daughters.
_____ краси́вые сыновья́. | _____ handsome sons.

Како́е краси́вое де́рево! | What a beautiful tree!
Како́й краси́вый ли́ст! | What a beautiful leaf!
Каки́е краси́вые дере́вья! | What beautiful trees!
Каки́е краси́вые ли́стья! | What beautiful leaves!

Та́м бы́ло мно́го ли́стьев. | There were lots of leaves there.
_____ дере́вьев. | _____ trees _____.

Я́ ви́дел в го́роде ва́шу до́чь. | I saw your daughter in town.
_____ ма́ть. | _____ mother _____.
_____ ва́шего сы́на. | _____ your son _____.
_____ дру́га. | _____ friend _____.
_____ и́х дочере́й. | _____ their daughters _____.
_____ матере́й. | _____ mothers _____.
_____ сынове́й. | _____ sons _____.
_____ друзе́й. | _____ friends _____.

Я́ говори́л с ва́шей до́черью. | I was talking to your daughter.
_____ ма́терью. | _____ mother.
_____ с ва́шим сы́ном. | _____ to your son.
_____ дру́гом. | _____ friend.
_____ с и́х дочерьми́. | _____ to their daughters.
_____ матеря́ми. | _____ mothers.
_____ сыновья́ми. | _____ sons.
_____ друзья́ми. | _____ friends.

Они́ живу́т у до́чери. | They live with their daughter.
_____ у ма́тери. | _____ mother.
_____ у сы́на. | _____ son.
_____ у дру́га. | _____ friend.
_____ у дочере́й. | _____ daughters.
_____ у матере́й. | _____ mothers.
_____ у сынове́й. | _____ sons.
_____ у друзе́й. | _____ friends.

1. *Is this your pen?*
   Are these your pens?
   Это ва́ше перо́?
   Это ва́ши пе́рья?
   Это ваш сту́л?
   Это ва́ши сту́лья?
   (ваша дочь, ваш брат, ваша мать, ваш муж, ваш сын, ваш друг)

2. *Don't forget about their mother.*
   Don't forget about their mothers.
   Не забу́дьте об и́х ма́тери.
   Не забу́дьте об и́х матеря́х.
   Не забу́дьте о ва́шем дру́ге.
   Не забу́дьте о ва́ших друзья́х.
   (о её сыне, об их дочери, о вашем брате, об этом дереве)

   Она́ е́дет к бра́ту.
   Они́ е́дут к бра́тьям.
   (к матери, к другу, к дочери, к мужу, к сыну, к брату)

3. *She's going to visit her son.*
   They're going to visit their sons.
   Она́ е́дет к сы́ну.
   Они́ е́дут к сыновья́м.

■ QUESTION-ANSWER DRILL

Where are their brothers?
I didn't see their brothers.
Где́ и́х бра́тья?
Я́ не ви́дел и́х бра́тьев.
Где́ и́х сыновья́?
Я́ не ви́дел и́х сынове́й.
(дочери, мужья, братья, матери, друзья)

■ RESPONSE DRILL

There's only one leaf here.
There are lots of leaves there.
Ту́т то́лько оди́н ли́ст.
А та́м мно́го ли́стьев.
Ту́т то́лько одно́ де́рево.
А та́м мно́го дере́вьев.
(один стул, одно перо, один лист, одно дерево)

■ SUBJECT REVERSAL DRILLS

1. *Their friends invited us to dinner.*
   We invited their friends to dinner.
   Их друзья́ пригласи́ли на́с на обе́д.
   Мы́ пригласи́ли их друзе́й на обе́д.
   Их сыновья́ пригласи́ли на́с на обе́д.
   Мы́ пригласи́ли их сынове́й на обе́д.
   (их матери, их друзья, их дочь, их братья, их мать, их дочери, их мужья)

2. *Her sons aren't acquainted with him.*
   He's not acquainted with her sons.
   Её сыновья́ с ни́м не знако́мы.
   Он не знако́м с её сыновья́ми.
   Её ма́ть с ни́м не знако́ма.
   О́н не знако́м с её ма́терью.
   (её дочь, её друзья, её муж, её дочери, её сын, её братья)

DISCUSSION

1. The nouns **ма́ть** *mother* and **до́чь** *daughter* are **две́рь**-nouns with an alternate stem for the nominative and accusative singular, as opposed to that of all the other cases singular and plural.

SINGULAR			PLURAL		
NOM-ACC	ма́ть	до́чь	**NOM**	ма́тери	до́чери
GEN-PREP-DAT	ма́тери	до́чери	**ACC-GEN**	матере́й	дочере́й
INSTR	ма́терью	до́черью	**PREP**	о матеря́х	о дочеря́х
			DAT	матеря́м	дочеря́м
			INSTR	матеря́ми	дочерьми́

Note that the instrumental plural of **до́чь** is **дочерьми́** (like **детьми́** and **людьми́**). An alternate form **дочеря́ми** also exists in conversational Russian.

2. The noun **сы́н** *son* has an expanded stem in the plural. It declines as a hard stem in the singular and as a soft stem in the plural.

SINGULAR		PLURAL	
NOM	сы́н	NOM	сыновья́
ACC-GEN	сы́на	ACC-GEN	сынове́й
PREP	о сы́не	PREP	о сыновья́х
DAT	сы́ну	DAT	сыновья́м
INSTR	сы́ном	INSTR	сыновья́ми

Note especially the genitive and accusative plural **сынове́й** with inserted vowel **е** and with the [j] of the plural stem written **й**.

3. The nouns **ли́ст** *leaf* and **де́рево** *tree* have expanded stems in the plural, following the declension pattern of **бра́т**, **сту́л**, and **перо́**; all such nouns decline as hard stems in the singular and as soft stems in the plural.

SINGULAR			PLURAL		
NOM-ACC	ли́ст	де́рево	NOM-ACC	ли́стья	дере́вья
GEN	листа́	де́рева	GEN	ли́стьев	дере́вьев
PREP	о листе́	о де́реве	PREP	о ли́стьях	о дере́вьях
DAT	листу́	де́реву	DAT	ли́стьям	дере́вьям
INSTR	листо́м	де́ревом	INSTR	ли́стьями	дере́вьями

Ли́ст also means *sheet*. In this meaning it has a regular plural, for example, **листы́**, **листо́в**, **о листа́х**: Да́йте мне́ не́сколько **листо́в** бума́ги. (Give me a few *sheets* of paper.)

ЧТЕ́НИЕ И ПИСЬМО́

Никола́й с Га́лей е́здили домо́й в колхо́з, где живу́т и рабо́тают их роди́тели. Э́то пятьдеся́т киломе́тров от го́рода. Колхо́з небольшо́й, то́лько не́сколько изб. За и́збами поля́, ле́с и небольшо́е о́зеро. В э́том о́зере ма́сса ры́бы. Бра́т и сестра́ лю́бят ходи́ть в ле́с и на о́зеро. Они́ всегда́ прино́сят мно́го грибо́в и ры́бы, и ма́ть ва́рит для ни́х уху́ и пече́т пироги́ с гриба́ми.

В лесу много грибов, только не всякий их найдёт. Иногда их под листьями сразу не увидишь. И надо знать, какие грибы хорошие, а какие плохие. Петя как раз этого не знает. Он увидел какие-то красные грибы с белыми точками и они ему понравились. Он взял их в руки и показал матери. Мать сказала, что они плохие и их надо выбросить. Вдруг Таня увидела в траве длинную чёрную змею. Петя хотел убить змею камнем или палкой. Но мать посоветовала детям не убивать её. Змея уползла. Петя рассердился на маму и долго не мог забыть об этом.

Николай и Галя приехали домой к родителям. Родители были рады видеть своих детей: ведь они ездят домой редко, только на каникулы. За обедом отец говорил о колхозных делах, спрашивал сына и дочь, как они живут в Москве. После обеда Галя с Николаем пошли к бабушке и дедушке в соседнее село.

— Я слышала, что вы с соседкой вчера ездили в лес за грибами.
— Да, с ней и с её дочерью.
— Вы на то же место ездили, где мы с вами были?
— Да.
— Ну как, много нашли грибов?
— О, да! Я сварила суп и даже испекла большой пирог.
— Вот как! Тогда мы тоже поедем в лес в следующее воскресенье.
— Только не ищите около озера: там грибов нет.
— Да, я знаю. Я там несколько раз искала и ничего не находила.

— Дети, покажите ваши грибы.
— Этот гриб я нашёл вон там, под деревом.
— Это как раз плохой. Выбрось его и вытри руки. А как твой дела, Таня?
— Я, кажется, нашла белые грибы — три больших и два маленьких. Вот, смотри.
— Нет, это не белые, но они тоже хорошие, возьмём их.
— Вот досада, что я таких не нашёл!
— Ничего, Петя, Мы ведь только что пришли в лес. Ты ещё найдёшь.

— Это бе́лый гри́б, ма́ма?

— Да́, Та́ня, это бе́лый. Посмотри́, Пе́тя. По́мнишь, мы́ ви́дели таки́е грибы́ в магази́не?

— Да́, по́мню. Они́ бы́ли о́чень дороги́е.

— И́х ведь тру́дно находи́ть.

— А где́ они́ расту́т?

— Под дере́вьями, но на́до зна́ть места́. Во́т бу́дем ходи́ть, и ты́ уви́дишь.

— Ма́ма, смотри́, уже́ о́зеро ви́дно.

— Где́? Я́ не ви́жу.

— Во́н та́м напра́во, за дере́вьями.

— Пойдём туда́, хорошо́?

— Я́ согла́сна, я́ уже́ уста́ла ходи́ть по́ лесу. А ка́к ты́, Та́ня?

— Я́ то́же. Пойдём отдохнём на траве́.

— То́лько возьмём с собо́й па́лку, та́м во́зле о́зера мно́го змей.

— Каки́х змей? Что́ ты́, Пе́тя, говори́шь глу́пости?

— Это не глу́пости, пра́вда, ма́ма?

— Я́ не зна́ю. Ты́ и́х ви́дел?

— Не́т, но мне́ дя́дя Алёша сказа́л.

— А́, е́сли дя́дя Алёша сказа́л, то это пра́вда.

— Ва́ля, что́ у на́с сего́дня на обе́д?

— Су́п с лапшо́й и ка́ша.

— Опя́ть? Неуже́ли ты́ не могла́ свари́ть что́-нибудь друго́е, наприме́р уху́?

— А отку́да я́ возьму́ ры́бу? Я́ два́ часа́ стоя́ла в магази́не, а когда́ пришла́ моя́ о́чередь, ры́бы уже́ не́ было.

— Во́т доса́да! Та́к хо́чется ры́бы! Я́ на э́ту ка́шу уже́ смотре́ть не могу́ — вчера́ ка́ша, сего́дня ка́ша. Я́ лу́чше совсе́м не бу́ду обе́дать.

— Ну́ не серди́сь, Алёша. Подожди́, я́ пойду́ к сосе́дке, мо́жет бы́ть она́ мне́ да́ст ры́бы. Я́ зна́ю, она́ доста́ла.

— Мне́ ну́жно зайти́ к Алёше Во́лкову. Пе́тя, пойдёшь со мно́й? Я́ тебя́ с ни́м познако́млю.

— А где́ о́н живёт?

— На у́лице Толсто́го.

— Это далеко́ отсю́да?

— Не́т, мину́т де́сять ну́жно идти́.

— Ну́, ла́дно, пойдём. Этот Во́лков, ка́жется, но́вый па́рень, из села́?

— Да́, о́н ме́сяц тому́ наза́д прие́хал в го́род. О́н мне́ нра́вится: просто́й тако́й и ви́дно, что с хоро́шей душо́й. Тако́му мо́жно ве́рить.

— Ну́, ты́ лу́чше бу́дь осторо́жен, ты́ ведь его́ ещё ма́ло зна́ешь.

— Да́, но я́ чу́вствую, что о́н хоро́ший челове́к. И, зна́ешь, всё вре́мя говори́ть себе́ «осторо́жно» — это ску́чно. Та́к жи́ть нельзя́. Это ра́ньше на́ши отцы́ боя́лись говори́ть откры́то, боя́лись люде́й, да́же бли́зких знако́мых. А тепе́рь ина́че, тепе́рь всё свобо́дно говоря́т то́, что ду́мают.

— Ну́, это ещё не совсе́м та́к, но, пожа́луй, ты́ пра́в. На́ши отцы́ боя́лись бо́льше, чем мы́.

— Скажи́те пожа́луйста, где́ кварти́ра Бори́са Миха́йловича Ку́рочкина?

— На пя́том этаже́. Я́ то́же та́м живу́. На́м на́до идти́ по ле́стнице, ли́фт не рабо́тает.

— А́, знако́мая исто́рия. У на́с в до́ме уже́ четы́ре ме́сяца ли́фт не рабо́тает: де́ти слома́ли две́рь. Я́ ка́ждый де́нь по́сле рабо́ты до́лжен ползти́ наве́рх на пя́тый эта́ж. Уже́ привы́к.

— А вы́ с Бори́сом Миха́йловичем вме́сте рабо́таете?

— Не́т, я́ то́лько что прие́хал из Москвы́. Мы́ с Бори́сом ста́рые друзья́. Я́ прие́хал сюда́ на неде́лю и во́т хочу́ его́ уви́деть.

— Ка́жется Бори́са Миха́йловича не́т до́ма. Стучу́ уже́ пя́ть мину́т и не́т отве́та.

— А́х, да́, о́н говори́л, что у ни́х сего́дня како́е-то собра́ние.

— Ничего́ не поде́лаешь. Придётся подожда́ть.

— Заходи́те ко мне́, е́сли хоти́те. Поговори́м, познако́мимся.

— Большо́е спаси́бо. А я́ ва́м не бу́ду меша́ть?

— Не́т, что вы́! Я́ бу́ду о́чень ра́д.

— Вы́ не зна́ете, почему́ Петро́в вчера́ и сего́дня не́ был на рабо́те?

— О́н о́чень бо́лен. Его́ жена́ звони́ла ча́с наза́д. Сказа́ла, что о́н и за́втра не придёт.

— Что́ с ни́м? Вы́ у него́ бы́ли?

— Не́т. Хочу́ зайти́ по́сле рабо́ты.

— А что́ его́ жена́ сказа́ла?

— Что у него́ всё боли́т.

— Ка́к всё? Не мо́жет бы́ть! Наве́рно, о́н про́сто хо́чет отдохну́ть.

— Что́ с ва́ми? У ва́с что́-нибудь боли́т?

— Я́ то́лько что упа́л и, ка́жется, слома́л себе́ ру́ку.

— Что́ вы́ говори́те! Иди́те скоре́е к врачу́. Хоти́те я́ ва́м помогу́?

— Да́, пожа́луйста. Позвони́те до́ктору О́сипову на кварти́ру. Его́ но́мер телефо́на два́-четы́ре-пя́ть-ше́сть.

— А вы́ ду́маете, о́н сейча́с до́ма?

— Да́. У него́ сего́дня свобо́дный де́нь.

— Я́ сейча́с позвоню́.

— Вчера́ мы́ бы́ли у сосе́дей на обе́де. У и́х до́чери Та́ни бы́л де́нь рожде́ния, и они́ на́с к себе́ пригласи́ли.

— Хоро́шии бы́л обе́д?

— Прекра́сный! Была́ уха́, пиро́г с гриба́ми, вку́сные бу́лочки, то́рт . . .

— Э́то действи́тельно обе́д!

— А каки́е пода́рки э́та Та́ня от свои́х роди́телей получи́ла! Вы́ да́же не пове́рите!

— Каки́е?

— Но́вый прои́грыватель, аппара́т «Зо́ркий» и авторучку!

— Всё сра́зу? Ну́, зна́ете, э́то да́же глу́по.

— Я́ с ва́ми согла́сен. Я́ свое́й до́чери никогда́ не покупа́ю та́к мно́го пода́рков.

PREPARATION FOR CONVERSATION   **Прощáй, шкóла!**

прощáй! прощáйте!
Прощáй, шкóла!
окóнчен, –а, –о, –ы
Вóт и окóнчена шкóла.

свобóда
чýвство   [čústvə]
Какóе чýвство свобóды!

поступи́ть (pfv II)
    поступлю́, постýпишь, –ят
вýз
Ты́ смóжешь срáзу в вýз поступи́ть.
отли́чник
**Ты́ отли́чник, смóжешь срáзу
в вýз поступи́ть.**
    захотéть (pfv *like* хотéть)
**Э́то для тебя́ свобóда: ты́
отли́чник, éсли захóчешь —
смóжешь срáзу в вýз поступи́ть.**

производство
рабóтать на производстве
**А я́ дóлжен рабóтать на
производстве.**
цéлый
**А я́ цéлые двá гóда дóлжен
рабóтать на производстве.**

тéхника

farewell! good-bye!
Farewell, school!
    finished, over, done with
Well, so school is finished.

    freedom, liberty
    feeling
What a feeling of freedom!

    to enter, enroll, join (an institution);
        to behave, act
    college
You can enter college immediately.
    "A" student
You're an "A" student; you can go
    straight on to college.
    to want, feel like
It's freedom for you: You're an "A"
    student; if you want, you can go straight
    on to college.

    production, manufacture
    to work in a factory
But I have to work in a factory.

    entire, whole
But I have to work two whole years in
    a factory.

    engineering, technology, technical things,
        equipment

интересова́ться (I) (*plus* instr)
   интересу́юсь, интересу́ешься, –ются

to be interested in

Ты́ всегда́ интересова́лся
те́хникой.

You've always been interested in technical
things.

**Но ведь, ты́ всегда́ интересова́лся
те́хникой.**

But you've always been interested in
technical things.

мя́со
мясокомбина́т

meat
meat-packing plant

А мясокомбина́т?

What about the meat-packing plant?

Подожди́, То́ля, а мясокомбина́т?

Wait a minute, Tolya; what about the meat-
packing plant?

дире́ктор
помо́щник
помо́щник дире́ктора

director
assistant, aide
assistant director

У тебя́ та́м е́сть знако́мый,
помо́щник дире́ктора.

You do have a friend there, the assistant
director.

са́м помо́щник дире́ктора

the assistant director himself

**У тебя́ та́м е́сть знако́мый,
са́м помо́щник дире́ктора.**

You do have a friend there, the assistant
director himself.

уже́ не́т (уже́ не)

no longer, not any longer (*or* more)

Его́ уже́ та́м не́т.
где́-то

He's not there anymore.
somewhere

**Его́ уже́ та́м не́т, где́-то
в друго́м ме́сте рабо́тает.**

He's not there anymore; he works somewhere
else.

научи́ться (pfv II) (*plus* dat)
   научу́сь, научи́шься, –атся

to learn

Чему́ я́ та́м научу́сь?
всё равно́

What will I learn there?
anyway, it doesn't matter

**И, всё равно́, чему́ я́ та́м
научу́сь?**

And anyway, what will I learn there?

рабо́чий, –его
просто́й рабо́чий

worker
unskilled worker, ordinary worker

**Ведь меня́ просты́м рабо́чим
пошлю́т.**

After all, they'll send me as an ordinary
worker.

весёлый (adv ве́село)
э́то ве́село

merry, lively, gay, jolly
it's fun

Да́, э́то не ве́село.
осо́бенный

Yes, that's no fun.
special, particular

Да́, э́то не осо́бенно ве́село.

Yes, that's no particular fun.

бы́стрый

quick, fast, rapid

**Ну, ничего́. Два́ го́да
пройду́т бы́стро.**

Well, never mind. Two years will go by
quickly.

жи́знь (f)
устро́ить (pfv II)
пото́м

life
to arrange, establish, organize, fix up
afterward, later on, then

**Пото́м ты́ устро́ишь свою́ жи́знь,
ка́к захо́чешь.**

Later on you'll arrange your life the
way you want to.

Что́ мне́ «пото́м»?	What good is "later on" to me?
учи́ться (II)	to learn, study
учи́ться в ву́зе	to go to college
Мне́ уже́ тепе́рь хо́чется учи́ться в ву́зе.	I want to go to college now.
профе́ссия	profession, calling, skill, trade
получи́ть профе́ссию	to enter a profession, learn a trade, acquire a skill
А каку́ю ты хо́чешь получи́ть профе́ссию?	What profession do you want to enter?
инжене́р	engineer
ста́ть (pfv I), ста́ну, ста́нешь, –ут	to become, get, grow; stop
Ты хо́чешь ста́ть инжене́ром?	Do you want to become an engineer?
Всё ещё хо́чешь ста́ть инжене́ром?	Do you still want to become an engineer?
мечта́ть (I)	to dream
Не́т, я́ об э́том бо́льше не мечта́ю.	No, I don't dream of that anymore.
чтобы [štóbi] or [štəbi]	in order to, to
Что́бы ста́ть инжене́ром, ну́жно пя́ть ле́т учи́ться.	In order to be an engineer you've got to study for five years.
сли́шком	too
Э́то сли́шком до́лго.	That's too long.
пра́ктика	practical experience, practice
Всё-таки полу́чишь пра́ктику.	Anyway, you'll gain practical experience.
да́ром	for nothing, gratis, with no return, in vain, to no avail
пропа́сть (pfv I) (*like* упа́сть)	to be lost, missing, wasted; to perish
Вре́мя не пропадёт да́ром	The time won't be totally wasted.
И заче́м тебе́ профе́ссия?	And what do you need a profession for?
месте́чко (var of ме́сто)	spot, place, job; small town
тёплое месте́чко	a soft spot, a nice cushy job
устро́иться (pfv II), устро́юсь, устро́ишься, –ятся	to get a job, to get settled, to get fixed up (*or* established)
Я́ хочу́ устро́иться на тёплое месте́чко.	I want to get myself a nice cushy job.
гла́вный	main, chief
гла́вное	the main thing
Гла́вное — устро́иться на тёплое месте́чко.	The main thing is to get yourself set up in a nice cushy job.
знако́мство	acquaintance, familiarity
по знако́мству	by knowing the right people, through friends
Гла́вное — устро́иться по знако́мству на тёплое месте́чко.	The main thing is to get yourself set up in a nice cushy job by knowing the right people.
нача́ть (pfv I) (past на́чал, –о, –и, [f] начала́; fut начну́, начнёшь, –у́т)	to start, begin
зараба́тывать (I)	to earn (*or* make) [money]

Мне́ хо́чется нача́ть зараба́тывать.	I want to start earning [money].
Гла́вное — устро́иться по знако́мству на тёплое месте́чко, нача́ть хорошо́ зараба́тывать.	The main thing is to get yourself set up in a nice cushy job by knowing the right people and start earning good [money].
серьёзный	serius
наде́яться (I) (на *plus* acc)	to hope, count on, rely on
Наде́юсь, ты́ э́то не серьёзно говори́шь.	I hope you're not serious in saying that.
Не́т, серьёзно.	Yes, I am.
Я́ са́м хочу́ та́к сде́лать.	I myself want to do just that.
Не́т, серьёзно. Я́ са́м хочу́ та́к сде́лать.	Yes, I am serious. That's what I want to do.
де́ньги, де́нег (pl only)	money
больши́е де́ньги	good money, lots of money
Я́ бу́ду зараба́тывать больши́е де́ньги.	I'll be gaking good money.
маши́на	car, machine
е́здить на маши́не	to drive a car, go by car
Я́ хочу́ е́здить на свое́й маши́не.	I want to drive my own car.
Бу́ду зараба́тывать больши́е де́ньги, е́здить на свое́й маши́не.	I'll be earning good money [and] driving my own car.
успе́х	success, luck
жела́ть (I)	to wish
жела́ть кому́-нибудь успе́ха	to wish someone luck
Ну, жела́ю тебе́ успе́ха.	Well, I wish you luck.

SUPPLEMENT

де́лать больши́е успе́хи	to do very well, to make excellent progress
О́н де́лает больши́е успе́хи в ру́сском языке.	He's doing very well in Russian.
мне́ всё равно́	I don't care, it's all the same to me, it makes no difference to me
Ты́ опозда́ешь на ле́кцию.	You'll be late to the lecture.
— Мне́ всё равно́.	I don't care.
ме́дленный	slow
Вре́мя шло́ та́к ме́дленно.	The time went very slowly.
занима́ться (I) (*plus* instr), занима́юсь, –ешься, –ются	to busy oneself, to occupy oneself, to study
О́н занима́ется ру́сским языко́м.	He's studying Russian.

Проща́й, шко́ла

В. — Ви́ктор   А. — Анато́лий (То́ля)   И. — И́горь

В.   1 Во́т и око́нчена шко́ла. Како́е чу́вство свобо́ды!

А.   2 Э́то для тебя́ свобо́да: ты́ отли́чник, е́сли захо́чешь — смо́жешь сра́зу в ву́з поступи́ть.[1] А я́ це́лые два́ го́да до́лжен ра́ньше рабо́тать на произво́дстве.[2]

В. 3 Но ведь ты́ всегда́ интересова́лся те́хникой.

И. 4 Подожди́, То́ля, а мясокомбина́т? У тебя́ та́м е́сть знако́мый, са́м помо́щник дире́ктора.

А. 5 Его́ уже́ та́м не́т, где́-то в друго́м ме́сто рабо́тает. И, всё равно́, чему́ я та́м научу́сь? Ведь меня́ просты́м рабо́чим пошлю́т.

В. 6 Да́, э́то не осо́бенно ве́село. Ну́, ничего́, два́ го́да пройду́т бы́стро, а пото́м устро́ишь свою́ жи́знь, ка́к захо́чешь.

А. 7 Что́ мне «пото́м»? Мне́ уже́ тепе́рь хо́чется учи́ться в ву́зе![3]

И. 8 А каку́ю ты́ хо́чешь получи́ть профе́ссию? Всё ещё хо́чешь ста́ть инжене́ром?

А. 9 Не́т, я об э́том бо́льше не мечта́ю. Что́бы ста́ть инжене́ром, ну́жно пя́ть ле́т учи́ться. Э́то сли́шком до́лго.

В. 10 Всё-таки полу́чишь пра́ктику — вре́мя не пропадёт да́ром.

И. 11 И заче́м тебе́ профе́ссия? Гла́вное — устро́иться по знако́мству на тёплое месте́чко, нача́ть хорошо́ зараба́тывать.[4]

А. 12 Наде́юсь, ты́ э́то не серьёзно говори́шь.

И. 13 Не́т, серьёзно. Я са́м хочу́ та́к сде́лать. Бу́ду зараба́тывать больши́е де́ньги, е́здить на свое́й маши́не.

В. 14 Ну́, жела́ю тебе́ успе́ха![5]

NOTES

[1] **Ву́з** is comparable to an American college or university; the word itself is another example of one formed from initial letters, in this case, **вы́сшее уче́бное заведе́ние** *higher educational institution*.

[2] All high school graduates with the exception of **отли́чники** *"A" students* are required to do two years of manual work, usually at a factory or kolkhoz, to which they are assigned by the government.

[3] Compare the three Russian verbs meaning *to study*: **учи́ть, учи́ться,** and **занима́ться**.

Я́ учу́ ру́сский язы́к.	I'm studying Russian.
Я́ учу́сь ру́сскому языку́.	I'm studying Russian.
Я́ занима́юсь ру́сским языко́м.	I'm studying Russian.

The verb **учи́ть** usually implies assiduous study and memorization, i.e., real effort: **Я́ учу́ э́ти ру́сские слова́** *I'm studying these Russian words*. The verb **учи́ться** is broader in its meaning: **Я́ учу́сь игра́ть в ша́хматы** *I'm learning how to play chess*; **Сы́н у́чится чита́ть** *My son is learning to read*. The verb **занима́ться** indicates study on a higher level, usually in connection with a specific field or discipline: **О́н занима́ется фи́зикой** *He's studying physics*; **О́н занима́ется исто́рией Кита́я** (or **О́н специали́ст по исто́рии Кита́я**) *He's doing research on the history of China* (or *He's a specialist in the history of China*).

Note that while **ходи́ть в шко́лу** may be used in the sense *to attend school*, one cannot use the verb **ходи́ть** in reference to a college or university. Compare **О́н** ýчится (*or* занима́ется) в ву́зе *He goes to college*; Óн у́чится (*or* занима́ется) в университе́те *He attends the university*; with Óн хо́дит в шко́лу *He goes to school.*

⁴ The notion of **тёплое месте́чко** means not only a *sinecure* or *easy job*, but often one in which the person can make a little extra money on the side through bribery or illegal dealings.

⁵ The verb **жела́ть** is used with the dative for the person (to whom it is wished) and with the genitive for the thing wished. Such expressions as **споко́йной но́чи, всего́ хоро́шего,** and **счастли́вого пути́** are all in the genitive case and have been shortened from the longer phrase containing the verb **жела́ть: Жела́ю ва́м (тебе́) споко́йной но́чи** *I wish you a restful night.*

PREPARATION FOR CONVERSATION   **Проща́льная вечери́нка**

вечери́нка	party (informal evening gathering)
проща́льный	farewell (adj)
проща́льная вечери́нка	farewell party
У на́с бу́дет проща́льная вечери́нка.	We're going to have a farewell party.
сбо́р	gathering, assembly
в сбо́ре	together, present, here
Ка́жется, всё уже́ в сбо́ре.	I guess everybody's here now.
Нéт, Óля ещё не пришла́.	No, Olya hasn't come yet.
Она́ звони́ла. Придёт немно́го по́зже.	She phoned. She'll come a little later.
жени́х, –а́; –и́, –о́в	fiancé, bridegroom-to-be
И зна́ете с ке́м? Со свои́м женихо́м.	And you know with whom? With her fiancé.
выходи́ть за́муж	to get married (said of women only)
Ра́зве она́ выхо́дит за́муж?	You mean she's getting married?
С женихо́м? Ра́зве она́ выхо́дит за́муж?	With her fiancé? You mean she's getting married?
Э́то и для меня́ но́вость.	That's news even to me.
сча́стье [ščáṣṭji]	happiness, luck
Дава́йте вы́пьем за её сча́стье.	Let's drink a toast to her happiness!
Вы́пьем.	Let's do that!
бу́дущее, –его	future
А тепе́рь — за на́ше бу́дущее.	And now, to our future.
вино́, –а́; ви́на, ви́н	wine
нали́ть (pfv I), налью́, нальёшь, –ю́т	to pour, fill (by pouring)
Нале́й мне́ ещё вина́, Ва́ня.	Pour me some more wine, Vanya!
фи́зик	physicist
собира́ться (I), собира́юсь, –ешься, –ются	to plan, intend, prepare, get ready; to gather, assemble
Мы́ собира́емся бы́ть фи́зиками.	We're planning to be physicists.
Мы́ с На́дей собира́емся бы́ть фи́зиками.	Nadya and I are planning to be physicists.
А ты́, Бо́ря, ке́м хо́чешь бы́ть?	How about you, Borya, what do you want to be?
учёный, –ого	scientist, scholar, learned man

А ты́, Бо́ря, ке́м хо́чешь бы́ть, учёным?

       космона́вт
Я́ хочу́ бы́ть космона́втом.
       хоте́л бы   [xaţélbi]
Я́ хоте́л бы бы́ть космона́втом.

       ма́сло
       переда́ть (pfv *like* да́ть) (past пе́редал,
         –о, –и; [f] –а́)
Переда́й мне́ ма́сло.
       колбаса́, –ы́; колба́сы, колба́с
Переда́й мне́ колбасу́.
Переда́й мне́ ма́сло и колбасу́.

       полете́ть (pfv II), полечу́, полети́шь, –я́т
       Ма́рс
Хо́чешь полете́ть на Ма́рс?
       земля́, –и́; зе́мли, земе́ль (acc sg зе́млю)
       вокру́г (*plus* gen)
Хо́чешь полете́ть вокру́г Земли́?
**Хо́чешь полете́ть вокру́г Земли́ и́ли пря́мо
   на Ма́рс?**

       не сто́ит
На Ма́рс не сто́ит, там то́же жи́зни не́т.

       шу́тка
Э́то уже́ ста́рая шу́тка.

       салфе́тка
Ви́тя, переда́й мне́ салфе́тки.

       лежа́ть (II), лежу́, лежи́шь, –а́т
       перед (*or* передо) (*plus* instr)
Они́ перед тобо́й лежа́т.

       проснỳться (pfv I), просну́сь,
        проснёшься, –у́тся
Ви́тя!!! Просни́сь!
       заду́маться (pfv I)

Ви́тя!!! Просни́сь! Ты́ о чём заду́мался?

       реши́ть (pfv II), решу́, реши́шь, –а́т
Да не могу́ реши́ть, куда́ мне́ идти́.
       ника́к (не)
Да ника́к не могу́ реши́ть, куда́ мне́ идти́.

       интересова́ть (I), интересу́ю,
        интересу́ешь, –ют
Меня́ всё интересу́ет.

How about you, Borya, what do you want to
  be, a scientist?

       astronaut, cosmonaut
I want to be a cosmonaut.
       would like
I'd like to be a cosmonaut.

       butter
       to pass, hand, give, pass on

Pass me the butter.
       sausage
Pass me the sausage.
Pass me the butter and sausage.

       to fly
       Mars
You want to fly to Mars?
       earth, land
       around
You want to fly around the Earth?
You want to fly around the Earth, or straight
  to Mars?

       it's not worthwhile, why bother, it's no use
No use going to Mars; there's no life there
  either.

       joke
That joke's already an old one.

       napkin
Vitya, hand me the napkins.

       to be lying
       in front of, before
They're lying in front of you.

       to wake up

Vitya, wake up!
       to become lost in thought, fall into
        reverie, daydream
Vitya, wake up! What were you daydreaming
  about?

       to decide, make a decision
Why, I can't decide where I ought to go.
       by no means, in no way (*lit.* nohow)
I can't for the life of me decide where I ought
  to go.

       to interest

Everything interests me.

институ́т	institute
пединститу́т [p̡edinsţitút]	teachers college
Поступа́й в пединститу́т.	Enroll in a teachers college.
литфа́к	department of literature
на литфа́к	to study literature
что́-ли	maybe, perhaps, possibly
Куда́ мне́ поступи́ть?	Where should I enroll?
В пединститу́т что́ ли, на литфа́к?	Perhaps in a teachers college, to study literature?
мысль (f)	idea, thought
Хоро́шая мы́сль.	That's a good idea.
Я́ то́же туда́ ду́маю.	I'm thinking of going there, too.
преподава́тель (m)	teacher, instructor
По-мо́ему, бы́ть преподава́телем о́чень интере́сно.	In my opinion, being a teacher is very interesting.

SUPPLEMENT

хи́мик	chemist
Я́ хочу́ ста́ь хи́миком.	I want to become a chemist.
исто́рик	historian
Я́ хочу́ ста́ть исто́риком.	I want to become a historian.
те́хник	technician
О́н ста́нет те́хником.	He'll be a technician.
нау́ка	science, knowledge, study, lesson
Меня́ интересу́ют то́чные нау́ки.	The exact sciences interest me.
Во́т тебе́ нау́ка!	Let that be a lesson to you!
нау́чный	scientific, scholarly
О́н пи́шет нау́чную рабо́ту.	He's writing a scientific (*or* scholarly) work.
преподава́ть (I) (*like* дава́ть)	to teach, instruct
О́н преподаёт ру́сский язы́к.	He teaches Russian.
око́нчить (pfv II)	to finish, graduate from
О́н око́нчил ву́з два́ го́да тому́ наза́д.	He graduated from college two years ago.
просыпа́ться (I)	to wake up
Я́ обы́чно просыпа́юсь в ше́сть.	I usually wake up at six.
про́шлый	past, last
Они́ прие́хали на про́шлой неде́ле.	They arrived last week.
про́шлое, –ого	the past
Забу́дь о про́шлом!	Forget about the past!
литерату́рный	literary
Вы́ чита́ете «Литерату́рную газе́ту»?	Do you read the *Literary Gazette*?

Проща́льная вечери́нка[1]

Надёжда (На́дя)   Ве́ра   Ива́н (Ва́ня)   Ви́ктор (Ви́тя)   Бори́с (Бо́ря)

На́дя   1   Ка́жется, всё уже́ в сбо́ре. Не́т, О́ля ещё не пришла́.

Ве́ра   2   Она́ звони́ла. Придёт немно́го по́зже. И зна́ете с ке́м? Со свои́м женихо́м.[2]

Ва́ня	3	С женихо́м? Ра́зве она́ выхо́дит за́муж?

Ва́ня 3 С женихо́м? Ра́зве она́ выхо́дит за́муж?

Ви́тя 4 Э́то и для меня́ но́вость. Дава́йте вы́пьем за её сча́стье.

Бо́ря 5 Вы́пьем. А тепе́рь — за на́ше бу́дущее. Налей мне ещё вина́, Ва́ня.[3]

Ва́ня 6 Во́т мы́ с На́дей собира́емся бы́ть фи́зиками.[4] А ты́, Бо́ря, ке́м хо́чешь бы́ть? Учёным?[5]

Бо́ря 7 Не́т, я хоте́л бы бы́ть космона́втом. Переда́й мне ма́сло и колбасу́. Спаси́бо.

На́дя 8 Космона́втом? Вокру́г Земли́ хо́чешь полете́ть и́ли пря́мо на Ма́рс?

Ва́ня 9 На Ма́рс не сто́ит, та́м то́же жи́зни не́т . . .

На́дя 10 Э́то уже́ ста́рая шу́тка.[6] Ви́тя, переда́й мне салфе́тки, они́ перед тобо́й лежа́т. Ви́тя!!! Просни́сь! Ты́ о чём заду́мался?

Ви́тя 11 Да ника́к не могу́ реши́ть, куда́ мне идти́: меня́ всё интересу́ет. В пединститу́т что́ ли, на литфа́к?[7]

Ве́ра 12 Хоро́шая мы́сль! Я́ то́же туда́ ду́маю. По-мо́ему, бы́ть преподава́телем о́чень интере́сно.[8]

NOTES

[1] Russians use the word **ве́чер** to mean both *evening* and *party*. In the latter sense, **ве́чер** refers to a formal or institutional evening gathering. For a private party, however, **вечери́нка** is more commonly used. The preposition **на** (*plus prepositional or accusative*) is used with both **ве́чер** and **вечери́нка** in this sense:

Я́ познако́мился с ни́м в клу́бе **на ве́чере.** I met him *at a party* at the club.

Приходи́те к на́м **на вечери́нку.** Come *to a party* at our place.

[2] The word **жени́х** *fiancé, bridegroom-to-be* and **неве́ста** *fiancée, bride-to-be* have come back into official usage, following the return of the tradition of engagements in the U.S.S.R. In an effort to discourage church weddings, the Soviet government has been trying to make civil wedding ceremonies more attractive and has even established special **дворцы́ сча́стья** *palaces of happiness*, one in Moscow and one in Leningrad. The whole ceremony—champagne included—takes about five minutes. There is always a waiting line of young couples, many of whom have traveled great distances in order to be married there.

[3] The Russian language is rich in variants of names which reflect the attitude or relationship of the speaker to the person named. Thus **Ви́ктор** may be called **Ви́тя** informally, **Ви́тька** to show superiority or contempt, or **Ви́тенька** to show affectionale regard. Similarly, **Ива́н** is called **Ва́ня, Ва́нька,** or **Ва́нечка**; **Никола́й** becomes **Ко́ля, Ко́лька,** and **Ко́лечка** (*or* **Ко́ленька**). **О́льга** is informally called **О́ля** and affectionately **О́лечка**; **Ве́ра** is affectionately **Ве́рочка,** but pejoratively **Ве́рка**; **Бори́с** is informally **Бо́ря,** pejoratively **Бо́рька,** and affectionately **Бо́речка.**

[4] Many **сто́л**-nouns designating professions may apply to women as well as to men:

Она́ фи́зик. She's a physicist.

Она́ хоро́ший вра́ч. She's a good physician.

Товарищ Орлова — профессор математики.	Comrade Orlov (f) is a professor of mathematics.
Она химик.	She's a chemist.
Она большой специалист.	She's a great specialist.

[5] Note that Russian uses the pronoun **кто** while English uses *what* in referring to work or professions:

Кто он, химик?	*What* is he, a chemist?
Кем ты хочешь быть?	*What* do you want to be?
Кем ты станешь, инженером?	*What* are you going to be, an engineer?

[6] "На Марсе **тоже жизни нет**" is the punch line from a recent space-age anti-Soviet joke. A cosmonaut, on returning from Mars, is asked if there is any life there and replies, "No, there's no life on Mars *either*."

[7] **Пединститут** (short for **педагогический институт**) serves the same function as an American teachers college. Students in the **пединститут** specialize in one field only. For example, Vera hopes to major in literature, i.e., enroll in the department of literature **поступить на литфак** (*full form* **литературный факультет**).

[8] The term **преподаватель** is applied to instructors at the secondary or university level. The rank of **преподаватель** is used at the university level for an instructor without an advanced degree who teaches basic or introductory courses.

The term **учитель**, on the other hand, is limited to the elementary and secondary-school levels, or refers to a teacher who gives private lessons, for example, in music or dancing.

Basic sentence patterns

1. Мой дядя был инженером.
   _____ химиком.
   _____ физиком.
   _____ историком.
   _____ директором
         пединститута.
   _____ преподавателем истории.

   My uncle was an engineer.
   _____ a chemist.
   _____ a physicist.
   _____ a historian
   _____ the director of a teacher's
                     college.
   _____ a history teacher.

2. Он был помощником директора.
   _____ профессора.
   _____ врача.

   He was the director's assistant.
   _____ the professor's assistant.
   _____ the doctor's assistant.

3. Ты интересуешься жизнью в колхозе?
   _____ историей?
   _____ химией?
   _____ географией?
   _____ физикой?
   _____ литературой?
   _____ этой работой?
   _____ работой на
         мясокомбинате?

   Are you interested in life on the kolkhoz?
   _____ history?
   _____ chemistry?
   _____ geography?
   _____ physics?
   _____ literature?
   _____ this work?
   _____ a job in the meat-
                     packing plant?

4. Я собира́юсь ста́ть врачо́м.   I plan to become a doctor.
_____ инжене́ром.   _____ an engineer.
_____ те́хником.   _____ a technician.
_____ космона́втом.   _____ a cosmonaut.
_____ преподава́телем.   _____ a teacher.
_____ учёным.   _____ a scientist.

5. Ке́м о́н рабо́тает?   What kind of work does he do?
— О́н рабо́тает вахтёром.   He works as a custodian.
_____ носи́льщиком.   _____ porter.
_____ шофёром.   _____ chauffeur.
_____ администра́тором.   _____ administrator.
_____ секретарём.   _____ secretary.

6. Я нахожу́ э́то интере́сным.   I find this interesting.
_____ тру́дным.   _____ difficult.
_____ лёгким.   _____ easy.
_____ возмо́жным.   _____ possible.
_____ невозмо́жным.   _____ impossible.

7. О́н каза́лся ста́рым.   He seemed old.
_____ молоды́м.   _____ young.
_____ симпати́чным.   _____ nice.
_____ стра́нным.   _____ strange.
_____ споко́йным.   _____ quiet.

8. Э́тот челове́к мне́ ка́жется глу́пым.   That man seems stupid to me.
_____ у́мным.   _____ intelligent __.
_____ безду́шным.   _____ heartless ___.
_____ симпати́чным.   _____ likable _____.
_____ несча́стным.   _____ unhappy ___.
_____ знако́мым.   _____ familiar _____.

9. Вода́ ста́ла холо́дной.   The water became (*or* turned) cold.
_____ горя́чей.   _____ hot.
_____ тёплой.   _____ warm.
_____ кра́сной.   _____ red.
_____ си́ней.   _____ blue.
_____ чёрной.   _____ black.

10. Они́ бы́ли молоды́ми врача́ми.   They were young doctors.
_____ хоро́шими специали́стами.   _____ good specialists.
_____ ста́рыми знако́мыми.   _____ old acquaintances.
_____ прекра́сными певца́ми.   _____ excellent singers.
_____ ста́рыми людьми́.   _____ old people.

11. О́н бы́л знако́м с Толсты́м.   He was acquainted with Tolstoy.
_____ с Чайко́вским.   _____ with Tschaikovsky.
_____ с Мая́ко́вским.   _____ with Mayakovsky.
_____ с Достое́вским.   _____ with Dostoevsky.
_____ с Го́рьким.   _____ with Gorky.
_____ с Толсты́ми.   _____ with the Tolstoys.
_____ с Достое́вскими.   _____ with the Dostoevskys.

12. Какого цвета ваша машина?	What color is your car?
— Чёрная с белым.	Black and white.
_____ с зелёным.	_____ green.
_____ с синим.	_____ blue.
_____ с жёлтым.	_____ yellow.

13. Какого цвета ваш костюм? — What color is your costume?
— Белый с красным. — White and (*or* with) red.
_____ с голубым. — _____ blue.
_____ с синим. — _____ dark blue.

14. Зайдите ко мне перед обедом. — Drop in to see me before dinner.
_____ перед экзаменом. — _____ before the exam.
_____ перед уроком. — _____ before the lesson.
_____ перед лекцией. — _____ before the lecture.
_____ перед концертом. — _____ before the concert.
_____ перед работой. — _____ before work.
_____ перед собранием. — _____ before the meeting.
_____ перед началом каникул. — _____ before the beginning of vacation.

15. Перед магазином масса людей. — There are lots of people in front of the store.
_____ зданием_____. — _____ the building.
_____ дверьми_____. — _____ the doors.
_____ домом _____. — _____ the house.
_____ кассой _____. — _____ the box office.
_____ горсоветом _____. — _____ the city hall.
_____ гостиницей _____. — _____ the hotel.

16. Как ты это устроил? — How did you arrange it?
_____ заработал? — _____ earn it?
_____ решил? — _____ decide (*or* solve) it?
_____ нашёл? — _____ find it?
_____ потерял? — _____ lose it?

17. Так ты никогда не научишься. — You'll never learn anything that way.
_____ устроишься. — _____ get a job _____.
_____ проснёшься. — _____ wake up _____.
_____ с ней не познакомишься. — _____ meet her _____.

18. Мне не хочется просыпаться. — I don't feel like waking up.
_____ собираться. — _____ getting ready.
_____ этим заниматься. — _____ doing (*or* studying) that.
_____ учиться. — _____ studying.
_____ возвращаться. — _____ going back.
_____ садиться. — _____ sitting down.
_____ с ней знакомиться. — _____ meeting her.

19. Я немного посплю. — I'll take a little nap.
Он _____ поспит. — He'll take _____.
Они _____ поспят. — They'll take_____.
Она немного поспала. — She took a little nap.
Он _____ поспал. — He took_____.

20. Когда́ вы́ обы́чно просыпа́етесь? | When do you usually wake up?
_____ ты́ _____ просыпа́ешься? | _____ do you _____ wake up?
Я обы́чно просыпа́юсь в се́мь. | I usually wake up at seven.
Мы́ _____ просыпа́емся _____. | We _____ wake up _____.
Они́ _____ просыпа́ются _____. | They __ wake up _____.

21. Он ско́ро проснётся. | He'll wake up soon.
Они́ _____ просну́тся. | They'll wake up _____.
Я то́лько что просну́лся. | I just woke up.
Она́ _____ просну́лась. | She _____ woke up.
Они́ _____ просну́лись. | They _____ woke up.

22. Порабо́тай немно́го! | Do a little bit of work!
Поспи́ немно́го! | Take a little nap!
Потанцу́й немно́го! | Dance a bit!
Поживи́ та́м немно́го! | Live there for a while!
Побу́дь со мно́й! | Stay with me!
Посиди́ немно́го! | Sit awhile! *or* Stay awhile!
Полежи́ немно́го! | Stay in bed awhile! *or* Lie down for awhile!
Погуля́й немно́го! | Go for a little stroll!
Походи́ немно́го! | Walk a bit!

23. Вы́ у́читесь ру́сскому языку́? | Are you studying (*or* learning) Russian?
Ты́ у́чишься_____? | Are you studying (*or* learning) _____?
Я учу́сь англи́йскому языку́. | I'm studying (*or* learning) English.
Он у́чится_____. | He's studying (*or* learning) _____.
Они́ у́чатся_____. | They're studying (*or* learning)_____.

24. Я мно́гое узна́л. | I found out a lot *or* I learned a lot.
Ты́ мно́гому научи́шься. | You'll learn a lot.
Мы́ о мно́гом говори́ли. | We talked about a lot of things.
Я ко мно́гому привы́к. | I'm used to a lot of things.
Она́ мно́гого бои́тся. | She's afraid of a lot of things.
Она́ со мно́гим не согла́сна. | There's a lot she doesn't agree with.

25. Я э́то переда́м ва́шему знако́мому. | I'll pass this on to your friend.
_____ ва́шим знако́мым. | _____ your friends.
_____ ва́шей знако́мой. | _____ your friend.
_____ на́шим рабо́чим. | _____ our workers.

Pronunciation practice: clusters beginning with the letters с and з

Clusters beginning with the letter с.

A. с + с = long с

[ssóṇij]   с Со́ней
with Sonya
[şşévəm]   с се́вом
with the sowing
[ssáləm]   с са́лом
with fat

[şşíṇij]   с си́ней
with blue
[ssúpəm]   с су́пом
with soup

B. с + з = long з

[z̧z̧imój] с зимо́й
with winter

[zzáḍi] сза́ди
from behind

[zzáɣiʂtju] с за́вистью
with envy

[zzólətəm] с зо́лотом
with gold

[zzóni] с зо́ны
from the zone

[zziváʈ] сзыва́ть
to call together

C. с + ш = long ш

[raššiḅítcə] расшиби́ться
to break to pieces

[ššíʈ] сши́ть
to sew

[ššárəm] с ша́ром
with a ball

[ššútkəj] с шу́ткой
with a joke

[ššíləm] с ши́лом
with an awl

[pəššibáʈ] посшиба́ть
to knock down

[ššápkəj] с ша́пкой
with a cap

[ššérʂtju] с ше́рстью
with wool

[ššiɹinój] с ширино́й
with the width

[raššítij] расши́тый
embroidered

D. с + ж = long ж

[žžíʈ] сжи́ть
worry to death

[žžárəm] с жа́ром
animatedly

[žžútkəj] с жу́ткой
with horrible

[žžírəm] с жи́ром
with fat

[pəžžímáʈ] посжима́ть
to squeeze together

[žžápkəj] с жа́бкой
with a small toad

[žžéʂtju] с же́стью
with a tin plate

[žžinój] с жено́й
with wife

E. с + ч = шч (щ)

[ščáʂtji] сча́стье
happiness

[ščitáʈ] счита́ть
to count

[naščót] насчёт
concerning

[iščiʂļáʈ] исчисля́ть
to calculate

[rəščisáʈ] расчеса́ть
to comb apart

[ščáškəj] с ча́шкой
with a cup

[ščužím] с чужи́м
with a foreign

[ščístim] с чи́стым
with clean

[ščimadánəm] с чемода́ном
with a suitcase

[ščilavékəm] с челове́ком
with a man

[ɲiščém] ни с че́м
with nothing

Clusters beginning with the letter з.

A. з + з = long з

[izzáɣiʂti] из за́висти
from envy

[izzóbə] из зо́ба
from the craw

[izzáɹivə] из за́рева
from the glow

[izzóni] из зо́ны
from the zone

[iz̧z̧irná] из зерна́
from grain

[raz̧z̧ivátcə] раззева́ться
to yawn

B. з + с = long с

[issádə] из са́да
from the orchard

[iʂʂéɱiɲi] из се́мени
from the seed

[issúpə] из су́па
from soup

[issarátəvə] из Сара́това
from Saratov

[issipúčij] из сыпу́чей
from the quicksand

[iʂʂól] из сёл
from villages

C. з + ж = long ж

[ižžáləşţi] из жáлости
from pity

[ižžáŗiţ] изжáрить
to fry

[ižžirlá] из жерлá
from the muzzle

[ižžógə] изжóга
heartburn

[ižžilútkə] из желýдка
from the stomach

[ražživáţ] разжевáть
to chew apart

D. з + ш = long ш

[iššerşţi] из шéрсти
from wool

[iššárə] из шáра
from a sphere

[iššólkə] из шёлка
from silk

[iššírmi] из шúрмы
from a screen

[iššútķi] из шýтки
from a joke

[iššitjá] из шитья́
from sewing

E. з + ч = шч (щ)

[iščásţi] из чáсти
from the part

[iščimadánə] из чемодáна
from the suitcase

[iščužóvə] из чужóго
from foreign

[iščášķi] из чáшки
from a cup

[iščislá] из числá
from the number

[iščivó] из чегó
from what

STRUCTURE AND DRILLS

Use of the instrumental in the predicate with verbs of *being* and *becoming*

MODELS

Óн бы́л дирéктором завóда.   He was plant director.

_____ дóктором.   _____ a doctor.

_____ преподавáтелем.   _____ an instructor.

_____ певцóм.   _____ a singer.

_____ учúтелем.   _____ a teacher.

_____ профéссором истóрии.   _____ a history professor.

_____ мойм сосéдом.   _____ my neighbor.

Онá былá фúзиком.   She was a physicist.

_____ хúмиком.   _____ a chemist.

_____ моéй сосéдкой.   _____ my neighbor.

_____ учúтельницей мýзыки.   _____ a music teacher.

_____ убóрщицей.   _____ a cleaning woman.

_____ продавщúцей.   _____ a saleslady.

_____ специалúстом в э́том дéле.   _____ a specialist in this field.

Я́ бýду врачóм.   I'm going to be a doctor.

_____ инженéром.   _____ an engineer.

_____ тéхником.   _____ a technician.

_____ истóриком.   _____ a historian.

_____ космонáвтом.   _____ an astronaut.

Она́ ста́нет инжене́ром. | She'll become an engineer.
_____ до́ктором. | _____ a doctor.
_____ певи́цей. | _____ a singer.
_____ учи́тельницей. | _____ a teacher.

Мы́ с сестро́й бу́дем фи́зиками. | My sister and I are going to be physicists.
_____ хи́миками. | _____ chemists.
_____ преподава́телями. | _____ instructors.
_____ учителя́ми. | _____ teachers.
_____ инжене́рами. | _____ engineers.
_____ доктора́ми. | _____ doctors.

■ REPETITION DRILL

Repeat the given models, noting that the instrumental case is used in the predicate after verbs such as **бы́ть** and **ста́ть** to describe what one was in the past or expects to be in the future.

■ STRUCTURE REPLACEMENT DRILLS

1. *She's a high-school teacher.*
   She was a high-school teacher.
   Она́ учи́тельница.
   Она́ была́ учи́тельницей.
   О́н помо́щник дире́ктора.
   О́н бы́л помо́щником дире́ктора.
   (он химик, она врач, он учитель, он директор завода, она певица, она моя соседка, они певцы, он отличник, она студентка)

2. *I'm a chemist.*
   I'm going to be a chemist.
   Я́ хи́мик.
   Я́ бу́ду хи́миком.
   Я́ до́ктор.
   Я́ бу́ду до́ктором.
   (певец, историк, директор фабрики, профессор химии, преподаватель музыки, учитель, студент вуза)

■ RESPONSE DRILLS

1. *My friend is a physicist.*
   His father also was a physicist.
   Мо́й дру́г фи́зик.
   Его́ оте́ц то́же бы́л фи́зиком.
   Мо́й дру́г учи́тель.
   Его́ оте́ц то́же бы́л учи́телем.
   (историк, техник, проводник, шофёр, носильщик, колхозник)

2. *I'm not a professor.*
   But I hope to become one.
   Я́ не профе́ссор.
   Но́ я́ наде́юсь ста́ть профе́ссором.
   Я́ не инжене́р.
   Но́ я́ наде́юсь ста́ть инжене́ром.
   (доктор, физик, космонавт, отличник, директор)

3. *I'm interested in the work of a doctor.*
   It's interesting to be a doctor.
   Я́ интересу́юсь рабо́той до́ктора.
   Интере́сно бы́ть до́ктором.
   Я́ интересу́юсь рабо́той инжене́ра.
   Интере́сно бы́ть инжене́ром.
   (техника, историка, химика, преподавателя, врача, учителя)

4. *A doctor's profession is very interesting.*
   I want to become a doctor.
   Профе́ссия врача́ о́чень интере́сна.
   Я́ хочу́ ста́ть врачо́м.
   Профе́ссия учи́теля о́чень интере́сна.
   Я́ хочу́ ста́ть учи́телем.
   (профессия инженера, профессия доктора, профессия химика, профессия физика, профессия историка)

(*cosmonauts*)   *What do they plan to become?*
                 Cosmonauts.
(космона́вты)   Ке́м они́ собира́ются бы́ть?
                 Космона́втами.
(инжене́р)   Ке́м о́н собира́ется бы́ть?
                 Инжене́ром.
(преподава́тели, учи́тельница,
инжене́ры, продавщи́ца, певе́ц,
учи́тель, врачи́, певи́ца)

■ QUESTION-ANSWER DRILLS

1. *Is she a physician?*
   Yes, and her sons will also be physicians.
   Она́ вра́ч?
   Да́, и её сыновья́ то́же бу́дут врача́ми.
   Она́ хи́мик?
   Да́, и её сыновья́ то́же бу́дут хи́миками.
   (инжене́р, фи́зик, до́ктор, те́хник,
   дире́ктор фа́брики)

2. *Was your son interested in technology?*
   Yes, and he became a technician.
   Ва́ш сы́н интересова́лся те́хникой?
   Да́, и о́н ста́л те́хником.
   Ва́ш сы́н интересова́лся пе́нием?
   Да́, и о́н ста́л певцо́м.
   (фи́зикой, хи́мией, исто́рией, ме́стом
   секретаря́, ме́стом помо́щника ди-
   ре́ктора)

3. *Is her daughter a college student?*
   Yes, she recently became one.
   Её до́чь — студе́нтка ву́за?
   Да́, она́ неда́вно ста́ла студе́нткой.
   Её до́чь — инжене́р?
   Да́, она́ неда́вно ста́ла инжене́ром.
   (убо́рщица, вра́ч, зао́чница, про-
   давщи́ца, профе́ссор хи́мии, учи́-
   тельница)

■ DISCUSSION

Whereas the nominative case is used in simple, definition statements in the present tense, the instrumental case is generally required in past or future definitions.

Compare	О́н инжене́р.	He's an engineer.
with	О́н бы́л инжене́ром.	He was an engineer.
	О́н ста́нет инжене́ром.	He'll become an engineer.
	О́н хо́чет бы́ть инжене́ром.	He wants to be an engineer.

In such instances, the instrumental usually describes a situation which is impermanent—one that was or is to become.

Note that one uses the nominative, however, if he views the situation described as permanent.

О́н бы́л америка́нец.	He was an American.
Э́та же́нщина была́ моя́ ма́ть.	That woman was my mother.

The instrumental of adjectives

THE ENDINGS		
SINGULAR		PLURAL
Masculine and Neuter	*Feminine*	
–ым, –им	–ой, –ей	–ыми, –ими

MODELS

Как ты́ мо́жешь бы́ть таки́м споко́й**ным**?   How can you be so calm?
_____ мя́гк**им**?   _____ soft?
_____ ску́чн**ым**?   _____ dull?
_____ холо́дн**ым**?   _____ cold?
_____ безду́шн**ым**?   _____ heartless?
_____ глу́п**ым**?   _____ silly?

О́зеро каза́лось споко́й**ным**.   The lake seemed calm.
_____ больши́**м**.   _____ large.
_____ си́н**им**.   _____ dark blue.
_____ зелён**ым**.   _____ green.

Вода́ ста́ла холо́дн**ой**.   The water's gotten cold.
_____ тёпл**ой**.   _____ warm.
_____ горя́ч**ей**.   _____ hot.

Она́ на́м ка́жется глу́п**ой**.   She seems silly to us.
_____ у́мн**ой**.   _____ intelligent _____.
_____ несча́стн**ой**.   _____ unhappy_____.
_____ симпати́чн**ой**.   _____ likeable _____.

Како́го цве́та ва́ш костю́м?   What color is your costume?
—Чёрный с бе́л**ым**.   Black and white.
_____ с кра́сн**ым**.   _____ red.
_____ с голубы́**м**.   _____ light blue.
_____ с жёлт**ым**.   _____ yellow.
_____ с си́н**им**.   _____ blue.

—Бе́лый с чёрн**ыми** то́чками.   White with black polka dots.
_____ с кра́сн**ыми** _____.   _____ red _____.
_____ с голубы́**ми** _____.   _____ light blue _____.
_____ с си́н**ими** _____.   _____ blue _____.
_____ с зелён**ыми** _____.   _____ green _____.

■ REPETITION DRILL

Repeat the given models, noting that the instrumental form of the adjective is often used to focus on a temporary condition.

1. *He's nice.*
He seems nice to me.
О́н симпати́чный.
О́н мне́ ка́жется симпати́чным.
Она́ ми́лая.
Она́ мне́ ка́жется ми́лой.
(они умные, он глупый, он умный,
они симпатичные, она холодная, она
скучная, они бездушные, он
спокойный)

2. *The lake is calm.*
The lake seems calm.
О́зеро споко́йное.
О́зеро ка́жется споко́йным.
Доро́га дли́нная.
Доро́га ка́жется дли́нной.
Ле́с большо́й.
У́лица споко́йная.
Село́ большо́е.
Доро́га коро́ткая.
Земля́ чёрная.
Хле́б вку́сный.

3. *The meeting was an interesting one.*
The meeting seemed interesting to me.
Собра́ние бы́ло интере́сное.
Собра́ние мне́ каза́лось интере́сным.
Экза́мен бы́л тру́дный.
Экза́мен мне́ каза́лся тру́дным.

Ле́кция была́ дли́нная.
Экза́мены бы́ли тру́дные.
Уро́к бы́л коро́ткий.
Результа́ты бы́ли интере́сные.

■ QUESTION-ANSWER DRILL

How do you find the soup?
I find it very delicious.
Ка́к вы́ нахо́дите су́п?
Я́ его́ нахожу́ о́чень вку́сным.
Ка́к вы́ нахо́дите пироги́?
Я́ и́х нахожу́ о́чень вку́сными.
(борщ, уху, торт, рыбу, печенье,
грибы, бульон, лапшу, булочки, пирог)

■ EXPANSION DRILL

Are you acquainted with her girl friend?
Are you acquainted with her nice girl friend?
Ты́ знако́м с её подру́гой?
Ты́ знако́м с её симпати́чной подру́гой?
Ты́ знако́м с э́тим па́рнем?
Ты́ знако́м с э́тим симпати́чным па́рнем?
(этими студентами, нашим
инженером, этой учительницей, этими
ребятами, этой продавщицей, её
женихом, этой женщиной)

■ RESPONSE DRILLS

1. *The chairs are old.*
They have to be replaced with new ones.
Сту́лья ста́рые.
И́х на́до замени́ть но́выми.
Ли́фт ста́рый.
Его́ на́до замени́ть но́вым.
(лестница, вилки, словарь, полка,
карты, атлас, пластинка, телефоны,
дверь)

2. *But these things are secondhand.*
They seem too expensive to me.
Ведь э́ти ве́щи поде́ржанные.
Они́ мне́ ка́жутся сли́шком дороги́ми.
Ведь э́тот костю́м поде́ржанный.
О́н мне́ ка́жется сли́шком дороги́м.
(эта вещь, этот стол, эта рубашка,
эти платья, эта шапка, эти стулья)

3. *He answered me in a direct way.*
I'm pleased with his direct answer.
О́н мне пря́мо отве́тил.
Я́ дово́лен его́ пря́мым отве́том.

О́н мне́ прекра́сно отве́тил.
Я́ дово́лен его́ прекра́сным отве́том.
(правильно, спокойно, быстро, хорошо,
просто, тепло, осторожно, коротко)

They were young men then.
He was a young man then.
Они́ тогда́ бы́ли молоды́ми людьми́.
Он тогда́ был молоды́м челове́ком.
Йх дя́ди бы́ли стра́нными.
Йх дя́дя был стра́нным.

Йх ба́бушки бы́ли о́чень ста́рыми.
Йх бра́тья бы́ли споко́йными людьми́.
Йх до́чери бы́ли ещё ма́ленькими.
Йх сыновья́ бы́ли ещё ма́ленькими.
Йх де́душки бы́ли симпати́чными людьми́.
Йх ма́тери бы́ли просты́ми же́нщинами.

SINGULAR				PLURAL	
Masculine and Neuter		*Feminine*			
–ым	**–им**	**–ой**	**–ей**	**–ыми**	**–ими**
молоды́м	си́ним	молодо́й	си́ней	молоды́ми	си́ними
но́вым	вече́рним	но́вой	вече́рней	ста́рыми	вече́рними
ста́рым	ру́сским	ста́рой	све́жей	но́выми	ру́сскими
	други́м	ру́сской	хоро́шей		други́ми
	све́жим	друго́й			больши́ми
	хоро́шим	больш́ой			све́жими
	больши́м				хоро́шими

DISTRIBUTION OF ENDINGS

1. In the masculine-neuter instrumental singular, the ending is spelled **–ым** for hard stems and **–им** for soft and mixed stems. Compare молоды́м, ста́рым with си́ним, други́м, ру́сским, хоро́шим, больши́м.

2. In the feminine instrumental singular, the ending is spelled **–ой** for hard stems and **–ей** for soft stems. Compare молодо́й, но́вой with си́ней, вече́рней. Mixed stems take the ending **–ой**, except where the ending is unstressed and preceded by **ш, ж, ч,** or **щ,** in which case it is spelled **–ей.** Compare ру́сской, друго́й, больш́ой with хоро́шей, све́жей.[1]

3. In the instrumental plural, the ending is spelled **–ыми** for hard stems and **–ими** for soft and mixed stems. Compare молоды́ми, но́выми with си́ними, больши́ми, хоро́шими, ру́сскими, други́ми.

Adjectives and pronouns (in adjectival form) which function as nouns

MODELS

Где́ столо́вая?
____ ва́нная?
____ убо́рная?
____ комиссио́нный?
Столо́вая уже́ откры́та.
В **столо́вой** опя́ть щи и ка́ша.
Пойдём в **столо́вую.**

Where's the *dining room* (or *dining hall*)?
_____ the *bathroom?*
_____ the *toilet?*
_____ the *commission store?*
The *dining hall* is already open.
Again, it's shchi and kasha at the *dining hall.*
Let's go to the *dining hall.*

---

[1] In addition to the regular feminine endings **–ой** and **–ей,** there are also longer endings **–ою** and **–ею,** found mostly in older literary works and in poetry.

Я ви́дел э́ти ве́щи в **комиссио́нном**.	I saw these things in the *commission store*.
Я доста́л э́ти ве́щи че́рез **знако́мых**.	I got these things through *friends*.
Óн мо́й хоро́ший **знако́мый**.	He's a close *acquaintance* of mine.
Онá моя́ хоро́шая **знако́мая**.	She's a close *acquaintance* of mine.
Вы́пьем за на́ше **бу́дущее**.	Let's drink to our *future*.
Забу́дь **про́шлое**, ду́май то́лько о **бу́дущем**!	Forget the *past*; think only of the *future!*
Ке́м ты́ хо́чешь бы́ть, **учёным**?	What do you want to be, a *scientist?*
Гла́вное — у него́ хоро́шее ме́сто.	The *main thing* is he has a good job.
Не́которые лю́бят ча́й с молоко́м.	*Some (people)* like tea with milk.
Вы́ ви́дите в лю́дях то́лько **хоро́шее**.	You see only the *good* in people.
_____ **плохо́е**.	_____ *bad* _____.
О чём же ты́ хо́чешь говори́ть?	What then do you want to talk about?
— О **мно́гом**.	About a *lot* of things.
— О **про́шлом**.	About *the past*.
— О **бу́дущем**.	About *the future*.
— О **друго́м**.	About *something else*.
Э́то со **вся́ким** мо́жет случи́ться.	That can happen to *anyone*.
Не **ка́ждый** мо́жет э́то сде́лать.	Not *everyone* can do that.
Я́ о́чень люблю́ **Толсто́го**.	I'm extremely fond of *Tolstoy*.
_____ **Достое́вского**.	_____ *Dostoevsky*.
_____ **Чайко́вского**.	_____ *Tschaikovsky*.
_____ **Страви́нского**.	_____ *Stravinsky*.
_____ **Гóрького**.	_____ *Gorky*.
_____ **Маяко́вского**.	_____ *Mayakovsky*.
Моя́ ба́бушка зна́ла **Толсту́ю**.	My grandmother knew *Mrs. Tolstoy*.
_____ **Достое́вскую**.	_____ *Dostoevsky*.
_____ **Страви́нскую**.	_____ *Stravinsky*.
_____ **Толсты́х**.	_____ *the Tolstoys*.
_____ **Достое́вских**.	_____ *Dostoevskys*.
_____ **Страви́нских**.	_____ *Stravinskys*.

■ CUED SUBSTITUTION DRILLS

1. (*our friends*)   *We had dinner at our friends' place.*
   (на́ши знако́мые)   Мы́ обе́дали у на́ших знако́мых.
   (э́ти ру́сские)   **Мы́ обе́дали у э́тих ру́сских.**
   (наш знакомый, этот учёный, этот рабочий, эти русские, наша знакомая)

2. (*dining hall*)   *He came out of the dining hall* (or *room*).
   (столо́вая)   Óн вы́шел из столо́вой.
   (ва́нная)   **Óн вы́шел из ва́нной.**
   (уборная, комиссионный, столовая, ванная)

3. (*the past*)   *It's not worth talking about the past.*
   (про́шлое)   Не сто́ит говори́ть о про́шлом.
   (бу́дущее)   **Не сто́ит говори́ть о бу́дущем.**
   (другое, многое, её знакомый, эти рабочие, его знакомые, этот учёный)

4. (*Mayakovsky*)   *Do you know this work of Mayakovsky's?*
   (Маяко́вский)   Вы́ зна́ете э́ту ве́щь Маяко́вского?
   (Достое́вский)   **Вы́ зна́ете э́ту ве́щь Достое́вского?**
   (Чайко́вский, Гóрький, Толсто́й, Страви́нский)

1. *They became scientists.*
   He became a scientist.
   Они́ ста́ли учёными.
   Он стал учёным.
   Бра́тья ста́ли рабо́чими.
   Брат стал рабо́чим.
   Э́ти америка́нки ста́ли на́шими
      знако́мыми.
   Э́ти студе́нты ста́ли на́шими знако́мыми.
   Её бра́тья ста́ли учёными.

2. *She met Mrs. Tolstoy.*
   She met the Tolstoys.
   Она́ познако́милась с Толсто́й.
   Она́ познако́милась с Толсты́ми.
   Она́ познако́милась со Страви́нским.
   Она́ познако́милась со Страви́нскими.
   (Маяко́вским, Достое́вской, Чай-
      ко́вским, Страви́нской, Толсты́м)

DISCUSSION

Many Russian adjectives function as nouns. This includes such names as **Толсто́й, Достое́вский, Чайко́вский, Маяко́вский, Страви́нский.** All such names have a feminine form ending in –ая and a plural form ending in –ые (or –ие): **Толста́я** *Miss or Mrs. Tolstoy,* **Толсты́е** *the Tolstoys;* **Достое́вская** *Miss or Mrs. Dostoevsky,* **Достое́вские** *the Dostoevskys.*

Those referring to persons may, but do not always, have feminine counterparts: **ру́сский** *Russian (man),* **ру́сская** *Russian (woman),* **больно́й** *sick man, patient,* **больна́я** *sick woman, patient* (f). The word **рабо́чий** *working man, laborer* is used only in the masculine form and refers only to a man. Compare it with **учёный,** which in its masculine form may also refer to a woman: **Она́ большо́й учёный.**

Besides the adjectives which function as nouns, there are a number of pronouns, adjectival in form, which also function as nouns, for example, **ка́ждый** *everyone,* **вся́кий** *anyone,* **не́которые** *some (people),* **мно́гое** *much,* **мно́гие** *many (people).*

The gender of such words is usually determined by the noun omitted or understood, for example, **столо́вая (столо́вая ко́мната), комиссио́нный (комисио́нный магази́н), про́шлое (про́шлое вре́мя), ка́ждый (ка́ждый челове́к).**

Some words referring to abstract concepts, however, are neuter and are not associated with any specific noun, for example, **но́вое** *that which is new,* **гла́вное** *the main thing,* **интере́сное** *that which is interesting.* Compare the neuter singular **мно́гое** *many things, a lot of things* with the plural **мно́гие** *many people.*

Reflexive verbs—part III

MODELS

Я́ интересу́юсь му́зыкой.   I'm interested in music.
Он интересу́ется _____.   He's interested in _____.
Мы́ интересу́емся _____.   We're interested in _____.
Вы́ интересу́етесь _____.   You're interested in _____.
Они́ интересу́ются _____.   They're interested in _____.
Ты́ интересу́ешься _____.   You're interested in _____.

Он интересова́лся хи́мией.   He was interested in chemistry.
Она́ интересова́лась _____.   She was interested in _____.
Они́ интересова́лись _____.   They were interested in _____.

Ты́ у́чишься англи́йскому языку́?	Are you studying (*or* learning) English?
Вы́ у́читесь _____?	Are you studying (*or* learning) _____?
Я учу́сь ру́сскому языку́.	I'm studying (*or* learning) Russian.
Она́ у́чится _____.	She's studying (*or* learning) _____.
Мы́ у́чимся _____.	We're studying (*or* leaning) _____.
Они́ у́чатся _____.	They're studying (*or* learning) ____.
Óн научи́лся е́здить на маши́не.	He learned to drive a car.
Она́ научи́лась _____.	She learned _____.
Они́ научи́лись _____.	They learned _____.
Ты́ собира́ешься уезжа́ть?	Are you getting ready (*or* planning) to go away?
Вы́ собира́етесь _____?	Are you getting ready (*or* planning) _____?
Я́ собира́юсь уезжа́ть.	I'm getting ready (*or* planning) to go away.
Óн собира́ется _____.	He's getting ready (*or* planning) _____.
Мы́ собира́емся _____.	We're getting ready (*or* planning) _____.
Студе́нты собира́ются.	The students are getting ready (*or* planning) ___.
Сего́дня óн просну́лся ра́но.	He woke up early today.
_____ она́ просну́лась _____.	She woke up _____.
_____ мы́ просну́лись _____.	We woke up _____.
Когда́ вы́ за́втра проснётесь?	When will you wake up tomorrow?
_____ ты́ _____ проснёшься?	_____ will you wake up_____?
За́втра я́ просну́сь ра́но.	Tomorrow I'll wake up early.
_____ она́ проснётся _____.	_____ she'll wake up _____.
_____ мы́ проснёмся _____.	_____ we'll wake up _____.
_____ они́ просну́тся _____.	_____ they'll wake up _____.
Я́ обы́чно просыпа́юсь в се́мь.	I usually wake up at seven.
Ты́ _____ просыпа́ешься _____.	You ___ wake up _____.
Óн _____ просыпа́ется _____.	He _____ wakes up _____.
Мы́ _____ просыпа́емся _____.	We _____ wake up_____.
Вы́ _____ просыпа́етесь _____.	You ___ wake up _____.
Они́ _____ просыпа́ются _____.	They ___ wake up_____.
Ты́ занима́ешься ру́сским языко́м?	Are you studying the Russian language?
Вы́ занима́етесь _____?	Are you studying _____?
Я́ занима́юсь ру́сским языко́м.	I'm studying the Russian language.
Óн занима́ется _____.	He's studying _____.
Мы́ занима́емся _____.	We're studying _____.
Они́ занима́ются _____.	They're studying _____.

■ STRUCTURE REPLACEMENT DRILLS

1. *I'm interested in geography.*
   I was interested in geography.
   Я интересу́юсь геогра́фией.
   Я интересова́лся геогра́фией.
   Я интересу́юсь геогра́фией.
   Я интересова́лась геогра́фией.
       (он, вы, они, она, мы, ты, он)

2. *I'm planning to enter college.*
   I was planning to enter college.
   Я собира́юсь поступи́ть в ву́з.
   Я собира́лся поступи́ть в ву́з.
   Я собира́юсь поступи́ть в ву́з.
   Я собира́лась поступи́ть в ву́з.
       (они, мы, Га́ля, Ви́тя, вы, он, она, ты)

3. *I'm studying physics.*
   I was studying physics.
   Я занимаюсь физикой.
   Я занимался физикой.
   Я занимаюсь физикой.
   Я занималась физикой.

   (вы, Надя, мы, они, Ваня, она, я, ты)

4. *I was learning how to play chess.*
   I learned how to play chess.
   Я учился играть в шахматы.
   Я научился играть в шахматы.
   Я училась играть в шахматы.
   Я научилась играть в шахматы.

   (сын, дочери, Наташа, мы, вы, он, ты, они)

5. *I wake up at seven.*
   I'll wake up at seven.
   Я просыпаюсь в семь.
   Я проснусь в семь.
   Она просыпается в семь.
   Она проснётся в семь.

   (мы, ты, вы, они, я, она)

6. *He got himself a nice soft job.*
   He'll get himself a nice soft job.
   Он устроился на тёплое местечко.
   Он устроится на тёплое местечко.
   Вы устроились на тёплое местечко.
   Вы устроитесь на тёплое местечко.

   (мы, ты, она, я, они, он, вы)

■ QUESTION-ANSWER DRILLS

1. *Would that seem interesting to you?*
   Yes, I'm interested in that.
   Тебе это будет интересно?
   Да, я этим интересуюсь.
   Ему это будет интересно?
   Да, он этим интересуется.

   (вам, им, ей, тебе, ему)

2. *Are you students?*
   Yes, we go to college.
   Вы студенты?
   Да, мы учимся в вузе.
   Она студентка?
   Да, она учится в вузе.

   (Они студенты? Она студентка? Вы студенты? Он студент? Ты студент? Они студенты?)

3. *Are you leaving already?*
   Yes, I'm getting ready to leave.
   Ты уже уезжаешь?
   Да, я собираюсь уезжать.
   Вы уже уезжаете?
   Да, мы собираемся уезжать.

   (она, ты, они, он, вы, она, они)

4. *Do you drive a car already?*
   Not yet, but I'll learn.
   Ты уже ездишь на машине?
   Нет ещё, но я научусь.
   Он уже ездит на машине?
   Нет ещё, но он научится.

   (вы, она, ты, они, он, вы, она)

■ MIXED STRUCTURE REPLACEMENT DRILLS

Plural to singular and vice versa.

1. *We'll wake up early.*
   I'll wake up early.
   Мы проснёмся рано.
   Я проснусь рано.
   Он проснётся рано.
   Они проснутся рано.

   (ты, мы, она, вы, я, он, мы, ты)

2. *What were you thinking about?*
   О чём ты задумался?
   О чём вы задумались?
   О чём девушки задумались?
   О чём девушка задумалась?

   (парни, она, он, вы, он, ты)

3. *I'm studying Russian.*
   We're studying Russian.
   Я занимаюсь русским языком.
   Мы занимаемся русским языком.

   Эта американка занимается русским языком.
   Эти американки занимаются русским языком.

   (вы, мы, ты, я, она, студенты)

4. *Wake up!*
Просыпа́йся!
Просыпа́йтесь!
Просни́сь!
Просни́тесь!

Учи́тесь ру́сскому языку́!
Занима́йся ру́сским языко́м!
Научи́тесь е́здить на маши́не!
Интересу́йся бо́льше заня́тиями!

■ RESPONSE DRILL

You're not awake yet?
Wake up!
Ты́ ещё не просну́лся?
Просни́сь!
Ты́ ещё не научи́лся?
Научи́сь!

Ты́ ещё не собира́ешься?
Ты́ с ни́м не познако́мился?
Ты́ не у́чишься?
Ты́ не занима́ешься?

DISCUSSION

The verb **интересова́ться** is accompanied by the instrumental case without a preposition to indicate the thing one becomes interested in: **Он интересу́ется ру́сской литерату́рой** *He's interested in Russian literature.*

The verb **занима́ться** is accompanied by the instrumental without a preposition to indicate the thing with which one is occupied or the thing one is studying: **Он занима́ется ру́сским языко́м** *He's studying Russian*; **Я́ занима́юсь чте́нием пи́сем** *I'm busy reading letters.*

Учи́ться and **научи́ться** are accompanied by the infinitive or the dative without a preposition to indicate the thing studied or learned: **Он у́чится ру́сскому языку́** *He's studying Russian*; **Она́ научи́лась говори́ть по-англи́йски** *She learned to speak English.*

The verb **устро́иться** is followed by **на** plus the accusative in the sense of getting established in a position or job: **Он устро́ился на хоро́шую рабо́ту** *He got himself a good job.* In describing the place where one works or settles, however, **в** or **на** plus the prepositional is used.

О́н устро́ился в Москве́.	He settled in Moscow *or* He got himself a job in Moscow.
Я́ устро́юсь на заво́де.	I'll get a job at a factory.
Она́ удо́бно устро́илась в но́вой кварти́ре.	She's comfortably settled in her new apartment.

Perfectivization by prefix по– to indicate a limited amount of the activity

MODELS

О́н рабо́тал це́лый де́нь.	He worked the whole day.
О́н порабо́тал полчаса́.	He did half an hour's work.
Мы́ мно́го танцева́ли.	We danced a lot.
Мы́ потанцева́ли немно́го.	We danced for awhile.
Она́ до́лго спала́.	She slept for a long time.
Она́ поспала́ о́коло ча́са.	She got about an hour's sleep.

Вы́ до́лго сиде́ли в па́рке?
—Не́т, мы́ посиде́ли о́коло ча́са, а пото́м
уе́хали.

Did you sit in the park long?
No, we sat about an hour and then drove away.

Ты́ до́лго стоя́ла в о́череди?
— Да́, мне́ пришло́сь постоя́ть мину́т
два́дцать.

Did you stand in line long?
Yes, I had to stand for about twenty minutes.

Вы́ до́лго иска́ли ша́пку?
— Не́т, мы́ поиска́ли мину́т де́сять и нашли́.

Did you spend a long time looking for the cap?
No, we hunted about ten minutes and found it.

О́н бы́л у на́с про́шлой зимо́й.
О́н побы́л у на́с два́ дня́ и уе́хал.

He was at our place last winter.
He spent two days with us and left.

Мы́ та́м жи́ли два́ го́да.
Мы́ та́м недо́лго пожи́ли, а пото́м нашли́
но́вую ко́мнату.

We lived there for two years.
We lived there for awhile, then found a new
    room.

Вы́ бу́дете игра́ть всё у́тро?
— Не́т, мы́ то́лько немно́го поигра́ем.

Will you be playing all morning?
No, we'll just play a little.

■ QUESTION-ANSWER DRILLS

1. *How much longer will I have to stand?*
   Stand a little longer.
   Ка́к до́лго мне́ ещё ну́жно стоя́ть?
   Посто́й ещё немно́го.
   Ка́к до́лго мне́ ещё ну́жно ходи́ть?
   Походи́ ещё немно́го.
       (работать, сидеть, стучать, мешать
       суп, заниматься, гулять, лежать)

2. *Were you able to get a good nap?*
   No, I only slept for half an hour.
   Вы́ смогли́ хорошо́ поспа́ть?
   Не́т, я́ поспа́л то́лько полчаса́.
   Вы́ смогли́ хорошо́ пое́здить?
   Не́т, я́ пое́здил то́лько полчаса́.
       (погулять, потанцевать, поработать,
       поспать, поездить)

3. *Are you off to look for work?*
   Yes, I'll go do a bit of looking.
   Ты́ идёшь иска́ть рабо́ту?
   Да́, пойду́ поищу́.
   Ты́ идёшь стира́ть?
   Да́, пойду́ постира́ю.

   (работать, играть в футбол, гулять,
   спать, смотреть на их игру, слушать
   новости)

■ STRUCTURE REPLACEMENT DRILLS

1. *We were strolling.*
   We strolled a bit.
   Мы́ гуля́ли.
   Мы́ немно́го погуля́ли.
   Мы́ рабо́тали.
   Мы́ немно́го порабо́тали.
       (стучали, спали, сидели, лежали,
       ездили на новой машине, стояли в
       очереди, слушали радио)

2. *I'll dance with her.*
   I'll dance with her awhile.
   Я́ бу́ду с не́й танцева́ть.
   Я́ с не́й потанцу́ю.
   Я́ бу́ду с не́й говори́ть.
   Я́ с не́й поговорю́.
   Я́ бу́ду здéсь сидéть.
   Я́ бу́ду здéсь стоя́ть.
   Я́ бу́ду с ва́ми рабо́тать.
   Я́ бу́ду с ва́ми гуля́ть.
   Я́ бу́ду с ва́ми слу́шать пласти́нки.
   Я́ бу́ду иска́ть ва́м ме́сто.

Although **по-** sometimes provides what may be considered the basic perfective for an imperfective verb **(смотре́ть, посмотре́ть)**, very often it is not the primary perfective, but rather a secondary perfective focusing on the limited duration of the activity.

Compare **чита́ть** (ipfv) *to read, to be reading*

прочита́ть (pfv) *to finish reading, read* (*through to the end*)

with **почита́ть** (pfv) *to do a bit of reading, read for a while*

Вы́ ко́нчили чита́ть э́ту газе́ту?	Have you finished reading this paper?
— Да́, я её уже́ прочита́л.	Yes, I've already read it.
— Не́т, я ещё не всю́ прочита́л.	No, I haven't read it all yet.
— Не́т, я ещё чита́ю.	No, I'm still reading it.
— Да́, я **почита́л** немно́го и уста́л.	Yes, I read awhile and got tired.

Among the verbs already encountered which may take perfectives with the prefix **по-** are the following: стоя́ть, сиде́ть, лежа́ть, говори́ть, ду́мать, слу́шать, рабо́тать, бы́ть, жи́ть, танцева́ть, иска́ть, стуча́ть, е́здить, ходи́ть, гуля́ть, спа́ть, пи́ть, игра́ть, стира́ть, занима́ться.

ЧТЕ́НИЕ И ПИСЬМО́

Шко́ла око́нчена. Де́сять лет прошли́ так бы́стро! Ви́ктор и Анато́лий учили́сь вме́сте и бы́ли больши́ми друзья́ми, но Ви́ктор был отли́чник, а Анато́лий – нет. Хорошо́ Ви́ктору: он мо́жет сра́зу поступи́ть в вуз. Анато́лий же до́лжен рабо́тать два го́да на произво́дстве просты́м рабо́чим. Э́то не осо́бенно ве́село. Но Ви́ктор говори́т Анато́лию, что ещё не всё пропа́ло: Анато́лий лю́бит те́хнику, вот э́ти два го́да и не пропаду́т, бу́дут хоро́шей пра́ктикой. А пото́м он смо́жет устро́ить свою́ жизнь, как ему́ нра́вится.

Ива́н хо́чет устро́иться на тёплое месте́чко, что́бы сра́зу нача́ть хорошо́ зараба́тывать, как говоря́т, стать на но́ги. Ра́ньше он хоте́л стать инжене́ром, но тепе́рь уже́ не мечта́ет об э́том: э́то сли́шком до́лго и тру́дно.

У него теперь другие планы: устроиться на хорошую работу. Тогда и профессия не будет нужна. Как устроиться? Очень просто: по знакомству. Виктор слушает и не верит, что Иван действительно мечтает об этом. Он его хорошо знает и понимает, что Иван не думает серьёзно о „тёплом местечке," а хотел бы тоже учиться дальше. Но Виктор всё-таки желает ему успеха.

На проща́льной вечери́нке все бы́ли в сбо́ре: На́дя, Ве́ра, Ва́ня, Бо́ря, Ви́тя. То́лько О́ля опозда́ла: она́ звони́ла Ве́ре и сказа́ла, что о́чень занята́ и придёт немно́го по́зже вме́сте со свои́м женихо́м. Все вы́пили за её сча́стье, а пото́м за своё бу́душее. Говори́ли о профе́ссиях, кто кем хо́чет бы́ть. Ва́ня с На́дей сказа́ли, что собира́ются бы́ть фи́зиками, а Бо́ря сказа́л, что хоте́л бы ста́ть космона́втом.

Ви́тя ника́к не мо́жет реши́ть, куда́ ему́ идти́: ему́ ка́жется всё интере́сным. Он не зна́ет, кем ста́ть. Ве́ра хо́чет поступи́ть в пединститу́т на литфа́к и сове́тует Ви́те то́же туда́ идти́. Она́ ду́мает, что преподава́ть о́чень интере́сно. Э́то она́ тепе́рь та́к ду́мает, когда́ шко́ла уже́ око́нчена. Тепе́рь все учителя́ ка́жутся таки́ми хоро́шими, а и́х рабо́та — тако́й интере́сной.

— Когда́ я бы́л ма́леньким, я о́чень люби́л чита́ть об Аме́рике. Я прочита́л все рома́ны Дже́ка Ло́ндона и Фенимо́ра Ку́пера.

— И, наве́рно, мечта́ли уе́хать в Аме́рику?

— Коне́чно. Я реши́л пое́хать пря́мо в Нью-Йо́рк. Но́чью вы́шел и́з дому, пошёл на вокза́л, купи́л биле́т до Ки́ева и пое́хал.

— Почему́ же до Ки́ева? На́до бы́ло до Владивосто́ка, ведь вы́ жи́ли в Ташке́нте?

— Да́. Как ви́дите, я пло́хо зна́л геогра́фию. По́зже наш учи́тель геогра́фии о́чень серди́лся и удивля́лся, что я та́к ма́ло научи́лся на его́ уро́ках.

— Ну́, и далеко́ вы́ уе́хали?

— Не́т, то́лько пятьдеся́т киломе́тров от Ташке́нта. Меня́ заме́тил проводни́к и спроси́л, куда́ я е́ду. Я сказа́л: «В Нью-Йо́рк, в Аме́рику». Он, коне́чно, позвони́л мое́й ма́тери, она́ прие́хала и взяла́ меня́ домо́й.

— Зна́ешь, Алёша, у нас тепе́рь но́вые сосе́ди Орло́вы: оте́ц, ма́ть и ма́ленькая до́чь.

— Да́, я с ни́м уже́ познако́мился. Он рабо́тает на мясокомбина́те помо́щником дире́ктора.

— Во́т как! А мне́ его́ жена́ сказа́ла, что он дире́ктор.

— Наве́рно она́ мечта́ет, что он ста́нет дире́ктором. Во́т ей и ка́жется, что он уже́ дире́ктор.

— Да, наве́рно. А зна́ешь, ке́м она́ рабо́тает? Продавщи́цей в кио́ске. Продаёт лимона́д.

— Что́? Жена́ помо́щника дире́ктора и рабо́тает продавщи́цей? Тру́дно пове́рить.

— Да, пра́вда, это немно́го стра́нно. Му́ж её хорошо́ зараба́тывает, у ни́х своя́ маши́на, шофёр.

— Подожди́, а кто́ тебе́ насчёт этого лимона́да сказа́л?

— И́х ма́ленькая до́чь Та́ня.

— Ну́, я ду́маю, что на́шей ма́ленькой сосе́дке не сли́шком мо́жно ве́рить.

— Да, пожа́луй. Познако́мимся с ни́ми как сле́дует, лу́чше и́х узна́ем. Мо́жет быть они́ и неплохи́е лю́ди.

— Да, наде́юсь, что мы́ бу́дем хоро́шими сосе́дями.

— Ка́к прошёл ве́чер у твои́х знако́мых?

— Ничего́, то́лько вы́пить как сле́дует нельзя́ бы́ло: да́ли не вино́, а каку́ю-то кра́сную во́ду. А о во́дке и не спра́шивай — не́ было совсе́м.

— А кто́ бы́л, интере́сно?

— Все́ на́ши ребя́та и ещё оди́н америка́нец.

— Како́й америка́нец?

— Фили́пп Гра́нт. О́н со мно́й на одно́м ку́рсе.

— А, Гра́нт! Я́ о нём слы́шал. Ка́к у него́ с ру́сским языко́м?

— Тепе́рь вполне́ хорошо́. Всё понима́ет и говори́т совсе́м свобо́дно.

— Скажи́те, до́ктор что́ я́ до́лжен де́лать?

— Лежа́ть, немно́го ходи́ть, и по утра́м де́лать масса́ж.

— О́х, ка́к не люблю́ масса́жа!

— Без масса́жа вы́ никогда́ не смо́жете хорошо́ ходи́ть.

— А ско́лько вре́мени мне́ ещё ну́жно сиде́ть до́ма?

— Ещё неде́лю, е́сли то́чно бу́дете де́лать всё, что я́ сказа́л. А е́сли не бу́дете, тогда́, пожа́луй, ещё две́ неде́ли не смо́жете ходи́ть на рабо́ту.

— Я́ не ду́мал, что это серьёзно.

— Ничего́, это ва́м бу́дет нау́ка.

— Да, в сле́дующий ра́з бу́ду осторо́жен.

— Стра́нно, я́ то́лько что до́ма пообе́дал и уже́ го́лоден.

— Неуже́ли? Хоти́те, я́ ва́м принесу́ немно́го борща́?

— Пожа́луйста. Я́ борща́ давно́ не ви́дел!

— Так сади́тесь. А ка́к насчёт ры́бы?

— Не́т, спаси́бо, не хо́чется.

— Хорошо́. Во́т бо́рщ, а во́т пироги́.

— Пироги́ я́ о́чень люблю́. О́, о́чень вку́сные!

— Я́ ра́да, что они́ ва́м нра́вятся. Бери́те ещё.

— Не́т, спаси́бо, уже́ дово́льно.

APPENDIX

Reference guide to the pronunciation of Cyrillic letters

The alphabet is given below in its conventional order, together with examples illustrating the various possible pronunciations of each letter and explanatory notes.

Notes

А
а	[a]	and, but
та́к	[ták]	so
ва́с	[vás]	you
ка́к	[kák]	how
да́	[dá]	yes
давно́	[davnó]	for long
куда́	[kudá]	where (to)
та́м	[tám]	there
авто́бус	[aftóbus]	bus
па́па	[pápə]	papa
ма́ма	[mámə]	mamma
по́чта	[póčtə]	post office

Russian **a** is pronounced with its full value [a] not only when it is stressed, but also in the syllable immediately before the stressed syllable and in the initial position. Otherwise it is reduced to [ə], the final sound in English so*f*a.

Б
ба́ба	[bábə]	old woman
ба́к	[bák]	tank
бы́ло	[bílə]	was
бы́л	[bíl]	was
рабо́та	[rabótə]	work
собра́ние	[sabráɲijə]	meeting
авто́бус	[aftóbus]	bus
бума́га	[bumágə]	paper
би́л	[ḅíl]	hit
бе́лая	[ḅéləjə]	white
обе́д	[aḅét]	dinner
в клу́бе	[fklúḅi]	at the club
на слу́жбе	[naslúžḅi]	on the job
бюро́	[ḅuró]	bureau
у тебя́	[uṭiḅá]	you have
клу́б	[klúp]	club
гри́б	[gɾíp]	mushroom
общежи́тие	[apščižíṭijə]	dormitory
коро́бка	[karópkə]	box

Before hard-series vowel letters (**а, э, о, ы, у**) the letter **б** is pronounced hard, somewhat like the *b* in English *b*ook. Before soft-series vowel letters (**я, е, и, ё, ю**) it is pronounced soft, somewhat like the *b* in *b*eauty.

In the final position and before certain consonants **б** is pronounced like the *p* in sto*p*, but without the puff of breath that accompanies the English sound.

В
ва́с	[vás]	you
вы́	[ví]	you

Before hard-series vowel letters the Russian **в** is pronounced hard, somewhat

448

завóд	[zavót]	plant, factory
здорóва	[zdaróvə]	healthy, well
вóт	[vót]	here, there
Ивáн	[iván]	Ivan
привéт	[pṛiγét]	greetings, regards
извинúте	[izγiṇíṭi]	excuse [me]
до свидáния	[dəsγidáṇijə]	good-bye
вчерá	[fčirá]	yesterday
автóбус	[aftóbus]	bus
в клýбе	[fklúḅi]	at the club
всё	[fṣó]	all
всю зúму	[fṣú zímu]	all winter
Лéв	[ḷéf]	Lev
здорóв	[zdaróf]	healthy, well

like the *v* in *v*ote. Before soft-series vowels it is pronounced soft, somewhat like the *v* in *v*iew.

Before certain consonants and at the end of a word **в** is pronounced like the *f* in *f*olk.

Г

гóрод	[górət]	city, town
Гáля	[gáḷə]	Galya
бумáга	[bumágə]	paper
газéта	[gaẓétə]	newspaper
ГУМ	[gúm]	GUM (dept. store)
дóлго	[dólgə]	long
никогдá	[ṇikagdá]	never
гимнáзия	[gimnáẓijə]	secondary school
Евгéний	[jivgéṇij]	Evgeny
Олéг	[aḷék]	Oleg
дрýг	[drúk]	friend
всегó	[fṣivó]	[of] all
хорóшего	[xaróšivə]	[of] good
Толстóго	[talstóvə]	[of] Tolstoy

Russian **г** is pronounced like the *g* in *g*oal before **о, а,** and **у** and like the *g* in ar*g*ue before **е** and **и.** (It is not written before **ё, я, ю, ы,** or **э.**)

Before certain consonants and at the end of a word **г** is pronounced like the *k* in s*k*ill.

Note: In the genitive case endings **–ого** and **–его, г** is pronounced like the *v* in *v*ote.

Д

дá	[dá]	yes
кудá	[kudá]	where (to)
идý	[idú]	I'm going
до свидáния	[dəsγidáṇijə]	good-bye
рáды	[rádi]	glad
дóлго	[dólgə]	long
идёт	[iḍót]	is going
на завóде	[nəzavóḍi]	at the plant
дéло	[ḍélə]	thing, matter
завóд	[zavót]	plant, factory
гóрод	[górət]	city
вóдка	[vótkə]	vodka

Before hard-series vowel letters the letter **д** is pronounced hard, somewhat like the *d* in English woo*d* but with the tongue touching the teeth. Before soft-series vowel letters it is pronounced soft, somewhat like the *d* in *d*uty (pronounced in the British way with a y-like glide).

At the end of a word and before certain consonants the letter **д** is pronounced like the *t* in s*t*ool.

Е

привéт	[pṛiγét]	greetings, regards
нéт	[ṇét]	no
пéния	[ṕéṇijə]	[of] singing
вчерá	[fčirá]	yesterday
в клýбе	[fklúḅi]	at the club
на завóде	[nəzavóḍi]	at the plant
всегó	[fṣivó]	[of] all
éсли	[jésḷi]	if
éсть	[jéṣṭ]	to eat
знáет	[znájit]	knows
рабóтает	[rabótəjit]	works

After a consonant Russian **е** is pronounced like the *e* in m*e*t or th*e*y only when it is stressed. Unstressed, it is pronounced more like the *e* in *e*mote or the *i* in *i*ndustrious. The consonant preceding **е** is typically pronounced soft. When **е** occurs in the initial position or immediately after a vowel it has the same vocalic value as elsewhere, but is preceded by the consonant [j] (as in *y*es).

Ё

всё	[fṣó]	all
Семён	[ṣiṃón]	Semyon
идёт	[iḍót]	is going
ещё	[jiščó]	yet, still
её	[jijó]	her
моё	[majó]	my
ёлка	[jólkə]	fir
ёж	[jóš]	hedgehog

After a consonant the letter **ё** is pronounced like *o* in sp*o*rt. The consonant preceding **ё** is typically pronounced soft. In the initial position or after another vowel **ё** is pronounced like the *yo* in *Yo*rk.[1]

---

[1] The letter **ё** always indicates a stressed syllable. When the stress shifts to another syllable **ё** is replaced by **е.** Compare **всё** [fṣó] with **всегó** [fṣivó].

Ж	скажи́те	[skažíṭi]	say! tell [me]!	The letter ж is pronounced somewhat like the s in leisure or pleasure, but is articulated farther back in the mouth than the English sound.
	уже́	[užé]	already, by now	
	жена́	[žiná]	wife	
	жёлтый	[žóltij]	yellow	
	на слу́жбе	[naslúžḅi]	on the job	In the final position and before certain consonants it is pronounced somewhat like the sh in shore. It is always pronounced hard, even when followed by e, ё, и, or ь, which normally indicate that a soft consonant precedes.
	мо́жно	[móžnə]	it's possible	
	у́ж	[uš]	already	
	му́ж	[múš]	husband	
	мужчи́на	[muščínə]	man	
	наре́жь	[naṛéš]	cut!	

З	заво́д	[zavót]	plant, factory	The Russian з is pronounced hard (as in zoo) before hard-series vowel letters and soft (somewhat like the s in the British pronunciation of resume) before soft-series vowel letters.
	здоро́ва	[zdaróvə]	healthy, well	
	за́втра	[záftrə]	tomorrow	
	зна́ете	[znájiṭi]	you know	
	зима́	[z̦imá]	winter	
	всю зи́му	[fṣú z̦ímu]	all winter	In the final position and before certain consonants з is pronounced like the s in swim.
	взял	[vzál]	took	
	зе́ркало	[z̦érkələ]	mirror	
	ра́з	[rás]	time, once	
	ска́зка	[skáskə]	tale	

И	и	[i]	and	Initially and after a consonant the letter и is pronounced like the i in machine or the e in emote.
	приве́т	[pṛiɣét]	greetings, regards	
	Ни́на	[ṇínə]	Nina	
	иду́	[idú]	I'm going	After a vowel it has the same vocalic value, but is preceded by the consonant [j] (as in yeast). In rapid speech, however, the [j] sound tends to disappear, especially in the combination ии.
	мои́	[mají]	my	
	сто́ило	[stójilə]	cost	
	в Росси́и	[vraṣí(j)i]	in Russia	

Й	домо́й	[damój]	home	The letter й sounds like the y in yes and boy. It occurs almost exclusively after a vowel letter when no vowel follows. It occurs between vowel letters only in words of foreign origin.
	мой	[mój]	my	
	поступа́йте	[pəstupájṭi]	enter, join	
	войти́	[vajṭí]	to come in	
	майо́р	[majór]	major	
	фойе́	[fojé]	foyer	

К	куда́	[kudá]	where (to)	The Russian к is pronounced like the k in skill before the letters о, а, and у, and like the k in askew before e and и. (It does not usually occur before ё, я, ю, ы, or э).
	уро́к	[urók]	lesson	
	ка́к	[kák]	how	
	Ко́ля	[kóḷə]	Kolya	
	Кири́лл	[ḳiṛíl]	Kirill	
	на по́лке	[napólḳi]	on the shelf	
	ви́лки	[ɣílḳi]	forks	

Л	дела́	[ḍilá]	things	The letter л is pronounced somewhat like the l in belt or middle before hard-series vowel letters and like l in milieu (or ll in million) before both soft-series vowel letters and ь.
	слы́шал	[slíšəl]	heard	
	бы́ло	[bílə]	was	
	бы́ли	[bíḷi]	were	
	на столе́	[nəstaḷé]	on the table	
	О́ля	[óḷə]	Olya	
	О́лю	[óḷu]	Olya	
	О́ле	[óḷi]	to Olya	
	бо́льше	[bóḷši]	more	
	портфе́ль	[partﬁéḷ]	briefcase	
	больны́	[baḷní]	sick	

М	письмо́	[ṗiṣmó]	letter	The Russian м is pronounced like the m in moose before hard-series vowel letters and like the m in amuse before both soft-series vowel letters and ь.
	мой	[mój]	my	
	та́м	[tám]	there	
	зи́му	[z̦ímu]	winter	
	мы	[mí]	we	
	Семён	[ṣiṃón]	Semyon	
	в ГУ́Ме	[vgúṃi]	in GUM	

Ми́ла	[m̦ílə]	Mila
меня́	[m̦iná]	me
вре́мя	[vr̦ém̦ə]	time
се́мь	[șém̦]	seven

Н

на уро́к	[nəurók]	to class
но	[no]	but
ну́	[nú]	well
студе́нт	[studént]	student
жёны	[žóni]	wives
Ни́на	[n̦ínə]	Nina
не́т	[n̦ét]	no
собра́ние	[sabrán̦ijə]	meeting
до свида́ния	[dəsv̦idán̦ijə]	good-bye
Ни́не	[n̦ín̦i]	for Nina
не́ было	[n̦ébilə]	there wasn't
извини́те	[izv̦in̦íţi]	excuse [me]
о́чень	[óčin̦]	very
де́нь	[d̦én̦]	day

Before hard-series vowel letters the Russian **н** is pronounced somewhat like the *n* in *n*oo*n* but with the tongue touching the teeth. Before soft-series vowel letters it is pronounced somewhat like the *ny* in ca*ny*on or the *n* in me*n*u.

О

О́ля	[ól̦ə]	Olya
уро́к	[urók]	lesson
на по́чту	[napóčtu]	to the post office
мо́й	[mój]	my
домо́й	[damój]	home
общежи́тие	[apščižíţijə]	dormitory
собра́ние	[sabrán̦ijə]	meeting
до свида́ния	[dəsv̦idán̦ijə]	good-bye
бы́ло	[bílə]	was
спаси́бо	[spaşíbə]	thanks

The Russian **о** is pronounced with its full value (like the *o* in p*o*rt) only when it is stressed. In the initial position and just before the stressed syllable it is pronounced [a]; otherwise it is reduced to [ə], the final sound in sof*a*.

П

по́чта	[póčtə]	post office
Па́вел	[páv̦il]	Pavel
су́пу	[súpu]	some soup
спаси́бо	[spaşíbə]	thanks
вполне́	[fpaln̦é]	completely
беспла́тно	[b̦isplátnə]	free
пра́вда	[právdə]	truth
ти́пы	[ţípi]	types
пе́ние	[p̦én̦ijə]	singing
тепе́рь	[ţip̦ér̦]	now
спешу́	[sp̦išú]	I'm hurrying
опя́ть	[ap̦áţ]	again
пёк	[p̦ók]	he baked
пи́ли	[p̦íl̦i]	drank
сте́пь	[sţép̦]	steppe

Before hard-series vowel letters **п** is pronounced somewhat like the *p* in *p*oor; before both soft-series vowel letters and **ь** it is pronounced more like the *p* in *p*ure.

Р

ра́д	[rát]	glad
уро́к	[urók]	lesson
вчера́	[fčirá]	yesterday
собра́ние	[sabrán̦ijə]	meeting
хорошо́	[xərašó]	good, well
конце́рт	[kancért]	concert
университе́т	[un̦iv̦írşiţét]	university
орёл	[ar̦ól]	eagle
ря́д	[r̦át]	row
приве́т	[pr̦iv̦ét]	greetings, regards
Кири́лл	[k̦ir̦íl]	Kirill
говоря́т	[gəvar̦át]	they say
тепе́рь	[ţip̦ér̦]	now
две́рь	[dv̦ér̦]	door

Before hard-series vowel letters the Russian **р** is pronounced with a tongue trill somewhat like the Scotch *r*. Before both soft-series vowel letters and **ь** it is pronounced trilled but soft, and it has somewhat the effect of a y-like glide following.

С

студе́нт	[studént]	student
студе́нтка	[studéntkə]	coed
собра́ние	[sabrán̦ijə]	meeting
ва́с	[vás]	you

Before hard-series vowel letters the Russian **с** is pronounced like the *s* in *s*oon. Before both soft-series vowels and **ь** it is pronounced somewhat like the *ss* in

интере́сно	[inṭiṛésnə]	interesting	assume (pronounced in the British way with a y-like glide).
су́п	[súp]	soup	
авто́бусы	[aftóbusi]	buses	
спаси́бо	[spaşíbə]	thanks	
Семён	[şiṃón]	Semyon	
всю́ зи́му	[fşú zímu]	all winter	
всё у́тро	[fşó útrə]	all morning	
ве́сь ве́чер	[γéş γéčir]	all evening	
письмо́	[ṗişmó]	letter	

Т

приве́т	[pṛiγét]	greetings, regards	Before hard-series vowel letters the Russian **т** is pronounced somewhat like the *t* in s*t*ool but with the tongue touching the teeth. Before both soft-series vowel letters and **ь,** it sounds somewhat like *t* with a y-like glide (as in the British cos*t*ume and *t*une).
та́м	[tám]	there	
на по́чту	[napóčtu]	to the post office	
ты́	[tí]	you	
авто́бус	[aftóbus]	bus	
идёте	[iḍóṭi]	you're going	
тепе́рь	[ṭiṗéṛ]	now	
хоти́те	[xaṭíṭi]	you want	
тётя	[ṭóṭə]	aunt	
слы́шать	[slíšət]	to hear	
посла́ть	[paslát]	to send	
опя́ть	[aṗáṭ]	again	

У

куда́	[kudá]	where (to)	The Russian **y** is pronounced everywhere somewhat like the *u* in Sch*u*bert. (It is never pronounced like the *u* in *u*niversity, i.e. with a [j] preceding it.)
уже́	[užé]	already, by now	
уро́к	[urók]	lesson	
иду́	[idú]	I'm going	
на по́чту	[napóčtu]	to the post office	
авто́бус	[aftóbus]	bus	

Ф

фа́кт	[fákt]	fact	The Russian **ф** is found mostly in words of foreign origin. It is pronounced hard (like the *f* in *f*arm) before hard-series vowel letters and soft (somewhat like the *f* in *f*ew) before both soft-series vowel letters and **ь.**
фо́рма	[fórmə]	form, uniform	
фами́лия	[faṃílijə]	last name	
жира́ф	[žiráf]	giraffe	
портфе́ль	[partféḷ]	briefcase	
Фили́пп	[fiḷíp]	Filipp	

Х

хорошо́	[xərašó]	good, well	The Russian **x** has no counterpart in English. Before **a, o,** and **y** it is pronounced hard, somewhat like the *ch* in German a*ch* and Ba*ch*; before **e** or **и** it is pronounced soft, somewhat like the *ch* in German i*ch*.
заходи́те	[zəxaḍíṭi]	drop in! come in!	
а́х	[áx]	oh!	
ху́же	[xúži]	worse	
хоти́те	[xaṭíṭi]	you want	
Хитро́в	[χitróf]	Khitrov	
бронхи́т	[branχít]	bronchitis	
схе́ма	[sχémə]	scheme, plan	

Ц

конце́рт	[kancért]	concert	The Russian **ц** is always pronounced hard (somewhat like the *ts* in ca*ts*), even when it is followed by **e** or **и,** which normally indicate that a soft consonant precedes.
Цара́пкин	[carápḳin]	Tsarapkin	
огурцы́	[agurcí]	cucumbers	
в канцеля́рии	[fkənciḷáṛiji]	in an office	
ца́рь	[cáṛ]	tsar	
оте́ц	[aṭéc]	father	

Ч

на по́чту	[napóčtu]	to the post office	The Russian **ч** is always pronounced soft (somewhat like the *ch* in *ch*eese), even when it is followed by **a, o,** or **y,** which normally indicate that a hard consonant precedes.
вчера́	[fčirá]	yesterday	
ча́й	[čáj]	tea	
«Óчи чёрные»	[óči čórnijə]	"Dark Eyes"	
о́чень	[óčiṇ]	very	
в о́череди	[vóčiṛiḍi]	in line	
плечо́	[pḷičó]	shoulder	
чу́дно	[čúdnə]	wonderful	

Ш

слы́шал	[slíšəl]	heard	The Russian **ш** is always pronounced hard (somewhat like the *sh* in *sh*ip but articulated farther back in the mouth), even when it is followed by **ь, e,** or **и,**
хорошо́	[xərašó]	good, well	
хоро́шего	[xaróšivə]	[of] good	
спешу́	[sṗišú]	I'm hurrying	

	спеши́те	[spišíti]	you're hurrying
	ка́ша	[káshə]	kasha
	ша́пка	[šápkə]	cap
	ше́сть	[šéṣṭ]	six

which normally indicate that a soft consonant precedes.

Щ	бо́рщ	[bóršč]	borsch
	ещё	[jiščó]	yet, still
	щи́	[ščí]	schi
	в я́щике	[vjáščiḳi]	in the drawer
	борща́	[barščá]	some borsch
	щу́ка	[ščúka]	pike

The Russian **щ** is a long, soft consonant pronounced somewhat like the *shch* in fre*sh ch*eese, spoken without a break. It is always pronounced soft, even when it is followed by **a** or **y,** which normally indicate that a hard consonant precedes.

Ъ	съе́л	[sjél]	ate
	отъе́зд	[atjést]	departure

The symbol **ъ** (hard sign) has no sound value of its own. It is used between prefixes that end in a consonant and word roots beginning with **e, я, ю,** or **ё** to indicate that these vowel letters are pronounced with a preceding [j] (as in *y*es).

Ы	ты́	[tí]	you
	вы́	[ví]	you
	бы́ло	[bílə]	was
	бы́л	[bíl]	was
	бы́ть	[bíṭ]	to be
	слы́шал	[slíšəl]	heard
	мы́	[mí]	we

The letter **ы** varies in pronunciation ranging from something like the vowel in b*i*t to the *i* of mach*i*ne. After lip consonants **б, в, п, ф,** and **м,** many speakers pronounce a w-like glide before **ы** so that it sounds somewhat like the English *we,* except shorter.

The letter **ы** never appears in the initial position in a word.

Ь	посла́ть	[paslát]	to send
	портфе́ль	[partféḷ]	briefcase
	письмо́	[ṗiṣmó]	letter
	бо́льше	[bóḷši]	more, bigger
	о́чень	[óčiṇ]	very
	семья́	[ṣiṃjá]	family

The symbol **ь** (soft sign) has no sound value of its own. It serves to indicate the softness of a preceding consonant at the end of a word or immediately before another consonant letter.

It also serves (like **ъ**) to indicate that the soft-series vowel letter which follows is pronounced with a preceding [j] (as in *y*es).

Э	э́то	[étə]	this
	э́тот	[étət]	this
	э́ти	[éṭi]	these
	экза́мен	[igzáṃin]	exam
	элеме́нт	[iḷiṃént]	element

The letter **э** occurs mostly in words of foreign origin, usually in the initial position. When stressed it is pronounced like the *e* in *E*ric; when not stressed it is apt to be pronounced like the *e* in *e*mote or the *i* in *i*llegal, although many speakers pronounce it as [e] wherever it occurs.

Ю	всю неде́лю	[fṣú ṇiḍéḷu]	all week
	говорю́	[gəvaṛú]	I speak
	стою́	[stajú]	I stand
	рабо́таю	[rabótəju]	I work
	пью́	[ṗjú]	I drink
	о́сенью	[óṣiṇju]	in the fall

The letter **ю,** both when stressed and unstressed, is pronounced like the *u* in t*u*ne after a consonant letter (which is pronounced soft); it is pronounced like the *u* in *u*nion after a vowel letter, **ъ,** or **ь,** or when it is in the initial position.

Я	говоря́т	[gəvaṛát]	they say
	опя́ть	[aṗáṭ]	again
	в канцеля́рии	[fkənciḷáṛiji]	in an office
	портфе́ля	[partféḷə]	[of the] briefcase
	стоя́ли	[stajáḷi]	stood
	до свида́ния	[dəsɣidáṇjə]	good-bye
	пе́ния	[ṗéṇijə]	[of] singing
	язы́к	[jizík]	language
	тяжело́	[ṭižiló]	hard

After a consonant the stressed letter **я** is pronounced somewhat like the *a* in f*a*r. In unstressed syllables **я** is usually pronounced like **и,** except in certain grammatical endings where it sounds like the *a* in English sof*a*. The consonant preceding **я** is always pronounced soft. When **я** occurs in the initial position or following a vowel, **ъ,** or **ь,** it has the same vocalic value as elsewhere, but is preceded by the consonant sound [j] (as in *y*es).

Noun declension

1. стóл-nouns

				SINGULAR			
	table	*city*	*knife*	*tea*	*student*	*teacher*	*day*
N	стóл	гóрод	нóж	чáй	студéнт	учúтель	дéнь
A	стóл	гóрод	нóж	чáй	студéнта	учúтеля	дéнь
G	столá	гóрода	ножá	чáя	студéнта	учúтеля	дня́
P	столé	гóроде	ножé	чáе	студéнте	учúтеле	дне́
D	столý	гóроду	ножý	чáю	студéнту	учúтелю	дню́
I	столóм	гóродом	ножóм	чáем	студéнтом	учúтелем	днём
				PLURAL			
N	столы́	городá	ножú	чаú	студéнты	учителя́	днú
A	столы́	городá	ножú	чаú	студéнтов	учителéй	днú
G	столóв	городóв	ножéй	чаёв	студéнтов	учителéй	днéй
P	столáх	городáх	ножáх	чая́х	студéнтах	учителя́х	дня́х
D	столáм	городáм	ножáм	чая́м	студéнтам	учителя́м	дня́м
I	столáми	городáми	ножáми	чая́ми	студéнтами	учителя́ми	дня́ми

2. окнó-nouns

			SINGULAR			
	window	*word*	*letter*	*meeting*	*dress*	*field*
N	окнó	слóво	письмó	собрáние	плáтье	пóле
A	окнó	слóво	письмó	собрáние	плáтье	пóле
G	окнá	слóва	письмá	собрáния	плáтья	пóля
P	окнé	слóве	письмé	собрáнии	плáтье	пóле
D	окнý	слóву	письмý	собрáнию	плáтью	пóлю
I	окнóм	слóвом	письмóм	собрáнием	плáтьем	пóлем
			PLURAL			
N	óкна	словá	пúсьма	собрáния	плáтья	поля́
A	óкна	словá	пúсьма	собрáния	плáтья	поля́
G	óкон	слóв	пúсем	собрáний	плáтьев	полéй
P	óкнах	словáх	пúсьмах	собрáниях	плáтьях	поля́х
D	óкнам	словáм	пúсьмам	собрáниям	плáтьям	поля́м
I	óкнами	словáми	пúсьмами	собрáниями	плáтьями	поля́ми

3. женá-nouns

				SINGULAR			
	wife	*girl*	*sister*	*street*	*earth, land*	*lecture*	*uncle*
N	женá	дéвушка	сестрá	ýлица	земля́	лéкция	дя́дя
A	женý	дéвушку	сестрý	ýлицу	зéмлю	лéкцию	дя́дю
G	жены́	дéвушки	сестры́	ýлицы	землú	лéкции	дя́ди
P	женé	дéвушке	сестрé	ýлице	землé	лéкции	дя́де
D	женé	дéвушке	сестрé	ýлице	землé	лéкции	дя́де
I	женóй	дéвушкой	сестрóй	ýлицей	землёй	лéкцией	дя́дей
				PLURAL			
N	жёны	дéвушки	сёстры	ýлицы	зéмли	лéкции	дя́ди
A	жён	дéвушек	сестёр	ýлицы	зéмли	лéкции	дя́дей
G	жён	дéвушек	сестёр	ýлиц	земéль	лéкций	дя́дей
P	жёнах	дéвушках	сёстрах	ýлицах	зéмлях	лéкциях	дя́дях
D	жёнам	дéвушкам	сёстрам	ýлицам	зéмлям	лéкциям	дя́дям
I	жёнами	дéвушками	сёстрами	ýлицами	зéмлями	лéкциями	дя́дями

4. двéрь-nouns

	door	notebook	line, turn	thing	mother	daughter
	SINGULAR					
	door	*notebook*	*line, turn*	*thing*	*mother*	*daughter*
N	двéрь	тетрáдь	óчередь	вéщь	мáть	дóчь
A	двéрь	тетрáдь	óчередь	вéщь	мáть	дóчь
G	двéри	тетрáди	óчереди	вéщи	мáтери	дóчери
P	двéри	тетрáди	óчереди	вéщи	мáтери	дóчери
D	двéри	тетрáди	óчереди	вéщи	мáтери	дóчери
I	двéрью	тетрáдью	óчередью	вéщью	мáтерью	дóчерью
	PLURAL					
N	двéри	тетрáди	óчереди	вéщи	мáтери	дóчери
A	двéри	тетрáди	óчереди	вéщи	матерéй	дочерéй
G	дверéй	тетрáдей	очередéй	вещéй	матерéй	дочерéй
P	дверя́х	тетрáдях	очередя́х	вещáх	матеря́х	дочеря́х
D	дверя́м	тетрáдям	очередя́м	вещáм	матеря́м	дочеря́м
I	дверя́ми / дверьми́	тетрáдями	очередя́ми	вещáми	матеря́ми	дочерьми́ / дочеря́ми

5. и́мя-nouns (neuter)

	SINGULAR			**PLURAL**	
	name	*time*		*names*	*times*
N	и́мя	врéмя	N	именá	временá
A	и́мя	врéмя	A	именá	временá
G	и́мени	врéмени	G	имён	времён
P	и́мени	врéмени	P	именáх	временáх
D	и́мени	врéмени	D	именáм	временáм
I	и́менем	врéменем	I	именáми	временáми

6. Nouns with declension irregularities

	church	neighbor	brother	chair	leaf	pen
	SINGULAR					
	church	*neighbor*	*brother*	*chair*	*leaf*	*pen*
N	цéрковь	сосéд	брáт	сту́л	ли́ст	перó
A	цéрковь	сосéда	брáта	сту́л	ли́ст	перó
G	цéркви	сосéда	брáта	сту́ла	листá	перá
P	цéркви	сосéде	брáте	сту́ле	листé	перé
D	цéркви	сосéду	брáту	сту́лу	листу́	перу́
I	цéрковью	сосéдом	брáтом	сту́лом	листóм	перóм
	PLURAL					
N	цéркви	сосéди	брáтья	сту́лья	ли́стья	пéрья
A	цéркви	сосéдей	брáтьев	сту́лья	ли́стья	пéрья
G	церквéй	сосéдей	брáтьев	сту́льев	ли́стьев	пéрьев
P	церквáх	сосéдях	брáтьях	сту́льях	ли́стьях	пéрьях
D	церквáм	сосéдям	брáтьям	сту́льям	ли́стьям	пéрьям
I	церквáми	сосéдями	брáтьями	сту́льями	ли́стьями	пéрьями

(*cont.*)

	SINGULAR				
	tree	*husband*	*son*	*friend*	*citizen*
N	де́рево	му́ж	сы́н	дру́г	граждани́н
A	де́рево	му́жа	сы́на	дру́га	граждани́на
G	де́рева	му́жа	сы́на	дру́га	граждани́на
P	де́реве	му́же	сы́не	дру́ге	граждани́не
D	де́реву	му́жу	сы́ну	дру́гу	граждани́ну
I	де́ревом	му́жем	сы́ном	дру́гом	граждани́ном
	PLURAL				
N	дере́вья	мужья́	сыновья́	друзья́	гра́ждане
A	дере́вья	муже́й	сынове́й	друзе́й	гра́ждан
G	дере́вьев	муже́й	сынове́й	друзе́й	гра́ждан
P	дере́вьях	мужья́х	сыновья́х	друзья́х	гра́жданах
D	дере́вьям	мужья́м	сыновья́м	друзья́м	гра́жданам
I	дере́вьями	мужья́ми	сыновья́ми	друзья́ми	гра́жданами

	SINGULAR			
	Mr.	*Georgian*	*man*	*baby, child*
N	господи́н	грузи́н	челове́к	ребёнок
A	господи́на	грузи́на	челове́ка	ребёнка
G	господи́на	грузи́на	челове́ка	ребёнка
P	господи́не	грузи́не	челове́ке	ребёнке
D	господи́ну	грузи́ну	челове́ку	ребёнку
I	господи́ном	грузи́ном	челове́ком	ребёнком
	PLURAL			
N	господа́	грузи́ны	лю́ди	де́ти
A	госпо́д	грузи́н	люде́й	дете́й
G	госпо́д	грузи́н	люде́й	дете́й
P	господа́х	грузи́нах	лю́дях	де́тях
D	господа́м	грузи́нам	лю́дям	де́тям
I	господа́ми	грузи́нами	людьми́	детьми́

7. Nouns used in the plural

	chess	*kids, guys*	*money*	*schi*
N	ша́хматы	ребя́та	де́ньги	щи́
A	ша́хматы	ребя́т	де́ньги	щи́
G	ша́хмат	ребя́т	де́нег	ще́й
P	ша́хматах	ребя́тах	деньга́х	ща́х
D	ша́хматам	ребя́там	деньга́м	ща́м
I	ша́хматами	ребя́тами	деньга́ми	ща́ми

Adjective declension

MASCULINE AND NEUTER				*Singular*			
N (*m*) но́вый	молодо́й	си́ний	друго́й	ру́сский	большо́й	хоро́ший
(*n*) но́вое	молодо́е	си́нее	друго́е	ру́сское	большо́е	хоро́шее
A (animate = genitive; inanimate = nominative)						
G но́вого	молодо́го	си́него	друго́го	ру́сского	большо́го	хоро́шего
P но́вом	молодо́м	си́нем	друго́м	ру́сском	большо́м	хоро́шем
D но́вому	молодо́му	си́нему	друго́му	ру́сскому	большо́му	хоро́шему
I но́вым	молоды́м	си́ним	други́м	ру́сским	больши́м	хоро́шим

FEMININE							
N но́вая	молода́я	си́няя	друга́я	ру́сская	больша́я	хоро́шая
A но́вую	молоду́ю	си́нюю	другу́ю	ру́сскую	большу́ю	хоро́шую
G, P, D, I но́вой	молодо́й	си́ней	друго́й	ру́сской	большо́й	хоро́шей

				Plural			
N но́вые	молоды́е	си́ние	други́е	ру́сские	больши́е	хоро́шие
A (animate = genitive; inanimate = nominative)						
G, P но́вых	молоды́х	си́них	други́х	ру́сских	больши́х	хоро́ших
D но́вым	молоды́м	си́ним	други́м	ру́сским	больши́м	хоро́шим
I но́выми	молоды́ми	си́ними	други́ми	ру́сскими	больши́ми	хоро́шими

Pronoun declension

1. Personal pronouns and interrogatives кто́ and что́

N	я́	ты́	о́н, оно́	она́	мы́	вы́	они́	кто́	что́
A	меня́	тебя́	его́, него́	её, неё	на́с	ва́с	и́х, ни́х	кого́	что́
G	меня́	тебя́	его́, него́	её, неё	на́с	ва́с	и́х, ни́х	кого́	чего́
P	мне́	тебе́	нём	не́й	на́с	ва́с	ни́х	ко́м	чём
D	мне́	тебе́	ему́, нему́	е́й, не́й	на́м	ва́м	и́м, ни́м	кому́	чему́
I	мно́й / мно́ю	тобо́й / тобо́ю	и́м, ни́м	е́й, не́й / е́ю, не́ю	на́ми	ва́ми	и́ми, ни́ми	ке́м	чём

Note: The reflexive personal pronoun **себя́** has no nominative form; it declines like **ты́: себя́, себе́, собо́й.**

2. Possessive pronoun modifiers and interrogative чей *whose*

MASCULINE AND NEUTER			*Singular*		
N (*m*) че́й	мо́й	тво́й	сво́й	на́ш	ва́ш
(*n*) чьё	моё	твоё	своё	на́ше	ва́ше
A (animate = genitive; inanimate = nominative)					
G чьего́	моего́	твоего́	своего́	на́шего	ва́шего
P чьём	моём	твоём	своём	на́шем	ва́шем
D чьему́	моему́	твоему́	своему́	на́шему	ва́шему
I чьи́м	мои́м	твои́м	свои́м	наши́м	ваши́м

FEMININE					
N чья́	моя́	твоя́	своя́	на́ша	ва́ша
A чью́	мою́	твою́	свою́	на́шу	ва́шу
G, P, D, I чье́й	мое́й	твое́й	свое́й	на́шей	ва́шей

			Plural			
N	чьй	мой	твой	свой	на́ши	ва́ши
A	(animate = genitive; inanimate = nominative)					
G } P }	чьйх	мойх	твойх	свойх	на́ших	ва́ших
D	чьйм	мойм	твойм	свойм	на́шим	ва́шим
I	чьйми	мойми	твойми	свойми	на́шими	ва́шими

Note: The third person possessives **его́, её,** and **йх** do not decline.

3. Declension of оди́н *one*, э́тот *this*, то́т *that*, and ве́сь *all*

	MASCULINE AND NEUTER		*Singular*		
N	(*m*)	оди́н	э́тот	то́т	ве́сь
	(*n*)	одно́	э́то	то́	всё
A	(animate = genitive; inanimate = nominative)				
G	одного́	э́того	того́	всего́	
P	одно́м	э́том	то́м	всём	
D	одному́	э́тому	тому́	всему́	
I	одни́м	э́тим	те́м	всем	

	FEMININE				
N	одна́	э́та	та́	вся́	
A	одну́	э́ту	ту́	всю́	
G } P } D } I }	одно́й	э́той	то́й	всей	

			Plural		
N	одни́	э́ти	те́	все́	
A	(animate = genitive; inanimate = nominative)				
G } P }	одни́х	э́тих	те́х	все́х	
D	одни́м	э́тим	те́м	всем	
I	одни́ми	э́тими	те́ми	всеми	

Verb conjugation

1. First conjugation verbs

	IMPERFECTIVE ASPECT					
INFINITIVE	чита́ть *read*	писа́ть *write*	ползти́ *crawl*	пе́чь *bake*	сове́товать *advise*	просыпа́ться *wake up*
PAST	чита́л чита́ла чита́ло чита́ли	писа́л писа́ла писа́ло писа́ли	по́лз ползла́ ползло́ ползли́	пёк пекла́ пекло́ пекли́	сове́товал сове́товала сове́товало сове́товали	просыпа́лся просыпа́лась просыпа́лось просыпа́лись
PRESENT	чита́ю чита́ешь чита́ет чита́ем чита́ете чита́ют	пишу́ пи́шешь пи́шет пи́шем пи́шете пи́шут	ползу́ ползёшь ползёт ползём ползёте ползу́т	пеку́ печёшь печёт печём печёте пеку́т	сове́тую сове́туешь сове́тует сове́туем сове́туете сове́туют	просыпа́юсь просыпа́ешься просыпа́ется просыпа́емся просыпа́етесь просыпа́ются
IMPERATIVE	чита́й чита́йте	пиши́ пиши́те	ползи́ ползи́те	пеки́ пеки́те	сове́туй сове́туйте	просыпа́йся просыпа́йтесь

Note: The imperfective future is formed by combining the future forms of **бы́ть** with the imperfective infinitive: **бу́ду чита́ть, бу́дешь чита́ть,** and so forth.

PERFECTIVE ASPECT						
INFINITIVE	прочита́ть *read*	написа́ть *write*	уползти́ *crawl away*	испе́чь *bake*	посове́товать *advise*	просну́ться *wake up*
PAST	прочита́л прочита́ла прочита́ло прочита́ли	написа́л написа́ла написа́ло написа́ли	упо́лз уползла́ уползло́ уползли́	испёк испекла́ испекло́ испекли́	посове́товал посове́товала посове́товало посове́товали	просну́лся просну́лась просну́лось просну́лись
FUTURE	прочита́ю прочита́ешь прочита́ет прочита́ем прочита́ете прочита́ют	напишу́ напи́шешь напи́шет напи́шем напи́шете напи́шут	уползу́ уползёшь уползёт уползём уползёте уползу́т	испеку́ испечёшь испечёт испечём испечёте испеку́т	посове́тую посове́туешь посове́тует посове́туем посове́туете посове́туют	просну́сь проснёшься проснётся проснёмся проснётесь просну́тся
IMPERATIVE	прочита́й прочита́йте	напиши́ напиши́те	уползи́ уползи́те	испеки́ испеки́те	посове́туй посове́туйте	просни́сь просни́тесь

Note: Perfective verbs are not used in the present tense.

2. Second conjugation verbs

IMPERFECTIVE ASPECT							
INFINITIVE	ве́рить *believe*	учи́ться *study*	смотре́ть *look*	стоя́ть *stand*	люби́ть *love*	проси́ть *ask*	серди́ться *be angry*
PAST	ве́рил ве́рила ве́рило ве́рили	учи́лся учи́лась учи́лось учи́лись	смотре́л смотре́ла смотре́ло смотре́ли	стоя́л стоя́ла стоя́ло стоя́ли	люби́л люби́ла люби́ло люби́ли	проси́л проси́ла проси́ло проси́ли	серди́лся серди́лась серди́лось серди́лись
PRESENT	ве́рю ве́ришь ве́рит ве́рим ве́рите ве́рят	учу́сь у́чишься у́чится у́чимся у́читесь у́чатся	смотрю́ смо́тришь смо́трит смо́трим смо́трите смо́трят	стою́ стои́шь стои́т стои́м стои́те стоя́т	люблю́ лю́бишь лю́бит лю́бим лю́бите лю́бят	прошу́ про́сишь про́сит про́сим про́сите про́сят	сержу́сь се́рдишься се́рдится се́рдимся се́рдитесь се́рдятся
IMPERATIVE	верь ве́рьте	учи́сь учи́тесь	смотри́ смотри́те	сто́й сто́йте	люби́ люби́те	проси́ проси́те	серди́сь серди́тесь

Note: The imperfective future is formed by combining the future forms of **быть** with the infinitive: **бу́ду ве́рить**, **бу́дешь ве́рить**, and so forth.

(cont.)

	PERFECTIVE ASPECT						
INFINITIVE	пове́рить *believe*	научи́ться *learn*	посмотре́ть *look*	постоя́ть *stand*	оста́вить *leave*	попроси́ть *ask*	рассерди́ться *become angry*
PAST	пове́рил пове́рила пове́рило пове́рили	научи́лся научи́лась научи́лось научи́лись	посмотре́л посмотре́ла посмотре́ло посмотре́ли	постоя́л постоя́ла постоя́ло постоя́ли	оста́вил оста́вила оста́вило оста́вили	попроси́л попроси́ла попроси́ло попроси́ли	рассерди́лся рассерди́лась рассерди́лось рассерди́лись
FUTURE	пове́рю пове́ришь пове́рит пове́рим пове́рите пове́рят	научу́сь научи́шься научи́тся научи́мся научи́тесь научатся	посмотрю́ посмо́тришь посмо́трит посмо́трим посмо́трите посмо́трят	постою́ постои́шь постои́т постои́м постои́те постоя́т	оста́влю оста́вишь оста́вит оста́вим оста́вите оста́вят	попрошу́ попро́сишь попро́сит попро́сим попро́сите попро́сят	рассержу́сь рассе́рдишься рассе́рдится рассе́рдимся рассе́рдитесь рассе́рдятся
IMPERATIVE	пове́рь пове́рьте	научи́сь научи́тесь	посмотри́ посмотри́те	постой посто́йте	оста́вь оста́вьте	попроси́ попроси́те	рассерди́сь рассерди́тесь

Note: Perfective verbs are not used in the present tense.

3. Irregular verbs

INFINITIVE	хоте́ть (ipfv) *want*		да́ть (pfv) *give*	
PAST	хоте́л хоте́ла хоте́ло хоте́ли		да́л дала́ да́ло да́ли	
PRESENT	хочу́ хо́чешь хо́чет хоти́м хоти́те хотя́т	**FUTURE**	да́м да́шь да́ст дади́м дади́те даду́т	
IMPERATIVE	(none)		да́й да́йте	

Other verbs conjugated similarly are: **захоте́ть** (pfv), **прода́ть** (pfv), **пода́ть** (pfv), **переда́ть** (pfv), and all other perfective verbs formed by adding prefixes to the above basic verbs.

Reference list of verbs[1]

Б
   би́ть I (pfv по-)   17   hit
   боле́ть II (pfv по-)   16   ache
   боя́ться II (pfv по-)   14   fear
   бра́ть I (pfv взя́ть)   13   take
   бы́ть (pfv по-)   4   be

В
   вари́ть II (pfv с-)   17   cook
   ве́рить II (pfv по-)   15   believe
   верну́ться I (ipfv возвраща́ться)   16   return
   взя́ть I (ipfv бра́ть)   6   take
   ви́деть II (pfv у-)   2, 6   see
   висе́ть II (pfv по-)   15   be hanging
   возвраща́ться I (pfv верну́ться)   16   return
   войти́ I (ipfv входи́ть)   4   enter
   встре́тить II (ipfv встреча́ть)   11   meet
   вы́бросить II (ipfv выбра́сывать)   17   discard, throw out
   вы́говорить II (ipfv выгова́ривать)   11   pronounce, utter
   вы́йти I (ipfv выходи́ть)   14   go (*or* come) out
   вы́пить I (ipfv пи́ть)   13   drink
   вы́тереть I (ipfv вытира́ть)   17   wipe
   выходи́ть II (pfv вы́йти)   14   go (*or* come) out
   выходи́ть (вы́йти) за́муж   18   get married

Г
   говори́ть II (pfv по- *or* сказа́ть)   1   speak, say
   гуля́ть I (pfv по-)   14   stroll

Д
   дава́ть I (pfv да́ть)   14   give
   да́ть (ipfv дава́ть)   13   give
   де́лать I (pfv с- *or* по-)   3   do, make
   договори́ться II (ipfv догова́риваться)   11   agree, come to terms
   достава́ть I (pfv доста́ть)   13   get hold of
   доста́ть I (ipfv достава́ть)   4   get hold of
   ду́мать I (pfv по-)   6   think

Е
   е́здить II (pfv по-)   12   go (by vehicle)
   е́хать I (pfv по-)   12   be going (by vehicle)

Ж
   жда́ть I (подо-)   9   wait
   жела́ть I (по-)   18   wish
   жи́ть I (по-)   9   live

З
   забыва́ть I (pfv забы́ть)   14   forget
   забы́ть I (ipfv забыва́ть)   7   forget
   заду́маться I (ipfv заду́мываться)   18   sink into reverie
   зайти́ I (ipfv заходи́ть)   13   drop in, go behind
   заказа́ть I (ipfv зака́зывать)   12   order
   закры́ть I (ipfv закрыва́ть)   3   close
   замени́ть II (ipfv заменя́ть)   4   replace
   заме́тить II (ipfv замеча́ть)   13   notice
   замо́лвить сло́во (*or* слове́чко) II (pfv)   9   put in a good word
   занима́ться I (pfv по- *or* заня́ться)   18   study, busy oneself
   заплати́ть II (ipfv плати́ть)   12   pay
   зараба́тывать I (pfv зарабо́тать)   18   earn
   заходи́ть II (pfv зайти́)   4   drop in, go behind
   захоте́ть II (ipfv хоте́ть)   18   want
   зва́ть I (pfv по-)   11   call
   звони́ть II (pfv по-)   7   phone
   зна́ть I (ipfv)   3   know

---

[1] Roman numerals I and II refer to the first and second conjugations. Arabic numerals refer to the lesson in which the verb was initially presented (usually in the Preparation for Conversation).

The other member of the aspect pair is indicated parenthetically; for the sake of completeness some verbs not formally presented or drilled in the text are included here. The translations given are the most basic ones.

И	игра́ть I (сыгра́ть *or* по-) 11	play
	идти́ I (pfv пойти́) 1	be going
	извини́ть II (ipfv извиня́ть) 1	excuse
	измени́ть II (ipfv изменя́ть) 4	change
	интересова́ть I (pfv за-) 18	interest
	интересова́ться I (pfv за-) 18	be interested
	иска́ть I (pfv по-) 12	seek
	испе́чь I (ipfv пе́чь) 17	bake
	итти́ I (*see* идти́) 1	be going
К	каза́ться I (pfv по-) 6	seem
	конча́ть I (pfv ко́нчить) 14	finish
	ко́нчить II (ipfv конча́ть) 14	finish
	купи́ть II (ipfv покупа́ть) 4	buy
Л	лежа́ть II (pfv по-) 18	lie
	люби́ть II (pfv по-) 10	love
М	мечта́ть I (pfv по-) 18	dream
	меша́ть I (pfv по-) 17	disturb, stir
	мо́чь I (pfv с-) 7	be able, can
Н	наде́яться I (pfv по-) 18	hope
	назва́ть I (ipfv называ́ть) 10	name
	назна́чить II (ipfv назнача́ть) 16	set, designate
	найти́ I (ipfv находи́ть) 17	find
	нали́ть I (ipfv налива́ть) 18	pour
	написа́ть I (ipfv писа́ть) 4, 7	write
	наре́зать I (ipfv нареза́ть) 5	slice
	научи́ться II (ipfv учи́ться) 18	learn
	находи́ть II (pfv найти́) 17	find
	находи́ться II (pfv найти́сь) 17	be situated
	нача́ть I (ipfv начина́ть) 18	begin
	носи́ть II (pfv по-) 15	carry
	нра́виться II (pfv по-) 11, 16	like
О	обе́дать I (pfv по-) 5	eat dinner
	обрати́ться II (ipfv обраща́ться) 16	consult
	обраща́ться I (pfv обрати́ться) 16	consult
	ожида́ть I (ipfv) 8	expect
	око́нчить II (ipfv ока́нчивать) 18	finish
	опа́здывать I (pfv опозда́ть) 11	be late
	опозда́ть I (ipfv опа́здывать) 11	be late
	оста́вить II (ipfv оставля́ть) 7	leave
	оста́ться I (ipfv остава́ться) 17	remain, be left
	отве́тить II (ipfv отвеча́ть) 3	answer
	отвеча́ть I (pfv отве́тить) 3	answer
	отдохну́ть I (ipfv отдыха́ть) 14	rest
	отдыха́ть I (pfv отдохну́ть) 14	rest
	открыва́ть I (pfv откры́ть) 11	open
	откры́ть I (pfv открыва́ть) 3, 7	open
П	переда́ть (ipfv передава́ть) 18	hand over, pass
	перейти́ I (ipfv переходи́ть) 14	cross, switch, go over
	переходи́ть II (pfv перейти́) 14	cross, switch, go over
	пе́ть (pfv с-) 13	sing
	пе́чь I (pfv ис- *or* с-) 17	bake
	писа́ть I (pfv на-) 4, 7	write
	пи́ть I (pfv вы́-) 5	drink
	плати́ть II (pfv за-) 12	pay
	побы́ть (ipfv бы́ть) 18	be (for a while)
	пове́рить II (ipfv ве́рить) 15	believe
	повтори́ть II (ipfv повторя́ть) 1	repeat
	поговори́ть II (ipfv говори́ть) 11	talk
	погуля́ть I (ipfv гуля́ть) 14	stroll
	пода́ть (ipfv подава́ть) 9	give, submit

поде́лать I (ipfv де́лать) 17	do
подожда́ть I (ipfv жда́ть) 8	wait
подойти́ I (ipfv подходи́ть) 7	approach
поду́мать I (ipfv ду́мать) 7	think
пое́здить II (ipfv е́здить) 18	drive (a bit)
пое́хать I (ipfv е́хать) 12	go (by vehicle)
пожи́ть I (ipfv жи́ть) 18	live (for a while)
позанима́ться I (ipfv занима́ться) 18	study, be busy (for a while)
позвони́ть II (ipfv звони́ть) 7	phone
познако́мить II (ipfv знако́мить) 10	introduce
познако́миться II (ipfv знако́миться) 6	meet
поигра́ть I (ipfv игра́ть) 18	play (for a while)
поиска́ть I (ipfv иска́ть) 18	look for
пойти́ I (ipfv идти́, итти́) 3	go
показа́ть I (ipfv пока́зывать) 15	show
пока́зывать I (pfv показа́ть) 15	show
покупа́ть I (pfv купи́ть) 4	buy
полежа́ть II (ipfv лежа́ть) 18	lie (for a while)
полете́ть II (ipfv лете́ть) 18	fly
ползти́ I (pfv по-) 17	be crawling
положи́ть II (ipfv кла́сть) 12	put, lay
получи́ть II (ipfv получа́ть) 9	get
по́мнить II (pfv вс-) 11	remember
помога́ть I (pfv помо́чь) 16	help
помо́чь I (ipfv помога́ть) 16	help
понима́ть I (pfv поня́ть) 6	understand
понра́виться II (ipfv нра́виться) 11	like
пообе́дать I (ipfv обе́дать) 5	eat dinner
попроси́ть II (ipfv проси́ть) 7	ask, request
порабо́тать I (ipfv рабо́тать) 18	work (for a while)
посиде́ть II (ipfv сиде́ть) 18	sit (for a while)
посла́ть I (ipfv посыла́ть) 1	send
послу́шать I (ipfv слу́шать) 13	listen
посмотре́ть II (ipfv смотре́ть) 4	take a look
посове́товать I (ipfv сове́товать) 13	advise
поспа́ть II (ipfv спа́ть) 18	sleep (for a while), take a nap
постира́ть I (ipfv стира́ть) 18	do the wash
постоя́ть II (ipfv стоя́ть) 18	stand (for a while)
постро́ить II (ipfv стро́ить) 15	build
поступа́ть I (pfv поступи́ть) 3	join, enroll; act, behave
поступи́ть II (ipfv поступа́ть) 18	join, enroll; act, behave
постуча́ть II (ipfv стуча́ть) 18	knock, rap
потанцева́ть I (ipfv танцева́ть) 18	dance (for a while)
потеря́ть I (ipfv теря́ть) 17	lose
походи́ть II (ipfv ходи́ть) 18	walk a bit
предлага́ть I (pfv предложи́ть) 14	suggest
предложи́ть II (ipfv предлага́ть) 9	suggest
предста́вить II (ipfv представля́ть) 16	present
представля́ть I (pfv предста́вить) 15	present
представля́ть (or предста́вить) себе́ 15	imagine
преподава́ть I (ipfv) 18	instruct
привы́кнуть I (ipfv привыка́ть) 14	get used to
пригласи́ть II (ipfv приглаша́ть) 15	invite
приглаша́ть I (pfv пригласи́ть) 15	invite
прие́хать I (ipfv приезжа́ть) 12	arrive (by vehicle)
прийти́ I (ipfv приходи́ть) 14	come, arrive
прийти́сь I (ipfv приходи́ться) 17	have to
принести́ I (ipfv приноси́ть) 8	bring
приноси́ть II (pfv принести́) 13	bring
приходи́ть II (pfv прийти́) 14	come, arrive
продава́ть I (pfv прода́ть) 13	sell
продолжа́ть I (pfv продо́лжить) 16	continue
пройти́ I (ipfv проходи́ть) 6	pass, go through
пропа́сть (ipfv пропада́ть) 18	vanish, be lost
проси́ть II (pfv по-) 12	request, ask
просну́ться I (ipfv просыпа́ться) 18	wake up

просыпа́ться I (pfv просну́ться) 18	wake up
проходи́ть II (pfv пройти́) 9	pass
прочита́ть I (ipfv чита́ть) 13	read

Р

рабо́тать I (pfv по-) 2	work
разреши́ть II (ipfv разреша́ть) 12	permit
рассерди́ться II (ipfv серди́ться) 16	become angry
расти́ I (pfv вы́-) 17	grow
реши́ть II (ipfv реша́ть) 18	decide, solve

С

сади́ться II (pfv се́сть) 14	sit down
свари́ть II (ipfv вари́ть) 17	cook
сде́лать I (ipfv де́лать) 9	do
серди́ться II (pfv рас-) 16	be angry
сиде́ть II (pfv по-) 10	sit
сказа́ть I (ipfv говори́ть) 1	say, tell
слома́ть I (ipfv лома́ть) 16	break
случи́ться II (ipfv случа́ться) 16	happen
слу́шать I (pfv по-) 7	listen
слы́шать II (pfv у-) 2	hear
смотре́ть II (pfv по-) 5	look
смо́чь I (ipfv мочь) 7	be able
снима́ть I (pfv сня́ть) 15	take off, take a picture
собира́ться I (pfv собра́ться) 18	gather, get ready, plan
сове́товать I (pfv по-) 13	advise
сойти́ I (ipfv сходи́ть) 16	go off, get off (or down)
спа́ть II (pfv по-) 12	sleep
спеши́ть II (pfv по-) 2	hurry
спра́шивать I (pfv спроси́ть) 8	ask, inquire
спроси́ть II (ipfv спра́шивать) 8	ask, inquire
станови́ться II (pfv ста́ть) 16	become, get, step, stand
ста́ть I (ipfv станови́ться) 18	become, get, step, stand
стира́ть I (pfv по- or вы́-) 17	wash, launder
сто́ить II (ipfv) 12	cost
стоя́ть II (pfv по-) 4	stand
стро́ить II (pfv по-) 15	build
стуча́ть II (pfv по-) 17	knock
счита́ть I (pfv со-) 10	count, consider
сыгра́ть I (ipfv игра́ть) 14	play

Т

танцева́ть I (pfv по-) 10	dance
теря́ть I (pfv по-) 17	lose

У

убива́ть I (pfv уби́ть) 17	kill
уви́деть II (ipfv ви́деть) 10	see
удивля́ться I (pfv удиви́ться) 12	be surprised
уезжа́ть I (pfv уе́хать) 16	go away (by vehicle)
уе́хать I (ipfv уезжа́ть) 16	go away (by vehicle)
узна́ть I (ipfv узнава́ть) 7	find out, recognize
упа́сть I (ipfv па́дать) 16	fall
уползти́ I (ipfv уполза́ть) 17	crawl away
услы́шать II (ipfv слы́шать) 13	hear
успе́ть I (ipfv успева́ть) 11	succeed, manage, have time
уста́ть I (ipfv устава́ть) 11	get (or be) tired
устро́ить II (ipfv устра́ивать) 18	arrange, set up
устро́иться II (ipfv устра́иваться) 18	be arranged, get settled
учи́ть II (pfv на-) 6	learn, teach
учи́ться II (pfv на-) 18	learn, study

Х

ходи́ть II (pfv по-) 11	go, walk, attend
хоте́ть (pfv за-) 3	want
хоте́ться (pfv за-) 5	feel like

Ч

чита́ть I (pfv про- or по-) 1	read
чу́вствовать I (pfv по-) 16	feel

Russian-English Vocabulary

Arabic numerals refer to the lesson in which the word was introduced or discussed.

Nouns are given in their nominative singular form, or, if used only in the plural, in their nominative plural form. Where an inserted vowel occurs in the nominative singular, the genitive singular is also indicated.

Verbs are given in their infinitive form, with the third person plural present-future sometimes also provided. Perfective verbs are marked pfv; imperfective verbs are not marked. Roman numerals I and II refer to the first and second conjugations.

Long-form adjectives are given only in the nominative singular masculine form except for soft stems, where feminine and neuter forms are also provided.

Prepositions are accompanied by a parenthetical indication of the case they require.

А а

а   and, but, by the way, how about 1
á   ah, oh 2
автóбус   bus 1
авторýчка   fountain pen 17
агá [ahá]   aha! ahhh! 7
администрáтор   clerk, administrator 12
Алёша (var. of Алексéй)   Alyosha (Alex) 17
аллó   hello (telephone only) 7
Амéрика   America 6
американец,–нца   American (m) 6
американка   American (f) 6
американский   American (adj) 6
Анатóлий   Anatoly (Anatole) 18
аппарáт   apparatus, camera 15
áтлас   atlas 8
аудитóрия   lecture room, auditorium, classroom 6
áх   oh! 4

Б б

бáбушка   grandmother 17
багáж   luggage, baggage 12
  багáжник   baggage compartment, trunk 12
без, безо (*plus* gen)   without 9
бездýшный   unfeeling, heartless 16
бейсбóл   baseball 11
бéлый   white 13
берý, берёшь (pres of брáть) 13
беспла́тно   free 3

библиотéка   library 6
билéт   ticket 12
бить, бьют (I)   to beat, hit, strike 17
близкий   close, near 15
Бóг   God 15
  Бóже мóй!   good heavens! my God! 16
бóлен, больнá, больны́   sick, ill 2, 3
болéть, боля́т (II)   to ache, hurt 16
больны́ (*see* бóлен) 2, 3
бóльше   more, bigger 5
  бóльше нéт   there isn't any more 5
большóй   large, big 6
  большóе спасибо   thanks very much 9
Бори́с   Boris 7
бóрщ   borsch (beet soup) 5
Бóря (var. of Бори́с)   Borya 18
боя́ться, боя́тся (II)   to be afraid 14
брáт   brother 6
брáть, берýт (I)   to take, get 13
брáтья (pl of брáт) 7
бýду, бýдешь (fut of бы́ть) 10
бýдущее   the future 18
бýлка   large roll, small loaf of French bread 17
бýлочка   roll, bun 17
бульóн   consommé, bouillon soup 17
буфéт   snack bar, sideboard 14
бы, б (conditional particle)   would 17
бы́л, былá, бы́ло, бы́ли (past tense of бы́ть) 1
бы́стрый   fast, quick, rapid 18
бы́ть   to be 4

В в

в, во (*plus* prep *or* acc) in, into, at, to 1
ваго́н railroad car 12
Ва́ля (var. of Валенти́на) Valya 17
вам, ва́ми (dat, instr of вы) 9, 12
ва́нная bathroom 12
Ва́ня (var. of Ива́н) Vanya (Johnny) 18
вари́ть (II) to cook (by boiling) 17
вас (acc, gen of вы) 2
вахтёр custodian (m) 7
вахтёрша custodian (f) 7
ваш, ва́ша, ва́ше, ва́ши your, yours 6
вдали́ in the distance 15
вдвоём two together 14
вдру́г suddenly 16
ведро́ pail, bucket 15
ведь after all, but, you know 9
везде́ everywhere 13
ве́ра faith, confidence 15
Ве́ра Vera 18
ве́рить (II) to believe, trust 15
верну́ться (pfv I) to come back, return 16
ве́рующий believer 15
ве́рхний, –яя, –ее, upper 12
весёлый merry, gay, jolly 18
 ве́село it's fun 18
весна́ spring 11
 весно́й in spring 11
ве́сь, вся, всё, все́ all, whole 2, 7
ве́чер evening, party (formal) 10
 по вечера́м in the evenings 16
вечери́нка party (informal) 18
вече́рний, –яя, –ее, evening (adj) 13
 «Вече́рняя Москва́» *Evening Moscow* (newspaper) 13
ве́чером in the evening 10
 сего́дня ве́чером this evening 10
ве́щь (f) thing 12
взя́ть, возьму́т (pfv I) to take, get 6
ви́д view, aspect 15
ви́дел, ви́дела, –о, –и (past of ви́деть) 2
ви́ден, видна́, –о, –ы visible, can be seen 15
ви́деть (II) to see 6
ви́жу (first person sg of ви́деть) 5
Ви́ктор Victor 18
ви́лка fork 5
вино́ wine 18
висе́ть (II) to be hanging 15
Ви́тя (var. of Ви́ктор) Vitya 18
вку́сный tasty, good, delicious 13
Владивосто́к Vladivostok 12
Влади́мир Vladimir 8
вме́сте together 10
 всё вме́сте all together 1
вме́сто (*plus* gen) instead of, in place of 14
вни́з down, downstairs 16
 внизу́ downstairs, below 12
вода́ water 12
водопрово́д running water, plumbing 15
возвраща́ться (I) to return, come (*or* go) back 16
во́здух air 14
возмо́жный possible 17
возьму́, возьмёшь (fut of взя́ть) 6
война́ war 10
войти́, войду́т (pfv I) to enter, come (*or* go) in 4
вокза́л station, terminal 12

вокру́г (*plus* gen) around 18
Во́лков Volkov (last name) 9
Воло́дя (var. of Влади́мир) Volodya 10
во́н there, yonder 6
 во́н та́м over there, over yonder 6
 во́н то́т that person over there 6
вообще́ in general, at all 16
во́семь eight 10
воскресе́нье Sunday 10
во́т here('s), there('s) 1
 во́т ка́к! is that so! 7
 во́т что́! so that's it! 9
вошёл, вошла́, –о́, –и́ (past tense of войти́) 15
вполне́ completely, fully 2
впро́чем however, but then again 14
вра́ч physician, doctor 16
вре́мени, вре́менем, etc. (*see* вре́мя) 10
вре́мя time 10
все, всё, вся, всю, etc. (*see* ве́сь) 2, 7
всё ещё still, yet 2
 всё равно́ anyway, it doesn't matter 18
всегда́ always 5
всего́ хоро́шего good-bye 2
всё-таки nevertheless, still, just the same 8
встре́тить (pfv II) to encounter, meet 11
всю, вся, etc. (*see* ве́сь) 2
вся́кий any, anyone, anybody 16
 во вся́ком слу́чае in any case 16
вто́рник Tuesday 10
ву́з college 18
вчера́ yesterday 1
вы́ you 1
вы́бросить (pfv II) to throw out, discard 17
вы́говорить (pfv II) to pronounce, say 11
вы́йти, вы́йдут (pfv I) to go out, get off 14
вы́пить, вы́пьют (pfv I) to drink, have a drink 13
вы́тереть, вы́трут (pfv I) to wipe, wipe off 17
выходи́ть (II) to go out, get off 14
 выходи́ть (вы́йти) за́муж to get married 18
вы́шел, вы́шла, etc. (past of вы́йти) 15

Г г

газе́та newspaper 13
Га́ля (var. of Гали́на) Galya 6
где́ where (at what place) 2
где́-нибудь anywhere 18
где́-то somewhere 18
геогра́фия geography 8
гла́вный main, chief 18
 гла́вное the main thing 18
гла́з eye 13
глу́пость (f) foolishness, stupidity 16
глу́пый foolish, stupid 16
говори́ть (II) to speak, talk 1, 6
го́д year 16
 в э́том году́ this year 16
го́лоден, голодна́, го́лодны hungry 5
голубо́й light blue 13
гора́здо by far, much, considerably 16
го́род city, town 4
 в го́род (*or* в го́роде) downtown 4
горсове́т gorsovet (city soviet *or* council) 2
горя́чий hot 12
господа́ ladies and gentlemen, everybody 3
господи́н Mr. 3

госпожа́ Miss, Mrs. 3
гости́ница hotel 12
гото́в ready 6
гра́ждане (pl of граждани́н) citizens 12
гри́б mushroom 17
гро́мче louder 1
грузи́н Georgian 7
гру́ппа group, section 7
гуля́ть (I) to stroll 14
ГУМ GUM (dept. store in Moscow) 4

Д д

да and 5
да́ yes 2
да ну́! no kidding! 13
дава́ть, даю́т (I) to give, let 14
давно́ for a long time, a long time ago 2
дади́м, дади́те, даду́т (see да́ть) 13
да́же even 5
да́й, да́йте (imper of да́ть) 13
далёкий far, far away, distant 15
да́льше further; continue! go on! 4
да́м, да́шь, да́ст (see да́ть) 13
да́ром gratis, for nothing 18
да́ть (pfv with irreg fut: да́м, да́шь, да́ст, дади́м, дади́те, даду́т) to give 13
два́, две́ two 6, 10
две́рь (f) door 4
дво́р courtyard, yard 14
  на дворе́ outdoors, outside, in the yard 14
двухчасово́й two-o'clock (adj) 17
де́вушка young lady, girl 9
де́вять nine 6
де́душка grandfather 17
действи́тельно really, indeed 16
де́лать (I) to do, make 3
де́ло thing, matter, business 2
  в чём де́ло? what's the matter? 7
де́нь, дня́ (m) day 4
де́нь рожде́ния birthday 4
де́ньги money 18
де́рево tree 17
дере́вья (pl of де́рево) 17
деревя́нный wooden 15
де́сять ten 10
де́ти children 17
джа́з jazz, American-style popular music 13
дире́ктор director 18
дли́нный long 17
для (plus gen) for 9
дни́ (pl of де́нь) 7
до (plus gen) before, until, up to 9
до свида́ния good-bye, I'll be seeing you 1
до́брый kind, good 11
  до́брый ве́чер good evening 11
дово́лен, –льна, etc. pleased 7
дово́льно rather, quite, enough 14
договори́ться (pfv II) to come to terms 11
до́ктор doctor 16
до́лго long, a long time 4
до́лжен, должна́, etc. must, have to 8
до́м house, building 9
дома́ (pl of до́м) 9
до́ма at home 10
домо́й home, homeward 1
доро́га road, way, route 15

доро́й expensive, dear 8
доса́да annoyance 5
  во́т доса́да! how annoying! what a nuisance! 5
доска́ board, blackboard 4
достава́ть, достаю́т (I) to get (hold of) 13
доста́ть, доста́нут (pfv I) to get (hold of) 4
до́чери, до́черью, etc. (see до́чь) 17
до́чь daughter 17
дру́г friend 9
друго́й other, different 5
друзья́ (pl of дру́г) 9
ду́мать (I) to think 6
душа́ soul, heart 16
дя́дя uncle 17

Е е

Евге́ний Evgeny (Eugene) 1
его́ him, it, his 6, 10
её her, it, hers 6, 10
е́здить (II) to go (by vehicle) 12
е́й (dat of она́) 14
ему́ (dat of о́н) 17
е́сли if 16
е́сть there is, there are 5
е́хать, е́дут (I) to be going (by vehicle) 12
ещё still, yet, more 5
  всё ещё still, yet 2
  ещё ка́к! and how! 14
  ещё ра́з once again, once more 1
е́ю (instr of она́) 17

Ё ё

ёлка fir tree, Christmas tree 17

Ж ж

жа́ль too bad, pity, sorry 15
жа́ркий hot 14
  жа́рко [it's] hot 14
жда́ть, жду́т (I) to wait 9
же (unstressed emphatic particle) but 5
жела́ть (I) to wish 18
жёлтый yellow 13
жена́ wife 2
жени́х fiancé, bridegroom 18
же́нщина woman 12
жёсткий hard 12
  жёсткий ваго́н second-class coach 12
жи́знь (f) life 18
жи́ть, живу́т (I) to live 9
журна́л magazine, journal 13

З з

за (acc, instr) for, at, behind, after 9
  за́ город (or за́ городом) out of town 17
  за меня́ for me, in my behalf 9
  за столо́м at the table 14
забыва́ть (I) to forget 14
забы́ть, забу́дут (pfv I) to forget 7
заво́д plant, factory 1
за́втра tomorrow 4
заду́маться (pfv I) to daydream 18
зайти́, зайду́т (pfv I) to drop in, stop by 13
заказа́ть, зака́жут (pfv I) to order 12

закры́ть, закро́ют (pfv I)   to close, shut 3
за́л   hall, room 6
замени́ть (pfv II)   to substitute 4
заме́тить (pfv II)   to notice 13
замо́лвить слове́чко   to put in a good word 9
занима́ться (I)   to occupy oneself, to study 18
за́нят, занята́, за́няты   busy, occupied 3
заня́тия   studies, classes 8
зао́чница (*full form* студе́нтка-зао́чница)   corres-
    pondence-school student (f) 9
за́перт, –а́, etc.   locked 4
заплати́ть (pfv II)   to pay 12
зараба́тывать (I)   to earn, make [money] 18
заходи́ть (II)   to drop in, stop by 4
захоте́ть, захотя́т (irreg)   to want, feel like 18
захочу́, захо́чешь, захо́чет, захоти́м, захоти́те, etc.
    (irreg fut of захоте́ть) 18
заче́м   why, what for 6
    заче́м тебе́   why do you need 6
заявле́ние   application 9
зва́ть, зову́т (I)   to call 11
    ка́к тебя́ (*or* ва́с) зову́т?   what's your name? 11
звони́ть (II)   to ring, phone 7
звоно́к, –нка́   bell 7
зда́ние   building 7
здесь   here 7
здоро́в, –а, –ы   healthy, well 2
здра́вствуй, здра́вствуйте   hello 3
зелёный   green 13
земля́   earth, land 18
зима́   winter 2
    зимо́й   in winter 11
Зи́на (var. of Зинаи́да)   Zina 10
змея́   snake 17
знако́м, –а, –ы   acquainted, familiar 10
знако́мство   acquaintance, familiarity 18
    по знако́мству   by knowing the right person,
        through friends 18
знако́мый (m), знако́мая (f)   [an] acquaintance,
    [a] friend 13
зна́ть (I)   to know 3
зна́чить (II)   to mean 10
    зна́чит   it means, so, then 10

И и

и   and, also, too 1
Ива́н   Ivan (John) 7
    Ива́нович (patronymic, son of Ива́н) 9
    Ива́новна (patronymic, daughter of Ива́н) 7
игра́   game, play 14
игра́ть (I)   to play 11
    игра́ть в ка́рты   to play cards 11
идём   let's go 5
идти́, иду́т (I)   to be going 1
из, изо (gen)   from, out of 9
изба́   hut, village house 15
изве́стия   news, news report 13
    «Изве́стия»   *Izvestia* (*News*) (newspaper) 13
извини́те   excuse [me] 1
измени́ть (pfv II)   to change 4
ико́на   holy picture, icon 15
и́ли or 10
    и́ли ... и́ли ...   either ... or 10
и́м (dat of они́, instr of о́н) 7, 14, 17
и́мени, и́менем, имена́, etc. (*see* и́мя) 11

и́мя   name, first name 11
ина́че (*or* и́наче)   otherwise, differently 15
инжене́р   engineer 18
иногда́   sometimes 3
иностра́нец, –нца   foreigner 15
институ́т   institute 18
интере́сно   [that's] interesting, [I] wonder 3
интересова́ть, –су́ют (I)   to interest 18
интересова́ться (I)   to be interested in 18
Ири́на   Irina (Irene) 9
иска́ть, и́щут (I)   to look for, seek 12
испе́чь, испеку́т (pfv I)   to bake 17
исполне́ние   performance 13
    в исполне́нии   performed by 13
исто́рик   historian 18
исто́рия   history 8
итти́ (var. of идти́) 1
и́х   their, them 6, 10

К к

к, ко (dat)   toward, to, to see 4, 7
ка́ждый   each, every 11
ка́жется   [it] seems 6
каза́ться, ка́жутся (I)   to seem 16
ка́к   how, as, like 2
    ка́к дела́?   how is everything? 2
    ка́к ра́з   just, it just happens, the very thing 5, 9
как то́лько   as soon as 17
како́й   what, which 9
како́й-то   some sort of, a, an, kind of 8, 16
ка́менный   [made of] stone, [made of] brick 15
ка́мень, ка́мня   stone, rock 17
кани́кулы (pl only)   vacation 15
каранда́ш   pencil 6
ка́рта   map, card 8
карти́на   picture 11
ка́сса   ticket window, box office, cash register 12
Ка́тя (var. of Екатери́на)   Katya (Kathy) 10
ка́ша   kasha (mush, cooked cereal) 5
кварти́ра   apartment 9
квита́нция   receipt, claim check 12
Ки́ев   Kiev 12
киломе́тр   kilometer (three-fifths of a mile) 15
кино́   movies, cinema 10
кио́ск   stand, newsstand 8
Кири́лл   Kirill (Cyril) 2
Кита́й   China 8
клу́б   club 1
клю́ч   key 7
кни́га   book 3
когда́   when, while 10
кого́ (gen, acc of кто́) 8
ко́е-что́   a thing or two 8
Козло́в   Kozlov (last name) 7
колбаса́   sausage 18
коло́дец, –дца   well 15
колхо́з   kolkhoz, collective farm 15
    колхо́зник   collective-farm worker (m) 15
    колхо́зница   collective-farm worker (f) 15
    колхо́зный   collective farm (adj) 15
Ко́ля (var. of Никола́й)   Kolya (Nick) 6
комиссио́нный (магази́н)   secondhand store 13
ко́мната   room 9
коне́ц, –нца́   end 16
    в конце́ концо́в   finally, in the end 16

конéчно   of course, sure, certainly 4
концéрт   concert 3
кончáть (I)   to finish, end 14
кóнчить (pfv II)   to finish, end 14
копéйка   kopeck 12
корóбка   box (cardboard) 4
корóткий   short 17
космонáвт   cosmonaut, astronaut 18
костю́м   suit, costume 4
котóрый   which, what, that 13
кóфе (indecl)   coffee 5
красúвый   lovely, pretty, handsome 4
крáсный   red 13
   крáсный уголóк   recreation room (*lit.* red corner) 13
кстáти   incidentally, apropos, by the way 3
ктó   who 4
кудá   where (to) 1
купé (indecl)   compartment 12
купúл, –а, etc. (past of купúть) 4
купúть (pfv II)   to buy 4
Кýрочкин   Kurochkin (last name) 7
кýрс   class (year), course 10
кусóк, кускá   piece, slice 8

Л л

лаборатóрия   laboratory 3
лáдно   O.K., fine, all right 14
лапшá   noodles 17
Лéв, Львá   Lev (Leo) 3
лёгкий   easy, light 13
   легкó   [it's] easy, easily 13
лежáть (II)   to be lying, to lie in bed 18
лéкция   lecture, class 6
Ленингрáд   Leningrad 12
лéс   forest, woods 15
лéстница   stairway, stairs, ladder 16
лéт (gen pl of гóд) 16
лéто   summer 11
   лéтом   in summer 11
ли   whether, if (question particle) 7
лимóн   lemon 17
лимонáд   lemonade, soft drink 14
лúст   leaf; sheet 17
листы́   sheets 17
лúстья   leaves 17
литератýра   literature 8
   литератýрный   literary, literature (adj) 18
литфáк   department of literature 18
лúфт   elevator 12
лóжка   spoon 5
лýчше   better, rather 1
лýчший   best, better 7
Лю́ба (var. of Любóвь)   Lyuba 17
любúть (II)   to love, like, to be fond of 10
любóвь, любвú (f)   love 17
Любóвь   Lyubov (Amy) 17
лю́ди   people 13
лю́кс   deluxe class 12

М м

магазúн   store 8
мáзь (f)   ointment, salve 16
мáленький   small, little 9

мáло   little, few, too little 10
мáма   mamma, mom 17
Марúя   Maria (Mary) 7
Мáрс   Mars 18
мáсло   butter, oil 18
мáсса   lots, mass, plenty 17
массáж   massage 16
мáт   checkmate 14
математика   mathematics 8
мáтери, матерéй, etc. (*see* мáть) 15
материáл   material 4
   материáл на костю́м   suit material 4
   материáл на плáтье   dress material 4
мáть, мáтери, etc.   mother 15
Мáша (var. of Марúя)   Masha 7
машúна   car, machine 18
мéдленный   slow 18
мéжду (*plus* instr)   between, among
   мéжду прóчим   by the way 13
мéл   chalk 17
мелóдия   melody, tune 13
меня́ (gen, acc of я́) 8
местéчко   spot, place, job, small town 18
   тёплое местéчко   a soft spot, a nice cushy job 18
мéсто   place, seat, berth, job 12
мéсяц   month; moon 16
мечтáть (I)   to dream 18
мешáть (I)   to disturb, hinder, mix 17
Мúла (var. of Людмúла)   Mila 3
мúлый   nice, kind, dear, darling 9
мúля   mile 15
минýтка   minute, moment 7
   [однý] минýтку   just a minute 7
мúр   peace, world 10
   «Войнá и мúр»   *War and Peace* 10
Михáйлович   (patronymic, son of Михаúл) 7
мнé (prep, dat of я́) 3
мнóго   a lot, lots, much 7
   мнóгое   many things, lots of things 11
могý, мóжешь, мóжет, etc. (pres of мóчь) 7
мóжет бы́ть   maybe, perhaps 6
мóжно   it's possible, one may 4
мой, моя́, моё, мой   my, mine 1, 6
молодéц, –дцá   one who does an outstanding job 7
молодóй   young 13
молокó   milk 5
Москвá   Moscow 9
мóчь, мóгут (I)   to be able, can 7
мýж   husband 2
мужчúна   man 12
мужья́ (pl of мýж) 7
мýзыка   music 13
мы́   we 1
мы́сль (f)   idea, thought 18
мя́гкий   soft 12
   мя́гкий вагóн   first-class coach 12
мя́со   meat 18
мясокомбинáт   meat-packing plant 18

Н н

на (*plus* acc *or* prep)   on, onto, to, at, in, for 1
навéрно   probably, likely 8
навéрх   up, upstairs 16
   наверхý   upstairs, on top, in the upper 12

надéжда   hope 18
Надéжда   Nadezhda (Hope) 18
надéяться, надéются (I)   to hope, count on 18
нáдо   [it's] necessary, one has to 9
  не нáдо!   don't! 15
Нáдя (var. of Надéжда)   Nadya 18
назáд   back, ago 17
  тому́ назáд   ago 17
назвáть, назову́т (pfv I)   to name 10
назнáчить (pfv II)   to set, designate, appoint 16
найти́, найду́т (pfv I)   to find 17
налéво   on the left, to the left 12
нали́ть, налью́т (pfv I)   to pour, fill 18
нáм (dat of мы́) 14
нáми (instr of мы́) 17
написáть, напи́шут (pfv I)   to write 4, 7, 12
напиши́те (imper of написáть) 4
напрáво   on (or to) the right 12
напримéр   for example 11
нарéжь, нарéжьте (imper of нарéзать) 5
нарéзать, нарéжут (pfv I)   to cut, slice 12
нарóд   people 7
  нарóдный   folk, popular, people's 13
нáс (gen, acc, prep of мы́) 5
  у нáс [éсть]   we have 5
насчёт (plus gen)   about 5
Натáша (var. of Натáлья)   Natasha 11
наýка   science, knowledge 18
  вóт тебé наýка!   let that be a lesson to you! 18
научи́ться (pfv II)   to learn 18
наýчный   scientific, scholarly 18
находи́ть (II)   to find 17
находи́ться (II)   to be located 17
начáло   beginning, start 16
начáть, начну́т (pfv I)   to start, begin 18
нáш, нáша, нáше, нáши   our, ours 5, 7
не   not (negative particle) 1
небольшóй   small, not large 12
невозмóжно   impossible 17
негó (gen, acc of óн and онó)
  у негó   he has, at his place 8
недáвно   recently, not long ago 5
недалекó   not far, close, near 15
недéля   week 8
недовóлен, –льна, etc.   dissatisfied, displeased 17
неё (gen, acc of онá) 4, 8, 10
  у неё [éсть]   she has 4, 7
нéй (prep, dat, instr of онá) 7, 14, 17
нéкоторый   some, certain 15
нельзя́   [it's] impossible, one can't 15
нём (prep of óн and онó) 7
немнóго   a little, somewhat 10
нему́ (dat of óн and онó) 14, 16
неплóхо   not badly 6
  неплохóй   not half bad, pretty good 7
непрáвильно   [it's] wrong, [it's] incorrect 3
несимпати́чный   not nice, not likable 16
нéсколько   several, some, a few 17
несчáстный   unhappy, unfortunate 16
  несчáстье   bad luck, misfortune, unhappiness 16
нéт   no; there's no, there isn't any 1, 7
неудóбный   uncomfortable, inconvenient 12
неужéли!   really! you don't say! 13
ни   not (negative particle) 13
  ни . . . ни . . .   neither . . . nor 13
нигдé   nowhere, not . . . anywhere 7

ни́жний, –яя, –ее,   lower 12
никáк   in no way, by no means 9
никакóй   not . . . any, none at all 15
Ники́тич (patronymic, son of Ники́та) 9
никогдá   never 3
Николáевич (patronymic, son of Николáй) 7
Николáй   Nikolay (Nicholas) 6
ни́м (dat of они́, instr of óн and онó) 10, 14
  с ни́м   with him (or it) 10
  к ни́м   to them 14
ни́ми (instr of они́) 10
  с ни́ми   with them 10
Ни́на   Nina 1
ни́х (gen, acc, prep of они́) 7, 8, 10
  у ни́х [éсть]   they have 8
ничегó   nothing; all right 4, 6
но   but 1
нóвость (f)   news, novelty 13
нóвый   new 13
  чтó нóвого?   what's new? 13
ногá   leg, foot 16
нóж   knife 5
нóмер   hotel room, issue, number 12
носи́льщик   porter 12
носи́ть   to carry, wear 15
нóчь (f)   night 11
  по ночáм   nights 16
  спокóйной нóчи   good night 11
  нóчью   at night, during the night 11
нрáвиться (II)   to like, please, appeal to 11, 16
ну́   well, why 1
  ну́, кáк?   well, how about it? 11
  ну́, чтó вы́!   why, what do you mean! 6
  ну́, чтó тáм!   whatever for! not at all! 9
ну́жен, нужнá, –о, –ы́   necessary 8
  мнé нужнá кáрта Еврóпы   I need a map of Europe 8

О о

о, об, обо (plus prep)   about, concerning 7
ó!   oh! 12
обéд   dinner, noon 5
  до обéда   before noon 9
  пóсле обéда   after noon, in the afternoon 9
обéдать (I)   to dine, eat dinner 5
обрати́ться (pfv II)   to consult, turn to 16
обращáться (I)   to consult, turn to 16
общежи́тие   dormitory 4
óбщий   general, over-all, common 15
объявлéние   notice, announcement 13
обы́чно   usually 15
обы́чный   usual 15
огонёк, –нькá   small light 13
  «Огонёк»   Ogonyok (magazine) 13
огурцы́ (pl of огурéц)   cucumbers 5
Одéсса   Odessa 12
одéт, –а, –ы   dressed 17
оди́н, однá, однó   one, a, one and the same, alone 6
ожидáние   waiting, wait, expectation 12
  зáл ожидáния   waiting room 12
ожидáть (I)   to expect, wait 8
óзеро   lake 15
окнó   window 5
óколо (plus gen)   near, by, about 9
окóнчен, –а, –о, –ы   finished, over, done with 18

оконча́ть (pfv II) to finish, graduate from 18
Оле́г Oleg 5
О́ля (var. of О́льга) Olya 4
о́н he, it 1
она́ she, it 1
они́ they 1
оно́ it 1
опа́здывать (I) to come (or be) late 11
опозда́ть (pfv I) to be late 11
опя́ть again 5
Орло́в Orlov (last name) 7
Орло́ва Miss Orlov, Mrs. Orlov 7
о́сень (f) fall, autumn 2
  о́сенью in fall, in autumn 11
О́сипов Osipov (last name) 16
осо́бенно especially, particularly 18
осо́бенный special, particular 18
оста́вить (pfv II) to leave 7
оста́ться, оста́нутся (pfv I) to remain, to be left 17
осторо́жен, –жна, etc. careful 16
осторо́жный careful 16
от, ото (plus gen) from, away from 9
отве́т answer 13
отве́тить (pfv II) to answer, reply 3
отвеча́ть (I) to answer, reply 3
отдохну́ть (pfv I) to rest 14
отдыха́ть (I) to rest 14
оте́ц, отца́ father 15
открыва́ть (I) to open 11
откры́т, –а, –о, –ы open, opened 5
откры́ть, откро́ют (pfv I) to open 3, 7
отку́да from where 9
отли́чник "A" student 18
отли́чно excellent, excellently 7
отсю́да from here, hence 15
отту́да from there 15
о́тчество patronymic 11
  ка́к ва́ше и́мя [и] о́тчество? what are your first name and patronymic? 11
о́чень very, very much, really 4
о́чередь (f) line, turn 4
о́черк sketch, essay, feature story 13
о́чи (poetic for глаза́) eyes 13
  «О́чи чёрные» "Dark Eyes" (song) 13
оши́бка mistake, error 12

П п

Па́влович (patronymic, son of Па́вел) 2
па́лка stick 17
па́рень, па́рня fellow, lad, boy 10
па́рк park 9
певе́ц, певца́ singer (m) 13
певи́ца singer (f) 13
пединситу́т teachers college 18
пе́й, пе́йте (imper of пи́ть) 13
пе́ние singing 1
  уро́к пе́ния singing lesson 1
пе́рвый first 6
пе́ред, пе́редо (plus instr) in front of, before 18
переда́ть, передаду́т (pfv irreg like да́ть) to pass, hand 18
перейти́, перейду́т (pfv I) to go across, go over, to switch 14
переходи́ть (II) to go across, go over 14
перо́ pen point, pen 6

пе́сня song 13
Пётр Pyotr (Peter) 9
Петро́в Petrov (last name) 11
Петро́ва Miss Petrov, Mrs. Petrov 7
Петро́вич (patronymic, son of Пётр) 11
Петро́вна (patronymic, daughter of Пётр) 9
пе́ть, пою́т (I) to sing 13
Пе́тя (var. of Пётр) Petya (Pete) 17
пече́нье cookies 17
пе́чь, пеку́т (I) to bake 17
пешко́м on foot 12
пиро́г pirog 17
писа́ть, пи́шут (I) to write 4, 7, 12
письмо́ letter, writing 1
пи́ть, пью́т (I) to drink 5, 12
пиши́те (imper of писа́ть) 4
пи́ща fare, food, diet 5
пла́н plan, map (of city) 15
пласти́нка record (phonograph) 13
плати́ть (II) to pay 12
плато́к, –тка́ handkerchief, kerchief 17
пла́тье dress 4
  материа́л на пла́тье dress material 4
пло́хо poorly 1
плохо́й poor, bad 14
по (plus dat) by, on, about, in, via, along, around, through 15
по-англи́йски [in] English 6
побы́ть, побу́дут (pfv I) to be, spend some time 18
пове́рить (pfv II) to believe 15
повтори́ть (pfv II) to repeat 1
поговори́ть (pfv II) to have a talk, talk 11
пого́да weather 14
погуля́ть (pfv I) to go for a walk, stroll 14
под, подо (plus instr or acc) under, underneath, beneath 17
пода́рок, –рка present, gift 4
пода́ть, подаду́т (pfv irreg like да́ть) to give, serve, submit 9
поде́лать (pfv I) to do 17
  что́ ж поде́лаешь! it can't be helped! what can you do! 17
поде́ржанный secondhand 13
подожда́ть, подожду́т (pfv I) to wait (for a while) 8
подойти́, подойду́т (pfv I) to go up to, come over to, approach 7
  подойди́те к телефо́ну! answer the phone! 7
подру́га girl friend 13
поду́мать (pfv I) to think 7
по́езд train 12
пое́здить, пое́здят (pfv II) to do some riding 18
поезжа́й! поезжа́йте! drive! go (by vehicle)! 12
пое́хать, пое́дут (pfv I) to go (by vehicle) 12
пожа́луй perhaps, that's an idea 14
пожа́луйста please, don't mention it, you first 1
пожи́ть, поживу́т (pfv I) to live (for a while) 18
позанима́ться (pfv I) to study 18
позвони́ть (pfv II) to call, to telephone 7
по́здно late 3
по́зже later, later on 16
познако́мить (pfv II) to introduce 10
познако́миться (pfv II) to meet, to be introduced 6
поигра́ть (pfv I) to play (for a while) 18
поиска́ть, поищут (pfv I) to look for 18
по́й, по́йте (imper of пе́ть) 15
пойдём let's go 10

пойти́, пойду́т (pfv I)   to go (on foot) 3, 6
пока́   so long; while, meanwhile 6
показа́ть, пока́жут (pfv I)   to show 15
пока́зывать (I)   to show 15
покупа́ть (I)   to buy 4
по́ле   field 15
полежа́ть (pfv II)   to lie down (for a while) 18
полете́ть (pfv II)   to fly 18
ползти́, ползу́т (I)   to be crawling, to be creeping 17
по́лка   shelf, bookcase 6
положи́ть (pfv II)   to put, lay 12
получи́ть (pfv II)   to receive, get 9
полчаса́   half an hour 16
по́мнить (II)   to remember 11
помога́ть (I)   to help 16
по-мо́ему   in my opinion, I think 7
помо́чь, помо́гут (pfv I)   to help 16
помо́щник   assistant, aide 18
понеде́льник   Monday 10
понима́ние   understanding, grasp 11
понима́ть (I)   to understand 3
понра́виться (pfv II)   to like 11, 16
пообе́дать (pfv I)   to eat dinner 5
попроси́ть (pfv II)   to ask, request 7
попу́тчик   traveling companion, fellow traveler 12
пора́   time, it's time 6
порабо́тать (pfv I)   to work (a bit) 18
портфе́ль (m)   briefcase 4
по-ру́сски   [in] Russian 6
поря́док, –дка   order, arrangement 6, 15
   всё в поря́дке   everything's O.K. 6
посиде́ть (pfv II)   to sit (for a while) 18
посла́ть, пошлю́т (pfv I)   to send 1, 12
по́сле (plus gen)   after 8
после́дний, –яя, –ее   last, latest 13
послеза́втра   day after tomorrow 10
послу́шать (pfv I)   to listen (to) 13
посмотре́ть (pfv II)   to take a look 4
посове́товать, –уют (pfv I)   to advise 13
посо́льство   embassy 13
поспа́ть, поспя́т (pfv II)   to sleep (for a while) 18
постира́ть (pfv I)   to do the wash 18
постоя́ть (pfv II)   to stand (for a while) 18
постро́ить (pfv II)   to build 15
поступа́ть (I)   to enroll, enter; behave 3
поступи́ть (pfv II)   to enroll, enter; behave 18
постуча́ть (pfv II)   to knock 18
потанцева́ть, –у́ют (pfv I)   to dance (for a while) 18
потеря́ть (pfv I)   to lose 17
пото́м   afterward, later on, then 18
походи́ть (pfv II)   to walk (a bit) 18
почему́?   why? 10
по́чта   post office, mail 1
почти́   almost 6
пошёл, пошла́, etc. (past of пойти́) 8, 15
пошли́!   let's go! 6
пою́, поёшь, etc. (pres of петь) 15
пра́в, –а́, –о, –ы   right 16
пра́вда   truth; that's true, isn't it, isn't that so 4, 6
   «Пра́вда»   Pravda (Truth) (newspaper) 13
пра́вильно   right, that's right 3
пра́ктика   practice, practical experience 18
предлага́ть (I)   to suggest, propose, offer 14
предложи́ть (pfv II)   to suggest, propose, offer 9
предста́вить (pfv II)   to present, introduce 16
   предста́вить себе́   to imagine 16

представля́ть (I)   to present, introduce 15
   представля́ть себе́   to imagine 15
прекра́сно   fine, excellent, splendid 12
преподава́тель (m)   instructor, teacher 18
преподава́ть, преподаю́т (I)   to instruct, teach 18
приве́т   greetings! regards! hi! 1
привы́к, –ла (past of привы́кнуть) 14
привы́кнуть (pfv I)   to get used to 14
привы́чка   habit 14
пригласи́ть (pfv II)   to invite 15
приглаша́ть (I)   to invite 15
прие́хать, прие́дут (pfv I)   to arrive (by vehicle) 12
прийти́, приду́т (pfv I)   to come, arrive (on foot) 14
прийти́сь (pfv I)   to have to, to be forced to 17
принести́, принесу́т (pfv I)   to bring (on foot) 8
приноси́ть (II)   to bring (on foot) 13
приходи́ть (II)   to come, arrive (on foot) 14
пришёл, пришла́, etc. (past of прийти́) 15
пришло́сь (past of прийти́сь) 17
прия́тно   pleased, [it's] nice 6
проводни́к   conductor, guide 12
продава́ть, продаю́т (I)   to sell 13
продавщи́ца   saleslady 8
продолжа́ть (I)   to continue, keep on 16
прои́грыватель (m)   record player 13
произво́дство   production, manufacture 18
   рабо́тать на произво́дстве   to work in a factory 18
происше́ствие   happening, occurrence, accident, event, incident 13
пройти́, пройду́т (pfv I)   to pass, go by 6
пропа́сть, пропаду́т (pfv I)   to be lost, to perish 18
про́пуск   pass, entry permit 13
проси́ть (II)   to request, ask for 12
просну́ться (pfv I)   to wake up 18
про́сто   just, simply 13
просто́й   simple 13
   просто́й рабо́чий   unskilled worker, ordinary worker 18
просыпа́ться (I)   to wake up 18
про́сьба   request, favor 9
про́тив (plus gen)   opposite, across from, against 6
профе́ссия   profession, calling 18
профе́ссор   professor 7
проходи́ть (II)   to pass, go by 9
прочита́ть (pfv I)   to read (through), finish reading 13
прошёл, прошла́, etc. (past of пройти́) 6
про́шлое   the past 18
про́шлый   past, last 18
   на про́шлой неде́ле   last week 18
проща́льный   farewell (adj) 18
проща́й, проща́йте   good-bye, farewell 18
пря́мо   straight, straight ahead, directly, just 12
пу́сть   let 17
пя́тница   Friday 10
пя́тый   fifth 12
пя́ть   five 10
пятьдеся́т   fifty 15

Р р

рабо́та   work, written paper 7
рабо́тать   to work 2
рабо́чий   worker 18
   просто́й рабо́чий   unskilled worker 18

рáд, –а, –ы glad 2, 3
рáдио (indecl) radio 13
рáз occasion, time; once 5
   как рáз just, it just happens 5
   на э́тот рáз this time 10
рáзве really; is it possible! 8
рáзве что unless maybe 11
разговóр conversation 4
разреше́ние permission, permit 15
разреши́ть (pfv II) to permit, allow 12
рáно early 3
рáньше earlier, before 16
распрóдан, –а, –о, –ы sold out 13
рассерди́ться (pfv II) to become angry, 16
расти́, расту́т (I) to grow 17
ребёнок, –нка baby, child 17
ребя́та kids, fellows, guys 5
ре́дко rarely, seldom 3
результáт result 7
реклáма advertisement, publicity 13
ре́ктор chancellor, president 6
ресторáн restaurant 9
реце́пт prescription, recipe 16
реши́ть (pfv II) to decide, solve 18
роди́тели parents 15
рожде́ние birth 4
   де́нь рожде́ния birthday 4
ромáн novel 10
ромáнс love song 13
рóс, рослá, etc. (irreg past of расти́) 17
руба́шка shirt, slip 17
ру́бль (m) ruble 12
рукá hand, arm 17
ру́сский Russian 6
ру́чка penholder, pen 6
ры́ба fish 5

С с

с, со (gen) since, from 2, 9
с, со (instr) with, together with 10, 17
сади́ться (II) to sit down 14
салфе́тка napkin 18
сам, –á, –ó, сáми oneself (myself, yourself, etc.) 15
сáхар sugar 17
Сáша (var. of Алексáндр, –дра) Sasha (Sandy) 4
сбóр gathering, assembly 18
   в сбóре together, present 18
свари́ть (pfv II) to cook (by boiling) 17
све́жий fresh 14
свежó cool, chilly, fresh 14
свобóда freedom, liberty 18
свобóдно freely, fluently 16
свобóдный free, unoccupied 14
свóй one's own (my own, your own, etc.) 7
сде́лать (pfv I) to do, get done 9, 11
себя́ oneself (reflexive personal pronoun) 9
   у себя́ in one's room (or office) 9
сегóдня today 5
сейчáс now, right away 6
секретáрь (m) secretary 9
селёдка herring 5
селó village 15
Семён Semyon (Simon) 2
Семёнов Semyonov (last name) 8
се́мь seven 10
семья́ family 15

Серге́й Sergey 16
серди́ться (II) to be angry, to be mad 16
серьёзный serious 18
сестрá sister 6
сиде́ть (II) to sit, to be sitting 10
симпати́чный nice, likable 16
си́ний, –яя, –ее dark blue 13
скажи́те (imper of сказáть) 1
сказáть, скáжут (pfv I) to say, tell 12
скóлько how much, how many 10
   во скóлько at what time 10
скоре́е, скоре́й quick, hurry up; sooner, faster 17
скóро soon 11
ску́чно dull, boring 3
сле́дующий next 8
   на сле́дующей неде́ле next week 8
сли́шком too, too much 18
словáрь (m) dictionary, vocabulary 8
слове́чко (var. of слóво) 9
   замóлвите за меня́ слове́чко! put in a good word for me! 9
слóво word 9
сломáть (pfv I) to break 16
слу́жба job, service, work 4
слу́чай case, occasion, incident, event, chance 16
   во вся́ком слу́чае in any case, in any event 16
случи́ться (pfv II) to happen 16
слу́шать (I) to listen 7
слу́шаю hello (on telephone) 7
слы́шать (II) to hear 2
смогу́, смóжешь, etc. (fut of смóчь) 7
смотре́ть (II) to look, see 5
смóчь, смóгут (pfv I) to be able, can 7
снимáть (I) to take off, take a picture 15
сни́мок, –мка snapshot, picture 15
собирáться (I) to gather; to plan 18
собрáние meeting, gathering, collection 1
совéтовать, совéтуют (I) to advise 13
совсе́м completely, quite, altogether 7
соглáсен, –сна, etc. agreed, agreeable 14
сойти́, сойду́т (pfv I) to go off, get off, come down, go down 16
   сойти́ с умá to be out of one's mind, to go crazy 16
   вы с умá сошли́! you're out of your mind! 16
сосе́д neighbor (m) 15
сосе́дка neighbor (f) 15
сосе́дний, –яя, –ее neighboring, next 15
сочине́ние composition 7
спаси́бо thanks, thank you 2
   большóе спаси́бо thanks very much 9
спáть, спя́т (II) to sleep, to be asleep 12, 13
специали́ст specialist 16
спеши́ть (II) to hurry 2
сплю́, спи́шь, спи́т, etc. (pres of спáть) 12, 13
спокóйный calm, quiet 11
   спокóйной нóчи good night 11
спрáшивать (I) to ask (a question), inquire 8
срáзу immediately, right 8
средá Wednesday 10
СССР (Сою́з Совéтских Социалисти́ческих Респу́блик) U.S.S.R. 7
стакáн glass 8
станови́ться (II) to stand, become, grow, get, step 16

ста́нция   station 12

ста́рый   old 9

стать, ста́нут (pfv I)   to stand, become, grow, get, step 18

стира́ть (I)   to launder, wash 17

стихи́   verses, poetry 10

сто́ить (II)   to cost 12

    ско́лько э́то сто́ит?   how much is this? 12

    не сто́ит   it's no use, it isn't worthwhile 18

стол   table, desk 5

столо́вая   dining hall, dining room, cafe 5

стоя́ть (II)   to be standing, to stand 4

страна́   country 15

стра́нный   strange 13

стро́ить (II)   to build 15

студе́нт   student (m) 1

студе́нтка   student (f), coed 1

стул   chair 7

сту́лья (pl of стул) 7

стуча́ть (II)   to knock, rap, pound 17

суббо́та   Saturday 10

суп   soup 17

сча́стье   happiness, luck 18

счита́ть (I)   to count, consider 10

США (Соединённые Шта́ты Аме́рики)   U.S.A. 13

сыгра́ть (pfv I)   to play a game 14

сын   son 17

сыновья́ (pl of сын) 17

сюда́   here, over here 10

Т т

так (unstressed)   then, in that case 3

та́к   so, as, that way, thus 3

та́к, ка́к   just as 16

тако́й   such, so 11

такси́ (indecl)   taxi 12

та́м   there 1

та́нец (sg of та́нцы) 10

танцева́ть, танцу́ют (I)   to dance 10

та́нцы   dance, dances, dancing 10

Та́ня (var. of Татья́на)   Tanya 17

Ташке́нт   Tashkent 12

твой, твоя́, твоё, твои́   your(s) 6

те́ (pl of тот) 13

те́ же   the same 13

теа́тр   theater 9

    театра́льный   theatrical, theater (adj) 13

тебе́ (prep, dat of ты) 6, 14

тебя́ (gen, acc of ты) 6, 9, 10

телефо́н   telephone, phone 7

    звони́т телефо́н   the phone's ringing 7

    звони́ть по телефо́ну   to phone 16

    подойди́(те) к телефо́ну!   answer the phone! 7

те́ннис   tennis 11

тепе́рь   now 2

тёплый   warm 14

    тепло́   [it's] warm 14

    тёплое месте́чко   a nice cushy job 18

теря́ть (I)   to lose 17

тетра́дь (f)   notebook 6

тётя   aunt 17

те́хник   technician 18

те́хника   technology, engineering 18

тобо́й (instr of ты) 17

това́рищ   comrade, friend, colleague 9

    това́рищ по ко́мнате   roommate 10

тогда́   then, in that case 6

то́же   too, also, either 2, 8

толку́чка   flea market, secondhand market 13

Толсто́й, Ле́в   Tolstoy, Leo (writer) 11

то́лько   only, just 5

    то́лько что   just, just now 8

То́ля (var. of Анато́лий)   Tolya 18

тому́ наза́д   ago 17

то́рт   cake 17

тот, та́, то́   that, that one, the one 6

то́т же, та́ же, то́ же   the same 13

то́чка   dot, point, period 17

то́чный   exact, precise 16

трава́   grass 17

три   three 10

три́дцать   thirty 12

тру́дный   hard, difficult 13

туда́   there, to that place 5

тури́ст   tourist 15

ту́т   here 4

ты   you 1

У у

у (plus gen)   at, by, on, from, at the place of 4

    у на́с [есть]   we have 5

    у него́ [есть]   he has 8

    у неё [есть]   she has 4

    у ни́х [есть]   they have 8

убива́ть (I)   to kill 17

убо́рная   toilet, lavatory 12

убо́рщица   cleaning woman 7

уви́деть (pfv II)   to see, catch sight of 10

у́гол, угла́   corner, angle 8

уголо́к, –лка́   little corner 13

    кра́сный уголо́к   recreation room (lit. red corner) 13

уда́ча   luck, good luck 11

удивля́ться (I)   to be surprised 12

удо́бный   convenient, comfortable 12

удо́бство   convenience, comfort 12

удово́льствие   pleasure 3

    с удово́льствием   with pleasure, gladly 3

уезжа́ть (I)   to go away (by vehicle) 16

уе́хать, уе́дут (pfv I)   to go away (by vehicle) 16

уже́   already, by now 2

    уже́ не   no longer, not . . . anymore 18

узна́ть (pfv I)   to find out, learn, recognize 7

«Украи́на»   The Ukraine (hotel) 12

украи́нец, –нца   Ukrainian 7

у́лица   street 13

у́м   mind, sense 16

    вы с ума́ сошли́!   you're out of your mind! 16

у́мный   wise, smart, intelligent 16

университе́т   university 3

упа́сть, упаду́т (pfv I)   to fall, fall down 16

уползти́, уползу́т (pfv I)   to crawl away, creep off 17

уро́к   lesson, class 1

услы́шать (pfv II)   to hear 13

успе́ть (pfv I)   to manage in time, succeed 11

успе́х   success, luck 18

    де́лать больши́е успе́хи   to do very well, make excellent progress 18

уста́ть, уста́нут (pfv I)   to be tired, to get tired 14

устро́ить (pfv II)   to arrange, fix up, organize 18

устро́иться (pfv II)   to get fixed up, get established, get settled 18

у́тро morning 4
  по утра́м in the mornings 16
уф! ugh! ooh! 14
уха́ fish soup, fish chowder 17
учёный scholar, learned man, scientist 18
учи́тель (m) teacher 7
учи́тельница teacher (f) 7
учи́ть (II) to teach; to study 6
учи́ться (II) to learn, study 18

Ф ф

фа́брика factory 9
факульте́т department 7
фами́лия last name, family name 11
фи́зик physicist 18
фи́зика physics 8
Фили́ппович (patronymic, son of Фили́пп) 2
фильм film, movie 10
фо́то photograph, picture 15
футбо́л soccer 11
  игра́ть в футбо́л to play soccer 11

Х х

Ха́рьков Kharkov 12
хи́мик chemist 18
хи́мия chemistry 8
Хитро́в Khitrov (last name) 2
хле́б bread 5
ходи́ть (II) to go, attend, walk 11
хокке́й hockey 11
холо́дный cold 14
  хо́лодно [it's] cold 14
хоро́ший good 9
хорошо́ good, fine, well, nice 1
хоте́ть (irreg pres: хочу́, хо́чешь, хо́чет, хоти́м,
  хоти́те, хотя́т) to want 3-5
хотя́ although 14
  хотя́ бы even if only 14
хо́чется [one] feels like 5
хочу́, хо́чешь, хо́чет, etc. (see хоте́ть) 3-5
ху́же worse 16

Ц ц

Цара́пкин Tsarapkin (last name) 2
цве́т color 13
  цветно́й in color, colored 15
це́лый entire, whole 18
це́рковь, це́ркви (f) church 15

Ч ч

ча́й tea 5
ча́с hour 10
ча́стный private, personal 13
ча́сто often, frequently 3
ча́шка cup 8
че́й, чья́, чьё, чьи́ whose 6
челове́к person, human being, man 13
че́м than 3
  лу́чше по́здно, че́м никогда́ better late than
  never 3

че́м (instr of что́) 17
че́рез (plus acc) through, across, in 13
  через ча́з in an hour 13
чёрный black 13
четве́рг Thursday 10
четы́ре four 10
чита́ть (I) to read 1, 10
что that, who, which 6
что́ what 3
  что́ вы́! you're not serious! 3
  что́ ли perhaps, possibly, maybe 18
  что́ но́вого? what's new? 13
  что́ это why is it, how come 16
чтобы in order to, to 18
что́-нибудь anything, something or other 9
что́-то something 14
чу́вство feeling 18
чу́вствовать, чу́вствуют (I) to feel 16
  чу́вствовать себя́ to be feeling 16
чу́ть не all but, darned near, almost 16
чьё (n of че́й) 6
чьи́ (pl of че́й) 6
чья́ (f of че́й) 6

Ш ш

ша́пка cap 17
ша́хматы chess, chess board 14
  игра́ть в ша́хматы to play chess 14
шёл, шла́, шло́, шли́ (past of идти́) 12, 15
шестна́дцать sixteen 16
ше́сть six 10
шка́ф cupboard, dresser 5
шко́ла school 6
шофёр driver (of car) 12
шу́тка joke 18

Щ щ

щи schi (cabbage or sauerkraut soup) 5

Э э

экза́мен examination, exam 7
электри́чество lights, electricity 15
эта́ж floor, story 12
э́ти these, those 6
э́то it, this, that 2
э́тот, э́та, э́то this, that 7

Ю ю

ю́бка skirt 17
Ю́рий Yury (George) 16

Я я

я I 1
язы́к language, tongue 6
яку́т Yakut 7
Я́лта Yalta 12
я́щик drawer, box (wooden) 5

INDEX

Russian words are in boldface and English translations in italics. The numbers refer to pages on which the items are discussed and drilled. The following abbreviations are used:

acc	accusative	m-d	multidirectional
adj	adjective, adjectival	N	note
adv	adverb, adverbial	n	neuter
aff	affirmative	neg	negative, negation, negated
asp	aspect	nom	nominative
con	consonant	obj	object
conj	conjugation	pers	person, personal
constr	construction	pfv	perfective
dat	dative	pl	plural
decl	declension, declensional	poss	possessive
demonstr	demonstrative	pred	predicate
dir obj	direct object	prep	preposition, prepositional
f	feminine	pres	present
fn	footnote	pres-fut	present-future
fut	future	pron	pronoun
gen	genitive	refl	reflexive
imper	imperative	reg	regular
impers	impersonal	sg	singular
indecl	indeclinable	subj	subject
inf	infinitive	u-d	unidirectional
instr	instrumental	var	variant
interrog	interrogative	vb	verb
ipfv	imperfective	vs	versus
irreg	irregular	vwl	vowel
m	masculine		

abbreviations: **Вуз (Высшее учебное заведение)** *college* 423 N; decl of abbreviations 115 N, 283 N; **ГУМ (Государственный универсальный магазин)** *GUM* 52 N; **СССР (Союз Советских Социалистических Республик)** *U.S.S.R.* 115 N; **США (Соединённые Штаты Америки)** *U.S.A.* 283 N

accent (*see also* stress): remarks on stress 7–8; use of acute to mark stress 5 fn

accusative case: acc for gen after neg vbs 247; acc of **кто, что,** and the pers prons 208–10; acc pl of nouns 243–45; acc sg of inanimate **стол–** and **окно–** nouns 57–58, 96; acc sg of **дверь–** nouns 96; acc sg of **жена–** nouns 96; acc sg of nouns 210–13; acc sg of nouns ending in **–а** and **–я** 95–96; decl of **чей** and poss modifiers 299–302; decl of adjs 295–99; primary function of 54; summary of noun endings in acc case 245; use of acc in time expressions 213

adjectives: dat sg and pl 378–80; formation of short-form adjs ending in **–о** from long-form adjs 330–31; hard stems, soft stems, and mixed stems defined 275; instr sg and pl 436–38; m, f, and pl short forms of **занят, рад, здоров, болен** 45–47; n short forms ending in **–о** used in impers constr 322–23; nom, acc, gen, and prep: sg and pl 295–99; nom sg and pl 272–75; that function as nouns 63 fn; 275; 438–40

adverbs: formation of from adjs 330–31; **куда** vs **где** *where* 20 fn; 218–21; placement of before vb 38 N

adverbial: expressions formed by prefixing **по–** 375

alphabet: formation of letters 29–32; handwritten 28; Russian (Cyrillic) and the writing system 5–7

alternation: in pres-fut of 2nd conj vbs 304–05; of stems in 1st pers sg of vb **видеть** *to see* 104–05; of voiced and voiceless consonants 39–43

animate (*see also* inanimate): use of gen case endings for

acc of all animate nouns in pl 245; use of gen case endings for acc of animate **стол**– nouns in sg 212

article: absence of definite and indefinite in Russian 10 fn

aspects *or* verbal aspects (*see also* imperfective aspect, perfective aspect): system of 38 N, 70–71

be **быть**: fut forms of 215–18; omission of in pres tense 22 N; past forms of 55–57; use of fut forms in building ipfv fut 215–18

capital letters: limited use of in Russian 31 fn; not used for nationalities 88 fn, 231 N

cardinal numerals: **1–10** 200; use of gen case with numbers 268–69

case system (*see also* accusative, dative, genitive, instrumental, nominative, prepositional cases): introductory remarks on 53–54

commands (*see also* imperative): formation of 2nd pers imper 290–95; use of ipfv aspect in neg commands 292; use of **не надо** in neg commands 352; use of unstressed suffix **–те** for pl-polite form of 2nd person imper 105

conjugation *or* verb conjugation (*see also* first conjugation, present-future, second conjugation, verb): 1st conj vbs with infs ending in **–авать** 327; of 1st conj vbs: **идти** *to be going* 14–17, 237, **мочь** and **смочь** *to be able* 188–90; of irreg vbs: **дать** *to give* 325–27, **хотеть** *to want* 75; of 2nd conj vbs: **видеть** *to see* 104–05, 215, **говорить** *to speak* 45, 97–98, 105, **слышать** *to hear* 45, 302, **спешить** *to hurry* 43–45, 105, **стоять** *to stand* 45, 302; of 2nd conj vbs with stem cons change in 1st pers sg 213–15; of two-stem 1st conj vbs 263–66; pres-fut of 1st conj vbs patterned like **работать** and **идти** 237–40; review of 2nd conj vbs 302–05; use of symbols I and II 109 fn

conjunctions: **и** vs **а** 13 N

consonants (*see also* alphabet, pronunciation, vowels): con sounds vs con letters 8–9, hard vs soft 3; neutral in terms of voice 40; omission of **д** and **т** between cons in pronunciation 35 fn; pronunciation of double 234; sounds 3–5; voiced vs voiceless 39–43, 371, 398–99

Cyrillic *or* Russian alphabet (*see also* Russian handwriting system): and the writing system 5–7

dative case: in impers constrs 320–23; of adjs, sg and pl 378–83; of **кто**, **что**, and the pers prons 318–20; of nouns, sg and pl 346–50; of **этот**, **чей**, and the poss modifiers 375–78; primary function of 54; with **надо** *it's necessary* 350–52; with **нужен** *necessary* 323–25; with preps **к** and **по** 371–75

days of week: 197; Monday considered as first 197 fn

declension (*see also* adjectives, nouns, pronouns): four noun decls 94; introductory remarks on Russian case system 53–54; nouns with decl irregularities 412–14; of abbreviations 115 N, 283 N; of titles of books, movies, plays 201

demonstrative *or* demonstrative pronoun: dat of **этот** 375–78; demonstr **этот** vs introductory **это** 250; instr of **этот** 406–08; nom, acc, gen, and prep of **этот** *this* 248–50

direct object (*see also* accusative case): occasional use of acc for gen after neg vbs 247; refl vbs never used with acc dir obj 382; use of acc to indicate 54, 213; use of gen for dir obj of neg vbs 246–47

directional *or* destinational: **куда** *where* (*to*) vs **где** *where* (*at*) 20 fn; vs locational concepts 218–21

endings (*see also* case system, declension, stems): concept of "zero" ending 54–55; m, f, and pl endings of short-form adjs 45–47; remarks on stems and 54–55

familiar (*see also* plural-polite): familiar sg **ты** vs pl-polite **вы** 11 fn, 55 fn; 2nd pers sg familiar imper as basic form 290–95

feminine (*see also* gender): **дверь**– nouns 94; **жена**– nouns 94; grammatical gender of nouns 69–70; identification of f nouns 10

first conjugation (*see also* conjugation, verbs): fut of **быть** *to be* 215–18; pfv fut of **пойти** *to go* and **взять** *to take* 102–03; pfv fut of **смочь** *to be able* 188–90; pres-fut of 1st conj vbs patterned like **работать** and **идти** 237–40; pres tense of **идти** *to be going* 14–17, 237, **мочь** *to be able* 188–90, **работать** *to work* 25–27, 237; two-stem 1st conj vbs 263–66; vbs with infs ending in **–авать** 327

first names (*see also* names): nicknames and vars of first names 52 N, 427 N

future (*see also* imperfective future, perfective future, present-future): of **не будет** constrs 245–46; of **быть** *to be* and formation of ipfv fut 215–18; of irreg pfv vb **дать** *to give* 325–27; use of in Russian where English uses pres or past 314 N

где vs **куда** *where:* 20 fn; in directional (destinational) vs locational concepts 218–21

gender *or* grammatical gender (*see also* feminine, masculine, neuter): of nouns 10, 69–70; use of m nouns for both men and women in professions 427–28 N

genitive case: after preps 151, 179–82, 182–85, 185–87; for dir obj of neg vbs 246–47; in fut **не будет** constrs 245–46; in parting wishes 226 fn, 424 N; in past **не было** constrs 160–63; in pres **нет** constrs 158–60; of adjs 295–99; of **кто**, **что**, and pers prons 156–58; of nouns in pl 240–43, 266–68; of nouns in sg 154–56; of **чей** and poss modifiers 299–302; primary function of 54, 156; used with numbers 268–69

go (*see also* verbs of motion): vbs indicating motion on foot: **идти**, **пойти**, **ходить** 14–17, 38, 102–03, 227 N, 237, 269–72; vbs indicating motion by vehicle: **ехать**, **поехать**, **ездить** 256 N, 269–72

handwriting: formation of capital letters 31–32; formation of small letters 29–31; Russian handwriting system 28–33; summary remarks on 32–33

hard consonants (*see also* pronunciation): always pronounced hard 5; and soft sign 10; use of "hard-series" vowel letters to indicate hardness of preceding con 8–9; vs soft cons 3–4

hard sign **твёрдый знак**: 7 fn; functions of 9–10

have: aff **у** constrs: in fut 246, in past 152–53, in pres 150–52; neg **у** constrs: in fut 245–46, in past 160–63, in pres 158–60

идти *to be going* (*see also* go, verbs of motion): past tense 269–72, 352–54; pres tense 14–17

imperative (*see also* commands): familiar vs pl-polite 2nd pers imper 105–06; formation of 2nd pers imper 290–95; suggestions that include the speaker 327–29, 355–356; use of **давай** and **давайте** in suggestions that include the speaker 329, 356

imperfective aspect: formation of ipfv fut 215–18; ipfv fut vs pfv fut 218; suggestions that include the speaker using ipfv vbs 355–56; use of in neg commands 292; use of past ipfv vb in neg answer to question using pfv past vb 190; vs pfv aspect 38 N, 70–71

imperfective future (*see also* future, perfective future): formation of 215–18; vs pfv fut 218

impersonal constructions: use of 2nd pers pfv fut vb without pron 230–31 N; use of subjectless 3rd pers pl vb 356–58; with dat case 320–23, with short-form n adj or inf 322–23

inanimate (*see also* animate): acc form of inanimate m and n nouns 57–58; summary of noun endings in acc case 245; vs animate forms of **стол**– nouns in acc sg 212